MURDERLAND

ALSO BY CAROLINE FRASER

God's Perfect Child
Rewilding the World
Prairie Fires

MURDERLAND

CRIME AND BLOODLUST IN THE
TIME OF SERIAL KILLERS

Caroline Fraser

FLEET

First published in the United States in 2025 by Penguin Press,
an imprint of Penguin Random House LLC
First published in Great Britain in 2025 by Fleet

1 3 5 7 9 10 8 6 4 2

Copyright © by Caroline Fraser

The moral right of the author has been asserted.

*All characters and events in this publication, other than those
clearly in the public domain, are fictitious and any resemblance
to real persons, living or dead, is purely coincidental.*

All rights reserved.
Penguin Random House values and supports copyright. Copyright fuels
creativity, encourages diverse voices, promotes free speech, and creates a vibrant culture.
Thank you for buying an authorized edition of this book and for complying with copyright
laws by not reproducing, scanning, or distributing any part of it in any form without permission.
You are supporting writers and allowing Penguin Random House to continue to publish books
for every reader. Please note that no part of this book may be used or reproduced in any
manner for the purpose of training artificial intelligence technologies or systems.

Image credits appear on page 453

Maps by Daniel Lagin

A CIP catalogue record for this book
is available from the British Library.

Hardback ISBN 978-0-349-12754-5
Trade paperback ISBN 978-0-349-12753-8

Book design by Amanda Dewey
Printed and bound in Great Britain by Clays Ltd, Elcograf S.p.A

Papers used by Fleet are from well-managed forests
and other responsible sources.

Fleet	The authorised representative
An imprint of	in the EEA is
Little, Brown Book Group	Hachette Ireland
Carmelite House	8 Castlecourt Centre
50 Victoria Embankment	Dublin 15, D15 XTP3, Ireland
London EC4Y 0DZ	(email: info@hbgi.ie)

An Hachette UK Company
www.hachette.co.uk

www.littlebrown.co.uk

For Island friends:

Jeff Dreiblatt
Sue Warner-Bean
Sheryl Verlaine Whitney

Here comes a candle to light you to bed,
And here comes a chopper to chop off your head.

TRADITIONAL

CONTENTS

Introduction. *Crime Scenes of the Pacific Northwest, or The Crazy Wall* 1

Maps 8

PART I. LITTLE DOMESDAY 13

Chapter 1. The Floating Bridge 15

Chapter 2. The Smelter 28

Chapter 3. The Reversible Lane 57

Chapter 4. The Island 68

Chapter 5. The Devil's Business 89

Chapter 6. The Daylight Basement 124

Chapter 7. The Bird's Nest 173

Interlude. *From Alamein to Zem Zem* 199

PART II. GREAT DOMESDAY 207

Chapter 8. The Lead Moon 209

Chapter 9. The Dutch Door 238

Chapter 10. The Volcano   *265*

Chapter 11. The Green River   *305*

Chapter 12. The Towering Inferno   *345*

Chapter 13. The Fog Warning   *371*

Acknowledgments 399

Notes   403

Image Credits   453

Index   455

MURDERLAND

INTRODUCTION

*Crime Scenes of the Pacific Northwest,
or The Crazy Wall*

The Pacific Northwest is known for five things: lumber, aircraft, tech, coffee, and crime. Weyerhaeuser, Boeing, Microsoft, Starbucks, and serial killers.

Every decade, the headlines. WHY ARE THERE SO MANY SERIAL KILLERS IN THE NORTHWEST?[1] There is no answer. There are just numbers. Per capita, Alaska is number one in the country, Washington five, Oregon six.[2]

"America's killing fields," it has been called, the home of the stranger, the lone wolf, the neighbor who's a little too quiet.[3] For some it's a hobby. For others, a career.

They have their own brands, but they're all different. The Want-Ad Killer, the Boxcar Killer, the Lust Killer, the Phantom Sniper, the Hillside Strangler, the Lewiston Valley Killer, the I-5 Killer, the Coin Shop Killer, the Dismemberment Murders, the Index Killer, the Happy Face Killer, the Eastside Killer, the Werewolf Butcher of Spokane. The Beast of British Columbia. The Green River Killer.[4] Weirdly, many of them are born in the same period, shortly before, during, or after World War II.

Amateur cartographer, I draw lines, making maps tied to timelines, maps of rural roads and kill sites and body dumps. Some of the maps are in my mind. I always consider the location of the scene of the crime. In a chaotic world, maps make sense. There are people who have gurus or crystals or graven images. I have maps. They tell a story. They make connections.

Here's one of my maps: It's August of 1961. I'm seven months old. There are three males who live in what you might call the neighborhood, within a circle whose center is Tacoma. Their names are Charles Manson, Ted Bundy, and Gary Ridgway.

What are the odds?

In 1961, Manson is twenty-six, serving a ten-year sentence in the federal prison on McNeil Island for forging a United States Treasury check. McNeil Island lies in Puget Sound, off the city of Tacoma.

Across the Sound, eight miles from Manson, Ted Bundy is fourteen, living at 658 North Skyline Drive, next to the approach to the Tacoma Narrows Bridge.

Gary Ridgway is twelve, residing north of Tacoma at 4404 South 175th Street, near SeaTac Airport, an address then considered to be in Seattle.

Eight years later, on August 9, 1969, Manson, gathering his followers, will urge them to murder everyone at 10050 Cielo Drive in Benedict Canyon on a night that will become a byword for inconceivable and random violence. The following night, they will kill Rosemary and Leno LaBianca.

Sometime in the 1970s or early 1980s, Gary Ridgway will begin killing women he picks up near the airport, blocks from where he grew up. He strangles prostitutes, runaways, and teenage girls. Dozens of them. At first he dumps their bodies in rivers, their hair rippling in the streamflow. Until 2001, when he's apprehended, he will be known to the public only as the Green River Killer.

But in the early morning hours of August 31, 1961, the one who gets the ball rolling—the prodigy, the polymath, the boy wonder—is Ted Bundy. That night, rain lashes the windows, and I'm a baby in a basket, teething, seething, rubbing my hair off on a fuzzy yellow blanket. That night, during a thunderstorm, in a neighborhood he knows only too well, Ted Bundy climbs through the living room window of a family named Burr. He used

INTRODUCTION

to live right around the corner. He has friends who know the Burrs. He finds Ann Marie, who is eight, wearing a blue-and-white flowered nightie, two religious medals, and a bracelet invoking the protection of Saint Christopher. Pied Piper of Tacoma, he spirits her out the front door. She is never seen again.

Now let's look at the map. If you take a ruler and lay it down in 1961 and connect the dots between Charles Manson, Ted Bundy, and Gary Ridgway, you can practically draw a straight line.

Is it chance? Is there a connection? Well, that's the question.

Here's another map.

They call it the OWL. The Olympic–Wallowa Lineament. Nobody knows what it is. It belongs to the geologists, and it could be either an optical illusion or a topographic feature of "unknown origin" or a "zone of crustal weakness."[5] Fault line or will-o'-the-wisp: take your pick.

If you're an earth scientist, the OWL suggests how the planet's rigid plates drift over the mantle. We live on top of rubble, not a solid foundation. If you're someone alert to the hazards beneath your feet, the OWL conveys the nature of the place, hinting that what lies beneath is dishonest, deceptive, given to the false front. The earth here looks safe, but it isn't. It has been hoodwinking people for thousands of years, for all of its conceivable life. The ground is unstable, volcanic, prone to sudden, startling fits of temper, to epic floods and rivers of fire, earthquakes and tsunamis, the theater of conspicuous collapse.

Think of what the place has been through. Burning, then freezing. Consider its proclivities: abusive and abused. Moisture seeps from every moss pore and lichen crevice. It has survived unspeakable pressures, once compressed by ice thousands of feet deep, sheets creeping across the surface, cresting in glacial slow motion every few thousand years and then falling back, drop by freezing drop. This is not terra firma. The longer we look, the more we see how it's broken. And where it will break again.

For the moment, the OWL is a cryptic line on a map, the faintest depression or fissure stretching for four hundred miles, slanting from northwest to southeast. Note, however, how it cuts across the landscape. See where it goes. It carves through America's killing fields, sites favored by murder's most devout practitioners. It falls along the future route of Interstate 90, expressway to hell.

Earthquakes are murderers, invisible until they strike. The OWL is Washington's shadow San Andreas, lying beneath bridges and tunnels, waiting to toss them like pick-up sticks. It intersects the seismically active Devil's Mountain Fault. If Devil's Mountain ruptures, it could cause a magnitude 7.5 event. Cry havoc.

The OWL stretches from Cape Flattery, the far northwest tip of Washington State, and skims across fathomless Lake Crescent, Elliott Bay, Seattle, the north shore of Mercer Island. Lake Sammamish. Issaquah. Remember these names, for we will see them again. From Issaquah it cuts through Stampede Pass and down the Wallula Gap on the Columbia River, through the Horse Heaven Hills and the south fork of the Walla Walla, flying past Cle Elum and Ellensburg. A route wreathed in bodies.

IT LOOKS INTENTIONAL. It's first mapped by Erwin Raisz, in 1945. Born in Hungary in 1893, Raisz practically invents geographical cartography, at a time when the field is only beginning to emerge from the days when men with feather pens drew outlines of continents freehand, seeding the oceans with compass roses and sea monsters rampant. He attends Budapest's Royal Joseph Polytechnic University, earning a degree in civil engineering and architecture. After serving in World War I, he immigrates to the United States in 1923, working for the Ohman Map Company and completing a Ph.D. at Columbia University. He becomes a gifted cartographer, informed by mathematical projections and block diagrams, drawing richly detailed maps of landforms, points of interest hand-labeled in even italic script, publishing in 1938 what would become the principal textbook for generations of mapmakers to come: *General Cartography*.

Raisz is the first to see the OWL. It emerges as he draws his "Landform

INTRODUCTION

Map of the Northwest States" (1:1,400,000), originally published in 1941. He proudly calls this creation "one of the most detailed maps of its kind," and it is indeed a map of great beauty.[6] Raisz spots the OWL by accident, he'll later say, when his map is finished in ink and he happens to glance across it sidelong: he's immediately struck by "a peculiar line stretching from Cape Flattery at the entrance of Juan de Fuca Strait to the Wallowa Mountains."[7]

Once seen, the OWL is impossible to unsee. "This line must be obvious," he writes, to anyone "looking at the map from [Washington's] northwestern corner toward the center." But then he runs into conjecture. "Apparently we may have here one of the major structural lines or lineaments," he suggests, supposing that it might be a geological fault line.[8] But where it comes from is anyone's guess. Like any scientist, Raisz wants to "return to the location" and study the actual landforms on the ground but is prevented by "wartime duties and travel restrictions."[9] So there the lineament lies.

Erwin Raisz dies of a cerebral hemorrhage in Bangkok on December 1, 1968, while traveling to New Delhi to deliver a paper, having drawn some five thousand maps that are said to be "accurate, consistent in style, and marvelously clear in intent."[10] His discovery remains a curiosity and a goad. Speculation runs wild, causing divisions in the geophysical community. The OWL is called "an outrageous hypothesis" and "a fictional structural element," perhaps an optical illusion like the Kanizsa triangle, a so-called contour illusion proposed by a psychologist in 1955, in which fragments of lines and partial pie shapes suggest the outline of a triangle that doesn't exist, a perceptual trick the eyes play on the brain.[11]

But as the years pass, science advances, fleshing out plate tectonics and limning faults and earthquakes, informed by new technologies that see through superficial layers of brush and soil, under beach sand and glacial drift and thick Quaternary deposits. Chief among these is lidar, ground-penetrating radar that exposes what lies beneath.

As these new technologies map the tantalizing outlines of what we can barely see with the naked eye—the history of a violent planet—scientists are coming to grips with the threat. But knowledge comes too late. No one in this era of hubris—erecting bridges, highways, and smelters—spares a thought for their future ruination.

The true crime lies in what we've done with the place. In 1945, the population of Washington is two million, but it grows, score by score. We are busy, busy bees, building houses not on rock but on sand. In the years since Raisz mapped it, we have swarmed all over his lethal line, but no matter. "Civilization exists by geologic consent," the historian says, "subject to change without notice."[12] Great will be the fall.

If we believe what it's telling us, the OWL says all of this and more. It's singing the old song of Bedlam: houses swallowed by mudslides, cliffs willfully caving in.[13] It's the crack in the teacup, the glacier in the cupboard, the line between life and the sudden lack of it.[14] Nature is a serial killer. Swift as death, the owl sweeps across the meadow, lifting a squirming ground squirrel in its talons. What no one tells you, what you cannot anticipate, is the screaming, all across the meadow and into the forest, fainter the farther away, sowing the air with sorrow, rage, and horror.

Whatever we build, however busy we become, the OWL is down there, indifferent, implacable. It is the fault line we cannot see, but we know it's there. It's the knife at the neck. It's the clean cut.

WELCOME TO THE CRAZY WALL.

What's a crazy wall? It's a real-life artifact of the mid-twentieth-century detective bureau. Cops push pins into wall maps, trying to find the pattern, to analyze, to snatch a cloud and pin it down. You can see versions of the real thing in photographs of police bureaus and their much-vaunted "task forces." The craziest wall of all may have been in Yorkshire in the 1970s, at the Millgarth Police Station in Leeds, where a regional task force trying to catch the Yorkshire Ripper is buried in clues, amassing an archive of tens of thousands of handwritten index cards attached to a carousel. The contraption gets so heavy the floor starts falling in.

Since then, the crazy wall has leapt into fiction, becoming a fixture of

INTRODUCTION

police procedurals, spy shows, and true crime. Every thriller from *The Usual Suspects* to *Fargo* includes a scene where the misunderstood, often alcoholic, and possibly delusional detective—Carrie Mathison in *Homeland*, Rustin Cohle in *True Detective*—stands in front of a bulletin board or whiteboard or chalkboard or wall and studies the entire mad mystery: suspects, clues, red herrings, Colonel Mustard and Professor Plum. Look out! There's someone in the library with a lead pipe.

Play along at home: connect the clues with string or yarn until the whole thing resembles a graph of sheer lunacy, a visual eruption of obsession. It's the big board in *Dr. Strangelove*, the 3D collage in *Sherlock*, the storage locker in *True Detective*. It's the inside of anybody's mind.

Spare some string for the smelters and smoke plumes, those insidious killers, shades of Hades. See how the Ripper glides through the alleys? His work is veiled by the fog of London "particulars," murky entrails of industrial stacks and coal fires.

Collect them all: compile a modern Domesday Book. William the Conqueror had one: a list of his holdings, the slaves, oxen, pigs, mills, weirs, iron ore works, and smelters in his mighty kingdom. He had to know everything to collect taxes. He kept two books, Little Domesday and Great Domesday, *dom* being Old English for "reckoning." According to the letter of the law, his reckoning will stand until the last trump shall sound, until the Day of Judgment.

Consider this a book of judgment. A guide to mayhem. A key, a trot, a crib, the CliffsNotes, the map with pins. Having compiled the data, I will show you my work, a master inventory. A timeline, with bodies. I have pictures—a smelter in the 1920s, a floating bridge in the 1940s, a boy on a beach in Ocean City, New Jersey. Maps of smoke and surveys of psychosis. I have a grid of the island I lived on with a pin in one serial killer's house, 1,232 yards from where I grew up.

Let's take a walk around the room. Let's have a look.

THE PACIFIC NORTHWEST

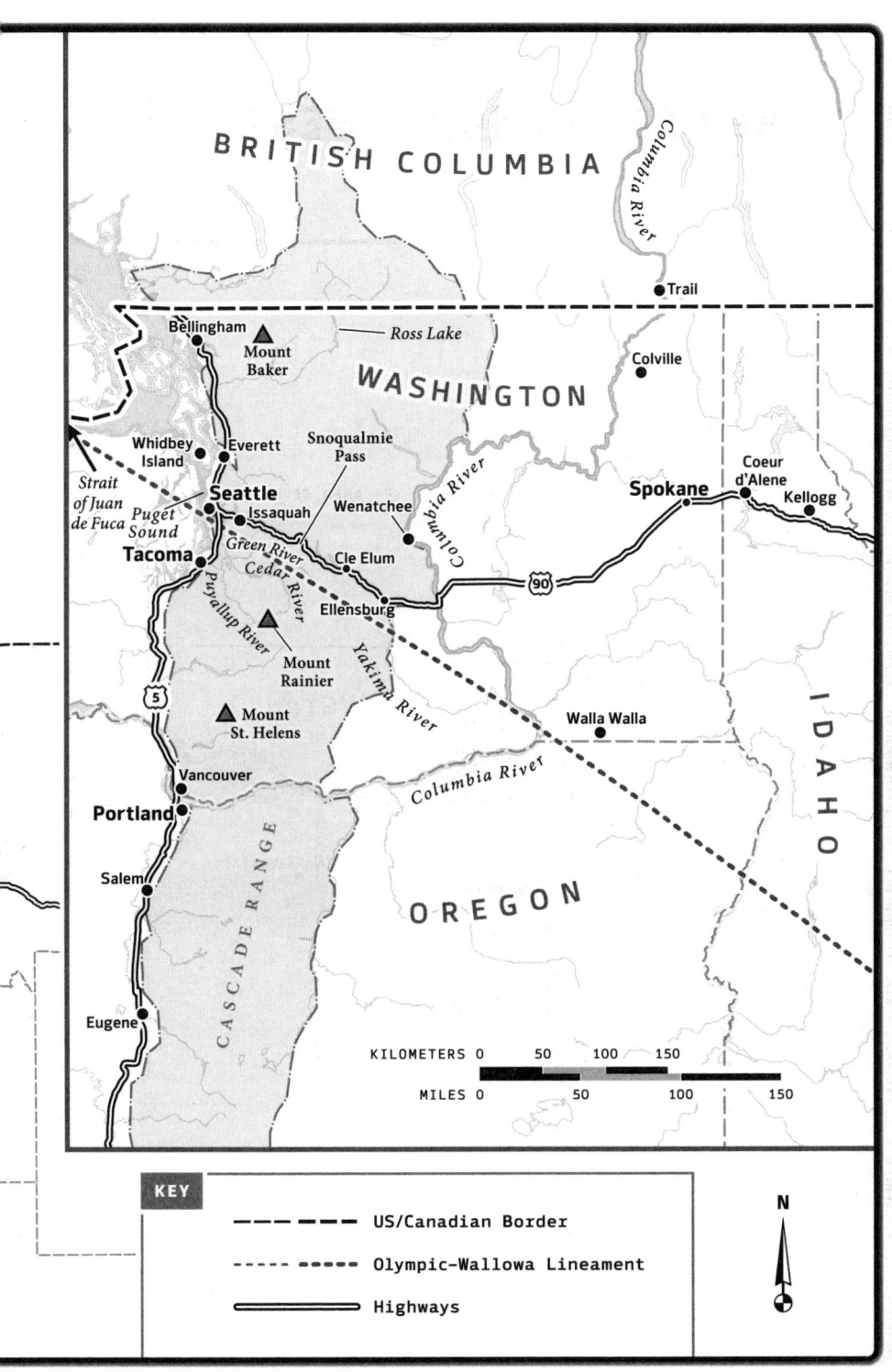

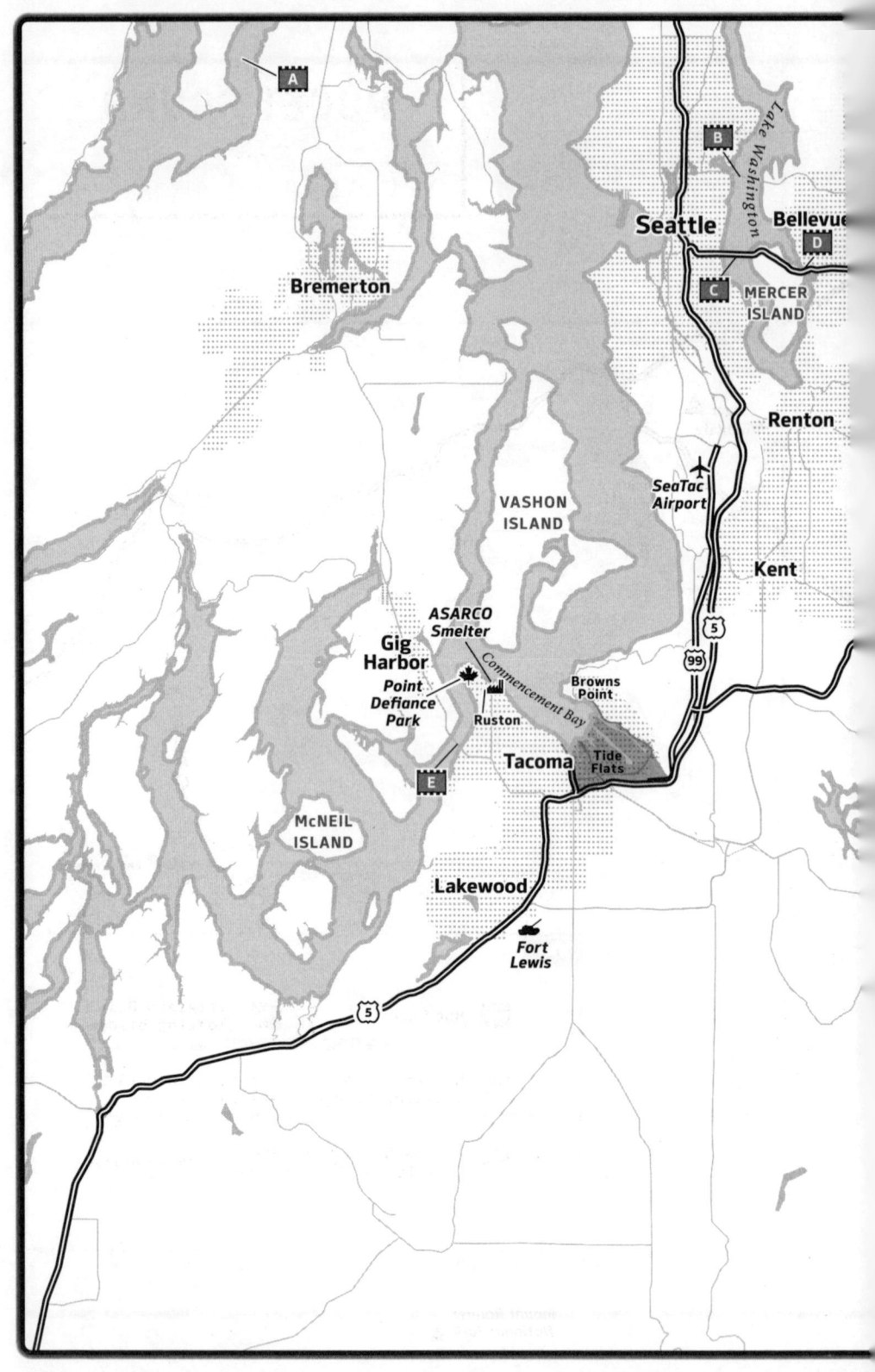

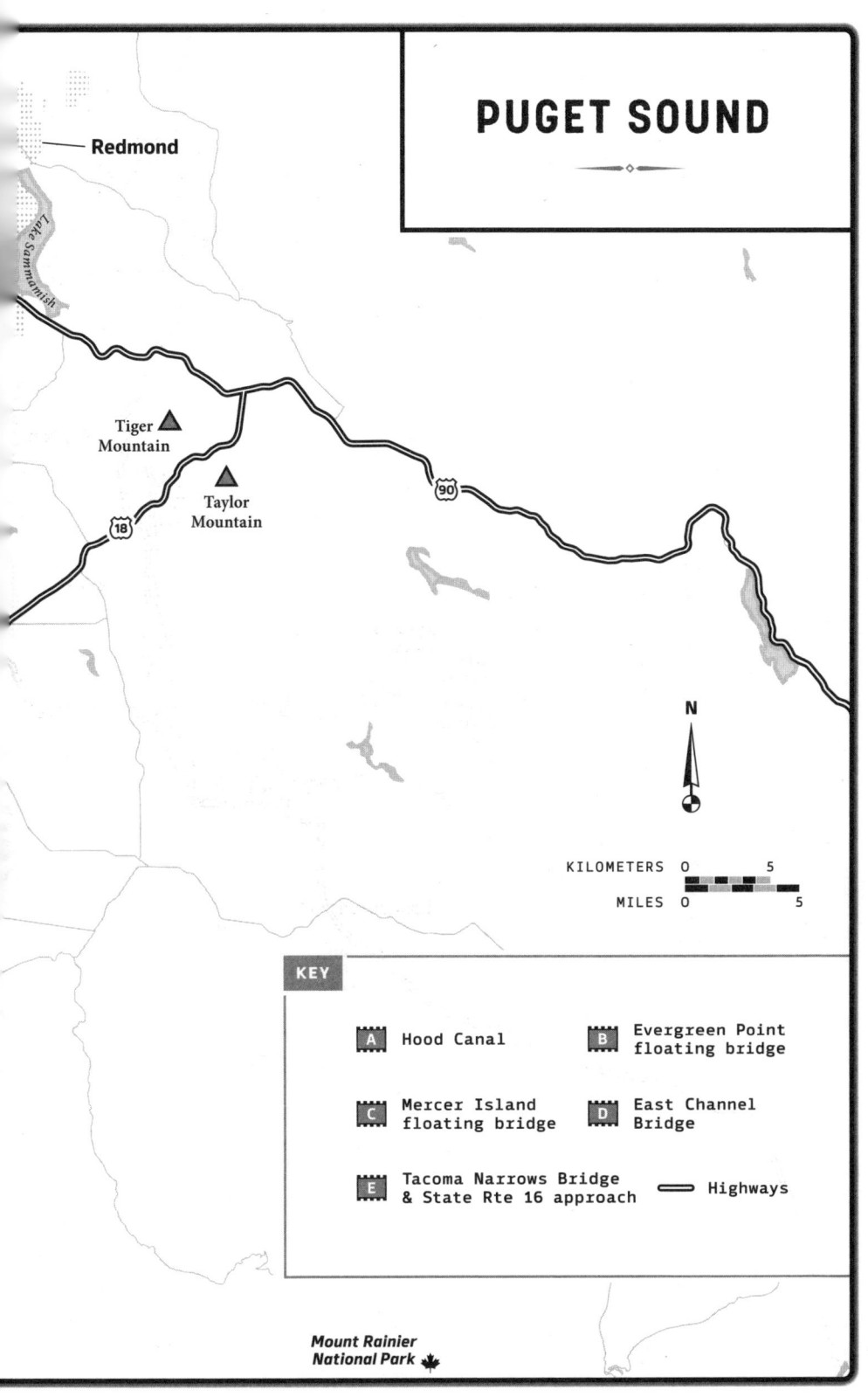

PART I
LITTLE DOMESDAY

Chapter 1

The Floating Bridge

Make a pact with the devil until you have crossed the bridge.

—Romanian proverb

Denn die Todten reiten schnell.
For the dead travel fast.

—Gottfried August Bürger, "Lenore"

Once upon a time, you could smell it, the salt water and the accelerants, the creosote, the diesel, and the benzene. Now people call it "Emerald City," unspeakable gall.[1] Back in the day, no one called it an emerald city.

It's dark. At forty-seven degrees, thirty-six minutes north of the equator, Seattle is the northernmost U.S. city with a population of over half a million, north of Boston and Burlington, north of Toronto, Montreal, and Ottawa, for that matter, and on the same latitude as Zurich, Switzerland. At the winter solstice in Seattle, there are eight hours and twenty-five minutes of daylight. When you're a kid, you're waiting for the bus in the dark and coming home near dusk.

All bridges lead to Seattle, but Seattle is a bit of spume, iridescent, evanescent, an oily bubble blowing atop the waves. It's a sad place in the 1970s, a place no one wants to be. A literal backwater. Someone puts up a billboard on the way to the airport: WILL THE LAST PERSON LEAVING SEATTLE TURN OUT THE LIGHTS.[2] The city lacks historical significance, confidence, political power, and pride of place. Its economy is boom and bust: Boeing and Weyerhaeuser, Weyerhaeuser and Boeing. Their contracts are always being canceled.

Its fortunes reflect the weather, a few fickle weeks of summer bracketed by months of overcast, the clouds clamping down, supplying mist and seeping rain and continuous bone-chilling cold. As a boy, my father learns by heart "The Cremation of Sam McGee," a Robert W. Service ballad inspired by the Alaska gold rush, and he recites it ever after by the campfire:

> *There are strange things done in the midnight sun*
>   *By the men who moil for gold;*
> *The Arctic trails have their secret tales*
>   *That would make your blood run cold;*
> *The Northern Lights have seen queer sights,*
>   *But the queerest they ever did see*
> *Was that night on the marge of Lake Lebarge*
>   *I cremated Sam McGee.*[3]

It's a funny poem about freezing to death.

BEHOLD A LETHAL GEOGRAPHY. A river of rock and ice carves the groove of Puget Sound between the mountains, gouging out Lake Washington and its mirror image, Lake Sammamish. Last gasp of the Ice Age, the Fraser Glaciation presses south down the Fraser Valley sometime between 25,000 and 10,000 years ago, five thousand feet thick where the town of Bellingham will be, thirty-five hundred feet at Seattle, two thousand at Tacoma. That's pressure. When the glaciers withdraw, they leave erratics in their wake. Erratics are boulders the size of buildings, calling cards of the apocalypse.

The ice leaves an erratic near what is currently the University of Washington campus, eighty feet in diameter and nineteen feet high. In times past, it was used by Native people as a landmark; later, mountain climbers began using it to train: Jim Whittaker, the first American to summit Everest, once scaled it. It is called the Wedgwood Erratic, and it lies becalmed between 28th Avenue Northeast and Northeast 72nd Street. Something, or someone, has left it there.

East across the mountains from Seattle, across the Cascades, we find a land of hanging valleys, scablands, and coulees, topographical anomalies so bizarre that geologists struggle to explain them. Unimaginable forces have been at work, violating everything known about natural erosion. What made these terrible scars? No one can say.

In 1927, a high school biology teacher in Seattle named J. Harlen Bretz delivers a paper at the Geological Society in Washington, D.C., theorizing that the weird distortions were carved by catastrophic flooding unleashed by the collapse of vast ice dams. His theory is called "preposterous." He is dismissed as "incompetent."[4]

He is, of course, correct.

Fifteen thousand years ago, there was an event so bizarre it inspired scenes in science fiction novels.[5] To the east, an ice dam formed between the mountains, stretching ten to thirty miles, creating Lake Missoula, a prehistoric body of water two thousand feet deep, covering three thousand square miles and holding five hundred cubic miles of water, exerting great pressure. At an unknown time, on an unspecified day, the ice dam failed and the water let fly.

No one alive has ever seen or heard anything like it. If there were hide-wearing humans in the area, pre-Clovis colonizers following their mammoth bliss, they likely did not survive to tell the tale. The hydraulic pressure of the flood ripped out bedrock, scouring the earth, changing the courses of great rivers, scoring the land, leaving massive rents that are still visible. Eddies of glacial silt washed up against mountainsides, still extant. Ice dams formed and failed again. The cycle was repeated dozens of times, perhaps once every half century over several thousand years. Geologists quibble, but they agree on one thing: All dams leak. All dams fail.

Spreading and contracting, glaciers leave the land black and blue, dominated by rock walls and harsh crags, lowlands covered in cedars and firs and primitive ferns the color of bruises. Rocked in the wind, the trees move of their own accord, swaying on unseen currents, lowering, watching, waiting.

The Northwest is biding its time, with five active volcanoes marching south down the Washington Cascades: Mount Baker, Glacier Peak, Mount Rainier, Mount Saint Helens, and Mount Adams. Each is an organic smelter, ready to bring forth gas, liquid rock, and ash. Civilization, such as it is, is erected on the back of this dragon, its bridges and tunnels as delicate as eggshell.

Magma, cataclysms. This is the natural path of the OWL, cutting through Seattle, passing north of Rainier, a forecast of disasters past and future. To the planet, it's all a game, Puget Sound just a "big hole" between two mountain ranges, a trough filled with immense crustal toy blocks.[6] There is a 45 percent probability that over the next fifty years the Juan de Fuca plate, lying offshore beneath the Pacific, will cause a "megathrust," a subduction earthquake of higher than 8.0 magnitude. It will do this by trying to force its way under the Cascadia continental plate.

Beneath us lies basement rock, the lowest layer above the earth's mantle, an unstable mélange, basalt and gabbro. Rock can change its spots. Put pressure on it and it goes through a phase change, compacting, tilting, sinking, deforming.

Geologists compare the slow-motion accident that is the Pacific Northwest to a train wreck or a jackknifing tractor trailer.[7] A block of rock we call "Washington" is hitting the wall, crumpling, folding, and faulting. Something temporarily known as "Oregon" is curling around it in clockwise rotation. A megathrust is expected every two hundred and forty years on average. It has been more than three hundred years since the last one. In the year 1700, there was a great calamity, a movement of the earth and everything upon it that caused the cedars and firs to slide upright off the island I come from. Someday, they may rise again.

"Faulting is complex and not yet understood," scientists say.[8]

Yet we know, don't we.

THE FLOATING BRIDGE

The earthquake to come is expected to bury the streets of downtown Seattle under eighty feet of broken glass and crack the Grand Coulee Dam, one of the largest concrete structures in the world. It will alter the topography of islands.

It will raise a tsunami to inundate the coasts of Washington, Oregon, and Japan. Rock, air, fire, and water: they will not take no for an answer.

The movement of the earth may or may not be related to melting under the continental crust and the long-expected lahar, in which hot gases and molten lava will flow from Mount Rainier, boiling the glaciers on its face, and mud and lava will pour out to sea, following the routes of rivers to the Sound.

It is more likely than not. The lahar has happened before, some sixty times, and is expected to happen every five hundred to a thousand years. The last time was six hundred years ago. Just a blink. That's when a ragged chunk of the mountain tore off. It still appears to be missing, near the top.

The next time the lahar happens, the Washington State Department of Natural Resources expects it will cost $6 billion and the lives of the 150,000 people living on top of old mudflows in nearby towns in the Puyallup Valley if they are not evacuated in time. Schoolchildren in the town of Orting, on the slopes of Rainier, are trained to run uphill, out of the valley, when sirens go off, triggered by trip wires and sensors.[9]

On a clear day, Rainier is stunning as seen from Seattle: star of picture postcards, a glittering, coveted view, a snow cone of brightest white against deepest blue. Diamonds, sapphires, and platinum. "The mountain is out," people say, self-satisfied, self-confident.

But it is all a facade. The mountain is admittedly "rotten inside."[10] Hollow, full of gas. A place where bad things happen.

Bad things can happen by accident. But sometimes they happen on purpose, and sometimes they are engineered. By engineers.

EVERY GREAT PSYCHOPATH wants a floating bridge. In Persia, Xerxes, King of Kings, orders his armies to cross the Hellespont on pontoon bridges made of flax and papyrus. When waters rise in a storm, sending his spans to eternity, he whips the water in retaliation. He beheads his engineers.

Sometime between AD 37 and 41, Caligula plans to ride across the Bay of Baiae by lashing together ships' hulls and laying a causeway upon them. No one today knows whether he built it or not.

Fleeing the Russians, Napoleon orders three floating spans across the Berezina. His Dutch builders tear down the houses of local people to build them, but the improvised pontoons are flimsy. In the chaos of combat, thousands of soldiers and civilians perish in the icy waters.

The Washington State Department of Transportation is no less grandiose. The growing city of Seattle is packed into a narrow north–south strip of land bordered on the west by saltwater Puget Sound and on the east by freshwater Lake Washington. The city can grow north and south, but a valuable expanse of land lies across the lake, on the east side. In the middle of the lake, a natural stepping stone, is Mercer Island.

A thirty-five-year-old engineer named Homer Hadley dreams of building a concrete floating bridge spanning Lake Washington from Seattle to Mercer Island. After traffic crosses the island, a shorter, conventional bridge on the isle's eastern shore will carry motorists to the east side of the lake. His critics call his vision "Hadley's Folly."

As early as 1920, Hadley is dreaming of his bridge. Concrete river barges come into vogue after World War I, when European cities run short of steel. During the next world war, concrete ships and barges ferry men and materiel across the English Channel on D-Day. They are deployed in the Pacific. Working for the Seattle Public School District's architectural office, Hadley proposes the idea in an earnest talk delivered to the American Society of Civil Engineers. At a time when the population is a few hundred thousand, he's pilloried by city fathers, editorials in *The Seattle Times*, and everyone who wants to preserve the aesthetic beauty of Lake Washington.

Mercer Island's first bridge, the East Channel Bridge, is constructed in

THE FLOATING BRIDGE

1923, but Hadley sees this as an insignificant span. Barely eighty feet long and made of wood, it connects the island to the east side of the lake and the rural town of Bellevue. It becomes so rickety that school bus drivers make children get out of the bus and walk on foot, a perilous crossing. "A tragedy occurred in 1937," says a local history, when a boy slipped through the railing and drowned in the East Channel.[11] Until a second bridge across the main channel is built, the structure still leaves islanders who want to get to Seattle having to take a passenger ferry or detour twenty-two miles around the south end of the lake.

Hadley is an outspoken critic of the New Deal and its architect, FDR. Nonetheless, he does not hesitate to pursue federal money, consulting with the director of the Washington State Department of Highways, Lacey V. Murrow. Lacey, the handsome brother of journalist and radio personality Edward R. Murrow, has joined the department as an engineer in his twenties. Dressed in sharp pinstriped suits and a camel-hair coat, his looks are compared favorably to those of Clark Gable. People laugh at Homer Hadley, a squinting, bespectacled man with receding hair, a geek, an egghead, an eighty-pound weakling. They don't laugh at Lacey V. Murrow.

Lacey is put in charge of the construction of two bridges, and they're both dedicated during the first two days of July 1940. This fact tends to be elided in later accounts. Because one of the bridges falls down.

The first to be dedicated is the Tacoma Narrows Bridge, a suspension toll bridge, thirty miles south of Seattle, spanning the slim arm of the Sound between the industrial city of Tacoma and the western peninsula, hosting Bremerton, a critical naval base. The ceremonial dedication of this crossing begins on July 1, under blue skies. Parades and floats file through downtown Tacoma, and ten thousand people crowd the shores to hear a nineteen-gun salute. The governor pays the first toll, and there stands Lacey V. Murrow, hailed by the press as a Horatio Alger.[12] He stands a little off to the side, jaunty straw hat in hand, his chest bifurcated by the ribbon about to be cut by officials from the Puget Sound Naval Shipyard.

He has just turned thirty-six, although his boss lies about his age. The press believes him to be forty-four. He is looking down, abashed. He should be.

On this celebratory day, Lacey receives a telegram from his younger brother, who's in London reporting on the Blitz for CBS Radio. Ed sends this terse message: CONGRATULATIONS HOPE YOU AND BRIDGES UPSTANDING.[13]

Ed may well have heard that the Tacoma Narrows Bridge has been fraught from funding to design. This bridge and the Lake Washington Pontoon Bridge are massive undertakings of Roosevelt's Public Works Administration, launched in the teeth of war. The impetus for the Tacoma bridge is military: the need for ready access to the Bremerton Navy Yard. But the original design put forward by Murrow's engineers, calling for heavy twenty-five-foot-deep deck trusses, is estimated to cost $11 million, deemed too high by federal authorities.

An East Coast engineer is brought in to redesign it. He drafts a thrillingly thin, graceful art deco suspension bridge: two lanes floating atop a light, eight-foot-deep deck, cutting the projected cost to $6.4 million. Washington State engineers examine the plan and declare it "fundamentally unsound."[14] Their concerns are dismissed. The first cable suspension bridge of its type in the world, it will be built quickly, in nineteen months, leaving no time for wind tunnel testing. It will become the third-longest suspension bridge in the world, after two far heavier bridges, San Francisco's Golden Gate and New York's George Washington.

It lasts four months. Problems are apparent during construction. Disconcerted workers feel the deck swaying and bouncing in the center of the span. Lacey Murrow is already aware of the flaw: University of Washington engineers are devising an emergency plan to anchor the deck to cement blocks on shore. Nonetheless, the bridge is felt to be cursed, dubbed "Galloping Gertie" for its horrific oscillation in even light breezes, as if it were a joke that men had spent millions of dollars building a bridge that might fly apart at the first gusts of wind.

At around 10:30 a.m. on November 7, 1940, those gusts arrive, exceeding forty miles per hour. The deck of the bridge begins whipping like a scarf, back and forth, up and down, a hallucinatory vision captured on sixteen-millimeter Kodachrome by the owner of a local camera shop.[15] The bridge is lashing itself into a self-perpetuating "aeroelastic flutter," a form of "self-excitation."[16]

That morning, Leonard Coatsworth, an editor at the Tacoma *News Tribune*, is driving across the bridge when the structure begins swaying violently, twisting in the wind "like a piece of taffy," according to news reports.[17] Lampposts are snapping off. "I jammed on the brakes," Coatsworth will say later, "and got out, only to be thrown onto my face against the curb. Around me I could hear concrete cracking. . . . The car itself began to slide from side to side of the roadway."[18]

Crawling on hands and knees, he makes it to the toll plaza. He saves himself, abandoning his daughter's three-legged black cocker spaniel, Tubby. A University of Washington professor filming the bridge in its final throes tries to lure Tubby to safety, but the dog panics, biting him on the knuckle. Nauseated, the professor retreats. At 11:02 a.m., Tubby vanishes with the car when the span twists up into the air, cables snapping like guitar strings, collapsing into Puget Sound, where great blocks of it remain today. The dog is the sole fatality, although two truck drivers barely survive.

Lacey V. Murrow appears at the site that day but is "too visibly shaken to remain."[19] He will not be beheaded, because he is no longer the director of highways. Dreading the inevitable, he resigned abruptly, two months earlier. In his defense he will say, "No one man can be blamed for the collapse," and the professor on the bridge will join him in the general self-exoneration, claiming that it was "a combination of conditions that no one anticipated."[20] Although they did.

The Tacoma Narrows Bridge is rebuilt to a sturdier design and will remain in use. Yet the original disaster stands as the most notorious bridge design failure in modern history, film of its demise studied frame by frame. Engineers are still arguing over the physics, because they're not as smart as they think they are.

LET US RETURN to the other bridge, the pontoon bridge to the north, across Lake Washington to Mercer Island, the bridge that will not fail four months and six days after its gala opening. On July 2, 1940, Murrow looks pensively at his second triumph too.

No one seems to know what this bridge will do—sink, swim, or float away. Families driving across it for the first time make their children don life jackets.[21] The U.S. Navy, which maintains a base at the south end of the lake, has opposed it, fearing it will interfere with seaplanes taking off and landing. People who live on or near the lakefront, a rural haven from downtown Seattle, dread the prospect of traffic, noise, and development. Banding together as the Lake Washington Protective Association, they denounce it in its planning stages as the work of a "cement trust," "a financial folly, an unnecessary tax burden, and a desecration of the lake."[22] For good measure, they predict that it will sink within five years. It will take a little longer than that.

It's the largest road project to date in Washington state history and involves far more than just the floating bridge. The plan calls for a six-and-a-half-mile-long highway across Mercer Island with on- and off-ramps and a rebuilt East Channel Bridge. To carry traffic into Seattle once it has crossed to the city side of the lake, the Mount Baker Tunnel is bored through the high bluff beside the lake. The builders drill 1,466 feet under an existing Seattle neighborhood, excavating two separate side-by-side tunnels, at the time the largest in diameter ever built.

No one knows what to call it. "The scow crossing" is among the less felicitous names. The State of Washington settles on "Lake Washington Floating Bridge," but everyone calls it the Mercer Island Floating Bridge. Graced by none of the poetry of a soaring suspension bridge, it just lies there, somnolent as a serpent on the water. Its grandeur lies in its ingenuity.

And its size. Unlike the wispy Tacoma Narrows, the Mercer Island Floating Bridge is overbuilt, monstrous, giving the impression not of delicate filigree but of immense weight and substance. It is the largest floating structure in the world, weighing as much as three battleships.

THE FLOATING BRIDGE

After it opens, the press, which once derided it as "a dangerous toy," hails this "Paul Bunyan achievement."[23] *The Seattle Times* is awestruck: "Resting on the bosom of Lake Washington are 100,000 tons of steel and concrete, stretching more than a mile between shores."[24] The publisher declares that "the beauty of the bridge is utterly amazing."[25]

Former skeptics greet it as the "new great wonder of the world."[26] Twenty concrete pontoons have been floated into position and anchored to the lake bed with sixty-five-ton reinforced concrete blocks. It is considered a civil engineering breakthrough, solving tricky dilemmas posed by the site. The lake is not only worryingly deep, at two hundred feet, but essentially has no fixed bottom, no floor except for a soggy miasma of silt that cannot support concrete pylons. The engineers are untroubled by local legends told by the Duwamish Tribe about the lake's habit of swallowing islands. They know better. Indeed, on November 7, 1940, when the Tacoma Narrows Bridge fails, employees at the floating bridge preen, boasting that the winds trouble it not at all, merely dashing dark waves against the concrete. It is "as solid as a rock," they say.[27]

But the planners have overlooked something incalculable by slide rule: human nature. The distracted drivers, the risk-takers, the hot rods, the hopped-up and harried and hysterical, the drunken and the drowsy. The hillbillies: one man causes a "chain-reaction" collision when he stops dead in the middle of a lane to retrieve a bedspring or screen door that flew off the roof of his vehicle.[28] Forty-five feet wide, the bridge stretches a mile and a half across the water: four lanes plus a four-foot span separating traffic heading east and west. There are four-foot-wide sidewalks but no room for error, no pullout, no breakdown lane, no shoulder. Beyond the traffic, there is water. Deep water.

The bridge is as straight as a string except for a protrusion, closer to Mercer Island. The "most novel feature of this novel structure" is a swelling, a bump on either side.[29] To accommodate ships too tall to fit under either of the elevated ends that rise up to meet the land, the bridge has been fitted with a flat, retractable drawspan, unique in all the world. The largest floating pontoon section contains within it an open rectangular well of water two hundred and twenty feet long and sixty feet wide.[30] The drawspan doesn't lift up into the air. To open the bridge for passing marine traffic, one section of the road surface is retracted so that it covers the top of the pool, leaving an opening in the roadway for boats to pass through.

Under normal conditions, when the bridge is not open, the traffic lanes separate around the pool, passing on either side. Cars and trucks must negotiate around that well of water at high speed, east- and westbound lanes each swerving in a semicircle to their right. People call it "the bulge."

In August 1945, World War II ends with the atomic bombs dropped on Hiroshima and Nagasaki. Gas rationing in Washington is canceled, and the thirty-five-mile-per-hour speed limit on most roads is cast to the winds. Within a month, traffic volume on the floating bridge doubles.[31] Accidents happen.

The bridge soon becomes notorious for a series of interestingly gruesome and abrupt mishaps, described by engineers as "sometimes fatal accidents."[32] The newspapers love them. For example, in September 1945, a month after the speed limit is lifted, Lee William Makarsky, a thirty-year-old Canadian Navy man, is killed when his car hurtles over the guardrail and into the water.[33]

Around the same time, the *Laura Lee*, a twenty-nine-foot cabin cruiser, breaks up when its engine fails during a storm and it's blown against the span's seven-and-a-half-foot-high concrete wall.[34] The boat's owner survives, after a leg is amputated.

In March 1949, a thirty-year-old Spokane woman, Judy Reed, speeding as she approaches the bulge, fails to straighten out after "starting the curve around the floating bridge draw span."[35] Striking the curb, the vehicle flies upward, landing astraddle the guardrail, skidding for ninety-five feet, "teetering first to one side, then the other," and ultimately toppling into the lake.[36] Reed's body is recovered by divers at a depth of eighty-four feet.

During a blizzard in January 1950, a forty-year-old man, Bert Heath, is "tossed into the lake in a crash of skidding vehicles."[37]

THE FLOATING BRIDGE

Yet these precipitate acts, these headlong high-speed depontisations, bodies sailing through air before sinking like skipped rocks, cannot erode the enduring popularity of the bridge, glorified for its convenience. It cuts a full hour off the commute between Seattle and the east side of the lake. It makes light work of walking on water. Within nine years, it has been crossed forty-four million times.[38]

Chapter 2

The Smelter

———◇———

> The gold, and the silver, the brass, the iron, the tin, and the lead, Every thing that may abide the fire, ye shall make it go through the fire, and it shall be clean.
>
> —Numbers 31:22–23

> He's composed of harshness.
>
> —Shakespeare, *The Tempest*

Let us linger for a moment in that frothy postwar fizz of euphoria, when people are eager to swallow the cost of progress. How bad can it be, after the world has gone to war? It is a time of celebration.

Just for a moment, if you will, let us float across the country in that effervescent bubble of champagne elation and planetary subjugation and heedless sexual entitlement to look down from our cloud somewhere above Philadelphia and witness the conception of a noteworthy child. At this time, a newly demobilized soldier or sailor or airman, identified tentatively in future years as either Lloyd Marshall, an Air Force or Navy man, or Jack Worthington, an Army veteran, hits the streets of the city after being sprung from his unit. Cocky and victorious, young Lloyd or Jack seeks his reward. Whoever he is, he finds it in twenty-two-year-old Louise Cowell.

She is named for her mother. The 1940 census finds Eleanor Louise, age fifteen and in her second year of high school, living at home with her parents, Samuel Knecht Cowell and Eleanor Cowell, and sisters, Audrey, eleven, and Julia, five, on West Shawmont Avenue in the Philadelphia neighborhood of Roxborough. Her nickname in the yearbook is "Weezie"; her stated ambition, college, but there's no money for that.[1] Samuel's occupation is listed as "gardener" for a "private family . . . working on own account."[2] Since he reports no regular salary, his income is zero.

Sometime in late February 1946, Lloyd or Jack encounters Louise, introduced by a friend. She is now a clerk in an insurance company, delicate, pretty, president of her church youth group. The circumstances of her seduction will remain purposefully vague. Is it a date? Drinks in a bar? Willing tryst or forcible deflowering? A knife in the alley, a hand over her mouth?

We have pins for our crazy wall: There is a Lloyd Marshall in Philadelphia, a sailor who served in the U.S. Navy from 1943 to 1946. He was demobilized on January 16, 1946, and lives three and a half miles from Louise Cowell. Another pin: Less than ten miles away is a John Worthington, an Army veteran released in September 1945. Two men. Years later, as journalists struggle to identify the father of Louise's child, these names are supplied to different parties on different occasions.[3]

Who is he really? Maybe she doesn't know. Whoever the father is, he takes her to a doctor, who gives her pills to make the baby fade away, but they don't work.[4] In September 1946, accompanied by a local minister's wife, she is conveyed north, seven months pregnant, to the Elizabeth Lund Home for Unwed Mothers in Burlington, Vermont, known to locals as "Lizzie Lund's Home for Naughty Ladies."[5] The unmarried Louise is, if not held captive, then self-confined for two months under conditions of societal reproach that Hester Prynne might recognize. Although her furtive removal has none of the open shame of the public stocks, it must feel, nonetheless, like punishment.

Let us assume the form of sad angels hovering in the chilly air of the Lund ward, looking down upon the consequence of Louise's tryst, following the long, trying hours of parturition on November 24, 1946. Perhaps she is sedated in the obstetrical fashion of the time, the nuns turning away, disapproving. Friendless, she bears the infant alone. He is a boy, full term, seven pounds and nine ounces, apparently normal. Legitimate? asks the birth certificate. No. Father? Unknown. She names him Theodore Robert Cowell.[6]

Then she leaves him, like a package at the train station, like lost luggage. Louise returns home. The baby remains at Lizzie Lund's for one month, two months, three. In the ward, babies are lined up in matching bassinets against a wall, fruits of the womb, observed by nuns who have taken vows of chastity, who have elected not to be mothers, who have chosen to upbraid those who have. Does he scream? Does he cry? Does anyone respond?

His mother does not. She does not return until three months after the birth, retrieving her son and once again returning to her parents' home. The story is given out, to neighbors, friends, and distant family, that her parents, Samuel and Eleanor, then forty-eight and forty-nine years old, respectively, have somehow adopted or acquired another child. There they live, Louise and baby Teddy and her parents and younger sisters, at 7202 Ridge Avenue, a mile from their former Shawmont residence. Within the family, according to Louise's sisters, the circumstances of the infant's arrival and the identity of his father are never discussed.

With men returning from war, Philadelphia has a housing shortage, and homes like the Cowells' are packed to the rafters with multiple generations. Throughout the war, the city's productivity has peaked, with steel mills running night and day, supplying shipyards and keeping destroyers, torpedoes, and antiaircraft guns rolling off assembly lines. Even after the war is over, the frenzy does not stop, not in Philadelphia. In the aftermath, the city becomes the "Workshop of the World," churning out metals, paints, soaps, batteries, bathtub enamel, ball bearings, railroad cars, tanks, and toys. The city is full of smelters.

What is a smelter? It is a commercial volcano, melting rocks for metal.

THE SMELTER

It is the Götterdämmerung. If you are one of those people who think rock is a solid, think again: it burns.

When Teddy comes home from Lizzie Lund's, Philadelphia boasts thirty-six lead smelters, more than any other American city.[7] Along the rivers, in crowded residential neighborhoods, furnaces burn raw ore until it flows, and their smokestacks pour the leftovers of that combustion into the air for all to breathe: tons of ultrafine particles that float and fall out and settle on the roofs and sidewalks, in the backyards and on the brick stoops and windowsills of the city. These clouds are poison, and their benign white visage cloaks the ghostly forms and features of uglier phantoms. Cadmium, mercury, and arsenic. Benzene, naphthalene, anthracene. Cyanide. Burned in the hellfire of private enterprise, set free on an unsuspecting world, they will have their revenge. The melting point of lead is 328 degrees Celsius—622.4 Fahrenheit. The closest smelter to the Cowell house is less than four miles away.[8]

Samuel Cowell is said to have a short fuse and a hot temper.[9] One of his daughters recalls him pulling her out of bed one morning for oversleeping and nearly throwing her down the stairs. Louise eventually admits he beat her mother.[10] The postwar boom has not reached him, and among his siblings he is notably less successful. His father is an optometrist. One of his brothers is a civil engineer; another, a talented musician. But S. K. Cowell struggles to make money, selling potted roses and Holland bulbs from his home nursery, advertising in *The Philadelphia Inquirer*. His bulbs are "dug to live for you."[11] Deacon at a Methodist church, he is said to hate Black people and Catholics. He keeps pornography in the potting shed.

There are photos of the boy. He is two, a toddler smelling an iris in his grandfather's garden, a heavy cable sweater buttoned fiercely up to his neck. The next year he's three, wearing shorts, shirtless, at the beach in Ocean City, New Jersey, a slice of the 14th Street Pier lying along the horizon in the background. The family has ties to Ocean City; his mother's grandfather owns a house near the boardwalk.[12] Teddy leans back against her body as her long, dark blunt-cut hair flies in the wind, her mouth dusky with lipstick. She is smiling; he is squinting, his brows knit. There is strain around the eyes. Same day, same beach: the boy and his grandfather stare down at the sand together as if transfixed, heads inclined toward each other in a strangely intimate moment. Samuel is slight, his arms ropy with muscle. The two could be father and son.

On October 6, 1950, when the boy is three, Louise goes to a Philadelphia courthouse to legally change her son's name to Theodore Robert Nelson.[13] She will call herself Louise Nelson, but there is no Nelson. She is effacing illegitimacy, erasing documentary evidence of sins past, and preparing to transport her son several thousand miles across the country, where they will start anew, staying with her uncle, her father's younger brother, John Cowell, a professor of music at the College of Puget Sound. She has decided to move to Tacoma, Washington.

TACOMA IS FAMOUS for one thing: its smell. If Seattle is considered a remote backwater in the 1950s—and it is—then Tacoma, poor sister to the south, is even more remote, more philistine, beneath contempt. Tacoma is Seattle's industrial flunky, the also-ran, the perennial embarrassment. Its setting once bore the rich grandeur of the Northwest, framed by mountains, royal robes of evergreens trailing into the placid harbor of Commencement Bay. Before white men arrived, it was a natural oasis, but Tacoma's forefathers took that charm and threw it away with both hands. In 1873, having commissioned a design by Frederick Law Olmsted laying out the town in a series of curvilinear terraces beautified with seven parks, city planners reacted with "a bemused blend of boosterism and dismay."[14] During a recession, they rejected Olmsted's vision.

Instead, the town on Commencement Bay, considered one of the five best natural harbors in the world, chooses industry at every turn, buoyed by a brief boom associated with the building out of the Northern Pacific Railway, battening on the smoke and stench of wood pulp and paper mills, lumberyards, oil refineries, chemical plants, rendering plants, sewage tanks, and smelters.[15] Soon their waste and effluent and slag heaps are strewn beside the bay and across the Tacoma tidal flats like offal dropped from a raptor's nest. Fifty-three industrial plants are invited to squat there, in the center of the city, and the smell of decomposition and putrefaction and acidification, a stew of sulfur, chlorine, lye, and ammonia, suffuses the air. The staggering odor is called, as early as 1901, "the aroma of Tacoma."

IT TAKES TWO great American family fortunes to build a city of serial killers: the Rockefellers and the Guggenheims.

The Guggenheims revere the power of metal. They first see it in Philadelphia, the city of smelters. Arriving there after a long sea voyage in 1848, Meyer Guggenheim, son of Simon, is a twenty-year-old immigrant from the Lengnau ghetto of Aargau, a canton in northern Switzerland. He begins peddling products door-to-door from a horse-drawn cart, including lace, one of the family's specialties in the old country.

But lace will take you only so far. Soon one of Meyer's bestselling goods partakes of the darker arts: stove black, a popular polish that he mixes himself after hiring a chemist to analyze a competitor's formulation.[16] The chief ingredient of stove black, he learns, is black lead, another term for graphite, also known by a more ancient name, plumbago. Graphite occurs in metamorphic rocks and has long been used to form crucibles in which steel is heated and refined. Vikings used the crucible process to make swords. This is Meyer's induction into the art of alchemy, turning base metals into money.

He realizes that women don't like powdered stove polish: it turns their hands black. Cleaning up one day after mixing the product, he observes that a jellylike paste has formed in the bottom of a soapy basin in which he's washed his hands.[17] It doesn't smear. He tries mixing soap into it, producing a thick blend that can be extruded in convenient lengths through a secondhand sausage maker and wrapped in a paper package. Voilà! A new and improved polish.

He marries Babette (later known as Barbara) Meyers, the daughter of a family who made the long transatlantic voyage with him. Selling goods from their grocery store at 443 Green Lane, they settle in the neighborhood of Roxborough, a few miles from where the Cowells will later live.[18] There the Guggenheims have the first of eleven children, including seven sons who survive to adulthood: Isaac, Daniel, Maurice, Solomon, Benjamin, John Simon, and William.

Meyer adapts and expands his business. In a crucial discovery, he finds that instead of buying expensive imported black lead, he can snap up broken crucibles from steel mills and use the scrap to make his polish. As the family's wealth begins to accrue, Meyer invests in spices, railroads, and lace factories. In 1880, a business associate asks Meyer to stake him to a silver mine in the Rocky Mountains of Colorado near a town called Leadville, elevation 10,154 feet. It yields little at first. But later that year, Meyer receives a telegram: RICH STRIKE. FIFTEEN OUNCES SILVER. SIXTY PERCENT LEAD.[19] The Guggenheims are minted, and Meyer soon envisions acquiring many more mines, enough to make all of his sons millionaires.

But the family has competition. Even as Meyer and his son Daniel invest heavily in mining and smelting, they begin sparring with the Rockefellers to wrest control of the lion's share of American minerals. William Rockefeller Jr., John D.'s younger brother, and H. H. Rogers—the family's "trust builder," an expert in crafting monopolies in oil, steel, gas, railroads, and banking—have already founded in 1889 a conglomerate, the American Smelting and Refining Company, designed to acquire "ores, minerals, metals" and control the smelting and refining thereof.[20]

But the Guggenheims fight them for it and, in the way of Gilded Age oligarchs, the two families eventually divide the world between them. In Montana, Rogers and William Rockefeller carve out the Amalgamated Copper Company (later Anaconda), but the arrangement is unstable. By 1901 the Guggenheim brothers have acquired a controlling interest in American Smelting and Refining. In future decades it will be better known as ASARCO, a behemoth operating as a near monopoly, one of the most economically and politically powerful entities in the world, governing 90 percent of American lead production.

Soon the Guggenheims have their eye on Tacoma, where the Northern Pacific promises access to "by far the best money making country in America," with "farming and mineral wealth in great profusion for millions of people."[21] There, one Dennis Ryan, who has gotten his start in "mineral wealth" in Saint Paul, establishes in 1888 the Tacoma Milling and Smelting Company on the shores of Commencement Bay. The company processes ores from local mines: gold, silver, and copper, but mainly lead. In 1890, Ryan hires as manager William Ross Rust, who then buys the company and changes its name to Tacoma Smelting and Refining. He employs fifty men and establishes a company town around the smelter. With a certain stolid literalism, it's called the "Smelter District."

Rust wants a company town as a tool. Its police force will smother unions and prevent the growth of lawless camps full of saloons and vice that usually spring up around mines, mills, and smelters, swarming with malcontents. He doubtless has in mind the open warfare that has broken out in Colorado, where one union, the Western Federation of Miners, urges every member to get himself a rifle.

By 1898, the Bunker Hill Company, which owns lead and silver mines in Idaho's Coeur d'Alene Mountains, has acquired a stake in the Tacoma smelter. The two companies' fortunes become inextricably entwined. The Idaho ores are among the richest veins of metal in the world, but Bunker Hill's labor battles are legendary for their violence.

After a series of gruesome accidents left men mangled in explosions and rockfalls, Bunker Hill workers burned the homes of several Idaho businessmen. In 1899 the company, soon to be known as "Uncle Bunker," refused to raise miners' pay by fifty cents a day. In retaliation, union men hijacked a train, engaged mine security in a gun battle, and dynamited the ore concentrator at the mill, a facility worth a quarter of a million dollars, blowing it to smithereens. A few years later, Fred Bradley, longtime Bunker Hill president, poured milk on his morning cereal, only to register an odd smell, which turned out to be strychnine. Within a month, a bomb went off outside Bradley's front door, leaving one of his ears hanging by a thread of skin. He was deaf and blind for two months and bore lifelong scars all over his body.

In 1903, John D. Rockefeller decides to unload the Northwest gold and silver operations he owns, selling his Monte Cristo mines in the Cascade Mountains and the associated smelter in Everett, north of Seattle. The Guggenheims snatch up the smelting facility, then add to their collection in 1905 by purchasing Rust's Tacoma smelter for five and a half million in cash, asking Rust to stay on as manager. The Tacoma plant is expanding, signing a twenty-five-year smelting contract with Bunker Hill while also beginning to process vast amounts of raw copper ore shipped from Alaska.

In Alaska's icebound Wrangell–St. Elias Mountains, prospectors hacking through the wilderness have spotted a grass-green meadow growing at an improbable elevation. The meadow is not paradise. It is not the Elysian Fields. It is a malachite wall, evidence of a mountain made of copper. At its base, the Guggenheim brothers build the mill town of Kennecott, alongside a massive glacier. Thanks to the magic wall, they will become the "Kings of Copper," shipping ores south to Tacoma.

Rust chooses not to live in the Smelter District, next to the Tacoma plant's monstrously shambolic and ever-expanding compound, crowded with sprawling industrial structures. He will spare himself the sight of the eight-hundred-foot-long Fine Ore Bins building where ores are sorted in batches by chemical composition. He will spare himself the cacophony and choking squalor of a maze of furnaces, chutes, gangways, chimneys, railcars, and jury-rigged docks and piers, covering some sixty-seven acres. Year by year, this industrial maelstrom seethes with smoke and dust, dangerous dust full of arsenic and lead.

Bringing his wife, Helen, and four-year-old son, Arthur, with him when he moves to Tacoma permanently in 1905, Rust builds the grandest house in the city's Old Town, a colonial revival mansion on I Street featuring eighteen rooms, four baths, eight fireplaces, mahogany staircases, and a fireproof terra-cotta roof. Known as the "White House," it is a visible monument to the money in smelting.

THE SMELTER

That same year, to vent noxious exhaust, a massive new smokestack is erected, towering above the smelter's older, squat chimneys. The people of Tacoma are inordinately proud. The smokestack represents jobs, food on the table, and children's school fees. There are picture postcards of it, tall and statuesque. It soars 307 feet in the air, hailed as one of "the most wonderful engineering feats known to the world."[22]

In 1906, on the fringes of Tacoma (population 36,000), William Rust now proposes to incorporate the Smelter District as a separate entity. With the company promising to pay nearly 90 percent of town taxes and improve its struggling sewer and water systems, residents eagerly agree, recognizing what one newspaper calls "the broad public spirit that has always governed that corporation."[23] They vote to change the name of their town to Ruston in his honor.

In 1911, Rust's older son, Howard, dies suddenly at the age of twenty-five. He is said to have had a heart attack or to have collapsed on the portico of the White House. Alternatively, he is reported to have died in Hanford, Washington, on a dude ranch where he had hopes of restoring his "shattered" health.[24] Rumors suggest suicide. After his death, his distraught parents sell the house for a song and build a second Rust mansion of nine thousand square feet with copper gutters, stained-glass windows, a basement ballroom, and enough Carrara marble to line the Roman baths.[25] The second mansion has a curious feature. Inside the front entrance, the vestibule's sealed interior door is designed as an air lock, presumably to prevent the aroma of Tacoma from seeping into the house.[26]

Another son is lost in 1912. In the early hours of April 15, the RMS *Titanic* hits an iceberg in the North Atlantic, and all the riches of its wealthiest passengers cannot keep it afloat. Among them are John Jacob Astor and Isidor Straus, owner of Macy's department store. Also Benjamin Guggenheim, the fifth of Meyer's seven surviving sons and himself father to three daughters, including thirteen-year-old Marguerite, known to the family as Peggy.

Benjamin sleeps through the initial brush with the berg. Awakened by his valet, he dresses as the ship begins listing, and the two men escort the party's maid to a lifeboat, helping women and children climb into the too few crafts. Then they return to the stateroom and Benjamin casts off his casual sweater for evening wear, adding a rose to his buttonhole. Thus attired, he says, "We've dressed up in our best and are prepared to go down like gentlemen."[27] He is last seen on deck as the final boats are lowered to the sea. His body and those of his valet and chauffeur are never found.

When news breaks that the White Star Line has failed to supply the magnificent liner with enough lifeboats, Daniel Guggenheim, head of the family enterprises, reacts angrily. "I feel very bitter against such a state of conditions which made this disaster possible," he tells *The New York Times*. "What we want," Daniel says, "is safety, safety, safety!"[28]

But safety is not a watchword in Ruston. In 1912, the Tacoma smelter switches from lead to copper, but the funny thing is, copper ores are streaked with other metals, including lead and the infamously malign chemical element arsenic. Thus, smelting copper yields a lucrative by-product: inorganic arsenic, which can be put to use in insecticides and herbicides. Ores smelted in Tacoma will be rich in the stuff. Why not catch some of that dust blowing out the smokestack? Why not capture and sell this valuable toxin?

In the manner of Meyer and his thrifty stove black, the sons of Guggenheim allow nothing to go to waste. When they close Rockefeller's former Everett smelter in 1912, they move its "arsenic kitchen"—a series of special brick rooms designed for condensing poison vapor—to Tacoma.[29] Many immigrants from Scandinavia, the Balkans, and other European countries are working at the plant, which employs 525 men. The fair-complected among them find that their skin cannot tolerate it. "They would get bad dermatitis and . . . little boils," recalls one worker, adding that "there was just a real bad reaction."[30]

Arsenic has many uses. It saves fruit orchards and cotton crops from the insect's tooth. In time, chromated copper arsenate, a toxic crystalline salt, will be used to suffuse pressure-treated lumber to kill wood-boring insects and prevent rot. In the damp Northwest, prone to mildew and decay, this is the wood people will use to build docks, decks, swing sets, playgrounds, fences, doghouses, picnic tables, and retaining walls. They will use the treated timbers to create raised beds for vegetable gardens. The copper arsenate gives the wood a pleasant verdant hue, that of Vienna green—a similar substance is marketed as "Paris green."

In 1917, Bunker Hill builds its own lead smelter, the largest in the world, and as if in response, the Tacoma smokestack is replaced again, the new stack reaching the extraordinary height of 571 feet, built with paving bricks from Seattle's streets.[31] For a time, it is the tallest stack in the world and the highest industrial structure on the West Coast. The taller it is, engineers promise, the less it will pollute. "Sulphurous fumes" will blow away in the wind.[32] That the solution to pollution is dilution is a truth universally acknowledged.

TACOMA'S POISON FACTORY IS INTERESTING INDUSTRY, the Tacoma *News Tribune* notes approvingly in 1927.[33] It is indeed. So much is already known. In 1913, chemist Frederick Gardner Cottrell delivers a paper on "The Problem of Smelter Smoke" to the Commonwealth Club of San Francisco, in a city where the Selby Lead and Silver Smelting Works has been pumping lead into the air since the 1870s. Selby is soon to be acquired by American Smelting and Refining.

Cottrell lays it out clearly: "The problem of smelter smoke is entirely distinct from that of ordinary city smoke," he says, explaining that the constituent parts "cannot be simply 'burnt up.'" The chief offenders, he admits, are these:

> **Sulphur**—Chiefly as sulphur dioxide, a colorless, invisible gas, but to some extent, as sulphuric acid, a liquid.
>
> **Arsenic**—Usually as the oxide, a white solid.
>
> **Lead**—Usually as the sulphate, a white solid, of the sulphide, a black solid; but sometimes the oxide, a yellowish solid.
>
> **Zinc**—Chiefly as the oxide of sulphate, white solids.[34]

IN THE 1920S, Tacoma's poison factory becomes one of the largest producers of highly refined colorless, tasteless inorganic white arsenic,* shipping it all over the country. It is one of the most hazardous substances known to man. In contrast to organic arsenic, a largely harmless compound commonly found in seafood, less than an eighth of a teaspoon of the inorganic powder can be fatal to an adult.

In 1923, the United States produces more than fourteen thousand tons of white arsenic domestically, but demand is so high that it must import ten thousand additional tons. Farmers dust those twenty-four thousand tons onto crops that year, killing codling moths and protecting stone fruit in the great growing regions: California's Central Valley, Oregon's Hood River Valley, and throughout eastern Washington.[35] Apple, apricot, peach, pear, and cherry trees are treated with it.

Meanwhile, the Guggenheim family is fruitful and multiplies. Rose Guggenheim, one of three daughters of Meyer and Barbara, marries Albert Loeb, son of a banker; her sister Cora marries Louis F. Rothschild, Loeb's banking and brokerage partner. Rose and Albert's eldest son, Harold Loeb, born in 1891, works for the Selby smelter in San Francisco for a short time but throws it over to hobnob with the avant-garde in Paris. In 1921 he starts a little magazine, *Broom*, which lasts for a few years, until his uncles turn down his request to endow it with smelting money. He drinks in cafés with Ernest Hemingway, then a newspaperman from Chicago, and goes to bullfights in Spain. All he gets for his trouble is an anti-Semitic caricature in the form of the hapless Robert Cohn in *The Sun Also Rises*.

In 1929, Harry Frank Guggenheim, son of Daniel and grandson of Meyer, creates an eponymous foundation, one of many philanthropic organizations spun off from the extraordinary wealth accrued by the family. Harry's institute is dedicated to examining and solving the urgent problem of violence and aggression in human society.

---

* "White arsenic" is a common name for arsenic trioxide, the most prevalent commercial compound.

THE SMELTER

Meanwhile, demand for the Guggenheims' products increases. During the searing droughts of the Dust Bowl, arsenic is sprayed alongside railroad tracks to keep down weeds, and the workers of the Civilian Conservation Corps distribute arsenic baits to kill cutworms and other pests. In 1938, USDA scientists marvel over swarms of migratory grasshoppers traveling startling distances. One swarm flies from northeastern South Dakota to Saskatchewan, a distance of 575 miles.

Here is a recipe for a delicious pesticide as recommended by South Dakota State University entomologists as part of the 1930s "War on Hoppers":

> 100 pounds wheat bran; 5 to 6 pounds white arsenic, or 4 pounds paris green; 1 or 1½ gallons cheap feeding molasses; 12 gallons water.
>
> Mix the white arsenic and wheat bran dry, spreading the bran out on a tight wagon box or floor and shaking the arsenic over it through a sieve, shoveling the bran over until thoroughly mixed. Dissolve the molasses in the water and add slowly to the poisoned bran while shoveling the bran or shaking it through a scoop fork. The mash should be as wet as possible without becoming sloppy.
>
> This bait can be mixed at home.[36]

Sure it can. Cook it up in the arsenic kitchen. The recipe, which recommends preserving the sweet bait in a "moist, succulent condition" to maintain its appeal to insects, is published in newspapers, including *The Daily Plainsman* in Huron, South Dakota.[37] It's commonly advised to add some lead arsenate, a leaded insecticide, to the Paris green.[38]

On January 31, 1939, a hundred miles north of Huron, not far from the town of Aberdeen, where the tornadoes of L. Frank Baum's *The Wonderful Wizard of Oz* roam, Mrs. Henry Brudos gives birth to her second son, Jerome, called Jerry. Jerry's father is an angry little man, five feet four, who is trying and failing to support his family on a South Dakota farm during this time of drought and grasshopper infestations. Decades later, farms to the north of his will form one of the largest Superfund sites in the Great Plains, the Arsenic Trioxide Site, covering twenty-six townships and 568 square miles, an area in which the poison has long since penetrated groundwater and seeped into wells. For years, it's not uncommon for South Dakota kids to uncover sacks of old grasshopper bait—arsenic or lead arsenate—in barns or old corncribs. Newspapers urge farmers to dispose of the stuff safely, lest it present a health hazard "to children, pets, and livestock."[39]

Little Jerry is "sickly."[40] He suffers from swollen glands, laryngitis, recurring sore throats, and fungal infections around his fingernails and toenails. He has migraines so severe they make him vomit and undergoes two operations to treat swelling in the veins of his legs. "Vague and slow," he fails the second grade.[41] Long-term exposure to the pesticide is associated with headaches, fungal infections, red and swollen skin, and sore throats.[42] Neurological effects, according to specialists, are "many and varied."[43]

Jerry also develops, as a young child, a strong and virtually irresistible attraction to women's high-heeled shoes. By his teens, having moved to the Pacific Northwest, he becomes known to local authorities for knocking women down on the street and stealing their footwear. How about a little arsenic, Scarecrow?

BY THE TIME the Depression rolls around, Tacoma is so steeped in violence that it has become a birthplace of noir. There, in 1920, a broken-down Pinkerton detective named Sam Hammett, exhausted by wrangling with union agitators in the mining towns of Montana and Idaho, is wiling away dull hours in a tubercular ward by reading the local newspapers, replete with vice and crime.

Later, using his middle name, Dashiell, Hammett begins his first novel with a description of a town he calls Poisonville:

> The city wasn't pretty.... The smelters whose brick stacks stuck up tall against a gloomy mountain to the south had yellow-smoked everything into uniform dinginess. The result was an ugly city of

forty thousand people. . . . Spread over this was a grimy sky that looked as if it had come out of the smelters' stacks.[44]

When he publishes his masterpiece, *The Maltese Falcon*, it contains a famous passage inspired by Tacoma.[45] The mysterious bird of the title, which costs so many lives, turns out to be fashioned not of jewels but of lead.

Dark doings—abductions, intrigues—fill the Tacoma papers. In 1921, Henry Arthur Rust, William Rust's twenty-year-old son, is picked up and held at gunpoint while walking to work. A bomb threat and ransom demand for $25,000 appears. But when Arthur is released unharmed, rumors fly that the whole thing was a plot contrived by the son to extort money from his father. The would-be kidnapper, Hugh Van Amburgh, whose father is a master mechanic at the Ruston smelter, knows Arthur and testifies to the hoax at his trial.[46] Conveniently for Arthur, however, Van Amburgh recants months later, pleading an overindulgence in "moonshine" and temporary insanity.[47]

The city gains national notoriety when nine-year-old George Weyerhaeuser, great-grandson of the timber dynasty's founder, is seized off the street on May 25, 1935, as he leaves school on his way to meet his sister. His parents receive a ransom letter demanding $200,000. Waiting for a response, the kidnappers stash the child, chained, in a hole they have dug near Issaquah, a small agricultural burg on the shores of Lake Sammamish surrounded by Cascade foothills—Tiger Mountain, Cougar Mountain—burying him alive.

Nervous that authorities may be closing in, they soon pull him out, driving him to Spokane and then back again. After they collect their money, they leave the boy standing on a logging road at midnight with a dollar and a blanket. After walking for miles, George finds a farmer's house and is restored to his family.

For George, it has a happier ending than the kidnapping that preceded it, that of the Lindbergh baby. But in turn it inspires another the following year. On the evening of December 27, 1936, a masked man begins pounding on the French doors of a Tudor mansion perched on the ridge overlooking Ruston and Commencement Bay, owned by a well-known and wealthy Tacoma physician.[48]

The children within are home alone, drinking root beer and eating popcorn in the living room: ten-year-old Charles Fletcher Mattson, his teenage siblings, and a friend. Terrified, they refuse to open the locked doors, but the intruder, armed with a revolver and described as "swarthy," breaks the glass, snatches Charles, and escapes, dashing down an embankment toward Ruston Way, along the edge of the harbor.[49]

J. Edgar Hoover sends forty agents to the scene, hoping to sort out a welter of confusing ransom notes demanding $28,000 in "old bills." But on January 11, 1937, a young man hunting rabbits south of Everett finds Charles's naked, battered body dumped in a thicket of alders, knifed in the back and beaten in the head with a blunt instrument.

National media coverage is so intense—the sense of outrage so unrelenting—that President Roosevelt issues a public statement the day after the discovery, announcing a $10,000 reward. "The murder of the little Mattson boy has shocked the nation," he says. "Every means at our command must be enlisted to capture and punish the perpetrator of this ghastly crime."[50] The kidnapper is never apprehended. The murder of Charles Mattson, a capital crime with no statute of limitations, remains an open case.

From here on, Tacoma cannot shake its reputation as the kidnapping capital of the West.

TIMES ARE HARD at the Ruston smelter, first unionized in 1914 and reorganized in the 1930s as Smeltermen's Local 25.[51] In 1937, a small earthquake knocks ten feet of bricks off the top of the smokestack. The following year, seventeen-year-old Joe Percich, son of Balkan immigrants, starts working at the plant.[52] His father has been laboring there since 1910. Young Joe is bullish on the company, saying, "I worked different places . . . but this place, they furnished you your shoes, your socks, everything, even your gloves. Everyday you got clean clothes. You got a bath every night."[53]

But the attire is merely the company's way of making more money. Clothes worn by workers in the arsenic plant and slimes house—where precious metals are skimmed out of the copper—are collected and burned in furnaces to strip them of every last ounce. On a sunny day, one worker says, you can see flakes of gold and silver floating through the air.[54]

Other workers are terrified by the conditions. Art Burgoyne begins as a temporary worker the same year as young Joe Percich and stays only five years, after working the most brutal jobs. He sees a co-worker lose an eye from a flying piece of hot slag and another man die after falling into a chemical tank. Art is a slight man, weighing 145 pounds, and a supervisor tells him that if he can't do the work, he's out, and they'll "hire the men standing outside the gate."[55]

Art hates the work, especially unloading boats full of dirty ore, the rocks full of minerals. It's a job rightfully belonging to the longshoremen who deliver it, but they refuse because it's "too nasty." It involves heaving sacks of graphite (now known to cause lung disease, silicosis, and cancer) off barges, a process so filthy and arduous that it makes Art feel as if he has been consigned to hard labor in hell, saying, "When I would put in eight hours a night dumping those sacks of ore, I thought I was made out of lead, I was so heavy inside. I'd spit up that black stuff for days on end."[56] He'd wash himself with soap and water over and over, he'll recall, and it still wouldn't come off.

As protection, workers are supplied with rags "made up like Kotex" to keep from breathing the dust. "They expected you to put that over your mouth," Art recalls. Other terrible jobs include transporting "blisters" of copper, weighing around a thousand pounds, and handling arsenic, which burns men's faces and hands. For that, he says, they had to wear special suits. "You'd work about ten minutes," he says, "and if you got a sweat up you'd have to stop, because the arsenic would get under your skin. . . . It burned into your inner skin. The outer skin would just peel off."[57]

At close of business on December 31, 1941, the American Smelting and

Refining Company is worth $185,452,053 ($3.9 billion in today's dollars). In 1943, Art quits and joins the Army.

THE GUGGENHEIMS HAVE an interesting war. They've already expanded into South America—Peru, Chile, Bolivia—building roads and mines, shipping the concentrated ores to Tacoma. There are rumors that they've dumped hundreds of ingots of copper in Commencement Bay to thwart FDR's wartime price controls.[58]

The family has bought its way into culture: Solomon, fourth son of Meyer, acquires old masters and modernists at the behest of a mistress, seeding a collection that will eventually fill a museum. Simon, sixth son and longtime president of ASARCO, establishes the John Simon Guggenheim Memorial Foundation in 1925 to memorialize his youngest son, dead at eighteen.

In Paris in August 1939, Peggy, daughter of the ill-fated Benjamin, with her 1919 inheritance of $450,000 (equivalent to more than $8 million today) opens a gallery for modern art in London, called Guggenheim Jeune.[59]

Undeterred by the coming war, she is determined to stay in Paris. She's buying a painting a day but is forced to interrupt her ambitious program as the Germans approach. During the lull of the "phony war," she resumes, acquiring forty works by Max Ernst, ten Picassos, eight Mirós, four Magrittes, three Man Rays, three Dalís, a Klee, and a Chagall.[60] When the Louvre declines to protect them, she spirits them out to New York two days before the Germans enter Paris. There she opens a new gallery, spinning lead into gold.

YEAR AFTER YEAR, lead is flying out of the smokestack. What is lead? It is a poison, second in toxicity only to arsenic. It is a chemical element bearing the atomic number 82 and the symbol Pb, from the Latin *plumbum*. In its solid phase, it is a shiny gunmetal gray, excruciatingly heavy. It burns with a white flame. It's resistant to corrosion. It never disappears. It enters the world in many ways, including but not limited to "oil-processing activities, agrochemicals, paint, smelting, mining, refining, informal recycling of lead, cosmetics, peeling window and door frames, jewelry, toys, ceramics, pottery, plumbing materials and alloys, water from old pipes, vinyl mini-blinds, stained glass, lead-glazed dishes, firearms with lead bullets, batteries, radiators for cars and trucks, and some colors of ink."[61] Lead is a vampire. Invite it in and it will drink your blood and live forever.

It tastes sweet. Chemically, it resembles calcium and is taken up rapidly in the bodies of children as their bones are forming. In ancient Rome, where winemakers boiled their grapes in great vats lined with lead for added sweetness, the diets of Nero and Caligula were rich in lead.[62] In Tacoma, decade after decade, it rises out of the smokestack, dust drifting and settling where it may—north, south, east, and west. The unwitting populace breathes it, eats it, drinks it, and becomes it.

As far as smelters go, Louise and her son Ted Nelson are now out of the frying pan and into the fire. When they arrive in Tacoma, they stay with her uncle John Cowell, three years her elder. John and Louise lived and played together as children. John is the social climber of the Cowell family. During World War II, he was seriously injured in a stateside training accident, preventing him from serving overseas. He recovered in time to earn bachelor's and master's degrees in music at Yale, marry an heiress, and encounter such musical stars as Leonard Bernstein and Paul Hindemith. In 1948, he accepted a position he felt was beneath him, at the School of Music of the College of Puget Sound, in Tacoma. In his memoir he'll write:

> The Seattle-Tacoma region was admittedly in the "minor leagues" musically, compared with the New York orbit we were so at home in. But it came to allow me to develop naturally as a composer and performer with freedom from the anxieties of the "big time" New York pressures.[63]

That tinge of self-satisfaction, pride in a former "New York orbit," will thoroughly impress young Teddy, and his status as poor relation will be impressed upon him by his cousin, the Cowells' young son, John, six months Ted's elder. The Cowells live at 1514 North Alder Street in Tacoma, a modest two-story frame house just across the street from the college campus.

Louise and Ted eventually move to a place in Browns Point, a nub of land on the far side of Commencement Bay, directly across from Ruston and the smelter. He is four, he is five, and the smokestack is filling the air with redolent particulates while he hunts for frogs in the local swamps. "I was somewhat of a champion frog catcher," he'll later say. "I was a frog man. Prided myself on my ability to spot that pair of bulging eyes, which would bob just above the surface of a murky pond."[64]

WHILE TEDDY IS MARINATING in Browns Point, Louise finds an office job as a secretary and dips her toe in the dating pool, attending a First Methodist Church social. There she meets another displaced soul struggling to make his way in the city, Johnnie Culpepper Bundy, an orphan from a backwoods North Carolina farm, one of a family of ten. Before Johnnie was a teen, his mother died and his father followed, drowning himself in the Pasquotank River in 1934, at the age of forty-eight. In the 1940s, Johnnie did what dirt-poor orphans from North Carolina usually did: he joined the Navy. After the war, he washed up out west, adrift in the turbid waters of Tacoma. Johnnie met Louise in 1951 and fastened upon her like a limpet. They married within months, on May 19, 1951, and Teddy stuck his hand in the wedding cake.[65]

Teddy doesn't like his new stepfather, who has a dorky Nash Rambler, a clown car, and works as a cook at the Fort Lewis military hospital south of town. Nonetheless, Johnnie adopts the boy, who, in his third larval stage, morphs into Ted Bundy. Teddy notes that Johnnie is passive, with little to say, deferring to Louise. Teddy prefers his uncle John, who drives foreign cars. He wants to be adopted by John Cowell and leave his mother behind; he wants to live with Roy Rogers and have his own pony; he wears a cowboy hat and a sweater appliquéd with bucking broncos, every button buttoned.

THE SMELTER

In 1953, Teddy's seventh year of life, six hundred and thirty tons of arsenic and a couple hundred tons of lead pour out of the Ruston stack.[66] No one knows it yet, but that's more airborne arsenic than anywhere else in the country. It's one of the largest sources of arsenic emissions in the world.[67]

That same year, the Bundys move to the Skyline neighborhood, all of them packed into a tiny cracker box of a house beside State Highway 16, which feeds traffic onto the Tacoma Narrows Bridge. The bridge has been rebuilt and painted with lead-based paint.[68]

Over the coming years, Louise has first one child, then another and another. Displaced by Bundy babies, Teddy joins the Boy Scouts and bicycles all over Tacoma, skimming through back alleys like a common tern, hovering outside windows, picking through garbage. He gets teased because of a mild speech impediment. At Scout camp, he can't get the hang of what the other kids are doing, can't tie the knots right, can't shoot the gun straight, and can't win the races. He gets angry and likes to scare people.[69] His elementary teachers note "boisterous" and "immature" behavior.[70]

He is ten, he is eleven. He has a paper route and a pocketknife and slashes the seats of an expensive convertible. He hits a fellow Scout over the head with a stick from behind. He is found undressed in a tent with a Scoutmaster. He runs up behind girls and pulls their pants down and likes to build "tiger traps" in the woods with his friends—pits covered with vegetation that hide sharpened sticks poking up from the bottom.[71] He never lives farther than five miles from the smokestack.[72]

Skyline is a new development. The city's population is burgeoning as tens of thousands of postwar hopefuls are drawn by jobs in the railyards, mills, and smelters. As old-growth forest is clear-cut, Skyline is bulldozed out of the "cut-over stump land," as the smelter manager puts it, and carved into minuscule lots.[73]

The manager tries to convince the city fathers not to turn Skyline into a human warren. The proposed suburban development, he warns, is just a few miles southwest of the Ruston smelter. It lies, he says, "in the heart of our smoke stream" and is "our area of greatest fumigation."[74] He knows that people will complain about the smell, for starters.

And they do. But it's not just the smell. For decades, nothing grows reliably, not trees, not the Douglas firs that spring up everywhere else like grass, not shrubs, not roses, not lawns. Gardens fail; crops die; bees die. Strange spots appear on the laundry hung to dry on the line. Small farmers sue. Every few years, the smelter "blows out" the smokestack, an expectorant form of industrial housecleaning, causing "arsenic showers."[75] When the smelter coughs, white ash falls all across town, snow made of lead and arsenic. Cats and dogs walk in it and try to lick it off their paws and collapse and die. It is known that smelter officials will pay a few dollars to replace them. Children have trouble breathing. They develop coughs and rashes and asthma. These are the diseases that can be seen.

The diseases that cannot be seen are different. These diseases constitute a category called the "late effects of lead poisoning on mental development," caused by infants chewing little flakes of lead paint off walls or the slats of their cribs or inhaling invisible particles out of the air or off windowsills or the steps to their homes. The late effects include "cruel, unreliable, impulsive behavior" and "extreme unpredictability" and have been documented since at least the 1920s,[76] when a physician wrote, with alarm, that children were living "in a lead world."[77] There's lead in the air, in soil, in paint, in pipes, in water, toys, food, and milk, but there are no federal standards governing lead levels in products, in the environment, or in the blood or bones of children.

The late effects of lead poisoning on children's moods and behavior stem from "gross evidence of cerebral damage."[78] These children act out. They are said to be "crazy-like."[79] They are irritable, nervous, inattentive, slow to learn. They have short attention spans. Sometimes they scream and bang their heads. Sometimes they set fires. Sometimes they wet the bed. They have dreams "bordering on hallucinations."[80] One boy, at six, sticks a fork into another boy's face, steals pencils and pens, and sets his apartment on fire twice.[81]

Lead can be seen in X-rays—deposited on the margins of children's long bones, or in opaque flakes of paint in their intestines, or in a blue-tinged "lead line" in their gums. Lead can be measured in human blood in

THE SMELTER

micrograms per deciliter. (A deciliter is a little less than half a cup.) In a child, blood lead levels of 125 micrograms per deciliter can cause acute swelling of the brain (encephalopathy) and death; over 80, kidney failure; over 60, stomach spasms; over 20, anemia and neuropathy.[82] Levels around 10 may be responsible for the loss of nine or ten IQ points.* There is no safe level of lead in the body, especially for children.

Industry and its spokesmen are quick to blame poor parenting for kids who eat paint, but it's not that simple. A major culprit emerges: leaded gas.

IN THE EARLY 1920S the fuel additive tetraethyl lead (TEL) is developed and marketed by General Motors and Standard Oil. It is designed to make automobile and airplane engines run without knocking. GM knows that an ideal antiknock solution already exists in ethyl alcohol, or ethanol. But virtually any hillbilly with a still can make ethanol from fermented fruit or corn.[83] No profits stand to be made from it. TEL, on the other hand, can be patented.

So tetraethyl lead is rebranded as "Ethyl," which sounds friendly, like a woman's name. Sales to the public begin on February 1, 1923, but the advertisements don't mention lead. On October 23, 1924, a Thursday, a man working at a Standard Oil TEL-refining plant in Elizabeth, New Jersey, is seeing things that aren't there. On Friday he begins screaming and running around the plant to escape imaginary pursuers. On Saturday he dies. Four others follow. Thirty-one workers are hospitalized with hallucinations and convulsions. The violent are placed in straitjackets.[84] Their symptoms are the result of acute lead poisoning, or saturnism.

At around the same time, hundreds of men begin hallucinating butterflies at a DuPont plant manufacturing TEL in Deepwater, New Jersey, swiping their hands through the air, trying to push winged insects away from their faces. But it isn't butterflies that are bothering them. It's lead. The hallucinations terminate in "violent insanity and death," according to

---

* As of 2024, the CDC has set the blood lead level of concern for children at 3.5 micrograms per deciliter.

The New York Times. Eight die. Three hundred fall ill. Some become permanently vacant.[85]

The fuel additive is the work of GM's mechanical engineer Thomas Midgley Jr., who invents not only leaded gasoline but chlorofluorocarbons, which will come to be regarded as two of the most harmful chemical compounds ever produced during the industrial age. Chlorofluorocarbons will destroy the atmosphere. Leaded gasoline will drive everyone mad, slowly, filling children's teeth with lead. Sometimes bad things are engineered by engineers.

Lead poisoning at refineries is one thing, but what about the chronic, day-by-day, breath-by-breath exposure caused by leaded gasoline? And smelter smoke? What about the need to breathe? American physicians raise concerns that lead particulates will blanket the nation's roads and highways, poisoning neighborhoods slowly and "insidiously." They call it "the greatest single question in the field of public health that has ever faced the American public."[86] Their concerns are swept aside, however, and Frank Howard, a vice president of the Ethyl Corporation, a joint venture between General Motors and Standard Oil, calls leaded gasoline a "gift of God."[87]

On October 30, 1924, untroubled by the hallucinations, convulsions, and straitjackets, Midgley, himself an Ethyl vice president, holds a press conference in the Chrysler Building in New York, and raises a tin of what he claims to be TEL in front of assembled journalists. He inhales deeply of the fumes and then, like Lady Macbeth, washes his hands in it, saying, "I'm not taking any chance whatever."[88] He has, in fact, begun wearing gloves religiously in his lab work. He knows that lead is absorbed through the skin. This has already happened to him: the year before, he was forced to take a long vacation in Miami to "cure" himself of lead poisoning.

In 1940, Midgley becomes paralyzed by what is said to be polio and contrives a Rube Goldberg device of pulleys and ropes to lift himself out of bed. In 1944 he strangles himself with his ropes, accidentally or on purpose.[89] The American Chemical Society bestows upon him the Priestley Medal, its highest award, because his achievements are lasting.

THE SMELTER

LEADED GAS FUMES drift through the Skyline neighborhood of Tacoma, where the Bundy family is perched right beside Highway 16, the busy roadway yards from their home, but it's nothing compared with the fumes and particulates from the Ruston smokestack.[90] Much of Tacoma, with a population approaching 150,000, will record high lead levels in neighborhood soils, but the Bundy family lives near a string of astonishingly high measurements of 280, 340, and 620 parts per million.[91] Lead occurs naturally in soil at trace levels of no more than fifteen to forty parts per million.*

In June 1961, Charlie Manson, a pimp, a thief, a violator of the Mann Act (transporting prostitutes across state lines), and a disciple of Dale Carnegie, is transferred to the federal penitentiary on McNeil Island, across from South Tacoma in the nether reaches of Puget Sound. Born to a fifteen-year-old girl, he spent his first years in a mining town in West Virginia, a product of broken homes, reform schools, and institutions. He never knew his father. Now twenty-six, he spends his days at McNeil sitting in a five-tier cellblock listening to the radio and studying Scientology and learning to play the guitar and writing songs and breathing the air from the Ruston smokestack.[92]

McNeil Island is proudly self-sustaining. Prisoners drink water from a well, grow crops, and tend a dairy herd, producing most of the food they eat. During his five years on the island, virtually everything Manson eats and drinks comes out of the earth, where particulates from the Ruston plume have been drifting down to the ground since 1890. He'll live on McNeil Island longer than he's lived in any place in his life. Later studies on McNeil find lead in soil ranging from a low of 19 parts per million (ppm) to a high of 190.[93] Helter smelter.

A few miles north of Tacoma, young Gary Ridgway is also growing up in the plume. Before settling there, his itinerant family moved all over the

---

* In 2024, the EPA lowered its level of concern for lead in soil at residential properties from 400 ppm to 200 ppm but prefers to use 100 ppm as a level of concern at properties with multiple sources of lead exposure from leaded paint and industry.

Intermountain West, and his older brother fondly recalls playing with Gary "in the slag pile from a copper mine" in Idaho.[94] The Ridgways live two miles east of the Seattle-Tacoma International Airport (SeaTac). That area, in addition to the Ruston plume, suffers powerful secondary exposures, trapped as it is between two of the most heavily traveled north–south routes in the region: Pacific Highway South (old Highway 99) and Interstate 5. The prevailing wind blows inland from the west, sweeping highway and jet fuel fumes across the neighborhood. Airplanes are flying on leaded gas. There is no lead limit for aircraft, but most mixes contain around 3 grams of lead per gallon, higher than the 1.10 grams in gasoline sold for cars and trucks.[95]

In 1960, annual lead emissions from the Tacoma smokestack are estimated at 226 tons.[96] In the summer of 1961, Gary is twelve and wets the bed. He is said to be "slow" and is held back a grade. "I wasn't learning good enough," he'll later say.[97] His mother, who has a habit of going about scantily clad and sunbathing nude in the backyard, scrubs his genitals to punish him for bed-wetting, and he finds himself beset by hallucinatory fantasies, simultaneously dreaming of having sex with his mother and of slitting her throat with a kitchen knife. His father drives buses but works part-time in a mortuary and relishes telling his family about a co-worker who has sex with corpses.[98]

On August 31, 1961, the number one hit song in America is "Wooden Heart," a song recorded the previous year by Elvis Presley, adapted from a German folk song. It has a pronounced oompah rhythm, accompanied by accordion. Elvis sings some of it in the original German, some in English, begging his lover to treat him good, because "I'm not made of wood / And I don't have a wooden heart."[99] For Pinocchio, for any puppet yearning to be a real boy, it is the perfect anthem.

In the heart of our smoke stream, Teddy is the boy with a wooden heart, a leaden heart, who goes out before dawn, working his paper route on his bicycle, escaping the house where his mother is heavily pregnant with the fourth Bundy baby.[100] He rides and rides and ends up at the Burr house, just around the corner from where his uncle John once lived. He has lately been prone to violent daydreams and night visions of an extreme sexual nature, fantasies and nocturnal emissions, strangulation married to ejaculation.[101]

He has seen exciting things in the true-crime detective magazines at the drugstore, in the pornography in other people's trash, and perhaps in his grandfather's potting shed, long ago. But seeing is not believing. He wants to act it out.

He is fourteen. He rides and rides in the dark night of August 31, peering into windows. The Burrs' living room window is cracked open to allow the TV antenna to snake outside. He drags a little bench over to the window and stands on it, pushing the sash up, leaving a footprint on the bench and another in a flower bed beside the basement door, the imprint of a teenager's tennis shoe.[102]

The Burrs live on North 14th Street. Next door to the Burrs' Tudor bungalow is old Mrs. Gustafson's orchard, a maze of apple trees and raspberry bushes frequented by neighborhood children. That summer, the street is upended by sewer construction: down the block yawn thirty-foot-deep trenches full of mud and rainwater.[103]

The Burr family is troubled that night. Eight-year-old Ann is sharing a bedroom with three-year-old Mary, who has a cast on her arm after falling off a playground slide. Mary keeps waking up because it is warm and humid. Half an inch of rain has fallen. For the past few nights, Ann's parents have thought they heard someone prowling in the yard. In the middle of the night, Mary starts crying: the skin under her cast is itching. Ann takes Mary to their mother, Bev. Bev shushes them and sends them back to bed. Their cocker spaniel, Barney, barks and barks, but Bev thinks that it's the wind and the rain.

It's not the wind and the rain. It's more than likely Ted Bundy, the paperboy, leaning in the living room window, asking Ann to open the front door, offering a combination of whispered persuasion or temptation or promises or threats that will never be known. Ann idolizes teenage boys and has a crush on one, calling him "lover boy."[104] She's pals with a girl named Sandi Holt. Sandi's older brother, Doug, is Ted's best friend.[105]

She leaves the door ajar as she goes, and her mother will find it standing open in the morning. Ted leads her into Mrs. Gustafson's orchard and, although no one will ever confirm exactly what happens there, he may well rape her and strangle her and throw her body like a rag into a pool of water at the bottom of a construction trench.[106] Later he will deny it but admit that the summer he was fourteen, "something happened."[107] It was something "autoerotic," he will say, something that involved an eight-year-old girl.[108]

Oh, and one other thing. She's still down there.

Chapter 3

The Reversible Lane

———◇———

Then kill, kill, kill, kill, kill, kill!

—Shakespeare, *King Lear*

It is the best of times. The lake is achingly beautiful—the water a sparkling marine blue. The bridge, the lady of the lake, is an ornamental chain laid upon the surface, a string of lights at night. Mercer Island is incorporated, the population is twelve thousand, and *House & Garden* declares it a star of "upper-level suburbia" where "a vacation-like atmosphere predominates."[1] Everyone loves the place.

During this era, she rides the waves, our bridge, the innocent if deadly star of every summer's Seafair festival, when the Blue Angels, the flying aerobatic squadron of the U.S. Navy, skim overhead and hydroplanes race across the surface sounding like demented mosquitoes. Floating femme fatale, she presides over mayhem as if she were born for it, designed for it, engineered for it. In 1961, the bridge kills more people than Ted Bundy.

She is federally indispensable. With the stroke of a pen in the late 1950s, old Highway 10—the central east–west route crossing the state from Spokane, climbing the Cascades through Snoqualmie Pass and sledding down the mountains to hop across Mercer Island to Seattle—is transformed into Interstate 90, the final segment of what will be one of the longest transcontinental highways in the country. The name change is just the beginning, however; major construction is needed to modernize I-90, particularly on the island, where on- and off-ramps are too short for traffic to merge safely at highway speeds. After construction is completed, I-90 is meant to join Interstate 5 at an interchange in Seattle, feeding onto the principal north–south highway of the West Coast, running from Canada to Mexico. These two highways are the state's arteries, pumping its economic lifeblood.

To accommodate rush hour traffic on the floating bridge and across the island, highway authorities add an additional feature at this time: the reversible lane. Signs are posted on on-ramps: DRIVE IN LANES WITH ↓ ONLY. During peak use, three lanes are dedicated to the most heavily traveled direction, a switch performed by means of lighted directional symbols mounted overhead: a green arrow or red X lights up above the reversible lane, which extends through the tunnels on the Seattle side all the way across the island to the east. On the floating bridge, however, where two lanes travel on either side of the bulge, one of the lanes confusingly diverts around the left side. The diversion causes a head-on collision in 1960 that leaves a Boeing flight engineer "invalided permanently," but no matter.[2] The reversible lane is instituted anyway, and the already impressive number of collisions on the bridge, in the tunnels, and on the island itself increases. People call it Suicide Lane.

On January 15, 1961, John E. Robinson causes a spectacular four-car pileup on the bridge, accidentally swerving into oncoming traffic, killing Thomas Simpson, a former policeman, and injuring himself, his daughter Linda, and seven other children in his vehicle.

My birth is sandwiched between bridge fatalities. On February 2, 1961, I am born on my father's birthday in Maynard Hospital in Seattle, which is named for Doc Maynard, an alcoholic justice of the peace, salmon packer, and doctor who arrived in Elliott Bay in 1852 in a canoe accompanied by Chief Seattle, leader of the Suquamish and Duwamish peoples. Shortly after appearing on the planet, I am driven home across the floating bridge in the first of what will be thousands of trips.

On April 18, 1961, thirty-one-year-old Robert Flanary is thrown from the passenger seat of a vehicle when it strikes the low curb around the bulge, and is somehow run over and killed by the same vehicle when it "climb[s] partly over the south guard rail of the bridge."³

The Northwest vogue for floating bridges continues: In August 1961, the Hood Canal Bridge opens, traversing a fjord in Puget Sound. It's the world's longest bridge crossing a tidal basin. That year, construction begins on a second floating span across Lake Washington, the Evergreen Point Floating Bridge. Designed to take pressure off the existing floating bridge, the Evergreen will serve burgeoning communities on the Eastside—Bellevue, Redmond, Issaquah. No one knows it yet, but there's a six-year-old growing up in Seattle whose company will transform the Eastside. His name is Bill Gates III, and he gets bullied a lot.

IN 1961, Jerry Brudos marries a seventeen-year-old in Corvallis, Oregon, asking her to do housework naked and in high heels. In the throes of his worst migraines, he begins to suffer from "blackouts."⁴

IN TACOMA, rumblings of dissatisfaction about air quality are beginning to be heard among the populace. ASARCO is unconcerned. There is as yet no Environmental Protection Agency, no Occupational Safety and Health Administration, and no federal standards governing workplace or industrial emissions of arsenic or lead. There's no consensus on how much airborne arsenic might harm a human being or how much lead might cause brain damage.*

For decades, virtually no oversight of such substances exists, and what does is piecemeal and ineffectual. In January 1941, the month that *Arsenic and Old Lace* (a black comedy about elderly spinsters who poison old men)

---

* In 2001, OSHA set the permissible workplace exposure limit for arsenic at no greater than ten micrograms of inorganic arsenic per cubic meter of air, averaged over an eight-hour period during a forty-hour workweek. There is no ambient air standard for arsenic set for the general public by the EPA, nor is there a standard set for arsenic in soil.

opens on Broadway, the U.S. Public Health Service blandly reports on the use of lead arsenate pesticides in Wenatchee, Washington, finding that orchard workers and their children bear high levels of lead and arsenic, but that there are no "adverse effects."[5] Lead arsenate pesticides, combining both chemical elements, continue to be used until the late 1940s, when DDT is invented. Not until 1958 does Congress pass an amendment prohibiting the FDA from approving food additives that cause cancer.

Nonetheless, throughout the 1950s physicians continue to treat afflicted children at the same time that smelters and leaded-gas lobbyists are insisting lead presents no health hazards. Making such claims is the industry's very own toxicologist, Robert A. Kehoe, a medical doctor who argues for decades that adults with blood lead levels measuring up to eighty micrograms per deciliter do just fine.* Moreover, he insists, lead at high levels in the environment and human bodies is "natural." Kehoe manufactures confusion over acceptable levels of lead for decades. He lies for General Motors, DuPont, the Ethyl Corporation, and the Lead Industries Association.

But then Clair Patterson comes along. He's a young geochemist who worked with uranium during the 1940s and on the development of the atomic bomb. After the war, he's set on determining the age of the earth by calculating how long it takes for uranium isotopes to decay into atoms of lead. In the process of working out these calculations, he realizes that his figures are corrupted by the fact that his laboratory as well as his own body are contaminated with the metal.

Studying lead levels in the oceans, polar ice, and atmosphere, he finds that high lead levels aren't "natural" at all but a by-product of industrial age pollution and leaded gas. At Caltech in the 1950s, he painstakingly creates a clean lab by ripping out lead pipes and eliminating every possible source of contamination, ultimately calculating that the earth is 4.5 billion years old, a billion and a half years older than everyone previously thought.

---

* Currently, a blood lead level of five micrograms per deciliter is considered elevated for an adult.

According to Patterson, the average American during the age of leaded gasoline is so filthy when it comes to lead contamination that he's comparable to Pig-Pen in the *Peanuts* comic strip. "That's what people look like with respect to lead," he says. "Everyone. The lead from your hair, when you walk into a superclean laboratory like mine, will contaminate the whole damn laboratory. Just from your hair."[6]

Not only that but Patterson calculates that the blood lead level of preindustrial humans would have been 0.016 micrograms per deciliter, far lower than that of anyone living in the industrial age. Americans, he concludes, are suffering from "enough partial brain dysfunction, that their lives are being adversely affected by loss of mental acuity and irrationality."[7] He devotes himself to campaigning against leaded gasoline and to proving that everything Robert Kehoe ever said or published about "normal levels" of lead in the blood is wrong.

Thanks to Kehoe, however, public confusion reigns throughout the 1960s as apprehension over pollution spikes. What's worse: lead, arsenic, insecticides, or sulfur dioxide?* Nobody seems to know. In 1960, for the first time the CDC issues an opinion suggesting that for children a blood lead level of sixty micrograms per deciliter might be a concern.[8]

In December 1961, Skyline resident Judy Alsos delivers a petition from the Citizens' Committee on Air Pollution, which has been trying for years to establish a dialogue with the Tacoma smelter. Judy is a mother whose son has trouble breathing and whose neighbor had three puppies that died after "arsenic showers" fell from the sky.[9] Amid a crowd of protesters singing and waving placards, she brings the letter to Governor Albert Rosellini at the Washington State Capitol. Signed by thirteen hundred people who live near the smelter, the petition demands that the state begin funding and staffing an air pollution program.

State health officials are finding it hard to determine the extent of re-

---

* Sulfur dioxide, a gaseous air pollutant composed of sulfur and oxygen, is a product of burning sulfur-containing fuels (oil, coal, diesel). The pollutant is notably high surrounding smelters and coal-fired power plants, and long-term exposure to emissions may have harmful effects on lungs, including respiratory distress, asthma, and lung cancer.

spiratory or other problems caused by the smelter, because, according to the director of the state health department, ASARCO has been "rather secretive" about the results of its own research.[10] The plant has placed seven sulfur dioxide monitoring stations around the city, but whatever it knows, it's not telling. It may not take a weatherman to say which way the wind blows, but the Ruston plant has two meteorologists on staff to study the entrails of the forecast and decide which children to poison on any given day.

To address these concerns, the smelter is recommending the construction of a "superstack," a smokestack that will top out at over a thousand feet.[11] Dr. Sherman Pinto, the physician at the Ruston plant, is establishing a reputation as one of the premier medical experts on arsenic in the world, publishing a 1963 study in the *Archives of Environmental Health* titled "Effect of Arsenic Trioxide Exposure on Mortality." The study examines the cause of death of 229 smelter workers, as reported by attending physicians, and concludes that the workers died of causes unrelated to their work. There is no evidence, Dr. Pinto writes, "that chronic arsenic trioxide exposure of the amount described in this study is a cause of systemic cancer in humans."[12]

Coincidentally, Dr. Pinto's 1963 study is published during the same year that the earliest version of the Clean Air Act is passed. For the first time, the federal government is setting itself up to control air pollution, authorizing research into how to monitor and address pollutants.

Around the same time, an official at the Tacoma plant laments to a colleague about how homes continue to be built on what the company calls the "waste land" of Skyline and the West End. *If only we had bought the land*, the official says, virtually wringing his hands, *we might have avoided this backlash*. Regretfully, he muses that it may not be possible to continue pumping arsenic into the air "for a great many more years."[13]

In the meantime, lead and arsenic are drifting across a remarkably wide area, reaching not only Seattle but as far north as British Columbia. Arsenic is found in sediments in Lake Washington.[14]

THE REVERSIBLE LANE

TIME IS FLYING. In 1963, I am two. With both hands I drink Darigold milk, delivered to our house in thick glass bottles topped with frilly paper caps. The Cascades' "Rhythm of the Rain" reaches number 3 on the *Billboard* Hot 100, and I stand before the mesh panel of my parents' hi-fi, ear against the speaker, carried away by the rain falling outside and the rain falling inside in the song.

It is February 13, 1963, and Hans Forster, general manager of Darigold Farms and survivor of an earlier head-on collision on the floating bridge in 1953, dies after a second crash, this one in the reversible lane on the island's East Channel Bridge to Bellevue.[15] Two weeks earlier, Forster removed the seat belts from his car, because the government can't tell him what to do.

The Evergreen Point Floating Bridge, crossing the northern part of Lake Washington from Seattle to the Eastside, is completed in 1963. It is more than 1.4 miles long, featuring thirty-three pontoons and fifty-eight anchors. It too has four lanes. East- and westbound traffic are separated, intermittently, by a small curb. As if in homage to established tradition, head-on collisions ensue. Within months, wave action at the north end of the lake is so violent that the pontoons and decking are beginning to crack. During storms, according to *The Seattle Times*, "bits of concrete" are "hurled like popcorn in a roaster."[16] Major modifications are in order.

The Evergreen bridge is soon awash in traffic, so the Highway Department revives the idea of building a third eight-lane floating bridge just north of the existing Mercer Island span.[17] There is talk of a fourth bridge, to be built to the south.

What's more, plans to improve the I-90 corridor crossing Mercer Island are becoming more complicated and expensive. The proposed solution to save island property values is a space-age "lid" featuring a park, tennis courts, and softball fields atop a section of the interstate's lanes, enclosed in a shallow tunnel. The price tag begins rising, from tens of millions to hundreds of millions of dollars.

THE AMERICAN SMELTING and Refining Company is like the little old lady who lives in a shoe and has so many smelters she doesn't know what to do. She has copper and zinc and asbestos mines and tailings and refining facilities and debris fields and cinder piles and slag heaps scattered all over the West and across the Great Plains: in Washington, California, Idaho, Montana, Utah, Nebraska, Colorado, Oklahoma, New Mexico, Texas, and Arizona. Many are conveniently located in and around major cities, including Tacoma, Everett, Omaha, San Francisco, Salt Lake City, and Amarillo. In the 1960s and '70s, copper smelters alone are pumping 1.4 million tons of sulfur oxides into the air of the western United States.[18] A group of molecules made of sulfur and oxygen atoms, sulfur oxides dissolve in water and are the main component of acid rain.

Seventeen hundred miles southeast of Tacoma, in El Paso, Texas, a boy named Ricardo Leyva Muñoz Ramirez is born on February 29, 1960, the youngest of five children of Julián and Mercedes Ramirez.

Mercedes, born in Colorado, is an American citizen, but Julián is a Mexican national and manual laborer who often works in construction, laying track for the Atchison, Topeka and Santa Fe Railway. His frustrations are many. His moods fluctuate from easygoing to violently angry. He has survived a childhood of hard labor on a farm, beaten routinely by his own father and grandfather. In turn, his family will suffer from his temper.

The children of Julián and Mercedes exhibit a bewildering variety of physical ailments. The eldest, Ruben, is born with "golfball-sized lumps" on the back of his head and neck and suffers such severe respiratory distress as an infant that he is administered last rites twice.[19] He rallies and survives.

Their second son, Joseph, cries piteously at six months. He is diagnosed with Köhler disease, a rare bone-growth disorder of the foot.[20] Over the years he will have fifteen operations to correct the curvature of his bones, eventually wearing special shoes that weigh four pounds each.[21]

Their third, Robert, appears healthy but at school is diagnosed with learning disabilities.

Their fourth child, Ruth, shares her father's disposition and becomes irrationally violent, at times breaking things and lashing out at people. "I'd just black out when I got mad," she'd say later. "There would . . . be an explosion inside of me, and I'd go off."[22]

Soon all the children have problems at school. When his eldest is sent home for stealing and doing drugs, Julián thrashes him with a water hose. He loses his temper even at himself. Once, to the consternation of everyone, he becomes frustrated trying to thread plumbing fittings underneath the kitchen sink and beats himself over the head with a hammer until blood runs down his face.

During these years, Mercedes is working at Tony Lama, the famous El Paso boot factory. She works seven hours a day, five days a week, standing at the back of the factory floor mixing pigments and chemicals, painting designs on distinctive Western cowboy boots and applying fixatives to the leather. The chemicals she works with contain benzene, toluene, and xylene, and there is no ventilation: no fans or suction or windows or masks. She often becomes dizzy, especially when she's pregnant.

During her last pregnancy, Mercedes becomes severely nauseated and faint at the boot factory and is forced to get injections to "retain the fetus."[23] Halfway through, she quits her job.

When Richie is born, the Ramirez family is living in El Paso's Segundo Barrio, the Second Ward.[24] It has been suggested to them by the town rumor mill that their children's difficulties may derive from the fallout of the Manhattan Project's Trinity test, the world's first detonation of a nuclear device, on July 16, 1945, 150 miles to the north in the Jornada del Muerto of New Mexico.

But the problem might lie closer to home, a home that is five miles downwind from the massive lead and copper smelter built in the Chihuahuan Desert on the Rio Grande, with a land grant signed over to the American Smelting and Refining Company by Mexican president Porfirio

Díaz on August 17, 1906.[25] The smelter sits virtually astride the border between the United States and Mexico and at the convergence of three states (Texas, New Mexico, and Chihuahua) and two cities, El Paso and Ciudad Juárez. Like Tacoma's, this plant dates back to the 1880s. It too boasts an enormous smokestack. Built in 1967, it's the tallest in the world at 828 feet, taller than the Woolworth Building in lower Manhattan, an early skyscraper—it's a stupendous landmark ringed in red and white stripes, visible for miles. This plant also hosts a company town nestled against the flank of the stack, called Smeltertown. Taking in raw ores from Arizona, it is burning rock to yield copper, lead, cadmium, zinc, and antimony.

Within a few years of Richie's birth, the Ramirez family buys a stucco house at 321 Ledo Street in El Paso's Lincoln Park, a neighborhood hard by the major interchange at Interstate 10 and near Catholic churches and the Concordia Cemetery, where the children play. This home too lies within the plume, with an additional light frosting of lead particulates from heavy highway traffic. Surface lead levels are somewhere between two hundred and six hundred ppm.[26]

At six, Richie falls off a swing and is unconscious for hours. At ten, he's suffering from petit mal seizures. He is diagnosed with epilepsy, but his parents are told that he will "grow out of it."[27] Sometimes he stares at the wall fixedly, without moving, for minutes at a time. Sometimes he falls to the floor, cursing and convulsing. Sometimes he sees monsters.

IT'S MAY 24, 1963, and a Kirkland movie projectionist who has threatened to quit his job because he hates driving in the reversible lane is killed in a head-on crash in the reversible lane.[28]

It's June 4, 1963, and two drivers approaching each other in the Mount Baker Tunnel collide head-on in the reversible lane but escape serious injury.[29]

It's December 20, 1963, and three are injured in a head-on collision in the reversible lane.[30]

It's 2:45 p.m. on February 5, 1964, and Mrs. Donna Doty, twenty, of

Issaquah, is driving her grandfather, Merton O. Smith, sixty-nine, of Mercer Island, across the East Channel Bridge when a car driven by Gerald Gjendem, twenty-nine, strikes a curb. Gjendem sideswipes an eastbound car and swerves directly into their path. After the collision, Mrs. Doty, mother of a thirteen-month-old son, and her grandfather are dead on arrival at Overlake Hospital. Gjendem, a boilermaker who has recently served a short sentence in the state reformatory for stealing a pickup truck, is badly hurt, with head and internal injuries, but survives.[31]

The following month, the State Highway Commission holds a meeting to discuss the reversible lane. After many near misses and collisions, drivers are pleading for it to be discontinued or its safety improved, writing to *The Seattle Times* to complain about the "semantic difficulty" presented by the signage. They ask that the reversible lane's X's and arrows be made to blink constantly while in use and that the speed limit on the floating bridge and its approaches be lowered.[32] In response, the committee recommends that the reversible lane remain in place, proposing that "all-white" safety vehicles patrol the bridge during rush hour to "make people more aware of their driving responsibilities."[33]

My mother is a confident driver, and we tool around happily on the island, stopping at her favorite stores, such as the one for witches: Bell, Book and Candle. It smells nice, and the door tinkles when it opens.

But anytime she drives over across the floating bridge, her hands tighten on the steering wheel when the tires emit a high-pitched whine as they fly over the steel mesh panel on the fixed decline. She hangs on like death in the slow right lane; she avoids the reversible lane. Her knuckles turn white as we steer around the bulge. This never changes.

Chapter 4

The Island

◆

> What is that sad, dark island?
>
> —Charles Baudelaire,
> "A Voyage to Cythera"

> What sort of place had I come to, and among what kind of people? What sort of grim adventure was it on which I had embarked?
>
> —Bram Stoker, *Dracula*

The island is a crime scene.

There are many islands in the Northwest, but this one is special. This one has quite the history. According to legend among the Duwamish, the lake swallows the island every night and spits it out again in the morning. At the highest point, an evil spirit is said to reside. Long ago, Native people would not stay past nightfall. During the day they picked salmonberries, gooseberries, thimbleberries, wild strawberries, and salal. They trapped weasels and dug wild potatoes. Then they left.[1]

They left because sometime in the past the lake swallowed the island, in whole or in part. This is true. Sunken forests lie offshore. More than a thousand years ago, Douglas fir trees slid off the south end, intact. There

THE ISLAND

they are still, a mummified forest underwater, standing upright. In sixty feet of water, their mineralized trunks reach toward the light.[2]

In 1953, twelve-year-old Brian Kirkpatrick pulls an arrowhead out of a pile of dirt in his backyard. It is two thousand years old. It breaks into pieces and is lost.

The island is made of blue clay, volcanic ash, and gravel predigested by nearby mountains. Its steep slopes and deep ravines are unstable, prone to landslides, riven by faults.[3] Earthquake activity is 276 percent higher than the national average. The OWL passes beneath its north shore.

On the morning of Thursday, April 29, 1965, at 8:28, Susie Warner's front yard begins jumping up and down.[4] We are four. We scarcely know what to do. When Susie's mother feels the house shaking, she herds us into the doorway while she prays aloud. Her name is Marvel.

The front yard is poised on a bluff, and Susie and I do not have a firm grasp on what is and is not normal. We do find it surprising that Marvel is praying out loud.

The earthquake is a natural disaster, a passing crime, a forty-five-second tantrum thrown by tectonic plates. Felt over 190,000 square miles, the magnitude 6.5 temblor breaks $28 million worth of buildings in Seattle, Tacoma, and Olympia, cities unaware of the seismic danger of an astonishing number of as-yet-unknown faults. It hurls down parapets, chimneys, and water towers. It kills seven. It frightens old people, who die of heart attacks, and cracks the state capitol. At Leschi Elementary, where my mother is teaching first grade, it knocks the gables onto the front stairs. This is how it starts.

IN AUGUST 1965, Frank Herbert, a forty-five-year-old newspaperman and pulp science fiction writer born in Tacoma, publishes *Dune*. One of the first works to popularize the term *ecology*, the novel is set in a wasteland covered in sand dunes after a planet's environment is decimated. As a youth, Herbert spent time exploring the waters of Puget Sound, regularly attempting to escape by sea the industrial despoliation of Commencement Bay, which receives 8.5 million gallons of smelter discharge per day, brimming with 2,500 pounds of toxic metals.[5] At age nine he rowed from the bay up to the San Juan Islands, sixty-seven nautical miles, occasionally grabbing on to the hull of a passing barge when he got tired.

Herbert's vision of desert wastes is drawn from the vast sand dunes on the Oregon coast, but the world he describes is inspired by Tacoma and its smelter. The air of his hometown, Herbert says, is "so thick you can chew it."[6]

IN THE EARLY morning hours of Thursday, June 23, 1966, Lisa Wick and Lonnie Trumbull are lying in twin beds in a basement apartment on Seattle's Queen Anne Hill.[7] Both are from Portland, Oregon, both twenty. They are newly graduated from stewardess training in Chicago and are on standby, slated to take their first flights for United Airlines in July. They have moved into the apartment on the first of the month. Lisa is wearing curlers in her hair, bulky rollers made of stiff wiry material. A third roommate, Joyce Bowe, is not home that night, staying with another stewardess.

Sometime between midnight and three in the morning, a man enters the apartment bearing a piece of lumber eighteen inches long and three inches square. He clubs Lonnie over the head, then turns to the other woman. The lights are out when he attacks Lisa, she'll later recall, and beats her over the head until she falls unconscious. There they lie until Joyce returns the following morning to find the door unlocked, the lights on, and blood sprayed across the walls. Lonnie is dead, Lisa unconscious. She will remain in a coma for several weeks. Police speculate that her life was saved by the curlers in her hair acting as a buffer, weakening the blows.

The attack takes place little more than a mile from where my grandmother lives, at the top of the hill. Police find the bloodstained weapon abandoned in a nearby vacant lot; they find the women's flight bags as well. They interview nearly a hundred neighbors, friends, and acquaintances of the victims, eliminating initial suspects. Six people pass polygraph tests.

After recovering consciousness, Lisa tells police that she was awake at the time of the assault, describing a white male with light-colored hair, five feet nine or ten, 165 pounds, wearing dark clothes. No one can explain how she's able to describe the suspect if the room was dark.[8] No one can explain why police fail to connect the attack to a series of rapes recently committed on Queen Anne Hill. In this case, the victims have not been raped.

The random viciousness sparks a national sensation, and the story is picked up by the Associated Press and United Press International, headlines appearing in newspapers from Alaska to New York City: STEWARDESSES PREY OF GRISLY CLUBBER (Springfield, Missouri), VICIOUS ATTACKER CLUBS TWO GIRLS (Fort Myers, Florida). To judge from the coverage, the most salient feature of the victims is their hair color. Trumbull is described as "dark-haired" or, in one instance, as a "pert brunette" (*New York Daily News*). Wick, invariably, is "blonde." The term *savagely beaten* appears in dozens of columns of type nationwide.

The summer is tense. In July, the mysterious attacker in Seattle is eclipsed when Richard Speck rapes and stabs and strangles eight student nurses in Chicago. Lisa is shown a photo of Speck by police but does not recognize him.

In Austin, Texas, that August, Charles Whitman knifes to death his wife and his mother, then shoots dozens from a sniper's nest atop the university tower, killing seventeen and wounding more than thirty.

Donovan sings creepy songs. "Season of the Witch." "Sunshine Superman."

At some point, my grandmother acquires a big black police whistle and begins sleeping with it under her pillow. A widow, she lives alone.

I HAVE MANY FRIENDS. Some are mine, some once belonged to my brother and sister: Raggedy Ann, an orange pig, a dark brown teddy bear wearing blue jeans stitched to his bottom, and Sophie, with green hair and button eyes. My sister sewed her for me out of two stuffed blobs. There is also

Sammy, a naked troll with carrot-colored hair flaring out of the top of his head. I cut his hair so that he will look like my father and my brother. It does not grow back.

I prefer these soft friends to real people because real people look angry. My father looks angry. He spanks my brother with a board for eating maraschino cherries without permission. My sister meets the same fate for taking crackers from the kitchen. I live in fear of this.

My favorite man lives in the City Dump. His name is Julius Pierpont Patches, and he has had a successful career with the Ding-A-Ling Brothers Circus. Every morning in TV land, at 7:30 a.m., he opens his door for Mr. Announcer Man to tell us the weather. When he asks what the forecast will be, someone throws a bucket of water in his face, because this is Seattle.

He has a rubber chicken and a Raggedy Ann doll just like mine, except his is called Esmeralda and she makes sounds on cue—a happy gurgle, a giggle, a sigh, and a full cry. He helps us tell the time and eats cornflakes with us and shows us Bugs Bunny and Bullwinkle and Looney Tunes cartoons that come flying out of his Cartoon Hat when he holds it up to the camera.

He has a girlfriend named Gertrude who's played by a man in a dress with a red mop on his head and a giant red mouth drawn on his face. They have no script. J. P. Patches and Gertrude make up stories every day, tripping over brooms and throwing whipped cream pies in each other's faces and hurling the rubber chicken around the room. The show is live, and sometimes the cameraman starts laughing.

I am a Patches Pal, but there are other things on TV. Jack LaLanne is bouncing up and down in a black leotard while my mother does jumping jacks in the living room.

On January 31, 1967, I am crouching before the TV watching the funeral procession of the Apollo 1 astronauts crawl across the screen. They have burned up inside a tin can shaped like a triangle. The can is scorched black.

THE ISLAND

On February 1, 1968, a Vietcong officer in his mid-thirties is captured by South Vietnamese forces. He is brought to the chief of police in Saigon just after the North has launched the Tet Offensive, a massive surprise attack during the Tet holiday, the Vietnamese Lunar New Year, in which Vietcong attacked dozens of South Vietnamese cities and towns simultaneously.

When the captured officer is brought before him, the police chief stiffly raises his sidearm, a .38 Special Smith & Wesson revolver manufactured in Springfield, Massachusetts, and shoots him point-blank in the head in a summary execution captured for posterity by an Associated Press photographer. The image of the man facing the camera, in the act of recoiling as the bullet is fired into the right side of his brain, appears on front pages of newspapers around the world the next day, February 2.

My name is Carrie, and February 2, 1968, is my seventh birthday.

I am in the first grade, and so is my best friend, Susie. Our lives are a mirror. Susie's birthday is a few weeks before mine. She has an older brother and an older sister. So do I. Our parents are friends. We go to the same church. As in a fairy tale, she is dark and I am fair. Rose Red and Snow White. A newspaper might call her a "pert brunette." She is cheerful, assertive, and outgoing. I am blond, quiet, and watchful.

By the age of two, I am routinely left at Susie's during the day while my mother goes to work, teaching in Seattle. My father threatens to leave her if she doesn't go back to work. The babysitting arrangement lasts, off and on, until we start school, and it is perhaps when I turn seven that my mother holds a small birthday party for me at home, the only one I recall. She bakes a pretty strawberry cake with sprinkles, and Susie is there. There are other little girls, but I only remember Susie.

Her brother, David, born in 1946, is fifteen years older than her. He graduates from high school in 1964, when we are three. He goes to college for a semester, then works a couple of casual odd jobs. In 1966, he enlists in the Marine Corps. After boot camp, he is assigned to a unit stationed in

Hawaii until the Fourth of July 1967, when he returns home on leave. In a photo taken in front of the Warners' doorway that summer, he stands in light green khakis with his sisters, who are dressed to go to church, both wearing beautiful pink-and-white Hawaiian leis he has brought them. He is a rangy young man with big ears and a broad grin. His father, Robert Warner, runs a coat factory in Tacoma and loves to play the electric organ and sing comic songs. Like him, David is good-looking and easygoing.

David arrives in Vietnam on August 1, 1967, assigned to Company G, "Golf" Company, 2nd Battalion, 5th Marines. He is one of 492,000 U.S. troops then "in-country," as they say. By the end of October, he's placed on light duty with a knee injury, assigned supply responsibilities at An Hoa. But when news breaks of the Tet Offensive and he learns that Golf Company is in the thick of the fighting in Hue, which has been captured by ten thousand North Vietnamese troops the Americans have failed to see coming, he asks to rejoin them. And he does, several days after the photograph of the execution appears on front pages, signaling a change in the national mood with regard to the war.

David Warner arrives in Hue on February 5, 1968, and by February 10 he is earning his first commendation. He leaves a protected position to help rescue two seriously injured Marine engineers pinned down under small arms and automatic weapons fire. He saves their lives.

Door-to-door urban fighting quickly becomes the stuff of legend in Hue, imperial capital of kings, its carved temples lining the Perfume River, as Vietcong battle to keep their hold on the Citadel, the stronghold north of the river. They are rounding up "cruel tyrants and reactionary elements" and executing them.[9] Marines fight to retake the city, block by block and building by building, suffering heavy casualties.

In the midst of it, David writes a letter to his family, full of pride in his fellow Marines, saying that his regimental commander has called Golf Company "the best damned bunch of street fighters he had ever seen," glorying in the fact that the company "has definitely won its fame in Hue."

Like scores of young fighting men, he captures the manic ebullience of combat while protecting his family from much else:

> The city was once beautiful but looks like hell now. All the buildings have been sacked and we've broken into all the houses. Most of the city [has been] damaged by artillery and mortars. . . . With all of this and all the casualties we've taken, we are very definitely winning. If Westmoreland was right . . . then they are hurting, and a truce of some kind should be in order before the summer's end. We have taken on their best and beat them.[10]

The letter arrives in the Warners' mailbox on the island on Monday, February 19. Later that day, two Marines appear in the doorway, an officer and a chaplain in the Class A uniform of midnight-blue jacket and trousers with the bright red stripe down the sides. It's the same doorway where Susie and I were standing during the earthquake, where David posed with his sisters in their leis, and the men tell Marvel Warner that her son is dead. Her husband is still at work at the coat factory. She does not call him. She waits until after he comes home and takes off his coat and sits down. Until after he reads his son's letter. Then she tells him.

That day, after the men leave, Susie feels as if she cannot remember David's face, and she walks around and around the house, room to room, looking at his photographs. The framed pictures are everywhere. Some are in her parents' bedroom, a room silent in the middle of the day, curtains drawn.

I look at them myself in the days and months and years to come: David manly and unsmiling in his various Marine uniforms. There's the one with the white cap and khaki shirt, the one with the camouflage battle helmet, and the one in dress blues.

I cannot make sense of them. He is as dead and alive as he ever was, all at the same time. On a rainy day, a stranger in a strange land, he is killed instantly on the porch of a house on the south side of the Perfume River by gunshot wounds to the head and body.¹¹ Yet here he is on the island, at home in his parents' sunny bedroom in Washington State, safe and sound.

ON APRIL 4, 1968, Martin Luther King Jr. is shot in Memphis at 6:01 p.m. central time. In Seattle it's 4:01 p.m., and my parents come home in the afternoon because of fear of rioting. They stand around the kitchen counter whispering, my mother wringing her hands. Three days later, ten thousand people march to the Seattle Center to mourn the assassination. My parents are not among them.

Riots are something on TV, on Walter Cronkite. On television, there is always Vietnam, and there are always riots and assassinations, so many that they are running together.

I am told not to talk about politics, because my brother said something about Nixon once at school and somebody punched him. My grandmother feels about Nixon the way she feels about the slugs she picks off her rose canes with a rusted kitchen fork and drops into a coffee can full of salt water to dissolve. "Nasty," she says, "just nasty." She is a Democratic precinct committeewoman, and she takes me door-to-door with her, handing out pamphlets. She is partial to Hubert Humphrey.

FROM APRIL 12 TO JULY 26, 1968, Ted Bundy is working at the Safeway on Queen Anne Hill as a night stocker.¹² My grandmother doesn't like Safeway. She likes Thriftway. She knows the fruit and vegetable man and the butcher and the cashiers and the baggers, and they all know her. They greet her and look the other way while she samples quite a few of the grapes. She introduces these men to me, one by one. "Here's my little granddaughter," she says, presenting me. "Tell them how old you are." I stare at my toes.

We walk slowly home along Howe Street, I in my brown Salt Water sandals, she in her black lace-up shoes, dragging the groceries in her two-wheeled cart, past the monkey puzzle tree, past the East Queen Anne Playground with its shallow cement wading pool, which to my sorrow is

THE ISLAND

empty of water almost all year. I play on the sidewalk in front of her house, pushing an old baby buggy that belonged to my mother. I have nagged her mercilessly to retrieve it from the attic crawl space. It is ancient and broken and squeaks, but I put the babies in, I take the babies out, I wheel them up and down the concrete, which is full of sparkly bits and smells good after the rain. Moss grows in the cracks, and I like to put my nose in my grandmother's roses and sniff, although there are earwigs crawling inside. If they get in your ear, they will eat whatever is inside your head.

At night, sleeping with her in the big bed in her bedroom, the police whistle under the pillow, I trace the pink and green pattern on her wallpaper with my fingers as bright white reflections slide across the mirror on the vanity, a car driving down the deserted block, the setting of the brake, the slamming of a steel door. Somebody's screen banging in the wind. A dog barking. Something rustling in the hydrangeas out front.

The brand-new Puget Sound Air Pollution Control Agency issues its first order to the local inferno to comply with its regulations for sulfur oxide emissions, but for everyone who's been breathing the air it's too late.

On November 5, 1968, when Hubert Humphrey loses the election to Richard Nixon, my grandmother hangs black crepe paper in the dining room in mourning.

ON THE MORNING of Wednesday, July 16, 1969, Apollo 11 lifts off, and the house up the street blows up. My sister and I run to the picture windows that look out over the lake, staring at the sky. We are home alone.

My sister thinks a plane from Boeing Field has made a sonic boom. This is the summer of sonic booms, the summer of "Sugar, Sugar" on the radio and on a record you can cut out from the back of the Alpha-Bits box. Boeing is planning the world's first "supersonic transport," after President Kennedy announced his plan to compete with the Concorde. The Seattle SuperSonics, the basketball team, is named for it. Whenever we hear a plane break the sound barrier, it makes a thud in our heads that spreads, the way footsteps on a dock sound when you are swimming underwater.

Then we see smoke. It is coming from the house up the block, a house on a rise on West Mercer Way overlooking the street. On an island of wooden houses, this one is clad in brick. In a neighborhood of modest, ranch-style structures, it seems high, not low. It looms. One of my third-grade classmates lives in that house, an eight-year-old girl named Jenny, who has two stiff straw-blond braids that spring out of the back of her head like Pippi Longstocking's.

The explosion is so powerful and the flames so intense that the fire chief thinks dynamite is involved. The local newspaper echoes my sister, reporting that "neighbors described the first blast 'like a sonic boom.'"[13]

It's not a sonic boom. It's not dynamite. It's something in the basement: a hissing propane gas container from a camp stove deliberately cocked on and placed next to the home's furnace by Jenny's father, Dr. Stephen L. Tope Jr., a thirty-four-year-old anesthesiologist and former lieutenant commander and medical officer in the Navy who has recently lost his job at Virginia Mason Hospital in Seattle. He has served multiple tours as a flight surgeon in Vietnam. He lets the basement fill with propane fumes, then turns the furnace on. In July.

The house explodes as he and his wife and two of his four fair daughters, aged five to eight, are upstairs, preparing to go on a trip to Blaine, on the Canadian border. The two other girls are outside, playing in the yard. He has a job interview in Blaine, and the house is for sale.

The floor upstairs billows, like a rug being shaken. Screaming, Dr. Tope's wife pushes her children out the door. He walks into the bedroom and fires a bullet into his right temple.

The house burns fiercely. Scorched black bricks blown twenty feet from the house are scattered beside the foundation when I walk past it on my way to school that fall. The doctor's body is found in that back bedroom. His wife and daughters are uninjured, but their dog, a Weimaraner, will not leave his master's side and dies in the fire.

After her father blows up her house, I never see Jenny again. When I hear "Blaine," I think *explosion, gunshot, dog*. I think, *That's what dads do*.

Dr. Tope misses the moon landing by four days. Chappaquiddick by two. In California, the Zodiac Killer is just getting warmed up.

In March of that year, a few months before his death, Stephen L. Tope wrote a letter that was published in *The Seattle Times*, protesting the inundation of the Marmes Rockshelter, the richest archaeological site ever found in the Pacific Northwest, located in southeastern Washington near the confluence of the Snake and Palouse Rivers.

First excavated in 1962, the site has yielded ten-thousand-year-old human remains, the oldest yet known in North America. Bone tools, hide scrapers, and arrowheads reveal a culture that spanned eight thousand years. Marmes's graves are accessorized with spearpoints and bead necklaces made of shells brought from the coast, several hundred miles away. Five matching knives carved from stone rest against a child's skeleton.

When the Lower Monumental Dam, nearing completion in 1968, threatens to flood the Marmes site, President Lyndon Johnson signs an executive order to build a levee to protect it. But the next spring the levee fails as the reservoir fills. Water seeps through the gravel under the barrier. Water always finds a way.

Several months before arranging the detonation of his family, Stephen Tope watches the Marmes destruction "with disbelief, dismay and disgust."[14] Archaeologists are the heroes of our time, he says, working "far away in obscure isolated parts of the world scratching in the dry earth, painstakingly salvaging ashes, seeds and bone fragments." He praises the Egyptians for protecting their heritage on the Nile. He laments the failure to protect the Marmes remains. He calls it "another miserable commentary on the price of progress."

"I am a disenchanted digger," he writes.

THE PARENT EARTHQUAKE. Landslides, tremors, glacial scour. Blind faults. Deep tectonic stresses. Certainly subduction, and the phase change of solid rock into something that looks and smells and acts like a gas. Basalt flows of fluidic lava. The disquieting behavior of what's underfoot.

MURDERLAND

IN THE FALL OF 1969, the third grade is learning the words to Joni Mitchell's "Both Sides Now" and singing from the bleachers in front of our parents in the East Seattle School gymnasium, across the street from the house that blew up. Mrs. Peacock, who has long hair like Joni Mitchell's, is standing in front of us, mouthing, "Bows and flows." It is a sad song, about not knowing clouds and love. We don't know anything either. We are still learning the multiplication tables, set to songs, and I can't remember any of the numbers above six. When we're supposed to stop singing at the end, Mrs. Peacock makes a circle with her hands.

Not long after we sing in the gymnasium, Mrs. Peacock doesn't come to school anymore. My mother tells me she took too many sleeping pills, and I have a pretty good idea what that means. *Barbiturates* is a word I know. I have studied an extensive *Life* photo spread about Judy Garland, who goes to sleep on a bathroom floor in London on June 22, 1969, and never wakes up. I find it astonishing that Judy Garland is somehow Dorothy in *The Wizard of Oz* and an old lady with a Seconal problem. She's alive, wearing a checked blue-and-white dress and saying there's no place like home. At the same time, she's dead.

There are lessons here. You can kill yourself on purpose or you can kill yourself by accident. Or, like Dorothy in Oz, you can kill someone else, such as a witch.

I am learning and learning.

Judy Garland reminds me of Emily Prestwich, our next-door neighbor. Emily Prestwich is old and smokes and her fluffy hair is orange, and she always has a green glass dish on her coffee table filled with desirable candy: black with red and yellow stripes or amber peanut shapes stamped with the exaggerated graph-like texture of a peanut shell.

Throughout the summer, the fake peanuts congeal into a bowl-shaped lump along with half-melted butterscotch drops and the black-and-yellow-striped tiles, and Emily Prestwich is generous about inviting us to sit on her weird knobby couch and peel these candies apart. Mrs. Prestwich is a good witch, but when I am sitting cross-legged in her front yard, poised over a bluff above the street, I think how quickly the Wicked Witch could appear in the sky, small at first and then larger and larger, and swoop down and carry me off.

If this happens, I wonder whether anyone will notice.

I AM NINE, I am ten. Off the island, I spend long stretches of time in Seattle, prone on my grandmother's couch, reading stacks of her magazines: *Redbook, Reader's Digest, Ladies' Home Journal, Better Homes & Gardens, Family Circle, Good Housekeeping.* She is not a good housekeeper. Her house is a comfortable mess. Piles of magazines and newspapers are stacked against the walls, serving as both insulation and entertainment. She's planning to read them when she gets old. She is already old and has her work cut out for her, so I'm helping. I can be helpful.

She is, as I say, a Democrat. She has white hair like George Washington, who I assume is also a Democrat, and in the corner there is a whatnot packed full of china teacups and ceramic donkeys, the Democrats' favorite animal. We while away our time drinking cups of coffee full of sugar. I dip sugar lumps in the coffee and watch the faint brown line creep up. I sniff Play-Doh and press wads of it onto the colored comic strips in the Sunday *Post-Intelligencer,* hoping to pull them away and find the comics imprinted on the dough, a magical thing. I like the regular features in *Reader's Digest,* "Humor in Uniform" and "Drama in Real Life." I like reading about bad things happening to other people. I study with awe the illustration of a giant rock falling down a mountainside and ripping off someone's arm.

My favorite feature in all of the magazines is the regular monthly installment in *Good Housekeeping* called "My Problem and How I Solved It."[15] There is the lady whose husband hits her. She decides not to complain about it because she understands that he needs to be in control. There are other ladies too, one whose son is a drug addict and another whose daughter gets pregnant in high school.

The Wicked Witch of the West is Dorothy's problem, and she solves it by melting her.

MURDERLAND

My problem is my father. He gets angry. He has high expectations and a hot temper. Sometimes, when he loses it, he has a look in his eyes, a blank look. His eyes are the color of mud. Our arms are for yanking, our heads for smacking with the handles of table knives, but he works mainly through threats. Words. *Stupid, lazy, spoiled brat. Crying like a baby. Don't do a half-assed job.*

My problem is my father, so I study the examples in *Good Housekeeping* and consider how to solve it. On the island, we live in his houses, houses he built, and he can throw us out. He has created us without meaning to. He can destroy us just the same.

He's an expert in elementary education. He has a Ph.D. specializing in discipline problems. His hair is a crew cut, from the Army. Under the stairs he keeps shoe polish and rat poison and slug bait. In the basement he has a windowless shop full of clamps and saws and routers and vises, jars of nails and screws and machine oil and gasoline. He has an axe.

We're living in the second house he's built, the gray one. He's built two on the island, and both have a daylight basement, popular in the Northwest: part of the space is underground and part above, gaining light through windows. My parents' bedroom is in the daylight basement.

At meals we are expected to sit still, with our feet on the floor, and keep quiet and eat everything put before us, including inedible things such as warm milk, egg salad, and flabby onions cooked with pot roast in the pressure cooker. We are expected to study the Bible and *Science and Health with Key to the Scriptures*, by Mary Baker Eddy, discoverer and founder of Christian Science, and pray a lot.

Christian Scientists don't go to doctors, don't wear seat belts, and don't believe in accidents. They hate materialism. Nothing is real, according to Mary Baker Eddy, not bodies, bones, brains, or eyes. We're supposed to know that, and if we really *know* it, we can heal anything. It works the other way, too. They're drilling us on the Ten Commandments in Sunday school. *Thou shalt not kill* is one, but somehow it emerges that it doesn't simply mean "Don't shoot somebody." It means you can murder people with your mind. If you're not careful.

THE ISLAND

In a world in which nothing is real, he can do whatever he wants. When I throw up in the car, I'm in big trouble, and he jerks me out, yelling that I have to learn not to get sick. I have to pray harder. I can tell he wants to leave me by the side of the road.

But instead of praying or reading *Science and Health*, I'm reading the story of Tanuki the Bad Badger, which my father brought back from Japan before I was born. Tanuki is a bad, bad badger who looks like a raccoon and lies to people and tricks them. He's a shape-shifter. He lives in an evil-smelling hole. After the old farmer catches him and ties him up, he lies to the farmer's wife to get her to free him and then hits her over the head with a mallet and kills her and cuts her up. Disguised as the old lady, wearing her clothes, Tanuki puts her in the soup and feeds her to her husband. Finally, a good rabbit tricks Tanuki and sends him out to sea in a boat made of earth. As Tanuki paddles far out, the boat breaks up and Tanuki sinks, his arms held high out of the water as he screams, punished for his wickedness.[16]

We are bad badgers, running with scissors, putting our feet on the couch and our elbows on the table, knocking over milk glasses, forgetting to be excused, shouting, tripping, falling on the stairs, practicing the piano in a loud and unmusical way, breaking the antenna on the portable TV (me), rocking so hard in the rocking chair after being told not to that it falls over backwards (also me), and, grievously, fouling the engine on the secondhand gas lawn mower (me again, since I was trying to kill a large black spider on the top of the mower by drowning it with the hose).

This figures among my more serious crimes, and the memorable part of it, an ancillary offense remembered by all involved, is that I allow my sister to take the blame, since by the time my father discovers the damage to the lawn mower he is sweating and swearing and yelling "Goddamn son of a bitch" so loud that I'm afraid he's going to throw somebody in the blackberry bushes. *Better not me* is what I think. I creep off, intent on survival.

My sister makes the mistake of laughing at him, and he's yelling "Do you think that's funny?" and jerking her by the arm and making her stand in the sun and pull the cord on the broken mower over and over again until she's shaking and crying, and then he runs off and comes back with a sledgehammer and beats the lawn mower with it and throws *it* in the blackberry bushes.

So my problem is my father. He appears to have embarked on a passive campaign to get rid of us through a series of near-death experiences—a car accident in Guadalajara, storms at sea in the family sailboat. When I'm a toddler, he orders my sister to watch me, perching us in thin air on an unsecured platform, the unfinished stairwell of the house he's building, telling us not to move.

After studying various examples, I begin to see how to get rid of him.

Potentially, there are any number of solutions. I am watching the four o'clock B movies on heavy rotation in Seattle, and I am alert to what these have to say about the disposal of bodies. For a time, I place a certain amount of hope in a letter opener.

Right between the eyes is the phrase. If I stab him *right between the eyes*, then he will be dead, and we can bury him in the vegetable garden, where the soil is soft. I experiment by pressing the point of the letter opener against the bone between my eyes and am dismayed by how hard the bone feels. As a practical matter, I'm not sure it will penetrate his head. What's more, I do not feel confident about enlisting my mother's cooperation. She is a kindergarten teacher. She is soft-spoken, patient, kind, but with unyielding views on what is and is not permissible. Divorce, for example, seems to be out of the question. She will not consider it. On the other hand, she seems pretty sick of him too.

Then I come up with a really good plan, such an excellent plan that it still seems viable.

Our boat is my father's pride, if not joy. A thirty-foot sailboat, a Mercator sloop with a fiberglass hull. We have built this boat, every member of our family, during years of weekends spent driving to an old barn full of fiberglass fumes outside Kent, a rural Eastside suburb where we stagger around in an epoxy fog, filling screw holes with wooden plugs. Our father installs teak trim and plumbing and builds out the cabin: the galley, the head, the bunk beds in the bow and alongside the engine. Laboriously, at home, working with stiff turquoise marine Naugahyde until her fingers crack, my mother sews cushions for the bunks and benches around the dining table. My brother, a teenager, runs the wiring.

The boat is launched on my mother's birthday, in a seeping, drenching rain. We carry heavy buckets full of ballast to fill the bilge: steel punchings. Sailing on a sunny day, I will learn, can be momentarily sparkling and glorious, but in the rain it is miserably cold, cold to the bone, water dripping from the hood of your rain jacket and pooling around your wet tennis shoes in the cockpit.

On a boat, there are endless ways to kill yourself or others. All seemingly by accident. There's drowning, the easiest and most popular approach, favored by weekend sailors who crowd Puget Sound by the hundreds every Saturday and Sunday, drinking and driving and pitching overboard at any errant wave. There are fumes in the bilge that can build up and explode, fires in the galley, carbon monoxide from a malfunctioning outboard. You can crack your skull on a bulkhead, or the boom might take a fast, silent swing across the cockpit, connecting with your head like a baseball bat. You can trip on piles of rope coiled on deck. You can catch an ankle in the anchor chain as it goes over the side. You would be surprised how fast things can go wrong.

Perennial errors of seamanship may prove useful: hitting a snag, or tearing out the hull against subterranean rocks, or knocking a hole below the waterline by ramming into one of many unseen tree trunks floating just beneath the surface, fallen overboard from freighters bound for China. Lost in the fog, you can be stove in by those freighters, or by Navy destroyers tearing along at high speed, or by speedboats with inattentive captains.

During my father's brief summer vacations, held as often as not in a steady, plodding, freezing gray rain, we sail drearily around the Sound or up north, in the islands. I sit in a puddle on the fiberglass bench in the cockpit, watching him stand with the tiller trapped between his legs, his hands shoved in his armpits. Rain drips off the end of his nose. We seek out cheap, isolated anchorages—he despises tourists—eating cold pot roast and onions from the pressure cooker, then wiping out the dishes with a dirty handkerchief because it's wasteful to use fresh water. On these trips we are plying narrows boiling with riptides (Deception Pass), skirting shallow peninsulas with rip currents (Point No Point), and traversing the wide-open strait that lies between Vancouver Island and the mainland—the Juan de Fuca Strait. This is a stretch of water so broad, with winds and rollers coming in off the Pacific, that its placid surface can whip into a maelstrom in a matter of minutes. The Strait of Juan de Fuca sees afternoon winds of twenty-five to forty miles an hour on a regular basis.

We motor through the locks that divide the Lake Washington Ship Canal from the Sound and then sail north: north to the strait, to the San Juans, to Canada. But one day, we head south. He stands at the tiller, unspeaking, his green windbreaker and khaki pants whipping in the wind.

Is it curiosity? He doesn't say. As we approach Tacoma, on our left, we hear a roar like fire, louder and louder, clouds rising from a smokestack. We see a line in the water, a visible demarcation. It's the water from the Puyallup River flowing past the smelter, and it is a completely different color than the water in the Sound: a light, murky, sediment-laden column so definitive that someone might have drawn it with a crayon. "What is it?" I ask. He doesn't answer, but we come about and sail away.

There's a lot of time to think on a boat. I spend long minutes studying the charts pinned to the galley wall, pondering the startling recorded fathoms beneath us. A fathom is six feet. One hundred and twenty-six fathoms lie off President Point. I can barely do the math, but that's 756 feet, higher than the Space Needle, higher than the Washington Monument, higher than the Golden Gate Bridge. Six millimeters of fiberglass between you and the end of the world. Look down into the water and sometimes it feels like looking into death itself, a place with no light, no definition, no bottom, just nothing. Leaves and feathers and branches sink into it—you've dropped them there—twirling, catching the light, wink-

THE ISLAND

ing, then disappearing, down, down, down. Down where the jellyfish drown. Never to be seen again.

My plan is to push him. Choose the right spot and no one will see. It will require split-second timing, careful consideration of distance from shore and of speed, momentum, and other boats: We will have to be moving fast enough to get far enough away from him before my mother can figure out what's happening and try to turn the boat around and go back. A crack on the head wouldn't hurt either. He can swim. We all know he can shout. It must look like an accident.

One shove. And overboard. He's my problem, and that's how I should solve it.

Later in life, one phrase will come to mind, after my father has died without much help from me. I'll think: *I should have killed him while I had the chance.* For years, years in which he does a lot of damage, I have means, motive, and opportunity. Yet I lack an essential quality: a single-minded commitment. Unaccountably, I fail to act. I am still sorry.

But not everyone holds back. Not everyone fails.

THERE ARE SO MANY. Skulls, skeletons. The disarticulated. Delicate bones cast in the leaf litter. Vine maple threading through the eye sockets. Silence in the duff. The recently dead waiting patiently in rivers, rigor long passed, facial effacement, hair weaving with the current. Bows, flows.

The places where these turn up make a map all their own. A map of lakes, forests, hillsides, highway turnouts, a skein of rivers plaited throughout Seattle and its satellite cities: the Cedar River, the Green River, the Duwamish. Within minutes, on any highway out of any outlying town, you can be steps from a wilderness, water running in unchecked torrents over great bulwarks. These rivers come fully furnished with boulders and downed trees, their trunks fallen like pillars in an antique land. Close by there are sheer rock cliffs and thousands of acres of Douglas firs, silver firs, western hemlocks, and cedars, logging roads frequented only occasionally by timber surveyors, telephone linemen, road workers, rail workers, rangers, and Eagle Scouts.

Off I-90, that ribbon of hot-mix asphalt running from Seattle to Boston, take any exit between Issaquah and Snoqualmie Pass and you are mere minutes from absolute isolation. You may lose yourself, and others, in the Cascade Range, the American Cordillera, the Ring of Fire. You may find yourself in seven hundred miles of contiguous fir-covered forests, a hushed textile web of giant sword ferns splayed over the forest floor, nurse logs quietly birthing new generations amid the general sorrow of weeping cedar boughs, deadwood, and widow-makers. Here sound is muted, dulled by centuries of accumulating duff—decaying forest matter—pine cones, pine needles, sloughed bark. It is as soft as a bed.

Here reigns the kingdom of the fungi, the yeasts, the rusts, the molds and mildews and mushrooms, shelflike sporophores marching up tree trunks and out of sight: stairways to heaven. You can enter the world of decomposition at any point, any trailhead, any overgrown pullout, at Tiger Mountain and Taylor Mountain and Mount Si, which has a face hidden in the side of its rock, right below the summit, the face of Snoqualm, the moon, who tries to steal the sun by tying it to a rope made out of cedar bark. Fox and Blue Jay steal it back from him and set it free. Snoqualm falls from his cedar rope and dies.[17]

This is where he brings them.

Chapter 5

The Devil's Business

> Think small.
>
> —1960 ADVERTISEMENT FOR THE
> VOLKSWAGEN BEETLE

Let's back up. It's the mid-1960s, sulfur wafting from the smelter's underworld.

In Tacoma, nineteen-year-old Rodger Jones is struggling to find a vocation. They don't know each other, but Rodger and Ted are part of the same cohort, the postwar baby boom. Born in 1945 in North Tacoma, Rodger has grown up here, attending Fife High School with the class of '64. Like Ted, he has been exposed to more than his fair share of lead and, while generally congenial, he too has acted out, getting into fights at school and attracting police attention. He's taken college courses at the local university but dropped out. In 1965, he accepts a job at the Ruston plant.

He's a skimmer in a hive of organized fire and brimstone. He learns that valuable minerals come from raw ore—rocks—which are crushed and then melted in a series of furnaces at the smelter twenty-four hours a day.[1] Given the venomous variety of metals that are veined throughout the ore, worker bees tending the first furnace, a roaster, are exposed to clouds of hazardous emissions. Refining metal always produces these toxic by-products, but Tacoma is one of the dirtiest plants in the world, smelting ores rich in arsenic.

Transferred to a second or "reverberatory" furnace, this commercial magma is heated to 2,800 degrees Fahrenheit, yielding a molten "matte" of copper and iron sulfides (a compound of iron and sulfur) that settles to the bottom of the heated vessel. What remains on top is a liquid slag full of impurities, which is poured off into ladles, gigantic seventeen-ton bucket-shaped vessels on railcars that are rolled out to Puget Sound. Their contents are dumped in the water, as slag has been for years. When the valuable matte is transferred from the bottom of the furnace to the converter, sulfur is burned off, producing more slag. After sulfur burns off, the melted "blister" of copper that remains is 98 or 99 percent pure.

But as the blister becomes pure, the men are becoming toxic. Shifts of workers tending the reverberatory furnace are exposed to lead, arsenic, copper, and cadmium. More shifts are laboring in the other divisions of the Tacoma compound, including a nickel plant, an acid plant, and a sulfur dioxide plant that was installed in 1949, capturing the gases generated by smelting copper. Just like arsenic, sulfur dioxide is a valuable product, added to foods, beverages, and soft drinks.

Nothing can be wasted. Blister copper is refined at the slimes house, where impurities are allowed to settle to the bottom of the tank. The material that settles is called "slimes," containing antimony, gold, silver, selenium, tellurium, and nickel sulfate. The slimes are leached with acid to remove impurities. Employees on day and night shifts are exposed to lead, arsenic, selenium, tellurium, silver, and gold.

All these products are worth more than individual lives. They are the essence of permanence, the stuff of bullion, wedding rings, coins, glassmaking, the gold leaf on church domes, the gilt on picture frames, and the gold of dental fillings. The Statue of Liberty is robed in copper. The luster is more precious than life.

Skimmers like Rodger wield a long rod, opening the furnace to drain off impurities. After skimming, the furnace must be closed and molten metal prevented from flowing out, overtopping the ladles and spilling onto the shop floor, incinerating everyone and everything in its path. If that happens, it's called a "runaway," and the things Rodger sees—steam explosions, accidents—will stay with him forever.[2]

They stay with Bill Baarsma too. Bill has also worked at the smelter in the '60s, during summers off from high school and college. He's grown up in Tacoma, and his father, Clarence Baarsma, is a foreman at the plant, renowned as a crane operator, a tricky job requiring finesse to maneuver ladles of lava. As a kid, Bill had to be deathly quiet during the day because his dad worked night shifts.

His dad is volatile. He drinks too much, he smokes, and, as a parlor trick, he can poke his finger in one nostril and out the other. There's a hole in his septum, something called "smelter nose."[3] He's so full of arsenic, Bill's dad, that he can taste it when he eats. It tastes like metal. "He had his demons," Bill says later.[4]

Bill sees disturbing things at the smelter. He starts outside, working in the yard for $1.25 an hour, sweeping up, looking for pieces of copper to collect in a wheelbarrow, watching out for the boxcars rolling in, filled with who knows what. Sometimes it's musical instruments. Sometimes it's pieces of weapons. Once it's the remains of a decommissioned Nike surface-to-air missile system.

Everything goes right into the converter to be melted down. Sometimes it sounds like popcorn—those are bullets, popping off. It's "Dante's Inferno," he says.[5]

He knows another young guy working there, a light-skinned Scandinavian who goes into the arsenic plant and comes out looking as if he has a deep tan. With blisters. Bill decides he's never going in there. As it is, Bill sometimes gets into the bathtub after work and the water turns green.

In the spring of 1965, Ted Bundy is a senior at Woodrow Wilson High School, and despite complaining of a certain malaise, socially and academically, he aspires to be a college boy, never entertaining a thought of joining the working-class milieu of the smelter. Ted has a B-plus average, which he feels is beneath him. "Something stunted my progress in high school," he'll later say, adding, "I was sort of just stuck."[6] Resentful about his family's poverty, he is unable to afford the skiing weekends of wealthy students. He goes skiing regardless, forging new dates on old ski passes to gain entry at Snoqualmie and other resorts. He steals ski boots, poles, and skis.

At some point, he has what he'll later call a "sexual encounter" with one of his sisters.[7]

He is held by police twice on suspicion of stealing a car, but his record is expunged when he turns eighteen.[8] On March 26, 1965, he claims to have been in a minor car crash and appears to have scratches on his face.[9] That summer, he works for Tacoma City Light, and with the money he saves he buys a vintage car, a 1933 Plymouth coupe.[10]

On a scholarship, he attends the University of Puget Sound (UPS) in Tacoma, and after classes are over, in April 1966, he sells the coupe and buys a 1958 Volkswagen Beetle.[11] Two months later, Lonnie Trumbull and Lisa Wick, the stewardesses on Queen Anne Hill, are bludgeoned and left for dead.

That summer, a mass of warm, stable air settles atop Tacoma like a smothering quilt, capturing and concentrating smelter fumes. Complaints flood into the company's office, which responds by sending a plane on "reconnaissance flights" overhead.[12] Observers report a plume of smoke "visible for about three miles out from the stack in a fan . . . two to three miles wide at its farthest point."[13] Once again, the smelter considers raising the height of the smokestack, this time to 813 feet.

In December, Lacey V. Murrow, a retired Air Force brigadier general, shoots himself in the chest with a twelve-gauge shotgun in his room at the Lord Baltimore Hotel in Baltimore. Soon after, Washington State bestows his name on the Mercer Island Floating Bridge. Like Ted, the bridge will have many names.

THE DEVIL'S BUSINESS

IN THE LATE '60S, my father buys a used off-white 1963 Volkswagen Beetle and then a black 1961 Beetle. Ted is twenty-one and bored at UPS. He transfers to the University of Washington and in March 1967, while skiing at Snoqualmie, meets a girl named Diane Edwards and falls in love. She's from San Francisco, scion of a wealthy, prominent family. He enrolls in summer classes at Stanford to be near her, studying intensive Chinese, but he can't concentrate and attends class fitfully. In July, Diane dumps him, and he gets a C in Chinese.

At the Ruston plant, Rodger Jones is having a very different experience. In 1967, he's seriously injured trying to stop a runaway on the plant floor and is forced to resign. That's the summer when the Tacoma City Council starts complaining about "the activities of the Smelter," and David Rowlands, the city manager, points out that more complaints about air pollution have been received "during the last five months than ever before," calling the situation "an emergency."[14] Company men are assigned to smother these concerns: the smelter manager, Robert Shinkoskey, and Sherman Pinto, the medical director. Their main suggestion, once again, is to raise the main stack.

It's 1967, the Summer of Love, and Charles Manson, formerly of McNeil Island, is free on parole, with thirty-five dollars in his pocket.

It's the Summer of Love, and because it's a groovy place, Washington State passes a Clean Air Act, establishing the Puget Sound Air Pollution Control Agency, part of a nationwide movement to protect the environment.

Ted, however, is a staunch Republican. He heads back to Washington and that fall works for a few months as a busboy at the Seattle Yacht Club, where he is befriended by Sybil Ferris, the pastry chef. She notices his manner: sometimes he speaks with a pronounced British accent, sometimes he pretends to be a politician. He borrows her Haviland china, sterling silver, and linen to host a dinner to reingratiate himself with Diane; he borrows her car to go on "night trips."[15] He borrows a hundred dollars and doesn't pay it back. She calls Ted's mother in Tacoma to ask her to intervene, but Louise Bundy says, "He doesn't live here anymore and we're not responsible for anything he does."[16] He is "let go" from the yacht club because he's always in the pantry eating whipped cream and "fancy foods" that employees aren't supposed to eat. He has an illicit key to a men's dormitory at the University of Washington; he sleeps on couches in the lounge. He wears an expensive Yankee Peddler overcoat with a fur collar, and the pastry chef at the yacht club has her suspicions about how he got his hands on it.

JANUARY 26, 1968, is a cold, rainy day, and nineteen-year-old Linda Kay Slawson is trudging down a street in Portland, Oregon, with a heavy case of encyclopedias for sale, going door-to-door in the neighborhood of Aloha. She has a piece of paper in her hand with the address of a potential customer, but it smudges in the rain. Hesitating, she sees a round-faced man in the front yard of a nearby home and asks if he's interested in encyclopedias. It's Jerry Brudos. He's moved to Portland, and he beckons her over, taking her arm, inviting her in out of the rain, into his garage workshop, telling her that his wife and children have company upstairs and he doesn't want to disturb them. She sits on a stool.

From behind, he strikes her over the head with a two-by-four, then strangles her. Stashing his prize in the basement, he sends his family off for hamburgers. He undresses and dresses the body, using the women's underwear he has collected. Eventually he reconciles himself to the fact that he must let go. He's right-handed, so he feels it makes sense to cut off her left foot. He stashes it in the freezer, for later. He ties the rest of her to an old engine part, drives to the St. Johns Bridge, and throws the body in the Willamette River, where she will vanish forever.[17]

Soon he will begin cutting the breasts off his victims, trying to fashion a mold. He wants to make a lead paperweight.[18]

THE DEVIL'S BUSINESS

It's January 1968, and Ted again registers for classes at the University of Washington but immediately withdraws, taking up traveling, sampling San Francisco, Denver, and Aspen, Colorado. He goes skiing. He drops by Fayetteville, Arkansas, to visit his uncle John, who teaches in the music department at the university. He asks his uncle for money. He visits relatives in Philadelphia, swinging north to Vermont to get a copy of his birth certificate.

In February, Sybil Ferris helps Ted get a job at the Olympic Hotel in downtown Seattle, the most expensive hotel in town. A month later, he's fired for stealing waiters' clothes out of their lockers. All in all, Ferris says, he is a "very weird boy."[19]

In April, working nights at the Queen Anne Safeway, he's appointed Seattle's assistant chairman of the New Majority for Nelson Rockefeller and wins a trip to the Republican convention in Miami in August, where he acquires a souvenir hat made of Styrofoam.[20] By July he's stopped showing up at Safeway.

Rockefeller loses to Nixon on the first ballot, but Ted is not discouraged. He is charming the movers and shakers among Seattle Republicans and working as a driver for Arthur Fletcher, a Republican nominee for lieutenant governor, and dating Cathy Swindler, daughter of Herb Swindler, the commander of the Seattle Police Department's Crimes Against Persons Unit. Cathy becomes deeply fond of Ted, saying, "I thought I loved Ted Bundy. Not totally in a romantic way . . . but in terms of being moved by what he said and his feelings for other human beings."[21]

I spend the day at the beach with my mother. I am reading *Pagoo*, the biography of a hermit crab, a wondrous creature, and I study the bright watercolor paintings of the venturesome young crustacean, who must find a series of sturdy shells of ever-increasing size to hide his vulnerable and rather obscene-looking tail. He searches and searches for temporary homes, fighting with his pincers to hold on to them.

MURDERLAND

At the climax of what is a thrilling story, he falls into a deep hole and is menaced by an octopus who seizes him, conveying him toward the terrifying parrotlike beak at the center of her being. "Can This Be the End of Pagoo?" is the title of this chapter, but it is not the end, because a moray eel arrives at just the right moment and nips off the tentacle ferrying the crab to his doom.[22]

On this day—a special day, because my mother works teaching other children and I rarely have her to myself—I have a bright yellow pail and a little blue plastic shovel, and I scrabble in the tidal pools, which are filling and emptying. The barnacles are waving infinitesimal feelers as the cold salt water flushes them and the pebbles and grains of sand are rolling back and forth and I suddenly find a hermit crab in one of these pools, a miracle, and I hold him covetously, filled with a desire to have this wonderful animal. To own him, to possess him.

My mother tells me and tells me that I may not bring him home to live in my room. Disobeying her, I hide him in my pocket and bring him home and try to keep him alive in a shoebox, secretly. But he cannot breathe, and he dies. All is ruined. My mother, who seems to know everything I do without my telling her, is exasperated. I bury him in the vacant lot next door, his limp little body still in his shell. The ground is cold and damp and it is the end of Pagoo.

THE YEAR 1968 is *Hair* and the dawning of the Age of Aquarius, and I am an Aquarius. I sing the song.

It is also the year of Martin Luther King Jr. on a motel balcony and Robert F. Kennedy in a hotel kitchen and the Boeing 747, which is so big. It's Jackie and Onassis. I know more about hermit crabs than I do about these people, but their names are washing past in waves, in snatches of conversations and clipped reports on *The Huntley-Brinkley Report* and in photographs in *Life* and *Look* and *The Saturday Evening Post* and the *Seattle Post-Intelligencer*. They are floating through the air as I lie on the

THE DEVIL'S BUSINESS

living room carpet studying my Golden Nature *Sea Shells of the World: A Guide to the Better-Known Species*, with 790 ILLUSTRATIONS IN FULL COLOR.

As we leave the UW bookstore, I study the frayed bell-bottoms and blackened naked feet of the girl walking down the sidewalk in front of us, the beaded curtains in the head shops, and the psychedelic colors on the record albums. I peer at the grungy laps of the kids sitting cross-legged on cobblestones at the Pike Place Market, playing the guitar, smoking fat cigarettes, and drinking Russian tea. My father hates my brother's long hair.

Meanwhile, my mother is living the Petula Clark lifestyle. Downtown, downtown! When we escape and go shopping, she's so happy. She loves movie matinees, shoes with bows, burnt sugar cake at the Frederick & Nelson bakery, and diet cola with lime. She's in love with Omar Sharif, so we see *Lawrence of Arabia* and *Doctor Zhivago* and anything else that helps us forget my father. He loves Mrs. Eddy and wants to break the chains of materialism, but I notice that he's very fond of money.

He has arranged for our purebred Siamese, Skoshi Toru, to be raped by a strange cat in the basement while she screams and growls in unholy rage. She has kittens on November 5, Election Day, and we name them Granko, Spiro T. Kitty, and Cassandra. When the kittens are old enough, he sells them.

In December there's "Sympathy for the Devil," and five days later there's *Oliver!* and my mother takes my sister to see it. I'm too young for this one. My sister happily tells me the whole story, about Oliver and Nancy and Fagin and the Dodger, and I'm excited to learn things I'm not supposed to know.

On Friday night, December 20, a man gets out of a parked car on a lovers' lane on Lake Herman Road, on the outskirts of Benicia, in the North Bay of San Francisco, and shoots two teenagers, David Arthur Faraday and Betty Lou Jensen, who are enjoying their first date in a Rambler station wagon.

As the crow flies, the distance from Lake Herman Road to the

ASARCO lead smelter at Selby, California, is around six miles. No one knows who the murderer, soon to become known as the Zodiac, might be, but he could live in Benicia or Vallejo, cheek by jowl with the smelter.[23]

IT IS ALSO in 1968 that Kenneth Nelson, vice president of environmental affairs for the American Smelting and Refining Company, writes to a colleague celebrating the fact that he and the plant's tame medico, Dr. Pinto, have "numerous trusted friends in State and Federal health agencies" who have passed them an advance copy of a paper attributing lung cancer among smelter workers to arsenic and sulfur dioxide.[24] "There are holes in the paper and in the author's reasoning," he says, and Pinto has produced two pages of "sharp, hard criticisms" with which to attack it.[25]

Sharp and hard they may be, but the paper is published the following year, revealing that the most highly exposed workers at an Anaconda copper smelter in Montana exhibit an eightfold higher risk of respiratory cancer.[26]

ON APRIL 16, 1969, in El Paso, Dr. John Abersold, the environmental scientist in charge of "air and agricultural research" for the smelter, tells members of the county board of health that 60 percent of the city's air pollution comes from traffic, including "dust released from wheels, particles from fumes and exhaust pipes and dust particles from the roads." It's the traffic, not the smelter. Whatever the smelter might contribute, he says, it is important to note that "El Paso is fortunate in that there is a lot of wind movement and high air velocity," adding that "the sunshine and dry climate are also factors in alleviating our problem."[27]

"Our problem," insofar as Dr. Abersold is concerned, remains undefined. As in Tacoma, ASARCO's El Paso smelter hosts multiple facilities making multiple products, and the good doctor makes reference to its several smokestacks, the enormous one for copper and smaller stacks for lead and zinc, as if they are a unique and enviable amenity, something any

THE DEVIL'S BUSINESS

community might covet, saying, "Tall stacks are an exclusive way to diffuse and control the emission of sulfur dioxide."

ON MEMORIAL DAY weekend of 1969, Ted either does or does not hitch a ride with two women college students heading out of Ocean City, New Jersey, where he once sat on the sand with his grandfather in a shared fugue state. He either does or does not get into the back seat of their open-top 1966 Marina Blue Chevrolet Impala convertible; he does or does not have a cast on his ankle; he does or does not convince the women to pull over on the Garden State Parkway just out of Somers Point and pull a knife on them and stab them to death and cover their bodies with leaves. Somebody does.[28]

Since January he's been living in Philadelphia with his aunt Audrey Tilden, one of his mother's younger sisters, and is enrolled at Temple University, where he is taking, among other courses, Human Behavior, Survey of English Literature, and Theater in Western Culture.[29] He has no money and no car and doesn't really like the East Coast because it's "crowded, dirty, with no forests."[30] On weekends he takes the commuter train to Times Square, at the time a den of "flesh shops," in his words, and goes to porn films. But they're not enough, although they offer "a sense of excitement, sense of control, a sense of domination."[31] He is, he'll later say, a "time bomb."[32]

In Ocean City, he walks the boardwalk, he walks the beach. Speaking of himself in the third person, he'll describe the smorgasbord of young bikini-clad women spread out on the sand as "an overwhelming vision." He lets himself go "tearing around that place for a couple of days," later admitting that, "without really planning anything, he picked up a couple of young girls. And ended up with the first time he had ever done it."[33] Does he mean murder? If so, it's not the first time, but it may feel as if it is.

At Temple University in Philadelphia in 1969 is Dr. Herbert Needleman, an internist, pediatrician, and child psychiatrist. He's noticed the large number of children from poor inner-city neighborhoods admitted to the hospital with lead poisoning: the homes where they live are permeated with lead. Out his window he watches children on a playground, struck by stark differences. Some are "strong and wild," others slow and stupefied.[34]

Needleman knows lead. In medical school, as a summer job, he worked at the Deepwater DuPont plant that manufactured tetraethyl lead. He shoveled chemicals. On smoking breaks, he saw a clot of older co-workers sitting together, not talking, staring into space. They were from the "House of Butterflies," he was told.[35] They were lead poisoned.

Needleman will devise an experiment, the Philadelphia Tooth Fairy Project, paying kids for their "deciduous teeth" to see how much lead they're carrying.[36] Soon he can tell what neighborhood kids are from just from their teeth. It's not only paint. He's spotted smokestacks next to St. Anne's, a Catholic school beside a convent and the National Lead Company. The nuns invite him for lunch, carefully brushing lead dust off the tables before they eat. Heading out to the street to take samples from the gutters, Needleman is approached by men from the factory. They tell him to "get the hell out of here."[37] The children's blood lead levels measure forty micrograms per deciliter, an amount that in future years will be shown to cause serious health issues and lower IQs.[38]

MEANWHILE, in the Portland area, Jerry Brudos has been busy. In late 1968 and early 1969, he cannot help himself from seizing Stephanie Vikko, sixteen; Jan Whitney, twenty-three; Karen Sprinker, nineteen; and Linda Dawn Salee, twenty-two, and strangling, smothering, or choking them. He hangs them on hooks and has sex with the bodies. In one case, he tries to reanimate a victim's corpse like Dr. Frankenstein, inserting hypodermic needles attached to electric leads into her rib cage.[39] He disposes of remains in wooded areas or, weighted with auto parts, in the Long Tom River. In May 1969, the bodies begin to come up.

Brudos is identified as a possible suspect by one of several students he's tried to snatch off the street or from parking lots. Police search his home in Salem, Oregon, on May 26, 1969. In the garage, a Corvallis detective notices an unusual knot in a rope, a knot he has seen on the ropes tying parts of women to parts of cars in the Long Tom River. Dubbed the Lust Killer, Brudos is arrested on June 3, 1969, and later that month pleads guilty to three murders.

By June, Ted is back in Tacoma, on the waterfront, working at Export Pacific, the historic Griggs lumber mill, known in its turn-of-the-century heyday as the St. Paul & Tacoma Lumber Company, one of the largest sawmill operations in the region. The vast mill property on the mudflats is just down the bay from the smelter, ideally situated for Ted to breathe the fortified air.

It's a perilous time to drop out of college: the Selective Service cancels his student deferment and classifies him I-A, available for immediate military service. But no matter: that summer, he's free and easy. He's renting an upstairs room in the southwest corner of a boardinghouse at 4143 12th Avenue Northeast, in Seattle's University District, owned by Freda and Ernst Rogers.[40] He is the cat among the pigeons.

IN 1969, there are seventeen accidents in the reversible lanes on the island's bridges.[41]

In the early morning hours of August 9, select members of Charles Manson's so-called family cut the phone lines at Sharon Tate's house above Beverly Hills, climb an embankment, and follow his instructions to "totally destroy" everyone within. During the beating, kicking, shooting, chasing, and stabbing that follows, little is said, apparently, but Tex Watson, tasked with the slaughter, is moved to declaim, "I am the devil, and I'm here to do the devil's business."[42]

At the end of September, Ted starts working as a process server. He meets twenty-five-year-old Elizabeth Kloepfer at the Sandpiper Tavern, near the university. They dance and drink some beers. She is a petite divorced mother of a three-year-old girl named Molly; she has long, shiny, light brown hair and a face of blank Botticellian innocence; she's a Mormon doctor's daughter from Ogden, Utah, north of Salt Lake City. Her ex-husband is out of her life, but she retains his name. She's recently moved to Seattle, and thus resembles Louise Bundy circa 1951, a single mother adrift in the big city and in need of a lifeline. They get drunk, and he comes back to her apartment with her. They fall asleep on her bed without having sex. During the night she becomes aware that he is moving around her room, looking at the perfume bottles and birth control pills on her dresser.[43]

In the morning, he makes breakfast for her and Molly: eggs and toast. Liz is embarrassed at getting drunk and avoids him for a day or so but then reverts to her initial enthusiasm, recognizing that he's older and more sophisticated than she feels herself to be. He has nice clothes, so she agrees to see him again. He tells her he's going to law school. He goes grocery shopping with her and buys steaks and French bread and wine and salad greens and makes her a nice meal. He reads a story about a teddy bear to her daughter, and they all fall in love.

Ted and Liz become deeply involved. She meets his parents at their home in Tacoma; they spend weekends at his parents' lakeside cabin, across the rebuilt Tacoma Narrows Bridge near Gig Harbor. He travels home with her at Christmas 1969. In January 1970 he helps her find a duplex apartment near Green Lake. Keeping his own place, he spends most of his time with her. They begin shopping for wedding rings and apply for a marriage license, but after an argument, he yanks his briefcase out of her VW, pulls out the license, and tears it up.

ON MARCH 8, 1970, the *San Francisco Examiner*, amid news on Nixon and Laos and POWs in Hanoi, runs a front-page story about the Selby smelter, which is releasing three to five pounds of lead dust every hour. The paper reports that lead may have caused the "mysterious" poisoning deaths of horses nearby since the early 1900s.[44]

The smelter is likely responsible for the deaths of eleven valuable Appaloosas on the ranch of B. George Wesner, near Benicia. A veterinary researcher at the University of California, Davis, performs necropsies and finds that the bodies contained eleven to seventeen ppm of lead, with twenty considered a lethal dose for an animal that size. The newspaper dredges up photos of Selby's towering smokestack and stories from 1913 in which local farmers claimed that crops and livestock were being "smeltered" to death, at which time the company dispatched agents to blame local oil refineries.[45]

Later that month, on the night of March 22, Kathleen Johns, twenty-two and seven months pregnant, is driving with her ten-month-old daughter from San Bernardino to Petaluma to visit her mother, a drive that proceeds without incident until a man in another car pulls alongside her and begins vehemently waving her off the road, indicating that there's something wrong with her vehicle. When she stops, he pulls up behind her and tells her that her left rear wheel is loose, offering to tighten it for her. She agrees, but when she pulls back onto the highway, the wheel falls off. The same man pulls her over again, offering to take her to the nearest gas station, but as they pass station after station she begins to fear the worst.

At the first intersection, Kathleen flees the vehicle, running into a field with her baby and crouching for more than an hour in the darkness as he searches the area with a flashlight. When her car is found, it has been set on fire. When she sees a composite sketch of the Zodiac suspect at the police station, she identifies him as her abductor. That summer, the Zodiac, perhaps high on the Selby supply, takes credit for terrorizing her.[46]

ON MAY 5, 1970, the day after four students are shot dead at Kent State University in Ohio during an anti-war protest, a thousand students and other protesters flood across the southbound lanes of I-5 in the University District, halting traffic. Ted is a counterprotester, waving his arms and shouting at the demonstrators to go home. He speaks out against the "radical socialist types who just were all for trashing the buildings and destroying the university."[47] Later, he tapes the handle of Liz's car jack so she can use it to "protect" herself.[48]

That same month, he's fired from the process server for missing work and begins a job at Pedline Surgical Supply, a medical wholesaler, delivering supplies such as plaster of paris to doctors' offices and hospitals. At some point prior to working for Pedline, he suffers a slip and fall, breaking his leg or spraining his ankle or suffering a similar injury that necessitates wearing a cast and using crutches—an injury that occurs at a convenient time for someone staving off the interest of the Selective Service.[49] In any event, he's lucky, drawing a winning number at the next draft lottery.

He's planning to apply to law school but performs poorly on the LSAT. He offers Liz vague excuses, saying Temple University has failed to supply his transcripts on time, slowing his admissions application. She realizes for the first time that he's lied to her and has not yet completed his undergraduate degree. He's skinny but so strong that he can sit cross-legged and hold four-year-old Molly in the air upside down by her ankles on Christmas Day.[50] "I Think I Love You" is the hit single.

OHIO'S CUYAHOGA RIVER spontaneously combusts in 1969, something it's done a dozen times before.[51] Think rivers can't burn? Sure they can, if they're covered in oil. With this symbol of environmental crisis fresh in the headlines, the 1970 Clean Air Act and Water Quality Improvement Act are passed, and federal and state bureaucracies must now limit hazardous emissions. For the first time, they must regulate lead and arsenic. The Environmental Protection Agency is created in December 1970 to wield these new powers. In 1971, the surgeon general declares that no child should have a blood lead level above forty micrograms per deciliter.[52]

WE HATE NIXON because he is trying to kill my brother with a lottery number for the draft. I overhear whispered conversations about running away to Canada. My mother wrings her hands.

THE DEVIL'S BUSINESS

My brother collects *Peanuts* cartoon books and lets me read them. He watches *The Fly* with me, in which Vincent Price turns into a housefly, and he chases me around making buzzing sounds and helps me hide my stuffed animals in his closet so my father can't take them.

Whenever my father leaves the house, my brother plays "Bridge Over Troubled Water" very loud on the record player. Over the summer, he finds our parents' marriage certificate and learns that my mother was seven months pregnant with him when she got married. There are no wedding photos, no frilly white dress: that's why. My brother leaves home and goes to university and doesn't ever come back to live with us again. His room is empty and there's no more bridge over troubled water.

In September 1971, Ted completes a forty-hour course in how to answer calls from people in crisis who may be in danger of suicide, part of a paid work-study stint at the Seattle Crisis Clinic in the Capitol Hill neighborhood. He becomes fast friends with an older woman volunteering on the Tuesday night shift, Ann Rule. Rule has family connections to law enforcement: her grandparents helped run a jail. She was briefly a policewoman in Seattle, but she quit when she failed her vision exam. Mother of two teenagers, in the midst of splitting up with her husband, she writes for detective magazines. The crisis hotline is cathartic for her: her only brother has recently committed suicide.

Alone in the clinic offices in a drafty old Victorian house, Rule spends long hours with Ted between calls, chatting about their personal troubles. She confides in him about the breakup of her marriage. He confesses his illegitimacy, telling her, "I only found out who I really am a year or so ago."[53] He's learned that he was born in a home for unwed mothers. When his mother brought him home, he says, she pretended he was her brother. "So I grew up believing that she was my sister," he says. Rule feels sorry for him, bringing sandwiches and cookies to share on Tuesday nights.

He admits he's been cooling on Liz and thinking of getting back together with his old girlfriend, Diane. He doesn't want to be tied down. Rule offers advice, suggesting that perhaps he cares more for Liz than he knows. She admires his courtly, old-fashioned manner with women, describing it later as "old-world gallantry."[54] After their shifts, he insists on escorting her to her car, watching until she's inside the vehicle with the doors locked and the engine started, waving her on her way. "Be careful," he says. "I don't want anything to happen to you."[55]

I AM NINE, I am ten, and I have never flown in an airplane. On November 24, 1971, a man giving his name as Dan Cooper boards Northwest Orient Airlines Flight 305 from Portland to Seattle, sits at the back of the plane, and hands the stewardess a note demanding a ransom. He shows her a bomb in his briefcase. He is matter-of-fact, calm, and polite. As the 727 circles over Puget Sound and the FBI assembles cash from local banks, he correctly identifies local landmarks, saying, "Looks like Tacoma down there."

After a stop at SeaTac Airport, where passengers are released, the plane takes off again, and "D. B. Cooper" (as he is dubbed, incorrectly, by the press) jumps out of the aft cockpit stairway with two parachutes and $200,000 in unmarked twenty-dollar bills somewhere over the Columbia River Gorge in southwestern Washington State. He vanishes forever.

I am eleven, and my father drains the oil out of my mother's car so she can't go anywhere.

In December, Ted leaves the job at the medical supply warehouse, taking with him some supplies of his own: bandages, a pair of crutches, and plaster of paris.

He's not the only one experimenting. On the morning of December 7, Jamie R. Grissim, sixteen, walks a few miles to Fort Vancouver High School, attends class, and is due to return home around 1:30 p.m. She writes poetry, loves horses, and is a diligent student.

That afternoon, she may or may not find herself in a van belonging to a twenty-two-year-old who graduated from Fort Vancouver a few years earlier, a man named Warren Leslie Forrest. He will later admit to picking up a sixteen-year-old girl at the time. He feels that hitchhikers are promiscuous bad girls and rape won't hurt them as much.[56]

Six months later, Jamie's purse and ID are found scattered beside a road north of Vancouver, Washington, 165 miles south of Seattle. She is nowhere to be found.[57]

EARLY IN 1972, Ted gets drunk one night and stalks a cafeteria worker at the University of Washington as she leaves work at midnight. He enters her basement apartment while she's in bed. He has followed her repeatedly. He knows the entry is often unlocked, perhaps because he has unlocked it himself. He jumps on her bed and tries to suffocate her with a pillow, but she screams and struggles. He runs away.[58]

For the winter and spring quarters of 1972, he reenrolls at the University of Washington, taking a two-part abnormal psychology course. He's again planning to apply to law schools. One day during class, the instructor, Joel Kestenbaum, is under seige by students demanding that grades be eliminated. Suddenly another student speaks up, and Kestenbaum takes in "this fellow, dressed in a tweed sport coat, button-down dress shirt, penny loafers," his cold, deep voice calmly rising above those of his fellow students, the "unwashed, unshaven hippies" who are challenging their instructor. Ted speaks sharply in favor of evaluating student work "properly." He seems, Kestenbaum feels, like "a very likable guy."[59]

Kestenbaum is not his only fan. Several professors in the psychology department are struck by him, including Patricia Lunneborg and Scott Fraser, who supervises Ted's honors thesis but is slightly put off when Ted writes a deceitful letter explaining his poor grades as a freshman and sophomore, saying that he's an orphan who has spent time in foster homes and suffers from emotional issues.[60]

Somewhere Ted acquires an old Ford pickup truck, and in April 1972 he drives all the way to Neah Bay near Cape Flattery, the westernmost point in the continental United States, a 150-mile, four- to five-hour drive from Seattle.

On May 12, 1972, Ted is rejected by the University of Utah law school, and that night Bonnie Jo Freeman, an attractive twenty-nine-year-old bank teller with curly brown hair, leaves her weekend job as a hostess at the Moose Lodge in Spokane around 11:00 p.m. Twice divorced, she has three daughters.[61] Her car is found, unlocked, in the parking lot.

Her body is spotted the following day by tourists taking in the view from the summit turnout in Idaho's Fourth of July Canyon, about an hour's drive east of Spokane and twenty miles east of Coeur d'Alene, off I-90. She's lying on a logging road in the canyon, having been manually strangled and pushed over an embankment in an area so remote, investigators say, that the perpetrator may have believed that "animals and rodents in the woods" would have destroyed the body before it was found.[62] The local pathologist finds no sign of rape.[63]

On May 18, Ted buys gas in Coeur d'Alene, Idaho.[64]

EL PASO AND THE STATE sue the ASARCO, a lawsuit initially focusing on sulfur dioxide emissions. During the discovery process, public officials are "surprised" to learn that "between 1969 and 1971 more than 1,100 tons of lead, 560 tons of zinc, 12 tons of cadmium, and more than 1 ton of arsenic" have been emitted from the smelter's smokestack.[65] In 1970, El Paso has a population of 340,000, so that works out to approximately six pounds of lead for every man, woman, and child in town. Ciudad Juárez is just across the border, and there's plenty to go around.

In 1972, tests reveal that five children living in Smeltertown, among a cluster of one hundred El Paso families housed in old adobes at the base of the smokestack, are suffering from lead poisoning. Hospitalized, they undergo painful chelation therapy, injected with a substance that binds to the lead. Another thirty are found to be suffering from chronic lead exposure, with symptoms including anemia, stomach pain, hyperactivity, and mental disabilities.[66] "We believe there are 40,000 children under the age of 6 in the El Paso area who should receive tests to determine whether dangerous levels of lead have built up in their organs and blood," says Dr. Bernard Rosenblum, director of the City-County Health Unit.[67]

Dr. Philip Landrigan, a pediatrician and epidemiologist, extends testing to a more affluent white area to stymie the corporation's inevitable temptation to blame poor victims for living in dirty housing.[68] The testing finds that 62 percent of children ten and under and 43 percent of everyone living within a mile of the smelter have elevated lead levels. In time, Smeltertown will be demolished and topsoil replaced, but the problem is far-reaching, extending well beyond a mile.

Some children's exposure may come from playing in dust, Rosenblum allows, but most comes from "the air they breathe." EL PASO FEARS "KILLER," reads the headline in a Texas newspaper, the killer being either lead or the smelter.[69]

ON MAY 9, 1972, Armand Labbe, Tacoma smelter manager, writes to his colleague Lee Travis, in ASARCO's Salt Lake City office, to report alarming data showing that children in Ruston are living and playing in a highly contaminated environment. After the dustup in El Paso, hair and urine samples have been taken from elementary schoolchildren in Ruston, as well as soil samples from vacant lots and playgrounds. It turns out that the Ruston soil is contaminated with lead to the tune of 70 to 4,800 ppm, with concentrations of arsenic measuring between 46 and 3,302 ppm.[70] Normally, Washington soil should have 24 ppm of lead and 7 of arsenic.[71]

A few days later, on May 15, Travis writes privately to Kenneth Nelson, the vice president of environmental affairs, brooding over how things look. He's been studying soil samples of lead and arsenic, remarking that "six areas are high enough to cause me some concern, but I don't know what to do about it. It seems to me we would stir up a lot of bad publicity if we tried to replace the soil like we did at El Paso and I am inclined to let the 'sleeping dog lie' unless some Agency calls the matter to our attention."[72] In Tacoma, the public is not informed. The sleeping dog lies.

Publicly, smelter officials deliver themselves of the opinion that arsenic is "not a strong carcinogenic agent."[73] In Tacoma, as in El Paso, they claim that whatever lead children may be picking up comes simply from playing in the dirt, not from breathing the air. If they play with dirt, if they put it in their mouths, that's their own fault.

On June 10, 1972, Ted receives his bachelor's degree in psychology from the University of Washington, graduating with honors. He stands unsmiling for a photo in cap and gown in the gray rain, hands hanging loosely at his sides. That summer, he completes an internship at Harborview Hospital's Mental Health Center, working with a caseload of twelve psychiatric outpatients, meeting with them, writing reports on their progress, and referring them to physicians for further evaluation.

All this compassion and responsibility bores him, so he begins having an affair with a Harborview co-worker, Sandy Gwinn, cheating on Liz. During one of their dates, he has her drive him around the shore of Lake Sammamish in Issaquah looking for the home of an imaginary elderly relative. He doesn't remember the address. On another, they drive a couple of hours west from Tacoma to Ocean Shores, on the Pacific. It's overcast on the shore, but Ted knows an isolated spot inland on the Humptulips River, which empties into the bay, where they picnic and go swimming. Ted repeatedly pushes Sandy's head underwater, pulling off her bikini top until she ties the strings in a knot to discourage him. Then he pulls off her bikini bottoms and has sex with her, pushing his forearm under her chin until she can't breathe. She keeps saying "I can't breathe" until he takes it away. She stops seeing him after that.[74]

Sometime that June, he may or may not catch sight of twenty-two-year-old Kerry May Hardy, a young woman with long copper-colored hair, follow her into the vestibule of an apartment building in Capitol Hill, not far from the Seattle Crisis Clinic, and club her from behind, admiring her where she lies, "her long hair spread out like a fan above her head."[75] He may or may not drag her into the weeds behind the building, depositing her remains in a shallow grave in a forested area near Cle Elum, on the eastern slopes of the Cascades, in an area later bulldozed to create a golf course, part of the Suncadia Resort.[76]

What is Cle Elum? It's a name belonging to the Kittitas people, meaning "swift water." It's a wide spot in the road and a way station on the Olympic–Wallowa Lineament. It's the "Heart of the Cascades," and nobody knows the Cascades like Ted Bundy.

On the Fourth of July, he's buying gas in Hoquiam, Washington, a small coastal city on Grays Harbor, where Billy Gohl, the "Ghoul of Grays Harbor," held sway. He was the state's first serial killer, murdering men during the Alaska gold rush by luring them to the local union building, shooting them, stripping them of valuables, and tipping their bodies through a trapdoor chute into the bay. Whatever Ted is doing in Hoquiam is Ted's business, but he always buys gas when he's hunting.

For the next few months, he's still working shifts at Harborview, and rumors begin circulating that he's stealing patient records.

THAT FALL, Ted is excited to get back into Republican politics. A neighbor down the street in the U District, Mary Ellen McCaffree, is an organizer for the 1972 campaign to reelect the governor of Washington, Dan Evans, and Ted hangs out at her house, where volunteers gather for leafleting and putting out yard signs.

In September he's hired by the campaign too, assigned to "shadow" Evans's chief opponent, Albert Rosellini, the former governor, and tasked with attending Rosellini's events and taping his speeches to analyze later. He enjoys putting on disguises to attend these appearances, wearing wigs and a false mustache, studying the ways in which actors transform themselves. During the first weekend of the month, he meets Richard Larsen, a *Seattle Times* reporter, at a special event, the grand opening of the North Cascades Highway, a controversial route through one of the most remote northern stretches of national forest in the United States.[77]

An enormous pair of shears is produced in front of a crowd of three thousand arrayed on bleachers in the town of Winthrop, on the eastern side of the mountain range. Evans cuts the ribbon, Ted hands out campaign buttons, and the governmental caravan makes its stately way west across Washington Pass and Rainy Pass. The next day, Ted is back on I-90, crossing the mountains at Snoqualmie Pass. He buys gas at Cle Elum.

In October, Ted is hired as an assistant director by the Seattle Crime Prevention Advisory Commission, the so-called Crime Commission. One of its members, University of Washington psychology professor Ezra Stotland, finds Ted so delightful, so utterly charming, that he invites him home for dinner with his family on several occasions, hoping that his sixteen-year-old daughter will find someone just like him to marry.[78] Ted is put to work assisting on a preliminary investigation for a study of assaults against women, part of a program called Speak Out on Rape.[79] When Dan Evans wins reelection in November, Ted applies for the position of commission director.

That December, Ann Rule gives Ted a call, asking if he'd like a ride to a Christmas party for current and former staff of the Crisis Clinic. Several times that night, she sees Ted staring at an expensively dressed woman with long, dark hair that's parted in the middle. He gets drunk and falls asleep in the car as she drives him back to his rooming house.

IN DECEMBER 1972, Rodger Jones begins his campaign as a gadfly and all-around thorn in the side of smelter management. After his earlier accident he's returned to work, becoming active in the union, which has become the Steelworkers Local 25. He begins publishing a typewritten and mimeographed newsletter, *The Smelterworker*, illustrated with hand-drawn cartoons and clip art. December's issue features an all-caps headline, ARSENIC: OUR PROBLEM, and reports on a pamphlet compiled that year by Dr. Pinto on plant workers at the smelter between 1949 and 1960, revealing a rate of deaths caused by respiratory lung cancer almost twice the state average. Despite this statistic, Dr. Samuel Milham, an epidemiologist at the state health department, states for the record that "we have absolutely no evidence that the amount of arsenic people are being exposed to around the smelter has caused any acute health effects at all."[80]

At the moment, no one's too worried about lead. The Ruston smokestack is still releasing tons of it per year, but the federal blood lead level is set so high during the 1970s—at forty micrograms per deciliter—that even heavily exposed children do not, on paper, appear to be poisoned. Jones quizzes Milham on the results of testing a small number of schoolchildren attending Ruston Elementary. They reveal elevated blood lead levels of more than fifteen micrograms per deciliter, but the health department shrugs its bureaucratic shoulders.[81] There's nothing they can do about it.

It's three-card monte, poison edition. Smelter officials are shuffling the cards. Now it's lead, now it's arsenic. Who knows anything, really, about arsenic? Dr. Pinto does, but he's not talking.

ON JANUARY 10, 1973, the EPA proposes a phaseout of leaded gasoline over the next five years, noting that a significant portion of the country's urban population, especially children, are "over-exposed" to lead, given that more than two hundred thousand tons is blowing out of tailpipes every year and the only safe level for lead is zero.[82] It will get around to arsenic later.

This is good news. But it's too late for Ted, who that month is passed over for directorship of the Crime Commission. He accepts instead a contract from the King County Law and Justice Planning Office to contribute to a study of recidivism associated with violent crimes, such as rape. Overseeing the project is Donna Schram, a psychologist in her thirties who is forging a career specializing in rape studies with a view to improving legislative and police responses. Early in 1973, Schram receives a call from Patricia Lunneborg, her mentor at the University of Washington, recommending a former student, Ted Bundy, who is applying to law schools but having trouble getting accepted because his early college grades were poor. His plan, Schram will recall, is "to meet people in the system and have recommendations to take with him on his next round of applications."[83] He's hired.

The project gives him access to thousands of individual criminal court records and an overview of how rape is investigated by police and prosecuted by courts. A draft of the resulting report will find that the rate of rape in Seattle has risen over the previous ten years by 420 percent and that "many rapists are multiple rapists."[84] Contributing to this data in more ways than one, Ted is fascinated to find that a number of offenders "do not seem to be 'sick people,' but individuals who believe that they can exert their will over others with impunity."[85] In other words, he's fine.

On the night of January 8, he chases a purse snatcher in the parking lot of Northgate Mall and catches him, recovering the victim's purse and thirty-four dollars. He accepts a commendation from the Seattle Police Department but does not reveal the reason why he hangs around the mall at night: he's parking his car in an underground tunnel near the loading dock, shoplifting tools, a television, clothes, and other items, and walking out unsuspected.

BY 1973, PEGGY REYNOLDS, editor, chief reporter, and photographer for the local paper, is incensed by the toll taken by the floating bridge. She makes a practice of running graphic photos of head-on collisions on the front page of the *Mercer Island Reporter* alongside incendiary headlines. On February 15, a crumpled Buick Skylark, its windshield crushed into the driver's seat, appears above FATALITY ADDS TO REVERSE LANE TOLL. Four women heading for the ski slopes in a Ford wagon survive; the Skylark's driver is "killed instantly."[86] In the first eleven months of 1972, there are twenty-six reversible lane accidents.

On March 1, 1973, the paper is virtually rolling its eyes, the latest crash earning the headline REVERSE LANES CHALK UP ANOTHER.[87]

THE DEVIL'S BUSINESS

WITH A LETTER of recommendation from Governor Evans, Ted reapplies to law school at the University of Utah in the spring of 1973 and is accepted for that fall.[88]

On a rainy day in March, he runs into Ann Rule outside the Seattle Public Safety Building and tells her he's studying rape victims and wants to see back issues of the stories she's written for *True Detective*. "It would help my research," he says.[89]

He buys a used 1968 Volkswagen Beetle, described variously as off-white, beige, tan, light brown, bronze, or light gray.[90] It is the chameleon of VWs, and it's white, exactly the same color as ours.

Liz's daughter, Molly, is seven, and one day she's home with Ted as her babysitter and they're playing hide-and-go-seek. She finds him in the living room with all the lights turned out, hiding naked under her grandmother's knitted afghan. "You're naked!" she says, and he takes off running for home base, where he sits cross-legged, hiding his crotch with both hands.[91] She pulls them off and sees he has an erection, "reddish-purple," something she's never seen before, and she asks him if it hurts.[92] He looks at her, and his eyes look funny.

She tries to run away from him, but he follows her into her bedroom and climbs into the top bunk bed with her, masturbating as he reads an Uncle Wiggily book to her. She accuses him of peeing on her bed. She's afraid of him now but doesn't tell her mother what he's done because she knows it's wrong and doesn't want him to get in trouble.

I AM TWELVE. *The Partridge Family* is the hit show. Richard Nixon is the president. The World Trade Center is under construction. David Cassidy is on the cover of *Tiger Beat* with his floppy hair and wicked grin. He looks like Jamie Castle, the blond troublemaker in our sixth-grade class who is dedicated to tormenting our teacher, Eddie De Rocco, who knows my father. Whenever Jamie does something unspeakable, like grab girls' crotches, Mr. De Rocco stands before us and says that the chickens will come home to roost.

In May 1973, the *Mercer Island Reporter* takes a picture of our School Safety Patrol, who are meant to guide younger kids across a busy street, West Mercer Way. I'm scowling in the back row, second from the left, with the rest of the girls.[93] The boys are in front. I'm behind the captain, Byron Blauman, a kid with a big round head and blond hair who looks like Charlie Brown. I'm not a fan of Byron, which may explain the scowl. He's always a leader of the kickball and softball teams, and when he picks his side, I'm always last and least desirable. "Fraser," he says, "easy out." I'm on the Safety Patrol, and I never feel safe.

One day in the spring of 1973 we arrive to find a new book on our desks. It's not a textbook. It's a spiral-bound stack of loose-leaf paper as big as a phone book. The mimeographed pages are thick with blurry purple type. It's all about drugs. I have not yet mastered the multiplication tables past six, but I will read anything put before me. I read this cover to cover.

It contains useful information, including nicknames. We are instructed to beware of anyone sidling up to us in the schoolyard and trying to sell us marijuana, dope, ganja, grass, reefer, weed, Mary Jane, Sweet Jane, Mary Ann, Jamaican Tea, Texas T, or Purple Haze. I look out the window at the East Seattle elementary playground, which takes up a full city block of heaving cracked cement ringed by deep green ditches overgrown with horsetails, the same ditches where, in first grade, we launched little grass boats. There isn't anyone out there trying to sell anything. There isn't anyone out there at all.

We learn about hash, hash oil, Thai sticks, cocaine, speed, amphetamines, heroin, LSD, acid, windowpanes, and microdots. LSD is something I know about from *Good Housekeeping*, the pages of which are filled with teenagers misbehaving, such as the daughter of Art Linkletter, the host of *Kids Say the Darndest Things*. I'm reading *Go Ask Alice*, inspired by Linkletter's daughter Diane. Everyone knows she jumped out a window high on acid, thinking she could fly.

THE DEVIL'S BUSINESS

It's the spring of 1973, and Ted is working for Ross Davis, chairman of the Republican Party in Washington State, a job he may or may not have acquired through his good friend Marlin Vortman, another Republican operative he knows from the Evans campaign. Vortman happens to own an off-white VW Beetle. Ted is driving back and forth from Seattle to the state capitol in Olympia, driving to Tumwater, driving to Tacoma, driving to Enumclaw, driving to Spokane, up and down and north and south and east and west, on every major interstate, on state roads and county roads and forest roads and frontage roads. He is buying gas, leaded gas, virtually every day of every month, and he doesn't register the fact that his Chevron credit card is making a map of his movements.

Sometimes Ted house-sits for Vortman and his wife, feeding their pets when they're away. Although he has his own car, he sometimes borrows their VW. He borrows Liz's VW as well.

In May he picks up a hitchhiker near Olympia and murders her and doesn't catch her name.[94]

On July 29, 1973, at 7:15 p.m., Rita Lorraine Jolly, a seventeen-year-old girl with chubby cheeks and long brown hair parted in the middle, leaves her apartment on Horton Road in the Portland suburb of West Linn, wearing a brown Pendleton shirt, army fatigue pants, and blue tennis shoes, and is never seen again.

On August 1, 1973, Clarence Baarsma, Bill Baarsma's father, a thirty-two-year veteran of the Tacoma smelter and the foreman of its smelting division, dies of esophageal cancer that has spread to his lungs. He's fifty-eight.

Ted is courting his old girlfriend from college, Diane, dallying with her in the Vortmans' apartment while they're away and not telling Liz. Liz's VW is stolen in August, reappearing on a nearby street a few days later. The only thing missing is a fancy "oriental" knife that Ted had been keeping in her glove compartment.

At some point that summer, Liz finds a brown bag full of women's clothing in Ted's apartment. He tells her it's junk he's getting rid of for his landlady.[95] When she confronts him about his shoplifting, scared that he'll get caught, calling him a thief, he grabs her arm and says, "If you ever tell anyone about this, I'll break your fucking neck."[96]

On August 20 in Eugene, Oregon, Vicki Lynn Hollar, a twenty-four-year-old woman with long, dark hair parted in the middle, walks with a colleague to her black 1965 Beetle. Wearing a pink dress, she has just left work at the Bon Marché. She gets in the car, and she and the vehicle disappear.[97]

ON AUGUST 29 Ted appears on the front page of *The Seattle Times*. A UPI reporter discovers that a Theodore Bundy is responsible for "dirty tricks" performed during Dan Evans's reelection campaign, when he posed as a college student working on a master's degree in political science while "secretly" reporting on the governor's rival.[98] He admits to being armed with a tape recorder while asking probing questions at press conferences. "I'm not the least bit uncomfortable with what went on," Ted says. "You have to know what your opposition is saying and doing."[99]

Dropping in on Donna Schram, his former boss, he brags about these escapades, saying he's modeled himself on Nixon attorney Donald Segretti. Schram is not impressed, having heard Ted bragging about stealing stuff from the campaign—a typewriter and paper, "everything he could get his hands on." She thinks, *I'm done with this guy*.[100]

News of Nixonian tactics in faraway Washington State is considered so startling that a local television news reporter tracks Ted down and interviews him. Shaking his head, his hair long and curly, he laughs heartily at his own hijinks, saying, "I'm embarrassed that I should be taking this publicity from it, really embarrassed."[101]

At the end of August, Ted stops by Ross Davis's house in Seattle and chats with Davis while rummaging through the trunk of his Beetle, tossing aside rags and tools. Davis happens to glance into the trunk and notices a pair of handcuffs.[102]

THE DEVIL'S BUSINESS

FOR SOME MYSTERIOUS REASON, Ted blows off law school at the University of Utah in the fall, writing the admissions office a letter explaining that he's suffered a serious car accident and is in the hospital. It's a lie.[103] He has sprained his ankle in a fender bender but is in no way incapacitated.

Instead, after a brief visit from Diane in early September, Ted starts taking night classes at the University of Puget Sound in Tacoma, a campus lacking in atmosphere and amenities. He can't concentrate and instead spends a lot of time in the law library, fantasizing about things that are more interesting to him.

Elaine Crafton, a nineteen-year-old from Tacoma, is walking down the street one afternoon near the UPS campus when a young man driving a VW Beetle abruptly pulls up to the curb next to her, waves her over to the window, and says, "Hi, I'm not from around here. Can you tell me where there are any parks near here?" He wants her to get in the car, and although she finds him a "very nice-looking individual who was very nice and clean-shaven, clean-cut," she listens to what she calls her "inner voice," which tells her not to get into a car with a stranger, a good-looking stranger who shouldn't need to hail girls off the street. She walks on.[104]

WHERE THERE'S SMOKE, there's fire: on September 3, 1973, a fire breaks out in the baghouse at the Bunker Hill lead smelter in Kellogg, Idaho. The baghouse building, which dates back to 1917, is the plant's chief pollution control. Before going up the smokestack, emissions from the plant are forced through twelve thousand tube-shaped wool-and-Orlon filter bags hanging from the ceiling, each thirty feet long and eighteen inches wide. Every one of the bags is full of lead dust. On September 3, twenty-eight hundred of the bags burn, along with a section of the roof.

The baghouse is now out of service. Before the fire, emissions not captured by the bags were running around 10 to 20 tons per month. After the fire, up to 160 tons per month—50 to 70 percent lead, along with arsenic, mercury, cadmium, and zinc—are pouring into the air.

But lead prices are climbing—they'll reach $479 per ton in October 1974.[105] Smelter officials are faced with a choice. Frank Woodruff, a company man who has climbed the copper ladder working at the Chino Mine in New Mexico, a hard man known for layoffs, has been elevated to vice president of Bunker Hill's new parent entity. It's now a wholly owned subsidiary of Gulf Resources and Chemical Corporation, based in Houston. He must help his overlords decide whether to shut the smelter down until the baghouse can be rebuilt, which could take six months. Other possibilities include keeping the facility open but reducing production. The most desirable option, however, is felt to be this: Continue production at current or greater levels while pumping unimaginable levels of lead into the community. Families live right next to the smelter, yards away, in a neighborhood called Deadwood Gulch.

Woodruff writes a memo to chew over with corporate. He and Gulf know all about El Paso and what children there were recently deemed to be worth, and they consider the costs as if weighing up pork by the pound. "El Paso—200 children—$5 to 10,000 [per] kid," he writes.[106] Another official at Bunker Hill works the math in a back-of-a-napkin calculation, estimating that the legal liability for poisoning five hundred children would amount to a mere "6–7 million."[107] If Gulf and Bunker Hill decide to keep running the smelter flat out, increasing production, they'll come out $10 million or $11 million ahead, even if compelled to pay an inflated $12,000 per child. The choice is children or profits. Guess which they choose.

For Woodruff and his colleagues, it's not a hard decision. They're doing the devil's business, which is no different from what Ted does. Like Ted, Bunker Hill has been killing people for years. It's second nature.

So the smelter does not shut down. Lead production is ramped up, for profit. The owners run the plant full bore, forcing their blast furnace smoke through the remains of the baghouse. When that slows them down, they release emissions directly into the air in what will amount to one of the largest lead-poisoning events in American history.

THE DEVIL'S BUSINESS

Bunker Hill is in a box canyon with narrow walls, prone to temperature inversions. Locals call the canyon "the Box." The Box is now filling with lead.

ON OCTOBER 15, Deborah Lee Tomlinson of Creswell, Oregon, just south of Eugene, a girl with shoulder-length light brown hair parted in the middle, runs away from home on her sixteenth birthday with another female friend. The two of them disappear.

EVERYTHING CHANGES and nothing does. We've moved back to the first house my father built, the ugly brown one. He's sold the other one. I take a school bus to a new school in the fall, a junior high with long, echoing corridors and metal lockers and clanging doors and crowds of students shouting and throwing things. At home, I am alone with my parents; my siblings have gone to college.

The bus feels like it's about to fly to pieces, with its rattling door and hard Naugahyde seats that have tears in them, metal springs poking out of the duct tape that somebody has pasted over the holes, but we listen to the radio and fall into a fugue state as we drive back and forth, listening, whether we like it or not, to the Top 40 hit songs of the fall of 1973, which are "Tie a Yellow Ribbon Round the Ole Oak Tree" and "Bad, Bad Leroy Brown" and "Let's Get It On" and "Crocodile Rock" and "Killing Me Softly with His Song."

We live on 72nd Avenue, where we lived after I was born. Straight down the hill, the street crosses over the top of the I-90 tunnel, a shallow trench excavated beneath the neighborhood and covered by a land bridge. Exhaust from the tunnel blows out of grates. If you walk on the lid atop the tunnel, you can feel the vibration and hear the roar, somewhere down there, underground.

On October 20, 1973, there's a Saturday Night Massacre, and my mother is whispering urgently about Nixon and Elliot Richardson and

Archibald Cox and William Ruckelshaus and impeachment. She sends me down to the shopping center the next day to buy a Sunday newspaper for thirty-five cents out of the coin-operated box in front of Ernst Hardware. "Ruckelshaus" sounds like "Rumpelstiltskin." I can tell that my mother is afraid of Nixon and afraid of my father, hiding her new shoes in my closet.

THERE'S AN OIL EMBARGO and a line of cars at the gas station at the bottom of the hill, and my mother is worried about having enough gas to get to work. It's a good thing Volkswagens get such good gas mileage, she says. She likes to look on the bright side.

During the Christmas holiday that year, Liz and Molly go home to Utah to visit her parents, and Ted invites Diane up from San Francisco and they spend Christmas week together in the Vortmans' apartment while the couple are vacationing in Hawaii. Ted and Diane are now "officially" engaged.[108]

THAT SAME WINTER, there is another young man, in the Midwest, in a state of readiness. Dennis Rader was born in 1945, the year before Ted, in Columbus, Kansas, a city in the far southeastern corner of the state, twenty-five miles from Pittsburg, Kansas. Pittsburg is named for coalpits, and that's where his mother and aunt take him, at age eight, to see a 3D movie, *House of Wax*, with Vincent Price, who is stealing women's bodies out of a cemetery and dipping them in wax and putting them on display in his museum.

Pittsburg is built on smelting. Lead and zinc in "payable quantities" are discovered there in 1850.[109] Robert Lanyon, a pioneer from across the state line in Missouri, begins smelting in Pittsburg in 1878, strip-mining coal shale and burning the coal to run the smelters. By 1890 Lanyon is smelting 188,000 pounds of zinc a week, running his plants in shifts, twenty-four hours a day, seven days a week. By 1893 there are six smelters in Pittsburg, population 6,697.[110]

THE DEVIL'S BUSINESS

Dennis grows up spending summers at his grandparents' farm outside Columbus, hunting and fishing and drinking water from a local well and swimming in old flooded "pit lakes" made from coalpits, collecting string, tying knots, and torturing cats in an abandoned barn. Like Ted, he loves Roy Rogers. "I *was* Roy Rogers," he later says.[111]

He is moody and a slow learner. By the sixth grade he is spying on a former teacher from a tree, planning to abduct her and "tie her up."[112] He loves watching horror movies and designing secret dungeons where he plots "death to pretty girls."[113] On hot days, he jumps in the cattle tank and ties himself up. "Sparky," his penis, is happy. He practices autoerotic asphyxiation in his basement and dreams of imprisoning Annette Funicello in a local sandpit. At fourteen, he's sexually excited by news that the victims of the Clutter murders in Kansas (later the subject of Truman Capote's *In Cold Blood*) were bound. He barely graduates from high school. In the future he idly plans to kill someone in Pittsburg.[114]

Later, remarking on his first crimes, he'll appeal to the god of fire:

> Compare it to a volcano. Early into its formation, a crack in the main structure occurs. Over the years, that crack produces more cracks and bad rock formations. All the time, pressure builds up in the main chamber, although there are no major eruptions. Some cracks let lava out to the surface and each time there is a cooling effect. Then in the fall of 1973, a major fault occurs, which led to the major eruption on January 15, 1974.[115]

It's as good an explanation as any for 1974.

Chapter 6

The Daylight Basement

—◇—

The sky was the color of lead.

—Vera Caspary, *Laura*

The sky is the color of lead because it's full of lead. The bluest skies you've ever seen might be in Seattle, but not in 1974.[1]

The Tacoma smelter, point source for sulfur dioxide pollution, controls the clouds. It influences the acidity of precipitation. Normal clean air has a pH level of 5.7. Normal clean rain has a pH level of 5.6. Below normal levels, salmon and rainbow trout fail to thrive, frogs' eggs die, tadpoles die, crayfish die, and mayflies die.

Rain near the smelter has a pH level below 4.[2] Rain in Seattle has a pH of 4.2 to 4.4 thanks to industry, cars, trucks, and planes.[3] ASARCO is picking up steam because its days are numbered.

The year 1974 is a very special one for the company, a major anniversary. In celebration, it issues a commemorative key chain with a brass fob. On the front is an illustration of a dump truck and an open-pit mine. On the back is a periodic table of the elements, with raised letters spelling out "75 Years of Progress in Metals 1899–1974."[4]

THE DAYLIGHT BASEMENT

On January 1, 1974, Diane Edwards flies back to San Francisco, still under the impression that she's Ted Bundy's fiancée. He's twenty-seven, and the minute he drops her off at the airport, he drives over to Liz Kloepfer's apartment, where Liz is cooking dinner for him, clad in an apron, and makes passionate love to her.[5] Diane will never see him again.

Around midnight on January 4, 1974, Karen Sparks turns off the TV in the living room and goes to bed. She is a strikingly beautiful twenty-one-year-old student at the University of Washington who shares a house with three male roommates at 4325 8th Avenue Northeast. She has long auburn hair parted in the middle, and the house, squarely within the U District, is half a mile by car from Ted Bundy's rooming house. It's less than that if you're slipping through alleyways and along back fences. She has recently noticed a man staring at her at the laundromat.[6]

She goes downstairs to her basement room, a messy student space with a mattress on the floor. Clothes, books, and records are propped against the walls or scattered on the floor. *Meet the Beatles* is leaning upside down by a bookcase. Crosby, Stills, Nash & Young. Creedence Clearwater. There is a bad moon rising, waxing gibbous.

Karen reads for a while and at one point thinks she sees a man peering in the window. But she isn't alarmed, feeling safe with her male roommates. She falls asleep.

At around 2 a.m. the man enters, probably through a door on the south side of the house that's often left unlocked. Wielding a piece of metal, perhaps a length of rebar left lying outside, he bludgeons the sleeping woman over the head and rapes her with it, jamming it so violently into her body that it splits her bladder in two. He pulls a quilt over her head and leaves her for dead.[7] At 2:30 the following afternoon, one of her roommates looks in, sees her in bed, and wonders why she's so tired.

Finally, at 7:30, growing concerned about her lying so still for so long, the roommate enters the room and pulls back the quilt, struck with horror to see that Karen, the sheets, and the mattress are soaked in blood. He calls 911, thinking that she has somehow been injured by falling down the stairs. Rushed to the hospital, she spends the next ten days in a coma, eventually recovering from her severe internal injuries. When she regains consciousness, she has no memory of the attack. She has lost 50 percent of her hearing and 40 percent of her vision and been left with permanent brain damage. She learns to speak again but for years will suffer from epileptic fits and ringing in her ears.[8]

ON JANUARY 15, 1974, I'm twelve, nodding, half asleep on the school bus, rocking along to Ringo Starr singing, "You're sixteen, you're beautiful, and you're mine."

In Wichita, Kansas, Dennis Rader has had enough of fantasies. He wants to kill somebody for real, and he knows who.

He's twenty-nine and has spent four years, from 1966 to 1970, in the Air Force. He's married to a woman named Paula and is a member of Christ Lutheran Church. During a recession, he's out of work, having lost a good job as a mechanic at Cessna. He's waiting for classes to start at Wichita State University, planning on a degree in criminal justice. He has nothing to do but indulge his incessant fantasies of bondage and murder.

He cuts pictures of women and children out of ads in magazines or newspapers, drawing bindings across their bodies and pasting them on his index cards. He invents names for these figures, such as "Monique." He calls them "slick ads." He calls the places where he hides them "hidey-holes"; he calls the barns and silos where he imagines holding women hostage "castles"; he calls his special treats, rape and bondage, "cookies." It's as if, inside his skull, there is a fifth grader operating the controls of a sexually deviant adult male.

He's seen an attractive Hispanic woman and her young daughter walking on the street, having spotted the woman before at the Coleman plant, where he used to work before Cessna. In Wichita, whoever doesn't work in aviation works at Coleman, the famous camping equipment brand, or for the Koch brothers. On several occasions, he follows the woman home and

THE DAYLIGHT BASEMENT

cases the house. He sees an adult male coming and going, noting the times he goes to work and when the children leave for school.

Dennis plans his "project," which he dubs "Little Mex," by drawing detailed descriptions in notebooks and on three-by-five-inch index cards, displaying the same limited vocabulary and poor spelling he had in elementary school. To prepare, he goes to the drugstore and buys a length of quarter-inch hemp rope. At 8:20 a.m. on January 15, after dropping his wife off at work and parking his car at a nearby store, he walks to the house owned by the Otero family. He likes this house because it's on a large corner lot, with no other house too close by.

He knows their names. He thinks the man, Joseph Otero, is off at work, the older children at school, the wife home with the youngest daughter. He's wearing his old Air Force parka, its pockets packed with a knife, a Colt .22 Woodsman handgun loaded with hollow-point bullets, lengths of pre-knotted rope and cord, adhesive tape, wire cutters, and gloves. It's a cold morning. He has had to scrape ice off the car windows.

He jumps the fence into the backyard. He's a Wichita lineman, as in the Glen Campbell song, so he cuts the telephone line to the house, and he sees a dog's paw prints on the snowy ground.[9] He almost runs off. He's sweating so much that the insides of his rubber gloves are wet. Suddenly a nine-year-old boy comes out the back door with the dog, a German shepherd mix, and everything's happening. Grabbing the kid, pulling his gun, leaving the dog in the backyard, he forces his way into the house, only to see that most of the family is at home: Joseph and Julie Otero, the parents; Joey, the boy; and Josephine, or Josie, the dark-haired eleven-year-old girl who's caught his eye and reminds him of his longtime dream victim, the belle of *Beach Blanket Bingo*, Annette Funicello. The Oteros are originally from Puerto Rico, and Joseph Otero, like Rader himself, has served in the Air Force.

When Dennis bursts into the house with Joey, Joseph comes from a back room, and Dennis holds the gun on him, telling the family the lies he's planned in advance. He says he's a wanted man who just needs to steal their car and some money. Joseph recognizes the jacket, and Dennis tells him he's AWOL. The two engage in "some friendly talk about the Air Force years."[10] The Oteros tell him their car is just about out of gas.

Next he moves the family to the back bedrooms, binding and gagging each of them, first with tape and then, when they complain about the tight restraints, with white cord, the kind used in venetian blinds. After tying them to the beds, he begins strangling them, Joseph first, then Julie. He hasn't realized how difficult it is to kill an adult human being who's fighting for life, how much strength and force it takes, how slippery the gloves become. "I had strangled cats, but had never strangled anyone before, so I really don't know how much pressure you had to put on a person or how long it would take," he'll say later.[11] He strangles Josie until she stops moving. The adults lose consciousness for a time but then begin to stir. Finally, he grabs some plastic bags and pillowcases, fitting them over the adults' heads, tying Joseph Otero's with a belt. Screaming and struggling as a bag is forced over her face, Julie Otero shouts, "May God have mercy on your soul!" before she succumbs.

Dennis smothers Joey with a plastic bag and a white T-shirt. Then he turns to Josie. "I wanted to hang her," he'll recall.[12] For this purpose, he has brought a rope noose. He searches the basement and finds a sturdy sewer pipe, attaching the hangman's noose to it. She's now awake but groggy. He carries her downstairs, pulls off her pants, pulls her panties down, and cuts her bra open. He asks if her parents have a camera, because he wants to take pictures. She says no. She asks what he's doing, and he tells her that she's going to go to sleep and wake up in heaven with her parents and brother. Her eyes are wide with shock. He puts her neck in the noose and lifts her, her toes barely off the floor, then pulls the rope, tightening it, fondling her breasts and masturbating as she dies.

He goes through the house, cleaning, drinking a glass of water, then carefully washing the glass, and turning up the thermostat to try to disguise the time of death, something he's read about in a thriller. He steals Joseph Otero's watch and a transistor radio. He wears the watch for years. He drives the Otero car, nearly out of gas as they'd said, to a department store and parks it, thinking it will make the scene look like a robbery.

THE DAYLIGHT BASEMENT

On his way back to his own car, he realizes he's forgotten his knife at the crime scene and swings by to get it. He finds it on the ground beneath the telephone line and drives home.

He packs up his notes and drawings and burns them in the woods, with leftover pieces of rope. When he's alone, he invents a name for himself, "BTK," which stands for "bind them, torture them, kill them." Once a murderer has a name, he reckons, "you have an identity."[13] In the coming days he buys a rubber ball and begins squeezing it religiously, as an exercise to strengthen his hands.

The bodies are not discovered until that afternoon, when Carmen, thirteen, Danny, fourteen, and the eldest, Charlie, fifteen, come home from school to find their parents and Joey lifeless, with bags on their heads. In the chaos that follows—the children screaming, frantically trying to free their parents, and running to the neighbors—Josie's whereabouts are not ascertained for some time. Her body is not located until a police officer, not wanting to touch the light switches, enters the dark basement with a flashlight and walks blindly into the corpse, seemingly standing upright. He has nightmares for years.[14]

Police are baffled by the scene, eventually developing theories about revenge schemes or drugs: in the Air Force, it turns out, Joseph Otero worked in Panama maintaining aircraft. But there is no evidence of drug running in the Otero family, and none of the scenarios make sense of the sexual element. Over the coming months, the police interview 780 people but are no closer to an answer.

MORE LEAD, MORE MURDER. In Tacoma, the crime rate rises 20 percent in 1974.[15]

The price of lead rises sharply during an unexpected commodities boom. In January 1973, lead is $286 a ton. By 1974 it's touching the sky, $400 a ton. Car batteries, paints, gasoline, electrical cables, solder used by telephone linemen, heavy vests used in shielding patients during X-rays: they all require lead. Lead means wealth. Miners at Bunker Hill are making $8,500 a year, better than the average annual mining wage of $5,756.[16] Smelters are running flat out.

Never has the number of violent crimes been higher, and FBI director J. Edgar Hoover boosts his agency by calculating the rise every decade: In 1960, crime grows an "astounding 98 percent" over the 1950s, nearly doubling again between the 1960s and the late 1970s.[17] Washington State is no exception, with 208,875 crimes in 1974, of which 12,036 are violent, up from 1,479 rapes, murders, robberies, and aggravated assaults in 1960.[18]

Meanwhile at *The Smelterworker*, Rodger Jones is keeping the pressure on, compiling a written record of the plant's accidents and exposures. MAN POISONED BY GAS is the opening gambit of the January 1974 issue, describing a harrowing incident in the nickel plant involving Lowell D. Binam, twenty-eight.[19] While attempting to clean scale off the inside of the nickel evaporator tank, Rodger reports, Binam set off a chemical reaction producing arsine, a highly toxic and flammable gas formed when arsenic comes into contact with an acid. Six hours of headaches and nausea later, Binam was startled to notice blood in his urine and was sent to Dr. Pinto, who had him moved to Tacoma General Hospital. He received an immediate blood transfusion and eventually recovered.

It is soon determined that the zinc metal coating of the galvanized bucket Binam was using had combined with sulfuric acid to create hydrogen gas, which, in the presence of arsenic, formed arsine. Galvanized buckets are removed from the plant by management, Rodger reports.

The Smelterworker is long on attitude if short on detail. Rodger follows up with a heated editorial denouncing the lax safety culture. Departmental safety meetings are limited to a crisp fifteen minutes, he says, and the company is refusing to disclose results of the previous year's air monitoring. In addition to Binam's misadventure, he describes another toxic gas crisis in the roaster department, in which the roastermen were forced to work an eight-hour shift while "barely able to see two feet in front of them."[20] Some kind of gas, Rodger explains, was pouring out of the "junction tower flu[e]" during repairs to a new flue system. He provides a cartoon drawing of roaster foreman Virgil Fallon showering naked in a gas mask.

THE DAYLIGHT BASEMENT

The newsletter's "Grievance Scorecard" tallies the results of recent arbitrations. Workers in the roaster department and the slimes house are feeling their grievances strongly. Notes on their health are alarming. Rags Stenstrom of the converters department and Slim McDowell of the carpentry shop are out with cancer, with Slim "presently in rather severe condition."[21] Readers are asked to remember him in their prayers. Rags dies a few weeks later, age sixty-two.[22] George Maas of the acid plant, an employee at the smelter since August 1964, has also died of cancer after a long illness, at the age of forty-nine.[23]

Elsewhere, on January 20, 1974, Harold Loeb, son of Rose Guggenheim, cousin of Peggy, and belittled by Hemingway, has died of a heart attack in Marrakesh, having lived to the ripe old age of eighty-two.

IN THE LAST round of the National Football League's 1974 draft, held on January 30 at the Americana Hotel in New York City, the Green Bay Packers choose Randall Woodfield with the 428th pick. From a middle-class family in Newport, Oregon, Randy is a student at Portland State and a leading wide receiver for their football team, the Vikings. He's an ardent member of the Campus Crusade for Christ and the Fellowship of Christian Athletes. He's said to have good hands and to run admirable routes on the field, and the Packers offer him a one-year contract at $16,000. He takes it.

What the Green Bay Packers don't know, however, is that Randy has been exposing his erect penis to females since junior high school, once standing on a bridge to do so. He too is in a state of readiness, pressure building, and when the team sends him a first-class ticket to their training camp in Wisconsin, he turns it down, preferring to drive his car, a Volkswagen Beetle. It's such a good vehicle, for so many things.

IT'S THURSDAY, JANUARY 31, 1974, and Lynda Ann Healy, twenty-one, rises before dawn. It's a dank Seattle winter morning, the forecast calling for highs in the upper forties, lows in the low forties, with periods of rain.

MURDERLAND

The papers that day are full of lies, danger, and death. Mount Etna has begun to erupt on its western flank, an event heralded by a series of explosions. Nixon is vowing never to resign. "One year of Watergate is enough," he says. "I have no intention whatever of ever walking away from the job that the people elected me to do."[24] Henry Kissinger predicts a quick end to the Arab oil boycott, and north of Seattle, in the mountains, a Greyhound bus with twenty souls is trapped for six hours by snowslides at the Stevens Pass summit. A Pan Am flight crashes on landing in Samoa in a thunderstorm, killing all but 10 of the 101 passengers. Rivers are rising and the Dow is down.

Lynda Ann Healy gets up early almost every morning, riding her bike a few blocks to the office of *Northwest Skier* magazine in order to compile and deliver the seven o'clock ski report on KVI Radio, a promotional spot. Conditions are good that day, at least for skiing. "Hi, skiers," she says.

> This is Lynda with your Cascade Mountain ski report for Thursday. All areas are operating and all areas are reporting new snow. Snoqualmie Pass is reporting eight inches of new snow for a sixty-eight inch total. Crystal Mountain reports ten inches of new snow.[25]

Lynda is a senior at the University of Washington, a singer, a skier, and a psychology major planning for a career in special education. She shares an older house at 5517 12th Avenue Northeast, in the U District, with four friends. It's a house like thousands of others in Seattle, built in the 1930s like my grandmother's, with a mountain ash tree in front, covered in hard orange berries. The house is six or seven blocks from Liz Kloepfer's. Lynda is living in an old-fashioned daylight basement, just like the Queen Anne Hill stewardesses, Karen Sparks, and the woman Ted tried to smother with a pillow.

The room is a reflection of the 1970s. There's a single window and no door to the basement corridor, just a curtain. The twin mattress rests on a frame with no headboard. Tacked to the wall at the head of the bed is a 1968 comic poster of the Seattle skyline drawn by a popular local artist, a good-natured lampoon of city landmarks: the Space Needle, Smith Tower, a fleet of ferries and fishermen bobbing in Elliott Bay.[26] On a narrow shelf above the bed, there's a candle stuck in an Italian wicker-covered wine bottle. Photographs of friends and family are pinned to the wall. On an exposed metal furnace duct, she's painted the initials B.F.D., for "Big Fucking Deal."[27] There's an Indian batik spread on the bed and pink flowered bedding, a pink satin case on the pillow.

Lynda is a talented, ambitious, busy, studious, and responsible young woman, and with her shining auburn hair and gorgeous smile she could sell Breck shampoo or just about anything else. Her path has occasionally crossed that of Ted Bundy. In 1972, both were enrolled in Psych 498 and 499, independent reading and lab courses with dozens of sections.[28] Ted's cousin Edna Cowell knows one of Lynda's housemates and has met Lynda once.

On the afternoon of January 31, Lynda is studying for a quiz in another psych class, wrapped in her blue afghan. She goes to chorus practice and stops at the grocery store. This is her week to cook for the house, and she's planning a special meal, beef stroganoff, for her parents, who are coming Friday night. She cashes a check at the nearby Safeway at 47th and Brooklyn, at almost the same time that Ted writes a check at the same store. He too is preparing for midterms, for law classes at the University of Puget Sound. The previous week, a prowler has tested the lock on a door at a nearby apartment house. Two nights earlier, an intruder was surprised in the basement of a house two doors down.

On Thursday night, Lynda and two of her housemates, Joanne Testa and Ginger Heath, meet their friend Pete at Dante's Tavern, a popular watering hole near their house, and share a pitcher of beer. It's a favorite spot of Ted's.[29] The three women walk home at around 9:30, and Lynda, who has to get up early, is in bed by midnight.

Sometime between midnight and 5:30 a.m., when Lynda's alarm goes off, Ted, who has coldly broken up with Diane by phone within the past few days, either jimmies the door or finds it unlocked or uses a key that he's stolen, silently descending the basement steps inside. He pushes through the beads into Lynda's bedroom and most likely strangles her to unconsciousness. Blood will later be found on the mattress, where her head would have been.[30] He removes her nightgown, stained with blood on one shoulder, and drapes it over the rod in the closet. He rapes her. Semen will be found. Photos on the wall next to the bed are knocked askew.

He fills her backpack with some of her clothing—a white peasant blouse, a pair of old jeans with a triangular patch on the back, and her wafflestomper boots—and wraps her naked body in a sheet. He pulls a pillowcase over her head. He makes the bed with hospital corners, a detail that will puzzle her roommates, because Lynda has never made her bed that way. Carrying her up four basement stairs and out the side door, he stashes her in the back seat of his VW, bound, gagged, and unconscious, covering her with something. He then drives across Mercer Island on I-90 and into the wilderness. On an isolated mountain hillside, where there is no one within screaming distance, he removes her from the car, rapes her again, and strangles her. He spends the night with her body.

When her alarm goes off that morning, there's no one to turn it off.

THE SEATTLE POLICE do not know what to make of Lynda Ann Healy's disappearance. While her mother and roommates insist that Lynda would never walk away from her life, miss work, or leave without notice, the first officers on the scene shrug. They think she's run off with a boyfriend. They cannot account for the fact that her wallet, coat, and bicycle are still in the house. They fail to notice the blood on the mattress or the missing sheet and pillowcase or the bloodstained nightgown or the semen. Or the fact that somebody, not Lynda, made the bed.

When these things are brought to their attention, they suggest she might have had a nosebleed or her period. Semen is neither collected nor tested.[31] The amount of blood—significant but less than what would suggest a life-threatening injury—doesn't look like anything to them. They do not connect the missing woman to the near-fatal attack earlier that month on Karen Sparks. Nor do they consider the fact that 1974 has just become—with the seizure on February 4 in Berkeley, California, of nineteen-year-old Patricia Hearst by the Symbionese Liberation Army—the most infamous year for kidnapping women in American history.

It is only as the days tick by, and as newspaper and television reporters begin covering the story heavily, that the official line changes. On February 13, 1974, *The Seattle Times* publishes a story with a hair-raising headline. No one who sees it will ever forget it: AFTER SHE PUT OUT THE LIGHT, WHAT EVIL CREPT IN?[32] It paints a portrait of a man entering Lynda's room and perhaps forcing her to dress and leave with him at knifepoint, a theory that may or may not take into account the bloody mattress, which has been shown on television. Detectives are finally willing to concede, thirteen days after Lynda's disappearance, that "grim speculation" may be warranted.[33]

Evil crept into the daylight basement, to be sure, but it was all around her, all her life, in one form or another. It was no big fucking deal until it was.

TWO DAYS AFTER the *Times* article, Ted is buying a new pair of shoes at the University branch of Nordstrom, my mother's favorite shoe store and her second-favorite department store, after Frederick & Nelson. Thanks to OPEC, the price of gasoline is reaching highs of more than two dollars a gallon, and my father is in a rage. But Ted is still topping up, a few dollars here, a few there. He's still attending night classes at UPS, an institution he considers beneath him.

On February 21, 1974, at 1:30 p.m., a four-year-old girl, Heidi Birgit Peterson, is taken from her Capitol Hill front yard, where she's been playing with her two-year-old brother, Carl. Asked what happened to his sister, Carl says, succinctly, "Heidi go."

As with Ann Marie Burr, the missing child sparks a citywide, then regional, then national manhunt. Police and volunteers beat the bushes in the little park across the street from Heidi's house, which lies within yards of I-5 and the approach to the Evergreen Bridge. Seattle printers vie with one another to donate time and materials to produce flyers—HAVE YOU SEEN HEIDI?—which are handed out around the city and enclosed with telephone bills and bank statements. Billboards are erected, rewards posted.

Heidi's mother says that the girl has been warned about strangers, and every block around her home, every blackberry patch and wooded area and highway median, is searched thoroughly and more than once. She is nowhere to be found.

On the night of Saturday, March 2, 1974, in a ground-floor apartment of a building three doors down from the rooming house where Ted lives, Mary Frank,* a twenty-year-old student at the university, goes to bed around 1:00 a.m. A few nights earlier, she had heard something and looked out the living room window, and on Friday, the day before, a friend of hers had noticed that her screen had been removed. On Saturday night, she forgets to put the wooden dowel in the window to lock it.

At 4:00 a.m., she's sound asleep but is awakened by the sound of the window moving. She opens her eyes and sees the profile of a man standing in the doorway, outlined by a light that's been left on in the living room. The man enters the dark room with a flashlight, leaving it shining from a nearby table. From his back pocket he pulls out a hunting knife with a carved bone handle. He tells her he won't use it unless she screams. He sits on the bed and says, "I'm not going to hurt you." Confused, she asks, "Where is the light coming from?" He says, "None of your business."

He's wearing a dark navy watch cap pulled over his head to below his chin, with slits for eyes and a white short-sleeved T-shirt and Levi's. He has no jacket, although the night is cold. She can't see his face or his hair but knows he's white because of his arms. His voice sounds like he's from the Northwest, and he seems well educated. She guesses he's a fellow student at UW, a young man in his early to mid-twenties, about 150 pounds and approximately five feet ten inches tall. He's been drinking, but he's not drunk.

---

* Not her real name.

THE DAYLIGHT BASEMENT

He talks to her for eight or ten minutes and then tapes her eyes, turns on her light, and takes off her clothes. He unzips his pants and rapes her. Then he tapes her arms and legs together. When she asks why, he says, "Just to slow you down." He turns off the light, covers her with a blanket, and says, "Now go back to sleep."

She hears him walk back through the living room and leave by the window. He takes his flashlight with him. She hears him running down the alleyway behind the building and listens for a car but doesn't hear an engine starting in the still night air.

Early the next morning, she calls Seattle Rape Relief, the first rape crisis center in the country, and reports the assault to two women, who arrange to take her for a physical exam. She calls the police later that evening, telling them she doesn't want her parents to know. She gives them a detailed report, noting that the rapist didn't ask for money and didn't touch valuable jewelry lying on a nearby table. In fact, she says, he didn't touch anything, except her. She says, "He was so calm and sure of himself I think he has done this before."[34]

FROM EVERY RADIO purls the Hollies song "The Air That I Breathe." It's already a hit in the United Kingdom and is released in the United States in March 1974. A classic ballad, it begins climbing the charts. A hallucinatory reverberatory guitar note held endlessly floats on the collective air that spring and summer, echoing out of the AM station on the school bus, eddying out of the windows of college dorms, and wafting across campus quads on clouds of cannabis smoke. Eric Clapton says the first note has more soul than anything he's ever heard, but it carries undertones of spacy menace.

In the Pacific Northwest, Ted is riding a doomsday high. After years of sporadic attacks on stewardesses and hitchhiking teenagers and random strangers, he is graduating to ever riskier pursuits, assaulting women in his own neighborhood, on his own street. His sorties are growing ever more complex as he enters the giddy-making higher atmosphere of the true aesthete, the collector, the marathon killer. He is what the police call a hot prowler, entering the homes of living prey to seize and possess and bear them away. Feeling magically immune to capture, he is becoming addicted to these activities, and, like any user, he is finding that it takes more and more product to meet his needs.

With each passing day, he is letting go of everything that keeps him marginally human—his girlfriends, his studies, his professional ambitions. He sees less and less of Liz Kloepfer and her daughter, Molly, becoming distant, distracted, and argumentative with the fragile little family he sought to create. Now he is his compulsions, driven by a mind rewired to crave the spectacular sexual highs of his childhood, running naked in the woods, reenacting the treasured detective magazine images of striking, raping, and strangling a bound and helpless form, then raping the dead body again and again. He can never get enough.

March 12, 1974, finds him on the Evergreen State College campus a few miles south of Olympia, the state capital. An alternative college that eschews grades and attracts free-spirited hippies and dope smokers to its hundred-acre campus enrobed in the color of its eponymous trees, Evergreen is easy pickings for Ted, with its heavily wooded trail between the dorms and the library. He parks on a side road. However long his wait, he is rewarded with Donna Gail Manson, nineteen, a slim girl, five feet tall, who is walking to a jazz concert set to begin in the lobby of the library at 8:00 p.m.

Donna is the definition of Evergreen, an enthusiastic pot smoker, a student of alchemy, and a hitchhiker, sleeping by day, partying by night, driving her staid roommate crazy. She has no reason to hitchhike that night, since she is mere steps from her destination, striding along the shadowy trail in specially selected green pants, an orange-and-green-striped pullover sweater, and a mod black maxi coat. She has long brown hair parted in the middle. She never gets where she's going. No molecule of her is ever found.[35]

Ted is experimenting with his trophies. Emboldened by his success at removing victims to a wilderness of his choosing, where he can revisit the

THE DAYLIGHT BASEMENT

remains, he is seeing that woodland creatures effortlessly work his will, taking parts for their own use, distributing and redistributing. Coyotes, foxes, and field mice. Ravens and crows. They all collect their tribute. Passerines take part, acquiring hair for their nests.[36] He does as they do, carving off pieces for himself. He begins taking heads.

IN THE SEVENTH GRADE, I'm preparing an oral report about the country of Turkey and a book report about Richard Bach's *Jonathan Livingston Seagull*, a book I like and dislike at the same time. I enjoy leafing through the pictures of flying birds and turning the filmy white interleaved sheets that cover them to create new gossamer images in which the gulls seem to fade into the sky.

But the story is weirdly familiar, because Jonathan Livingston Seagull appears to be a Christian Scientist.[37] He's intent on rejecting the materialism of all the other gulls, who only care about eating gross things like garbage. Yearning to overcome the "lead weights" of a merely physical existence, Jonathan flies higher and higher into the upper atmosphere until he dematerializes into a perfect spiritual realm where nothing exists.[38] Seagulls, he learns from two magical spirit fowl, are not real. They're only an idea, the perfect image of "the Great Gull."

I already know this stuff from Sunday school, where we learn that we don't really exist but are in fact shadows of a bunch of other things: God, love, blah, blah, blah. We are forced to memorize lists of these things, and it bores the pants off me.

Gulls do love garbage. They're everywhere, screaming and mobbing. If you eat at the takeout bar of Ivar's Acres of Clams on Elliott Bay and stand at the end of the pier and throw french fries into the air, they catch them, every time, and it's thrilling because they have long, sharp bills with a red spot on the lower half, and they could snap your finger right off.

I learn in English class that other people have strong feelings about *Jonathan Livingston Seagull*. I get into an argument with a boy about what the story does and doesn't mean. I say something sarcastic, and when I'm not looking he comes up behind me and hits me hard over the head with an encyclopedia. I see stars.

ON MARCH 17, the OPEC oil embargo comes to an end. Liz Kloepfer returns from a skiing weekend to find Ted in her apartment, weeping. He doesn't have a key, but he's begged the landlord to let him in because he has to see her. He's doing badly in law school and has decided to drop out. He looks drained, and she holds his head in her lap, soothing him as he cries. He says he's afraid he isn't "going to make it."[39]

He buys gas on March 19, 25, and 29 and April 1.

ON APRIL 3, 1974, the most violent tornado outbreak yet recorded in human history erupts across the Interior Plains of North America. Over a twenty-four-hour period, 148 tornadoes spin across thirteen states, killing 319, from Alabama and Georgia in the South all the way north to Ontario. Propelled by a midlatitude low-pressure center over Kansas, the storms sweep north and east, leaving the Land of Oz untouched.

A day later, in Wichita, there is another kind of outbreak. On the afternoon of April 4, less than three months after killing four members of the Otero family, Dennis Rader feels the itch. He has been stalking twenty-one-year-old Kathryn Bright, an attractive young woman who works at the Coleman plant and lives alone. She fits his fantasy profile: "a coed, dishwater blond, small."[40] Watching her from his car, he admires her bohemian denim outfits and beaded purse.[41]

That afternoon, he breaks into Kathy's house while she's still at work. He has again prepared extensively in the manner of a Boy Scout, and he's armed with two guns—a .357 Magnum and the Woodsman target pistol—extra rounds, two knives, a pair of leather golf gloves, and two stocking caps. He has seen a movie starring Jack Nicholson as a hit man who wears golf gloves. He shatters a window at the back of the house and crawls

THE DAYLIGHT BASEMENT

through, searching for items to tie up his victim with. He finds nylon stockings and a blue scarf to use for a gag.

Things go wrong from the start. When Kathy arrives home at 2:00 p.m., she's not alone. Her brother, Kevin, nineteen, is with her. When they enter the house, Dennis waves a gun at them, telling them he only needs cash and a car, marching them into a bedroom. He ties up Kevin, moving Kathy to another bedroom, where he ties her to a chair, hoping for an opportunity to play out his sexual bondage fantasies.

In the fracas that ensues, Kevin breaks his bonds. Dennis shoots him in the forehead, grazing him, then returns to attack Kathy. Kevin runs in, getting a grip on the Magnum. The gun jams. Dennis pulls out the Colt, shooting him in the mouth. Kevin falls.

Dennis is now fighting with Kathy, who has slipped out of her gag and half out of her bindings. Physically unable to strangle her, he stabs her eleven times across the front and back of her abdomen with an eight-inch Buck knife, covering his clothes and his Hush Puppies in blood. Hearing Kevin running out the front door, he flees.

By the time police arrive at the house, Kathy is still alive but in terrible pain. She tells them her name before the ambulance arrives but can barely speak. She dies at the hospital.

Having tried and failed to steal the pickup truck in the driveway—it won't start—Dennis rushes home. His wife is still at work. He cleans himself up and within days has burned his bloody pants, gloves, and shoes. His parents live nearby, and he hides the guns in their basement. He has stolen Kathy's driver's license, a prize he will take at many murder scenes, calling them "trophies for my Hidey Holes."[42]

Seriously injured, Kevin pulls through and is able to provide a description. A police sketch appears in the newspaper. Dennis finds it suggestive of his own features, and it makes him uncomfortable. But the police are convinced that there cannot be a link between the attack on the Brights and the Otero murders.

The day after Dennis kills Kathy Bright, a high school teacher in Maine publishes his debut novel, about a girl who can murder people with her mind. She has my name.

ON APRIL 11, Ted buys gas twice, for a total of almost nine and a half gallons, and on April 12 he buys gas again.

On Sunday, April 14, Jane Curtis, a student at Central Washington University in Ellensburg, an agricultural town just east of the Cascades and a straight shot across the mountains on I-90, encounters a good-looking man in his twenties outside the campus library, struggling to carry an armful of books. He has one arm in a sling and a metal brace on his finger.[43] He asks her to help him carry the books to his car, which, it transpires, is a VW Beetle parked in a dark spot around three hundred yards past a railroad trestle, near a student parking lot. As they walk through the underpass beneath the tracks, they chat about skiing at Crystal Mountain, a resort in the foothills of Mount Rainier, but when they reach the car she can see that the front passenger seat is missing. Suddenly the hair stands up on the back of her neck. He asks her to start the car for him. He tells her, "Get in."[44] She says no, drops his books, and runs.

ON APRIL 15, Patty Hearst is captured on a surveillance camera in the Sunset District branch of the Hibernia Bank in San Francisco, swinging an M1 carbine while yelling, "Up, up, up against the wall, motherfuckers!"[45] Which is itself a line from a 1969 Jefferson Airplane song, "We Can Be Together," about anarchy and the need to redistribute private property.

Presently known as Tania, Patty is or is not an enthusiastic member of the group that kidnapped her on February 4, the Symbionese Liberation Army (SLA), which isn't an army at all but a motley group of radicals headed by an escapee from Soledad Prison, Donald DeFreeze. As a child in Cleveland, he had both of his arms broken multiple times by his father and developed a fascination with firearms, fireworks, and explosives.

THE DAYLIGHT BASEMENT

TED HAS TWO old Tacoma friends in Ellensburg, Terry Storwick and Jerry Bullat, and he stops by to visit them sometime in April 1974. They can't remember exactly when or why.

He's secretly reapplying to the University of Utah's law school without telling Liz, embroidering his résumé by implying that he's the author of Donna Schram's rape study.[46]

Back in Seattle, he's buying more gas and getting a new muffler put on the car, and on Wednesday, April 17, he runs errands: grocery shopping, writing a check at Ernst Hardware, and buying more gas. At 9:30 that night he's in Ellensburg again, and Kathleen D'Olivo, a twenty-one-year-old student at Central Washington State, runs into a man outside the library. He's dropping things, his right arm in a sling. This time it's an awkward assortment of packages, including several books wrapped in butcher paper. Thinking he's going into the library, she offers to help, but he explains that he's trying to get to his car. She agrees to walk with him, carrying his packages, but is struck by the appearance of his elaborate cloth sling, one or two fingers strapped in a metal brace. There's something off about it: it looks sloppy and unprofessional. He's speaking softly, explaining that the injury is the result of a skiing accident, but she feels wary.

Passing over a pedestrian bridge and under the railway trestle, they reach the car, parked in a dark area beside a log. He drops his keys in the dirt and tries to feel around for them but says he can't find them because of the brace. He asks her to do it. Not wanting to bend over in front of him, she says, "Maybe if we stand back, we can see the light shining on them."[47] The keys glimmer. She sweeps them up, hands them over, and takes off.

That same night, Susan Rancourt, an eighteen-year-old freshman, is dealing with her own errands. In high school, she was an outstanding student, a cheerleader, and the homecoming queen. In a family with six kids, she's taken on two jobs to afford college, working in a nursing home full-time the summer before college. She has blond hair, blue eyes, and a bridge in her teeth. To maintain the expensive dental work, she's fanatical about brushing and flossing. At home, she's such a straight arrow that her family nickname is Miss Prudence Pureheart.[48] She's ambitious and smart, majoring in biology, maintaining a 4.0. She's slight, at five foot two and less than 120 pounds, but sturdy and fit: She jogs every morning. She jogs with the campus police. She jogs in a group with another student named Terry Storwick, which may or may not be relevant.[49]

At 8:00 p.m., Susan starts a load of clothes in a washing machine in one of the dorms and hurries off to an advisers' meeting at Munson Hall, hoping to qualify as a dorm counselor, a job that will lower her living expenses. She's wearing a sunny yellow coat over a yellow short-sleeved sweater and gray corduroy pants. On her feet, brown Hush Puppy shoes.

After the meeting, she's going to join a friend to see a German film at Barto Hall but plans to stop by the laundry room to put her clothes in the dryer. Her route takes her past the library. Susan is nearsighted, but for some reason, that night she's not wearing her glasses or contact lenses. For some reason, she never returns to the dorm, never collects her clothes, never reenters her life. She's gone.

ON APRIL 25, 1974, Robert Lee Yates Jr., a young gun enthusiast, buys a Ruger .357 handgun with a six-inch barrel at PayLess Drug in Walla Walla, Washington.[50] It's not the most powerful handgun in the world—that's the .44 Magnum wielded by Clint Eastwood in *Dirty Harry* in 1971—but it's close. It's powerful enough to bring down large game.

ON MONDAY, MAY 6, 1974, Ted buys gas twice, about four gallons total, writes a check at Safeway and another at Pay 'n Save, and heads south on I-5. He's got some driving to do.

At the same time, sitting in her dorm room at Oregon State University in Corvallis, Roberta Kathleen Parks—everyone calls her Kathy—is feeling blue. She's been brooding over an argument she had with her father a couple of days earlier. On Monday she learns that he's had a heart attack, and although her sister reassures her that he's likely to survive, she has

THE DAYLIGHT BASEMENT

trouble concentrating. She's twenty and tall at five foot seven, with serious blue eyes and long ash-blond hair falling to her waist, framing a delicate, narrow face and high forehead. Wearing a navy-blue top, blue pants, a white corduroy coat, and platform sandals, carrying a purse with fifteen dollars, she leaves the dorm around eleven that night and heads over to the cafeteria for coffee and a snack.

While Kathy is drinking her coffee, a nice-looking guy approaches her and sits down for a chat. He asks if she might like to go to a bar in Corvallis for a drink, and she accepts. But once she's in the VW, he remembers he's got to pick up a finished copy of his thesis from a typist. However implausible that might seem at midnight, there's not much she can do about it, and he drives her down a deserted road to a remote location. At a dark spot, he pulls over and yanks her, protesting, out of the car, easily overpowering her, telling her to be quiet, to submit, and he won't hurt her. He may or may not threaten her with a knife or a tire iron. He tells her to take off her clothes, watching, then he rapes her.

Repeating his threats and promises, he ties her up and drives her, still alive, for hours up north, to Taylor Mountain, an 1,100-foot hump of a foothill near Issaquah with a view of Mount Rainier from the top, dominated by mature red alders and skirted by poorly frequented trails, a link between Seattle's Cedar River watershed and Tiger Mountain State Forest. He pulls off Highway 18 on a power-line access road and drags her out of the car. He rapes her again. "Why not?" he'll say later, having gone to all the trouble. Why not "give it another lick?"[51] He may strangle her as he rapes her. He may crush her skull with the tire iron.

ON MAY 20, 1974, Patty Hearst's distraught parents are pleading with her to give herself up after she's seen a few days earlier pumping lead from an automatic rifle into a Los Angeles sporting goods store in defense of her former SLA captors. At the same time, news breaks in Tacoma that the smelter has begun selling the six hundred tons of slag that it produces each day. Before this, slag has been dumped into the bay, because nobody wants it: it's black rock with high concentrations of lead, arsenic, and cadmium.

But in 1974, the government orders the smelter to stop throwing it overboard. In the face of such harsh environmental restrictions, ASARCO suddenly realizes the "growing economic value" of contaminated gravel.[52] Now the slag will be hauled away by truck and rail and barged to Seattle and Vancouver, British Columbia, where it will be commercially marketed for the first time. "We've had to overcome preconceived ideas about slag being ugly and undesirable," says one of the entrepreneurs.[53]

Soon people can't get enough of this good slag. It's considered to be high-quality, inexpensive fill material, and people living throughout North Tacoma use it to line their residential driveways. It's trucked across the Tacoma Narrows Bridge to the town of Gig Harbor and used to surface the car wash at Gig Harbor Ford. It's snapped up by construction companies, who lay it in roadbeds and pipe trenches and use it to create ornamental berms. Over the coming years, a lumberyard adjacent to Commencement Bay will strew it across places where heavy machinery needs traction. The acids in the wood will leach metals out of the slag, contaminating the site with arsenic and lead.[54]

Because the slag is sold by the smelter to a private company for resale, no one knows where it goes or what it does. Nobody keeps records. The name of the company taking this commodity off the smelter's hands is Black Knight.[55]

ON MAY 20, *The Seattle Times* prints a hopeful column by Herb Robinson about long-debated safety concerns on the Mercer Island Floating Bridge. E. I. Roberts, a district highway engineer for the Transportation Department, goes on record promising "to eliminate the bulge as soon as we can."[56] There's no longer any question that it's causing accidents, but the future of the bridge is mired in political and legal turmoil over the completion of the last mile or so of the ill-fated Interstate 90 project, which seems to become more expensive with every minute.

THE DAYLIGHT BASEMENT

The accident rate on the bridge in its current configuration is "twice that of comparable highways elsewhere in the state."[57] Roberts, the engineer, doesn't know it yet, but it will be years before the bulge is removed.

TED IS ONCE again accepted at the University of Utah's law school and starts a new summer job on May 23, 1974, in Olympia at the Department of Emergency Services, the state agency tasked with responding to health crises, natural disasters, and the gas shortage caused by the OPEC oil embargo. DES is responsible for allocating the state's scarce fuel resources. Ted is hired by Tom Sampson, former director of the Seattle Crime Prevention Advisory Commission, to help prepare their annual budget. It's a job with a deadline. The budget must be completed before Ted leaves in September to move to Utah.

Many of his new colleagues are deeply impressed by the handsome young recruit. He becomes friendly with Carole Ann Boone, a recent divorcée and single mother. Like Ann Rule and Liz Kloepfer, she enjoys buttonholing Ted to talk about her relationship troubles and listens sympathetically as he fields irate calls from Liz, complaining about his inaccessibility. She feels that Ted is "a shy person with a lot more going on under the surface."[58] She's sure he wants to date her, but somehow it never happens.

The job puts him on the road constantly, commuting between Seattle and the state capital. As co-workers in Olympia, Ted and Tom meet once or twice at Evergreen State College, a few miles away, to play racquetball.[59] Among the responsibilities of DES is coordinating search and rescue teams for missing persons, such as Lynda Healy, Donna Manson, and Susan Rancourt.[60]

ON MAY 29, 1974, fourteen-year-old Diane Gilchrist, four foot ten and a hundred pounds, leaves her home in Vancouver, Washington. Vancouver is the city where Jamie Grissim disappeared in 1971, and it boasts a three-hundred-acre Alcoa aluminum smelter three miles northwest of downtown, a site contaminated by decades of dumping. Its soil and groundwater are saturated with 66,000 tons of petroleum hydrocarbons, organic chemicals, cyanide, and metals.[61] Diane is mad at her parents; she's running away. She's seen getting into a van, and then never again.

Warren Leslie Forrest, born in 1949, grows up in the immediate vicinity, five miles east of the Alcoa smelter, and excels on the varsity cross-country team at Fort Vancouver High School.[62] By age fifteen, he already has troubling predilections and extreme sexual fantasies he just can't shake. He returns after serving in Vietnam as a Specialist 5 Missile Crew Service gunner to work for the Clark County Parks Department. He has a key to every park in the county. He drives a 1973 Ford van.

ON THE EVENING of May 31, 1974, a Friday, Liz Kloepfer's parents are in town, visiting from Utah, and Ted takes them all out for pizza. They return to Liz's apartment at around ten o'clock that night, and Liz is bothered by the fact that Ted is eager to leave.[63] They have a big day planned for Saturday, when Liz's father is to baptize Molly in a Mormon ceremony.

But Ted has plans too, and they do not include getting to bed early. Phyllis Armstrong is a freshman at the University of Washington with long brunette hair. Originally from the Tacoma suburb of Sumner, she now lives in the Kappa Alpha Theta house, a sorority on Greek Row. The Row runs along 17th Avenue Northeast, across the street from the campus. She rooms with her best friend, Georgann Hawkins. At eleven o'clock, Phyllis walks down the front stairs toward a man at the foot of the steps. He's standing there on crutches with his leg in a cast, holding a gas can. He says, "Can you help me?"[64]

She says, "Sure!" He asks her to carry the can to a VW Beetle parked on the street, sit in the driver's seat, and press a button under the dash while he pours fuel into the vehicle. Chattering nervously, he says he works in Olympia and lives in a rooming house nearby. He's been

THE DAYLIGHT BASEMENT

drinking—she can smell it. After a minute or two of sitting in the car, she gets what she'll describe as a "cold chill," a feeling that something's not right. She jumps out and takes off running, saying, "Sorry—bye!"[65]

Nothing is wrong with his car, so Ted drives south, ending up at the Flame Tavern in Burien, a sketchy dive bar on a commercial strip near SeaTac Airport, an area he knows from commuting between Tacoma and Seattle. That afternoon, twenty-two-year-old Brenda Carol Ball, short and slight at five foot three and 112 pounds, with long, swinging brunette hair, recently a student at Highline Community College, had told her roommates that she was headed to the Flame. She's spent the whole night there, drinking until closing time at 2:00 a.m. She asks a musician in the band if she can catch a ride home with him, but he's heading elsewhere. She's last seen in the parking lot, talking to a man with curly brown hair who may or may not have a cast on one arm.

He invites her to his place at the Rogerses' rooming house, and the two of them drink themselves silly, perhaps indulging in Mickey's Big Mouth, a malt liquor that is a particular favorite of Ted's ("That stuff makes me nasty"), and they have sex that may or may not be consensual.[66] Brenda passes out. As he watches her sleeping, he becomes aroused again and his sexual excitement merges with another desire, and he strangles and rapes her where she lies. He keeps her for a while, leaving her in bed, then stashes her body in the closet. "No one's coming in," he says.[67]

The following day, Ted doesn't show up at church for Molly's baptism, instead joining the family two hours late. Liz is angry. No one reports Brenda missing for nineteen days.

ON THE SAME NIGHT that Ted and Brenda get together, May 31, 1974, Gloria Knutson is celebrating at the Red Caboose, a bar in downtown Vancouver, Washington. She is set to graduate from Hudson's Bay High School the next day. She has long blond hair and a winning smile. She tries to hitchhike home. She disappears.

ON JUNE 2, 1974, Uncle Bunker is suspected of killing horses in Kellogg, Idaho. Bunker Hill officials deny that the lead smelter has anything to do with the dead animals, but they do admit that they've recently bought two carcasses "as a public relations gesture," to appease the owners.[68] But there are not just two dead horses. There are nine.

Weird things are happening. Evergreen trees in the valley have been dying for years, and bridges near Kellogg are corroding faster than anywhere else in the state, pitted by acid.[69]

Four days later, news breaks that two Kellogg preschoolers are being treated by private physicians for lead poisoning. Despite the fact that Bunker Hill has been running the smelter flat out without filtration since the baghouse fire in 1973, a spokesman confidently asserts that "we've had a smelter since 1917 and there has never been any problem with lead poisoning."[70] For the first time, Idaho state health officials don't accept the smelter's word. They announce an expanded study, in which nurses will collect blood samples from preschool and older schoolchildren to test for heavy metals exposure in the Coeur d'Alene Mining District.

ON JUNE 11, Ted returns to Greek Row and approaches a girl from Tacoma. She's Phyllis Armstrong's roommate at Kappa Alpha Theta, Georgann Hawkins. Phyllis hasn't told anyone about the ten nights earlier when she encountered the man with the gas can and the VW. Nothing happened, so what's to tell?

Everybody calls her George, and she's the quintessential freshman sorority girl, a confection of bright golden hair, a brilliant smile, and a bubbly personality. She's from Lakewood, a neighborhood in South Tacoma, and a graduate of Lakes High, where she was a cheerleader. In 1973 she was chosen as a Daffodil Princess, celebrating the bulb industry in the Puyallup Valley since 1925. She rode in the Daffodil Parade, with Phyllis as one of her attendants. Beaming, she walked into the state legislature on the arm of a handsome young legislator and stood at a dais bearing the

THE DAYLIGHT BASEMENT

seal of Washington's lieutenant governor, Johnny Cherberg, the apple of my Democratic grandmother's eye, to give a speech.

June 11 is the Tuesday night of finals week at the University of Washington. It's unusually warm for Seattle, following a sunny day, seventy-five degrees. The imminence of summer break makes it hard to concentrate. Georgann goes to a party near the sorority, leaving at midnight to return to her room to study. She has a Spanish test in the morning. On the way, she stops at Beta Theta Phi to spend a few minutes with her boyfriend, Marvin, then skips down the back stairs into the alley behind Greek Row. One of her boyfriend's frat brothers, Duane, leans out an upstairs window and asks whether she's ready for her test. She takes a moment to chat. Everybody's up late.

She walks down the lighted trough of the alleyway, past rows of windows and toward the back stairs of her own sorority. Duane watches for a moment before pulling his head back in. She's forty feet from her door when someone walking toward her from the end of the alley catches her eye. He's struggling to walk on crutches, carrying a heavy briefcase packed with books. She's a Daffodil Princess and nothing if not obliging. She walks toward him. He asks for help, and she gives it with a smile, saying, "They call me George."[71]

She carries the bag of books to his VW, parked in a dirt lot beyond the alley, behind a convenient bunch of spiny ragweed, shielding it from the street. At the car, she turns her back to him, bending over to put the bag in the car, and he grabs the crowbar he's left beside one wheel and cracks her over the head with it, hitting her so hard that one of her shoes flies off, as do both of her earrings. She falls, unconscious. He handcuffs her and loads her onto the floor of the passenger side of the car—the seat has been removed for this purpose—and takes I-5 south to I-90, crossing the Mercer Island Floating Bridge. Heading for Issaquah, he must take this bridge and not the Evergreen, which is closer to the U District, because that one still has a tollbooth staffed by a human being. And there's a body in the car.

But Georgann is not dead. As he's driving across the floating bridge, she wakes up, opening her eyes and talking about her Spanish test, somehow believing in her concussed state that Ted Bundy is her Spanish tutor and has come to help her. She's murmuring about this as he drives her across Mercer Island, a few hundred yards from where I am asleep in bed in my room next to the carport and our own VWs. Once he's crossed the island, he drives a mile past Issaquah.

It's the middle of the night and there's not much traffic, so he can easily pull a U-turn in the middle of I-90, cross the westbound lanes, and pull off onto a completely deserted side road that takes him uphill to a grassy knoll in the forest. He pulls her out of the car. She's "quite lucid," Ted will recall, as he strips off her clothes—navy-blue cotton bell-bottom slacks, a long-sleeved, sheer red-white-and-blue flowered shirt over a sleeveless white halter top, and her one remaining white patent leather clog.[72] In the spotlight of the VW's headlamps, he carefully undoes the safety pin fastening her pants at the waist because they're a bit too big. Either before or after he takes off her clothes and rapes her, he hits her again with the crowbar and breaks her jaw and strangles her with a piece of rope, raping her body all night until the sun comes up, although the only witness attesting to this sequence of events is wholly unreliable.[73]

THE MOST UNCANNY things we see from the sailboat always occur in the Strait of Juan de Fuca, where the land on all sides fades into a haze of sun and clouds. In the strait, it's often sunny and deceptively warm in early afternoon, but then the wind comes up off the Pacific and begins lashing everything into a frenzy. Sometimes we see out there in broad daylight things that would make your blood run cold.

Once, out of the clear blue silence, practically becalmed, our sails listlessly catching and losing pockets of lazy air, the halyards barely slapping the mast, we hear a whoosh, an exhalation, as if from a hose spewing air and spray. A pod of killer whales is surfacing beside the boat, their black-and-white backs rising and falling. Their dorsal fins look like knives. They are close enough to touch. They are a visitation from another world. They are here and they are gone.

Another time, it's cold and foggy, and the silence is like a seizure of air, a supernatural deadness, a vacuum. Any movement on board—footsteps, or the clink on deck of the metal crank for winding the winch—sounds like a gunshot. In this stasis, out of the water rises an apparition of black steel, first the periscope and antennae and conning tower and then the hull of a ballistic missile submarine. As it surfaces, sheets of water pour off it. It looks demonic, like a killer whale made out of metal.

It's from Naval Submarine Base Bangor on Hood Canal, where submarines are serviced and nuclear warheads are stored along with vast tanks full of enough fuel to blow the Northwest to kingdom come. In 1973, the Navy had announced that Bangor will be the home of the new Ohio-class Trident fleet ballistic missile submarines. This is considered a great honor. When the submarine surfaces before us, we just stare, speechless.

On the naval charts clipped to the wall of the galley are any number of warnings regarding the Navy, which also maintains a major air station at Oak Harbor on Whidbey Island, the long island that forms a backstop to the Strait of Juan de Fuca. On charts of the strait are shipping lanes and no-man's-lands, "Operating Areas" and "Precautionary Areas" and "Restricted Areas." On one occasion we sail obliviously into a restricted area and notice that the water around us is dyed a venomous neon green.[74]

We hear a helicopter overhead. We hear gunfire and splashing. It's one of the big helicopters you see in Vietnam on the news, the Chinook. It has big tandem rotors, one at each end, and we can see strobing orange explosive flowers blooming from the open door. There are bursts in the water. My mother is wringing her hands the way she does when she's really worried, and my father takes a good, long upward squint and says, "That's live ammo." He's been in the Army. He comes about and beats it out of there, but I'm wondering if the men firing the guns can see us and whether they care if they hit us or not.

MURDERLAND

ON THE FRONT page of *The Seattle Times* on Wednesday, June 12, 1974—beneath a photo of Nixon and Anwar Sadat in the back of a convertible, waving to two million Egyptians in Cairo—is another headline: U.W. COED, 18, DISAPPEARS ON WAY TO SORORITY HOUSE. Below the fold, there's Georgann Hawkins, smiling, a daffodil pinned in her hair.[75]

That same day, the *Idaho State Journal* publishes the third in a series of articles on pollution, asserting that some of Idaho's lakes are "virtual cesspools and others pristine jewels."[76] The cesspools include several small lakes connected to Lake Coeur d'Alene: raw sewage is piped into these only a few yards offshore, leading to the growth of algae.

All of these bodies of water are lined with lead. Bunker Hill has been dumping metals into the South Fork Coeur d'Alene River for seventy-five years, along with sewage from dozens of mining camps. It all leaches into the lake. Locals have long described the South Fork as "too thick to drink and too thin to plow."[77] They call it "Lead Creek." The branch that flows past the Silver King School in Kellogg glows light green, and any rubber balls that fall in must be retrieved immediately, lest they melt.[78] Kids on the playground taste metal in their mouths, and teachers are often so alarmed at the "heavy, blue smoke" enveloping the building that they run out of classrooms thinking the school's on fire.[79] It's not. It's just the smelter.

A Bunker Hill spokesman tells the reporter that a new $1.3 million aerator and sewer system installed by the company will filter out particles of heavy metals entering the atmosphere. It's a pity they have to clean up the water, he adds, since the zinc in the lake is actually helping to "disinfect" the raw sewage. Zinc does have antibacterial properties. It's added to toothpaste and mouth rinses, but you wouldn't want to brush your teeth in Lake Coeur d'Alene. The article mentions the dead horses and the two children who have symptoms "resembling lead poisoning."[80]

That morning, at daybreak, Ted leaves the Issaquah site in a state of panic, throwing Georgann's clothes out the window of the VW as he

THE DAYLIGHT BASEMENT

drives, tossing out the crowbar, crutches, briefcase, and handcuffs. No worries—he'll be back.

At five o'clock in the afternoon, Ted gets on his bike and rides over to the parking lot where he attacked Georgann the night before. He sees cops scouring the area, but they're in all the wrong places, blindly combing parks and campus walkways. He's able to easily spot Georgann's missing white clog and her earrings—two little hoops—and scoop them up and take off. He's afraid that Phyllis, Georgann's roommate, whom he tried to abduct two weeks earlier, might tell what she knows; he's afraid someone might have seen his car. But the cops find nothing and learn nothing. To them, it's as if Georgann has simply vanished into thin air.

He buys gas in Olympia on June 12, 13, and 14. Perhaps every one of those nights, he returns to Georgann's body on the Issaquah hillside and has his way with it. Always with him, he has stashed in the forward trunk of the VW a tool kit with everything needed to repair a Beetle but also other things, including handcuffs, an army shovel, plastic bags, strips of bedsheet, a mask made out of pantyhose, a knit ski mask, and a hacksaw. On one of Ted's visits, he beheads the corpse. He may or may not take the head home with him, perhaps in a gym bag; he may or may not bury it farther uphill.[81] He'll recall feeling a certain "possessiveness."[82]

As the April cover story in *True Detective* has it: THERE IS RAPE AFTER DEATH![83]

WATER SPORTS ARE HIGH on Ted's list of favorite pastimes. Ted, Liz, and Molly have often vacationed at Flaming Gorge, Utah, boating, waterskiing, and swimming. In Seattle, they frequent Green Lake on the weekends, a small lake and surrounding park near the zoo. Ted once saved a toddler there, a three-year-old girl struggling in the water.[84] For Christmas in 1973, Liz gave him a yellow inflatable raft.

On June 29, 1974, a week after his last visit to Georgann's remains, Ted packs up the raft and drives a woman named Becky, a new acquisition he's met through friends, over his well-traveled trail across Snoqualmie Pass, past Cle Elum, and down the eastern side of the Cascades. They've slept together several times. They're meeting Larry Voshall, a friend of Ted's from the Republican Party, and Larry's date, Susan, at a rafting spot on the Yakima River, just off I-90. The four of them had dinner together the night before. They're planning to head downriver about ten miles to a diversion dam, a float trip of around five or six hours. Ted knows the area well. The Yakima River flows over the OWL, passing Cle Elum, passing Ellensburg. Let's put a pin in it.

The weather is perfect, hot and clear, but the outing is overshadowed by Ted's behavior. Larry, who met Ted a year ago, has always thought of him as suave, debonair, well-dressed, and personable. But after they shove off, Ted seems to have put off his manners along with most of his clothes.

He boasts about skiing at Vail and Aspen and describes himself as an expert rafter, mocking the others as amateurs. He ties an inner tube to the back of the raft and puts Becky in it, aware that she can't swim. In a wide part of the river, where there's plenty of room for safe passage, he steers deliberately beneath a waterfall, allowing Becky to drift under, nearly overwhelming her. He puts his own head under it, almost upsetting the raft.

At one point Larry looks over to see that Ted has untied the top of Becky's halter-style bathing suit, causing it to drop off. Ted clearly enjoys her humiliation. After they pull the raft out, Ted goes off by himself to collect the other car, disappearing for an hour and a half. During the two-hour drive home and their dinner in North Bend, he doesn't say a word. It's as if, Larry says, he's become a completely different person.[85]

He becomes a different person with Liz as well, when he goes rafting with her on July 6, over the Fourth of July holiday, again on the Yakima River. At first they're in good spirits. They're alone: Molly is staying with her grandparents for the month. They stash their bikes in bushes downriver, then drive back upstream with the raft. They've done this half a dozen times before and, for a time, the two enjoy the hot, silent day, drinking cold beer. They pull over on a small island and have a picnic lunch, then push off again.[86]

THE DAYLIGHT BASEMENT

An hour later, Liz is sitting peaceably on the edge of the raft, watching the world float by, when suddenly Ted lunges, shoving her overboard. The water is ice-cold, snowmelt from the Cascades. She can barely breathe from the shock of it but grabs a rope on the side of the raft, staring upward into Ted's eyes. They're dead and blank, she sees. He's expressionless.

Panting, she heaves herself back in, saying, "Why do you have to ruin everything?" He says nothing. Then he says it's no big deal: "Can't you take a joke?"[87]

The next day, July 7, he buys gas in the morning in Seattle and drives to Lake Sammamish, where he's seen wandering by himself along the shoreline. He buys gas that afternoon on Mercer Island. He buys gas on July 9 and 10. On July 11, he calls in sick to work and buys gas twice.

ON JULY 11, Krista Kay Blake, nineteen, a single mother, is seen getting into a blue Econoline van driven by a white male near the intersection of 29th and K Streets in Vancouver, Washington. She's met the driver, a County Parks employee, who has promised to take her to Portland. Instead he steers north to Tukes Mountain Park, a largely undeveloped county park made up of open fields surrounded by forest south of Mount Saint Helens.[88] He chats with her, beats her, and hog-ties her, perhaps holding a knife to her neck, perhaps raping her. He certainly murders her. He absolutely buries her body in a shallow grave.

The next day, July 12, Warren Leslie Forrest leaves for a vacation at the shore in Long Beach, Washington, with his wife, Sharon. Even though their marriage is, in her words, "rocky," and he's struck her on two occasions and he's mentioned having frequent blackouts that summer, she describes his demeanor while on vacation as "very relaxed."[89]

LAKE SAMMAMISH IS THE LITTLE sister to Lake Washington, a glacial gouge, a slit filled with water. I-90 cuts Lake Washington in half but runs just south of Sammamish, kissing its southern rim, inviting drivers to an off-ramp to the state park that cups its soft sand beach.

The lake is surrounded by cedars and Douglas firs. In 1892, the Lake Sammamish Lumber and Shingle Company made short work of all that timber, cutting seven million shingles. Then the mill burned down. Resorts popped up, cabins, lodges, dance halls. Nearby, somebody built a fake "Frontier Town" and dude ranch complete with saloon, bunkhouse, and blacksmith shop. Celebrities plied the region, including Roy Rogers, Texas governor John Connally, and astronaut Wally Schirra. During the summer of 1953, a young Clint Eastwood trained lifeguards at nearby Beaver Lake.

Lake Sammamish is thus associated, above all, with the strenuous pursuit of recreation. On the night of Saturday, July 13, Liz calls Ted, who's at his parents' house in Tacoma, to see if he wants to do something the next day. He says no: he can't go anywhere with her, because he has "other things to do."[90]

When she asks what, he says, "Just things, Liz."[91] But the next morning, as she's getting ready to go to church, Ted waltzes in as if that cold rejection had never happened. Her feelings are still hurt, and they have a fight. He wants to know what she's planning to do later on; she says she's going to the beach. "Which beach?" he asks; Carkeek Park, she says, referring to a strip of sand between Puget Sound and the railroad tracks. Despite their troubles, she hopes he'll join her later. After church, she lies there reading *All the President's Men*, waiting for Ted. He never shows.

He has, in fact, gone to Lake Sammamish. Why there? Let's ask the OWL, because the Olympic–Wallowa Lineament skims its southern shore, which from this day forth will be marked by the devil. Its capacious lawns are teeming with sun worshippers, picnickers on blankets, and youthful revelers clad in little more than shorts and bikinis. The skies are bright blue, the temperature headed above ninety. Rainier Brewery, a Seattle institution, is holding its annual "beer bust" at the state park, featuring a Dixieland-style band, men in red-and-white-striped vests with Styrofoam straw boater hats and white pants playing banjos. There are three-legged

THE DAYLIGHT BASEMENT

races and a keg-throwing contest, with girls in precarious halters perched on their boyfriends' shoulders.

Alongside the beer enthusiasts, the Seattle Police Athletic Association is having a summer picnic. There are forty thousand people at the lake that day, and the parking lot behind the beach is packed. There's someone walking around filming with a sixteen-millimeter camera.

Ted arrives early, looking for a good parking place. Janice Graham, twenty-two, five foot six, with long blond hair parted in the middle, arrives around 11:30. She's wearing sunglasses and a short green halter dress. First she looks for a picnic table but can't find one, so she heads over to the Rainier Beer races and joins the watching crowd. A man approaches her and says hello. She says hello back but edges away from him. He asks if she can help him lift his sailboat onto his car. His left arm is in a sling, and he's cradling it, so she says, "Sure."[92]

He has a nice smile. He's white, five foot eight or ten inches tall, 160 pounds, around twenty-five, wearing a white T-shirt with a crew neckline lined with red trim. They walk past the bandstand and the restrooms toward the parking lot, and he keeps up a continual patter. She tells him she's waiting for her husband and parents, and he says, "This is out of sight; there are so many people."[93] He keeps cradling his arm. He says he hurt it playing racquetball. He asks if she's ever played it, says that it's a lot of fun. She tells him she lives in Bellevue and works at Boeing.

When they get to the Volkswagen, which she later describes inaccurately as metallic brown, she doesn't see a sailboat and asks where it is. The sailboat is a lie, although Ted does love sailing. He says it's at his folks' house, just up the hill. He motions toward the passenger-side door, encouraging her to get in, but she asks what time it is. It's 12:20, so she has to go meet her parents. He apologizes and says, "I should have told you it wasn't in the parking lot."[94] He thanks her repeatedly.

Meanwhile, at around 12:15, Sylvia Valint, fifteen, is lying on the beach with two friends, a couple hundred yards in front of the restroom. All of them watch as an attractive young woman, five feet tall, a hundred pounds, long blond hair falling down her back, arrives, wheeling a yellow women's

Tiger brand 10-speed with curved handles wrapped in black vinyl. She takes off her Levi's cutoffs and yellow midriff shirt, revealing a black bikini. Men watch appreciatively. She lies down on a towel to sunbathe, applying cocoa butter. Like Janice Graham, she's wearing a wedding ring. A half hour later, a man with his arm in a sling walks over and asks if she can help him.

There are varying accounts of their conversation, one from Sylvia Valint, who's closest, and others from people in the vicinity. Valint doesn't remember a sling; others do. He's wearing tennis whites: white crew shirt, white shorts, white tennis shoes. The woman in the black bikini invites the man to sit down. "Let's talk about it," she says, seemingly reluctant.[95] He tells her that the boat is at his parents' house, up the hill in Issaquah. She asks if there's room in his car for her bike; he says he can put it in the trunk. She eventually agrees after he says his parents are at home, but only "under one condition, that I get a ride in the sailboat."[96] As they talk, Valint hears her say that her name is Jan. His name, he says, is Ted.

As they walk to the Volkswagen, Janice Graham sees them go by, thinking to herself, *That was fast work.* She wonders where he'll put the bike.

The woman's name is Janice Ott, and she's a caseworker in the probation department of the King County Youth Services Center in Seattle. Working with troubled kids in juvenile detention, she's trained in handling antisocial behavior. Her husband, Jim, is in California that weekend, finishing a course in the design of prosthetic limbs for the disabled. She has a dazzling smile and green eyes.

Ted drives about three miles, up a hill past Issaquah, talking about the weather and pretending to be a good guy. He knows where he's going. There's a deserted cabin up there, and once he's pulled off onto the final approach to a grassy area, north of an abandoned railroad line and State Highway 10, north of East Fork Issaquah Creek, it's too late for her to do anything. There's no one around, no one to hear.

He brandishes a knife or a gun, and she tries to talk him out of it, rallying her professional manner. She thinks he means to rape her, but he's

THE DAYLIGHT BASEMENT

not talking anymore. He ties her up, sexually assaults her, and gags her. Does he keep her alive? Later, he'll say he did. He's in a state of extremity, "overexcited, over-aroused, driven, compulsive."[97] He has to have more.

He may be picturing two issues of his favorite magazines—*Inside Detective* from September 1973 and *True Detective* from the following month—describing in detail the sex murders in Florida committed by one Gerard John Schaefer, who loved "doubles," capturing two teenaged girls at once and taking them out into the wilderness and torturing and murdering them in front of each other.[98] A TRAIL OF BUTCHERED GIRLS, promises the cover of *Inside Detective*, a girl in a green halter top hanging by her wrists, screaming as a man advances. "Brutal sex acts with captives," it vows. Ted likes doubles too.

He's in a state of wild stress and sexual pressure that has built and built. He is suffering, he'll later say, from "periodic fluctuations" of tensions that are "more biologically or biochemically based," feelings that come in waves "with a rise in intensity."[99] Such episodes have no regularity, he'll say, but there's something clearly escalating. It's been more than a month since he seized Georgann Hawkins, parts of whose body, unbeknownst to Janice Ott, are nearby.

Shortly before four o'clock, leaving Janice Ott tied up but alive, he returns to Lake Sammamish. He approaches Sindi Siebenbaum, a sixteen-year-old with long, gleaming brown hair, as she's walking back from the restroom. He hails her by saying, jauntily, "Excuse me, young lady, could you help me launch my sailboat?"[100] She looks him over and asks what he's done to his arm. He says he sprained it. He's nervous, talking rapidly. His pupils are small. When Sindi tells him she can't help, he plucks at her arm and she shakes him off.

Next he targets Patricia Turner, eighteen, with long brown hair parted in the middle, wearing Levi's and a black flowered halter top. He tells her, "I need to ask a really big favor of you," talking about his sailboat and saying his brother would usually help him but he's too busy. Pat brushes him off, saying "Sorry," and walks away.[101]

He tries Jacqueline Plischke, twenty, with long blond hair, wearing a pink bikini top and cutoffs, who has noticed him staring at her near the waterskiing launch, a man with a beige sling on his left arm. He asks if she can help with his sailboat and she says, "I'm not very strong."[102] He says, puzzlingly, "It's better that I asked someone who was alone." She says she's waiting for someone. He says, "Oh, I see," and turns and walks away.

Meanwhile, Denise Naslund, eighteen, 110 pounds, with long dark brown hair parted in the middle, is reclining on the lawn with her boyfriend and another couple near one end of the parking lot. Denise is studying to be a computer programmer and has driven the group in her beige 1963 Chevrolet Impala, of which she's inordinately fond. It's a birthday present from her mother. The two couples have been there since one o'clock, watching the keg toss, drinking beer, and smoking dope. They're in a mood, since Denise has brought her dog and the dog has run off and is missing.

At four, one of the guys fetches hot dogs and hamburgers from the concession stand. After they eat, both boys fall asleep. Denise tells her friend Nancy that she's feeling high. On the way to the park, she and the boys have each taken four Valiums.

At around 4:30, she gets up and walks away, toward the cinder-block bathrooms. Her purse is locked in the trunk of her car. A Seattle Police Department employee sees her in the restroom, talking to another woman in a knit maroon bikini as they walk out, but Denise never returns to the lawn.[103]

That's because she's left with Ted Bundy, who is driving her to the logging road off Highway 10 where Janice Ott is still conscious. Terrified, the two women can see each other as he ties up and attacks Denise in front of Janice.[104] Then he strangles them and has sex with their corpses. He drives their bodies up the road. He may or may not cut off their heads with a hacksaw, then or later.[105]

On this single day in July he has exposed himself in ways he can never undo. He has approached multiple women within earshot of witnesses. At least one of them has heard him say his name is Ted. But in the moment, it doesn't matter. He's possessed by a powerful feeling of invincibility, con-

THE DAYLIGHT BASEMENT

vinced he can never be caught. The women he takes will not be missed, or so he feels. "I mean, there are *so* many people," he would argue later. "It shouldn't be a problem."[106]

He's too tired to spend the night with them. Instead he calls Liz and asks her out to dinner, arriving at her house after six, wearing a gray turtleneck and long pants. They drive to the Green Lake Bowl Cafe, a bowling alley a block from Green Lake, said to have the best hamburgers in town. The burgers are enormous, and Liz can barely finish one. Ravenous, he eats two. For dessert they go to Farrell's Ice Cream Parlour, a faux nineteenth-century soda fountain chain popular for its ice cream floats and fancy sundaes. The waiters wear barbershop quartet–type costumes and Styrofoam straw boaters. Liz sees that Ted's eyes are puffy and are positioned close together, something she hasn't noticed before.[107]

When they return to her place, he seems exhausted and complains of getting a cold. Nonetheless, he insists on removing Liz's ski rack from the back of his VW and putting it on hers, changing the appearance of a vehicle that was doubtless seen. It's dark by the time he's finished. He calls in sick to work for the next two days.

Back at Lake Sammamish, after Denise fails to return from the restroom, her friends are alarmed. Eventually, hers is the only car left in the lot. They've been searching for her, and they find her dog but not her. At 8:30, they flag down a park ranger to say that she's missing.

Janice Ott's husband, Jim, has been calling her basement apartment in Issaquah since four o'clock that afternoon. She'd promised to call him then. The phone rings and rings.

ON MONDAY, JULY 15, the United Steelworkers go on strike, idling a thousand workers at the Tacoma smelter and halting installation of the pollution controls mandated by the state. It's the third strike in five years.

On Tuesday, July 16, a state highway employee pulls over on a logging road north of Highway 10 outside Issaquah, planning to have lunch. But as he rolls down the window, he smells something putrid. He walks a few dozen feet into the underbrush to see what's there and glimpses something pale, something he takes for the carcass of a deer. He decides to eat lunch somewhere else.

PANIC ERUPTS AFTER the disappearances at Lake Sammamish. Janice Ott, newspapers report, was "last seen with a 'smooth talking' man named Ted who had a cast on his left arm."[108] There's something so malignant and brazen about someone trolling for women, taking not one but two in a single day, that it's virtually all anyone can talk about.

Police assure the public that there appears to be "no connection" between the disappearances of Janice Ott and Denise Naslund and the five coeds missing from area universities, but the public is not reassured. Rumors fly about "demon cults" and Satanic worship.[109] Psychics pop up like mushrooms.

Over the next few days, rewards are issued and maps of the locations of the missing women in relation to the suspect's car are published. No fewer than three composite sketches of the suspect are issued.[110] For months to come, they will adorn telephone poles and bulletin boards. They're all over Mercer Island.

Divers search the lake bottom. Park rangers and volunteers comb the park and forested areas throughout Issaquah, joined by sixty Explorer Scouts training with a local search and rescue team. Twenty-six pairs of women's panties are found at sites around the lake, none of them apparently belonging to the missing victims.[111]

Among the young detectives assigned to interview witnesses at the lake that day is Robert Keppel, thirty, from Spokane, where his father was a fixture in the sheriff's office. As a teenager, he helped his dad run down shoplifters. Avoiding the draft, he finished a master's degree in the police science program at Washington State University and became a patrolman in King County.

Then he got drafted. He earned a commission as an officer in the U.S. Army Military Police Corps. In Vietnam, he saw every kind of crime:

"drug overdoses, suicides, murders, hostage situations in villages." He describes it as "a great police experience."[112]

In 1974, he's just started working again for the King County Sheriff's Office. He heads out to Lake Sammamish during his second week as a major crimes detective.

IT'S STILL HOT on Wednesday, July 17, three days after the Lake Sammamish abductions, when Norma Countryman, a fifteen-year-old girl, is sitting by the side of the road in Ridgefield, Washington, a town off I-5 just north of Vancouver. She's smoking a cigarette when a guy in a blue van pulls over and offers her a ride. He's been picking up some treated lumber. She hesitates, but the guy is friendly and seems nice. Eventually she climbs in.

He holds a knife to her throat and drives her to Tukes Mountain Park. There he drags her into the woods, punches her in the face, gags her with her bra, hog-ties her, and secures her between two trees with a length of rope. Then he leaves.[113]

Norma doesn't know it, but the body of Krista Kay Blake is buried 167 feet away. Alone, she gnaws on the ropes binding her. After hours of tearing at them with her teeth, she frees herself from the trees, but her ankles and wrists are still tied. Hopping and stumbling through the woods, she hears furtive sounds and freezes, terrified that her abductor has returned. She waits for two hours before moving again.

At dawn, she staggers out of the woods, finding herself at a deserted Clark County Parks building, waiting until an employee pulls up in a truck. It's Jim Bellew, who is startled at the apparition before him: a young girl with her lips half chewed off and a rope burn up one side of her face, her clothes hanging off her. "What happened to you?" he asks, and she tells him it was a guy with a mustache driving a blue van.[114]

Later, Bellew jokes with his colleague Warren Leslie Forrest about Warren's blue van and long handlebar mustache, and Warren says he'll have to go home and shave and get his van painted a different color.

As *The Seattle Times* rolls out the composite sketches of "Ted," there are a number of people who are either intrigued or terrified, depending on the nature of their relationship to Ted Bundy.[115] Ted's old boss at the Pedline medical supply company is struck by the resemblance as soon as he sees it but doesn't mention it to anyone.[116] On July 22, while Liz Kloepfer is at work, a colleague hands her that day's *Times*, saying, "Don't you think this looks like someone you know? Doesn't your Ted have a VW?"[117] She feels sick to her stomach but takes comfort from reports that the VW at Lake Sammamish is said to be bronze or metallic brown. Her Ted's car is tan.

The comfort doesn't last, though, because her mind is racing with other thoughts. She studies the jawline in the sketches, comparing it with photos of Ted, seeing the similarity. She thinks about the container of plaster of paris and the crutches he kept from his medical supply job. She thinks about his eyes when he pushed her into the river, about his threatening to break her fucking neck.[118] About the sack of women's clothing in his apartment.

On July 25, Ted visits a rug repair shop to drop off a small Oriental rug for cleaning, the origin of its stain unknown. That same day, Joel Kestenbaum, the instructor of the UW abnormal psych class who had once appreciated his student's support during a contentious discussion, calls Keppel to say that a couple of years ago he had a "weird guy in my class who drives a 1968 VW and matches the composite drawing from your office."[119] The problem is, the police are receiving thousands of calls and tips. They lack the technology and manpower to sort through them.

Ted has long since dropped off Janice Ott's bike at the Washington Park Arboretum, the 230-acre botanical garden and preserve run by the University of Washington minutes from his rooming house.

At midnight on July 30, Rebecca S., a student at Evergreen, is doing her laundry in the student housing commons when she notices a man, five foot eight and 160 pounds, with long dirty blond hair, who is standing rigidly, partly concealed by the door to the room, staring at her. He says, "Hello

THE DAYLIGHT BASEMENT

there, are you doing your laundry?"[120] At that point, another woman comes into the room to remove her bicycle, and he holds the door for her, leaving briefly.

Moments later, Rebecca looks up and sees that he's back, staring, and seems "really impatient," as if waiting for her to be done folding her clothes. His manner, she says, "is quick . . . sure of himself." She pushes her way past him and runs. Two days later, she sees a composite of "Ted" in the newspaper and tells police she's "positive" the man in the laundry room was him.[121]

DURING THE FIRST week of August, Liz flies to Salt Lake City to visit her family, and while she's there Ted asks her to find him an apartment for the fall.[122] Having spent so much time during the summer murdering people, he's behind on preparing the Department of Emergency Services' budget and must put in extra hours at work while at the same time packing and preparing to move.

Liz finds a nice place near the University of Utah in a neighborhood called the Avenues. When Ted arrives at SeaTac to pick up her and Molly, she's surprised to see that he's had his hair cut so short that he's almost unrecognizable. That afternoon they take Molly to Green Lake. While reaching under the seat of his VW to retrieve one of Molly's socks, Liz feels something else under there and pulls out a hatchet.[123] He says he was using it to cut down a tree.

ANN RULE HAS been thinking about the composite too. She feels guilty for suspecting her old friend Ted but finally breaks down and calls a source in the police department. She asks if he can check Ted Bundy's car registration; she's not sure if he even has a car. The source calls back to tell her that Ted owns a 1968 VW Beetle, and at first Rule thinks he's teasing. He's not. She asks him to keep her report anonymous.[124]

She's planning to write a book about the missing women, building on her busy career writing for *True Detective* as the magazine's Northwest specialist on serial rapes and murders. She's writing as "Andy Stack" or "Alan Stackhouse," and there are so many horrific stories on her beat that she's supporting her children with them.

In "Teen Beauty Shot Three Times after Rape Ordeal!" she covers Rodger Thompson, an eighteen-year-old soldier on leave from Fort Lewis in 1973, who picks up a hitchhiking fifteen-year-old girl, rapes her repeatedly, then shoots her three times. Unbelievably, the girl survives.[125]

In "Case of the Two Virgins and the Insatiable Sex Freak," she documents the career of Carl Harp, a shoe repairman at Bon Marché in the Southcenter Mall and a dead ringer for John Denver, with shiny blond hair and round granny glasses. In the summer of 1973, he stands in the woods beside the northbound lanes of the 405 in Bellevue and fires into oncoming vehicles, killing one man and grievously wounding another. Hiding out near the town of Gold Bar in the Cascades, he follows up by raping two women at gunpoint. Afterwards he tells them, "That wasn't so bad, was it?"[126]

In "Murder for the Hell of It!" she tracks the exploits of Phillip Van Hillman, a twenty-year-old Seattle man and Vietnam veteran who—barely a week after Ted lets loose at Lake Sammamish—shoots an elderly man at a Cascades campground for no reason, threatening to shoot another family nearby.[127] Arrested, he pleads guilty, and prison psychologists say he has a "Jekyll and Hyde personality."[128]

The case that truly haunts her, however, is that of Charles Rodman Campbell, who—also in 1974—begins a series of frenzied rapes and murders that will stretch across the years. That year, Charles, a twenty-year-old red-haired felon with a taste for methamphetamine, spots Renae Wicklund in her front yard in rural Clearview, Washington, south of Everett. Renae is twenty-three, washing windows on a rare sunny day and singing to her year-old daughter, Shannah, when Charles comes running down her driveway, pulls a knife on her, threatens to kill the baby, and forces her to perform oral sex on him. When he leaves, she goes to a neighbor, Barbara Hendrickson, reports the crime, and identifies the suspect from a photo lineup.

A fugitive for thirteen months, Charles snatches Hallie Ann Seaman, a UW student working on a master's degree in architecture, from a campus building on the night of April 29, 1975; her body is found the next day. She's been raped and stabbed repeatedly, and the case will not be solved until DNA testing in 2023. Charles himself is not apprehended until 1976, when he's convicted and sentenced to forty-five years for the attack on Renae Wicklund. Barbara Hendrickson testifies against him.[129]

In the humble pages of pulp magazines, Ann Rule is cataloging a rising tide of inconceivable deviance. One thing she never asks herself is, *Why here? Why now?*

DONNA SCHRAM, Ted's old boss at the King County Law and Justice Planning Office, writes a psychological profile of the offender for the police, who keep it confidential. Whoever is taking the women, she tells them, doesn't care whether they consent or not. He's fully expecting to "overcome and overpower" them.[130] His world revolves around women, and she lists as his likely characteristics:

- exhibitionist
- in trouble, but never arrested as an adult
- manipulative
- graduate student
- middle, upper class
- frequent contact with parents
- first or only [child]
- pampered by women
- difficulty forming relationships, but efficient and could be successful professionally
- relatively little basis for interaction with men with the possible exception of athletics (doesn't drink, smoke, probably doesn't use drugs at all)

- able to delay gratification, not sexually excited by the approach but by something else after the initial interaction
- after a "type," but the "type" is related more to inexperience or naiveté, rather than sexuality or high probability of consensual sexual intercourse
- lives alone[131]

She's describing Ted but doesn't know it. Her list is accurate, with a few exceptions—Ted does drink and use drugs. But she doesn't look at the police sketches and think of him, failing to recognize the troubled young man whose boasting, lying, and stealing offended her. Whose name is Ted.

ON AUGUST 2, Carol Valenzuela, eighteen, with long blond hair parted in the middle, is last seen hitchhiking from her home in Camas, a community on the Columbia River, to downtown Vancouver, Washington. Married to Robert Valenzuela, formerly employed at the Camas paper mill, she is the mother of ten-month-old twins and, unfortunately, she accepts a ride from a man named Warren Leslie Forrest.

SPURRED ON BY her best friend and by the incessant coverage in Seattle newspapers, Liz Kloepfer drops a dime on Ted. It's not the first occasion. After Lake Sammamish, she and her friend had called information from a pay phone in the parking lot of a Green Lake grocery store and asked for the number for the "Ted" police hotline. Anonymously, her friend asked about the color of the VW at Lake Sammamish and was told it was metallic. She hung up without asking anything else. Liz called back and asked if the suspect was wearing a watch on his right arm, the way Ted does, but the officer didn't know. Liz was not relieved.[132]

But on August 8 she calls again from a pay phone. Weeping, she pours out her fears that her boyfriend matches the description, that he talks in a

THE DAYLIGHT BASEMENT

funny English accent, that he lies and shoplifts, that he owns crutches and plaster of paris and drives a VW. The officer asks for her boyfriend's name and tells her to come in and fill out a report. She hangs up.[133]

AT SIX O'CLOCK that same evening, it's broad daylight. I'm standing in the empty lounge of the student union at Western Washington State College in Bellingham, craning my neck to watch the television bolted to the wall. My sister is working at the candy counter nearby, but there aren't any customers, because school hasn't started yet.

My mouth is open. Richard Nixon is resigning. He says he's made the world a "safer place," but that's a lie.[134] I hate him and his spatula nose, but since he's leaving, my hate has nowhere to go, a disorienting feeling, as if the world is subtly shifting, melting like a piece of cake in the rain, as a popular song has it.[135]

LATER THAT MONTH, on August 21, *The Seattle Times* announces that a grant of $335,000 has been awarded for a rape study to the Battelle Human Affairs Research Center, headquartered in Seattle, a project for which nearly half a million dollars has now been raised. Donna Schram tells the newspaper that Seattle "probably has the best rape program in the country."[136] That's a good thing, because it also has the best rapist.

The timing is ironic, however, since August is the first month that year that Ted doesn't stalk and abduct and rape and murder anyone. He's too busy finishing the DES budget while at the same time preparing to skip town.

On Labor Day weekend, Liz and Molly drive down to Olympia to help him. Liz brings her TV set so Molly can watch it while Ted dictates notes for Liz to type. They finish at midnight, and Ted leaves the budget on his boss's desk, tied with a red ribbon, along with a sarcastic handwritten note dated August 30, 1974, saying:

> It is with some regret, not much, but some regret that I submit this my final resignation. Try to persuade me to stay. Bribe me. Slash my tires . . . But the world needs me.
>
> The experience I gained here is without value. Invaluable. And the people I've worked with here are, with a bad moment here and there, are fine and enjoyable people.
>
> This was a good summer.
>
>   Theodore Bundy

Caution. Tears will run the ink.[137]

On September 2, 1974, Labor Day morning, he has breakfast with Liz and Molly. A friend takes his picture as he stands beside his white VW Beetle, dressed in his tennis clothes, the car parked under the Aurora Bridge, next to Lake Union and the Burke-Gilman Trail, his bike strapped to the back like Janice Ott's. He buys gas in Seattle, one last time. Then in Yakima. Then again in Pendleton, Oregon, on the shortcut through eastern Oregon to pick up Interstate 84 through southern Idaho. In Nampa, twenty miles west of Boise, he calls Liz to tell her he loves her.

Somewhere on the outskirts of Boise, as darkness falls, he picks up a hitchhiker, sixteen to eighteen years old, with light brown hair, about five foot six, carrying a large green backpack. She's running away from home, possibly heading for Montana. Taking an off-ramp, he rapes and murders her near a railroad trestle and throws her body into a river—the Snake or the Boise, he's not sure which.[138]

Gordon Lightfoot is singing "Carefree Highway" on the radio, a hit on the *Billboard* Hot 100 that summer, as Ted drives south to Salt Lake City, looking forward to better skiing and hunting in Utah and Colorado. He finds it.

Chapter 7

The Bird's Nest

> I knew myself, at the first breath of this new life, to be more wicked, tenfold more wicked... and the thought, in that moment, braced and delighted me like wine.
>
> —ROBERT LOUIS STEVENSON, *THE STRANGE CASE OF DR. JEKYLL AND MR. HYDE*

On Thursday, September 5, 1974, Dr. James Bax, Idaho state health and welfare director, announces that 98 percent of 175 blood samples collected from children living within a mile of the Bunker Hill smelter outside Kellogg, show "dangerous lead concentrations" of forty, sixty, seventy, and even ninety micrograms per deciliter.[1] Spokesmen for the smelter immediately dispute the findings, saying that their "private surveys" have found no such poisoning.[2]

Some of the highest readings are recorded in Deadwood Gulch, a neighborhood deep in Smelterville, two miles west of Kellogg. Mary Shields, who shares a small house in Deadwood with her three children, her husband, and another family of six, tells an Associated Press reporter, "It gets pretty thick here. Sometimes we have to put all the babies in one room and turn up the fan to keep the air clear. It takes their breath away. It just about kills them."[3] A smelter worker points to his hutch and says,

"Look at my rabbits. They just sit and don't hop."[4] A local veterinarian says as many as a hundred horses have died in recent years, and children taunt one another with cries of "leaded," meaning dumb.

There are kids who can't sit up, kids with kidney damage who can't control their urination, kids who can't walk. All three children in the Cutchins family, a quarter mile from the Bunker Hill stack, are suffering. Baby Stacey, born after her father moved the family there to take a mining job in 1972, has fevers, headaches, and a perpetual cold. Her older brother, Robert, endures constant stomach pains and headaches, yanking on his hair to indicate distress. Her sister Emily's head hurts too. She "squeezes" it in pain.[5]

The Idaho governor swings by the hospital to visit fifteen-month-old Arlene Yoss, whose infant body has been found to contain a higher concentration of lead than any other living human being. No one knows whether she will survive. She's undergoing chelation therapy, the procedure involving injecting a chemical into the body to bind to the lead so that it can be excreted in urine. It's a dangerous treatment, damaging to kidneys and excruciating to bones. Near the smokestack, which is visible everywhere in Kellogg, the governor stands on his hind legs and says it's too soon to "pinpoint the source of this trouble" but promises that the state will get to the bottom of it.[6] He has no plans to talk to company officials.

Arlene's father, Bill Yoss, sues Bunker Hill, and the company sues him back, calling him a "squatter" and implying that his family is poor, shiftless trailer trash. Eventually there will be a settlement throwing some $9 million to the Yoss family and other victims, and the *Seattle Post-Intelligencer* runs an editorial cartoon with two panels, the first showing a demon threatening a child with a hypodermic needle, the second an infernal smoke cloud pouring out of a smokestack. The captions read, IF A PERVERT POISONS A CHILD . . . THAT'S CALLED CHILD ABUSE. IF A CORPORATION POISONS A CHILD, THAT'S CALLED MAXIMIZING PROFITS.[7]

Researchers empowered by the creation of the EPA have been systematically analyzing Tacoma gardens, sifting soil and testing winds, measuring "elevated concentrations" of just about every heavy metal imaginable.

Dust from the smelter is found to contain 30 to 40 percent arsenic and 20 to 30 percent lead, with a soupçon of zinc, copper, mercury, and other metals.[8] Total mass emission rates from the smelter's roaster, reverberatory furnace, and converter gas streams are measured in pounds per hour: arsenic at 58.05 pounds; lead at 24.65; zinc, 15.7; copper, 4.825; cadmium, 1.32; and chromium, 0.065.[9]

Smelter officials, however, are less concerned with what's going up the chimney than with what may or may not be hidden in workers' lunch boxes. Workers are certainly taking home arsenic and lead in their lungs and on their skin. But what their bosses want to know is this: Are they stealing silver and gold in their lunch pails? *The Smelterworker* glumly admits that searches are allowed under the law because these are precious metals.[10]

SEPTEMBER 7, 1974, is the first day of grouse-hunting season in King County, and two men are driving a Jeep on a dirt track off old Highway 10. They're looking for the spot where they bagged a couple of birds the year before, but as they bushwhack up the hillside, following animal trails, they spot part of a skeleton lying on top of the ground and then, several feet away, a human skull with "a little reddish brown tint to it."[11]

They don't know it, but they've just encountered Denise Naslund. They're walking back to the Jeep when they run into a couple of young target shooters, who are skeptical that the remains are human. They offer to show them, and on the way back to the skull they find a "clump of long black hair ... fresh and shiny ... about two feet long."[12] They drive the few miles back into Issaquah to tell authorities.

BONES NOT MISSING WOMEN'S reports *The Seattle Times* the next day, inaccurately, because a lieutenant with the King County Police Department has told reporters that the skull can't belong to one of the Lake Sammamish victims.[13] That skull, along with a spine, rib cage, and two leg bones, are documented and collected immediately. "We're so very glad, so relieved," says Denise's mother, Eleanor Rose, on learning that it's probably not Denise. Mrs. Rose has been frantically imploring the police to provide her with news.

Bob Keppel, the King County homicide detective, is off work that Saturday, down in Tacoma with his partner, Roger Dunn, where they're buying railroad ties soaked in creosote for landscaping projects around their homes. Keppel's knee is burning as they load them into the back of Dunn's pickup. He's injured it playing basketball and is slated for surgery. Heading back north on I-5, they hear on the radio that police are investigating the discovery of skeletal remains east of Issaquah.

Dropping off the ties at home, Keppel arrives at the scene at four that afternoon, limping, bedraggled, and embarrassed to be stinking of creosote. Having actually studied the dental records, he's dismayed by the lieutenant's public insistence that there's no connection to the Lake Sammamish victims. He's not so sure.

Keppel is ordered to return at dawn the next morning with a team from an Explorer Search and Rescue unit, teenagers, many of them Eagle Scouts, who take a keen interest in law enforcement and are training to locate lost hikers and accident victims in the wilderness. Some of them are fifteen or sixteen years old.

When Keppel shows up the next morning, he can smell gunpowder in the air. The lone patrolman on guard duty has fired his weapon, suffering from frayed nerves and exhaustion after listening to animals in the underbrush all night. Before long, news blares out the car radio: the skull does belong to Denise Naslund.

The ESAR team of fifty volunteers, mostly boys and a few girls, are instructed to lay out grids, using string to mark off quadrants across the forest floor, as in an archaeological dig. They search each quadrant on hands and knees, shoulder to shoulder, examining every inch, lifting every leaf and stone on the dark, wet earth, navigating through dense thickets of blackberries and crawling through stinging nettles. They begin at 8:50 a.m. At 9:08, they find human hair. At 9:20, a leather sheath for a machete, two feet long. Three minutes later, a screwdriver. A minute after that, blond hair. At 9:50, a rib bone; 10:12, a jawbone; 10:50, more blond hair, along an

THE BIRD'S NEST

animal trail. At 11:10, blond hair woven into a bird's nest. At 11:15, coyote dung with a small hand bone.[14] The search goes on for seven days.

They find Denise's spinal column and rib cage, Janice's lower jawbone, and other parts of their cadavers, disassembled and widely scattered across the hillside: vertebrae, decayed flesh, and teeth. Leg bones, a pelvis, fingernails. It has been less than two months since the women were abducted.

Also included among the more than four hundred items of evidence are a gold earring, women's underwear (not belonging to any of the victims), a turquoise comb, and a tire iron. Using an antiquated press camera from the 1950s, Keppel crawls around after the teenagers, taking photographs of their discoveries.

Janice's skull is never found. There are, Keppel reckons, three sites of decomposition on top of the ground, with extra leg bones and vertebrae belonging to a third victim. For all the meticulous searching, day by day, hour by hour, the police and the searchers fail to consider one possibility: Additional bodies may be present but buried. If they dig, they might find more. They might find the skull of Georgann Hawkins.[15]

As a young, inexperienced detective, Keppel is used to examining crime scenes where evidence is hours old. He's distressed by the advanced decay, human bones in the coyote feces, and the extra skeletal scraps—evidence of a third victim, which will "rattle" in his mind for years.[16] He's haunted not only by the violence of the crimes but by the blond hair in the bird's nest, the indifferent dismantling of once vibrant young women, now reduced to disparate objects.

Kleptotrichy, they call it: the stealing of hair by birds.[17] The tufted titmouse is so partial to mammal fur—or, say, to the long, bright hair of a Georgann Hawkins or a Janice Ott—that it will pluck strands from a dead woman. Nature, knitting them back into the bigger picture. The OWL at work.

As it is, the scene is overwhelming. The team searches 130,000 square feet of hillside over thirteen days and 4,887 hours, the largest such operation to date in King County.[18]

Keppel begins to realize how carefully it was chosen. Only a mile from a populated area, it's nonetheless remote, and the quiet hillside affords advance notice of anyone approaching.

The absence of Janice Ott's skull may be significant, suggesting that it was deliberately moved or removed by the killer. Small animals are likely to scavenge minor bones first—hands, feet, ribs, sternum, and clavicle—detaching and dragging them away. Human skulls, however, weigh eight to eleven pounds and are generally the last body parts to be scattered or taken, if taken at all. Nearly 90 percent are found where the body was left. Few creatures aside from bears, coyotes, and dogs can easily drag them; few natural predators are motivated to remove them.[19] MISSING BONES HINT OF BEHEADING, a later headline will read.[20]

I AM THRILLED to learn that a new show, *Kolchak: The Night Stalker*, will premiere on September 13, 1974, starring Darren McGavin as Carl Kolchak, a disheveled fedora-wearing wire service reporter on the trail of supernatural serial murderers. It's based on previous made-for-TV movies—*The Night Stalker* and *The Night Strangler*. Through some miracle of parental inattention I've watched *The Night Strangler*, which aired in 1973. The movie was covered heavily in the Seattle press, because it's set in and around Seattle, with a credit sequence featuring the Space Needle. It tells the story of an ageless serial killer who reemerges every twenty-one years to strangle young women and drain them of their blood, which keeps him alive. Kolchak is sent to the area to cover the Daffodil Festival.[21]

The series promises all manner of nightmarish intoxication and unbearable excitement. Over the course of its single season, it will feature a reincarnation of Jack the Ripper, vampires, witches, werewolves, mummies, voodoo, an alien who sucks the bone marrow out of its victims, and a politician who forges a pact with Satan and turns into a rabid dog.

The only problem is, I'm not allowed to watch it. Mary Baker Eddy tells us to denounce on a more or less daily basis "Ancient and Modern Necromancy, alias Mesmerism and Hypnotism." My father takes this to mean anything that smacks of the supernatural. For the next few months, on Fridays at nine, which is technically past my bedtime anyway, I sulk out of the living room, hoping that he'll drop dead of a heart attack.

What he doesn't know is that I am already a secret fan of reruns of *Dark Shadows*, which air at four in the afternoon, before he gets home. At that hour, I can sit in solitude, inches from the screen, with my hand on the dial and watch vampires and werewolves, and there's nothing he can do about it. If I hear his VW on the gravel, I can switch it off, leaving only the dying crackle of static and the telltale warmth of the box, which he somehow never picks up on. In these moments, he is powerless.

I love monsters. The salt monster on *Star Trek*. The Human Fly. Barnabas Collins, of course. In the Northwest in 1974, vampires are abroad in the land. Everyone knows it. I can feel in my bones that *The Night Stalker* will explain everything. There *is* a night stalker, there *is* a night strangler. He's out there, and how will I escape if I can't see him coming?

OCTOBER IS THE DEADLIEST MONTH. On October 1, 1974, twenty-year-old Daria Wightman is standing on a street corner in downtown Portland when a man driving a blue van pulls over. He tells her that he's hoping to hire a model for a photography class he's taking at Seattle University. He agrees to pay her ten dollars an hour, and they drive to Washington Park, the 410-acre public park that's home to the Portland Zoo, a rose garden, a Japanese garden, tennis courts, and an archery range.

Parked on a dead-end road at the park's periphery, he pulls a knife on Daria and binds her with tape, forcing her into the back of the van for the twenty-five-mile drive to Lacamas Park in Clark County, where he unlocks the park gate with his key. He drags her into the woods, shoots her multiple times in the chest with a dart gun, inserts plastic tubing into her vagina, and rapes her. He ties a slipknot around her neck, dragging her farther into the forest and then choking her until she passes out. When she wakes up, she finds herself naked, lying next to a log and covered with brush and leaves, having been left for dead.[22]

Bleeding from the wounds on her chest, she is nonetheless able to stagger out of the forest to the park entrance, where she is discovered at around 6:00 p.m. and taken to a hospital.[23] Questioned by police, she describes her assailant, and the police in turn contact a Clark County Parks official. He tells them that Warren Leslie Forrest is the only employee matching Daria's description who owns a blue van and has a key to Lacamas Park. Warren is arrested early the following morning. Between the ages of twenty and twenty-five, he's raped eight women, torturing one of them by sticking pins in her breasts.[24] He's been murdering women since he was twenty-two. He's been fantasizing about it since he was fifteen.[25]

Like Ted Bundy, he's an attractive young white male with an impressive record: an honors student and captain of the high school track team. In the Fort Vancouver High School yearbooks he's a stunner, with floppy light brown hair, blue eyes, and an easy grin. As people say about Ted, he's clean-cut.

HOURS AFTER WARREN Leslie Forrest is arrested, on the night of October 2, Ted is driving through the dark, deserted streets of Holladay, a suburb of Salt Lake City, and spots a sixteen-year-old girl, Nancy Wilcox, walking alone.[26] She's a student at Olympus High School, a bouncy, popular girl, five foot six, 120 pounds, with cascades of curly blond hair. On that evening, she's impulsively left her house after an argument with her parents, apparently intending to meet her boyfriend.

Nancy has a part-time job selling burgers and ice cream at a local Arctic Circle drive-in, where she's recently been seen chatting with a handsome older man who seems to fancy her. Friends will recall seeing her with a man in a VW.[27] She may or may not already know Ted. Newly freed from the surveillance of Liz Kloepfer back in Seattle, he is cultivating and stalking new friends and girlfriends in the social rounds of campus life and law school and the guilelessly friendly Mormon neighborhoods of the city. Some of these friends he will date. Some he will murder.

On that night, just a little over eight miles from his apartment, Ted is watching Nancy Wilcox as she walks down the street toward an orchard some five hundred feet from her house. He's been drinking. He hops out of the car and runs up behind her, perhaps holding a knife. He'll later say he "restrained" her, possibly by bashing her over the head with a blunt object or throttling her or both, perhaps raping her in the orchard for starters, then carrying her to the car and driving her, still alive, to his apartment.[28]

There he spends the night raping her. He murders her the next day, dumping her body somewhere in the vast Utah wilderness, perhaps near Capitol Reef National Park, a stunning stretch of rugged red-rock canyons and ridges that lies a four-hour drive south of Salt Lake City. Her remains are never found.[29]

ON THE SAME DAY that Ted murders Nancy Wilcox, the Bunker Hill Company holds a public meeting in front of a hundred concerned citizens to announce that it will shut down operations for two weeks. High levels of lead have turned up in preliminary testing of dirt, vegetation, and air near the smelter, as well as in the blood of children. Of 333 children tested, 300 are found to have abnormal levels of lead.[30]

Dr. Bax, Idaho state health officer, observes that airborne lead concentrations have increased four times in Kellogg since 1971. High levels of other metals are also found: cadmium and antimony. He advises parents to mop their floors.

For its part, Bunker Hill says it will continue with its own studies, to be performed by a research group affiliated with the lead and zinc industry. The shutdown will not be immediate—perhaps in the next two months or so, officials say. There's no hurry.

ON OCTOBER 11, Ted buys gas twice in Salt Lake City.

The next day, his doppelgänger's deeds continue to come to light when, on the first day of deer hunting season, the skull of Carol Valenzuela, last seen in August hitching a ride from Camas, Washington, to Portland, is stumbled upon by hunters in the Dole Valley, a heavily forested area twenty miles northeast of Vancouver and south of Mount Saint Helens. It's an area frequented by Warren Leslie Forrest.

Her skeleton lies near that of another woman whose identity will remain a mystery for years and whose age is estimated as twenty to twenty-five, her height five foot five to five foot seven, her hair dark brown. When Valenzuela's identification is confirmed, her husband, Robert, is taken into custody as a "material witness," although police are unable to interview him. When they arrive at the Valenzuela residence, they find that he's taken a large quantity of aspirin tablets and must be rushed to the hospital.[31]

ON OCTOBER 13, Ted calls Liz Kloepfer shortly after 3:00 a.m. He's settling into the apartment Liz found for him at 565 First Avenue in a second-floor unit of a big Dutch Colonial house carved into student flats. He's hanging out with Margith Maughan, the twenty-seven-year-old downstairs neighbor, who moved in shortly before he did. Margith is from a well-known Mormon family, daughter of a Utah Supreme Court justice and a graduate of the University of Utah who's done a stint in the Peace Corps. However upright her family, she enjoys drinking beer with Ted, who seems nothing if not respectable. Soon he will become the on-site manager of the house, with access to the basement. Soon he will take a night job at Ballif Hall, a dormitory, while attending classes only sporadically.

He grows a mustache and in mid-October, buying gas frequently, begins haunting the area around a junior high school in Midvale, another suburb of the sprawling city, bifurcated by Interstate 15, the main north–south highway.

The great central valley of Utah is a trough between the Wasatch Range to the east, looming jagged and uncompromising above the headquarters of the Latter-day Saints in Temple Square, and a smaller mountain range across the valley to the west. Towns and offshoots of Salt Lake are dotted all down the valley, from Bountiful and Ogden in the north to Murray, Holladay, Midvale, American Fork, Provo, and Spanish Fork in the south. At Spanish Fork, a major highway climbs through the Wasatch to the east.

Ted feels right at home in his new hunting ground, which extends through the valley and into the mountains and is dotted with nearly a hundred smelters—some built by Rockefeller and ASARCO, a few recently decommissioned, many long defunct.[32] The properties are surrounded by smokestacks and hills of slag, dust eddying on the wind, particulates enriched with highlights of gold, silver, copper, lead, zinc, and arsenic.

Back home in the Northwest, Phillip Van Hillman, star of one of Ann Rule's *True Detective* profiles, is sentenced to twenty years in prison on October 15, a day when the air pollution in Seattle is so bad that the Puget Sound Air Pollution Control Agency announces that it might have to order industries to curtail production.[33] Officials say that the air might be even dirtier the following day.[34] A temperature inversion is causing stagnant conditions, and the air quality index measures 35 in Seattle and 33 in Tacoma. The agency is required to issue emergency alerts when it reaches 50.

On October 18, Melissa Smith, a seventeen-year-old living in Midvale, has been on the phone, counseling a friend with boyfriend trouble. She agrees to meet the friend where the girl works, the Pepperoni, a local pizza joint about a mile away. Melissa is the daughter of the Midvale police chief, Louis Smith. She has long dark hair parted in the middle and is a savvy child. But she's not savvier than Ted Bundy.

On foot, she takes the quickest route to the Pepperoni, walking under the I-15 and the railroad overpass, and hangs out with her friend until around ten. Then she heads home, stopping for a few minutes to talk to a cousin who lives nearby. At a quarter past ten, the wife of a police dispatcher who lives in the area hears a scream.[35] The scream may come from Melissa, walking through the dark underpass, attacked from behind by her assailant.

His victim unconscious, Ted loads her into his car and takes her to his apartment, where he calls Liz Kloepfer at 11:17 p.m. He keeps Melissa or her body there for somewhere between twenty-four hours and a week. The day after abducting Melissa, Ted goes hunting with Liz's father.

DOWN IN WICHITA, Dennis Rader is growing restive. He's agitated about the fact that police are questioning three suspects, men involved in sex crimes, for the Otero murders. These are his murders, and he doesn't want anyone else taking the credit. On October 22 he places a call to Don Granger, a columnist at *The Wichita Eagle*. Speaking in a low, rough voice with an exaggerated midwestern accent, he tells Granger to go to the public library and locate a specific volume, *Applied Engineering Mechanics*. Inside the book, he says, will be a letter containing details that only the murderer could know.

Granger supplies the tip to the police, and they find the letter. It does indeed contain details, unpublicized facts concerning the positions of the bodies and what was done to them. Its weird tone, combining spelling errors and subliterate grammar and narcissistic self-justification, is reminiscent of a recent horror movie, *The Exorcist*, in which a child speaks in the voice of a demon:

> I'm sorry this happen to the society . . . It hard to control myself. [. . .] Where this monster enter my brain I will never know. But, it here to stay. How does one cure himself? If you ask for help, that you have killed four people, they will laugh or hit the panic button and call the cops.
>
> I can't stop it so, the monster goes on, and hurt me as wall as society. Society can be thankfull that there are ways for people like me to relieve myself [. . .]. It a big compicated game my friend of the monster [. . .] waiting in the dark, waiting, waiting . . . the pressure is great and somt-times he run the game to his liking. Maybe you can stop him. I can't.[36]

Admitting to only the Otero murders and not to the attack on Kathy Bright and her brother, Rader adds a postscript announcing his moniker:

"Since sex criminals do not change their M.O. or by nature cannot do so, I will not change mine. The code words for me will be . . . bind them, torture them, kill them, B.T.K., you see he at it again. They will be on the next victim."

He has arrived.

ON SUNDAY, OCTOBER 27, nine days after her abduction, the nude body of Melissa Smith is discovered by deer hunters on a Wasatch mountainside covered in heavy scrub oak brush and small pines near a new development east of Salt Lake City. Captain Pete Hayward and Detective Ben Forbes respond. This is the first time that a body of one of Ted's victims has been found so soon—the first time that police and forensic investigators can see what he's done before the veil of decomposition has been drawn.

The body of the "young female American," as she's described in Forbes's initial report prior to identification, is an "obvious homicide," lying on her stomach with her right arm extended and her left folded beneath her.[37] There are heavy abrasions across her back, her buttocks, and the backs of her legs, the skin obscured by dirt and scrape marks. Around her throat is a man's navy-blue knit sock, tied at the back of the neck, interspersed with strands of the victim's hair and a single string of wooden beads, yellow, blue, and red. At the back of her head is a deep puncture wound, mistaken at first for a bullet hole. There is no blood at the scene. A portable deck chair is found nearby.

Once the body is removed and autopsied by the state medical examiner, however, the gaping wound, extending through the scalp to the skull, is determined to have been caused not by a bullet but by a sharp object, causing a skull fracture and brain hemorrhage.[38] The abrasions on her back are postmortem. A single false eyelash is found adhered to her right leg, although a friend later says Melissa never wore false eyelashes.

Hemorrhaging is visible due to the neck injury, caused by strangulation with the sock. There is sperm in the vagina, sperm in the rectum, and sperm, along with a wad of bubble gum, in the girl's mouth. Her stomach is full—she drank a milkshake—but her body has been drained of ten pints of blood.[39]

Louis Smith, Midvale police chief and the girl's father, is brought in to identify the body, and he recognizes the necklace. But the condition of the corpse is such that he thinks it's his daughter but is just not sure. Local dentists who have done work on Melissa's teeth are brought in; they examine her and identify the dental work as their own. Just as they're rendering their opinion, the medical examiner spots a small birthmark on the lower left back of the victim, previously described by Melissa's mother, and the identification is complete.

The time of death given by the examiner is forty-eighty to seventy-two hours before the discovery of the body. If this is accurate, it means that Melissa was alive for days after her abduction. But the calculation may be flawed. There are no signs of her wrists or ankles being bound: if she was held, she must have been unconscious. What's more, the body was found on a shaded north slope at an altitude of around seven thousand feet, where temperatures at night drop to freezing. That, and bloodlessness, may have preserved the remains.

The day that Melissa's body is found, Liz's best friend is in Utah and hears the news on the radio. She flies back to Seattle that day and tells Liz that it's happening again. "It's happening in Utah right now," she says.[40] The next morning, Liz calls the King County Police again, and this time she screws up her courage to the sticking point. She talks to Randy "Hergy" Hergesheimer of the Major Crimes Unit and convinces him to call the police in Salt Lake for more details. Later that afternoon, she meets him in the parking lot of a Herfy's Burgers and pours out her list of the nightmarish similarities between "Ted" and Ted. He asks her about their sex life; he asks if her Ted has ever been violent. No, she says, but then admits that they once had a fight in this very parking lot and Ted slapped her. That he threatened to break her fucking neck. She tells him about the crutches and the plaster of paris.

She doesn't want to reveal his full name, but Hergesheimer feeds it to her himself, because Ted Bundy is on their list. He's already been checked out, the officer tells her, and he's probably not the guy.

The day that Melissa's body is found, Ted is buying gas in Bountiful, Utah.

HE'S STARTING TO make mistakes. Utah Ted is a little sloppier than Washington Ted. He's losing focus. He doesn't know the terrain and back roads as intimately. Tree cover is not as dense. He's not at home anymore.

He's aware there's something wrong, something inside. Later he'll refer to himself as an "organism," always seeking to "relieve tension."[41] "It starts early," he'll say. "A guy who abducts girls like that, that comes from something, some incident that manifests itself very early in life."[42] He muses on circuits and wiring, the mysterious workings of the things behind our eyes, the things that get crossed:

> The younger that a person . . . that he or she was when they manifested abnormal behavior or thought pattern . . . the more likely it was that there was going to be a condition that would be lasting. And, uh, permanent. A chronic disorder . . .
>
> Let's consider the possibility that this person suffered from some sort of an acute onset of a desire that resulted in the pattern of, of, of, *killing* young girls. And that there was no other explanation for that, other than it was some sort of genetic or even congenital condition whose time had come . . . that, uh, I mean, that unless you could get it under an electron microscope somewhere and you could understand the complex circuitry of the brain, you'd never know just why, because there'd never be a satisfactory explanation. Everything in the person's background might be known, but how do you account for it?[43]

How indeed? Ted puts his exploratory finger on something substantial:

> So you'd have to . . . somewhere in the chemical, uh, finery of the brain, something went wrong . . . some chemical imbalance or

some genetic switch gone wrong . . . a predisposition, you might call it a condition . . . a weakness or predisposition, which, absent certain stresses and certain environmental conditions, would never have resulted in this behavior but *did*. . . . We do know that it's environmental, it's specific to an environment.[44]

It is specific to an environment, the imbalance in the chemicals. He just doesn't know how. He will never know.

ON OCTOBER 30, 1974, Stephen King checks into the Stanley Hotel in Estes, Colorado, for a night, among the last guests of the season.[45] When he writes the book he dreams of that night, he puts his madman behind the wheel of a VW Beetle. Red in color.

TED CAN'T STOP. He's been hanging around Lehi since September. Lehi is named for the prophet in the Book of Mormon who gets out of Jerusalem before the Babylonians go ape, and it squats at the northern end of Utah Lake. I-15 swings by Lehi on the route south from Murray to American Fork. Intoxicated by the teen scene at the Knotty Pine Cafe in Lehi, Ted does the stupidest thing a serial killer can do: he gets to know a girl before he kills her.

He gets to know Laura Aime. Laura's a seventeen-year-old with long brown hair who stands nearly six feet tall. She's physically confident from her work on the family farm, where she tends cows, horses, goats, sheep, and flocks of chickens and turkeys. She has her own horse named Arab, a big Arabian stallion, and often goes deer hunting with her father, who works at U.S. Steel in Provo. She has scars on the inside of her left forearm from barbed wire, from the time her horse threw her.

Teased about her height, Laura drops out of high school but continues to hang out with her friends. One day in late fall 1974, she's sitting around on the grass at school when an older man, a "college guy" who seems familiar with Laura already, gets out of his VW and strolls over to her, protesting when one of her friends, a boy, shoves a handful of grass into her halter top. "She's mine," the college guy says. Laura tells him, "Get screwed," leaving him speechless.[46]

The guy in the VW begins showing up in Lehi regularly, looking for Laura, stopping by the Knotty Pine Cafe on the main street and drinking coffee and flirting with her and her girlfriends. One night at the restaurant, he blocks her into a booth, refusing to let her out. "I'm ready to go," she says, but the man says, "You can't. I'm going to rape you." She laughs and pushes him away.

He's seen driving by her house or her friends' houses when she's there, and she's spotted on the street arguing with him. He wants to date her, but she doesn't want to date him. She's heard saying, "Get the fuck out of here. I don't want to see you no more."[47]

In October 1974, the Aime family is renting a house in Provo, a few miles downshore from Lehi and a shorter commute to U.S. Steel. It's easy for a girl to hitchhike between Lehi and Provo and all over the valley. The valley is safe—it's full of Mormons. Laura's mother, Shirleen, begs her not to do it anymore after news breaks of the discovery of Melissa Smith's body, but Laura shrugs it off, saying, "I'm a big girl. I can take care of myself."[48]

On Halloween night, Laura is hanging out with friends at a house party in Orem, just north of Provo. She's drinking a lot. Sometime between ten o'clock and midnight, heavily intoxicated, she gets up and announces that she's going to hitchhike to American Fork to buy some cigarettes. She's wearing a halter top and blue Levi's with patches on the rear and silver cross earrings and a thin chain around her neck. Her fingernails are painted black. No one goes with her.

LAURA AIME IS THE THIRD woman Ted has murdered that month. He calls Liz at 12:44 a.m. that night.

He's busy during the week with law school and dorm duties and socializing with Margith and his other friends and housemates at 565 First Avenue, where he's constantly getting high and drinking beer. He sleeps with Margith a couple of times but loses interest in November, to her dismay.

Nonetheless, he likes to scare her, hiding in the bushes or behind her car, jumping out as she walks by. He likes to walk past her apartment at night, peering in her window until she sees him and screams. He likes to come into her apartment during the day and at night, unannounced. "I would turn around and he would be standing there," she'll recall.[49]

On Friday, November 8, he puts on green pants and a sports jacket and shiny black patent leather shoes, arms himself with a small handgun and a badge, and heads to the Fashion Place Mall in Murray to go shopping.

Carol DaRonch is also shopping that night, although she's looking for something different. She's a stunning girl with big brown eyes and masses of long brown hair curling around her shoulders. She could be a model or a movie star. She's eighteen and graduated from high school that June. She has a job with Mountain Bell Telephone. She still lives with her parents, Fred and Beth DaRonch, in a rambler a few doors down from Fred's brother, who works for Kennecott Copper. He's a foreman at the Bingham Canyon Mine, thought to be the deepest open-pit mine in the world, two and a half miles wide, previously owned, of course, by ASARCO. Their home is near the carcass of the old Murray lead smelter at State Street and 53rd, mothballed since 1949. Another serial killer who grows up playing near the Murray smelter will ultimately say of his victims, in self-justification, "They don't know they're dead."[50]

Carol is a shy, quiet, happy girl, proud of her car, a maroon late-model Camaro. After work that Friday, she heads to the mall, arriving around 7:00 p.m., planning to look for a present for one of her cousins. It's dark and rainy that night, and she parks near Sears and dashes in, cutting through the store to the main corridors, heading for Auerbach's, a department store. She runs into some of her cousins and stops to chat. Moving on, a book about cats in the Waldenbooks window strikes her eye, and when she pauses to check it out, a man in green pants and shiny black patent leather shoes approaches her.

It's Officer Roseland, a handsome man with wavy hair and a neatly trimmed mustache. He asks her if she has a car parked in the Sears lot, requesting the license plate number in an official manner, and tells her that there's been an attempted break-in. He wants her to tell him if anything's missing.[51]

She goes with him, but she's dubious, somehow, about his manner. She asks to see his identification, and when he laughs at her, she doesn't insist. Outside, standing beside her car, she looks in the window and can see that nothing's wrong. The car is untouched, and nothing's missing. She says so, and he asks her to open the door anyway, but she resists. She sees something shiny in his pocket. Handcuffs.

He asks her to accompany him to the police substation in the mall, where he says the suspect is being held. They walk through the mall and out again, to a door near a laundromat, which he tries to open. It's locked.

"What did you say your name was?" she asks him. "Officer Roseland," he says, and instructs her to come with him to police headquarters to help fill out a report. He guides her to his car, a light-colored VW that's seen better days. She's surprised at how ratty it is, with a tear across the top of the rear seat. She asks to see his ID again, and he whips out his wallet and flashes a gold badge at her. She gets in the car. He asks her to put her seat belt on, and she refuses.

He drives off, making a U-turn, and Carol can see that he's not heading to State Street, in the direction of the police station. She begins to smell alcohol on his breath. A half mile from the mall, he veers over into the bus lane near McMillan Elementary School and abruptly pulls up onto a curb, stopping the VW. She says, "What are we doing?" He doesn't say anything but grabs her left arm and snaps the handcuffs on her wrist. Now she's screaming, "What are you doing?" She's terrified, trying to get the car door open as he's grabbing her around the neck with his right arm.

The door falls opens and she jams her foot out. He pulls a gun and says he's going to blow her head off. It's small, it's black, it's pointing at her body, but she's fighting and screaming, thinking that if he drives off with her, her parents will never understand what happened. She's somehow outside the car, and so is he, and he's raising a weapon over his head, and she grabs it with her left hand. It's a crowbar, a six- or eight-sided solid metal rod, and she pushes against it with all her might, trying to keep him from hitting her over the head.

Headlights come flashing along, an oncoming vehicle, and she breaks free, running madly into the street, waving and jumping up and down, and when the car stops she piles in on top of the woman in the passenger seat, shaking and hysterical, saying, "He was trying to kill me. He was trying to kill me." She still has the handcuffs on, fastened twice to the same wrist, and is missing a shoe. As they drive past, she sees her assailant driving off in the opposite direction.

The couple who pick her up immediately take her to the police station where she's so overcome by terror and adrenaline and the aftereffects of fighting for her life that she cannot even walk into the building without help. She's beside herself for some time but gradually recovers her wits and gives the police a description of the man. She looks at pictures of possible suspects.

By that time, the man in the shiny black shoes is long gone. He's on his way north, to Bountiful.

HE WAS IN BOUNTIFUL a few days earlier, getting gas and casing Viewmont High School, picking up a brochure for the school's upcoming production of *Redhead*, a musical set in 1880s London, during the era of Jack the Ripper.[52] Vehicle for the popular dancer Gwen Verdon and choreographer Bob Fosse, the 1959 Broadway original was a hit, winning multiple Tony Awards, including Best Musical.

The Mormon kids are putting on a play about a serial killer. As it opens, Ruth LaRue, a gorgeous actress, is strangled in her dressing room by a psychopath with a yen for artistes. Verdon played a girl who works in a waxworks museum tasked with recreating a tableau of the attack, and it attracts the murderer's attention. Trying to uncover his identity, she too is assaulted but survives.

THE BIRD'S NEST

Frustrated and angry after his struggle with Carol DaRonch, Ted drives directly to Viewmont High for his second attempt of the evening. The school is abuzz with excitement, family members and friends taking their seats in the auditorium.

Raelynne Shepherd, the teacher in charge of dance for the production, is racing back and forth through a hallway between the dressing room—where she's helping students with costumes and wigs—and the ticket booth, checking on the crowd in the auditorium. At a few minutes before 8:00, when the performance will begin, she's approached in the hallway by a handsome man with patent leather shoes who says, "Excuse me, but could you come out to the parking lot and try and identify a car for me?"[53] Raelynne, who is twenty-four and beautiful, says she's busy but she can find somebody to help him. He keeps trying to persuade her. Annoyed, she says, "I'm sorry," turns her back on him, and goes into the dressing room.

A half hour later, he's still in the hallway, and she asks if he's found anyone to help. He doesn't answer. He just stares at her.

She watches the play until it's time for the next costume change, when she sees him again in the hallway. He walks toward her, saying, "Hey, um, you really look nice."[54] "Thanks," she says. Again he asks for help, saying it will take only a few seconds. She offers to send her husband to help. He ignores that, bending his face next to hers and saying, "Do you know if Brent Olsen is around here?" It's a made-up name.

He watches the play as a string of teenage girls pirouette across the stage in see-through tutus and tights, their shadows cast on the curtain behind them.[55] At intermission, around 9:30 p.m., Raelynne sees him leave the auditorium. At 9:50 p.m., another young woman attending the play is approached in the parking lot by a handsome man around thirty years old with wavy dark hair. He asks if she knows someone, a name she doesn't recognize. The man says it's his brother and asks if she can help him fix something on his car. She says no and returns to the auditorium.

At 10:10 p.m., Dean Kent, an oil executive who's attending the play with his wife and his daughter Debi, a seventeen-year-old Viewmont student, hands Debi the keys to their car so she can pick up her younger brothers at the roller skating rink. Debi is a small girl, five feet one inches tall and 110 pounds, with long brown hair, chubby cheeks, and a cherubic smile. She's wearing a blue sweater or sweatshirt with a flower on the front, white slacks, a waist-length blue coat, a gold chain, silver hoop earrings, and a 1975 Viewmont High class ring. At around this time, the man who's been trying to convince Raelynne Shepherd to go outside with him is seen at the back of the auditorium, standing around as if he were an usher.

A few minutes later, at 10:20 p.m., nearby residents hear screams and a loud banging noise coming from the parking lot. To one witness, the screams sound "desperate."[56] A neighbor comes out to investigate but can't see anything.

At 10:40 p.m., Raelynne sees the man again, leaning over a railing at the back of the auditorium. He's breathing heavily. His hair is mussed, and he appears to be upset. He sits down in the aisle across from her and her husband, but as the curtain falls and the applause extends through several curtain calls, he gets up and leaves.

When the Viewmont High School yearbook appears the following spring, it describes the attentive audience at *Redhead* as having been "captured by the shrill but effective scream of Ruth LaRue as she was strangled."[57] The write-up does not mention the fact that a student was abducted in the parking lot during the play. Her scream was shrill but not effective.

Debi's purse and keys are discovered that night on the ground next to the family car, still in the parking lot. Also found is a key to a pair of handcuffs, later determined to unlock those on Carol DaRonch's wrist. The Kents report their daughter missing at 11:55 p.m.

Ted drives Debi to his apartment, where he keeps her for twenty-four hours. She's alive for half of it.[58]

Three days after Debi Kent goes missing, Margith Maughan is in Ted's apartment, which she's noticed he keeps very, very clean, and they're watching the six o'clock news. A report on the Kent case comes up, and Margith says she's worried about her safety with a guy like that running around. "Why would a girl let something like that happen to her?" she asks. She adds, "I'd kill him."

Unbeknownst to Ted, Margith has been carrying a hammer in her purse for self-defense. Ted looks surprised to learn this, his eyes widening. He says, "You'd kill him?" She says, "Yeah, I'd kill him."

He says, "Well, you don't have to worry about that."[59]

GULF RESOURCES CHAIRMAN Robert Allen boasts that profits at Bunker Hill are sky-high, topping $25.9 million in 1974, after losses of $9 million the previous year.[60] It's the best year in Gulf's history, but Allen sends a memo to Bunker Hill warning against spending too much time on environmental issues. Financial planning, he says, is more important.[61]

ON NOVEMBER 19, 1974, *The Seattle Times* reports on a letter recently written by local resident Joanne Werner to the mayor of Mercer Island. The mayor is her husband, Ben Werner, and she's complaining about a recent accident on one of the island's I-90 on-ramps, an accident in which her car was totaled. People who live here shouldn't have to risk their lives every time they leave the island, she writes, adding, "The odds are such that when we die, it will probably be on I-90."[62]

She has a point, the reporter notes, because the accident rate on the bridge and its approaches is three times as high as on other urban freeways, a statistic confirmed by state highway officials. Traffic comes across the bridge at fifty miles an hour, the article says. That's what Mark Twain would call a stretcher. Try sixty. Try seventy.

Mayor Werner, who has no power to regulate speed limits on a federal highway, tells the *Times* that some residents are so "intimidated" by the prospect of merging with high-speed traffic that they're afraid to leave the island. What he doesn't say is that Mercer Island is now locked in lawsuits over the fate of the I-90 expansion that could address the dangerous on-ramps, the bridge bulge, and the reversible lane.

The project calls for fourteen lanes of traffic, wider than a football field, crossing this bucolic suburb, elevated on fifty-foot pylons. Robert Moses, notorious urban planner and despoiler of neighborhoods, has erected such monstrosities throughout New York City on the backs of the poorest and least influential, razing homes and dividing minority communities. Mercer Island, by contrast, is the whitest and wealthiest neighborhood ever to be asked to host a federal highway. It digs in its gilded heels.

Werner's predecessor has reacted to the I-90 proposal by saying of the interstate, "We don't want to see it, smell it, or hear it."[63] The island newspaper runs a "Name the Monster" contest for the project—"Gasper" is the winner—and the head of the state highway department is hanged in effigy from a streetlamp.[64]

THE DAY BEFORE Thanksgiving, a couple of students from Brigham Young University are hiking in American Fork Canyon, northeast of Provo, up in the Wasatch. Gazing down across a stream as they walk, they're looking for fossils and rocks for a geology class when they see a pale form, thinking at first it's a deer. To their horror, they suddenly realize it's the body of a naked woman, and she's dead. They're stricken by the sight, which they describe later as "really grotesque." They see blood around the woman's neck and breasts. Earlier they saw a light-colored VW in the area and are terrified that the killer might be nearby. They run across the creek and back to their car and drive to the nearest ranger station.

In Utah, the canyon is usually snow-covered by Thanksgiving, but winter has been late to arrive. At first, county sheriffs from Provo who rush to the scene are thinking that they've found Debi Kent. When Shirleen Aime calls to ask if it's Laura, they say no. Absolutely not.

But it is Laura Aime. There's not a stitch on her, except for her ring and gold chain, caught up in strands of her hair and in the brown nylon stocking tied tight around her neck, knotted at the back. Like Melissa Smith, she's been dragged through leaves, twigs, dirt, and mud. Like Melissa Smith, she's been killed somewhere else. There are abrasions below one breast and on her thighs, but the most extensive damage is to her head, which has been savagely beaten, causing deep lacerations, a depressed fracture of the skull, and multiple contusions and hemorrhages. Anus and vagina are positive for semen.[65]

Jim Aime comes to identify the body with his wife. Wanting to spare her, he goes in alone. The damage to Laura's head is so extensive that he can't recognize his daughter, but when he asks to see the inside of her left arm, scarred by the barbed wire from her horse-riding accident, he is sure. Outside in the hall, when she hears him screaming, Shirleen Aime knows.[66]

Contrary to what Ted has been able to achieve in the Pacific Northwest, where he has broken women down into their constituent parts and scattered them across mountainsides, the women of Utah are testifying with their entire bodies, revealing a virulent late twentieth-century case of Dr. Jekyll and Mr. Hyde.

In his sunny daylight guise, Ted can summon the affable professional—desirable, persuasive, fluent. But when the chemical finery comes into play, he morphs into another being, wordless and barely human: he's the invisible worm that flies in the night in the howling storm.[67] He's a modern monstrosity who, "for all his energy of life," is something "not only hellish but inorganic."[68] A sexual virus masquerading as a person, usurping "the offices of life."[69] As with Robert Louis Stevenson's shape-shifter, the horror within is "closer than a wife, closer than an eye . . . caged in his flesh," and it's working its way out every week or two, cyclically, as the entity rejoices in beating and choking females to death, ejaculating in every orifice of their unconscious bodies.[70]

Ted, our latter-day Hyde, is inarticulate, his face contorted. Witnesses will see blue eyes shifting to black, a dead white spot indented in his cheek like the stamp of Satan.[71] They will feel the chill of an acquisitive gaze.

What follows must be identical to the galvanizing moment when Dr. Jekyll swallows the pure potent powders that trigger his transformation:

> Instantly the spirit of hell awoke in me and raged. With a transport of glee, I mauled the unresisting body, tasting delight from every blow; and it was not till weariness had begun to succeed, that I was suddenly, in the top fit of my delirium, struck through the heart by a cold thrill of terror.[72]

It is the taste of metal, metal with the tang of fire. It is the lead within and the lead without. It is "the slime of the pit."[73]

Interlude

From Alamein to Zem Zem

> Nature does not know extinction; all it knows is transformation.
>
> —Wernher von Braun

O f arms and the murderer I sing.
Here's a picture for you. It's late October 1942, and on the desert ridges outside the Egyptian town of El Alamein, on the Mediterranean, columns of tanks face one another, hundreds upon hundreds. The Axis forces are led by the Desert Fox, Erwin Rommel, whose Panzer Army has been tearing successfully across North Africa. They have 547 tanks. The Allies, led by Field Marshal Bernard Law Montgomery, have 1,029. Each side's tank formations are bolstered by hundreds of armored cars, aircraft, artillery pieces, and anti-tank guns. For the Allies, to lose El Alamein is to lose Alexandria, Cairo, the Suez Canal, and its shipments of fuel. Lose the Suez, lose the war.

Around four o'clock in the morning of each day's battle, drivers start their tank engines. According to an eyewitness account, in the half-light of dawn, the cold tanks seem "to crouch, still but alive, like toads."[1] As they're fired up, the engines grow warm, the machines "half-hidden in clouds of blue smoke."[2] Men are moving silently in the stench and exhaust fumes, because "the engine drowns all other noises except explosions.... Men shout, vehicles move, aeroplanes fly over, and all soundlessly: the noise of the tank being continuous, perhaps for hours on end, the effect is of silence."[3] During the fighting itself, as tanks are hit, "expanding columns of black smoke slant [ ] ... across the orange sky."[4] That smoke is the fog of war. The smog of war.

This picture comes to you by way of Captain Keith Douglas, twenty-two, of Tunbridge Wells, Kent. He captures it in three ways: in prose description in his memoir *Alamein to Zem Zem*; in poems; and in his battlefield drawings, scratchy sketches of exploded tanks and dead bodies torqued by rigor.

What he's recording is the battle. But he's also after something more: the engine of war and what it runs on.

For the British, it runs on tea. How often do they brew up? Every chance they get. They're in the middle of a desert, and they're thirsty. They're young, and many of them are going to die. The only thing that makes them feel better is drinking tea. Like all soldiers, they spend the majority of their time waiting. Throughout the forward area, there are signs, all in caps: WHEN IN DOUBT BREW-UP.[5] It becomes a joke: when a tank catches fire, it's said to have "brewed up."

To boil tea during the Western Desert campaign, British soldiers assemble what's called the "Benghazi boiler," a cooker fashioned from an empty four-gallon fuel can, holes poked in the sides, the bottom filled partly with sand and petrol and then set on fire.[6] A second fuel can, placed atop the cooker, becomes the teapot. Water supplied to the front lines is also transported in fuel cans, and the foul taste of gasoline is masked by strongly brewed black tea.

The engine of war also runs on petrol, and everything is cooked in leftover gas tins: tea, coffee, and tinned meat. Adjusting to his new life as cannon fodder, Keith Douglas says he has never before realized "the immense moral satisfaction and recreation of brewing up."[7] Nor has he realized the importance of petrol. To the gods of war, it is mother's milk, ferried everywhere by three-ton supply lorries. At night, crews lie beside

INTERLUDE

their tanks, "petrol fires everywhere."[8] Every part of the can is used. Whatever's in it—they're breathing it, drinking it, and eating it.

What's in the fuel that fills the cans? Lead. Metal wins the war: iron, lead, steel, copper, and aluminum. This truth is elemental. Battleships, bullets, aircraft, bombs, grenades, torpedoes, tanks: it's a war of metals and chemicals and new formulations of fuels, of rubber, nylon, and plastics. Of molecules, remixed. An American armored division goes through sixty thousand gallons of gasoline a day.[9] When heavy bombers and fast fighter planes take to the skies with their new one-hundred-octane super-leaded fuel, their speed, maneuverability, and prodigious loads "delivered destruction."[10]

There's a poster: two soldiers in the foreground, firing their weapons, more parachuting through the skies. "They've got the GUTS," the poster reads. "Back 'em up with MORE METAL."[11]

It's easy to lose sight of the metal, because there are more dramatic aspects of World War II. The rise and fall of the Third Reich. The battles, the generals, the pincer movements, the personalities. Rommel, Eisenhower, Monty, Patton, Churchill, FDR, Stalin. The spies and the betrayals, the self-sacrifice and the heroism, the Battle of Britain, the Battle of the Bulge, and the Battle of the Pacific. The death camps, the labor camps, the prison camps, the ghettos. The Holocaust.

But metal is inescapable. Stalin knows it. At a four-day conference in Tehran in 1943, he toasts Churchill on the prime minister's sixty-ninth birthday, raising a glass of champagne and sending a nod Roosevelt's way, saying, "This is a war of engines and octanes. I drink to the American auto industry and the American oil industry."[12]

Carrying some twenty pounds of miscellaneous metal, soldiers' lives depend on it:

> They strapped a pound and a half of bullet and shrapnel repellent steel to their heads. They also carried a nine-pound semiautomatic rifle containing metal parts made of about five pounds of various alloys of steel and copper. Capable of emptying an eight-cartridge

magazine as quickly as the trigger could be pulled, the semiautomatic rifle gave American soldiers the advantage of moving metal more quickly into the battlefield conflict. Each soldier also carried another eight pounds of iron, copper, and lead alloyed cartridges in belts slung across their shoulders or wrapped around their waists. They carried a pound and a half of steel in the spade attached to a backpack in which food rations were sealed in about a half-pound of tin. Another pound or two of iron and lead alloys were fabricated into the hand grenades attached to most of their belts, riveted with ounces of brass and steel. Those soldiers assigned communication roles often carried another 30 to 40 pounds of copper and iron alloys in radio equipment.[13]

The metal being produced on the American home front exceeds the levels of every other industrialized nation. The United States had begun with deficiencies, until the Bureau of Mines stepped in, cataloging every domestic mine producing copper, lead, iron, manganese, tungsten, and zinc and offering them support. The bureau has financed ASARCO and Anaconda all over the West, building roads, bulldozing, and drilling in Arizona, Idaho, Oregon, Nevada, Montana, and Wyoming, testing new methods of exploration, extraction, and transportation, substituting nimble trucks for slower trains.[14]

The state of Washington benefits enormously. During the war, the government appropriates $2 billion to increase the generating capacity of the mighty hydroelectric dams on the Columbia "by six-fold," according to historians, "enabling the operation of new government-owned aluminum smelters in Spokane and Tacoma . . . and Troutdale, Oregon."[15] According to one estimate, the Grand Coulee alone produces the power to make the aluminum used in a third of the planes built during the war. At Hanford, also on the Columbia, land is acquisitioned and plutonium teased into existence. Not for many years will Hanford's casual waste disposal, in which chemicals and radioactive materials are thrown into pits or released into the air or hurled into the river, be deemed "inadequate."

Pouring government money into open-pit mines, the United States

INTERLUDE

makes up for its early shortages in spades, stripping every ounce of metal from its own mines and those it controls in South America. During the war, the American military consumes "827 million tons of iron, 22 million tons of copper, 9 million tons of lead, 9 million tons of manganese, 8 million tons of chromite, 300 thousand tons of antimony, and 70 tons of tungsten . . . enough material to fill ten football-field-sized rectangles *almost one mile high*."[16] These cosmic quantities of raw and manufactured resources will, historians say, eventually "overwhelm the Axis," a suite of enemies well supplied themselves.

Copper is essential. The Department of the Interior calls it "literally the nervous system of a warring nation."[17] Copper wiring starts the engines on all those tanks, trucks, jeeps, planes, and ships.

Lead is "the useful metal."[18] An alloy of lead and antimony is molded into the soft bullets that deform flesh. The fusing systems in Fat Man, the nuclear bomb detonated by the United States over Nagasaki, Japan, on August 9, 1945, are powered by lead-acid batteries.

Where does all this metal go? What isn't used is stockpiled; some is recycled. But often enough, metal simply falls where it may. After the bombs explode and the bodies decompose, the lead lies upon the earth and enters the groundwater. It doesn't go anywhere. It becomes where we live. It becomes the foundation of daily life. It becomes us.

The scale of environmental devastation caused by the industrialization of World War II exceeds anything the planet has ever seen. Cities are transformed by the war: Baltimore, Philadelphia, Chicago, Cleveland, Cincinnati, and Detroit. So is the Ohio River Valley. The sleepy stretch from Baton Rouge south to New Orleans soon bristles with oil and gas infrastructure. By 1945, Pittsburgh, the dirty steel mill city long called "Hell with the lid off," has to turn on streetlights at ten o'clock in the morning because the smog from coal-fired smelters and iron and steel plants is so thick. In Los Angeles in July 1943, a synthetic rubber plant creates the first pall of smoke to bedevil the city, a "gas attack" that blankets the downtown area, sending people to the hospital with ragged throats and streaming eyes. "It's just industrial gases," says the city health department.[19]

MURDERLAND

Love Canal, a waterway in Niagara Falls, New York, is purchased by the Hooker Chemical Company in 1941 as a repository for the dumping of tons of wastes produced by manufacturing solvents for war matériel: rubber, synthetic resins, epoxy, arsenic trichloride, and hexachlorobenzene. After the war, the company covers the dump in concrete and sells it to the city's school district, which builds an elementary school on top of it. The concrete crumbles during heavy rains. Children enjoy playing in the black puddles around exposed fifty-five-gallon drums full of poison.

It's a good war until it isn't. Love Canal gives rise to the Superfund program, and virtually every Superfund site in the country dates back to the Second World War or the Cold War. What do they care? Boeing, Rocketdyne, Raytheon, Aerojet, GE, DuPont, and every other corporate arm of the defense industry make billions off the war. It's too much trouble for them to figure out what to do with their leftovers: acids, effluents, and explosives. They'll think about it later or, if not later, never.

World War II is the Doomsday Machine from *Dr. Strangelove*, a diabolical engine unleashed by blowing up a million bombs and shooting bullets in a million places, leaving ineradicable swaths of heavy metals and chemicals that last forever. It's the whole alphabet, from Alamein to Zem Zem, from arsenic to zinc. We're waging war on ourselves, and we're winning.

As the war rages to its conclusion, monsters are coming to life, animated. The greatest generation of serial killers comes out of the war: Richard Speck and Fred West are born in 1941; Ted Kaczynski, John Wayne Gacy, James Homer Elledge, and the rare female lust murderer Carol Bundy (no relation to Ted) in 1942; Gary Heidnik and Rodney Alcala in 1943; Dennis Rader, Joseph DeAngelo, Randy Kraft, Leonard Lake, and Arthur Shawcross in 1945; William Earl Cosden Jr., Ted Bundy, Gerard John Schaefer, Richard Cottingham, John Linley Frazier, and Peter Sutcliffe in 1946; Herbert Mullin in 1947; Ed Kemper in 1948; Gary Ridgway, Robert Pickton, and Warren Leslie Forrest in 1949.

Recipes for making a serial killer may vary, including such ingredients as poverty, crude forceps delivery, poor diet, physical and sexual abuse,

INTERLUDE

brain damage, and neglect.[20] Many horrors play a role in warping these tortured souls, but what happens if we add a light dusting from the periodic table on top of all that trauma? How about a little lead in your tea?

Criminologists reach for explanations, each less convincing than the last, suggesting that this so-called epidemic of serial murder might be put down to "group neurosis" or "combat stress" or bad mothers or the crimes committed by American, British, and French soldiers, believed to have raped thousands of women in Germany during the postwar era.[21] But there may be something else at work, something basic.

As for Captain Keith Douglas, in the window of time between the Desert Campaign, which he survives, and the invasion of Normandy, which he does not, he writes a poem called "Simplify Me When I'm Dead." He is twenty-four years old when he is himself simplified on June 9, 1944, near Bayeux, after his skull encounters mere metal in the form of an insignificant scrap of shrapnel. He sees it coming. "Take the brown hair and blue eye," he writes, generously, as if he has a choice.[22]

PART II
GREAT DOMESDAY

Chapter 8

The Lead Moon

———◆———

> Ye shall scent out all the places—whether in church, bedchamber, street, field, or forest—where crime has been committed, and shall exult to behold the whole earth one stain of guilt, one mighty blood spot.
>
> —Nathaniel Hawthorne,
> "Young Goodman Brown"

*T*ick tock, tick tock, says the cuckoo clock. The iron pine cone pendants hang. The copper-bottomed kettle screams.

We have always had the kettle, part of my mother's set of Revere Ware. Who makes Revere Ware? ASARCO.[1]

We have always had the clock. It's a Swiss German relic of my father's mother's family, and I have been told so many times never to touch it that I loathe it. Only my father is allowed to wind it. Susie Warner always wants to see it when she comes to our house—trying to catch sight of the little carved bird poking its head out the door on the hour. I couldn't care less. I am beginning to count the minutes, hours, days, and years that I will live in this house.

My father winds the clock weekly, grinding his teeth with irritation and concentration, pulling the chains with their heavy weights. If he winds the mechanism too tight, it will break. He's wound too tight, and the weekly chore is a battle between his will and the physical world, which according to his religion isn't supposed to exist.

Ladies' Home Journal declares Mercer Island one of the fifteen most "livable" suburbs in the country.[2] In one of my classes I meet a short kid with floppy hair who brings his Elton John albums to school. On the cover of *Goodbye Yellow Brick Road* Elton wears sparkly platform shoes and outrageous neon-colored glasses and glitter, and I don't know what to make of it.

My mom and I are waiting until my father leaves the house and then we're jumping in the white VW and driving to Bellevue to shop at Nordstrom and have tea and toasted nut bread in the café and swing by Calico Corners to flip through the Butterick patterns and buy cotton yardage in pretty prints on sale to make summer shifts. When we get home, we hide everything in the closets, because my father doesn't want us to buy anything. Materialism.

Susie and I are learning the theme from *Exodus* arranged for four hands, and we're writing a novel about a land we've invented called Burodeen—part Hobbit, part Narnia, part everything else we're reading at the Mercer Island Public Library. In grammar class, I'm learning how to parse sentences, and it's intensely satisfying to draw lines and separate clauses. I'm parsing people too, slotting everything and everyone into different lines of communication, keeping them in different closets. My mom is one, and Susie is another, and the short kid with the floppy hair, whose name is Jeff and who is the friendliest person I've ever met, is another. Who knows where to put Elton John. He's a dangler.

ON JANUARY 1, 1975, the American Smelting and Refining Company officially changes its name to ASARCO. The United Nations declares it the first International Women's Year, with plans to eliminate discrimination. On January 2, Nixon's henchmen, Haldeman and Ehrlichman—both Christian Scientists and hence accomplished liars—are convicted for the Watergate cover-up. Ehrlichman's uncle lives on Mercer Island. Pol Pot is tuning up in Cambodia. Select members of the Baader–Meinhof Gang are about to go on trial for murder and attempted murder after taking hostages at the Swedish embassy.

The year 1975 looks to be difficult economically, because the hot market for lead, copper, and aluminum is cooling off in the teeth of recession. Housing starts, plywood, and auto sales are sliding. It's the year that a federal standard for inorganic arsenic in the workplace is proposed.[3]

The aroma of Tacoma remains eye-wateringly strong. On January 3, the Tacoma *News Tribune* reports that employment is solid: the ASARCO smelter's production of copper and slag is robust, and Kaiser, which has been smelting aluminum on the tidal flats since the 1940s, is stockpiling metal. Western Plastics, which set a record for production in 1974, is laying off only a few employees; Pacific Resins and Chemicals is bullish. Nalley's Fine Foods, owned by W. R. Grace & Company and located in South Tacoma, in an area called the "Nalley Valley," is cautiously optimistic.[4]

DOES LEAD CREATE CRIMINALS? asks *The Ecologist*, a British journal founded in 1970 after Rachel Carson's *Silent Spring* heightened concerns about chemicals.[5] Lead emissions may play a role, the cover story suggests, in the rise of juvenile delinquency, adult crime rates, admissions to mental hospitals, aggressive behavior, muggings, and "football hooliganism."[6] It quotes from a rash of new scientific papers exploring the threat of lead in pipes, paint, soil, air, water, and gasoline, noting that a recent study has found that there's enough lead in vegetation growing "beside a secondary highway to abort a cow subsisting on that vegetation."[7] The lead in vehicle exhaust is, an expert says, "peculiarly suited for retention by the lung."[8]

Children exposed to lead in utero or during their first years of life might display a dizzying array of symptoms, the expert reports. Some are mentally dull, suffering from difficulties in reading and writing similar to what's seen in dyslexia. Others are bright but hyperactive, with short attention spans. Some are impulsive, some violent.

The FBI's *Uniform Crime Reports* for 1974 reveals that crime in Washington State is up 29.2 percent, nearly three times the national average, which has increased by 11.3 percent. Murder in Washington is up 30.6 percent, as compared with 5.5 percent nationally. Asked why this might be happening, the special agent in charge of Seattle's FBI office says, "It's anybody's guess."[9]

Detectives throughout the West are fresh off their Intermountain Crime Conference, held in Stateline, Nevada, on December 12, 1974, where Bob Keppel, of the Seattle task force, talked about all things "Ted" and Utah detectives working on the cases of Carol DaRonch, Melissa Smith, Laura Aime, and Debi Kent swapped details of abductions and murders. The name Ted sticks in everybody's minds, including that of the Salt Lake detective assigned to investigate Melissa Smith's case, Jerry Thompson.

Everywhere Ted goes, that productive son of Tacoma leaves women dead in his wake the way ASARCO blows smoke. Northwest automatons are busy with their business. They will not stop until somebody puts a stop to them.

Ted is only one among many. Little Domesday records his doings, but now we're going to need a bigger book. We need Great Domesday, a ledger tracking those permeated with heavy metals, volatile chemicals, tar, creosote, chromium, arsenic, carcinogens, mutagens, and whatever's leaching out of pressure-treated lumber. Dr. Jekyll has been at work here for a long time, nearly a hundred years, and his experiments are about to yield results. Spectacular results.

Ted feels like Utah is becoming a little crowded for him, a little soiled; he's left corpses hither and yon. Sometime during the winter of 1975, he asks Margith Maughan if she's ever driven to Lamb's Canyon, east of Salt Lake City, along the same route where Melissa Smith's body was found. It's a beautiful place, he says. He was up there in the fall, just before the snow fell. It seems to Margith that he's been gone almost every weekend.

After a Christmas visit from Liz, Ted doesn't know that she called the

Cover of a 1911 booklet promoting Tacoma, Washington, celebrating the industrial development and pollution of its waterfront, known for "the aroma of Tacoma."

An early photograph of the American Smelting and Refining Company's Tacoma smelter before a series of ever-higher smokestacks was constructed. The caption, from a 1906 promotional book, reads "Tacoma Smelter by moonlight—the fires are never extinguished."

Hat in hand, handsome young highway director Lacey V. Murrow stands at left with dignitaries at the July 1, 1940, ribbon cutting at the ill-fated Tacoma Narrows Bridge.

A day later, on July 2, 1940, Murrow poses at the opening of the Lake Washington Bridge, the largest object afloat in the world at that time. Its flawed design would cause numerous accidents in decades to come.

The Tacoma Narrows Bridge, called "Galloping Gertie" for its disconcerting vibrations, collapsed on November 7, 1940.

A 1943 U.S. government–issued poster urged Americans to support a war effort heavily reliant on copper, lead, and other metals.

In 1949, executives celebrated ASARCO's fiftieth anniversary at the Tacoma Smelter.

Louise Cowell and her son, Teddy, at Ocean City, New Jersey, circa 1949.

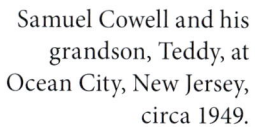

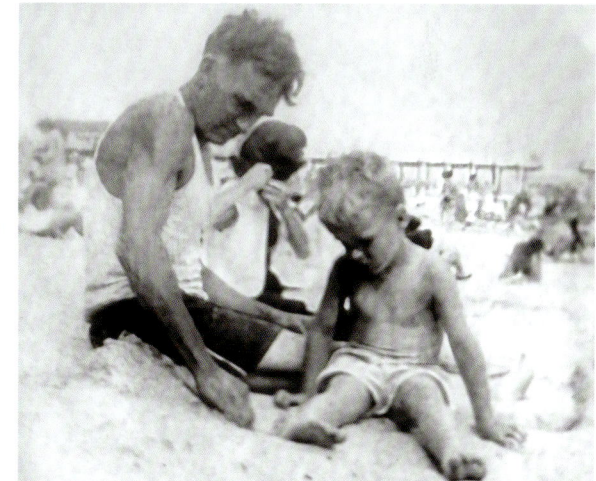

Samuel Cowell and his grandson, Teddy, at Ocean City, New Jersey, circa 1949.

An appeal to MASTER DETECTIVE readers:

CAN YOU HELP FIND ANN MARIE BURR?

Tacoma, Washington police, and the family of a pretty little girl who vanished in the night, urgently request the aid of any alert reader who thinks he or she might have information that could possibly unravel the mystery of this tragic and baffling disappearance...

by ROBERT COUR

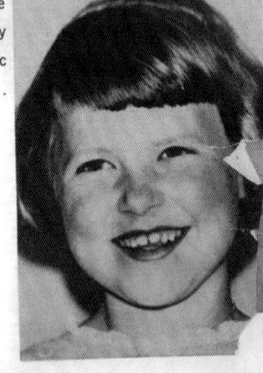

In 1966, several years after the 1961 disappearance of Ann Marie Burr from her home in Tacoma, *Master Detective* magazine ran an appeal to readers.

Ted Bundy, age sixteen, towers over his four half siblings in this photograph in Tacoma, circa 1963. By this point, he may already have committed his first murder.

Lynda Healy, a psychology student at the University of Washington, believed to have been Bundy's first murder victim of 1974, was attacked and abducted from a basement room in a house she shared with roommates.

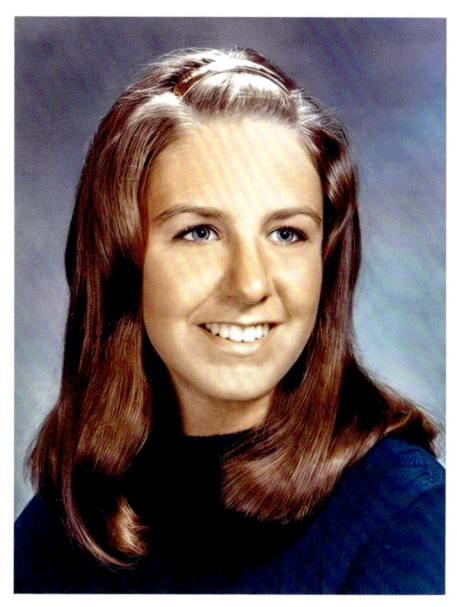

Georgann Hawkins, the Daffodil Princess from Tacoma, disappeared from an alleyway behind the Kappa Alpha Theta sorority on June 11, 1974.

Janice Ott, one of two women abducted by Bundy from Lake Sammamish State Park on the afternoon of July 14, 1974.

Ted Bundy and his Volkswagen Beetle at Lake Union, September 2, 1974, the day he left Seattle to attend law school in Salt Lake City, Utah.

Volunteers search the Issaquah site for human remains, September 1974.

Warren Leslie Forrest of Vancouver, Washington, was one of half a dozen serial killers active in Washington State in 1974.

Dennis Rader as a boy, when he had already begun to fantasize about rape and torture.

Dennis Rader at eighteen in 1963, in the Wichita Heights High School yearbook.

Ted Bundy wanted poster, issued by the FBI in 1978 after his second escape from a jail in Colorado.

On July 30, 1979, a *Miami Herald* photographer caught Bundy's distorted grimace after the Chi Omega jury recommended the death penalty for his 1978 murders of Margaret Bowman and Lisa Levy.

On May 18, 1980, Mount St. Helens exploded in the most catastrophic volcanic eruption in American history to date, killing fifty-seven.

The notorious bulge on the Lacey V. Murrow Floating Bridge. Under repairs, the bridge would sink on Thanksgiving weekend, 1990.

Gary Ridgway, seen in a 1982 mug shot after an early arrest for solicitation, was poised to begin murdering scores of women and girls.

Randy Woodfield, the I-5 Killer, one of many serial rapists and murderers who frequented the interstate highways, in his 1981 mug shot.

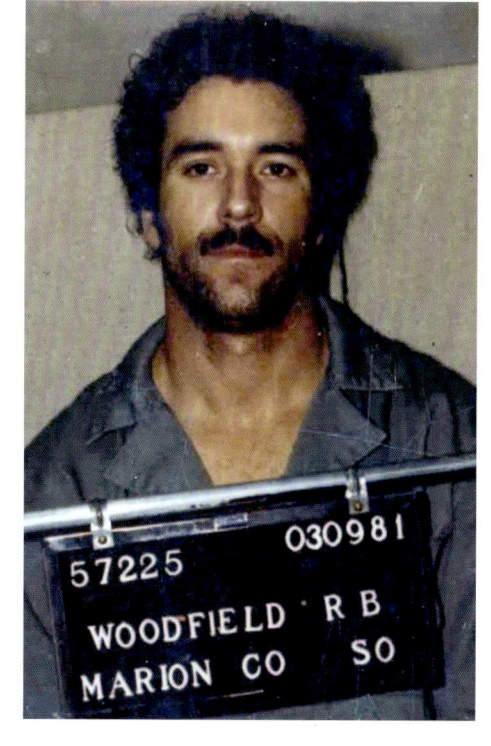

Shawnda Summers, age seventeen, was picked up and murdered by Ridgway on October 9, 1982. Her remains were found north of SeaTac Airport ten months later.

Marie Malvar, from the Philippines, was eighteen on April 30, 1983, when she disappeared. Although family tracked her to Ridgway's house, police failed to investigate. Her remains would not be found until 2003.

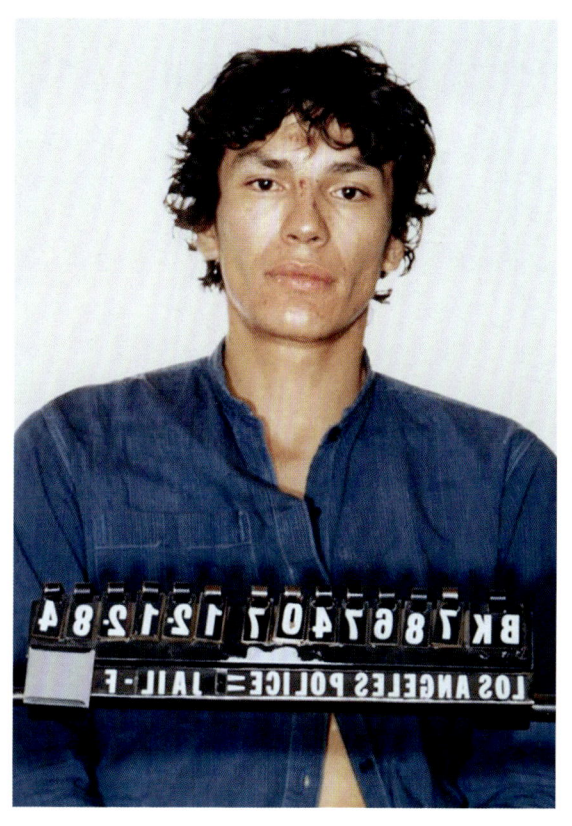

Richard Ramirez, the so-called Night Stalker, after his 1985 arrest for a frenzied rape and murder spree that paralyzed Los Angeles neighborhoods for months.

Israel Keyes, in an undated photo distributed by the FBI.

Children playing beside the ASARCO smelter smokestack in Ruston, Washington, August 1972. The stack was demolished on January 17, 1993.

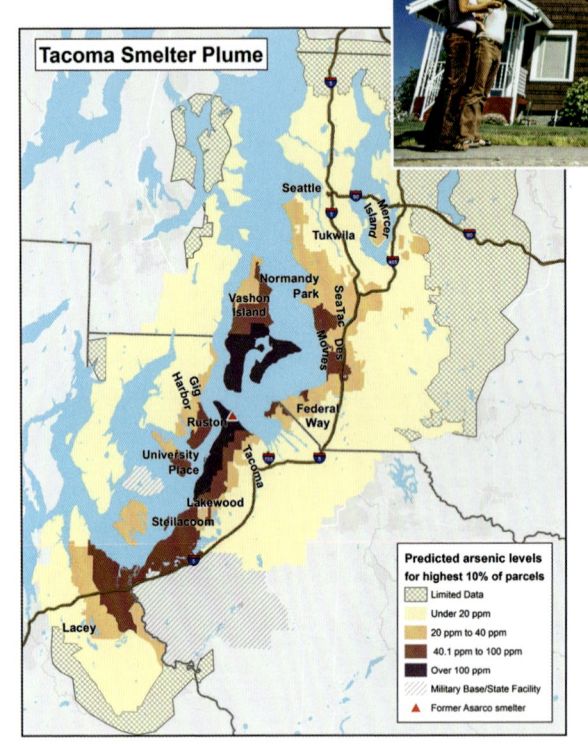

"Dirt Alert," a program mapping the Tacoma smelter plume. Its lead and arsenic pollution settled on more than a thousand square miles of the Puget Sound region.

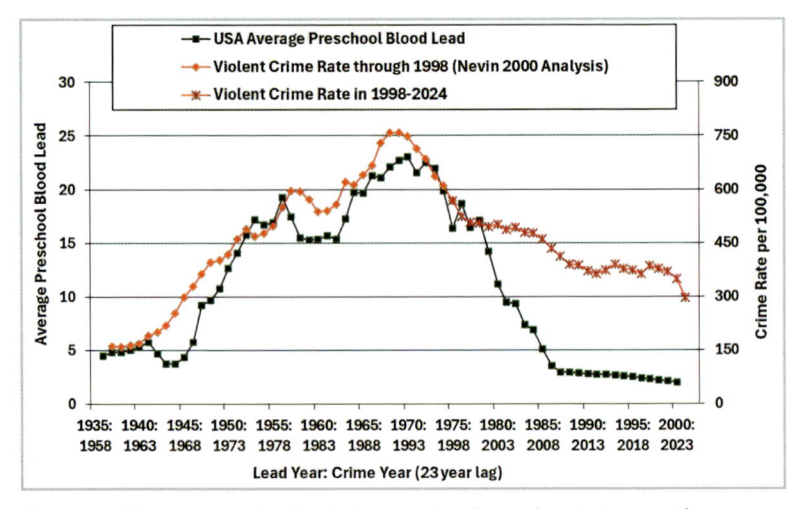

Young children exposed to leaded gas and industrial emissions in the post–World War II era were more likely to commit violent crimes as adults, as seen in this updated graph of USA Average Preschool Blood Lead Trends from Rick Nevin's *Lucifer Curves: The Legacy of Lead Poisoning*.

Salt Lake police on December 29 and told them she's concerned about the possibility that her boyfriend may be a killer. They assured her that they've checked him out and there's nothing to worry about.[10] He, on the other hand, is so lonely and distraught when she leaves that he plans a spur-of-the-moment trip to Seattle.

On January 3, heading to the airport, Ted calls Liz in tears, saying, "There's something wrong with me."[11] By the time he gets off the plane, however, his mood has lifted. He's "happy and confident," bringing along a brochure on ski resorts in Colorado.[12] After the discovery of the bodies of Smith and Laura Aime, he decides to venture farther afield, to a lodge in his brochure. He draws an X next to its name.

It's the Wildwood Inn, a resort in Snowmass Village, Colorado, at an elevation of 8,209 feet, in the Roaring Fork Valley.

On Saturday, January 11, he finds himself in Glenwood Springs, Colorado, on I-70, only forty miles from Wildwood, hours from Salt Lake. He's buying gas and sleeping overnight in his car. The next day, Sunday, he buys more gas before reaching the resort. It's rustic: several stories of wood and stone, its corridors outside the building to protect floors from wet ski boots. Nearby, a big heated swimming pool fills the air with steam.

Caryn Campbell, a twenty-three-year-old nurse from Farmington, Michigan, is staying at the Wildwood with her boyfriend, who is a doctor, and his two kids while he attends a medical convention. Shortly after 7:30 that evening, she's heading back to her room to fetch a magazine while the doctor waits by the lobby fire. She's a cheerful beauty with long, shiny brown hair, and when she sees a handsome stranger struggling along the corridor with an awkward hold on his ski boots, claiming some kind of disability, some need for help getting to his car, she lends a hand. In the parking lot, as she's bending over, he captures her, handcuffs her, loads her into the VW, and drives off.[13]

The whole thing is hurried and botched. There is a struggle. At some point, she rakes his face and neck with her fingernails, perhaps as he strangles her. Her left ear is split. After a relatively short time, he tips her body over a guardrail on Owl Creek Road, which runs past the Wildwood and out into the mountains. Covered in snow and ice, the remains freeze into an embankment.

He drives back to Utah, where an acquaintance in one of his classes, Wynn Bartholomew, notes that his friend Ted looks "haggard," with bags under his eyes and "crimson red scratches branded across his cheeks and neck."[14] Bartholomew asks if he had a rough weekend. Ted says he ran into some tree branches.

On February 17, her body is found.

THE NATIONAL SEARCH for four-year-old Heidi Peterson, missing since February 21, 1974, ends nearly a year later. On Friday, January 24, 1975, skeletal remains and fragments of clothing are found by a Seattle Parks Department employee trying to retrieve a garbage can that's fallen down a slope. The hillside, across the shipping canal from the University of Washington campus, is two blocks from her Capitol Hill home. The area had been thoroughly searched months earlier, after her disappearance, by volunteers, Boy Scouts, and dogs. In the ensuing months, blackberries have grown ten feet tall, shielding the slope from view.[15]

Rumors are flying.[16] Heidi was not accustomed, says Captain Herb Swindler, whose daughter once dated Ted Bundy, to crossing the street by herself.[17] Cause of death is never determined. But either before or after her death, which occurred within two months of her abduction, her skull was fractured.

NEWS OF THE RECOVERY of Heidi's body drops from the headlines on Saturday, March 1, when two forestry students at Green River Community College, tramping through the woods surveying timber for a class project, stumble across more remains. Bob Keppel takes the call from a police radio room operator who tells him, "You have a found skull off Highway 18." He's told to meet the students "where the power lines cross, four miles south of I-90."[18]

THE LEAD MOON

The OWL knows this place. It's familiar territory to Keppel and the Explorer Scouts who months earlier groped their way across a grid outside Issaquah where the bones of Janice Ott and Denise Naslund were found. George Weyerhaeuser, the little kidnapping victim who spent a cold night in 1935 buried in a hole in the woods, would recognize the spot too. Highway 18, also known as the Echo Lake Cutoff, is the back road that cuts south from Snoqualmie to Tacoma. A dark road, it runs down the valley between Tiger Mountain and Taylor Mountain, and it's still a lonely road in 1975, with few houses and little traffic. It's eleven miles from the Issaquah body site.

"Desolate," Keppel says of the place.[19] "Dismal," he calls the day.[20] It's raining heavily when he arrives, and he follows the students a thousand feet into the woods, a distance so far he can barely imagine anyone walking it while carrying a body. The students have marked the path back to the scene with fluorescent tape, and they haven't touched the skull. As soon as Keppel sees it, he recognizes a distinctive pattern of silver dental work. It's Brenda Ball, from Ted's late night at the Flame Tavern. Keppel has dental charts and images of the missing woman's teeth, and he's been studying them for months.

The skull is a fallen bowl full of maple leaves. The ground where it lies is an evergreen mosaic of ferns, mosses, and rotting vegetation. A spider's web stretches across the fracture on its right side, a break so massive he assumes it's been made postmortem, by animals. He later learns that may not be true.

Keppel returns the next day with six German shepherds and their handlers, specialists in locating cadavers, and they search for the rest of Brenda. He splits off from the dog team and immediately gets lost, flailing down a crevice between two slopes. When he hears shouting, he stumbles and falls on his face in the soaking leaves and strangling undergrowth. Struggling to his knees, he finds himself staring at another fractured skull a few feet away, bleached clean, a sapling growing through the facial bones. He instantly recognizes the uniquely identifiable bridgework of Susan Rancourt, the student from Ellensburg, last seen heading to the laundry room to put her clothes in the dryer. She has been lost since April 17, 1974. Now she is found.

As one of the dogs comes running, its paw falls on another human jawbone, sending it flying into the air. To the east, a third skull is located, belonging to Kathy Parks, formerly of Oregon State University in Corvallis, who once agreed to go for a drink with a nice-looking young man. Once more, the teenage crews of the Explorer Search and Rescue group are mobilized. Once more, they board a vintage green Chevy bus to head into the wilderness, where they crawl in the dark over sodden earth, combing through leaves and vine maple for fragments of women.

Scott Brainerd is sixteen. He has a driver's license and a 1963 VW Beetle and lives in Tacoma, where he goes to Lakes High School, which Georgann Hawkins also attended. Everybody at the school knew her or knew someone who knew her. Everybody has heard of "Ted." Being on the ESAR crew makes him feel important, he'll later say, but it's also creepy to be spending an entire week on Taylor Mountain, sleeping in pup tents by night, conducting grid searches by day. It rains all week, and the mountain is "foggy . . . dank and dark," he'll recall, with "an oppressive feel to it."[21] Several hundred strong, team members wear rain gear, thick rubber gloves over wool mittens, stocking caps under plastic helmets, and heavy hiking boots.[22] They're in a somber mood. He finds the search "cold, exhausting, and depressing," the dark broken only intermittently by flashbulbs going off somewhere down the line of searchers.[23]

The skulls that Keppel found are removed early, and the team sifts through dirt hoping to uncover the kinds of additional fragments yielded by the Issaquah site—hair, loose teeth, bits of fingernail, jewelry. A few bones are found, but the search is frustrating. Besides the Ann heavily damaged craniums of three women—Ball, Rancourt, and Parks—little turns up. A clump of Susan Rancourt's blond hair. One tooth. Lynda Ann Healy's mandible is discovered, but nothing else that can be immediately identified as hers. Kathy Parks's facial bones are missing. All the skulls seem to have been deposited at the same time, since the leaf litter and vine growth atop them are uniform. When hardly anything more of their skeletons is found, Keppel speculates that the perpetrator moved the skulls from another site, as yet undiscovered. He wonders about intentional decapitation.[24]

THE LEAD MOON

But in addition to the limited human remains, the ESAR team finds and removes from the mountain an enormous quantity of women's clothing, shoes, and pornographic materials, enough to make a pile six feet high and twenty feet wide. The Explorers are told that these items have no relevance to the search. Nevertheless, Scott lies in his tent at night, wondering about the state of humanity.

Taylor Mountain represents a substantial breakthrough, establishing that Healy, Parks, Rancourt, and Ball were killed by the same person, likely the person who murdered the women at Lake Sammamish. Nonetheless, the investigation stalls. The "Ted" Task Force has been shuffling through more than two thousand tips on potential suspects, as well as a list of 916 registered VW owners in Washington State, a list that doubtless includes my father.[25]

The lack of progress stirs up a certain desperation, a willingness to entertain weird theories and experimental methods. There are plans to put Karen Sparks, the surviving rape victim, under hypnosis. A California detective keeps calling with a hot tip about the phases of the moon tying together unsolved murders in Washington, Utah, Colorado, and New Mexico. Herb Swindler and Ann Rule kick around the astrological views of a friend of hers, suggesting that the killer strikes only when the moon is in Taurus, Scorpio, or Pisces.[26] Swindler meets a psychic at Taylor Mountain at dawn to pierce the earth with a pole and examine its shadows.[27]

None of these methods yields useful information, but the task force office is struck dumb when a deputy brings in something found on the mountain amid the litter of women's clothing. It's a crude figure fashioned out of a stick bound with twine topped by a shrunken monkey's head, its teeth intact, its eyes replaced with turquoise chips. Below the head, the monkey's paws are lashed to the wood.[28]

AROUND NOON ON MARCH 5, 1975, Annette Jolin, thirty, working on a career as a criminologist, is walking through Duniway Park in Portland,

Oregon, when she hears breathing at her back and is seized from behind. She feels a knife blade at her neck.

Jolin, however, is not without resources. She's one of several policewomen in Portland, hired in 1973 by a new female police chief, and she activates the signaling device she's been given. She's undercover, walking through the park as a decoy to catch the man with a knife who's been assaulting women in the park, fondling them, forcing them to fellate him, and stealing their purses.

The muscle-bound man who's grabbed her quickly gropes her breasts and demands money. She gives him eight dollars in marked bills. He pauses, as if tempted to do more, but then takes off and is quickly seized by Jolin's fellow officers. His name, he says, is Randall Woodfield, a recent draft pick of the Green Bay Packers.

What the police don't know is that Randy was born in Salem, Oregon, on December 26, 1950, and lived in his infancy in the plume of the decades-old Oregon Pulp and Paper Company, a sawmill, foundry, and pulp producer on the banks of the Willamette.[29] Later acquired by Boise Cascade, the mill is a major emitter of sulfur dioxide. After its closure, the property will be classified as a contaminated brownfield with an accumulation of hazardous substances, including petroleum hydrocarbons, arsenic, barium, cyanide, chromium, lead, manganese, dioxins, and PCBs.[30]

Randy's time with the Green Bay Packers has ended in ignominy. After training camp, the Packers drop him, having learned that he's exposed himself repeatedly. A Wisconsin official comments that he just can't "keep the thing in his pants."[31]

Randy drives a special car, a gold 1974 "Champagne Edition" Volkswagen Beetle, which is his pride and joy. As soon as he gets out of jail, he'll try not to make the mistake of leaving witnesses alive.

ON MARCH 10, 1975, a worker checking on conditions at a dam built below Mount Baker—the 10,786-foot snowcapped, glacier-covered stratovolcano that punctuates the North Cascades thirty miles east of Bellingham—

notices a dark column of steam coming out of the mountain. So-called wisps have been seen wafting from Baker before, but these aren't wisps. These are fumaroles, high-energy vents.

Park employees, state workers, and U.S. Geological Survey scientists scramble to investigate, finding a number of high-pressure steam vents blasting through solid rock and ice, sounding "like several jet engines running at full throttle."[32] The steam is full of sulfur, a ton and a half of which is being emitted per hour. Scientists hasten to install new monitoring devices to detect the risk of potential earthquakes and eruptions. They must wear gas masks.

The steam has created dozens of holes and crevices across the snow-covered face of the Sherman Crater, nine hundred feet below Baker's summit, forming a shallow bubbling lake of snowmelt heated by the magma below. These subterranean forces raise concerns about the potential for a lahar sending tons of meltwater, mud, trees, and boulders hurtling downstream into reservoirs and dams. Experts are beginning to question the wisdom of building dams at the base of an active volcano.

That summer, the U.S. Forest Service closes popular shorelines and campgrounds at Baker Lake, some distance down the mountain. Residents of the nearby town of Concrete and resort owners who rely on income from tourists and fishermen are outraged.[33] "All this steam business is a lot of hot air," says the publisher of *The Concrete Herald*.[34]

THE SEARCH AT TAYLOR MOUNTAIN concludes on the night of Saturday, March 8, 1975. That's the first International Women's Day, a day on which Ted Bundy buys gas three times in Salt Lake City.

Ted and the smelter seem to be acting together, as if in concert, on a two-week cycle governed by what you might call the Lead Moon.[35] On March 15, he buys gas in Silverthorne, Colorado, deep in the Rockies. He backtracks thirty miles west to Vail, the ski mecca. After shoveling his VW out of a snowdrift, he walks down the main street. He's hobbling on crutches and fumbling with a ski boot tree, and he hails a young woman,

Julie Cunningham, a twenty-six-year-old ski instructor on her way to have drinks and dinner with friends. She has long dark hair and is wearing a brown suede jacket, blue jeans, a ski cap, and boots. She offers to help him carry his boots to the parking lot but first runs to a mailbox to post some letters.

When they get to his car, he grabs a crowbar he's propped up by the back bumper and strikes her over the head. She falls like a stone. He lifts her into the car, handcuffs her, and heads west on I-70, toward Glenwood Springs.

Like Georgann Hawkins, Julie regains consciousness in the car and starts talking to him, asking where he's from. He's not saying anything. Twenty-five miles west of Glenwood Springs, he pulls off at Rifle, looking for a side road. She asks him to loosen the handcuffs, since they're hurting her, and he does. As he's circling the car, she makes a break for it, somehow opening the car door, and there's a struggle. He hits her again with the crowbar, rapes her, and strangles her with a cord, then drags her body under a bush.

Also on March 15, news breaks that ASARCO is asking the EPA for permission to fill with slag another fourteen acres of Commencement Bay, south of the smelter, along Ruston Way.[36] They need more space to construct their pollution abatement facilities, officials say, which were supposed to be up and running by now but have been delayed numerous times, the subject of multiple variances applied for and received.

On April 6, a warm Sunday afternoon in Grand Junction, Colorado, Denise Oliverson, twenty-four, with long brown hair parted in the middle, is riding her bike to the park to hang out with friends. The next day, when she doesn't turn up to meet them and never comes home, her boyfriend reports her missing. After searching for a few hours, police find her yellow bicycle and red sandals on railroad tracks beneath an overpass. She's never seen again.

The following day, despite the pleas of local residents, the Tacoma City Planning Commission votes 3–1 to approve ASARCO's permit to fill more of the bay with slag. During the comment period, resident Harold Simonson begs officials to "think of this in human terms instead of chemical terms."[37] Fifteen-year-old Christine Gregorich agrees, saying that she likes to ride her bike and walk along the beach. "If this is allowed to go on," she asks, "what will happen to the waterfront during my generation?"

ON MARCH 19, 1975, at 6:02 p.m., Liz Schensted, a writer and editor at the *Mercer Island Reporter*, is driving west on I-90, preparing to exit at Southeast 24th Street, the exit below the hill I live on, one that leads to the island's shopping district. The reversible lane has just switched off post–rush hour. Out of the corner of her eye, she sees a gray shape flying toward her, and within seconds her car, a yellow Dodge Dart, is hurtling over a thirty-foot embankment.

Trapped, bleeding from a head injury, she loses consciousness briefly but is aware of emergency workers struggling to extricate her for half an hour. Her pelvis is broken in two places; her left leg is broken. She has a broken toe, a broken rib, facial lacerations, and a deep cut over her left eye. For days she suffers from excruciating involuntary muscle contractions and convulsions. Assigned to cover I-90, she's usually the one to call the state patrol every Wednesday to get the latest tally of serious accidents, of which there are around two hundred a year on the six-mile stretch of highway from Bellevue to Seattle.[38]

It takes her months to recover, and during that time her mother dies of cancer. In articles she writes later, she points out that the reversible lane was responsible for her injuries: concrete Jersey barriers between east- and westbound lanes would have prevented the accident. "The nightmare," she says, "goes on ... and on."[39]

DOWN SOUTH in the well-leaded town of El Paso, on May 4, 1975, Richie Ramirez is fifteen and sitting in the kitchen of his cousin Miguel's house, watching an argument between Miguel and his wife, Josefina. Miguel is a Green Beret, home from Vietnam with four medals and a handful of

Polaroids and eight shrunken heads of Vietnamese women. When his wife argues with him about why he's keeping a gun in the freezer, he grabs it and shoots her in the face. She lingers for eleven days and then dies.[40]

Nationally, and in El Paso, violent crime is on the rise.[41]

SOMETIME AROUND THE END of April or the beginning of May, Ted Bundy returns to the body of Julie Cunningham, near Rifle, Colorado, and buries it in a shallow grave. It takes him hours to find the remains, and he is surprised to discover that they're largely intact, preserved by aridity and cold temperatures. "I had never seen somebody who'd been out that long who was not . . . eaten," he would say later.[42]

On May 5 he drives two and a half hours north from Salt Lake to Pocatello, Idaho, and checks into the Holiday Inn. Casing the women's dormitory on the campus of Idaho State University, he's confronted by a security guard who orders him to leave but does not report the encounter to police.

Around noon the next day, May 6, he drives by Alameda Junior High School, a couple of miles from the motel. He picks out a girl from a crowd of students milling around outside and offers a ride to Lynnette Culver. She's twelve, has big blue eyes, and weighs 110 pounds. She's wearing blue jeans, a red-checked shirt, and a maroon jacket with a fur-trimmed hood. A couple of years earlier, in her school picture, she was sporting blond pigtails and bangs.

They chat. She admits she's in trouble for skipping school sometimes, as she's doing now. She tells him that she has relatives in Seattle and is about to move to a bigger house so her grandmother can live with her family. He takes her to the Holiday Inn and strips her, rapes her, and drowns her in the bathtub, not necessarily in that order. Then he puts her body back in the VW and drives north. Somewhere between the town of Blackfoot and Massacre Rocks, a state park on the Oregon Trail, he tosses her in the Snake.

Meanwhile, on the same day, ASARCO is demanding that county commissioners in Helena, Montana, issue $45 million in revenue bonds to pay for $35 million in state-required pollution controls for its lead smelter, in operation there since 1888. (The extra $10 million is for "unforeseen contingencies that inevitably occur," according to the corporation.) Pollution controls involve building a sulfuric acid plant, a gas cleaning system, and modifications to its sinter plant, which yields nuggets of iron ore that are used to convert iron into steel.

The acid plant will convert the sulfur dioxide that has been poisoning the air of East Helena to sulfuric acid, a corrosive substance destructive to human skin, teeth, eyes, and lungs. Sulfuric acid can in turn be sold to petroleum refineries or industries producing fertilizers, explosives, glue, or lead batteries. ASARCO will subsidize the bonds but wants the lower interest rates it can get through their issuance. ASARCO is the victim here, it feels. "The citizens of this state have forced this pollution control on us," the plant manager says.[43]

But if ASARCO is a victim, it's also a perpetrator. Young Ed Kemper, the "Co-Ed Killer," who slaughtered his grandparents, his mother, and six young women in Santa Cruz, California, between 1964 and 1973, spent his formative years here, breathing the air and playing "gas chamber" with his sister and decapitating the family pet, a Siamese cat, with a bayonet.[44]

FUTURE CLOUDED FOR TACOMA SMELTER, says the *News Tribune*.[45]

On May 15, a hundred people turn up at a six-hour meeting to protest the extension of the arsenic pollution variance applied for by ASARCO. Armand Labbe, the Ruston plant manager, flatly states that the smelter can never meet OSHA's recommended standard, which would allow workers to breathe only four micrograms of arsenic per cubic meter of air averaged over an eight-hour period. He produces two University of California professors who claim that the poison does not cause cancer. A representative of the Washington Thoracic Society states that it does, citing

OSHA studies establishing that smelter workers develop lung cancer at a rate three times that of other occupations. The Puget Sound Air Pollution Control Agency votes to deny the variance.

Ted's been going to Mormon prayer meetings. He surprises Liz by driving to Seattle the first week of June and showing up without telling her, convincing Molly to lead her mother into a bedroom, where he grabs Liz from behind. "For a split second I froze in terror," she'll later say.[46] She notices that his license plate has been removed and propped up inside the car. He tells her it fell off.

A few weeks later, on the balmy summer night of June 27, Susan Curtis, a fifteen-year-old high school student with long brown hair, is attending the Bountiful Orchard Youth Conference held at the Provo campus of Brigham Young University. Susan has new braces, and after dinner she wants to go back to the dorm room to brush her teeth. Like Debi Kent, she's from Bountiful, and like Debi Kent, she attended *Redhead* at Viewmont High School the night of November 8. Ted grabs her, rapes her, kills her, and buries her somewhere along U.S. Route 6 in the middle of Utah, between Price and Green River.[47] He doesn't get her name.

He may or may not pick up a hitchhiker, twenty-four-year-old Shelley Robertson, in Golden, Colorado, on June 29.

At 5:45 p.m. on the night of the Fourth of July, Nancy Baird, mother of a four-year-old son, disappears from a Fina gas station in Farmington, Utah. Farmington is just north of Bountiful. Nancy has long, shiny blond hair. She's wearing a blue halter top and shorts, and a smock with the Fina logo. She will never be found.[48]

The following night, Peter Sutcliffe, a truck driver who lives in the city of Bradford in West Yorkshire, England, attacks a woman walking alone, hitting her over the head from behind with a hammer and slashing her stomach with a knife. The woman, Anna Rogulskyj, survives, but with severe head injuries.

Born in June 1946, seven months before Ted Bundy, Peter grew up a weak and sickly child in an area of England suffering some of the worst air pollution recorded in the country outside of London. Lead mining and smelting had been going on in West Yorkshire since the Roman era. Blocks of lead, called "pigs," have been found near local bridges, stamped in Latin, and the region has a long history of coal and pit mines, textile mills, and tanneries.

Peter's mother worked in a munitions factory, his father in a bakery and a textile mill. The textile mills filled the Yorkshire air with chemicals wrought from dyes, starch, and mothproofing, an aromatic stew of bleach, formaldehyde, lead, and mercury. As early as the 1700s, the mills were known for producing "factory cripples" suffering from "mill fever," caused by breathing air full of dust and lime.[49]

By the 2000s, the counties of South and West Yorkshire, comprising the cities of Bradford, Sheffield, Leeds, Halifax, and Huddersfield, have ties to at least eight serial killers, more than any other area of the U.K. In addition to Sutcliffe, the "Yorkshire Ripper," they include Harold Shipman, "Dr. Death," a family practitioner believed to have "euthanized" more than two hundred of his patients, and Ian Brady and Myra Hindley, the so-called Moors Murderers, who killed five young children between the ages of ten and seventeen.[50]

As a young man, Peter worked as a gravedigger and had a vision that a tombstone was speaking to him in Polish, a language he didn't know. Like Ted, as a teenager he became an avid voyeur, developing an overwhelming urge to hit women over the head from behind. While working as a truck driver, a vocation strongly associated with serial murder, he killed approximately thirteen women.

ON JULY 13, 1975, Susan Savage and Patrick Oliver, two childhood friends in their early twenties, go on a picnic. They've grown up in Walla Walla, Washington, a name that serves as a gag line in old cartoons and movies: the town so nice they named it twice. It's a small agricultural mecca in southeastern Washington that grows apples and onions. To the Nez Perce the name means "Place of Many Waters," and various creeks wend their way through town on their way to the Columbia. On that sunny Sunday afternoon, Susan and Patrick drive in his Mercury Cougar to their favorite spot, on Mill Creek near the Wickersham Bridge. They leave home at a quarter after two, telling their families they'll be back in time for dinner.

They never return. By the following afternoon, Patrick's family are so worried that they send Dan, the missing boy's brother, to look in the couple's favorite places, accompanied by the boys' uncle. They find the Mercury Cougar parked on the roadside near the bridge. Spotting a pile of debris down by the creek, they investigate, seeing a tarp weighed down by a tire. Underneath the tarp are the bodies of Susan and Patrick. Both of them have been shot—Patrick three times, once through the heart, and Susan twice. Susan is naked from the waist down, her halter top yanked up to expose her breasts, and there is a "substance" observed on her body.[51] It's never tested, however, because it's washed off at the funeral home before the crime is investigated.

Horrified, the community raises a $5,000 reward for information. The Oliver family is well known in Walla Walla, having suffered a previous tragedy several years earlier, when another of Patrick and Dan's brothers was killed in a Fourth of July car crash. Susan, who recently got a college degree in interior design and a job as a graphic designer, has long been a favorite babysitter. But aside from a sighting of a sporty red car near the scene, no useful leads are forthcoming.

The two victims have been shot with a Ruger .357-caliber handgun with a six-inch barrel. No one knows it yet, but the gun was purchased at the PayLess Drug in Walla Walla the previous year by an employee at the nearby Washington State Penitentiary, the oldest men's prison in the state and the site of its death row. His name is Robert Lee Yates Jr., and he has a pale, pasty face like a lump of dough. He owns a red Dodge Dart, and his favorite spot for target practice is the Wickersham Bridge over Mill Creek.

MEANWHILE IN WICHITA, Dennis Rader is taking time off from killing, since he has a new job. He's working for ADT, installing security and fire

THE LEAD MOON

alarms in residential and commercial buildings, which provides excellent cover for casing new victims. His first child, a son, is born on July 26, 1975, and Dennis is thrilled to be starting a family.

Established in August 1874, ADT stands for American District Telegraph. It's a company that originally specialized in establishing telegraph-enabled call boxes to report neighborhood emergencies, an early version of the 911 system. Its employees, according to advertisements, are "dedicated to your safety."[52]

IS THE SMELTER A MENACE? asks the Tacoma *News Tribune* on July 27 as the Puget Sound Air Pollution Control Agency threatens its future. Someone's finally asking the right question, and the answer is yes. The Ruston plant is emitting seven hundred pounds of arsenic a day, along with 150 tons of sulfur dioxide, at maximum production.[53]

Every time the Tacoma smelter comes under fire, ASARCO, like a sulking child, threatens to take its toys and go away. The smelter's 1974 payroll in Tacoma is $16 million. The company pays more than $1 million per year in state and local taxes. Of its property taxes in 1974, more than $300,000, or nearly a third, goes to city schools. Its shipping supports the Port of Tacoma and longshoremen. Whole industries are reliant upon it, including the Burlington Northern Railroad; Foss Tug, a major West Coast maritime tugboat company; and a silica plant in Wenatchee. Seven percent of U.S. copper comes from the smelter.

At such critical junctures, ASARCO often trots out a live worker whose robust good health after working in the plant for decades is considered a testament to its safety. This time it's Owen Gallagher, sixty, born four blocks from the smelter. In 1934 he followed his father, who emigrated from Ireland in 1908, into the plant.[54] Gallagher himself, however, doesn't work in the roaster department, the slimes house, or the arsenic kitchen. He works in personnel. He works in an office.[55] He'll serve as mayor of Ruston for twenty years.

Despite Gallagher's good health, the Tacoma smelter must contend with the proven fact that the urine of Ruston schoolchildren contains fifteen times more arsenic than normal—as much as smelter workers.[56]

All of these issues and more are raised in the *News Tribune* article, perhaps the most comprehensive public airing of debate about the smelter in years.

But for some reason, no one is talking about lead. No one's talking about it, but everybody's breathing it.

ONE CHILD INHALING lead in Tacoma in 1975 is Joseph Edward Duncan III, who is twelve. The fourth of five children of Joseph Edward Duncan Jr. and Lillian Mae Duncan, he was born in 1963 at a hospital near Fort Bragg, outside Fayetteville, North Carolina. Joe has curly brown hair, misaligned front teeth, and eyes set far apart. He grew up an Army brat, moving every two years and living at different bases at home and abroad until his father retired from the service to become a postal worker, moving his family to Tacoma in the mid-1970s.

In 1975, Joe commits the first of many rapes of younger children, forcing a five-year-old boy to fellate him.

TWO DAYS LATER, Ted is driving around. It's two thirty in the morning on August 16, 1975, in a suburb of Salt Lake called Granger. He's looking for somebody. He has the front passenger seat pulled out and placed on the back seat, making a handy space to stash a body. There's a gym bag, open, where the seat should be. In it are a ski mask, a pair of pantyhose with slits cut for eyes, and an ice pick. On the floor behind the driver's seat is a crowbar.

His VW is spotted by Sergeant Robert Hayward, a longtime member of the Utah Highway Patrol. Having just spent hours staking out taverns as part of a team targeting drunk drivers, Hayward is sitting in his unmarked car, a green 1974 Plymouth Fury, on his own street, in front of his own house. He's seen a couple of other vehicles pass by whose owners he knows, but when he sees the VW he doesn't recognize it. There have recently been burglaries in the area.

His superior calls for assistance on another matter, but when Hayward pulls out of his driveway, his headlights pick up the gray or white VW again, parked a block away from his home and in front of his neighbors' house. He knows the couple who live there. They're out of town, and their two teenage daughters are home alone.[57] The VW suddenly takes off at a high speed, its headlights off. Hayward follows.

He sees the VW run a stop sign and turns his red spotlight on the car, matching its speed. Finally it pulls into a parking lot. Before Hayward can exit his car, the driver jumps out and approaches him, already talking and apologizing. Hayward demands his driver's license. The sergeant finds he's dealing with a Theodore Robert Bundy of 565 First Avenue, Salt Lake City, a man dressed entirely in dark clothing: a long-sleeved black turtleneck, dark pants, and sneakers. He says he's a law student. He claims to be lost.

Hayward lets his flashlight play over the interior of the car, seeing the passenger seat pulled out and the bag on the floor. He asks if he can look inside, and Ted says yes. Hayward sorts through the ski mask, the pantyhose, and the ice pick. He finds additional items: a flashlight, rope, a length of electrical cord, and strips of a torn bedsheet. He calls for an additional patrol car and is joined by two deputies and a sergeant.

The officers again request to search the car, and again Ted says yes. In the trunk they find handcuffs. Behind the seat, the crowbar. Asked what the cuffs are for, Ted says he uses them in his law classes. They ask why the seat is pulled out, and he says it's broken. They think he's a burglar, suspecting that the stuff in the bag may be burglars' tools. As they question him, things just get stranger and stranger, as Hayward will say later.

What is he doing in a quiet residential neighborhood in the middle of the night, ten miles from his apartment? He says he went to a movie. When they ask which one, he tells them *The Towering Inferno*, at the

Valley Vu Drive-In. The cops know exactly what's playing at the Valley Vu, having spent their shifts driving past it numerous times. It's not *The Towering Inferno*. It's three Westerns.

When they confront Ted with his lie, he changes his story, saying he was lost and alarmed at the sudden pursuit. They arrest him for evading an officer and take him to the station for booking. What Ted doesn't know is that Sergeant Robert Hayward's brother is Pete Hayward, the Salt Lake County sheriff, who months earlier responded to the call about Melissa Smith's body.

FOR TED, things are taking a turn. With bail set at $500, he's released on his own recognizance on August 17. The next day, Detective Jerry Thompson is looking over a list of the weekend's arrest records when the name Ted jumps out at him. At a meeting of local law enforcement run by Pete Hayward the next day, Ted's arrest is discussed further. Ben Forbes, the detective who wrote the report on Melissa Smith's body, calls the Seattle Police Department, promising to send them Ted's mug shot.[58]

On August 20, Forbes follows up with an official letter to Bob Keppel, describing the "burglary tools" found in the VW. Keppel has been spearheading a newfangled experiment, instructing a computer to cross-check multiple lists of suspects, including VW owners, mental patients released from facilities, people who received traffic citations in areas near where women disappeared, classmates of Lynda Ann Healy, etc. Ted is one of twenty-five names appearing on four or more lists.[59]

On August 21, Ted is picked up by Forbes, taken to the downtown police station, fingerprinted, photographed, and booked on possession of burglary tools, although he supplies an anodyne excuse for each one. Cooperative to a fault, he stands around joking with Forbes, saying he found the handcuffs in a bag of garbage. The pantyhose are for skiing, he says, for wearing against the cold, under his ski mask, and he uses rope and strips of sheet to tie his raft to the top of the car. He shrugs off the ice pick and crowbar as "common pieces of household equipment."[60] When Jerry

THE LEAD MOON

Thompson arrives, he asks Ted if they can search his apartment. Ted readily agrees, saying, "I have nothing to hide."[61]

At 565 First Avenue, Ted watches them search, unperturbed. The apartment, Forbes will tell Keppel later, is "very immaculate," but Thompson and the other detectives nonetheless find a few intriguing things: a Colorado Ski Country guide from 1974–1975 with an *X* penned next to the name of the Wildwood Inn; a pamphlet from Bountiful; and credit card gas receipts. Ted gives permission to take them. They find a copy of *The Joy of Sex* and a pair of black patent leather shoes in the closet. The shoes are not taken into evidence.

They search thoroughly, but what they don't know is that Ted, as the apartment house manager, has keys to a utility shed and the cellar, accessed through a set of underground stairs next to the building, under a heavy wooden hatch. Somewhere in the cellar or elsewhere on the property, Ted has concealed a stack of Polaroids. Some of the pictures were taken in the last moments of his victims' lives; some of them, perhaps, past that point. Within the next few days, the Polaroids will vanish.

What has not disappeared, however, are the remains of Shelley Robertson, the woman who vanished while hitchhiking in Golden, Colorado, in June. On the day that Ted's apartment is searched, her nude body is discovered by a group of mining students exploring a mine shaft in Berthoud Pass, Colorado. Her skull shows severe injuries to the back of the cranium.

A few months before her disappearance, the February issue of *True Detective* featured a graphic article about Robert Garrow, a pedophile, rapist, and murderer who killed a number of people back east in 1973, including a woman, Susan Petz. He stabbed her and hid the body in an abandoned mine shaft in Mineville, New York, a town near his childhood home that's famous for its pile of iron ore tailings.[62] Did Ted read about the mine shaft? *True Detective* has always been one of his favorite magazines.

HIS CONVICTION that he is invulnerable has led him to allow the police to search his apartment and to question him. He thinks cops are dumb, not without reason, since they've never come close to catching him before. They're not so dumb, however, that they don't start thinking about his handcuffs, his crowbar, and Carol DaRonch.

Yet Ted is nothing if not devoted to his own welfare. The next day, he retains John O'Connell, a renowned young criminal attorney in Salt Lake who styles himself like Kris Kristofferson with a heavy beard and mustache, his long hair topped with a ten-gallon Stetson.[63] On August 22, O'Connell tells the Salt Lake City Police Department that his client will have nothing further to say.

A day later, Detective Jerry Thompson calls Mike Fisher, the investigator working on Caryn Campbell's murder in Colorado, and tells him about the X written in the margin of Ted's ski guide, next to the Wildwood Inn. Fisher explodes with excitement, yelling, "Jesus Christ, Jesus Christ!"[64]

On August 30, Ted is baptized into the Church of Jesus Christ of Latter-day Saints. He tells anybody who'll listen that he has nothing to hide, while at the same time he's hiding things. Planning to sell his car, he's combing junkyards for VW parts. He finds and installs a new back seat, without a tear across the top, and has the vehicle repainted from off-white to light brown. He's ordained into the lower priesthood of his new faith as the police subpoena his law school records, gas credit card records, and bank statements.

The police ask Raelynne Shepherd, the dance teacher at Viewmont High in Bountiful, who saw Ted on the night Debi Kent disappeared, to look at a photo lineup. She picks a clean-shaven image of Ted, saying if you put a mustache on him, he'd be the guy. They show the photos to Carol DaRonch. She pulls out the photo of Ted and says she's sure it looks like the man she remembers, except that he had a mustache.[65]

On September 10, the police begin running twenty-four-hour-a-day surveillance on Ted, who quickly spots them and surveils them in return, writing down their license plate numbers. They interview Liz Kloepfer's father, Dr. Russell Hirst, who tells them that in his opinion Ted is a "schizophrenic," pleasant and helpful one minute, "extremely moody" the next.[66] Detectives fly to Seattle to interview Liz. She tells them the stories she's been telling all along—the crutches, the "oriental" knife, the plaster of paris.

They ask Liz about Ted's sexual preferences. She tells them about *The Joy of Sex*, which he bought sometime in 1972 or 1973, and how she agreed to let him tie her arms and legs to the bedposts with nylon stockings twice before having intercourse, but hated it and wouldn't do it again. She's angry that Ted has just asked her to loan him $700 to pay his lawyer. She's so nervous during the interview that she smokes an entire pack of cigarettes.

On September 19, Ted sells his VW for $700 to a high school student at Salt Lake's Hillcrest High, the same school Melissa Smith went to, without telling him that a bail bondsman holds the title. To close the deal, Ted forges a duplicate title.

A week later, Ted moves to a different apartment, and on October 1 Detective Thompson arrives to deliver a subpoena to appear in a lineup. The subpoena concerns only the attempted kidnapping of Carol DaRonch, and Ted is so relieved there's no murder charge that he says, "Oh God, is that all?" Thompson says, "You were waiting for Murder One, weren't you, Ted?"[67]

The next day, October 2, Ted appears for the lineup with his hair cut short. He looks different, having changed the part in his hair from right to left. Carol DaRonch is there, as are Raelynne Shepherd and another woman who saw Ted at the performance of *Redhead*. They're all afraid that he might see them through the glass.

Each man in the lineup is assigned a number and asked to step forward, turn to the left and to the right, and repeat several phrases: "Would you like to come to the station with me?" and "Could you come outside and identify a car for me? It'll just take a minute" and "I'm a police officer. Your car has been broken into."[68] Ted is number seven.

Each woman is given a piece of paper and asked to write down the number if they recognize one of the men. By the time the exercise is over, all three women have written down the number seven.

Ted is arrested on charges of aggravated kidnapping and attempted murder. Bail is set at $100,000. Again his mug shot is taken, and he's detained in the Salt Lake County Jail.

When news breaks that a Ted has been arrested on serious charges, a Ted who hails from Seattle, all hell breaks loose. It's front-page news in Seattle, Tacoma, Olympia, Spokane: FORMER EVANS AIDE CHARGED IN KIDNAP CASE; TED, KIDNAP SUSPECT, LINKED TO KILLINGS; DEATH LINK SOUGHT.[69] It's news in Oregon, Utah, Idaho, Colorado, New York, and all across the country. I'm reading it in my grandmother's *Seattle Post-Intelligencer*: IS UTAH "TED" THE SEATTLE "TED"?[70]

Ann Rule gasps when she hears the news on the radio as she's driving her son home from a junior high football game. It's not a complete surprise. Ted called her in September to tell her that she might be reading about him in the papers, but she's still shocked.[71] Richard Larsen, the *Seattle Times* reporter who met Ted at the opening of the North Cascades Highway, hears it in a Portland hotel lobby at the Western States Republican Conference. He's told the news by Ross Davis, chairman of the Washington State Republican Party. Davis has an odd smile on his face as he describes a phone call he's just received from another reporter. He says that Ted Bundy has been arrested, and there must be some mistake.

Larsen says, "Ted doesn't drive a Volkswagen, does he?"

Ross Davis stops smiling and says, "Yes, he does."[72] In the coming days, Davis is quoted as saying, "It's unbelievable. You're kidding. That just sort of floors me. I can't imagine it. His whole approach was nothing but ethics."[73] To another reporter, he describes his protégé as "such a neat guy. There has to be a mistake.... It's not the same guy I knew."[74]

No one who knows Ted can believe it. A neighbor who lives near the UW rooming house talks to an Associated Press reporter, saying that when he came by in June, "he was very suntanned and talked a lot about how beautiful the Utah desert is in the spring because of all the blooming flowers."[75]

Louise Bundy expresses astonishment. "Could my son do these things?

Of course not," she says. "What a stupid thing to ask a mother. In no way could he do those things."[76]

He's now a suspect, however, in eleven murders in the Northwest, in addition to those in Utah and Colorado. The sheer number of crimes laid at his feet is so astounding that it obliterates everything else. The enormity of it is like a klieg light washing out the serial rapes and murders committed by other men in the region—Warren Leslie Forrest, for example, or Gary Addison Taylor, the so-called Phantom Sniper, who has Elvis lips, a pompadour, and an "irresistible urge" to kill women.[77] Taylor took a fancy to his next-door neighbor near SeaTac, Vonnie Stuth, nineteen and a newlywed. He shot her in 1974 while she was at home making a Jell-O salad for Thanksgiving and buried her. After she disappeared, everyone thought it was "Ted."[78]

Other men's murders are often attributed to him. Bob Keppel and Ann Rule will come to believe that Ted is responsible for raping and murdering Katherine Merry Devine, a fourteen-year-old Seattle child abducted while hitchhiking in December 1973, found with her throat cut in a state forest near Olympia, and Brenda Joy Baker, also fourteen, also hitchhiking, found with her throat cut in Millersylvania State Park, south of Olympia, in June 1974. But it's not Ted. It's another serial murderer: William Earl Cosden Jr., who's moved to Olympia after being found not guilty by reason of insanity for murdering a woman in Maryland in 1967.[79] He works in his father's truck stop. In 1974, there are at least half a dozen serial killers operating in Washington.[80] Nobody can see the forest for the trees.

In 1975, violent crime is up 14 percent in Washington's three largest cities: Seattle, Tacoma, and Spokane. Tacoma records a 62 percent rise in murder (compared with single-digit increases in the two other cities) and a 28 percent rise in rape.[81] No one knows why. Later that month, James Reston, a syndicated columnist for *The New York Times*, muses on "mindless violence," including some fifty bombings in California alone, blaming political turmoil and the dissolution of the family and the pernicious influence of television.[82] He doesn't consider the fact that the concentration of a heavy metal associated with heightened aggression has risen 300 percent in Greenland ice cores since leaded gasoline became ubiquitous.[83]

TED IS NOT released from jail until November 20, when a judge reduces his bail to $15,000. His parents put up their house as collateral. Meanwhile, there are more than a dozen cops in several states working on his case, and they hold another multistate conference, this time in Aspen, to share information. Salt Lake police have seized Ted's Volkswagen from the high school student who bought it, stripping it down to the bare metal, vacuuming it, and sending the detritus to the FBI for analysis.

Ted has spent his time in jail writing self-pitying letters to Liz and Ann Rule. He told Rule that he felt like he was "in the eye of a hurrican[e]." "My world is [a] cage," he complained.[84] Released, he flies to Seattle for Thanksgiving, persuading Liz anew that he had nothing to do with any crimes.

Keppel and his team are canvassing Bundy's family and friends. They learn from Ted's cousin John Cowell that Ted loves the area around Taylor Mountain. The two of them have hiked there repeatedly. They talk to his cousin Edna and discover that she knew Lynda Ann Healy. Ted's Republican cronies admit that they saw him at Lake Sammamish the week before the July 1974 murders, wandering on the beach by himself. Lacking enough evidence to charge him, the Seattle cops tail him throughout his visit, if only to prevent further attacks. He delights in taunting them, trying to ditch them in the Volkswagen he's borrowed from his friend Marlin Vortman, the same color as his own.

After Thanksgiving, Ted meets Rule at the Brasserie Pittsbourg, a French restaurant in the basement of a building in Seattle's Pioneer Square, and they have a long, boozy lunch in a back room, with a couple of carafes of Chablis, while rain pours down the windows. He's dismissive of the charges against him, insisting that they won't come to anything. She's as disarmed by him as Liz is, scarcely able to believe he could be guilty. Yet as a crime reporter, she has doubts. She asks if he was aware of the missing women the previous year. He's uncomfortable with the question, telling

THE LEAD MOON

her he was too busy with law school and never read the papers. He can't look her in the eye while he's saying it.[85]

On December 10, 1975, the Tacoma *News Tribune* publishes an article on psychologist Donna Schram, Ted's former boss, who has issued the conclusions of a yearlong study on rape in Seattle and King County. Of 308 reported rapes or attempted rapes in 1974, only 6 have resulted in convictions. More than 59 percent involved strangers, and 35 percent of the victims suffered injuries, ranging from beatings to stab wounds. King County prosecutors require women to show that they resisted an attack, but victims trained in self-defense say that it doesn't help, that physical resistance tends to provoke violence.[86]

In most cases, the study finds, rapists are entering victims' homes through unlocked doors and windows.

Chapter 9

The Dutch Door

―◆―

Lying is a delightful thing, for it leads to truth.

—Fyodor Dostoevsky,
Crime and Punishment

We live on the island, and the island is safe. Our doors and windows are often unlocked.

Doors are utilitarian for my father, who built the house. He doesn't care how they look. He doesn't care about security. He cares about cost. Our front door is the cheapest of all available alternatives aside from, say, a tent flap. It's a hollow core door, interior grade, with a simple lock. A child could break into it. A child has.

Doors are lies. Open and closed, in and out, predator and prey. Janus-faced, they keep no one safe.

Our upstairs door is painted turquoise, from the same can of paint he used to paint turquoise squares on the cement floor in the daylight basement, which has never been finished. The downstairs door, from basement to backyard, is a Dutch door, farmhouse-style, two halves with nine little windows up top. The top swings open.

Dutch doors are meant to keep farm animals in the barn, like Mister

THE DUTCH DOOR

Ed, the talking horse on TV. I'm studying the photos in *Life* magazine from Cielo Drive after the Manson family is done with it. The living room's open-beam ceiling is like ours, but a rope dangles from a beam. The front door is a faux Dutch door with nine windows on top and the word PIG at the bottom, written in Sharon Tate's blood.

I'm watching the werewolf on *Dark Shadows* circling outside the saloon while the barmaid is closing up. She locks the Dutch door, with its nine windows. Beside it is a wall of glass windows, but windows don't stop a werewolf. He leaps through, raising his claws. She screams and screams, and the screen goes black.

NO ONE FEELS SAFE. On January 1, 1976, the *Mercer Island Reporter* asks, WILL BRIDGE KEEP AFLOAT? The Mercer Island Floating Bridge is nearing the end of its lifespan. Unless the highway department is allowed to close it to replace the decking and reinforce the pontoons, it's anyone's guess what might happen. If nothing is done in the next five years, an engineer muses, "we might get a bit of list."[1]

And who's the petty thief on the island who's becoming a one-man crime wave, stealing license plates, boosting cars, joyriding, prowling, and lifting stuff from friends' houses: bicycles, rings, watches, down jackets, cigarettes, loose change? Just up the street, a thief breaks into a van to steal a tape deck but abandons it when it's found to be engraved with the owner's driver's license number.[2]

Odds are it's George Waterfield Russell Jr.

George lives down the street, and since he's a few years ahead of me at school, I've doubtless seen him on the bus, at the Pay 'n Save, at the grocery store, walking down the street, riding a bike. The population of Mercer Island in 1975 is pushing twenty thousand, but most people in the north end are recognizable, George perhaps more than most because he's Black, on an island with relatively few Black families. When he was younger, he delivered newspapers and hung around with local cops, doing odd jobs at the station. The cops liked this little kid, who was a cheerful, chattering presence. They bought him soda pop and showed him how to take fingerprints. They called him their mascot.

Russell is a name on the island, because Bill Russell, the famous basketball player for the Boston Celtics, recently moved here to coach the Seattle SuperSonics. George Russell is not related to him. George is the stepson of Dr. Wonzel Mobley, a dentist who lives on the island but practices in Seattle. Born in Florida in 1958, George is the biological son of Dr. Mobley's wife, Joyce, and George Waterfield Russell Sr., who drove a hearse in West Palm Beach.

George's childhood was fractured by benign neglect, his mother leaving him with her mother and younger sisters when he was a few months old to attend Florida A&M University in Tallahassee. The grandmother, sisters, and George moved periodically, spending time in Fernandina Beach, a coastal community in Florida's far north. His mother called him once during his youngest years, when he had chicken pox. He never knew his father.

When he was six, his mother married Wonzel, from Orlando, and the couple picked up George in a U-Haul. They drove across the country to Fort Lewis in Tacoma, where Wonzel finished a stint in the Army and where on-base housing was painted with lead-based paint. The soil and water were contaminated with lead, arsenic, chloroform, mercury, cadmium, battery acid, and barium.[3]

The Mobleys then moved to Seattle, where Joyce, having earned a master's degree, taught college and Wonzel worked as a temp on a project to clean up algae in Lake Washington. Then they moved to Washington, D.C., where Wonzel went to dental school, returning to the Pacific Northwest when George was ten. They moved to Mercer Island and soon another child was born, a daughter.

According to George, Wonzel became good friends with Bill Russell and other players: Downtown Freddie Brown and J. J. Johnson. The Mobleys had parties; they were successful. But in 1975, when George was a junior at Mercer Island High School, his parents split up and his mother left him again, moving to Maryland and taking her daughter, the preferred child, with her. She didn't take George. She left him behind with his stepfather, who was no longer related to him.

His stepfather remarried, beginning a new family. The Mobley home is at 7244 North Mercer Way, yards from the capped I-90 tunnel. Massive exhaust fans pull air out of the tunnel and expel it, full of particulates, full of lead, from leaded gasoline. George, a troubled boy with a troubled past, drops out of high school.

After stealing pills from his stepfather's dental supplies and making sexual moves on his stepmother, he ends up homeless on the island, living in Luther Burbank Park, establishing secret hidey-holes in vacant lots and forested areas—holes to bury his treasure, the things he steals from his friends, from his friends' parents, and, soon enough, from any house or car or pool house or boathouse or business he can break into. He's the rustling in the bushes, the Peeping Tom, the hot prowler. The cops don't like him anymore.

ON THE MORNING of January 28, 1976, Salt Lake detective Jerry Thompson answers a call from an FBI analyst. The Bureau has completed its forensic analysis of material vacuumed out of Ted's VW. Three human hairs match two victims, the report concludes: two head hairs are thought to be "microscopically identical" to Caryn Campbell's hair, and a pubic hair matches those of Melissa Smith. Nobody knows it yet, but hair analysis will ultimately be deemed of dubious value.

Ted is outraged by the findings. He has cleaned that car so thoroughly, so many times, that he's absolutely sure the hairs have been planted, even though he's well aware that both women were in the vehicle. He can't say that, so he just fumes.

He sighs and shakes his head throughout his February trial, presided over solely by a judge. Ted has waived his right to a jury, although Marlin Vortman tells him that's "nuts."[4] It's as if, Vortman will say later, Ted believes that his trial is "a *Perry Mason* episode." Ted stares at Carol

DaRonch during her testimony, unnerving her, but is himself unnerved by the stares of two mothers, Shirleen Aime and Belva Kent, and a father, Louis Smith. In the corridor, he laughs and jokes with the press, dismissive of the charges, confident of success.

But in court, deprived of handcuffs and crowbar, his wiles are weakened. He has only his lies, and these, it turns out, are no match for professionals. Believing that an expert on the fallibility of human memory may sway a judge, if not a jury, the defense calls Elizabeth Loftus, an associate professor in the Department of Psychology at the University of Washington, who is at the beginning of her career. Had circumstances been different, she might have once been a colleague of Ted's. As it is, however, Loftus testifies that experiments have shown that the memories of an eyewitness can be swayed and altered by any number of factors, including the passage of time.

Carol DaRonch's testimony exhibits issues raised by Dr. Loftus, having changed on points regarding the VW and its license plate, the badge shown to her by "Officer Roseland," the type of jacket Ted was wearing, and his mustache. She weeps and grows confused as O'Connell cross-examines her, trying to catch her out. In his opening statement, he plays to stereotypes, painting the victim as "immature," "sheltered," "unsophisticated," "unobservant," "submissive to authority," and suffering from a "malleable memory."[5]

What never changes, however, is her identification of Ted Bundy. On the night in question, November 8, 1974, she walked with him, talked to him, asked for his identification, saw the handcuffs in his pocket, got in his car, smelled the alcohol on his breath, and was attacked by him. She fought with him as he threatened to kill her. She remembers him. On redirect, the prosecutor asks her if she knew immediately on seeing Ted in the lineup that it was him. She says, emphatically, "Yes." He asks if she's positive today and she says, "Yes."

At the close of the case, when the judge, Stewart Hanson Jr., must render his decision, he takes into account her positive identification and the fact that Ted has lied continually since his arrest. He's lied about his black patent leather shoes, worn the night of DaRonch's assault, denying that he ever owned them. Police saw a pair during the search of his apartment but failed to take them into evidence. Prosecutors, however, find neighbors who live across the hall who testify that they've seen him wearing them.

He's lied to the police about what he was doing the night of his arrest, saying he'd gone to see *The Towering Inferno*. To account for that lie, he makes up another one, saying he was just out driving, hoping to see a part of Salt Lake he'd never seen before. But the neighborhood where he was arrested is not a scenic one, and he had no reason to be there in the middle of the night with masks, rope, garbage bags, and a crowbar. During the trial, to explain the initial lies, he's fabricated another story, saying he was smoking marijuana in his car and that's why he fled. But the cops know what marijuana smells like, and they testify that there was no odor in the car or on his person when he was arrested.

It's possible that a jury might have weighed Carol DaRonch's confusion against Ted Bundy's shifting story and decided that there was cause for reasonable doubt. Juries can be unobservant, unsophisticated, malleable, and submissive to authority. But Ted Bundy has chosen to be judged by a judge.

On the afternoon of March 1, 1976, court reconvenes. In a hushed room, in front of Ted's parents, Liz Kloepfer, Carol DaRonch, and the parents of other victims, the judge renders his verdict, finding Theodore Robert Bundy guilty of aggravated kidnapping, a first-degree felony. He has not, as yet, been charged with any murders.

The judge orders a presentence investigation report to include a battery of physical and mental evaluations, citing the need to consider the "safety of the Defendant," among other issues.[6] Thanks to unceasing reporting, he is now one of the most notorious convicted criminals in the United States.

ON MARCH 10, ASARCO officials in Tacoma announce that they've dropped plans to create new slag-land along Ruston Way south of the smelter. Copper prices are dropping, and the idea is shelved "indefinitely."[7]

Two days later, having just worked the overnight swing shift at the Ruston plant, Loy McDonald, sixty-two, is preparing to work overtime at 7:30 a.m. He's sent to work on the high-voltage Cottrell electrostatic precipitator, a massive piece of pollution control equipment some two stories high. It was invented in 1907 by Frederick Gardner Cottrell—author of "The Problem of Smelter Smoke," delivered at San Francisco's Commonwealth Club—to charge particles of valuable minerals or chemical compounds that would otherwise pass through an industrial smokestack. The charged particles can be collected, retrieved, and sold.

After a series of layoffs at the plant, Loy is working alone on a two-man job, and the switches on the Cottrell are a little sticky. One switch does not engage properly. Men in the control room hear a moan. The electricity shorts out. Electrocuted, Loy dies an hour later in a Tacoma hospital. He's worked for ASARCO since 1948.

His union brothers do not mince words. DEATH AT THE SMELTER, reads their flyer. "Brother McDonald's death was industrial murder for profit," they say, denouncing attempts to pin the blame on the victim.[8] "Loy McDonald was killed by ASARCO," they say, and his "blood is on the company's hands and we are not going to wait until the next man dies to do something about it!"[9]

They don't wait. In the mid-1970s, union members acquire a "death list" tallying recent lung cancer fatalities among ASARCO workers and retirees.[10] Most men are in their sixties and seventies, but others are in their thirties, forties, or fifties, such as the youngest, Victor Joseph Hrvatin, born in Ruston, who died in 1959 at age thirty-six. A converter man, James R. Todd, died in 1971 at forty-four; a mason, Robert Mataya, in 1974 at fifty; a retired crane operator, Allen E. Staples, in 1973 at sixty-five.[11] Clarence Baarsma, Bill's father, who could put a finger through his septum, is on the list. There are fifty deaths in all, five each in 1973 and 1974, and the union calls out Dr. Sherman Pinto, "the plant quack," for covering them up.[12]

Pinto, in his publications, has been lying, attributing excess lung cancer deaths to pneumonia.[13] According to the state average, as the union points out, one excess death a year from lung cancer caused by cigarette smoking or pollution at the smelter would be the norm; ASARCO has racked up ten in the past two years. "These men were killed by management just as surely as if a ladle of hot copper had been dropped on their heads," they write.[14]

In 1977, Dr. Pinto is forced to revise his 1963 arsenic study, and this time he grudgingly admits something closer to the truth. Considering 527 retirees, he and his co-authors find that overall mortality at the Tacoma smelter is 12.2 percent higher than average, largely due to respiratory diseases and lung cancer caused by arsenic.[15]

Pinto dies five years later of a cerebral hemorrhage at age seventy-five.

AFTER AN EIGHT-WEEK TRIAL, on March 20, 1976, Patty Hearst is found guilty of the armed robbery of the Hibernia Bank. In the courtroom, as the verdict is read, her mother and sisters weep, and her father, Randolph Hearst, says, "Oh Christ."[16] Patty herself is dry-eyed.

I, too, am becoming bad, causing disruption in Sunday school. The teacher asks me to read the title of the Lesson-Sermon, one of Mary Baker Eddy's rhetorical devices—"Are Sin, Disease, and Death Real?"—and tosses me the ball. I say, "no," which is the expected response, but then add "supposedly," causing a sharp intake of breath and excited glances among the children of the faithful. I feel gleeful.

Things are starting to come out of my mouth, surprising me and others. Rude things, contentious things, the darndest things.

I'm reading about Patty Hearst in *People* magazine and thinking about lies. My father lies: he says nothing is real. My mother lies to my father. Everybody's lying to everybody else.

If everyone can lie, I'm thinking, *why oh why can't I?*

FOR HIS PRESENTENCING REPORT, Donald M. Hull, an investigator for Utah's Adult Probation and Parole Department, interviews Ted, Ted's mother, his neighbors and classmates, Liz Kloepfer, and former girlfriends in Seattle and Salt Lake City, including Sandy Gwinn and Margith Maughan. He compiles accounts of Ted's educational background and employment history, taking notes on the subject's religious affiliations, financial status, sexual experience, habits, and hobbies. He receives letters of support from Ted's siblings. He reinterviews Carol DaRonch and the couple who rescued her on the night of her assault and drove her to the police station.

Hull finds Bundy "very controlled and calm" as he vehemently asserts his innocence, suggesting that someone else attacked Carol DaRonch. She was "pressured" to identify him by overzealous law enforcement, he tells Hull.[17]

As for the defendant's family, Ted expresses concern for his mother and indifference toward his stepfather. ("I learned to love him," he says.) He shows "marked signs of hostility" when queried about his real father. Asked where that man might be, Ted's face becomes "quite contorted and reddened," Hull remarks. After an internal struggle, he regains his composure and says dryly, "You might say that he left my mother and me and never rejoined the family."[18]

Hull reviews Ted's middling grades, spotty attendance record, and incompletes at virtually every institution he has attended, which includes five universities. His tendency to drop out. His employment history, listing a dozen jobs that rarely lasted more than a few months. His petty thefts and heavy drinking and moodiness.

He hears from fellow high school students who recall Ted being uninterested in dating and masturbating in a broom closet. Ted denies it.

Medical testing reveals Ted to be, at the age of twenty-nine, a paragon of ruddy good health, at five foot eleven and 170 pounds. His resting heart rate is a rock-solid 66; his blood pressure exemplary at 110/60. As a child, he had chicken pox, German measles, and mumps. As an adult, a fractured ankle. Everything appears normal.

But there's one unusual finding. An X-ray of his skull shows "some nonunion of coronal suture," according to the radiologist.[19] In medical parlance, "nonunion" refers to a break in a bone that fails to heal.

THE DUTCH DOOR

The coronal suture is a zipper across the top of the cranium, a "dense and fibrous association" of connective tissue between the frontal and parietal bones. At birth, its flexibility allows the baby's head to pass through the birth canal; during childhood, it allows the brain to grow rapidly. The coronal suture typically fuses by around age twenty-four.

Nonunion of the suture can be caused by trauma or vitamin and mineral deficiencies in the diet. In children, lead exposure interferes with the ordinary uptake of vitamins and nutrients such as vitamin D and iron. In Ted's case, there is no knowing what caused it. Forceps in delivery. A blow. A little too much lead. All of the above. The radiologist, however, observing no evidence of "increased pressure or calcification," moves on.

THE EPA BEGINS the phaseout of leaded gasoline in April 1976. Its industry opponents lose lawsuits, one after another, filed against the proposed federal regulations, which have already been watered down at the request of corporate titans and Nixon's White House. Lawrence Blanchard Jr., vice-chair of the Ethyl Corporation, which remains one of three chief American suppliers of tetraethyl, the additive that crippled and perhaps killed its inventor, is apoplectic, comparing the regulations to "the worst example of fanaticism since the New England witch hunts in the 17th Century."[20]

Blanchard claims, although he must know it to be a lie, that "no person has ever been found having an identifiable toxic effect from the amount of lead in the atmosphere today."[21] He might want to pay a visit to three-year-old Arlene Yoss, still in pain after treatment for the lead poisoning she received from breathing the air at Bunker Hill, or to anyone living in the smelter plumes in Tacoma, El Paso, or Ciudad Juárez.

Everyone's mad and getting madder. By the spring of 1976, residents within whiffing distance of the Tacoma smelter are fomenting dissension, colluding with the Sierra Club, Greenpeace, Friends of the Earth, and local rabble-rousers such as GASP (Group Against Smog Pollution) and IRATE (Island Residents Against Toxic Emissions). The most irate live on Vashon Island, directly across Puget Sound from the Ruston smokestack.

It's been collecting arsenic the way a magnet collects iron filings. There's talk of lawsuits. There's pressure.

Bending to it, ASARCO agrees to work with the Washington State Department of Health to test the concentration of arsenic in children's urine on Vashon. In late June, the health department finds that there are no instances of "abnormal urinary excretion" in its samples, although island children aged five to seven are, in fact, averaging thirty micrograms of arsenic per liter, and for ten-year-olds it's even higher: thirty-six.[22] That's twice what's considered normal, and five to six times higher than in children not exposed.*

Meanwhile, Rustonians have formed a committee to beautify their streets for the upcoming bicentennial celebrations on the Fourth of July. To counter their "smelter town" image, they're planning to hang flower boxes. The flowers will have to be artificial. Mildred Parker of the beautification committee assures the local newspaper that they've chosen the plastic flowers not because of ASARCO and its caustic showers of arsenic. It's simply too messy to water flowers, she says. But everyone knows.

"You always hear something bad about the smelter," Mrs. Parker remarks sadly.[23]

AFTER DONALD HULL completes his report, a team of Utah prison psychologists goes to work on Ted. The tests they administer include the California Psychological Inventory, the Minnesota Multiphasic Personality Inventory, the Hooper Visual Organization Test, the TWIST Assessment (Two Word Incomplete Sentences Test), and a Rorschach test.

Dr. Evan Lewis finds Ted to be in the highest 10 percent of the population intellectually, with well-developed verbal skills. But he's troubled by Ted's compulsive response to testing, noting that Ted insists on keeping a record of how he responds to every one of the four hundred items on the Minnesota Multiphasic, "a behavior which I have never seen before" and

---

* There was no federal health standard for arsenic in urine. Researchers in this case assumed, based on an earlier study, that fourteen micrograms per liter was normal for children.

THE DUTCH DOOR

one that is indicative of the "rigid control Mr. Bundy was exerting over his emotional responsiveness."[24]

He notes that the patient is sometimes "fastidious" in appearance and at other times "slovenly," a pattern that jibes with Ted's tendency to vacillate, to shift between the goals of an ambitious young Republican striver and the largely menial jobs he's sought. Dr. Lewis speculates that the crimes against women of which Ted is accused are "calculated" and senses "an aberrant feeling toward females" emerging during the Rorschach: ambivalence, withdrawal, and hostility.

But it's Dr. Al Carlisle who puts the final nail in Ted's Utah coffin. A thirty-nine-year-old clinical psychologist with a Ph.D. from Brigham Young University, Carlisle is friendly and earnest and has never met anyone like Ted before. His office in the Utah State Prison in Draper has a beautiful view of the Wasatch Range. He ponders Hull's report, but not too closely: he wants to bring a fresh mind to the case. His job, as the judge has defined it, is to determine whether Ted has the capacity for homicidal violence.

Carlisle is initially charmed by the prisoner, who greets him on first meeting by walking up to him, putting out his hand, and saying, "Hi, I'm Ted!" The psychologist spends hours with him, reviewing his arrest and life history. He reinterviews many of the people Hull has turned up, as well as new sources. He talks to Sybil Ferris, the elderly woman who worked at the Seattle Yacht Club and who loaned Ted money and a car and found him jobs. Her account begins to reveal a secretive side to Ted.

She tells Carlisle that in her experience he's "a very, very peculiar boy," "a very weird boy," given to telling lies and stealing things and "sneaking around."[25] She's come to be afraid of Ted and recalls seeing him in an Albertsons near Green Lake with a cast on his arm. The attributes she describes—constant lying and a propensity to steal without remorse—unveil what Carlisle believes are "psychopathic personality traits."[26]

There are flashes of anger. When he asks Ted about his reactions to fear and punishment, he touches a nerve. Loudly, Ted says, "I don't have fears! Fear, pain, and punishment don't stick with me!"[27] The psychologist notes that Ted has volatile feelings about his illegitimacy, logging his subject's remarks about his juvenile sexuality. He's startled by Ted's description of his fourth-grade teacher as a "voluptuous disciplinarian," observing dryly that "it is uncommon for people to attribute sexual concepts to adults they knew as children."[28] He believes that something may have happened around Ted's middle teen years, when he failed to respond to girls who were interested in him.

Prompted by a conversation with Dick Larsen of *The Seattle Times*, Carlisle asks Ted about the 1961 disappearance of Ann Marie Burr. Ted says flatly, "I didn't know anything about it."[29] Given that it was the talk of Tacoma, Carlisle expresses surprise, and Ted says, "I was so involved in my school activities I didn't pay much attention to it."[30] The doctor is skeptical.

Asked to describe the winter and spring of 1974, a time when Ted was constantly in motion, driving hundreds of miles and buying tank after tank of gas, the prisoner offers one word. The year 1974, he says, was "uneventful."[31]

Carlisle talks to Sandy Gwinn about her rapey sex with Ted on the beach. He talks to Larry Voshall about the catastrophic river rafting trip, and Larry tells him that Ted just seemed to "enjoy seeing people frightened."[32] He talks to Diane Edwards about Ted's "vituperative" act, dumping her after their brief engagement. He's learning that Ted, despite his assertions of normality, has "a very dark side to him."[33] He comes to believe that Ted Bundy does have the capacity for "extreme anger and violence," and reports as much.[34]

Ted writes to Ann Rule to complain about the bias of the investigators and psychologists, suggesting that they, too, have been skewed by the bad press he's getting. "The report," he tells her, "seems to be focusing on the Jekel and Hyde theory [sic]."[35]

During the sentencing hearing before Judge Hanson on June 30, 1976, Ted appears as his own attorney, exhausted and unkempt, wearing a T-shirt with the word DIAGNOSTIC across the chest. He rails against the assessments, denying that he's callous, hostile, passive-aggressive, or "de-

THE DUTCH DOOR

pendent on women."[36] He's already written lengthy, self-pitying letters to the judge, pleading his innocence and complaining about the "abject loneliness" he's suffering.[37] He goes on and on, sniffling and finally breaking down into sobs. Knowing full well that he's already abducted, raped, and murdered more than a dozen women in Washington, Oregon, Idaho, Utah, Colorado, and perhaps other states, he suggests that in five or ten years the judge should ask himself whether "the sacrifice of my life [is] worth it."[38] The judge sentences Theodore Robert Bundy to one to fifteen years.

Ted is now forcibly becalmed at the Utah State Prison, Point of the Mountain, just north of American Fork and beside Highway 15. The carefree highway is running along without him. All he has is the air that he breathes and the view east from the prison yard into the cleft of the mountains where he took Laura Aime.

MERCER ISLAND HAS ITS OWN bicentennial committees, lots of them: a Heritage Committee, a Horizons Committee, a Finance Committee. A weekend of festivities is planned: a festival, a parade, fireworks, and the dedication of Bicentennial Park in the business center. The festival is a revival of Mercerfair, a formerly annual event lost years ago to apathy. It promises concerts, parachutists, a Frisbee contest, a duck pond, a fishpond, a bowling game, a beanbag toss, and a wheel of fortune. All booths are to be manned by the Masons, Lions, Job's Daughters, Rotary, Kiwanis, and Veterans of Foreign Wars.

Christian Scientists aren't big joiners, and I don't belong to anything. But I'm caught up in the festival excitement, idly hoping that I might win a plastic bag with a goldfish in it, a perennial dream. I'm captivated by the spectacle of tall ships, which are arriving by the day in the waters of Lake Washington and Puget Sound—gorgeous wooden schooners and brigs and barques flying their sails and flags like the pirate fleet in *Treasure Island*.

Mercer Island feels benign at this moment, sparkling in the fine July weather. There's much to do down in the center—grocery shopping at Art's Food Center and bagels at Mama Reuben's Bakery and sandwiches at Alpenland, my mother's favorite place for lunch. There's Mercer Island Cyclery, full of new bikes that smell deliciously of rubber, and Chick's Shoe Service, where my mother gets her shoes reheeled, and Look's Pharmacy, which has paperbacks and comics on a revolving rack. Sometimes I'm allowed to walk down the hill to the center by myself, along a hidden path between banks of blackberry bushes.

But the island is not as nice as it looks. Hidden in the back pages of the *Mercer Island Reporter* on July 1, 1976, is news of a GIRL RAPED AT BURBANK, a fourteen-year-old attacked by a man with a knife who offered to help her fix her bike.[39] There's an item about Bob Tall, sixteen, who dies in a boat accident on Lake Washington, and news of vandals breaking fourteen windows in local schools, including my old school, East Seattle. There's a report of a man exposing himself to five kids at Island Crest Children's Park.

On the Fourth, we stroll through the new park, which is about as big as a handkerchief. Later, we barbecue hot dogs in our backyard and see fireworks over the tops of the trees. During the parade, a sixteen-year-old girl is arrested for toasting a passing police officer with a bottle of beer. The next week, after the celebrations, there's more school vandalism and an exploding mailbox. Jewelry is stolen, cars are ransacked, and the paper reports the heist of eight cases of fireworks, worth $474.24. A seventeen-year-old "youth" wipes out three bollards on Island Crest Way.[40]

Two doctors who live next to the Mercer Island Floating Bridge write an angry letter to the paper attacking opposition to the I-90 project, which is languishing in the courts during a decade-long dispute over its environmental impact statement. Failure to fix I-90 and the bridge is contributing to the decline of the neighborhood, they say, as if the deteriorating corridor amounts to a giant pothole for which everything is to blame: "slum"-style incidents, "prowlers, burglaries, a few fires . . . uncontrolled barking dogs, abandoned automobiles, etc."[41] How many of these might be the responsibility of George Waterfield Russell Jr. remains unknown.

They complain about "numerous awful automobile wrecks with frequent explosions on the highway and bridge right next to us." Alarming,

THE DUTCH DOOR

to be sure, but these accidents represent a professional opportunity for one island boy. In the coming years, Owen Blauman, enterprising younger brother of my classmate Byron, whose family lives next to the bridge, will hear the crashes and sirens and run up the hill to the bridge deck with his camera to take pictures of the carnage for the *Mercer Island Reporter*.

ON JULY 15, 1976, ASARCO issues a press release, "Tacoma Smelter Arsenic Emissions Pose No Threat to Maury and Vashon Island Residents." This is a bald-faced lie, but since ASARCO has taken over state testing of affected children, it can say whatever it likes. The corporation, through the smelter's "environmental specialist," begins communicating directly with parents, issuing calming statements claiming that "small amounts" of arsenic may show up in children's urine and then be rapidly and completely eliminated.[42] It's all just part of the "normal function" of the human body, the specialist says, although at least one child has been exposed to an arsenic concentration of 184 micrograms per liter, an amount then considered to be more than ten times normal.[43]

ON OCTOBER 22, 1976, Ted Bundy is formally charged with the murder of Caryn Campbell, a case based largely on the two hairs found in his VW and gas receipts placing him in the vicinity. He's been held in maximum security in the state prison ever since it was discovered that he was planning an escape, having acquired fake identification papers while working in the prison's printing department, as well as a schedule of flights to Portland and Seattle.[44]

In order to be present for the upcoming hearings, motions, and trial, he will be extradited to Colorado.

ON ONE OF HIS RARE forays back home, my brother has gotten married, to a classmate he met as a child at East Seattle School, and they are leaving the island forever. My sister is planning to get married too, just as soon as she graduates from college the coming spring.

As I see her engineering her escape, the question arises: How am *I* going to get out of here? Who am *I* going to marry? I look around. There's no one. I've never been on a date.

I'm in high school, so I pick someone who appeals to me: Neil Diamond. I don't know him, but that seems like a minor issue, easily solved. He's always on the radio, and I have one of his cassettes, which I listen to over and over on a tape recorder my father has borrowed from work. *Cherry, cherry.* My name is Caroline, and he's written a song just for me. It's a famous song, and it must mean something.

I write him a letter explaining my feelings, suggesting that he come and pick me up. I mail it to him at the address on the cassette, an address for Columbia Records on Wilshire Boulevard in Los Angeles. And then I wait.

I'm glad to skip the dating phase. Listening to girls sitting around me in Spanish class, everybody knows somebody who knows somebody who almost went out with Ted Bundy. It's a mark of distinction, a brush with celebrity, but we also know that someone's been snatching girls off the street and taking them into the mountains and cutting their heads off. So where does that leave us?

I'm doing well enough in English and Spanish but am unable to grasp the complexities of genetics in biology class. I ask the teacher, Mr. Gaylord Hall, if I can talk to him after class. My heart pounding, I lay before him an incoherent tissue of lies—that I cannot be expected to study genetics because of my Christian Science background, that I must be extended some kind of exemption. I hint that I may not be around much longer (I'm planning to skip town with Neil Diamond), and I see waves of distaste, confusion, and suspicion flashing across his face.

Mr. Hall is the father of one of my longtime classmates. She's an awkward and vulnerable presence, often bullied, who has never learned to scowl as repressively as I have. I have avoided his daughter, lest her unpopularity attach itself to me, and yet I've been to his house. He puts me off, suggesting that he'll consider it, and nothing ever happens. Neil Diamond never arrives. I receive a poor grade in biology and from then on avoid the entire hallway where Mr. Hall holds sway.

ON JANUARY 12, 1977, Bunker Hill officials announce a partial shutdown of operations at its blast furnace, fuming plant, lead refinery, electric furnace, and baghouse because of "stagnant air."[45] Just how bad could it be to justify the decision to shut down the plant? No one's saying.

LATER THAT MONTH, I attend the 1977 Star Trek Convention at the Olympic Hotel, an event studded with "11 Guest Celebrities, 9 Fan-Oriented Contests, 8 Star Trek Episodes, 2 Animated Episodes, and 16 Major Motion Pictures." Guests include Robbie the Robot from *Forbidden Planet*, sci-fi writers Robert A. Heinlein and Harlan Ellison, George "Sulu" Takei, and the guy who wrote the "Trouble with Tribbles" episode, in which Captain Kirk finds his ship overwhelmed by rapidly reproducing guinea pig–like space creatures.

I've been invited by my friend Jeff. He's rented a room in the Olympic Hotel with a bunch of friends and conference organizers, including a nineteen-year-old woman who ends up spending the weekend with Harlan Ellison. It's not lost on me that male celebrities, whether they're Elvis or Ellison or Ted Bundy, prefer girls on the younger side, and the affair becomes the talk of the con, bestowing a nebulous form of status on the chosen one.

The whole thing feels faintly ridiculous. Wandering the halls are kids with rubber Spock ears and Captain Kirk shirts. Robbie the Robot is imposing, but all he can do is rotate his metal chest and wave his flipper-like arms. Still, attending is another way of annoying my father, who can't seem to muster doctrinal objections to this latest bizarre development.

What he doesn't know is that I've also joined Jeff at the convention's on-site Red Cross blood donation drive, fascinated to watch a needle dipping into my vein. I proudly collect a little cup of orange juice.

What I love is the movies, shown in hushed auditoriums—*2001: A Space Odyssey*, *Fantastic Planet*, *The War of the Worlds*—and *Star Trek* episodes, especially "The City on the Edge of Forever," written and ultimately reviled by Ellison. It's a romantic episode in which Captain Kirk, Spock, and Dr. McCoy travel back in a time machine to Depression-era New York City, where Kirk falls in love with a soup kitchen worker played by Joan Collins. In a tragic twist, Kirk is forced to sacrifice his one true love: she must die in a traffic accident in order to prevent changes to future time, such as Nazi Germany acquiring the atom bomb and winning the war.

After seeing this episode, I dedicate myself to reading everything Harlan Ellison has ever written. Pyramid, a publisher of cheap paperbacks, has seen fit to reproduce much of the writer's prodigious output: *Deathbird Stories*, *Love Ain't Nothing But Sex Misspelled*, *Gentleman Junkie*, and my favorite, *I Have No Mouth & I Must Scream*, the title story devoted to a grotesquely dystopian future in which humans have lost a genocidal war to an Allied Mastercomputer, which keeps a few specimens alive to amuse itself by torturing them forever.

I acquire these books, with their transgressive titles and lurid covers, and hide them behind *Little House on the Prairie* and other things with a higher parental acceptance value. In church, sitting on a wooden pew during the Wednesday evening testimony meetings or the even more deadly, if rare, Christian Science lecture, I hunker into myself and think vengefully, over and over, *I have no mouth and I must scream*.

What interests me most about Harlan Ellison is his ruminations on how he, a small Jewish boy growing up as a pariah in Painesville, Ohio, became a writer, earning pennies a word from pulp magazines and then graduating to the big time as a scriptwriter in Hollywood. He lays it all out in the essays he writes for the *Los Angeles Free Press*, collected in *The Glass Teat* and *The Other Glass Teat*. I adopt this as my new career path. This is how I'm going to get out.

THE DUTCH DOOR

DOWN IN WICHITA, after a long absence, Dennis Rader returns to the killing field. He has been casing houses and working up a number of potential victims. But for one reason or another—barking dogs, nobody home when he comes calling—he has not been successful in bringing any of his "projects" to completion.

Growing agitated, he strikes at random on March 17, 1977, parking his car at Dillons grocery store, where he shoplifts film for his camera and buys true-crime magazines and uses the copy machine to make his homemade pornography. He follows a young boy walking down a nearby residential street. Dennis stops the child to ask if he recognizes the people in the photo he pulls from his wallet, who happen to be his own wife and baby. The boy says no and continues to his own house as Dennis watches.

Dennis then knocks on the door, and the boy, six, and his eight-year-old brother open it. They're watching cartoons. Their mother is sick in bed with a stomach flu. Wearing what he calls his "James Bond jacket" and "nice shoes," carrying a small suitcase with his murder kit, Dennis forces his way in, pretending to be a private detective. When the boys' mother, Shirley Vian, twenty-four, comes out of her bedroom, wearing a robe and a pink nightgown, he pulls out his .357 Magnum. He tries to tie up the boys, but they start screaming. He enlists Shirley's help in forcing them, along with their younger sister, into the bathroom, tying the doorknob to a pipe under the sink and barring the door by shoving a bed in front of it. He's already planning to do to Shirley Vian's daughter what he did to the Oteros' youngest girl.

He proceeds to hog-tie Shirley in the bedroom, stripping her and binding her with black electrical tape. At one point she vomits, and he gets her a glass of water from the kitchen. According to his own recollection, he comforts her "a little bit," boasting that "this compassion runs in most of my crimes."[46] Then he places a large white plastic garbage bag over her head and strangles her with her own nightgown and a piece of parachute cord he's brought with him.

The children, who have managed to force a small opening in the bathroom door, can see some of what's happening and are screaming and crying. Dennis is unable to complete his planned activities because of their racket. A ringing telephone alarms him, putting him off his game, so he throws his gun and the rest of his items back in his suitcase and takes off.

In the next few minutes, one of the boys succeeds in breaking the bathroom window and alerting neighbors, but when the EMTs arrive, it's too late. Dennis doesn't care. Messy as it was, the project was a triumph as far as he's concerned, because he has succeeded in killing Shirley Vian and stealing her underwear.

ON APRIL 23, 1977, I attend another festival on the island: Circus McGurkus. The name comes from nursery school books by Dr. Seuss, and the homemade food, booths, and games are meant for children three to eight years old. It's a fundraiser for the preschool association, set up outdoors on the Mercer Island High School campus. Some of my friends are working the booths, and I stroll around, wistfully watching the goldfish toss. If you win, you get a chit for a live goldfish at Island Pets.

I'm too old for goldfish now, my mother has told me, although I would still like one. Instead I get chicken pox, and I instantly assume it came from the Paint-the-Face booth, where sticky toddlers have their faces painted like Indian chiefs while eating snow cones. Later that afternoon, sitting on the couch with my mother, she begins looking at my face and tells me to go to bed in the middle of the day. I can't imagine what she's talking about, but I do it anyway. Soon I'm very hot, and the bed has inexplicably turned into *Death Valley Days*. I'm crossing the desert with the Borax Twenty Mule Team, watching what's happening like a movie in my mind. The movie lasts for hours, days, but I'm cautioned against coughing, because I'm not supposed to disturb my father. He doesn't want to know that I'm sick. My mother slips me a couple of orange-flavored children's aspirin on the sly.

THE DUTCH DOOR

THE WEEK I'M IN BED with the chicken pox, a 1975 Ford van, going eastbound on the Mercer Island floating bridge, loses control and bounces across the road, striking the south curb. It lands on the bridge railing before skidding another thirty to forty feet and flipping over and striking a bridge stanchion, crushing the van's roof to within two inches of the floor and killing two of the passengers behind the driver's seat. The van severs a bridge cable and damages an electrical box housing the reverse lane signals. The *Mercer Island Reporter*'s full coverage, BULGE TAKES TWO LIVES and TWO KILLED ON BRIDGE, features photographs and gory descriptions of the crushed van and the damaged bridge right beside a photo of Circus McGurkus.[47]

At some point during 1977, after years in which his island peccadilloes were brushed aside, George Waterfield Russell Jr. is convicted of possession of marijuana and criminal trespass.

ON MAY 23, 1977, the same day that he pleads not guilty to the murder of Caryn Campbell, Ted writes a personal note to law enforcement in an old Filofax datebook: "Now what's a nice F.B.I. agent like you doing snooping in a book like this. Best Regards, Never Again, ted."[48] He makes a habit of signing his name with a lowercase *t*, which he believes expresses humility. But the "Never Again" is suggestive of the fact that Ted is planning to go on the lam.

In January, Utah lent Ted to the State of Colorado as if he were a library book, and Colorado has promptly mislaid him. He is housed in the state's Garfield County Jail but regularly attends hearings at the courthouse in Aspen. As his own attorney, Ted demands the right to do research in the law library, upstairs on the second floor. The library has large, unsecured sash windows.

On June 7, unshackled, asking to use the phone in the library, he watches as his guard steps away to smoke a cigarette. Then he opens the window, twenty-five feet off the ground, and jumps out. He's planned ahead and is wearing two layers of clothes and a heavy sweater; he's been practicing by leaping off the top bunk in his cell. He sprains an ankle, but that doesn't stop him from running through town and up into the hills.

It's cold in the mountains at night, as Ted has reason to know. He finds an empty cabin where he hides briefly. After several days of walking in circles, he becomes weak and hypothermic and returns to Aspen. Trailed by men, dogs, and helicopters, he's apprehended at around two o'clock in the morning on June 13, behind the wheel of a blue Cadillac he's trying to steal.

ON THE ISLAND, things are getting frenzied, the youth more unruly, the parties more raucous, the accidents more extreme. Community meetings are held about drug use at the schools. Experts inform concerned parents that the "pushers" are their own children, which is true.[49]

On the night of June 24, Craig Nelson and Greg Slater, both twenty-one, are driving a 1974 four-door Datsun sedan at a high speed on a curving stretch of West Mercer Way after drinking too much, and the car leaves the roadway. Both survive, but Nelson is cited for reckless driving and driving without a license.

The following night there's a more spectacular crash, also on West Mercer Way, killing two passengers. A Volkswagen Beetle driven by twenty-year-old Mitchell Guy "Mad Dog" Maddock swerves onto the shoulder, overcorrects, crosses the centerline, and rolls, sliding seventy-eight feet on its roof before hitting a power pole. During these maneuvers, a passenger in the back seat, Thomas Olson, twenty, is thrown through the rear window, but his foot catches in the frame and he's dragged for a considerable distance to his death. Another passenger, Kevin Harris, twenty-two, dies of severe head injuries. Mad Dog survives with head lacerations and contusions.[50]

The community is staggered as well by the fate of Mercer Island track star Pete Dawson, eighteen. After a senior beer bash held on May 20 near Bremerton, a party attended by some three hundred minors, Dawson is blinded when the motorcycle he's riding collides head-on with another

THE DUTCH DOOR

motorcycle. A bitter debate over irresponsible teenage drinking ensues. Dawson and his parents, however, take a more measured tone, asserting that everyone must take responsibility for themselves. Dawson's father tells the newspaper, "We live in a violent age."[51]

We certainly do. By 1977, more than half of the children in the country have what are termed "very high blood lead levels," and island youth, bathed in leaded gas and fallout from the smelter plume, may have higher levels than most.[52]

IN EL PASO, where the smelter is still smoking away, levels are certainly high. Richard Ramirez is registered at Jefferson High School, but he isn't doing a lot of studying. He's a known truant. He's breaking into neighborhood houses and apartments at night, learning how to be a hot prowler from his brother-in-law Roberto. They like standing in bedrooms staring at sleeping couples. It gives them a thrill.

Richard has a .22 rifle, given to him by his father, and he enjoys going out in the desert and shooting coyotes, rabbits, and birds. He's an excellent shot and becomes proficient at stalking animals quietly. He loves eviscerating the bodies with a knife, feeding the entrails to his dog, Indio. He sleeps in the cemetery often and has persistent sexual fantasies about sadism and bondage. Resentful of his parents' Catholic teachings, he becomes interested in Satan.

While still in high school, he gets a job at a Holiday Inn as a maintenance man and begins pilfering wallets and jewelry, using his passkey to walk into bedrooms while guests are asleep. On other occasions he stares through bathroom windows at women as they undress. One night, watching a buxom woman enter a bathroom, he sneaks around to the room's front door, enters with the key, and hides in a closet, springing on her from behind as she comes out. He rips off her underwear and ties her up with it, but her husband returns and swiftly beats Richard unconscious. It's Richard's first arrest for a violent crime, but for some reason the couple at the Holiday Inn decide not to press charges.

MURDERLAND

On October 17, 1977, the naked body of Yolanda Washington is found dead just outside Forest Lawn Memorial Park, cemetery to the stars in the Hollywood Hills. At nineteen, she was said to be the most gorgeous woman working on the Sunset Strip. There are ligature marks on her neck, wrists, and ankles; her legs are posed akimbo; and she's been raped.

The day after Halloween, the naked body of Judith Miller, fifteen, a former student at Hollywood High School, is found in a neighborhood north of downtown L.A., showing the same kinds of marks. She has been raped and sodomized.

Not long after, Catharine Lorre, twenty-four-year-old daughter of actor Peter Lorre, is walking with a friend near the corner of Hawthorne and Highland, a few blocks from the Musso & Frank Grill on Hollywood Boulevard. Two men in a car pull alongside them, flashing badges, claiming to be vice cops, demanding identification.

Born in Germany, Catharine pulls papers out of her purse, and the men see photos of her father. He starred in Fritz Lang's *M* in 1931, about a serial murderer of girls. Cornered at the end, Lorre's character cries out, "I cannot help myself! I have no control over this evil thing that is inside me—the fire, the voices, the torment!"

The men are Angelo Buono and Kenneth Bianchi, and together they are the entity known as the Hillside Strangler. They let Catharine walk on.

In November, working at night, Ted begins furtively sawing an opening in the ceiling around a square metal plate securing the light fixture in his cell at the Garfield County Jail. He's using a hacksaw blade acquired from another inmate. Despite his successful escape at the courthouse, he's still being held at this old and poorly maintained facility. Repairs are scheduled for the electrical system and light fixtures, but no one's gotten around to it.

During preparation for the first attempt, he lost twenty-five pounds. After he's recaptured, he begins skipping breakfast and loses five more.

THE DUTCH DOOR

He's working out. He's prevailed upon Ann Rule and his latest female acolyte, his Olympia friend Carole Ann Boone, to send him packages of protein powder, vitamins, nuts, and dried fruit. He has hundreds of items in his cell, so much miscellaneous crap that it hides a multitude of sins. There's a typewriter, legal files, civilian clothes, blankets, a small metal Christmas tree with five candy canes, three pine cones, and seven Christmas tree ornaments. Soap, a cigar, packs of Salem Lights, and a screwdriver. In a well-run jail, much of this would be contraband.

He has a radio from Kmart and stacks of magazines (*Time, Rolling Stone, Esquire, Penthouse, Playboy, People, The New Yorker*), volumes of *Criminal Law Digest*, and books by Hunter S. Thompson and Pearl S. Buck. He has *Shōgun* and *Tai-Pan*, by James Clavell; *Julian*, by Gore Vidal; and *The Gulag Archipelago*, by Aleksandr Solzhenitsyn. *The Return of the King*, by J. R. R. Tolkien. *Zen and the Art of Motorcycle Maintenance. Understanding Media*, by Marshall McLuhan. *Human Hair Analysis and Comparison.* Norman Vincent Peale and Edgar Cayce. A police supply catalog.

He has a copy of his favorite book, Henri Charrière's *Papillon*, THE SENSATIONAL BEST SELLER OF A MAGNIFICENT REBEL WHO WOULD LIVE FREE—OR NOT AT ALL.

He has safety razors and Mennen aftershave and Chanel for Men. He has a jar of Vaseline, which, among other things, may ease his exfiltration through the narrow hole in the ceiling.[53]

IN KANSAS, researchers will eventually complain that there is a "paucity" of research on elevated blood lead levels statewide. But findings ultimately show that the highest such levels historically are found in southeastern Kansas, part of the midwestern "lead belt."[54] Where Dennis Rader spent much of his formative years.

But Dennis Rader has never really grown up and still talks like a child in a man's body. On December 8, 1977, he embarks on what he calls PJ Foxtail, or Project Fox, at a duplex apartment at 843 South Pershing in

Wichita, an address belonging to Nancy Fox, twenty-five, who works in a jewelry store. He likes the fact that the word *fox* has three letters and sounds like *sex*.

No door, no window can keep him out. While Nancy Fox is at work, he cuts the phone line, scores a hole in the glass of a double-hung window at the back of her house, and enters, waiting for her to return. When you're breaking and entering, he says, "there's a powerful feeling as you enter someone's territory, the smell and fixtures surround you [and there are] unexplored parts of the house, with treasures to find and keep. It is a violation to them, yes, sort of mental rape."[55]

This project goes more smoothly than earlier ones. When Fox arrives, he pulls a gun on her and tells her that he has a sexual problem. He wants to tie her up and take pictures. She's upset, so he allows her to smoke a cigarette and go to the bathroom, where he directs her to disrobe. He handcuffs her with her hands behind her back, then ties her up. He strangles her with a belt until she passes out, then revives her, whispering in her ear that he's BTK, that he's a bad man. "That's my torture," he'll say later.[56] Then he strangles her again, with pantyhose, masturbating and ejaculating into her blue nightgown as she dies. Blue is one of his favorite colors.

He takes lingerie, a necklace, and her driver's license as his trophies. He hides them in his hidey-holes.

IN THE LAST TWO WEEKS of December, Ted Bundy is able to squeeze through the twelve-by-twelve-inch opening several times and explore the crawl space above, but he's terrified that the hole will be discovered. He's on the cusp of being transferred to another facility, since the judge has granted a change of venue to Colorado Springs.

On the night of December 30, the jailer who lives in the apartment above the cells goes to a movie with his wife, and Ted Bundy slides through the hole, emerging in a closet in their apartment. He's out the door, and he's free.

Chapter 10

The Volcano

———◇———

Indian legends tell of a great eruption.
—*Rules and Regulations: Mount Rainier*
National Park, 1924

On January 7, 1978, a child is born. Not in a manger, exactly, but close. Israel Keyes enters the world in Cove, a census-designated spot on the map in the northernmost reaches of the state of Utah, north of Logan and almost at the Idaho state line, with a population of only a few hundred remote souls.

His parents, Jeff Keyes and Heidi Haakanson, are both in their twenties, both Mormons from Los Angeles. The child is born at home, as was their first, Israel's older sister, America, who arrived in 1976. Jeff hates doctors. He has never been immunized. He doesn't trust modern medicine and will not enter a hospital. He doesn't believe in birth certificates or Social Security numbers. He is a loner and a God-botherer. He's about to move his family to Washington State.

Reborn out of the Garfield County jailer's closet and dressed in the man's clothes, Ted drives out of Glenwood Springs in an MG Midget he finds with the keys in the ignition.

He makes it halfway to Vail, around thirty miles, before getting stuck in the snow. Hitchhiking the rest of the way, he asks a cop where he can wait until the weather clears. The cop suggests the Holiday Inn. Thanks to the criminal incompetence of Garfield County specifically and the State of Colorado generally, as well as the pile of books he's concealed under a blanket back in his cell, no one realizes he's missing.

He has $500 in cash, saved from the largesse of family and friends. He asks for rides from folks in the hotel lounge but finally shells out for a Trailways bus ticket to Denver. There he catches a flight to Chicago, then takes the train to Ann Arbor, Michigan, where he stays in a YMCA on the University of Michigan campus. He's always liked college campuses.

No one knows he's missing until lunchtime on December 31, by which point he's in Chicago and on to points east. At the YMCA, he shaves off the beard but not the mustache. He gets his hair cut short. On January 2, 1978, he watches the Washington Huskies defeat Michigan in the Rose Bowl in a college bar and drinks so much he throws up in the bathroom. The next day, he's looking for a car to steal.

On January 4 he finds one and drives to Atlanta, eager to get out of the cold. Once there, he goes to a sporting goods store, steals a sleeping bag, wipes down the car, and abandons it. Then he goes to the Omni Center to see *The Sting*, a movie celebrating an elaborate plot devised by two cunning and attractive con men, played by Paul Newman and Robert Redford. Later, he boards a bus to Tallahassee, Florida.

Okay, let's take out the map. Run a ruler or a straightedge or a piece of yarn along the OWL. Run it clear down through the country on the diagonal, slicing the United States in two, southeast through the Tetons and the cornfields of Kansas and the black soil of Arkansas. It'll come out somewhere in the Southeast. Say, Tallahassee. If you're an animal on the run and your frontal cortex is picking up weaknesses in the continental crust, singing sensations of fault zones and hot spots, movements in the lithosphere that ping the lead in your brain and speak to you through the nonunion of your coronal suture, these messages may well urge you to go to the Florida State University campus and kill women.

THE VOLCANO

After Ted's arrival, he lasts nine days before he explodes. He spends that time renting a room furnished with a table, chair, chest of drawers, and bare mattress at the Oaks, a once gracious old three-story Florida mansion carved into a rooming house for students. In the front yard is a five-hundred-year-old specimen. He gives his name as Chris Hagen.

The Oaks is called "the Oak Club" by residents, a name full of irony, given what's to come.[1] It's reminiscent of the popular Tony Orlando song from a few years earlier, "Tie a Yellow Ribbon Round the Ole Oak Tree." It's about a man who's getting out of prison and wants to know if his girlfriend still loves him. For him, it's been three long years. For Ted, it's not even two.

He occupies himself by hanging around the registrar's office, the main FSU library, and local businesses. He steals things, nice things: a red Raleigh bicycle, a Smith Corona typewriter, a portable Panasonic TV for his room, a Sony transistor radio, a license plate, and a golf umbrella. He steals a student identification card in the name of Kenneth Misner and uses the typewriter to request a copy of Misner's birth certificate. He steals money out of women's purses at the grocery store. He shoplifts food. At night he drinks a quart of beer and watches TV and then heads out into the night. He pretends he's jogging.

He has reason to be concerned. His latest escape will eventually earn him a place on the FBI's Ten Most Wanted Fugitives list and become national news, the stuff of legend and late-night comedy routines. People have T-shirts made up that say, RUN, TED, RUN. People think it's funny.

ON JANUARY 10, 1978, an electrical power failure occurs at the ASARCO smelter in El Paso, forcing an emergency shutdown and causing a massive, gaseous cloud of sulfur trioxide to belch out of its new acid plant, float across I-10, and hover over downtown.* The county chief of environmental health services, Ruben Kretzschmar, is unable to tell the public how

---

* Sulfur trioxide is a strongly acidic corrosive gas or liquid used in making detergents. In manufacturing, SO_3 gives off irritating toxic fumes.

damaging the gas might be to their health, venturing a guess that it might cause lung problems. It certainly might: it's corrosive and carcinogenic. A precursor to sulfuric acid and a component of acid rain, it can, in sufficient quantities, cause death. It comes out of industrial smokestacks, volcanoes, and hell.

Kretzschmar, however, is quick to absolve ASARCO of any blame, saying, "It was one of those things that nobody could have avoided. It was just something they could not control."[2]

ON SATURDAY, JANUARY 14, Ted steals chicken and potato salad from a convenience store for lunch and eats it at a local schoolyard. By that evening he's wearing a dark navy-blue jacket, tan or light-colored pants, and a dark knit cap over his hair. He's actually wearing two sets of clothing, one atop the other, and carrying three pairs of women's pantyhose, stolen from a laundromat or off a clothesline. Two of them have been altered to serve as ligatures, the right leg cut off and the left looped through the hole. The third pair is a mask, with holes cut for eyes and mouth. It's a cold night for Tallahassee, below freezing.

At around 9:00 p.m., several girls are walking on campus when a man in a dark jacket, light pants, and a dark hat starts following them. They walk faster. He calls out, "Hey girls!" They run.

At quarter past nine, he's casing the apartment of Cheryl Thomas, twenty-one, an FSU dance student who lives alone in half of a ground-floor duplex on Dunwoody Street, ten blocks from the Oaks. He watches as she leaves for the night, then enters the apartment, leaving a kitchen window cracked open. Then he heads back toward the Oaks.

On his way, he passes the Chi Omega sorority house. The Oaks is four blocks from Chi Omega, which is itself next door to Sherrod's, a popular nightclub. It's Saturday night, and Sherrod's is hopping, the dance floor packed. Sorority girls are coming and going, stopping at the club before heading out with friends to other parties on campus. Several notice a man who's older than the college-age clientele, a man in a dark jacket with a hat, standing with his arms folded, staring at girls. He asks one of them to dance and she turns to her friend and says, "Look at this guy I'm getting ready to dance with. He looks like an ex-con."[3] Whatever superficial polish he once possessed is gone. Now he's just a creep.

Shortly after midnight, Ted returns to Dunwoody Street and sees a light on: Cheryl Thomas has just gotten home.[4] Once again, he heads back in the direction of the Oaks, planning to drink more before returning. He wants to enter when the light is off, when the woman inside is asleep.

At 1:15 a.m. the morning of January 15, FSU student Cheryl Rafferty parks her car in a campus lot a couple of blocks from the Chi Omega house. She gets out and locks the door, only to be startled when a man in a dark jacket, khaki-colored pants, and a dark ski hat comes out of the bushes near her. She begins walking; he follows. She starts running, dashing into a campus building across the street.

Sherrod's nightclub closes at two, and most of the sorority sisters have returned to the Chi Omega house by three. Most are asleep.

Shortly after three, Ted picks up a heavy oak log about two feet long off a woodpile next to the Chi Omega building and pulls open a back door with a combination lock. Either it's been left open or the lock fails. He runs silently upstairs to the second floor. Near the end of the hall is the room where Margaret Bowman, twenty-one, a woman with long dark hair, is sleeping; her roommate is away. He beats her unmercifully over the right forehead, crushing her skull. Bark from the log flies around the room and catches in her hair. He strangles her with one of his pantyhose ligatures, accidentally dropping the other one on the empty bed next to her, then pulls the bedspread over her body.

In the room next to Margaret he finds two women, also asleep, Karen Chandler and Kathy Kleiner, and lays into them with the log, breaking their jaws. Across the hall, he darts into another room where Lisa Levy, twenty-one, lies sleeping. He beats her and strangles her, biting the nipple off her right breast and twice sinking his teeth deep into her left buttock, leaving livid tooth marks. He grabs a Clairol hair spray bottle and uses it to sodomize her rectum and vagina. He then covers her with a sheet and makes his way down the stairs.[5]

On his way out, he is seen. Nita Neary, twenty, is returning home from a date after 3:15 a.m. and notices that the side door is unlocked. She's downstairs, turning off lights that have been left on in the living room and foyer, when she hears someone descending the stairs and sees a man hunched by the front door. She catches sight of his profile as he's opening the door and gains an impression of his long, straight, pointed nose and thin lips. She sees that he's wearing a dark ski-type cap pulled low over his forehead, a dark jacket, and light-colored pants. In his right hand he's carrying a thick, dark club. Then he's out the door.

Nita Neary is scandalized and alarmed. Men aren't allowed on the second floor, and the year before, her former roommate was attacked and beaten in the woods nearby, a case that remains unsolved. She runs upstairs and wakes the Chi Omega house president, but just as she's finishing relating news of the intruder, Karen Chandler stumbles out of her room. At first the sisters assume she's drunk, but then they see blood on her face. Kathy Kleiner is found huddled on her bed, bleeding from the mouth and moaning. The walls of their room are spattered with blood, and the house is in an uproar, but Margaret Bowman and Lisa Levy have not appeared.

Police are called and arrive at 3:22 a.m. They check all the rooms, finding Margaret's dead body. Lisa Levy has a faint pulse, and EMTs attempt to revive her, but she is dead on arrival at the hospital.

In the meantime, Ted is heading to his next appointment. He's seen by eyewitnesses, who notice a man walking surreptitiously, carrying a long, dark club next to his leg. He returns to Cheryl Thomas's duplex on Dunwoody Street, crawling in the kitchen window. He knocks a potted plant to the floor, waking Cheryl, who thinks it's her cat, then springs on her, beating her with a club, either the same oak club brought from Chi Omega or a different heavy object. He ejaculates onto the bedsheet. The beating is so loud that Cheryl's two women friends who live in the other half of the duplex hear thunderous banging and whimpering through the wall. They have an agreement with Cheryl that if they're ever anxious about security, they'll call each other, even if it's the middle of the night. The women call Cheryl's number. When there's no response, they call 911 at 4:37 a.m.

The first call likely saves her life. Ted is alarmed by the ringing phone. In the melee, his pantyhose mask is pulled off and left in the bed, with several of his hairs.[6] He shoves the kitchen table over to the window and jumps out, likely discarding his weapon somewhere in the heavy growth that surrounds much of the campus. It's never found.

As police race from the Chi Omega scene to her apartment, Cheryl Thomas is groaning and writhing in pain. The sweater she was wearing in bed has been ripped off, and her severe injuries include five skull fractures, multiple contusions, a broken jaw, and a dislocated shoulder. One of her cranial nerves is severed. She will suffer profound hearing loss in her left ear and persistent problems with balance and equilibrium. She will no longer be able to dance.

Karen Chandler has suffered a broken jaw, a broken arm, and a crushed finger. Her teeth have been knocked out, and numerous facial bones crushed. Kathy Kleiner likewise has serious facial injuries, her jaw broken in three places. She's suffering from whiplash in her neck and lacerations on her shoulder. Both women are hospitalized, undergoing multiple surgeries.

When the news hits Seattle, everyone knows.

IN THE NEW YEAR on Mercer Island, adults are preoccupied with juvenile crime, vandalism, and property destruction involving multiple cases of felony arson. Throughout the 1970s, a number of serious and potentially life-threatening fires are set, presumably by island children. A portable building at an elementary school is burned, totaling $22,500; a fire at South Mercer Junior High costs $70,000; another at Mercer Crest, $20,000.[7]

Professor Ellis Evans, an expert on adolescent development at the

University of Washington, is brought in to tell parents that "national trends show steady increases in the number of youthful offenders each year this decade."[8] He talks about drugs and alcohol and how they alter the nervous system, but he doesn't talk about other substances in the air and the water. He doesn't talk about lead in the lake or arsenic accumulating in the needles of pine trees.

Much of the vandalism remains trivial, if expensive and annoying—kids kicking in lockers, breaking windows and lights, and applying graffiti to walls. An elaborate mural of marijuana leaves and bong pipes appears at Lakeridge Elementary. The district supervisor of grounds and maintenance notes dryly that "the spelling has improved over the years," but decries the constant thieving of costly lighted exit signs, stolen to decorate rebellious teens' rooms.

I don't steal signs, but I am fixated on preparing my own exit. I too am a prowler. If I wait until my parents are asleep, I find that I can creep into the living room by keeping to the side of the hall, where the carpeted floor doesn't squeak. There I can write in my notebook, look out into the night, and even watch television with the sound tuned as low as it will go, my ear pressed against the speaker. In this way I am able to see many valuable episodes of *Star Trek*, including "The Menagerie," in which Captain Pike and the woman Vina are kept in cages by a superior race of beings. The humans don't know it, but they're disfigured and dying. They can't see it because their minds have been taken over by a powerful reality distortion field. They escape, but in the end choose to return to their captors, wrapped in the soothing illusion that they are whole and well.

Dystopia appeals to me, and I'm quietly contemplating the end of human civilization.

On January 31, 1978, Dennis Rader sends a poem about "Shirley Locks," inspired by Shirley Vian, to *The Wichita Eagle*, written out on one of the three-by-five cards he uses to make homemade "slick ads," or pornographic pictures. The newspaper, however, takes no notice of the item, throwing it in a mail file and causing deep frustration to its author.

Soon he begins working on another poem, titled "Oh! Death to Nancy," an homage to his murder of Nancy Fox. It's a weird parody of an old Appalachian folk song, "O Death," which he's read in a library book. As with all his communications, it includes a number of discomfiting errors, and after the first five lines it shifts violently from the victim's perspective to the murderer's:

> *What is this taht I can see*
> *Cold icy hands taking hold of me*
> *for Death has come, you all can see.*
> *Hell has open it,s gate to trick me.*
> *Oh! Death, Oh! Death, can't you spare me, over for another year!*
> *I'll stuff your jaws till you can't talk*
> *I'll blind your leg's till you can't walk*
> *I'll tie your hands till you can't make a stand.*
> *And finally I'll close your eyes so you can't see*
> *I'll bring sexual death unto you for me.*[9]

Dennis fancies himself something of a poet. Many of his favorite women—his mother, his grandmother, his cousin's wife Betty—read poetry to him. His favorite poem as a child was "The Spider and the Fly."[10]

IN THE AFTERMATH of his night of murder and mayhem, Ted goes on a shopping spree, using money and credit cards stolen from wallets and purses at local grocery stores and bars, brazenly returning to Sherrod's nightclub to steal more. Many belong to women but carry a man's name, because 1970s corporate policy requires women to obtain a husband's or father's permission to apply.

He dines at the Tallahassee Holiday Inn and a local deli. He spends hundreds of dollars on clothes, socks, pajamas, tennis gear, luggage, sheets and towels, and smokers' paraphernalia, including a pipe, tobacco, and lighter. In arrears on his rent at the Oaks, he's erecting the scaffolding of a normal life out of possessions more suited to a Waspy New Englander than a felon whose résumé includes rape, murder, and necrophilia.

For several days, having earlier swiped a set of keys to a white van off the board in the media center, he's been trying to steal the van itself but has been frustrated. Alerted by the missing keys, students have deliberately been blocking it in with other vehicles. Studying the situation, Ted has copies made of the keys, then leaves the original set on the van's dashboard. Students remove the blocking vehicles. On February 5, he steals the van.[11]

He's seen buying gas in Lake City with a stolen credit card on February 7, his hands shaking. Lake City is around a hundred miles east of Tallahassee, a straight shot toward Jacksonville and the coast.

He drives to Jacksonville, enjoying a sumptuous meal at a Holiday Inn: shrimp cocktail, steak and lobster, blueberry pie with ice cream. After midnight, he checks into a different Holiday Inn.

On February 8, he leaves the hotel without checking out, buys more gas, and stops that afternoon at Green Acres Sporting Goods. He examines several knives before selecting a Buck 120 General hunting knife in the style of a Bowie, with a blade around six to eight inches long, for twenty-six dollars. Back in the van, he peels the price tag off and it falls to the floor.

Fifteen minutes later and a few miles away, he pulls up next to Leslie Ann Parmenter, a fourteen-year-old girl who's just left J. E. B. Stuart Middle School. Her brother is scheduled to pick her up, but Leslie misses him when she goes back into the school to fetch something from her locker. She's alone, walking through the parking lot of the Kmart adjacent to the school property, when Ted gets out of the van and approaches her. He's wearing a blue coat with a name tag on it that reads RICHARD BURTON, FIRE DEPARTMENT. He's unshaven, his hair unkempt, and Leslie is alarmed when he tries to talk to her, asking if she's going to Kmart. At that moment, Leslie's brother Danny, who is tall, older, and well-muscled, drives up in his pickup truck. The Parmenters' father is a homicide detective with the Jacksonville Sheriff's Office.

"Can I help you?" Danny demands aggressively. Ted gets back in the van and drives off, and Danny follows. The van gets away, but Danny writes down the license plate number. Ted flees west, back to Lake City. He stays at yet another Holiday Inn, charging a meal, four gins, and a draft beer. The desk clerk notes his appearance, which is slovenly and dazed.

The next morning, February 9, he's trolling another middle school, Lake City Junior High. It's a cold, rainy morning. Kim Leach, a twelve-year-old with bouncy shoulder-length brown hair, is talking to her friends in homeroom while buying a ticket to the Valentine's Day ball. When the bell rings, she walks to her next class, which is PE. Carrying her books, she forgets her purse. The homeroom teacher sends a note, asking her to come back and retrieve it. Outside, the student delivering the message sees a man standing across the street, staring. Kim heads back to homeroom and is recrossing the campus lawn when she's intercepted. She's wearing blue jeans, a blue football jersey with the number 83 on the front, a brown fur-lined coat, and Hush Puppies. Underneath her jersey is a white turtleneck.

An emergency medical technician who works at the Lake City Fire Department is leaving the night shift at the fire station and driving past the front of the junior high when he sees a white van stopped in the westbound lane, traffic backing up behind it. He watches as a man in his early thirties, around five foot ten with wavy brown hair, leads a young girl to the van, pulling her by the arm. The man is scowling, and the girl looks as if she's been crying. He assumes it's a father and daughter. He sees them drive off.

Farther along, another driver is forced to veer nearly off U.S. 90 when a white van swerves into her lane. She gets a glimpse of the man at the wheel, who seems to be shouting at someone in the passenger seat.

In the swampy wastes and scrublands outside Lake City, Ted turns off the main highway, finding cover. There, wherever that is, he assaults Kim Leach inside the back of the van, raping her and cutting her throat with the knife he bought the day before. He leaves her body in a hogpen with a collapsed tin roof, surrounded by fields, sinkholes, swampland, and woods, off a dirt road across from Suwanee River State Park. Departing from his longtime practice of disposing of personal items away from the body of his victim, a practice that has protected him for years, he deposits the rest of her clothing beside her. The garment left on her body is the white turtleneck, saturated with blood. She will not be found for fifty-seven days.

ON FEBRUARY 10, the same day that the FBI adds Bundy to its Most Wanted list, a receptionist at KAKE-TV in Wichita opens a letter from the BTK killer. It contains the Nancy Fox poem, a drawing of nooses, and a long missive claiming credit for the murders of Fox, the Otero family, Shirley Vian, and another, unnamed victim, likely Kathy Bright.

Dennis is frustrated with the police for suppressing news of his doings: "How many do I have to Kill before I get a name in the paper or some national attention. . . . Look a pattern is developing."[12] He supplies requisite details, adding hair-raising remarks about his thwarted intentions at some of the scenes. Shirley Vian's children were "very lucky," he observes, adding that he was going to bind the boys with black electrical tape, smother them with plastic bags, and then hang the girl. "God-oh God what a beautiful sexual relief that would have been," he writes.[13]

But despite Dennis's being, as he himself acknowledges, "a psycho," he raises important questions. Recalling his enjoyment of what he did to Josephine Otero, he talks about the mystery of what drives him:

> You don't understand these things because your not under the influence of factor X. The same thing that made Son of Sam, Jack the Ripper, Havery Glatman [sic], Boston Strangler, Dr. H. H. Holmes Panty Hose Strangler of Florida, Hillside Strangler, Ted of the West Coast and many more infamous character kill. Which seem s senseless, but we cannot help it. There is no help, no cure, except death or being caught and put away. It a terrible nightmarebut, you see I don't lose any sleep over it.[14]

How many people *does* he have to kill before somebody asks why? What *is* happening? What is "factor X"?

THE VOLCANO

Dennis doesn't know that "Ted of the West Coast" and the "Panty Hose Strangler of Florida," whose doings he has tracked with avidity, are the same person, but there are, in fact, a remarkable number of serial killings occurring simultaneously in the 1970s, many of them clustered in the Northwest or anywhere there are smelters or heavy traffic or both.

He's been following with pleasure and admiration the development of the man or men dubbed the "Hillside Strangler" in Los Angeles, an entity leaving numerous bodies of women and girls—some sex workers, some not—throughout Los Angeles in October and November 1977. Most of the bodies bear the marks of ligatures at the neck, wrists, and ankles; most are raped. There's Elissa "Lissa" Kastin, twenty-one, a professional dancer. There are two young girls, Dolores "Dolly" Cepeda, twelve, and Sonja Johnson, fourteen, last seen boarding a bus heading home. The girls' decomposing bodies, strangled and raped, are found by a nine-year-old boy picking through a trash heap near Dodger Stadium in November 1977.

There's Kristina Weckler, a twenty-year-old honors student at the Art Center College of Design, who's been raped, sodomized, and injected with Windex; Evelyn King, twenty-eight, an aspiring actress; and Lauren Wagner, eighteen, a business student who lives with her parents in the San Fernando Valley and whose body bears burn marks on her hands. There's Kimberly Martin, seventeen, a sex worker who's recently signed up with a call girl agency rather than work the streets on her own; she's afraid of the Hillside Strangler.

Dennis Rader is aware that there's a pattern to his own behavior but senses a larger pattern as well, one involving multiple serial rapists and killers operating all over the country, displaying versions of his pathology and variations of factor X.

As if to underline his point, on February 17, 1978, an orange Datsun, the wrecked car of the final California victim of the Strangler, is spotted by a helicopter pilot halfway down a cliff on the Angeles Crest Highway. Inside the trunk is the body of Cindy Hudspeth, twenty, a student and waitress who has been tied up, raped, tortured, and strangled, then placed in her car before it's pushed off a cliff. The Hillside Strangler, or at least one of them, is headed north, to Washington State.

ON FEBRUARY 10, Ted returns to the Oaks and goes on a dinner date with another resident, Frances Messier. They enjoy steaks at Chez Pierre, drinking two bottles of champagne. They return to his room to watch *The Rockford Files*. In the early hours of the following morning, he's caught trying to break into a green Toyota by a sheriff's deputy who notices that the Toyota is parked next to a white van. As the deputy is checking on his radio to see if the car is stolen, Ted runs for it, hiding in shrubbery nearby.

On February 12, Ted steals a couple of other cars but discovers they're unsafe at highway speeds. He finally finds an orange 1972 VW Beetle parked with its keys in the ignition. He steals it, returning to the Oaks to collect his belongings, which include twenty-two pairs of socks and four cheerleader magazines. He wipes down his room, having already scrubbed the inside of the white van with a rag dipped in Coca-Cola. Driving west to Pensacola, he tries to check into a hotel, but his stolen credit card is refused. On Valentine's Day, he drinks heavily, spends the day at a beach, and is briefly detained by a security guard that night after trying to lift a wallet from a woman's purse at a bar. When nothing is found to be missing, he's released.

In the early hours of February 15, he's pulling into a restaurant parking lot when he's spotted by a Pensacola patrolman, David Lee, who calls in the orange VW's plates to learn that it's been stolen. Lee turns on his flashers and a chase ensues, but Ted eventually pulls over and gets out of the car. Ordered to lie on the pavement, he waits until one handcuff is snapped on his wrist, then kicks Lee's ankles and runs. Lee fires a shot in the air, then another. Ted falls to the ground but is uninjured. He continues fighting as Lee attempts to handcuff him, but the patrolman gets the upper hand, cuffing and arresting him. When they arrive at the Pensacola police station, Ted gives his name as Kenneth Misner. In the mug shot, his face is puffy and swollen.

Inside a suitcase in the VW, among a litter of socks and boxer shorts, is a selection of books, including *Navigation the Easy Way* and *Piloting, Seamanship, and Small Boat Handling*. Escape by sea. In a briefcase is a Saint Christopher's medal.[15]

Over the next few days, he refuses to admit his real identity, and Florida officials are unsure who they're holding. Ted is on the ragged edge of sanity, exhausted, confused, and in alcohol withdrawal. He stumbles closer to honesty than he ever has before. He weeps. He makes veiled references to his "problem" and his "fantasies."[16] He tells one investigator that he drives around at night and feels "like a vampire."[17] He says, "I really can't talk about it," but urges detectives to keep looking. He says, "The evidence is there. Keep digging."[18] He suggests that they make a deal, offering his confessions in exchange for being sent to an institution in the Pacific Northwest. He wants to get out of Florida.

He calls John Henry Browne, a flamboyant Seattle defense attorney. He calls Liz and weeps some more, all but confessing to her, saying, "There is something the matter with me. It wasn't you. It was me. I just couldn't contain it. I've fought it for a long, long time."[19]

She's upset that the police are claiming that the murders started when she first met Ted, in 1969, but he says that the police "are years off." He tells her that he doesn't have a split personality or blackouts. "I remember everything I've ever done," he says.[20]

IN APRIL 1978, taking a step that seems only too tentative, the Centers for Disease Control lowers its definition of lead toxicity in children from an astonishingly high forty micrograms per deciliter of whole blood to the only slightly lower level of thirty. The ruling notes that "lead toxicity is defined as biochemical . . . or functional derangements caused by lead. Undue lead absorption refers to excess lead in the blood with evidence of biochemical derangements in the absence of clinical symptoms."[21]

The CDC doesn't know it, but functional derangements caused by lead are being seen all over the country, wherever men are repeatedly beating, raping, strangling, stabbing, and smothering women and children, as if compelled by some force as implacable as gravity.

A STATE TROOPER with the Florida Highway Patrol finds Kim Leach's body on April 7. The trooper has spotted a pile of cigarette butts dumped by the side of the highway, butts that resemble those recovered during the search of the white van, which has been located in Tallahassee. Combing the area, he discovers the badly decomposed remains.

According to a jailer at the county lockup, Ted begins hyperventilating when he hears the news, pacing and muttering. He's having trouble breathing until someone brings him a paper bag. He knows what he did.

ON APRIL 19, 1978, my grandmother Ruth Webb dies. She's eighty-two and hasn't been well all spring. She's had diabetes for years. A few days earlier, she'd suffered a stroke or the beginnings of a stroke. She's taken to Swedish Hospital, where I am not allowed to visit her, and she has a second stroke, which is fatal.

My mother's name is the same as her mother's, although everyone calls my mother Ruthie. Ruthie was her mother's only child, doted upon, photographed at every milestone, and lavished with love, affection, and pride. Her educational accomplishments, a college degree and a master's degree, are seen by my grandmother, whose rural schooling stopped at the fourth grade, as miraculous. She dies the day before Ruthie's fifty-first birthday.

My mother is devastated, as upset as I've ever seen her, telling me that my father refused to wait in the hospital with her, that he told her that her mother died because she didn't pray hard enough. She keeps calling her mother "Mama," which I haven't heard before. She makes me go to school the day her mother dies.

I'm stopped in the hallway that morning by one of my English teachers, who has taken it upon herself to give me college counseling and urge

THE VOLCANO

me to enter writing contests. She asks me what's wrong, and I'm surprised that anyone can see it in my face. I feel like a block of wood.

There's no funeral, no memorial, and no service. This is my father's doing, I'm sure of it, because Christian Scientists don't have funerals. It feels all wrong, because my grandmother was loved. My mother loved her, I loved her, my brother and sister loved her. The only job she ever held was as a ticket taker on a streetcar, but she worked all her life. She worked on the farm from the time she could walk, baking bread, taking care of her younger siblings, and feeding Weyerhaeuser lumbermen for twenty-five cents a plate, even though they were fresh. She never spoke of a secret tragedy, the day her father hanged himself in the barn in 1917. She kept that a secret all her life.

She worked to make a home for her husband, a World War I veteran, and her beautiful daughter. She was an extraordinary cook, known throughout the state for her angel food cakes, which were raffled off for her beloved Democrats. She idolized Harry Truman, serving as a Democratic precinct committeewoman for years. Johnny Cherberg, the lieutenant governor who once squired a Daffodil Princess, loved her angel food. She always made one big cake and several little ones, for us. She arrived at every family dinner with these cakes, and with mason jars full of crisp celery and carrot sticks in chilled water. In summer, she brought jars of blooming roses.

Two days after my grandmother dies, a staff assistant in the White House writes a letter to my grandmother, saying that President Carter has asked him to congratulate her upon her retirement after "44 years of service to your party and your country" and sending her the president's warm personal regards and best wishes "for days filled with life's greatest blessings."[22] She never gets to read it.

Several months after my grandmother's death, my mother and I are sifting through decades of flotsam in my grandmother's house on Queen Anne Hill, finding all manner of startling wreckage: twenty-dollar bills beneath the floorboards, empty liquor bottles hidden in the basement, rotting if triumphant newspapers—JAPS SURRENDER. My father is insistent that the house be cleaned and rented, and I think I know why. It's my mother's house, not his, and he doesn't want her to have it. He doesn't belong here. My siblings and I have been urging her to leave him and move into this house.

He's disposing of things and selling the furniture. He's remorseless. I want to push him out the window. He's somewhere downstairs when my mother and I are pulling things out of a bedroom closet, a narrow space under the eaves. I try not to look at my grandmother's dresses, hanging on the back of the closet door, dresses that hold her shape and her smell, and that she will not wear again.

Later that afternoon, my friend Jeff comes by to pick me up in his Dodge Dart. We're going to see the most popular art exhibit ever, an international sensation and the talk of every town: *The Treasures of Tutankhamun*. Packed with objects never before allowed out of Egypt, the show has finally arrived at the Seattle Center after visiting Washington, D.C., Chicago, and other cities. Waiting in a long line outside, we shuffle forward with hundreds of others to enter the many dark rooms of the tomb, seeing photographs of the unwrapped mummy of the boy king. His death mask is sparkling gold—copper-alloyed twenty-three-karat gold with royal insignia of the cobra and vulture and eyes of volcanic obsidian. We see caskets fashioned to hold his organs and intestines. His golden sandals. An alabaster chalice glowing from within.

We are a horde of heathens luxuriating in the opulent death of this boy who perished at nineteen, perhaps from a blow to the head. There is said to be a curse.

There is a spell inscribed in Egyptian hieroglyphics across the back and sides of the death mask, a script from the Book of the Dead. It seeks to protect his right eye, his left eye, his forehead, the nape of his neck, and the locks of his hair. But the power of the spell wanes, and when British archaeologists force their way into his tomb three thousand years later and tear the bright mask from his mummy, they break almost every bone in his body.[23]

THE VOLCANO

It's a bad summer on the floating bridge, a summer of spectacular accidents involving heavy machinery. On June 27, 1978, the bed of a dump truck inexplicably rises to its upright position while crossing the bridge, crashing into an overhead structure supporting lane-directional signals and knocking it onto the pickup truck behind it, killing Kevin Grund, sixteen, and David Caldwell, twenty-eight, of Grund & Co., a painting contractor.[24]

On August 29, the driver of a stolen 1964 Oldsmobile Cutlass decides to make a U-turn near the western end of the bridge, striking a cement truck head-on, and is then struck from behind by another vehicle, causing a five-car pileup. The cement truck veers across the span, breaching the cement railing, the cab dangling above the lake. Its engine catches fire. David Sprague, a seventeen-year-old Mercer Island High School student, jumps off a bus, climbs across the shaft between the cab of the cement truck and the trailer, and pulls the driver to safety. The driver of the stolen vehicle and her passenger—both juvenile females—sprint off the bridge and are arrested later.

That incident ends without fatalities, but between 1970 and 1976, 2,660 accidents and sixteen deaths occur along the I-90 traffic corridor that includes the bridge, according to a study conducted by the state's Department of Transportation. That's twice the rate of accidents on I-5. Clifford Bascom, an island resident, speaks to a reporter for *The Seattle Times*, describing a head-on collision he and his son suffered two days before Christmas the previous year, headlined POSTCARD-PRETTY ROAD IS A SORE SPOT FOR MANY:

> We were coming home just after dark, going into I-90 from Bellevue Way. I don't remember anything after that. The cops said the other driver was in the reversible lane, hit some gravel and skidded.
>
> He hit us head on. I had a bad head injury. I had all my ribs broken in one side, an arm broken, both legs broken. My right ankle

was smashed up. My face still is pretty numb because of nerve damage. Other than that, I'm O.K.

My son lost his spleen and a kidney. We were both lucky, I guess. We could have been killed.[25]

He adds: "The Mercer Island Bridge, that whole stretch of highway along there, is a treacherous thing."

ON DECEMBER 10, 1978, a feature in *The New York Times Magazine* describes Ted Bundy as an "all-American boy," a "terrific looking man," and "Kennedyesque," while misspelling the names of two of his victims.[26]

Not everyone has Ted's appeal. On December 20, a drunk, disheveled, and disoriented killer by the name of John Wayne Gacy begins confessing in Chicago to the murders of more than thirty boys and young men, many of whom he has lured to their deaths at his home, strangling or asphyxiating them, waking from an alcoholic stupor to find their handcuffed bodies on the floor. Gacy lives at 8213 West Summerdale Avenue in Norwood Park, three miles due east of O'Hare International Airport, swept by the purifying fumes of leaded jet fuel, a gift of the prevailing winds.[27]

Born a few years before Bundy, in 1942, Gacy is a longtime member of the Elks Lodge and appears in full regalia as "Pogo" with the Elks' Jolly Joker clown club despite a prior conviction for sodomizing a teenage boy. Bodies are found interred in the crawl space beneath his home, covered in lime. Earlier that year, Gacy, a Democratic precinct captain, was photographed shaking the hand of First Lady Rosalynn Carter.

Even though he's confessed and has drawn the police a schematic map of the remains in his crawl space, he's resentful when they retrieve them, a process that takes weeks. He tells a psychiatrist, "It was a hiding place. It was a secret place. Those are my bodies. That's where I wanted to keep them. They had no right to touch them."[28] That same year, an Ohio boy named Jeffrey Dahmer has graduated from high school and three weeks later murdered his first victim.

THE VOLCANO

By the late 1970s, "the golden age of serial murderers," as a crime historian will call it, is well underway.[29] In earlier decades, these perpetrators could be measured in the double digits, but the numbers climb sharply after World War II, along with the lead in gas tanks and bloodstreams. There are 55 serial killers in 1940, 72 in 1950, 217 in 1960. By 1970 there are 605. By 1980, 768.[30] Body counts of individual killers are rising.

COLLEGE APPLICATIONS ARE DUE at the end of 1978, and I'm excited about applying to UCLA. Jeff and I are planning to move to Los Angeles and become screenwriters. I fantasize about sun, palm trees, and the smell of coconut oil, yearning to be warm.

That fall quarter, the creative writing class offered at UCLA is in poetry: I will have to submit poems to apply. *How hard can it be?* I think. I've read T. S. Eliot. I've read Sylvia Plath.

I write what I know. I write about creosote and murder. I write about the devil.

In the Night, What Things Move

Telephone poles' high wire connections swoop
and glide in the quiet and highly still
air of morning. Any noise, my cat moving
between the leaves of the table, another cat
outside, fighting for life in the bushes, or, maybe,
love, any noise enters the skin. Anyone
looking in from the outside sees me faded
like a photo or an ancient religious image, black
and white, scraped, a bit, around the edges.

Someone, and who knows really
who it is, walks nightly in the street,
outside, someone not an animal, sounding
like leaves, dried and loud, blown downwind.
Shoes might make that noise, but neither nails

nor padded soles shod such a one, bowing
and scraping every night, somewhere
in back of my head, beyond where eye
can see. The moon's light circle caught between

two legs of two telephone poles, in a groin
of dark wood so tarred and sticky it never dries
in damp weather, spurs him on. These sheets,
these things I find myself between, keep
tangling. One siren sleeves the spine
in shivers, one candle sheets the window
in a red tide of warning, he's coming, coming
and in my dream, morning comes at night,

and what moves, he moves, what bleeds, he bleeds.[31]

FOR SOME REASON that puzzles authorities, the Hillside Strangler has stopped doing what he's been doing in Los Angeles. On January 12, 1979, two women in Bellingham, students at Western Washington University, the school my brother and sister attended, are reported missing: Diane Wilder, twenty-seven, and Karen Mandic, twenty-two. They're roommates, Wilder majoring in dance and Mandic in business administration.

Working her way through college, Mandic has a part-time job at the Fred Meyer Super Shopping Center, just past I-5 from her apartment. Kenneth Bianchi, twenty-seven, works there too, in the security office, employed by the Whatcom Security Agency. He's taking police courses so he can apply for a job at the Whatcom County Sheriff's Department.

Bianchi was born in Rochester, New York, in 1951, to a seventeen-year-old alcoholic sex worker. At three months of age, he was adopted as an only child by Nicholas Bianchi and his wife, Frances.

Nicholas Bianchi worked at the American Brake Shoe Foundry, producing brake shoes for railroad cars. These so-called friction products were made of cast iron and asbestos, the latter a substance that, in addition to causing cancer, will be implicated in central nervous system damage, including memory problems and disturbances in gait, posture, and fine movements. The wives, children, and dogs of workers have been affected by asbestos fibers brought home on workers' clothing.[32]

Whether it was the lingering effects of his birth to an alcoholic mother or the brake shoes or both, the Bianchis' child soon appeared to be defective. His eyes rolled back in his head. He was examined for urinary dribbling and petit mal seizures.[33] For years he wet the bed, and his mother made him wear sanitary napkins. From the time he could speak, he lied constantly. At the age of eight, he was examined for psychiatric issues. His IQ was above average, but he was removed from school twice for aggressive behavior. By age twelve he was yanking pants off younger girls. When he was thirteen, his father died suddenly.

As an older teen, Kenny told a girlfriend that he had killed a man and was a suspect in the Alphabet Murders, a series of child murders in Rochester between 1971 and 1973 in which three girls were strangled manually or with a ligature. All were raped. At the time, he was working in the area as an ice cream vendor.

Kenny had an older cousin from Rochester, Angelo Buono Jr., who moved to Glendale, California, northeast of Hollywood, established a thriving car upholstery business in a garage behind his home, and became an enthusiastic rapist while inhaling daily the heavy metals and chemicals familiar to Richie Ramirez's mother. In 1975, Kenny joined him in L.A.

Shortly after the women's disappearance in Bellingham, Bianchi becomes a suspect when investigators learn that he's been in touch with the women, asking them to house-sit at a residence while the alarm system is under repair. The home, at 334 Bayside Road, is owned by William Catlow, a former Georgia-Pacific Corporation executive. The view overlooks Chuckanut Bay, well south of Bellingham and away from the sulfurous odor of the Georgia-Pacific paper mill that has been polluting Bellingham

Bay with mercury, petroleum compounds, and a variety of metals for decades. The Catlows are away on vacation.

The day after the women go missing, a resident in the Catlows' neighborhood spots a car parked in the woods off a cul-de-sac. In the back are the bodies of Wilder and Mandic, beaten, raped, and strangled with a ligature. Bianchi is arrested after supplying a series of contradictory alibis. Noting his California driver's license, Bellingham police call the L.A. County Sheriff's Department to inquire about his background. By happenstance, they speak to a member of the Hillside Strangler Task Force, who observes that the address on Bianchi's license is right next door to one of the victims. Someone puts a pin in a map.

THE HOOD CANAL BRIDGE, on Puget Sound sinks on February 13, 1979.

Catastrophic failure occurs during a storm with sustained winds of 85 miles per hour and gusts up to 120. Waves ten to fifteen feet high pound the structure for hours. By 7:30 a.m. on February 13, three massive anchors attached to the floating bridge via cables three feet thick are coming loose, and the span is closed to traffic. The cables snap, and the bridge sags like a string. It descends into the abyss.

They rebuild it.

IT DOESN'T TAKE a gale to kill yourself on the island. Light rain and a high rate of speed will do. In the early morning hours of February 26, twenty-two-year-old Jeffrey A. Gumm of Renton crashes into the bulge, flies from his car into Lake Washington, and drowns. His 1977 Camaro is found "crumpled like a tin can" in the eastbound lanes, according to police on the scene.[34] After a shoe and wallet are spotted in the water, his body is retrieved later that day.

Spring of my senior year is marked by deadly events: At 2:50 a.m. on March 15, Jon Toledo, eighteen, is driving a 1973 Oldsmobile Cutlass sedan on I-90, returning from Bellevue, when he takes an exit at eighty or ninety miles per hour, loses control, and wraps his car around a reversible-lane standard.[35]

The impact is so violent that the engine flies across the highway, littering the roadway with car parts. Alcohol may or may not be a factor. The driver and his two passengers, Greg Kinney, sixteen, and George W. Russell, twenty, are killed. This George W. Russell is different from George Waterfield Russell Jr.; otherwise the future, as in Harlan Ellison's *Star Trek* episode, might well have turned out to be different.

Two more die on May 2, at around 11:30 p.m., when my classmates Michael Zwang, nineteen, and Brenda Poole, eighteen, plow a 1975 Harley-Davidson at high speed into the rear of a Volkswagen driven by twenty-four-year-old Gregory Courson of Issaquah. Neither Zwang nor Poole is wearing a helmet.[36] Both perish. They join others who won't make it to graduation: Jeff Nelsen, dispatched in a crash in the San Juans in 1978, and Shelley McMillan, victim of a freak accident in an all-terrain vehicle.[37]

We don't know it yet, but in future years one of our fellow students will murder his mail-order bride.[38]

I'm co-editor of the Mercer Island High School newspaper, fondly known as the *High Times*, and presumably the paper of record takes notice of these calamities. But I'm distracted, wielding my newfound power in an editorial vendetta against the island's school superintendent, a proxy for my father, who is the assistant superintendent of the Seattle Public School System. I barely register others' upheavals—Susie moves to Wenatchee after her father unaccountably buys an apple orchard. I'm caught up with Sheryl, a new friend. We're in American Studies together, reading *Moby-Dick* and learning what's wrong with this country, although something in her eyes tells me she already knows. She's beautiful and solemn, and loves to go fast in her Pontiac GTO. I'm beginning to believe we're going to get out of this place.

Jeff and I spend a lot of time driving around in the Dart, and we're often high, listening to the Beatles' "Revolution," from *The White Album*. Sometimes we're dropping acid. Sometimes we're reading Mao's Little Red

Book. One day, I'm trying to explain Christian Science to him and he says, "But you don't believe that, do you?" And whatever's left of the theology pops like one of the soap bubbles Susie and I used to blow in her backyard.

One weekend, we drive a few hours up to Ross Lake and meet his friends from Lakeside, an expensive prep school, and take a smorgasbord of assorted pharmaceuticals laid out on a picnic table.

It's too cold to swim. Ross Lake is a reservoir created by a dam impounding the Skagit River and surrounded by forbidding mountains, such as Desolation Peak. The reservoir is twenty-three miles long and 540 feet deep, a distance greater than the height of Smith Tower, Seattle's first skyscraper, or the Space Needle. We don't care. The color of the water is milky green, and in our minds we're floating like tops in the biggest bathtub on earth.

But we're not degenerates. We never drive drunk.

AT FOUR IN THE MORNING on March 28, 1979, an accident in the Unit 2 reactor at the Three Mile Island nuclear facility causes the core to overheat and begin melting, releasing radioactive gases and iodine. Over the coming days, weeks, and months, the plant's owner, Metropolitan Edison, and experts from the Nuclear Regulatory Commission swear up and down that there's no hazard to human health or safety. They're lying.

Years later, an attorney investigating the incident says, "What the industry learned from this is that you can lie, cheat, falsify documents, intimidate and harass workers, be convicted of a crime, and you can get a license to operate a nuclear reactor. That's the lesson of Three Mile Island."[39]

IN APRIL, the Tacoma *News Tribune* is crowing about how Tacoma's air is now cleaner than Seattle's, pointing out that smelter emissions have been reduced over the past two years, thanks to recent technological improvements. Meanwhile, Seattle traffic is getting steadily worse, and the editorial boasts that "we in Tacoma are indeed favored with a clean, moist, moving marine air."[40]

That same month, however, the New York–based nonprofit group Inform, Inc., funded by Ford Foundation grants, issues a thousand-page report, compiled over three and a half years, on the hazards of the copper industry. It has nothing nice to say about the Tacoma smelter, rating it "poor" in industrial hygiene and engineering controls and only "fair" in safety, medical services, and workers' rights.[41] "All copper-production workers at Tacoma have hazardous arsenic exposures," it determines, with some 85 percent exposed to very high arsenic content and 70 percent to high levels of copper dust and copper fumes.[42] Workers might also be in contact with cadmium and lead levels above proposed and present OSHA standards. Inform concludes that workers will die of lung cancer at rates exceeding the statewide average.

The smelter begs to differ. A spokesman tells the local paper, "Numerous ventilation systems have been installed."[43]

JOSEPH EDWARD DUNCAN III, now fifteen, is arrested in 1979 after a high-speed car chase in which he attempts to smash through a police roadblock in a stolen vehicle.

He's sent to Tacoma's Jessie Dyslin Boys Ranch, a state-run orphanage and group home, an institution later implicated in widespread sexual abuse.[44] There he tells a therapist that he has tied up and assaulted six boys and raped thirteen. His deep-set eyes are growing ever crazier.

Released after a few months, he steals a gun from a neighbor's house. The following year, he uses it to abduct a fourteen-year-old boy on his way to school, forcing the child to undress and fellate him. He burns the boy with a cigarette and beats him with a piece of wood. Identified later that night, Joe is arrested and eventually put away for twenty years.[45]

ON MAY 31, 1979, Ted Bundy rejects a plea deal that has been painstakingly negotiated by state-appointed attorneys. He has led everyone to believe that he will plead guilty to the Chi Omega killings and Kim Leach's murder, accepting three twenty-five-year sentences, to be served consecutively, in exchange for taking the death penalty off the table.

Physical evidence in the Chi Omega case is thin; prosecutors have little more than Nita Neary's eyewitness glimpse and circumstantial evidence. The plea deal will save his life. Privately, according to Florida's deputy state attorney, Ted has admitted guilt: when he enters the court that day, he's carrying a written admission. In the courtroom, however, he rebukes his lawyers and tears up the papers. There will be a trial.

ON JULY 6, Randy Woodfield is paroled. He has served only four years of a ten-year sentence after pleading guilty to second-degree robbery. In his 1975 plea agreement, first-degree robbery and oral sodomy charges were dropped. He has lied to the state psychologist, saying how sorry he is, how he's reformed, how he's become a Christian. After his release, he cycles through a series of jobs, bartending, compiling a little black book of hundreds of women's names, and contracting herpes.[46]

ON JULY 9, Stacy Sparks, eighteen, goes missing. This is familiar. A recent high school graduate and waitress at the Little Pebble at Shilshole Bay Marina, she's last seen leaving the Raintree Restaurant in Lynnwood, a neighborhood in North Seattle, at 9:30 p.m.

There are several Raintrees in the area, but the Lynnwood Raintree at 145th and 15th Streets, which features a glass-enclosed slice of a tree at the entrance, with simulated rain showering on it and reflected by strips of mirror, has a distinct reputation. It's known locally as the "hump and dump" or "the Wet Bush" or a "meat market," where you can listen to live music, play pool, pick up girls, grill your own steaks, and get a baked potato wrapped in foil. On Tequila Tuesdays, it's a dollar a shot. Such are the delights of 1979.

But the night Stacy Sparks stops by is a Monday, and she's having an innocent drink with her girlfriends. They call her "Spacy Stacy." She's five foot two, with short, curly blond hair, and she's wearing jeans and a pale yellow T-shirt with a rose on the front and driving a light blue 1978 Plymouth Arrow two-door hatchback with white stripes. She's apparently heading to her boyfriend's place in West Seattle, but police hear rumors that she might have been planning to visit an older man, a secret lover on Mercer Island. Over the coming months, scores of volunteers and members of a National Guard division comb the woods searching for her. "People just don't disappear like that," says a detective with the Lynnwood police.[47] In fact, they do.

Psychics are consulted, including one who sees the victim being driven past the famous Boehm's Candies in Issaquah and up into the mountains on I-90, held against her will in a deserted cabin on a dirt road and injected with heroin by three people, including a man named Tom who is "part Indian."[48] He gives Stacy three days to live. Peter Hurkos, a famous clairvoyant associated with the Boston Strangler case, charges the family several thousand dollars for a consultation. He clutches a pair of her earrings matching the rose pendant on a necklace she was wearing that night. Stacy loves roses. Hurkos feels she's dead in a ditch, covered in leaves.[49]

This is the summer when I'm getting ready to leave my mother to her own defenses, something I can scarcely bear to think about. I'm afraid for her but also consumed with impatience. Why won't she leave him? Sometimes I want to yell at her, *Do you want to spend the rest of your life in the daylight basement?*

One morning shortly before I depart for good, I'm asleep in bed, past the time my father deems appropriate. He steals into my room quietly, holding a feather, and rubs it across my eyelashes until I'm startled awake. It turns out that I do have a mouth, and I can scream.

AFTER A COMPETENCY HEARING, Ted Bundy is appointed co-counsel in charge of his defense, but his attorneys find him "erratic, impulsive, and strange."[50] He is acting in multiple roles at his trial—as witness, attorney, and defendant, a situation considered unprecedented by local court watchers—and virtually every decision he makes on his own behalf undercuts his defense.[51] In a nod to the publicity that the proceedings have attracted, the judge rules that the trial, which has been moved to Miami, will be among the first to be televised nationally.

In the courtroom, Ted is a peacock, mugging for photos, delighted by the cameras. Agitated, he's on Ativan and a revolving cocktail of other drugs administered in the county jail to calm him down, and his public defenders, who believe he's mentally ill, give him stacks of legal briefs to carry around to "keep him occupied."[52]

On July 9, the prosecutor briskly questions the Florida State University officer who was first on the scene at the Chi Omega house, Officer Raymond Crew. Asked to describe the condition of Lisa Levy's body as he discovered it, Crew says, "Initially I observed a puncture wound through the nipple on the right breast. When the sheet was pulled off of her and she was moved to the floor, I observed a bloody mark on her right buttocks."[53]

After Crew's testimony, so disturbing that it makes a female juror feel ill and require a cup of water, Ted, seated at the end of the counsel table, jumps up, preempting his defense attorney from conducting the cross-examination. Wielding a yellow legal pad and fidgeting with a pen, he stands at the podium. It's his first performance as an attorney in front of the jury, and it will become one of the most bizarre moments in American jurisprudence. Speaking slowly and in an almost trancelike fashion, Ted proceeds to elicit from Officer Crew, "to the best of your recollection and step by step," a more graphic and damning description than the one he's already given.[54] Despite objections from the district attorney that this reiteration is "repetitively gruesome," the judge allows it, handing Ted plenty of rope to hang himself.

THE VOLCANO

And he does, drawing out a ghastly picture of the appearance of Margaret Bowman: "Her mouth was open. Her eyes were open. There was what appeared to be a nylon stocking knotted around her neck, and her head was bloated, discolored." Ted then lingers over Lisa Levy's body, asking specifically about "the position of her legs." Described in newspaper accounts as "detached, cool, and seemingly confident," he appears to be savoring the clinical depiction of his handiwork.[55] The camera watches the jury. He does not. He's reliving a moment of profound sexual gratification.

Jurors are openly aghast, with one alternate staring at him fixedly. The district attorney says later, "I've never seen anything like it in my career as a lawyer. You would never want your client to cross-examine a crime scene witness. He was bringing out the gore he had left there."[56] For Ted, that's the point.

Whenever his defense attorneys make progress, he upstages them. One of his lawyers competently questions Nita Neary, emphasizing how brief was her side view of the perpetrator, leaving a momentary impression only of the profile of his nose and lips. When he's done, Ted demands that the lawyer be fired.

He's outraged by Neary and by the testimony of an enterprising odontologist, Dr. Richard Souviron, who claims that he can accurately identify the bite marks on Lisa Levy's buttock as belonging to Ted. This is the first time that bite mark evidence has been allowed in a court of law, and it will be challenged in future years as junk science.

But what Ted cannot grasp is that the problem is not Dr. Souviron or bite marks or Nita Neary. The problem is Ted. His arrogance, narcissism, and grandiosity are obvious to everyone, including his own attorneys. In some indefinable if not legally admissible way, he is insane. The case against him is flimsy, and if he stays silent and allows his attorneys to do their jobs, it's possible he might be acquitted.

As it is, on July 24, 1979, after a mere six and a half hours of deliberation, he's convicted of the murders of Margaret Bowman and Lisa Levy.

His mother, who cannot believe he's guilty, begs for his life. A week later, he's sentenced to death.

THE ISLAND REMAINS a crime scene. In 1979, 7 people are killed in accidents on the floating bridge or its I-90 approaches.[57] In 266 accidents, 204 are injured, with property damage reaching $607,057. There are 157 rear-end collisions, 25 sideswipes, 5 overturned vehicles, and 38 incidents in which a single vehicle strikes a "fixed object such as the guardrail, curbstone, bulge wall, or stanchions."[58] Of the 20 most serious accidents, 12 occur on the floating bridge, eight at the bulge.

Byron Blauman's little brother Owen is in high school, moonlighting as a photographer at baseball games and bridge carnage. He's there after a station wagon is involved in a five-car collision. He's there an hour later when a Ford Pinto is totaled after crossing all three eastbound lanes and plowing head-on into a Peterbilt semi.[59] He's there when a car is fished out of the lake like a salmon by a tow truck. The driver of that vehicle, twenty-four-year-old Taryn Marr Nakamichi, is heading eastbound at 1:20 a.m. when she hits the bulge, swerves across the bridge, and pitches over the guardrail. She drowns.[60]

In the fall of 1979, after I've left for college, somebody places explosives in a drainpipe at the base of one of the concrete supports holding up an I-90 ramp above the Mercer Slough. It is thought to be "one of the biggest bombs ever exploded in Bellevue."[61] The detonation is perhaps masked by the roar of traffic on the highway itself, and the destruction is not discovered until November 12. "Whoever did it might have thought they could have brought the whole road down," says a lieutenant with the Bellevue Police Department's bomb squad. There's no note, no phone call claiming responsibility.

Soon a suspect emerges. John Stickney, eighteen, a tall blond guy and one of my former classmates at Mercer Island High School, has dropped out before graduation. He's still in love with a former girlfriend, Lisa Clark. She's gone to college at Washington State University in Pullman, almost all the way to Idaho, south of Spokane. She's broken up with him, but he can't accept it. He works as a blaster's helper for Industrial Rock Products, Inc., blowing up rocks at a quarry outside Monroe, a town in the foothills of the Cascades, northeast of Seattle. He's worked for the company since he was twelve.

John's family lives at the south end of the island, and he blows things up "just for the hell of it," a friend says.[62] Teri Gregory, another girl in our class and Lisa's roommate at WSU, has seen him pouring gasoline over a wrecked vehicle and lighting it on fire.[63] He has a temper, threatening Lisa with a rifle, threatening suicide.[64]

That winter, John stalks Lisa, showing up at her college dorm unexpectedly even though she begs him not to, making it clear they're no longer dating. On Monday, December 17, he works all day. No one knows that he's stolen fifty pounds of dynamite and a number of commercial blasting caps. He gets in his car and starts driving east, across the Cascades through Snoqualmie Pass, where it's snowing and icy, crossing barren scablands and featureless agricultural prairies.

Once at Perham Hall, he tries repeatedly to confront Lisa, eventually tracking her down at her dorm room, trying to kick the door in. "I have a bomb," he says. "Someone's going to get hurt if you don't let me in."[65]

Lisa and her roommate decide to make a run for it, throwing open the door and screaming, "He has a bomb!" They run to safety as campus officers arrive, clearing students off the floor. John does indeed have a bomb: a metal pipe or cylinder packed with dynamite. He's holding wires connected to a battery, and two officers—David Trimble, twenty-six, and Michael Kenney, thirty-five—approach him, pleading with him to put it down. After a brief struggle, John turns his back and walks away, holding the bomb against his stomach. It explodes.

There is a shattering blast that sounds like a sonic boom.[66] The floor trembles as if it will collapse. All the windows on the fifth floor blow out; the rooms closest to the explosion are pulverized. Police on the scene fear that Trimble and Kenney are dead. Rushed to the hospital, Trimble suffers first- and second-degree burns on his face and puncture wounds on his hands, chest, and abdomen. Both his eardrums are ruptured, as are Kenney's. Three students are treated for minor injuries.

John Stickney is dead. The story is so bizarre it's covered nationally, turning up in *The New York Times*. For the island, it's just the beginning.

ON DECEMBER 23, 1979, Peggy Guggenheim dies of a stroke in Italy at the age of eighty-one. She's lived much of her adult life in a palazzo in Venice, a patron of the arts, sleeping under a silver headboard fashioned by Alexander Calder, attended by Lhasa apsos and feted by celebrities who flock to her cocktail parties. She's said to have slept with a thousand men.

Meyer's money keeps throwing off culture the way clay flies off a potter's wheel, obliterating any association with slag and smoke. His dreams of legacy have given rise to generations of attenuation and mediocrity and the usual self-indulgent eccentrics, dilettantes, and sybarites. Within the family, this is blamed on "too many daughters," although Peggy is one of the few who distinguishes herself.[67] William Guggenheim III, great-grandson of Meyer, publishes a sex manual in 1973 and, after receiving messages from beyond the grave, founds the "After-Death Communications Project."[68]

Lead and arsenic have supported Peggy in style. For years she maintains a gondola with two gondoliers, but later in life—driven by extreme parsimoniousness—she cuts back to one.[69]

THE TRIAL OF TED BUNDY for the murder of Kimberly Leach begins on January 7, 1980, and this time physical evidence ties him to the crime. In addition to eyewitnesses, there are credit card receipts, bloodstains in the white van, and fiber evidence connecting Ted's clothing to Kim Leach's and to the van's carpeted floor. There's the price tag peeled off the knife, found in the van where he dropped it. When the prosecuting attorney

THE VOLCANO

holds up the white turtleneck left on Kim's body, stained with a giant bib of rust red below her neck, the courtroom gasps.

Ted reconciles himself to accepting legal representation, to no avail. Again he's convicted and again sentenced to death. During the penalty phase, he wrests control once more, questioning Carole Ann Boone, his former colleague and devoted groupie. In a bizarre stunt, taking advantage of a statute in Florida law, he asks her to marry him while she's on the stand and declares their marriage accomplished by the court.

Ted is then consigned to the lower circles of penal hell at the Florida State Prison in Starke, confined in the "DEATH HOUSE," as his medical records have it. There he will stay for the duration: Washington, Utah, and Colorado relinquish their cases once Florida convicts him on multiple capital murder counts.

During the trial and for weeks following, Ted sits for a series of jailhouse interviews with Hugh Aynesworth, a Dallas-based investigator for the ABC program *20/20*, a newsmagazine show on the model of CBS's *60 Minutes*, and Stephen G. Michaud, a former *Newsweek* reporter who has covered serial killings in the past, notably those committed by Dean Corll, the so-called Candy Man who handed out free sweets and with accomplices murdered at least twenty-eight teenage boys in Houston between 1970 and 1973. Ted steadfastly maintains his innocence. Their arrangement is that while Michaud interviews Ted, Aynesworth will reinvestigate the murders of which he is accused in the western states, looking for a potential alibi that could exonerate him.

Michaud develops a rapport with Ted, in part because of shared history. Like Ted, Michaud was born in Burlington, Vermont, and moved to Tacoma with his mother as a youngster. Neither knew his father; both attended Tacoma public schools. Both are left-handed. In their hometown, Michaud would later write, they were "swept by the same local fads . . . drank the same regional beers, and knew the same kind of girl."[70] There, however, the similarities end.

The interviews get off to a rocky start, because Ted can't find a way of discussing what he's done without confessing or implicating himself. Soon Michaud hits upon a solution, encouraging his subject to speak about a hypothetical third-person killer and what that killer might have done. Revelations ensue.

As Aynesworth follows Ted's trail through Washington, Utah, and Colorado, he begins to see that their subject is no criminal mastermind. Investigating murder after murder, he learns that Ted hasn't thought to establish an alibi for a single one of them.

I'M IN LOS ANGELES. I'm off the OWL and out of the centrifugal pull of the island, but I have nowhere to live. I'm from out of state and don't qualify for a dorm. First I camp in an unsustainably expensive apartment for a month, sleeping on the floor because I have no furniture. Through a friend I meet in poetry class I am invited to be a boarder in a sorority house. I don't pledge, I simply pay, and it's cheap.

It's not Chi Omega. It's a new house, down on its luck. It cannot pay its bills. Sorority houses are built from copycat plans, and I live in the Lisa Levy room. It looks out onto Hilgard Avenue, the eastern boundary of the UCLA campus, perched above the spiky palms and fleshy red tubelike flowers of the university's botanical garden. When I run upstairs I think of the hallway schematic from the Ted trial, but I'm too busy to be worried. It's ten years later and two miles as the crow flies from 10050 Cielo Drive.

I'm smoking Benson & Hedges menthols, scanning lines in Elizabeth Bishop, writing poetry, and practicing piano in soundproof rooms. I'm memorizing lyrics to Elvis Costello, smoking dope, dropping acid with Jeff on Venice Boulevard, eating the free vegetarian food the Hare Krishnas are giving away and Twinkies from the campus vending machines, getting drunk at the Sunset Marquis, absorbing maraschino cherries while chatting with the bartender at the Whisky a Go Go, and spending hours in language labs with headphones on, practicing French. The teaching assistant is from France, and her face is half-frozen because of a nuclear accident.

THE VOLCANO

My best friend in class is a tall, blond Aryan with blue eyes who I'm guessing is gay; he's writing short stories about a boy in love with his molester and collecting rare editions. The Aryan and I are working eight, twelve, sixteen, twenty hours a week in the basement of the research library in a hive of typing bees digitizing the card catalog, inputting information in many languages requiring tricky diacritical marks, and doing lines of coke off the top of the toilets to stay awake.

In Los Angeles, 100 percent of the folding money has touched cocaine. It binds to the green dye.

I HAVE ESCAPED, but not everyone can. In the early hours of the morning on May 12, 1980, Jason Perrine, sixteen, a freshman at Mercer Island High School, revs the engine on his girlfriend's sister's 1972 Chevy Camaro and blasts Lynyrd Skynyrd's "Free Bird" on the car stereo. Sitting in the passenger seat is his fifteen-year-old girlfriend, Dawn Swisher.

Jason is estranged from his parents and living at Dawn's house. He's planning to drop out of school and start a new job at Jack in the Box, but then he decides that's a stupid plan. So he revs the engine and drives the Camaro at 110 miles per hour into the gymnasium wall at North Mercer Junior High, the school where I studied grammar and wrote about *Jonathan Livingston Seagull*. Jason is killed instantly. Dawn ducks under the dashboard and survives, albeit with serious injuries. The gym is totaled.

Jason, it transpires, has been troubled by *Jonathan Livingston Seagull* and Richard Bach's latest regurgitation of Mary Baker Eddy's thoughts, titled *Illusions: The Adventures of a Reluctant Messiah*. The book is about a guru who teaches the author that nothing is real. Everything is an illusion, and no one ever dies. It's exactly what my father believes, but Jason has decided to put it to the test. When I hear this story, whispered by my mother from her refuge in the laundry room, I feel a sneaking admiration.

Jason's explosive act inspires international press coverage and endless editorial hand-wringing over teen angst, peer pressure, overindulgent parents, and a culture of permissiveness. After some time has passed, Jason's anguished father puts it down to his son being "a casualty of . . . the breakdown of the family, the drug culture . . . and the violence and brutality in society."[71] Asked for his response, Richard Bach declares himself indifferent, because, he says, nothing is real.[72]

HERE'S REAL FOR YOU. Six days later, on May 18 at 8:32 a.m., Mount Saint Helens blows her head off.

The mountain has long been admired for its beautifully conical snow-capped form. But beginning in March, this demure peak appears determined to destroy all illusions, building on a long mythology of terror. The Cowlitz people call her Loowit or Lawetlat'la, "Smoking Mountain."[73] Lethal spirits live there, high up in Spirit Lake, where a demon drags fishermen to the bottomless depths and eats them.

She puts on a long tease. In March, a 4.6 earthquake strikes, followed by weeks and weeks of temblors. A gashlike crater opens near the peak. Steam is emitted. Beginning in April and increasingly in May, a bulge grows near the summit, to the north, pushing out at the rate of five or six feet a day until the swelling extends some three hundred feet. It's magma.

Throughout March and April and into May, the National Forest Service and Washington's Department of Emergency Services, for which Ted Bundy once worked, fitfully discourage people from getting too close. The agencies try to exclude sightseers, photographers, recreationists, and those who live on the mountain, including a cantankerous old drunk named Harry Truman, who's been renting out boats on Spirit Lake at his Mt. St. Helens Lodge since the 1930s. A committee of state and federal officials declares a "red zone" around areas of the greatest volcanic activity.

Harry Truman, who's eighty-three and keeps sixteen cats and drinks Schenley whiskey and Coke all day, ignores the red zone. The Weyerhaeuser Timber Company lobbies for exemptions. It has three hundred loggers working in the surrounding Gifford Pinchot National Forest and pressures officials to keep the roads open.[74]

Closures mean that tourist revenue is being lost. Thousands want to gawk, putting bumper stickers on their cars: LAVA OR LEAVE IT.[75] Enterprising souls are selling ash by the Ziploc bag. By May, people are so tired of the restrictions that they begin ignoring them.

On May 18 the summit begins to move. Magma and boiling gas blow out, traveling three hundred miles per hour at a temperature of 660 degrees Fahrenheit. A hellish landslide of ash, snow, ice, rock, and mud hurtles down the north flank of the mountain, carrying all before it, following the path of the North Fork Toutle River. Thousands of two-hundred-foot Douglas firs are reduced to kindling. As earth drives through Spirit Lake, the water flies out.

Fifty-seven people are killed. Harry Truman and his sixteen cats are vaporized. David Johnston, a USGS volcanologist stationed at an observation post six miles north of the blast, has only enough time to radio his colleagues, shouting "Vancouver! Vancouver! This is it!"[76] He vanishes. Camping four miles northwest of the summit, Day Bradley Karr, thirty-seven, and his sons Andy, eleven, and Mike, nine, are asphyxiated. They were hoping to take pictures.

It is the end of the known world. A tremendous Plinian column of black smoke and ash punches through the sky, rising eighty thousand feet into the stratosphere in a visible monument to anger at the core. In less than five minutes, the initial blast has traveled twenty-three miles, killing every tree and scrap of vegetation and hundreds of thousands of animals, covering the mountain in an ash avalanche six hundred feet deep. Eleven of the dead are loggers. Ash blows throughout the state and into Oregon, Idaho, Montana, Wyoming, Colorado, and the Dakotas, and drifts around the globe for days, carried by the prevailing winds.

Several inches of ash blanket the as yet undiscovered bodies of two young women, Marsha Ann Weatter, eighteen, and Katherine Jean Allen, twenty, of Fairbanks, Alaska. They're resting in a field of grass and sagebrush 150 yards north of I-90 near Moses Lake, 150 miles northeast of Mount Saint Helens. Six weeks before the eruption they were on their way home, hitchhiking from Missoula to Seattle. They've both been shot once.[77]

Seventy-five miles north of Mount Saint Helens in Auburn, people on the highway pull over, gobsmacked. "Everyone just stared with their mouths open with shock," a man tells the *Seattle Post-Intelligencer*. "I was late for work because I just couldn't pull myself away from the sight. You could feel the tension [and] excitement that rolled off everyone. It was so thick in the air."[78] A mountain climber on nearby Mount Adams falls over backwards in astonishment at the spectacle, an image captured by her husband.

Like everyone, I am astounded, struck dumb with awe and admiration. I feel obscurely as if I have been waiting for this all my life. I'm not the only one. Dixy Lee Ray, the governor of Washington, born in Tacoma and a biologist, tells a newspaper, "I've always said, for many years, that I hoped I lived long enough to see one of our volcanoes erupt."[79]

The mountain is glorious in her destruction. All I can think is, *What took you so long?*

Chapter 11

The Green River

> When I receive newspapers or clippings from the Pacific Northwest, I read of the bodies of young women turning up with relative frequency. And I don't know what it is. I don't know if it's just because I'm paying so much attention to the Pacific Northwest or if there's something about the Pacific Northwest that seems to encourage this kind of activity.
>
> —Ted Bundy in *The Riverman*, by Robert D. Keppel and William J. Birnes

Murder Incorporated is in its death throes. No one knows it yet, but by 1980 the Tacoma smelter has six years left. Still, as with any archfiend chained on a burning lake, wrapped in dark designs and contemplating damnation, the fiery furnace remains parlous. Its entrails are combustible, its singed bottom steeped in stench and smoke.[1] It is irredeemable and, in some manner unfathomable to us, eternal.

In January and again in March 1981, a warning is raised when, on three different occasions, a monitoring station at North 37th and Vassault Streets records sulfur dioxide exceeding 0.25 ppm at a time when the government has decreed that the pollutant not exceed 0.14 ppm over a twenty-four-hour period.² The gas, currently being reassessed by a federal commission, may be "more harmful" than previously thought.³ Considering that the smelter is emitting on average 14 tons of sulfur dioxide every hour—230 tons per day—these alarms are perhaps not surprising, but the smelter is handed a relaxed deadline to cut its emissions by half: 1987.⁴

In July, a University of Washington biologist completes a study, sampling water from sixty-eight lakes in the Alpine Lakes Wilderness in the central Cascades, a gorgeous and remote stretch of backcountry traversed by the Pacific Crest Trail. Judging by the data, the biologist concludes that acid rain is killing fish in seven of the lakes. Two bodies of water are so chemically unbalanced that severe fish kills are presumed to have occurred already.

The sources of the acid are assumed to be the smelter and a coal-fired power plant south of Olympia supplying power to Tacoma and its smelter. Tom White, ASARCO superintendent, thinks not. "If you look at our stacks," he says, "you'll see that none of our plumes go anywhere near the Alpine Lakes area."⁵ This is a lie, but White proposes another culprit. "Mother Nature," he says, could be "contributing to the acidity in these lakes. It's very difficult to determine where these things start." It's not. It's Murder Incorporated.

Crying lead tears, our Beelzebub, Bunker Hill, is closed in 1981 due to the slump in the housing and auto industries. "Smelting in the whole U.S. has practically been destroyed," laments the western editor for *Engineering & Mining Journal*. "There is no money in smelting nowadays."⁶ No one's planning new smelters, and no one who's writing Uncle Bunker's obituary thinks to mention Arlene Yoss or her lead-poisoned siblings or the infants smothered in Deadwood Gulch, the box canyon where you can cripple a kid for $12,000.

RANDY WOODFIELD, erstwhile draft pick of the Green Bay Packers, goes on a months-long crime spree in his gold Volkswagen. On October 9,

1980, he shows up at the home of a former classmate, Cherie Lynn Ayers, twenty-nine, whom he knew from second grade through high school, and corners her in her bedroom, beating and stabbing her to death.[7] A month later, on November 27, Thanksgiving Day, he murders one of his friend's ex-girlfriends, Darcey Renee Fix, twenty-two, and her boyfriend, Douglas Altig, twenty-four, at her home in North Portland. Both are shot, Darcey multiple times. The murders, the local newspaper reports, are the latest in "an extraordinary year for murder in the city," with forty-eight homicides, more than in any year since 1975.[8]

Between October 1980 and the end of February 1981, Randy is driving north and south on I-5, robbing, raping, and murdering along the heavily traveled corridor between Northern California, Oregon, and Washington. Fake beards and a strip of athletic tape across his nose disguise his face. He becomes known as the I-5 Bandit or the I-5 Killer, the latest in a series of highway slayers ranging from Ted Bundy to a lengthening list of truckers preying on hitchhikers and truck-stop prostitutes, a phenomenon so pronounced that the FBI eventually launches a Highway Serial Killings Initiative.[9] The agency publishes a U.S. map with dots representing bodies along highways, spreading "across the nation like a pathogen carried by car."[10] Or, perhaps, leaded gas.

Randy robs gas stations, ice cream parlors, and drive-ins. If girls or women are working alone, he fondles and rapes them. He muscles a waitress into a bathroom at a restaurant in Seattle, forcing her to masturbate him at gunpoint. He murders a mother and her fourteen-year-old daughter in their bed outside Redding, sodomizing the girl. He invades a home in Corvallis, where two sisters, ten and eight, are alone, demanding that they strip naked and fellate him. North of Salem, he sexually assaults and shoots Shari Hull and Lisa Garcia, both twenty, working as cleaners at night in an office building. Garcia survives, despite being shot in the head.

In less than five months, he rapes and kills scores of women and girls: he's suspected of some sixty sexual assaults and perhaps as many as forty-four murders.[11] Arrested in March 1981, after being identified by several victims, he goes on trial for the murder of Shari Hull and the attempted murder of Lisa Garcia. He is convicted later that year.

On September 14, 1981, they find Stacy Sparks. She's been under the floating bridge all this time. It killed her.

Divers find the wreck of a blue Plymouth Arrow with white racing stripes at the bottom of the lake, beneath the bulge, which is finally being removed. The roof is pancaked, and in the back seat is a skeleton wearing a pale yellow T-shirt with a rose on it and a necklace with two carved roses. Reconstructing the accident, investigators determine that Stacy was coming from Mercer Island and hit the bulge at high speed, the vehicle flying through the air and into the water, unseen by anybody in the middle of the night. No one can imagine what she was doing on the island, although rumors persist that she was visiting an older man.

As for the bulge itself, serial killer, it will not go quietly. The plan is to replace the infamous section requiring motorists to swerve and negotiate tight curves at speed, often in the dark and the rain, lashed by wind and waves. But as workers prepare to remove it, a construction barge crossing through the opening in the bridge snags on an underwater power cable, cutting power. The span is stuck open for hours, traffic backing up for miles.

The divers who retrieve Stacy Sparks from the bottom describe "a veritable junkyard" on the lake floor, littered with a trailer hitch, hubcaps, and other detritus.[12] One of the bridge's anchor cables is hooked to the axle of her car, as if reluctant to let go.

In October, two Greenpeace protesters climb the Ruston smokestack and unfurl a banner reading, after the last tree is cut, the last river poisoned, the last fish dead, you will find that you can't eat money.[13] However hackneyed, it's a sentiment that gains additional

THE GREEN RIVER

piquancy on January 8, 1982, when a dozen people, including a six-week-old infant and four policemen, are hospitalized after the Ruston smelter "coughs dust on the road."[14]

During the incident, according to one account, several hundred pounds of arsenic dust "escaped from a bin," as if assuming human form. The cloud covers a section of Ruston Way with an inch of particulates, covering at least one car. "We thought we would be smothered and buried alive," says Mary Catalinich, whose vehicle is afflicted. Her husband, James, compares the experience to the eruption of Mount Saint Helens. "It just rolled down on us," he says. In the hospital, the couple are clutching their dust-laden coats, consigned to plastic bags.

Three Mile Island is still fresh in everyone's minds. Another man caught in the dust storm says he feared that "the smelter was going to explode. I felt the end was near." Smelter officials reckon that the dust is perhaps 15 to 50 percent arsenic, mixed with additional smelting by-products such as zinc, gold, and copper. The smelter manager who speaks to the newspaper has a gas mask dangling around his neck.

AFTER A STINT IN THE NAVY, where he contracts gonorrhea, and two brief failed marriages that each produce a son, Gary Ridgway joins Parents Without Partners in 1981. The support group meets at the White Shutter Inn, a bar on the Highline, also called the Pac Highway or Old Highway 99 or the SeaTac Strip. The Highline runs past the airport and the neighborhood where Gary grew up. Bars line the roadway next to hot-sheet motels. Women walk up and down all day and night, asking men who pull over if they want a date, if they want to party. It's an ugly stretch of road, swept by jet fumes and littered with condoms, beer cans, needles, and bottles. The Flame Tavern, where Ted's late-night trophy Brenda Ball disappeared in 1974, is near the Highline.

Gary dates dozens of women he meets at Parents Without Partners. His ex-wives and girlfriends will describe him as "sexually insatiable," demanding sex several times a day. He has a pronounced preference for having sex outside, in the woods or in public parks. Such places are easy to find, since he's lived in a series of neighborhoods, including Auburn, Kent, Burien, and Maple Valley, that lie south of Seattle proper and are still partly rural and heavily wooded, full of dim old logging roads, shady fishing spots, highway turnouts, and desolate ravines where people dump trash.

After leaving the Navy in 1971, Gary returned to Kenworth Truck Company, where he'd worked briefly in his twenties and where he would remain for decades, spray-painting the cabs of big rigs. Sandwiched between Highway 99 and historic Boeing Field on the east, the Kenworth plant squats in a zone of heavy industry hugging the southern flanks of Lake Washington.[15] During World War II, the company built tank retrievers—"wreckers"—and bomber nose cones. In 1945 it was acquired by Pacific Car & Foundry Co. (PACCAR), a railcar manufacturer housed nearby on an eighty-two-acre facility in Renton, south of the lake. PACCAR built Sherman tanks during World War II and fabricated the legs of Seattle's most recognizable symbol, the Space Needle. North of PACCAR's campus and adjacent to the lake was the Boeing plant where, between 1941 and 1962, the U.S. Air Force manufactured planes.

When Gary went back to the truck plant, the neighborhood surrounding Kenworth and PACCAR already had one notable serial killer associated with it, also named Gary. Between 1969 and 1971, Gary Gene Grant, a troubled youth who'd washed out of the military and lived in a trailer park on the most polluted end of the lake, murdered four, stabbing and strangling two young women, having sex with their bodies, and beating, stabbing, and strangling two six-year-old boys. Shortly after killing the boys, he confessed to all of the murders.

Industrial paint formulations are exempt from lead regulations, and during Gary Ridgway's career at Kenworth he routinely gets paint all over his face and clothing. On December 4, 1981, he meets his latest Parents Without Partners girlfriend and seems upset. He tells her he "just nearly killed a woman."[16] She thinks he's talking about a close call, some kind of traffic accident. He's not.

THE GREEN RIVER

REMEMBER CHARLES RODMAN CAMPBELL, redheaded rapist of Renae Wicklund? He's out on work release for good behavior on April 14, 1982, when he returns to Renae's house in Clearview, where he attacks her. This time he beats her, breaking her jaw, her nose, and a rib, strangles her, and cuts her throat. He rapes the body with a blunt instrument. When her neighbor, Barbara Hendrickson, fifty-one, arrives, planning to make Jell-O for Renae, who's been sick with strep, he slits Barbara's throat from ear to ear. When Renae's daughter, Shannah, now eight, returns from school, he beats her too, stabbing her five times, cutting her throat, and nearly decapitating her.[17]

Arrested for the triple murder, Charles becomes the prime suspect for a mysterious 1977 attack on Renae's former husband: at Christmastime that year, a complete stranger (perhaps a former fellow inmate of Campbell's) entered Jack Wicklund's West Seattle home, tied Jack to a chair, poured gasoline over him, and set him on fire. Jack survived with severe burns and died the next year in a one-car accident.[18]

Charles grew up in Edmonds, living just east of Highway 99, where he was beaten regularly by his father, a former Marine who worked as a truck driver. Yet he hated not his father but his mother, who punished him for playing with matches. He tells a psychiatrist, "The world has created me and I am free to do what I want."[19] On death row, asked whether he has regrets, he laughs.

ON JUNE 22, 1982, Ted Bundy tells prison guards that he needs to talk to a psychologist, telling them, "I am going crazy." In the coming months he will complain of headaches, a stiff neck, nausea, dizzy spells, sensitivity to sound, fatigue, a burning sensation in the back of his neck, sharp pains in the back of his skull, ringing in his ears, and fear of death. He tells a prison doctor that he keeps having flashbacks, which cause "acute distress when they occur at unpredictable times."[20] He doesn't say what, exactly, he's flashing back to.

MURDERLAND

IN THE SUMMER OF 1982, women are turning up in the Green River. The river becomes the Duwamish in its final miles, draining into Elliott Bay and Puget Sound after it curls down out of the Cascades, off the foothills of Rainier, wending its way from high in the Green River Valley and Stampede Pass down into the lowlands around Kent.

First is Wendy Coffield, sixteen, who lived with her impoverished mother in Puyallup but more recently was a runaway from a juvenile detention center in Tacoma where she'd been sent for stealing food stamps. She disappeared on July 8 and is found in the river on July 15, not drowned but deliberately placed there. She has five tattoos of hearts and butterflies and a unicorn and has been strangled with her own jeans.[21] Someone has stripped her clothes off and then re-dressed her.

On the afternoon of August 12, Frank Linard, an employee at P. D. & J. Meats, a slaughterhouse outside Kent, is taking a break from hosing down blood and leftover scraps of cattle flesh. Standing atop a truck behind the plant, smoking a cigar, he's staring down at the Green River, at what he thinks is an accumulation of foam. The longer he looks, however, the more he starts to suspect it's something more solid. At first he thinks it's a deer carcass, but then he realizes it's a woman.

He climbs off the truck to walk down the riverbank and get a better look. She has a heart tattoo. She's naked, caught on a log, her arms waving in the moving water, hair rippling. From the side he can see her face, and her eyes are dark pools with no pupils.[22]

It's Debra "Dub" Bonner, twenty-three, who's been missing from Tacoma for several weeks. She, too, has died not from drowning but from strangulation.

A few days later, on August 15, a treasure hunter floating downstream on the Green River, searching for antique bottles, spots two more bodies. Cynthia Hinds, seventeen, and Marcia Chapman, thirty-one, are underwater, their chests and abdomens weighted with boulders. Detective Dave Reichert responds to the call, and as he is making his way down the steep, slippery grass bank to the river, he almost falls onto the body of Opal Mills, sixteen, left on the riverbank.

Marcia, better known as "Tiny" for her petite frame, has left behind three young children she was supporting by working the streets. Cynthia, who was called "Cookie," had also been working the Highline. Opal was friends with Cookie and was heading out to paint houses with her when she was last heard from; she has no apparent connection to prostitution. Named for her aunt Opal, who was murdered in Oakland, California—a crime that has never been solved—"Little Opal," as she was known, was a sweet, cheerful, chubby girl from a religious family who lived in Kent. She had memorized many Bible verses and named all of her stuffed animals.[23]

All three of the latest victims are Black. Two of them are naked but for bras pulled above their breasts. Like Wendy Coffield, Opal has been strangled with her own pants. Pink particles are found on her body, and triangular-shaped stones have been forced into the vaginas of some of these women so firmly that at autopsy they must be surgically removed.[24]

With the discovery of five victims in or near the river, there is intense coverage from local TV, radio, and newspapers. The requisite police task force is formed the next day. This killer is so prolific, however, that officers assigned to the case can barely handle the processing of the reports of missing women, not to mention the bodies as they're found, weeks, months, or years later.

After Marcia Chapman, Cynthia Hinds, and Opal Mills are found, the killer realizes that his modus operandi needs refreshing. He moves away from the river, utilizing ravines, trash piles, and logging roads. Between July 8, the day of Wendy Coffield's death, and December 24, 1982, he kills fifteen women—two or three per month. He's fond of ghost towns: the empty streets north and south of SeaTac Airport, right off the Highline, where the Port of Seattle has been buying and condemning houses since 1977 in order to expand, adding first a second and then a third runway.[25] The northernmost of these abandoned neighborhoods, studded with patchy wooded areas, backs onto a Little League field around South 146th Street, and local kids like to dodge around the barriers and ride into the deserted area on their bikes. They call this creepy street "Raper's Road."[26] They're on to something.

What better place to throttle a person than under the deafening roar of jumbo jets? One such girl is Gisele Lovvorn, seventeen, who has escaped from the San Fernando Valley and a school that she hates and is roaming the country wearing long hippie skirts. She has a case of wanderlust and a bad boyfriend. She loves to read, loves the Grateful Dead, and loves hitchhiking.[27] She has a tiny tattoo of a bird on her right breast, and her badly decomposed remains are found on abandoned property south of the airport about a month after she was last seen.

Another is Shawnda Leea Summers, seventeen, a working girl from Bellevue with a beautiful heart-shaped face. She goes missing on October 9, 1982, and her mother flies up from California to search for her. Residents using Raper's Road as a shortcut report a powerful odor of decomposition, but the smell is attributed by police to the dumping of rotten fish. Her bones are not found until the following summer, when they're spotted in a vacant lot by an apple picker. A fresh crop of Explorer Scouts is brought in to continue the search, and a dog belonging to the baseball field's caretaker comes home with a human femur. It belongs to a woman who will never be identified.[28]

Gary is not Ted Bundy, who chooses uniformly white victims, fancying himself a connoisseur, collecting Breck girls and coeds. He's not Dennis Rader, who stalks victims for days or weeks while making up outlandish names for his "projects." He has no forethought and no imagination. He kills women the way other men eat potato chips or wash their cars or clip their toenails. One after another. Doesn't matter what they look like, how old they are, what color skin or hair they have. They can be fifteen; they can be forty. They can be white, Black, Native American, Hispanic, or Asian American, and they are. Prostitutes and drugs are all the media can talk about with regard to this killer, but the one thing—the only thing—his victims have in common is that they are female. The sight of these women walking on a street, Gary will say later, is to him "like candy in a dish."[29]

IF NOT FOR THE GREEN River Killer, murder would be down in Seattle in 1983. Except for that relentlessly single-minded and importunate reaper who's snatching two, three, or four women a month, crime overall appears to be in decline, and officials are happy to pat themselves on the back. Eugene Cotton, executive director of the Washington Association of Sheriffs and Police Chiefs, says proudly, "The effort we are putting into crime prevention is beginning to pay off."[30]

On April 30, eighteen-year-old Marie Malvar disappears after her boyfriend sees her climbing into a crummy old maroon pickup with a distinctive blotch of white paint on the passenger door. Several days later, the boyfriend spots the truck at Ridgway's house and alerts the authorities. While the police ask their questions, Ridgway leans against a fence, hiding the deep scratches Marie made on his arm.

ON THE ISLAND, reflecting the inconstancy of the OWL, George Waterfield Russell Jr. is taking a sharp turn toward the felonious. Taken into custody on May 21 on charges of car prowling, possession of marijuana, possession of a weapon, and malicious mischief, he breaks the glass in a police station window with a phone book and jumps out.[31] He bops all over the north end and the tony Newport neighborhood in Bellevue, just across the East Channel Bridge, where one of my Sunday school teachers used to live.

Chewed out by his supervisor, the officer responsible for the escape begins beating the bushes. He hears from informants that George is hiding in a boat or living under someone's house or holed up in a cave. George can't run fast because he has pins in his hip from a joyriding accident, but every time the cops spot him, he slips away into the woods. They post a $500 reward.

They hear he's at Denny's, the island's hangout for dope smokers and dodgy types; he's at Safeway; he's catching rays at Clarke Beach, at the south end.[32] They search for two weeks with the aid of three additional law enforcement agencies, the KIRO-TV helicopter, and K-9 units. When they finally catch up with him at a friend's house, he's booked on all the original charges and felony escape. He spends ten months in the county jail.

AFTER GEORGE IS RECAPTURED, there's another incident at the smelter. In June, residents of North Tacoma are complaining that "black particles" are pitting the paint on their homes, cars, and lawn furniture. Larry Lindquist, the ASARCO plant manager, admits that it's a "granular substance of arsenic, iron, and copper" from the Ruston smokestack.[33] He claims it can easily be cleaned off.

Mark Giske, who lives about a mile south of the smelter, says he's seen it coming out of the smokestack every night for a week. The stuff is "highly caustic and looks like soot," he says. "It must be something acidic because it eats through wax, paint, anything. And it won't come off either."[34] A smelter representative gives him a coupon for a free car wash.

Another resident complains that it's been "raining tar" since the end of April, saying that "the stuff just pours out of there" before sunset every night. The Puget Sound Air Pollution Control Agency, when asked to comment, says that ASARCO has recently admitted to having problems with its metallic arsenic and acid plants. But no one's asking the obvious question: If the stuff coming out of the stack can eat through paint, what can it do to your skin, your lungs, your blood, or your brain?

In July, it's the owners of 250 boats and a hundred cars parked at the Tacoma Yacht Club who are outraged when a "purple acid-like substance" is found eating through the fiberglass on their boats and the paint on their cars. This should perhaps not come as a complete surprise, given that the marina was built from slag and is yards away from the smelter. But you don't mess with a man's boat, and the yacht owners are hopping mad.

THE GREEN RIVER

A Ruston superintendent allows that acid might well be falling from the skies because the smelter has been fired up recently from "a dead cold start."[35] The marina manager shrugs, suggesting it's not that bad, but a boat owner says, "I can't get the stuff off. It looks like ink, and it's eating right into the gel," the coating on the fiberglass.[36] Another man, who's moored a fifty-foot yacht at the club for two nights, says he was horrified to wake up and find goo dissolving the finish on his boat. "It's got to be acid-based," he says.

On June 8, 1983, the first day that Tacoma residents are complaining of black grit, the Green River Killer abducts nineteen-year-old Constance Naon, who's been living in her fifteen-year-old Camaro, working at a sausage factory, and turning tricks out of the Red Lion Inn parking lot. She won't allow him to touch her breasts, so he strangles her, bites her on the breast, rapes her, and pushes a rock into her vagina.[37] She will be found months later just south of SeaTac, under the flight path. According to what police know, which isn't much, she's victim number seventeen.

Embedded in her scalp and in the soil beneath her are minuscule pink glass particles, similar to ones found on the body of Opal Mills. Police hope they have a clue, but they don't. The pink beads turn out to be garnets, volcanic in origin, a gift of Mount Saint Helens.[38]

WHILE ACID IS EATING through the yachts, William Ruckelshaus launches the "Tacoma process." Ruckelshaus was the first director of the EPA, tapped by Nixon to put out the fire on Ohio's Cuyahoga River. He takes over again in 1983 to put out the public relations flames lit by Ronald Reagan's first, controversial EPA director, Anne Gorsuch, who has gutted the agency and its Superfund program.

Representative of the Sagebrush Rebellion, a movement in western states to privatize federal land, and a chain-smoker of Marlboros (themselves an excellent source of cadmium, arsenic, and lead), Gorsuch is a firm believer in the benefits of pesticides.[39] She has promised an oil refinery in New Mexico that she won't enforce regulations limiting the amount of lead in gasoline, and she's working behind the scenes to relax the EPA's proposed standards, allowing small refineries to ignore them. This irritates larger corporations, such as Exxon, that are already in compliance.

Dr. Herbert Needleman of the Tooth Fairy study, now a professor of pediatrics at the University of Pittsburgh School of Medicine, points out, with others, that lead remains poisonous to children and that the $100 million a year that the refineries might save by keeping lead in fuel would be offset by the $140 million to $1.4 billion it would cost to treat the 200,000 to 500,000 children who would get lead poisoning.[40] But no one cares.

Reagan has already tipped his hand. During his first campaign, he's ginned up a scare over a potential "resource war" with the Soviet Union that could block American access to "strategic"—i.e., military-related—metals. As soon as he's elected, he establishes a Strategic Minerals Task Force to curry favor with mining and smelting interests, staffing it with top executives from ASARCO, Kennecott, and other corporations.[41]

He's steering attention away from leaded fuel by wringing his hands over inner-city welfare queens, the ones who bear "out-of-wedlock" children in subpar housing where the windowsills are covered in chalky, disintegrating lead paint.[42] If you blame lead paint, then you can blame bad mothers in Black neighborhoods—not ASARCO, not Exxon, and not refineries, with their sweet, sweet lead-lined political donations. In fact, although children in poor urban neighborhoods have multiple heavy exposures from industry, tailpipes, and paint, every child in America, rich or poor, has been exposed to lead from gasoline.

Gorsuch is full of good ideas. She yearns to incinerate toxic waste at sea, off the Maryland-Delaware coast. She's forced to resign after being cited for contempt of Congress for refusing to divulge Superfund records, but not before the chairman of the Puget Sound Air Pollution Control Agency writes to her to say, "The tens of thousands of persons living within 16 kilometers of the Tacoma smelter deserve better treatment of this issue by EPA than EPA headquarters apparently proposes."[43]

In her wake, Ruckelshaus, who has lived in Seattle for some time, is drawn into the Ruston maelstrom. Since 1970, the Clean Air Act has tasked the EPA with setting air quality standards for six common air pollutants, including lead and sulfur dioxide. But the agency drags its bureaucratic feet on a poison not on that list, arsenic, delaying a long-awaited federal standard determining whether and how much of it might cause cancer. Ruckelshaus isn't comfortable making the decision on how much arsenic people should be breathing or whether to put a stake in the black heart of the smelter, killing its six hundred jobs. He decides to leave it to the victims: they shall decide their own fate, he decrees, and they shall do it in a public comment period before the court-ordered deadline of July 11, 1983.

ASARCO deploys Hill & Knowlton, a powerful public relations firm, to whip up support. Polls are taken. Meetings are held. Buttons are worn. Some of them read HEALTH; others, JOBS. Some read BOTH. Seventy-two percent of those living near the smelter consider the facility an environmental health hazard.[44]

Greenpeace rallies. At meetings, intemperate remarks are made, and Mount Saint Helens is accused of releasing more arsenic than the smelter ever could. (It did not.) Fish are said to contain arsenic. Elderly smelter veteran Doss Bridges offers himself as evidence for the defense, saying, "I worked at that plant until I retired. I'm 88 years old and still breathing!" Another man says that cancer is caused by stress, and the EPA causes stress. One woman says, "Our town, Ruston, is all green and flowered."[45]

In the end, the debate having been turned away from lead and toward arsenic—a substance surrounded by scientific uncertainty engineered by ASARCO itself, which has stifled and distorted investigation—nothing happens. The EPA decides not to regulate arsenic emissions from the Ruston smelter. In the meantime, copper prices are plunging, and with unemployment at 7.5 percent, ASARCO announces in June 1984 that it will close the smelter within a year.

THAT SAME SUMMER, I'm supposed to be finishing my master's degree at Harvard, but instead I'm taking a semester off and living in a studio apartment in West Hollywood with my boyfriend. He's been almost catatonically silent since his father was murdered a few years earlier in a drug deal gone bad. We've cheated on each other. I have been open about it; he has not. Somehow my betrayal is felt to be more devious than his. He holds my hand and starts squeezing it until he's crushing it. I think uneasily about the time he tried to strangle me on a ferry in Greece.

I'm working as a secretarial assistant to an emeritus professor at UCLA who has something to do with the development of the scanning electron microscope. I'm secretly writing letters to my other boyfriend back at Harvard and torturing the one I'm with by playing Marvin Gaye singing "I Heard It Through the Grapevine" at top volume on the stereo. I'm not sorry.

In the apartment house, I'm climbing the back stairs after the little boy who lives next door. He wears a single white glove and blasts Michael Jackson singing "Billie Jean" at all hours, so I learn all the words to *Thriller* while lying in the bathtub reading *Democracy*, by Joan Didion.

Democracy is a story about Hawaii; the Harvard boyfriend is from Hawaii. It's a story about Inez Victor, who's married to a congressman running for president, a stand-in for some hypocritical loser like Ted Kennedy. Inez maintains a largely unrequitable passion for a cynical CIA fixer named Jack Lovett (*love it*: get it?) who deflowered her when she was a teen and is always turning up doing amoral Graham Greene–style things in Southeast Asia while delivering lines I admire, such as "I believe some human rights are being violated on the verandah."[46]

I don't have the faintest idea what my human rights are, and my Hollywood boyfriend can't decide whether to fuck me or kill me. When it comes to Los Angeles, I've threaded the needle, spending my last months there in the providential span between the Hillside Strangler and the Night Stalker.

LITTLE RICHIE RAMIREZ is all grown up and fancies himself a Satanist. He makes a pilgrimage to San Francisco to meet Anton LaVey, huckster founder of the Church of Satan and author of *The Satanic Bible* who, it's rumored, played the devil in *Rosemary's Baby*. Rick, as he's called, is impressed by LaVey and draws pentagrams on his arms, but he isn't much of a joiner.

Over the past few years, he's been spending his time in a seedy downtown Los Angeles apartment near the bus station, stealing cars, breaking and entering, and injecting cocaine. He rapes the woman who lives downstairs. His parents and his sister beg him to return to El Paso, and he travels back and forth via Greyhound. But El Paso holds little charm for an anonymous Satan worshipper who wants to prowl the highways all night.

He's six foot one, wears black, and never smiles. He has a dead stare, like a shark. He doesn't bathe. He has bad teeth. He's about to go berserk.

ON THE NIGHT of March 16, 1984, more than four hundred women march through a chilly downpour in Seattle bearing signs saying TAKE BACK THE NIGHT, making their way from the Pike Place Market to the county courthouse. Speakers accuse the police of undercounting the number of missing and murdered women while failing to provide the kind of major investigation that was organized during the Ted murders. "If 52 white middle-class college girls were missing or dead, there'd be an entirely different response," says Cookie Hunt of the Women's Coalition to Stop the Green River Murders.[47] She tells the crowd that the police major in charge of the Criminal Investigation Division has said they should "carry a whistle" to protect themselves. A woman yells in response, "Take away his gun and let HIM carry a whistle."[48]

The women are more right than they know about the police. Gary Ridgway has left microscopic spheres of DuPont Imron paint on his earliest victims, and he works at the only company in Seattle that's using that paint.[49] It contains lead.[50] The Green River Task Force has the evidence but never takes notice. More women will die as a result.

Others criticize a recent prostitution "bounty" law proposed in the state legislature that would offer a hundred dollars to anyone turning in a streetwalker to the authorities. A woman tells *The Seattle Times*, "Violence against women is an All American sport."[51]

Between 1974 and 1984, alarm grows over the phenomenon of serial killers, the "new murderers."[52] Apprehension is sparked in part by the FBI itself: Its Behavioral Sciences Unit is jockeying for funding, trying to pump up internal bureaucratic and public support. Its representatives have been feeding the press alarming statistics and gruesome details, claiming that there are around five thousand "unexplained murders" a year.[53] There are thirty-eight active serial killers in custody, but "there could be hundreds" at large.[54]

The press runs with it, grasping at vague references to "chromosome abnormalities or hormone imbalances."[55] Experts are marshaled: Dr. Park Dietz, associate professor of law and psychiatry at the University of Virginia School of Law and a future courtroom sage on the topic, speaks solemnly of sexual sadists and antisocial personalities who fantasize about torture "on nearly a daily basis since age 12."[56] The articles imply that the G-men have a handle on it. Yet because the killers are "much smarter than we give them credit for," the National Center for the Analysis of Violent Crime in Quantico, Virginia, will require additional funding.[57]

When it comes to serial killers, 1984 is shaping up to be what one scholar will later call "a moral panic."[58] In the Pacific Northwest, however, it's difficult to tell what distinguishes a moral panic from a real one.

ON APRIL 10, Richard Ramirez boards a Greyhound bus to San Francisco, staying in an apartment in the Tenderloin. On the street he spots nine-year-old Mei "Linda" Leung, a little girl with long dark hair and bangs. She's pacing the block with her eight-year-old brother, looking for a lost dollar bill. Rick tells the girl to follow him into the basement of his building to find the dollar. That's where he beats her and rapes her. He stabs her to death with a switchblade and leaves her body hanging from a pipe by her blouse. Her brother, who's wandered off, eventually goes into the basement and finds her there.

Then Rick returns to Los Angeles, where, two and a half months later, on June 28, he cases an apartment building in a working-class neighborhood north of Dodger Stadium, removing a screen from a downstairs bedroom window and crawling in. Jennie Vincow, seventy-nine, is asleep in bed. Wearing gloves, he tosses the place, searching for jewelry, cash, or valuables, and finds nothing. Frustrated, he takes his hunting knife and stabs her repeatedly, easily overpowering her when she wakes up screaming. He's sexually excited by her terror and slashes her throat, nearly severing her head. He steals a portable radio.

ON JULY 18, 1984, while Geraldine Ferraro is preparing to accept the nomination as Walter Mondale's vice presidential running mate at the Democratic National Convention in San Francisco, James Oliver Huberty, forty-one, a balding white "loner" who has apocalyptic fantasies and hoards guns, goes to the San Diego Zoo with his wife, Etna, and their older daughter, who is twelve. They live in San Ysidro, California, a suburb of San Diego that's home to the biggest border crossing with Mexico.

Some months earlier, the family moved from Canton, Ohio, to the West Coast after Huberty lost his job as a welder at Union Metal, a utility plant owned by Babcock & Wilcox, a corporation with a hand in everything from the Manhattan Project to New York's Indian Point: a major producer of boilers, nuclear steam generators, commercial nuclear reactors, fast breeder reactors, nuclear-powered submarines, and petrochemical refineries. In an exit interview, he told his employer he believed that the cadmium fumes he inhaled on the job were "making me crazy."[59]

Out of work, he's become despondent and suicidal. A week before visiting the zoo, he was fired from his job as a security guard. Returning from the zoo outing, Huberty, who has been trying and failing to make an appointment at a mental health facility, dresses in camouflage and collects a pistol, a shotgun, a nine-millimeter semiautomatic Uzi, and 257 rounds of ammunition. He goes to a crowded McDonald's nearby. He's hearing voices. Although he's never served in the armed forces, he starts yelling about how he's killed thousands in Vietnam and wants to kill more. He kills twenty-one people, including an eight-month-old infant and several children, while also injuring nineteen. Finally a SWAT team sniper shoots him from the roof of a neighboring building. At the time, it's considered the worst mass slaying in U.S. history.

MASSACRE AT MCDONALD'S: WHY? asks the *Los Angeles Times*, and many others attempt to probe the "mystery" of why this man went on a rampage. "Perhaps there was something inside James Huberty that made his explosion inevitable," one writer remarks.[60]

There is something inside. An analysis of his hair at autopsy reveals that it contains extraordinarily high levels of lead and cadmium. "He had the highest cadmium level we have ever seen in a human being," notes the chemical engineer who performs the analysis, adding that Huberty's kidneys nearly failed twice from the exposure.[61] Cadmium, like lead, is associated with violent behavior.[62]

DOWN IN FLORIDA, on the same day as the mass shooting, Ted Bundy is found to have cut through a corroded cell bar with two hacksaw blades bought from a guard for four dollars apiece, gaining access to an interior corridor. In this escape attempt, he has partnered with the quiet, Cuban-born Manuel Valle, who is on death row for having killed a cop in 1978 during a traffic stop in Coral Gables while driving a stolen Camaro. The exterior wall of Valle's second-floor cell is located in a blind spot shielded from the guards' view at night. It features a steel mesh grating that, if removed, could provide access to the prison yard.

Through the opening in his cell, Ted crawls into the corridor at night, joining Valle in his nearby cell. The two hide the alterations to their doors by smearing the damaged bars with a mixture of soap, toothpaste, foot powder, and paint. They spend their evenings sawing away at Valle's grating. They have acquired gloves, skullcaps, and a flashlight, fashioning a rope out of strips of sheet and planning to throw a large rubberized floor mat over the razor wire when they climb the fences. Should they succeed, they'll run through the woods using a compass and meet an accomplice who will drive them to the airport, where they'll head for Mexico.

THE GREEN RIVER

But on the night of their planned escape, guards are tipped off by an informant and arrive to search Ted's cell, discovering the cut bar within seconds. During the subsequent lockdown, all cells are searched, and two guards are arrested for smuggling contraband, including dozens of rounds of live ammunition, to multiple prisoners.[63]

Members of the FBI and the Florida State Attorney's Office interview Ted, finding him unrepentant. He's tried to escape from every prison he's been locked up in. As another serial rapist and murderer from Washington will say, "If I do escape, I promise you I will kill and rape again, and I will enjoy every minute of it."[64]

For ninety days, Ted is segregated in a separate wing and subjected to fifteen-minute checks. He loses yard privileges.[65] Resented by other inmates for the disruption to their lives, he stays out of the showers for months, electing to take "bird baths" in his cell, but retributory justice is said to catch up with him in the form of a prison gang, which rapes him.[66]

By October 1984, Ted is finding time to write to the Green River Task Force and offer his services in apprehending the killer he calls "the Riverman."[67] He has a subscription to the Tacoma *News Tribune*, and when the newspaper runs descriptions of the sites where bodies were left, he has a pretty good idea what's going on. He writes to Bob Keppel, who initiates first a lengthy correspondence and then a series of interviews with Ted in Florida, ostensibly to develop a profile of the killer but also to pick Ted's brain about his own murders. Ted demands details. He wants to see pictures.

He believes that this creature is, like him, from the Tacoma area, based on where he's leaving the bodies. The Riverman, Ted tells Keppel, is revisiting his bodies and lavishing affection on them, and cops should try to stake out the places where he's left them. These places, Ted suggests, will become sacred to the killer, and he's right.[68] One necrophile recognizes another.

AT THE END OF MARCH 1985, the Ruston smelter banks its fires permanently after ninety-five years in operation to little fanfare but much local distress. On March 18, five hundred workers at the Ruston plant are laid off. As the fires die, the community loses not only jobs and a unique if precarious sense of self but also the uninterrupted stream of copper, lead, and arsenic particulates the stack has bestowed on them for nearly a hundred years.

Union workers are granted thirty-nine weeks of unemployment benefits but denied an additional $1.5 million in federal benefits that they asked for. Thirty workers retrain by taking computer classes at Tacoma Community College. Others plan to become truck drivers. The volunteer fire department is dissolved and its steam whistle, long powered by the plant's boiler, falls silent. Dropped from the corporate teat, a reluctant Ruston is forced to rely on Tacoma not only for fire protection but for water, electric services, and schools. It loses two of its six police officers.

Some thirty to forty buildings contaminated with heavy metals remain to be dismantled. Ruston town clerk Loretta Prettyman is overwhelmed at the prospect, telling the newspaper, "I'm getting to the point of being lost."[69] The mayor, Peter Brudevold, is "hoping and praying that in the future, other industries will come and be located around the smelter."[70]

BUT 1985 BELONGS to the Night Stalker, Richard Ramirez, initially known as the Valley Intruder or the Walk-In Killer. The press is running out of names for these guys whose behavior is more bizarre than anyone can comprehend.

Graduate of the school of ASARCO and an intravenous cocaine addict, Rick becomes completely unhinged in March, leaving a trail of destruction across a wide swath of communities north, east, and west of downtown Los Angeles. On March 17, he follows Maria Hernandez, twenty, who is driving her gold Camaro to her condominium in Rosemead. As she gets out of the car in the parking garage, he walks toward her, carrying a .22 revolver at his side. He's dressed entirely in black, wearing an AC/DC baseball cap. He's been listening to "Highway to Hell" over and over on his Walkman.

Maria is carrying her keys and a purse. She presses a button on the wall to close the garage door, and Rick ducks under it, his cap falling off. She's unlocking the door of her condo when she hears a noise and turns to see him raising the gun to shoot her. She blocks her face defensively with her hand, and the bullet hits the keys, ricocheting into the garage. Bleeding, she falls and plays dead. Only her right hand is injured.

Rick mounts the stairs to the now unlocked door to Maria's house and enters it. In the kitchen is her roommate, Dayle Okazaki, thirty-four, who ducks beneath the counter when she sees him. She's heard the shot in the garage. She waits, then gradually lifts her head to see if he's still there. He shoots her in the forehead.

He sees Maria again, on the street, where she's run out of the garage, and points the gun at her. She dives behind a Volkswagen. He drives off but has left his cap and an eyewitness.

On the freeway again, he follows another woman, who exits at Monterey Park. It's thirty-year-old Tsai-Lian Yu, also called Veronica. She sees him following her and maneuvers behind him, hoping to get his license plate number. At a red light, he gets out of his car and walks over to her, and she angrily confronts him through the window. He tries to grab her and pull her out. Her driver's-side door is locked, and she's screaming as he jumps over the hood of the car and yanks open the unlocked passenger door. He gets in and shoots her twice in the side. She staggers into the street and dies.

It's only just begun, as the song says. Over the coming summer months, in May, July, and August, he will enter, at night, a dozen homes in Whittier, Monterey Park, Monrovia, Burbank, Arcadia, Sierra Madre, Glendale, Sun Valley, Northridge, Diamond Bar, and Mission Viejo, shooting, knifing, beating, stomping, strangling, and raping the inhabitants and, on occasion, mutilating their bodies. He draws pentagrams on walls. He cuts the eyes out of a woman after he shoots her and takes them with him in a jewelry box. They're brown.

He ransacks the houses, stealing cash, coins, diamonds, cameras, VCRs, watches, rings, and necklaces, carrying the loot off in bloody pillowcases. He makes the women swear on Satan that they've told him where all the valuables are. He will utilize his .22 as well as knives, a machete, telephone and electrical cords, neckties, handcuffs, thumb cuffs, a tire iron, and his own fists and feet. His victims are men, women, and children, ranging in age from three to eighty-three. He rapes an eighty-one-year-old invalid and draws a pentagram on her thigh with lipstick.

Some of those he attacks will survive. He tends to shoot the men in the head; they generally do not survive. His modus operandi is that he has none. He employs every conceivable method of violence and assault. He is without form. He is void.

Los Angeles loses its mind. It's an oppressively hot summer, with temperatures routinely over a hundred in the San Gabriel Valley. By July it's obvious to the press and the public alike that a serial murderer of unparalleled viciousness rules the city. In Arcadia, requests for police security checks are up 400 percent over the previous month. Newspapers advise homeowners to install outside lighting, alarms, window gates, and deadbolts and to get rid of louvered windows. In sweltering weather, people are told to keep their windows nailed shut and their curtains closed. They're told to practice dialing 911 in the dark. They line up to buy guns and guard dogs. Frank Salerno, the hardened detective for the Los Angeles County Sheriff's Department who handled the Hillside Strangler case, is assigned to investigate, and even he's sleeping with a gun by his bed. Not since the summer of Charles Manson has the city been so transfixed by dread.

Rick Ramirez doesn't know it yet, but Salerno and his partner, Detective Gil Carrillo, are working promising leads. Creeping around back bedroom windows and sliding doors, he has left shoe prints in flower beds, as well as in pools of blood inside homes, and police have traced the make and model of the sneaker. It's an Avia aerobic shoe with a distinctive waffle design on the sole, size 11½. Contacting the shoe's manufacturer and designer, police learn that very few pairs were made and sold, so few, in fact, that only a single pair in a size 11½ has ever been sold in California.

The shoe is a unicorn, and police keep the information confidential so the perpetrator will not destroy the best physical evidence against him.

There are also his teeth. In pain, Rick has been seeking out dentists. He's always had bad teeth: Cocaine wears down enamel when smoked or snorted. Lead exposure causes dental disease as well, replacing calcium in tooth enamel, resulting in a thin, deficient layer that's easily worn away. When police locate a stolen vehicle that Rick has been using, they find a slip of paper with a dentist appointment on it, and they stake it out. Virtually every surviving victim has mentioned his disgusting mouth.

He doesn't show up for his appointment. He skips town, going to San Francisco, where he shoots a couple in their sixties, killing the man and raping the woman, who survives. At a press conference, Mayor Dianne Feinstein publicly reveals the information about the Avia shoe, earning the lasting enmity of police throughout the state. Rick Ramirez goes to the Golden Gate Bridge that night and throws his pair in the water. On August 25 he returns to Los Angeles, where he beats and shoots another couple in Mission Viejo. He's not aware that police have finally identified him based on a single fingerprint in one of the cars he has stolen. They've leaned on his fences and drug associates. They release his mug shot to the press on August 29, 1985.

Unaware of this development, he takes a bus to Tucson the next day to visit his brother Robert. When he returns to L.A. the next morning, he's staring back at himself from the cover of every Spanish and English newspaper in the city. He is no longer an anonymous devil: Invasor Nocturno, El Matador, the Night Stalker, the Killer. He's Richard Ramirez. Panicking in East Los Angeles, he tries to carjack first one vehicle, then another, and people scream when they see him. A crowd begins chasing him through Boyle Heights, ballooning from dozens to several hundred, men grabbing pipes and fence posts. When they catch up to him, they beat him without mercy, but he's saved by the police.

In the midst of such high drama, it's hard to see his crimes for what they are: the exposed tip of a mammoth iceberg. In 1985, 95,908 violent crimes are committed in Los Angeles County, including more than 1,000 homicides and 4,448 rapes.[71]

Leaded gasoline won't be fully banned in California until 1992. The CDC again revises its definition of an "elevated blood lead level in children," this time to twenty-five micrograms per deciliter.[72]

No one has taken Dennis Rader off the board. He's still running around in Wichita and the suburb of Park City, working for ADT and fantasizing about how a neighbor, Marine Hedge, fifty-three, a single woman who works at a coffee shop in a nearby medical center, would look with a rope around her neck. He's a Boy Scout leader and the president of Christ Lutheran Church. He refers to these roles as his "white hat" activities, but his habits bleed into one another.

When, on April 27, 1985, he puts on his "black hat" and kills Marine Hedge by strangling her in the middle of the night, he strips her, ties her up in a bondage position, and drives her to his church, where he poses her dead body and takes Polaroid pictures. "I did not use the altar," he'll say later. "I was bad and disturbed, but I still had respect for some items of God's house."[73]

After he's finished his photo shoot, he dumps her in a ditch.

Back in the Northwest, in 1986, George Waterfield Russell Jr. seduces an impressionable fourteen-year-old girl on the island, climbing in her window to spend nights with her. She doesn't find out until later that he's twenty-eight. He gets her pregnant before her fifteenth birthday, and while he's in jail for stealing a TV and selling beer to minors, she has an abortion. Then she drops him.

Tacoma's reputation for violent crime remains intact, and the region has long been developing a remarkable subspeciality, producing boys bent on committing sexual crimes with a peculiar woodland kink. Gary Ridgway, who loves to have sex outdoors, covers the wall behind the headboard of his bed with silk-screened wallpaper depicting a forest scene so that when he rapes and murders women at home, he can enjoy the view.

Gerald Friend, born in 1937 in Puyallup, had moved into the Tacoma smelter plume by the age of twelve and began fantasizing about sexual torture, much as Gary and Ted would. At fifteen he abducted a seven-year-old boy, stripped him, and tied him to a tree in the woods. He pinched the boy's genitals with pliers, cut off his hair, and forced him to roll in nettles before releasing him, naked. He was convicted of rape in 1960 after abducting a twelve-year-old girl, threatening to kill her, raping her twice, and cutting her hair in a wilderness area near Mount Rainier.[74] The girl escaped by swimming across the Carbon River when he fell asleep.[75]

Released on parole in 1984 despite two successful escape attempts, in which he remained at large for weeks before recapture, Friend reoffends on June 5, 1987, by offering a ride to a fourteen-year-old girl, driving her to his mobile home, hanging her from a pulley attached to the ceiling in his bedroom, whipping her, cutting her with a knife and razor, burning her with hot wax and a propane torch, and raping her repeatedly. He's driving her into the Cascade Mountains near Mount Rainier when she's finally able to slip away at a gas station.[76] When police search his bedroom, they find a gym bag full of "miscellaneous women's panties," twenty-two pornographic magazines, and a Barbie doll handcuffed with chains.[77]

Friend is a suspect in the Green River killings, and his name is placed near the top of a list of some twenty thousand men under suspicion. He becomes a person of interest in the murder of Michella Welch, twelve, snatched on March 26, 1986, while riding her bike in Puget Park, a heavily wooded ravine just south of Ruston. She's been beaten and sexually assaulted and had her throat slashed with a knife. He's suspected in the murder of Jennifer Bastian, age thirteen, sexually assaulted and strangled on August 4, 1986, while riding her new Schwinn bike in Point Defiance Park, the peninsular park adjacent to the Ruston smelter. So many crimes, so many suspects.

Indeed, Tacoma is so crime-ridden that it's been dubbed "Little Detroit of the West."[78] Los Angeles gangs the Bloods and the Kitchen Crips are sending representatives north, contesting territory with a spinoff group, the Hilltop Crips. Crips and Bloods are forcibly recruiting kids of eleven and twelve to sell crack cocaine in Hilltop, a historically Black neighborhood in Tacoma settled by men who since the 1930s and '40s have served tours at nearby Fort Lewis. Due to redlining and discriminatory lending, housing has been largely unavailable to their families in Tacoma outside Hilltop and a few other neighborhoods.[79]

Because of the proximity of Fort Lewis, the percentage of Black people in Tacoma is higher than in cities of comparable size in the Northwest, such as Everett and Spokane. But in the wake of recessions throughout the 1970s and '80s, good jobs, schools, and housing are not available to them. During the Reagan years especially, this is said to be their own fault, as if somehow Black communities in every major city in the country—Philadelphia, Baltimore, Chicago, Cleveland, Cincinnati, New Orleans, Los Angeles, Tacoma—have chosen to live in the poorest housing available, invariably distinguished by flaking lead paint and in neighborhoods adjoining major industrial sources of pollution, such as smelters, oil refineries, and lead battery recycling plants.

In line with national trends, by the late '80s, drive-by shootings, carjackings, armed robberies, and hostage situations are skyrocketing not only in Hilltop and the Eastside but throughout northern Tacoma, central Tacoma, local shopping districts, Tacoma Mall, Lakeside Mall, and in what's called "the ring around the bases," the strip malls and cheap apartments and substandard housing surrounding Fort Lewis–McChord Air Force Base.[80]

What is geographically unique is this: a decades-old smelter plume falls across the most heavily populated area of Pierce County, from Tacoma down to the state capital of Olympia, ten miles outside the county, clinging to the southern reaches of Puget Sound like a dirty bathtub ring.[81]

AT A FEW MINUTES before noon on September 16, 1986, in Wichita, Bill Wegerle comes home for lunch to find his twenty-eight-year-old wife,

Vicki, dead on the bedroom floor, tied up and strangled with a nylon stocking. Their two-year-old son is unharmed in a playpen.

Dennis Rader has accessed the house by pretending to be a telephone repairman. He's wearing "technician-type clothes" adorned with a Southwestern Bell Telephone logo that he's cut out of a phone book and taped to a hard hat.[82] He picked Vicki Wegerle because he liked her deep front porch and the piano music he heard her practicing. He loves organ and piano music and finds the score from *The Phantom of the Opera* sexually arousing. He fantasizes about murdering the organist at his church but can't figure how to do it without getting caught.

Bill Wegerle becomes the chief suspect in his wife's murder. That same year, DNA is first introduced as evidence in the American criminal court system.

ON AUGUST 29, 1988, St. Martin's publishes the second novel by Thomas Harris, *The Silence of the Lambs*, featuring what *Kirkus Reviews* calls "one of the great villains of thrillerdom," Dr. Hannibal Lecter. Having appeared briefly in Harris's earlier novel, *Red Dragon*, Lecter is said to be based in part on the uncanny charisma of Ted Bundy, although the author has substituted cannibalism as a perhaps more socially acceptable alternative to Ted's appetite for sex with dead bodies.[83]

I have encountered Hannibal Lecter in *Manhunter*, the first movie version of Harris's *Red Dragon*, directed by Michael Mann and released in 1986 at the height of the "moral panic" over serial killers. I see the movie in a seedy Boston theater on a side street yards away from the Christian Science Mother Church, which looms out of the lowlands of the Back Bay like a goiter. The movie stars William Petersen as Will Graham, a detective similar to Bob Keppel, who interviews Lecter (spelled "Lecktor" in the film) as a means of getting inside the mind of a serial killer. At the conclusion of their interview, held in a jarringly white cell in an asylum for the criminally insane, Graham, who's had a nervous breakdown after successfully investigating and arresting the good doctor, tells him, "I know that I'm not smarter than you."

Lecktor replies, "Then how did you catch me?"

Graham says, "You had disadvantages."

"What disadvantages?" asks Lecktor.

Graham says, "You're insane."[84]

I'm supposed to be working on my dissertation, but I've gone to this movie alone, ducking into the theater. It feels vaguely pornographic but also like a documentary. The movie is accurate. Ted Bundy's death row attorneys are desperately trying to prove that he's insane: mentally incompetent and incapable of assisting his lawyers in his own defense. It hardly matters whether it's true; in Florida, it's a hard sell.

"BLOODY TACOMA" is what the headlines call the first weeks of 1988, with six people slain by February 15.[85] Police blame drugs, guns, and rock cocaine, pointing the finger at Hilltop, around six miles southeast of the smelter, prone to gang activity. There, bullets are flying through residents' bedroom walls. "There's shooting up here every night," says a Hilltop woman who's found a stray bullet on her mattress, adding, "It's got a lot to do with all the crack houses."[86] In the first few weeks of the year, a cocaine user is shot in front of the Blue Bird Tavern, and the body of a suspected dealer is dumped in the middle of an intersection south of the Tacoma Mall.

But it's not all drugs. On the morning of Sunday, January 17, 1988, Peter Brudevold, the mayor of Ruston, who was hoping and praying for heavy industry to rescue his town, is found in his backyard, face down in a pool of blood. He's been manually strangled and beaten multiple times in the head with a hammer. He dies the day before his sixty-second birthday.

Former manager of a drive-in and a bowling alley, Brudevold had been known to "cut a mean rug" at the Big Bad Wolf Tavern and had always been a bit of a drinker, often arriving at his Ruston home in the wee hours with noisy friends in tow.[87] He'd been cited for driving under the influence after tying one on at the Ruston Inn. But he's also remembered fondly for helping neighbors, leaving buckets of mussels, flats of strawberries, or bouquets of roses from his garden on the front steps of those in need.

Less than a week after his murder, one of his friends, Eddie Wayne Bell, forty, is pulled out of the basement of his estranged wife's home in the Eastside neighborhood of Tacoma. He's been wielding a knife and has swallowed three bottles of aspirin in an attempt to commit suicide. Police find a note signed "Ed," saying he's sorry for killing "Pete." They also find a bloody hammer and a pack of cigarettes tying him to the mayor's murder.[88]

Bell, a longtime Tacoma resident, has served prison terms for burglary and rape and later claims that on that fateful Sunday, Mayor Brudevold grabbed his crotch and tried to kiss him. After Bell's trial and second-degree murder conviction, the judge sentences him to the maximum sentence of eighteen years, citing the fact that he can become "unpredictably violent" when provoked.[89]

ON DECEMBER 28, 1988, the skeletal remains of Stacy Elizabeth Hawn, age twenty-three, are found in Skagit County, Washington. Last seen alive on July 7, Stacy, while working as a prostitute, has had the misfortune of encountering Robert Lee Yates Jr., currently thirty-six, married to his second wife, Linda, and the father of two daughters. A warrant officer in the U.S. Army, he was stationed in Germany from 1980 to 1984, but, beginning with the murder of Stacy, he has returned to the United States, where he'll be flying helicopters and killing prostitutes for the foreseeable future.

BY JANUARY 1989, Ted Bundy has evaded the death penalty for a decade. He's guarded his history, clutching his killings close to his chest, admitting them to no one. To Stephen Michaud and Bob Keppel he has spoken in coy hypotheticals. Throughout 1988, he has weighed the idea of confessing to Keppel, repeatedly changing an appointment with the detective, but his attorneys have advised him not to give incriminating statements.

He believes that when his appeals have run their course, he may be able to leverage information on the missing women for an extension of his life, trading "bones for time." Georgann Hawkins has never been found. Neither has Donna Manson or many victims in Utah and other states.

Working pro bono, his two appellate attorneys, James Coleman Jr. and Polly Nelson of the Washington, D.C., firm of Wilmer, Cutler & Pickering, arrange to have first a psychologist, Dr. Art Norman, and then a psychiatrist, Dr. Dorothy Otnow Lewis, evaluate their client for mental incompetence. Dr. Norman disappoints them, finding neither mental illness nor brain damage.[90] In his view, Bundy is a classic sociopath, someone who enjoys killing.

Dr. Lewis, on the other hand, supplies everything they might have hoped for. A graduate of Radcliffe and the Yale School of Medicine, she specializes in multiple personality disorder and has assessed clients in high-profile criminal cases, including Arthur Shawcross, a serial killer in Rochester, New York, and Mark David Chapman, the man who shot John Lennon. In multiple studies, often written with her collaborator, Dr. Jonathan Pincus, she has traced the fantasies of serial murderers back to episodes of sexual and physical abuse in childhood. She pays particular attention to damage to the frontal cortex, which results in aggression and impulsivity. She's testified in multiple trials and has been criticized by her peers for employing hypnosis and planting false memories.

Alongside Polly Nelson, she interviews Ted at length and learns that he was hit over the head with a two-by-four in an apparent accident when he was six. Approaching family members, she hears that Samuel Cowell, Ted's grandfather, was prone to violence—throwing one of his daughters down the stairs, kicking pets—and that his wife, Ted's grandmother, suffered from mental illness and received electroshock therapy. From one of Louise Bundy's younger sisters she hears a remarkable story about something Ted did as a toddler in Philadelphia: one night he went into the kitchen, gathered a number of knives, and arranged them next to his aunt in her bed.[91]

She learns of Ted's episodes of depression, in which he felt unable to attend classes and couldn't hold down a job, followed by periods of mania, in which he felt energetic and euphoric, successfully completing a degree and working on political campaigns. Citing his mood shifts during the Florida trials and his tendency to undermine his own defense, she diagnoses him as bipolar.

None of it makes any difference: Florida courts assert that Ted was competent to stand trial and assist in his defense, and after a few final legal maneuvers, including an appeal to the Supreme Court, his execution is all but certain. He begins confessing, in the most tortured and circuitous fashion, to Nelson, Lewis, and, in the final hours of his life, a series of lawmen, including Bob Keppel, FBI agent William Hagmaier, and sheriffs from Utah, Colorado, and Idaho. Like mendicants before a guru, they shuffle in to see him, imploring him for details, names, places where missing bodies can be found. But most of them haven't thought to bring the most basic vehicle of enlightenment: maps.

He's telling different stories to different people. He cannot bear to admit, even to hardened investigators such as Keppel and Hagmaier, the full extent of his violence, necrophilia, and mutilation of bodies. While confessing to thirty murders, he acknowledges to the FBI man that he cut off the heads of half a dozen of his victims and kept them, for a time, perhaps in his boardinghouse room.[92] For what purpose, he doesn't say.

He refuses to clarify when he began killing. Over the years, when asked specifically about his first murder, he's offered a mass of contradictions and equivocations. He tells Dr. Norman that he picked up a couple of girls near Ocean City, New Jersey, in 1969, which was "the first time he had ever done it."[93] He tells Hagmaier he started killing in May 1973, when he picked up a hitchhiker near Olympia, contradicting what he earlier told Stephen Michaud, to whom he insisted that 1973 was a "dormant stage."[94] He's also mentioned 1972. He's implied to Michaud that he was voyeuristically canvassing neighborhoods in 1966 or 1967, a time corresponding to the attack on the two stewardesses on Queen Anne Hill.[95]

According to Dr. Ronald Holmes, a University of Louisville professor of criminal justice, Ted has suggested that he might have started killing at age fourteen, an admission supported by his telling Lewis, in his final hours, that "something happened" the summer he was "thirteen, fourteen."[96] Both Lewis and Al Carlisle, who assessed Ted in 1976, are intrigued by his teen years, deeming suspicious his self-professed ignorance of the disappearance of Ann Marie Burr.

In his last moments with Ted, Keppel asks directly if he killed Burr in 1961. His denial is a model of indirection and special pleading. He doesn't say no. He says he couldn't have done it, because he was too young and the Burr house was too far from his home. "Never went to that area," he says, which is a lie, because his uncle lived around the corner. "Never had any occasion to go there. It was just, just another part of the forest."[97] He's told Keppel that there are some murders to which people like him will never confess. Keppel believes this is one of them.

In the days leading up to the execution, the scene outside the prison becomes medieval. Crowds gather outside the prison yard, frat boys from Gainesville baying for blood and wearing TGIFRYDAY shirts, performing for their girlfriends and television news vans. To add to the festivities, two local men burn an effigy of Ted tied to a kitchen chair, lighting candles on its head as if it were a birthday cake.

The night before his execution, Ted gives a self-pitying interview to the unctuous television evangelist James Dobson, headliner of Focus on the Family, blaming his crimes on pornography. It will air after he's dead. Then he calls his mother in Tacoma. He says, "I'm so sorry I've given you all such grief . . . but a part of me was hidden all the time."[98] Nonetheless, he assures her, "the Ted Bundy you knew also existed."

Louise Bundy is now living in a house only a few blocks from where Ann Marie Burr vanished. Standing at her dining room table, clutching a pencil, she tells the boy born out of wedlock in a foundling home, the one she abandoned before retrieving him: "You'll always be my precious son."[99]

He's written a last letter to Liz Kloepfer, who hasn't had any contact with him for years. The letter is intercepted by her daughter, Molly, who destroys it.[100]

THE GREEN RIVER

At 7:06 a.m. on Tuesday, January 24, 1989, Ted Bundy is electrocuted in the death chamber of the Florida State Prison in Starke. The person who throws the switch, never identified, is said to have been a woman.

In February, the tabloid *Weekly World News* publishes illicit photos of Ted Bundy's body, apparently taken in the funeral home. His eyes are frozen open.

That same month, *The New Yorker* runs a Talk of the Town comment by Roger Angell on the spectacle. The Waspy New Englander gently tut-tuts at the pornographic nature of Dobson's prurient interest and the "complicit knowledge" of a television audience that tunes in to watch a dead man.[101]

"I don't believe that Ted Bundy or anyone else understood what made him commit and repeat the crimes he confessed to," Angell writes, "which were rape murders of an unimaginable violence and cruelty."[102] I'm a fact-checker at *The New Yorker*, and I solemnly confirm these words.

IN ANOTHER PART OF THE FOREST, George Waterfield Russell Jr. is approaching criticality. He's still breaking and entering and staring at sleeping women on the island, but he's also working the Eastside suburbs. He's spending a lot of time across the bridge in Bellevue, hanging out at the Black Angus, a popular steakhouse and nightclub. He acts as if it's his office, setting up shop in a booth, placing a police scanner on the table, reading a newspaper, and pretending to be a policeman or an informer. He wears a navy-blue Seattle Police Department cap.[103] Sometimes he's clutching a textbook: *Crime Scene Search and Physical Evidence Handbook*. At night, out prowling, he carries two knives. At some point in 1990 he steals a Smith & Wesson pistol.[104]

At the steakhouse, he meets and seduces a woman, Mindy Charley, and moves in with her, without asking. He tells her he's an undercover policeman and can't talk about his job. After a tumultuous monthslong, on-again off-again romance, Mindy orders him to move out, tossing his stuff out the door. In a rage, he beats her up, smashing everything in her apartment, including the furniture, and is arrested the next day, February 12,

1990, at his stepfather's house on Mercer Island. Out on parole, he's reported for casing houses on 72nd Street, where my parents live.[105] On March 21 he's brought up on an outstanding warrant, as well as charges of criminal trespass and obstruction of justice. He gets four days.

After harassing a waitress, calling her a bitch and threatening to kill her, he's banned from the Black Angus.[106] He has an answer to this. He creates a tableau vivant, or more like the opposite of *vivant*. On the night of June 28, he beats and strangles Mary Ann Pohlreich, twenty-seven, a woman he met recently while clubbing at Papagayo's Cantina, another Bellevue nightspot. He kills her in his friend's pickup truck when she refuses to have sex with him and then spends several hours with her body, penetrating her vaginally and anally.

He drives her body to the Black Angus, around the back where the trash is taken out, leaving her naked on the ground, elaborately posed, left foot crossed over the right ankle, hands crossed over her stomach, left over right. He places a Douglas fir cone inside her cupped hand. Over her right eye he balances the plastic lid from a container of Frito-Lay dip. He sweeps a small pile of trash next to her head and props the broom nearby.[107] At autopsy, the as yet unknown offender is labeled a "sadistic necrophile."[108]

There's no identification on the body, and it takes a couple of days before Mary Ann's roommate, away that weekend, reports her missing.

Over the next six weeks, George meets up with another group of women roommates and begins hanging out with this new harem, napping in their beds while they're at work. On August 9, less than two miles from the Bellevue Black Angus, he murders Carol Beethe, thirty-six, in the bedroom of her Bellevue home. A veteran bartender, she serves drinks at a place called Cucina! Cucina!, supporting her two daughters; she's probably run into George Russell on the nightclub circuit. Whether he follows her home or has staked her out before this, he turns up in her bedroom and beats her to death with an unidentified blunt object. Defensive wounds are minimal: he knocks her out early on but then beats her and beats her and beats her, far more than is required to kill her.

He spends considerable time with her acquiescent form. He positions her in bed, placing her head in a plastic dry-cleaning bag and then resting a pillow over her face. He puts red high-heeled shoes on her feet and splays her legs open. He inserts a rifle into her vagina, its stock supported by her feet, facing the doorway of her room. He locks the door.[109]

Her daughter sees the silhouette of a man wielding a flashlight moving through the hallway that night and thinks it's her mother's boyfriend. It's not.

Now he's the "Eastside Killer," and less than a month later, on September 3, he murders Andrea "Randi" Levine, twenty-four, a secretary at a business services center. He's met her casually, through friends. Before this night, her landlords have noticed a prowler in the backyard. She, too, is found on top of her bed, posed, a white dildo in her mouth, a copy of *More Joy of Sex* propped on her left arm, her legs akimbo. Similar to Carol Beethe, she's been beaten in what police call a "blitz" attack, and was probably asleep when attacked and killed, although the killer continued to bludgeon her repeatedly and with great force.[110] Once she was dead, he cut her more than 230 times over the surface of her body, including the bottoms of her feet.[111] The anger he's acting out on the bodies of his victims is meant to be shocking, and it is. After years of being everybody's friend, palling around with the police, moving in with acquaintances, putting one over on everybody, he's finally broken through to say what he really feels about white women. He feels like beating them to death, raping them, and posing them in sexually degrading positions. In George Waterfield Russell Jr., the Pacific Northwest has produced another in a long line of outlandishly wanton necrophiliac killers who've lived, at one time or another, within the Tacoma smelter plume.

BRIDGES IN THE PACIFIC Northwest never stay upstanding for long, and in November 1990 the Lacey V. Murrow Memorial Bridge—the Mercer Island bridge that has been an accessory to Ted Bundy's crimes and seen all manner of dump trucks, cement trucks, pickup trucks, and passenger cars fly through the air, seeking shelter in the bosom of Lake Washington—is fifty years old. It's the oldest floating bridge in the world.

Finally, it is being resurfaced with a brand-new deck. It's been closed to traffic for nearly two years, after a new floating span was built alongside. In its wisdom, the Washington State Department of Transportation, along with its Indiana-based contractor, Traylor Bros., decides to remove the old concrete sidewalks on the bridge by using high-pressure hoses, a practice called hydrodemolition. The Department of Ecology will not permit dirty demolition water to run off into the lake. So the contractor elects to store the wastewater in the hollow concrete pontoons of the bridge itself, until such time as it can be pumped into water trucks and disposed of elsewhere.

Someone is forgetting what every hiker learns: how heavy water is. It's as heavy as a body.

The work is being performed in November, a month in which it not uncommonly rains in Seattle, a time when winter storms sweep in off the Pacific. Yet, over the Thanksgiving holiday, workers are a little neglectful. They've left the hatchways in some of the pontoons open. They've blasted holes in the concrete and failed to seal them. When a severe storm begins to blow, the bridge is open to the elements.

It rains and rains. Rivers in the Snoqualmie Valley, flood-prone, begin to overflow their banks. On the night of Saturday, November 24, on what would have been Ted Bundy's forty-fourth birthday, the pontoons begin to fill. Wind whips across the old span. Whitecaps churn, spume flies, and the waves beat and beat and beat.

The month of November delivers a record-breaking rainfall of 10.05 inches, and during the twenty-four-hour period ending on Saturday, some 3.56 inches falls, topping a record set in 1959. Emergencies are declared in eighteen of Washington's thirty-nine counties. The state runs out of sandbags and has to import more from New York. Sixteen state highways are closed, and more than two thousand people are evacuated.

At nine in the morning on Sunday, November 25, a KIRO Radio traffic helicopter is up in the air reporting on the Snoqualmie Valley flooding.

THE GREEN RIVER

It's piloted by Paul Brendle, and he hears that something's happening to the floating bridge. Workers are frantically trying to pump the water out, but then they run for their lives. The bridge is riding low. It's breaking up. On the beaches and shorelines, people stand and point, hands over their mouths.

By the time Brendle arrives overhead, a third of the bridge has broken away from the west end, closest to Seattle, "and has drifted out to an angle [of] approximately twenty degrees," he reports.[112] He calls the scene as if it were a baseball game, delivering a play-by-play to KIRO anchor Rick Van Cise:

> And here it goes now. There's a huge yellow crane, one of those big construction cranes. And when I made the last pass over a few moments ago, Rick, it was in fact high and dry. And now it's up to the top of its wheels. So this crane will be pitching over in any moment and going underwater. It will also go to the bottom of Lake Washington.
>
> And another section of the bridge is now giving away, breaking up. As I'm watching it right now, the concrete is bubbling. Now it lifts up. The entire section is canted about a forty-degree angle, just like a big battleship rolling over and getting ready to pitch straight down. The crane is gone now.[113]

The bridge isn't content to sink by itself. It tries to take the new one with it. As the old span tears away, it snaps twelve of the fifty-eight cables anchoring the new bridge, and tugboats rush to stabilize it. Fresh storms are in the offing. Billy J. Hartz, a University of Washington civil engineering professor who's been brought in to assess the Hood Canal debacle, says of the Department of Transportation and Traylor Bros., "These people just don't seem to understand marine design. I just couldn't believe they'd do it again."[114]

It's not hard to believe. For some reason, people here seem to have a hard time learning things.

The enfeebled new bridge must be closed while traffic is routed to the

Evergreen Point Floating Bridge or south, skirting Lake Washington, routes that are soon stalled in gridlock. A COMMUTER'S NIGHTMARE, screams *The Seattle Times*: I-90 MAY BE CLOSED FOR WEEKS. Nobody talks about hubris or human stupidity, although everybody wants to blame the Traylor Bros. Surveying the damage from another helicopter, Governor Booth Gardner says, "My state is falling apart on me."[115]

Engineers around the world marvel over the catastrophe, pointing out that there's pretty much one way to sink a floating bridge and that's to fill it with water, the way a child sinks a toy boat in a bathtub.[116] Divers begin searching the lake bed for keys to the mystery, while an anonymous expert rolls his eyes. "If it sank, it got water in it," he says. "It's that simple."[117] Washington State is "the floating-bridge capital of the world," *The Seattle Times* notes, but it "could as easily these days be called the sinking-bridge capital of the world."[118]

Why the surprise? The malevolence has never been in question: It was in the men who made it. It was their design. It's been killing people from the beginning. The bulge, the reversible lane—the whole contraption has been a serial menace, like something Stephen King thought up.

Somewhere, Stacy Sparks is smiling.

Chapter 12

The Towering Inferno

> The world has many times been turned to chaos.
> And at that moment this ancient rock,
> here and elsewhere, fell broken into pieces.
>
> —Dante, The Inferno[1]

The story begins with the discovery of a body on February 24, 1988, in a fictitious town five miles south of the Canadian border, twelve miles west of the state line, not far from Lewis Fork, off Highway 2.[2] The fisherman who finds her is wearing the same red-checked lumberjack coat my father used to wear, a coat seen on searchers in photos after the disappearance of Ann Marie Burr.

From the opening moments of *Twin Peaks*, which airs on April 8, 1990, I am transfixed. I know this place. David Lynch has seen it: cedar boughs blowing in the wind, mill stacks wafting white smoke. Owls, staring. Under the ponderous soundtrack, there's Mount Si, which my father has climbed to prove he will never die. There's a girl's body wrapped in plastic on a beach, sand peppering her dead skin.

In the establishing shot of the Mar-T Cafe, an off-white VW like the one last seen driven by Ted Bundy pulls into the parking lot.

As news of the death of Laura Palmer breaks across town, there is more screaming and weeping than has ever been heard in any episode of network television. It's as if the collective mourning that never found expression in the real world in 1974 has suddenly broken free of whatever restrained it and is sailing out over the airwaves, curling through Douglas fir needles and drifting like smoke over the water.

"Here in Twin Peaks," someone says, "health and industry go hand in hand."[3]

MIKE WEISENBURGH, a clerk at PayLess Drug on Mercer Island and a former friend of George Waterfield Russell Jr., tips off the authorities. In September 1990, after pondering the fact that he and another friend had introduced George to Andrea Levine—and that Andrea had subsequently said something about George stealing fifty dollars from her purse—he calls the King County Police Department.[4]

Mike's story is only the latest item tying George to the murders of the three women. Cops have been interviewing Mindy Charley and other former girlfriends; they learn that George was at Papagayo's the night of the first murder and was seen leaving with a woman.

On September 12, George is arrested and questioned as a suspect. He giggles during the interview, denying everything. He claims he knows dozens of cops. He says he used to work for the Mercer Island Police Department. He stops laughing only when they ask for samples of his hair, blood, and saliva. Then he wants an attorney.

On January 11, 1991, after lab tests match his DNA to semen found on Mary Anne Pohlreich, he's charged with her murder.

Asked for his recollections, Bill Stewart, assistant principal at Mercer Island High School, where George should have graduated with the class of 1976, calls him "a likable and friendly kid who also was devious and skipped school too often," a description that fits virtually everyone I knew in high school including myself, except I wasn't that friendly.

THE TOWERING INFERNO

Eight days after George is arrested, Dennis Rader murders Dolores "Dee" Davis, sixty-two. She's a grandmother and, according to her family, a wonderful cook who makes everything from scratch, including casseroles, ham loaf, and red velvet cake.[5] Dennis is looking forward to killing someone after getting very excited during his last "Big Bondage Outdoor Event," in which he camped alone and tied himself up.[6]

At night, after his victim has turned out her lights, he throws a cinder block through her sliding glass doors. When she runs out to ask if he's hit her house with his car, he tells her he's on the run. He has a club, a knife, and a gun. "Cooperate and no one gets hurt," he tells her. He ties her up. He strangles her with her pantyhose.

After fantasizing about hanging her in various positions in a barn, he stashes her body in a rural road culvert, placing a porcelain mask over her face "for a more female look."[7]

In 1991, the CDC decides that a childhood blood lead level of ten micrograms per deciliter is cause for concern.[8]

The day of the demolition of the ASARCO smokestack dawns bright, clear, and cold. It's a festive occasion: one hundred thousand people turn out to bear witness on January 17, 1993. In one of the largest crowds assembled in Tacoma since the ribbon-cutting at the ill-fated Narrows Bridge, they pack rooftops, sit in deck chairs on lawns, line bridges and streets, and crowd onto fifteen hundred boats out in the bay. They drink so much coffee that Don, of Don's Ruston Market, laments not renting another espresso machine.

Rustonites remain weirdly attached to the 562-foot-tall landmark that has been poisoning them for generations. Maria Bradley, who's contracted breast cancer in her forties after living within a half mile of the smelter for four years, says, "Even if it kills me, I don't care. I don't want to see it go."[9] While acknowledging that two other women on her street have gotten cancer and one has died, she nonetheless calls the smelter "the most amazing thing I'd ever seen." Another neighbor, Judy Sherwood, also grows emotional, saying, "That was safety. We're losing a part of our heritage."[10]

Others are less nostalgic. Ruston native Tom Harmon recalls waking at three o'clock in the morning as a child and "choking on it when they used to crank that sucker up. When the wind didn't blow, the stuff went straight up and then straight right down on us."[11] Gregory Tanbara says that, growing up in the North End of Tacoma, "on certain days, I could feel the arsenic in the air. It was like playing tennis with a match head in your mouth."[12]

A local boy has been chosen to push the plunger. Shortly after half past noon, a demolition specialist starts the countdown, and 12,700 tons of bricks fall in eight seconds. Souvenir seekers are forbidden from collecting them for fear of lead and arsenic contamination. The pile will instead be bulldozed into a 360-foot trench.[13] Jenny Puz, who lives a few blocks from the chimney, says, "My heart went with that stack."[14]

All goes as planned, and a sprinkler system is in place to tamp down dust. Nonetheless, a massive cloud of particulates forms seconds after the implosion, panicking some in the crowd, who begin running. Only a few are wearing masks. Seventy smelter buildings remain to be razed, and a Superfund plan is in the offing.

LET'S NOT LOSE sight of young Israel Keyes. When last spotted, he was rusticating as an infant in rural Utah, but when he reaches the age of three or four, Jeff and Heidi Keyes cast their eyes on Washington State as a place offering even greater isolation from society. They move to a one-room cabin on a heavily forested mountainside north of Colville, a town of a few thousand in the sparsely populated northeast fastness of the state, somewhere near Twin Peaks. Jeff Keyes has bought 160 acres, but the cabin has no electricity and no running water. No plumbing and no heat.

What there is, is a smelter. As the crow flies, forty miles north of Colville in British Columbia is the town of Trail. There lies the Cominco plant, one of the largest lead and zinc smelters in the world, a major producer of said metals and of cadmium, arsenic, mercury, chromium, and manganese. Since 1896 the smelter has been releasing tons of wastes into the air and flushing them down the nearest river, which happens to be the Columbia. Cominco's black slag heavily pollutes the banks of the river beside the American town of Northport, thirteen miles south of the smelter. Drifting across the forests by air and pouring down the Columbia and its tributaries, poisons from Cominco make their way to Lake Roosevelt, the impoundment of the Columbia above the Grand Coulee Dam, one hundred miles southwest of and downstream from the smelter, where they enter the bodies of living creatures, including fish, bears, deer, rabbits, squirrels, and humans, notably members of the Confederated Tribes of the Colville Reservation, who fish as part of a traditional subsistence lifestyle.[15]

Growing up, the Keyeses are dependent on whatever they can shoot, fish, or scavenge: fishing is critical to survivalist families who shun regular employment and the associated taxes. Jeff is not an ideal provider, wandering into the wilderness for days on end to commune with his Lord. In his absence, Israel takes his father's place, helping his mother give birth to subsequent siblings. The children, who will eventually number ten, live much of the year in a tent. They do not attend school. They receive no medical care and have no birth certificates or Social Security numbers. Their chief contact with the outside world, aside from winter visits to California to see grandparents, is at the Ark, a church in Colville promoting Christian Identity theology, preaching that whites are the chosen race and Jews are direct biological descendants of Satan.

There, Israel meets two other boys, Chevie and Cheyne Kehoe, who live a half mile from the Keyeses' property, part of another large homeschooled family of zealots, living off the grid while their father, in the tradition of Charles Manson, plans for a coming race war. Chevie is named for the car. Israel and the Kehoe boys bond over their intense love of firearms, and the three of them begin stealing, trading, and selling them.

During the last years of the twentieth century, the Colville tribes learn that since the 1980s the Cominco smelter has been daily dumping into the river up to 40 pounds of arsenic, 136 pounds of cadmium, and 440 pounds of lead. Every year between 1990 and 2000, the corporation has reported repeated "accidental" but nonetheless massive releases into the Columbia of arsenic, mercury, sulfuric acid, lead, zinc, and cadmium. From 1994 to 1997, the smelter's spills of lead, cadmium, and arsenic amount to more than all U.S. companies reporting discharges combined. A tribal spokesman calls the spills "a cause for concern" not only for their population but for "anyone who eats more fish than folks in Iowa."[16]

ON SEPTEMBER 17, 1994, a nine-year-old girl named Penny Davis is playing with her seven-year-old brother and one of her friends near her home outside Tonasket, a remote town of around 850 people in north-central Washington, on the banks of the Okanogan River. The hamlet once produced a Nobel Prize–winning physicist, Walter Houser Brattain, credited with helping to invent the transistor in 1947, but most of the town lives below the poverty line.

The Davis home is out in the country and has no electricity, no running water, and no telephone. Dana Davis, a thirty-three-year-old single mother of four, bought the shack and twenty acres for a $1,000 down payment and moved her brood there the previous year. She relocated from Hilltop, hoping to protect herself and her kids from the guns, drugs, and violence in Tacoma.

Around dinnertime on September 17, Penny wanders away from her little brother and her friend. They've been pretending to camp in a dry creek bed, but Penny has been fighting with her friend all afternoon and is growing frustrated. By 7:00 p.m., after shouting her name for some time, Dana Davis rides around on horseback for hours, calling for her. At 11:00 p.m. she drives into Tonasket, almost twenty miles, to alert the police.

That night, as Okanogan County sheriff's deputies drive along Patterson Creek Road, where the Davis property is, they encounter one of the neighbors Dana has recruited to help search for her daughter. His name is Jack Spillman, and he, like Dana, grew up in Tacoma.

After learning that Spillman has a history as a sex offender, the deputies return in the middle of the night to interview him, rousting him at his girlfriend's mother's house, not far from the Davis home. Spillman, it turns out, has on occasion lived with Dana Davis and her children. When the deputies wake him, they note that his demeanor upon being questioned about Penny is "dead calm."[17]

THE SKY IN THE NORTHWEST is growing brighter. It's as if someone has removed a scrim of gray across the sun, a dirty transparency that's been shrouding the light for decades. The phaseout of leaded gasoline that began in 1973 is nearing completion. New cars beginning with model year 1975 are outfitted with catalytic converters, equipment destroyed by leaded fuel. By the mid-1980s, most gasoline sold in the United States is unleaded, with leaded banned completely by 1996. Smog also lifts in other major cities, including Los Angeles.

Measuring blood lead levels, scientists are studying the shift in air quality in real time as smelters continue to shut down, their profitability slashed by falling prices and by EPA regulations destroying their long-cherished impunity to environmental laws. In 1994, *The Journal of the American Medical Association* publishes a study of national surveys finding that the mean blood lead level of people aged one to seventy-four has dropped 78 percent from 1976 to 1991. For children aged one to five, it has dropped 77 percent.[18] The cause is believed to be the withdrawal of 99.8 percent of lead from gasoline and the removal of lead from soldered cans.

This is progress, but lead particulates have been soaring out of smokestacks since the late 1800s and drifting off highways since the invention of tetraethyl in 1921. Whatever's left in the environment is still there. It coats the medians and byways of every major interstate. It lies athwart rooftops and nestles into the yards of every community near freeways. It's in the vicinity of every urban smelter and battery recycler, whether the plants are still running or not. It's in the dusty attics of houses, in parks and baseball diamonds and soccer fields and elementary school playgrounds.[19] It's in the bodies and bones and teeth of everyone who grew up with it. Every once in a while, it sets loose another Frankenstein's monster.

TAKE CIUDAD JUÁREZ, for example. The border city has always shared what natural resource specialists call a "common air shed" with El Paso, sharing as well the fallout from the ASARCO smelter.[20] The two cities lie in a valley between the Franklin Mountains of Texas and the Sierra de Juarez Mountains in Mexico, separated by the channelized Rio Grande, or, as it's called in Mexico, the Río Bravo. In the spring, the valley and its conjoined cities are scoured by swirling sandstorms.

We've seen what a fetal diet of lead, benzene, and boot fixatives did for Richie Ramirez. We've seen how sleeping in a dusty cemetery adjacent to major highway interchanges in El Paso catalyzed his urges. Now look: what happened to Ramirez begins happening at scale in Ciudad Juárez.

Throughout the 1980s and '90s, the border city is ballooning. Several hundred maquiladoras, or factories, are springing up around town, producing appliances, electronics, automotive parts, medical devices, and clothing. The population jumps from 250,000 in 1960 to more than 800,000 in 1990. Soon it will top a million.

Air pollution in Juárez has always been worse than in El Paso. In the city south of the border, total suspended particulates in the form of dust, pollen, and chemicals disgorged by industrial sources and open burning are completely unregulated. In the early 1980s, benzene solubles found in those particulates are measured at 3.9 for El Paso and 28.8 for Juárez.[21] Smog trapped by winter temperature inversions is heavier on the southern side of the border, where people burn anything to stay warm. There, cars and trucks are older, and leaded gasoline, buoyed by government price supports, is far cheaper than unleaded. Mexico's phaseout of leaded fuel won't begin until 1990 and will not be completed until 1997.

The aroma of Juárez would not be unfamiliar to residents of Tacoma, from the ASARCO smelter as well as the Chevron and Texaco refineries separating sweet and sour crudes near the border.[22] There's lead, arsenic, and cadmium for all, but always more for Juárez. In 1977, after the dusty shacks of Smeltertown are torn down, the levels of lead in El Paso fall. But even so, according to Dr. Philip Landrigan, the CDC epidemiologist who ran field survey teams there in 1972 and 1977, El Paso still has the fifth-highest lead levels in the United States. For cadmium and arsenic, it ranks among the top two or three.[23] Across the river in Juárez, it's undoubtedly even worse.

In 1993, the bodies of young women begin turning up in Juárez in startling numbers and with horrific injuries. Femicides, they're called. Some are students, some workers. The maquiladoras preferentially hire young women, who are more reliable and punctual than men, less likely to use drugs and commit crimes.[24] Women are working for a minimum wage of around $4.50 a day, and they're facing long, dangerous commutes across the city, walking and taking company buses. They disappear off these buses or off the streets, never returning from their jobs or schools.

When their bodies are found, if they're found at all, they bear the marks of rape, torture, and dismemberment, shot, beaten, stabbed, or strangled. Some are burned. Some are hanged from electrical cords.

Many are teenagers. One is two months old. The eldest is ninety-one. They're dumped in the desert. They're found in their homes. They're thrown from moving vehicles. They're left in dumpsters.[25] Multiple serial killers are believed to be at work.

No one ever cleans up one molecule of lead in Juárez. The city becomes "the ghastly, premier center of female homicides in the twenty-first century."[26] Over a ten-year period, between 1993 and 2003, some 370 women are killed, and the femicides on a map of Juárez form an unmistakable stain along the border, a patch spreading from northwest to southeast, following the prevailing winds blowing the plume from the ASARCO smokestack.[27] Year after year, the crime rate lands Juárez at the top of lists of the most dangerous cities in the world. The El Paso smelter is shut down in 1999.

VIOLENCE DOMINATES THE 1980S. As the postwar generations of the age of the automobile reach maturity, crime sets new records, and the homicide rate climbs above 10 per 100,000 for the first time in American history.[28] There is a significant rise in the number of victims killed by strangers in the 1980s and another such rise in the 1990s.

Therefore, President Bill Clinton, during his first term, sees crime as a political opportunity to cement his centrist credentials. In September 1994 he signs into law the Violent Crime Control and Law Enforcement Act, the largest of its kind in history, expanding offenses listed under the Federal Death Penalty Act to include not only homicide, espionage, and treason, but also non-homicide narcotics offenses such as large-scale drug trafficking. The act encourages states to build more prisons and to pass laws establishing mandatory minimum sentences. Incarceration metastasizes.

The Clintons are quite proud of it. The law takes effect as *The Bell Curve* is published. Authored by political scientist Charles Murray and the late Richard J. Herrnstein, a Harvard psychologist, the book argues that intelligence as measured by IQ tests is heritable and unchanging, determining everything from an individual's health and income to their predilection to commit crime. Basing their argument on assumptions about genetic differences between races, they assert that gaps in IQ may be impossible to eradicate. Murray and Herrnstein are suggesting that white people are smarter than Black people and always will be, because they're born that way.

The book, whose inherent racism is debated and debunked, is published at a moment of overweening concern about crime. It feeds into a growing concern over "superpredators," a term coined by conservative writer John Dilulio in a 1995 essay in the neoconservative *The Weekly Standard* and adopted by Hillary Clinton. The article expatiates on "violent drug kingpins" and "urban street criminals" growing up in what is described as moral poverty, "fatherless, Godless, and jobless."[29] Dilulio bases his analysis of "scientific kiddie-crime literature" on a study of ten

THE TOWERING INFERNO

thousand boys born in 1945 and living in Philadelphia, a year when a third of males between ten and eighteen had at least one arrest.[30] The author appears to be unaware that in 1945 Philadelphia was the smelter capital of the country or that neighborhoods such as East Baltimore are being called "Zombieland" because one in five children there have lead poisoning.[31]

There are, in fact, superpredators, but they're not Black kids in Harlem or Hilltop. They're largely white males. Murderers, yes, but also serial rapists, torturers, mutilators, and necrophiles. Quite a few of them hail from Washington, Idaho, Oregon, and British Columbia, where they leave strings of bodies alongside highways or discarded in woods and rivers.

WHAT ARE THE ODDS that Mercer Island, a most livable suburb according to *Ladies' Home Journal*, would spawn both a serial killer and a mass murderer? Pretty good, apparently. George Waterfield Russell Jr. and Martin Pang have grown up within blocks of each other and of the I-90 tunnel.

On January 5, 1995, Pang, thirty-nine, a 1974 graduate of Mercer Island High School with an extensive history of domestic violence and death threats, sets fire to the family's frozen food warehouse in Seattle's Chinatown. At the five-alarm blaze, four firemen die in flames stoked up by Pang's high-octane leaded racing fuel stored in the basement, and a fifth from a related heart attack the following year. It's the worst loss in Seattle firefighting history.

At his sentencing, friends and relatives of his victims speak of Pang's "sociopathic behavior."[32] It seems to be going around.

YOU CAN CATCH it in Tacoma. Jack Owen Spillman III grows up in the heart of it. He's born Roy Wilson on August 20, 1969, in Spokane, to Thelma Faye Wilson, a woman who marries with casual frequency. Originally Thelma Durrett, she becomes Thelma Scott (in 1959), then Thelma Wilson (in 1960), Thelma Talbott (in 1962), Thelma Wilson again (remarrying

Wilson in February of 1969), Thelma Milner (in 1972), and Thelma Spillman (in 1976) when she marries Jack Owen Spillman Jr.

Roy is raised first in Wenatchee, the agricultural mecca in central Washington known for apple orchards huddled alongside the river and for a heavy early reliance on lead arsenate pesticides—so heavy that the area will ultimately be recognized for its own plume.[33] When he's three years old, Roy's mother is married to an orchard hand, and they live for a time near contaminated orchard property.[34]

Roy's early life is marked by what will later be described as physical and sexual abuse by one of his stepfathers, a man said to be "very violent."[35] At age seven he moves to Tacoma to live with his mother and Spillman, her latest husband, just in time for the last lead flowering of the Ruston smelter. Spillman is Roy's favorite stepfather, so he takes his name—last and first—and the family resides at 1309 South 45th Street, six miles from the smokestack, from 1976 to 1982.

Tacoma is where Jack Owen Spillman III will commit the first of many recorded crimes, which range from petty thefts at age thirteen, when he drops out of school, to burglary, public indecency, malicious mischief, car theft, and—in 1985, when he is sixteen—taking indecent liberties with a minor child. For that charge he spends two years in a juvenile facility. He has an IQ of 87.

In 1993 he's arrested for raping a woman in Spokane, spending four months in jail. The charges are later dropped.

He works as a butcher and likes to kill animals. One of his favorite things to do is read about Ted Bundy.

After Penny Davis disappears in Tonasket in September 1994, Jack moves back to Wenatchee, where he lives with his mother. That winter, he wins several thousand dollars playing bingo and uses the money to buy a distinctive Chevy pickup truck with hefty tires and a chrome roll bar.

On March 29, 1995, hikers in a canyon twelve miles from where Penny was last seen find a child's jawbone. Soon after, deputies unearth her body from a shallow grave. The cause of death is unclear due to decomposition, but evidence indicates that the body has been moved.

THE TOWERING INFERNO

Two days later, when the news breaks, a Wenatchee woman reports that someone has broken into her apartment through an unlocked window and killed her children's hamster, spraying the walls with its blood and leaving a stuffed panda bear impaled by a bloody knife.

Working as an itinerant roofer, Jack is often unemployed and occupies himself by stalking females, peeping, exposing himself, and attacking women in their yards. He makes obscene phone calls. He watches young girls from his pickup truck, killing and mutilating a cat belonging to one of them. He commits other rapes, attacking a mother and daughter in an apartment building.

In April he begins stalking Rita Huffman, forty-eight, a single mother. When Rita moved to town, she first worked in Wenatchee's apple-packing sheds, then began selling cars at local dealerships. Rita has recently rebuffed Jack at a local bar, where he tried to grab her arm, the briefest passing contact. She lives with her youngest child, Amanda, or Mandy, who is fifteen and attends high school. They live in a rural area of East Wenatchee.

On the night of April 12, 1995, Jack breaks into the Huffmans' home through an unlocked sliding door at the back of the house, wearing a ski mask. He kills Mandy by hitting her over the head with a baseball bat. He kills Rita after a struggle, leaving defensive wounds on her arms and wrists, stabbing her thirty-one times. Although Mandy is already dead from massive cerebral contusions, he stabs her sixteen times in the neck. He strips and eviscerates both women. He rapes Mandy, jamming the baseball bat into her vaginal cavity; he places genital skin across her face. He cuts off Rita's breasts, distributing them near her daughter. He spends hours at the scene, drinking the victims' blood, having sex with the bodies, and posing them provocatively. Hours later, Rita's older daughter discovers her mother and sister after trying and failing to reach them on the telephone.[36]

Although Jack Owen Spillman III fancies himself skilled in the arts of serial murder, he leaves many clues. His vehicle is seen by the Huffmans' neighbors. Police begin surveilling him, watching as he discards his ski mask, soaked in blood around the mouth, in the dumpster outside his apartment.³⁷ His knife is discovered in a trash can in the parking lot of the local VFW post, where his truck has also been seen.³⁸ He's arrested on April 19. He's twenty-five years old.

He refuses to make a statement, but police match DNA on the knife to the victims, finding more evidence in his truck. They interview his cellmate, who's been listening to Jack bragging incessantly about the murders in such harrowing detail that the man, who has no knowledge of the facts otherwise, can describe them. Jack has told him that he's been yearning to find underground caves in the woods where he can keep victims alive while torturing them, hoping to become the best serial killer in the world. He likes to imagine he's a werewolf and becomes known as the "Werewolf Butcher."

Confronted with the evidence, Jack pleads guilty, confessing also to the murder of Penny Davis, the nine-year-old he tied to a tree and tortured with a knife before killing her. He had sex with her dead body too, which he moved many times, first placing it in a river, then digging it up again and again to defile it.

Four months after his plea bargain, he's interviewed by Bob Keppel, now an investigator for the state attorney general's office. Keppel believes that Jack has agreed to the interview solely because he knows that Keppel interviewed Ted, his hero, on death row. He tells Keppel that he hopes to follow in Ted's footsteps.

Speaking to a Wenatchee newspaper, Keppel notes that killers like Spillman, mutilators who commit cannibalism, vampirism, and necrophilia, are exceptionally rare, representing less than a tenth of 1 percent of all murderers.³⁹ He does not address the fact that so many of this rare breed—Bundy, Ridgway, Spillman, and Yates, among others—have spent quality time in Tacoma, a place where paraphilias flourish like fungi.

INTERESTING THAT ROY WILSON takes the name Jack. Who else do we know who likes to eviscerate women and goes by Jack? Spring-heeled Jack. Saucy Jacky. Jack the Ripper.

THE TOWERING INFERNO

We don't know who Jack the Ripper is, but he's breathing the air in London Town in the winter of 1888, when millions are burning bituminous coal with a high volatile content, coal that produces prodigious amounts of soot, smoke, gas, and ash. In October 1888, the Ripper sends half of a human kidney preserved in wine to George Lusk, chairman of the Whitechapel Vigilance Committee, accompanied by a brief note:

> From hell.
>
> Mr Lusk,
> Sir
>
> I send you half the Kidne I took from one woman prasarved it for you. tother piece I fried and ate it was very nise. I may send you the bloody knif that took it out if you only wate a whil longer
>
> signed
>
> Catch me when
> you can
> Mishter Lusk[40]

Hell indeed. Here's how Alexis de Tocqueville describes Manchester:

> A sort of black smoke covers the city....
> ... From this foul drain the greatest stream of human industry flows out to fertilise the whole world. From this filthy sewer pure gold flows. Here humanity attains its most complete development and its most brutish; here civilisation works its miracles, and civilised man is turned back almost into a savage.[41]

Charles Dickens, who reports as a journalist on the poisoning of workers in the city's white lead mills, likewise summons London's infernal November skies in *Bleak House*:

> Smoke lowering down from chimney-pots, making a soft black drizzle, with flakes of soot in it as big as full-grown snow-flakes—gone into mourning, one might imagine, for the death of the sun. . . .
>
> Fog everywhere. Fog up the river, where it flows among green aits [isles] and meadows; fog down the river, where it rolls defiled among the tiers of shipping, and the waterside pollutions of a great (and dirty) city. . . . Fog in the eyes and throats.[42]

For *fog*, read *smog*. Burn bituminous coal and you breathe its impurities: arsenic, mercury, and trace metals, such as lead.[43] In the 1800s, coal is ubiquitous. So is the Dutch process for producing white lead paint, a product so popular that Britain smelts more and more lead in the early decades of the century: in 1810, 12,500 tons, rising to a peak of 73,000 in 1856. The tonnage falls thereafter, but even in the 1870s and '80s lead production is high, at 54,000 tons.[44] The rise in lead coincides with a parallel jump in juvenile delinquency and property crime. London is Tacoma before Tacoma is even a gleam in a Guggenheim's eye.

We pay attention to the wrong things. We make a mystery of Jack the Ripper. It's not a mystery. It's history.

THERE'S SOMETHING WRONG with my mother. She can't make change anymore. Standing at a bus stop, she stares at the coins in her palm, baffled, unable to pick out four quarters to make a dollar. I lose patience with her as she holds out her hand for help, the woman who has patiently corrected my math for decades.

I don't know it yet, but something is making her disappear around the edges. It's what I've always feared. By the time I've discovered that she's an individual, someone who is more than just my mother, she's not there. It's too late to say I'm sorry, as the Zombies say.[45] Perhaps I should have killed him when I had the chance, but I'm not as smart as I think I am.

THE TOWERING INFERNO

IN 1996, Herbert Needleman—he of the Philadelphia Tooth Fairy study looking at lead in children's teeth (the serial killer in Harris's *Red Dragon* is called the Tooth Fairy)—publishes a new study of several hundred boys in the Pittsburgh public school system, establishing a strong association between students with high lead levels in their bones and juvenile delinquency. Examining reports from parents and teachers, the study finds that children with higher lead levels are more aggressive, prone to anxiety, depression, social problems, and difficulty paying attention. Children deemed "troublesome" at age eight by their teachers are "significantly more likely" to be delinquent at eighteen and convicted of a violent crime by thirty-two.[46]

Having interviewed scores of families whose children are being treated for lead poisoning, Needleman says, "If you listen to parents with lead-poisoned kids, they tell you that the biggest thing is that the kids' behavior changes—they become dangerous."[47]

IN THE EARLY 1990S it's discovered that areas of Snohomish County, the Snohomish River, and Everett are heavily contaminated with lead, cadmium, and arsenic from the Rockefellers' old smelter, which was processing ores from the Cascades' Monte Cristo mines from 1894 to 1912, stripping them for gold, silver, copper, lead, and zinc.

Developers have since built dozens of houses on top of where the old arsenic kitchen had been, the one the Guggenheims bought and moved to Tacoma. The state Department of Ecology will later discover homes where arsenic levels are twenty-five times the minimum cleanup level of twenty ppm, finding cadmium and lead in the soil fifteen feet below the surface.[48] Parks, overlooks, intersections, and areas of the river will be found to be heavily contaminated.

Snohomish County, of course, was home to Charles Rodman Campbell, the triple murderer who slit the throats of two women and a child, but by May 27, 1994, he's past caring. That's when the State of Washington hangs him by the neck.

OUT IN THE WOODS north of Colville, Israel Keyes is heavily armed. He's a good shot. "I would hunt anything with a heartbeat," he says.[49]

At fourteen, he swears vengeance on one of the family cats that's gotten into the garbage too many times. Out in the woods, he ties it to a tree with parachute line and shoots it in the stomach with a .22, watching as it careens around and around and finally vomits and dies.

A friend who's with him is traumatized. Word gets around, and nobody goes out in the woods with Israel anymore.[50]

At fifteen, rebelling against his parents, he starts building his own cabin, financing it with construction work done for fellow Ark members. At sixteen, estranged from his parents and forbidden to talk to his siblings, he moves into the cabin and lives by himself. He stalks things in the woods. He stalks people.

On March 2, 1996, when Israel is eighteen, twelve-year-old Julie Harris, who lives in Colville and stands five foot one and weighs 115 pounds, has a fight with her mom's boyfriend about doing her homework. She creeps out of her home early the next morning with nothing more than four slices of pizza. She's reported as a runaway.[51]

Julie is in the seventh grade. Born with a blood disorder, she's a double amputee and gets around on two prosthetic feet and braces. Her room at home is full of comic books, mystery stories, and sports trophies: she's recently won a gold medal in downhill skiing at the Special Olympics. A month after she goes missing, her prosthetic feet are found washed up at the confluence of the Columbia and Colville Rivers and she is presumed dead. The following spring, her skeletal remains are discovered by children near Kettle Falls, on the Columbia.

Weeks after Julie's bones are found, another twelve-year-old girl goes missing in Colville. Cassie Emerson, daughter of Marlene Emerson, twenty-nine, is feared abducted or worse when Marlene's body is found in their burned-out trailer after an arson fire on June 27, 1997. A month later, Cassie's decomposed remains are found by horseback riders around five miles from the trailer, off a logging road, scattered and scavenged by animals.

Local police see no connection between the two cases. They're looking at the mothers' boyfriends. They're certainly not looking at Israel Keyes.

Meanwhile, Israel's teenage pals the Kehoe brothers, weaned on the daft backwoods fumes of white supremacy and Cominco, have launched a Bonnie and Clyde–style war, putting Colville on a bizarre crime map all its own. Chevie Kehoe, a polygamist who has ordered the murder of a man in order to acquire his wife, has devoted himself to establishing an Aryan Peoples Republic. He's infuriated by the 1993 Branch Davidian siege in Waco, Texas, and is bent on revenge, planning to assassinate federal judges and bomb federal buildings in the hopes of destabilizing the U.S. government. He kidnaps and robs a couple in Colville and plants a bomb outside Spokane City Hall.[52]

In January 1996, Chevie recruits a fellow skinhead to travel to Arkansas with him to settle a beef he's had with a gun dealer, William Frederick Mueller. After bullying their way into the Mueller home by impersonating FBI agents, Chevie and his friend overpower Mueller, his wife, and Mueller's eight-year-old stepdaughter, Sarah Elizabeth Powell. They torture Sarah with an electric cattle prod to force her to reveal the location of her stepfather's stash of gold, firearms, and other valuables. Then they tie plastic bags over the heads of the couple and the child, suffocating them and dumping the bodies in a local bayou. Stolen weapons and ammunition from the $37,000 heist turn up in multiple robberies in the Midwest. Some are found in the hands of other members of the Aryan Peoples Republic, and federal agents trace the arms back to the Kehoes.

By February 15, 1997, the brothers are on the run, stopped by law enforcement in Ohio for driving with expired Washington plates. They start firing and escape, only to engage in another gun battle the next day. They escape again, but after hiding out in rural Utah for a few months, the brothers fall out. Cheyne turns himself in to Washington police, telling them where to find Chevie, who is arrested as well.

Israel has no such apocalyptic plans at the moment. His goals, while grand, are more self-oriented. During the summer of 1997, while Chevie is under federal indictment for fifty-seven crimes, including five murders, as well as kidnappings, robberies, racketeering, and interstate transportation of stolen property, the Keyes family makes another move, this time to eastern Oregon. Temporarily restored to the family and unclear about what to do with his future, Israel accompanies them.

On a hot day, he's tubing on the Deschutes River near Maupin, a town of a few hundred people in the middle of nowhere. Throughout the late afternoon, he watches from the trees as the number of folks on the river dwindles. He sees a teenage girl floating by, out of sight of her friends. He jumps out of the bushes, grabs her, and hauls her into a pit-style outhouse, the kind maintained by the Forest Service or the Bureau of Land Management, furnished with a massive concrete waste tank underneath. He lashes her arms to the bars on either side of the toilet installed for use by the disabled. He ties a rope around her neck, bends her face down over the closed toilet seat, and rapes her. He's planning to kill her and dump her body in the tank, where, he reckons, it may not be found for months, if ever.[53] He's the undead Ted.

But the girl talks to him. He's stunned by the fact that she seems relatively calm, stoic even, as if something similar has happened to her before. She tells him her first name and scolds him, saying he's so good-looking, he could get girls like her to go out with him. In the end, he doesn't kill her. He drags her back to the river, pops her in her inner tube, and pushes her out on the water. The crime is never reported.

Later that year, Israel buys ten acres and a cabin outside Constable, New York, a rural property so far north that it's five miles from the Canadian border, offering excellent escape routes if, say, you're a fugitive.

On July 9, 1998, Israel Keyes enlists in the U.S. Army, spending part of a three-year stint at Fort Lewis.

The following year, ASARCO cuts off one of its own heads, selling itself to its former subsidiary, Grupo México, for $1.24 billion in cash.⁵⁴ By this time, however, it is a full-grown hydra and simply grows another. Controlled by the secretive Mexican billionaire Germán Larrea Mota-Velasco, Grupo México is the largest mining outfit in Mexico and the third-largest copper producer in the world. In this way, the corporation attempts to protect its assets from hundreds of pending lawsuits.

ROBERT LEE YATES JR. is becoming an old hand at Fort Lewis, where he reports for National Guard training in 1997. Born May 27, 1952, on Whidbey, the long, thin island that puts a stop to the Strait of Juan de Fuca, he's been raised in a devout family with a history of violence.

On October 13, 1945, seven years before Bobby is born, his grandmother Novella Johnson Yates, fifty-four, wakes early in her farmhouse on Bone Cave Road in rural Van Buren County, Tennessee. She's a mother of ten. Barefoot, she goes to the woodshed, fetches a double-edged axe, and returns to the house, where her husband, John Taylor Yates, fifty-five, is still asleep. She hits him over the head four times, penetrating his skull with the fourth blow. He dies six days later, and Novella is consigned to a mental institution. Bobby Yates's father, Robert Lee Yates Sr., is fifteen at the time and will later say that he heard the blows from another room, finding his mother after the attack sitting calmly in a straight chair. "She simply broke," he'll say.⁵⁵

After his mother murders his father, Robert Yates Sr. becomes a solid citizen, moving to Oak Harbor, Washington, a naval base and a town of less than five thousand. He works in civilian jobs at the Whidbey Island Naval Air Station, coaches Little League, and worships in the Seventh-Day Adventist Church, serving as an elder. His son Bobby, a Boy Scout and Little Leaguer, is close to his parents, but they don't know that he's being sexually molested at age six by an older neighbor boy. His little white face is so pale, he looks like a ghost.

The family lives near the Seaplane Base, commissioned in 1942, a time when citizens on the West Coast were convinced that the Japanese would soon attack.⁵⁶ After the war, the base was upgraded to support the Pacific Fleet, providing aircraft and vehicle maintenance, painting and paint stripping, and machine and boat shop activities. The waste generated included solvents, zinc chromate, lead paint, lead-based sealants, and thinners. Soil, groundwater, and surface water at the base were contaminated.⁵⁷

Like his grandmother, Bobby is broken too, perhaps for different reasons. In high school, he's moody. He has an excellent throwing arm but refuses to play football during his senior year. He has trouble settling down, attending college for a couple of years, marrying, then marrying again before divorcing his first wife. He and his second wife have four girls and a boy. He teaches his children how to clean his many guns: the .357 handgun, a .410, a 12-gauge shotgun, a 30.06 rifle, and an AR-15 semiautomatic assault weapon. He shows them how to melt lead to make bullets.⁵⁸ In family snapshots, he appears without affect, unsmiling.

He can't control his temper and loves killing things. He spends a rocky 1975 working as a security guard at Walla Walla State Penitentiary and at Pantrol, a manufacturing company in Spokane. This is the period when he shoots Susan Savage and Patrick Oliver from the Wickersham Bridge and, after a fight with a Pantrol co-worker, spreads his feces on a company door.

After a childhood living next to the Seaplane Base, Bobby becomes a flyboy, enlisting in the U.S. Army in 1977 to become a helicopter pilot. That year he shoots a swan and cuts off its wings so his three-year-old daughter, Sasha, can wear them and look like an "angel."⁵⁹ He kills Stacy Hawn in Skagit County in 1988, and is long suspected of shooting three more women in 1990—Yolanda Sapp, twenty-six; Nickie Lowe, thirty-four; and Kathy Brisbois, thirty-eight—their bodies found stripped near the Spokane River. But it turns out that was another serial killer.

Yates serves in Desert Storm in 1991. After he's stationed at Fort Rucker, Alabama, in 1995, the body of a trans woman sex worker, Tarayon Corbitt, eighteen, turns up near the fort. Amid rumors, Yates the Army in 1996. Honorably discharged, he returns to Spokane with his family and gets a job at a Spokane smelter, Kaiser Aluminum, filling in as a carbon setter, changing burned anodes and wielding a sandblasting hose.

While busy, he nonetheless finds time to kill ten Spokane women, including Jennifer Joseph, who's sixteen. In order to keep his car clean, he's putting plastic bags over their heads before shooting them, often using Walmart bags with a big yellow smiley face. This earns him the moniker "the Smiley Face Killer," an irony, given that he never smiles if he can help it. He returns to the bodies, bestowing oral, anal, and vaginal acts upon the dead, leaving them in ditches or burying them in shallow graves or dumping them off an embankment beside a sewage treatment plant. Semen is recovered. His car, a white Corvette, is seen near sites where the murdered women were working the streets.

He's joined the National Guard, spending weekends at Fort Lewis training helicopter pilots for the Guard's 66th Aviation Brigade. He kills two women in South Tacoma: Melinda Mercer, twenty-four, in 1997 and Connie LaFontaine Ellis, thirty-five, in 1998.

After the second Tacoma murder, two of his daughters, tired of being slapped around, report him for domestic violence. Nervous that cops are showing an interest in his activities, he sells the Corvette. It's seized from its new owner, and blood, fibers, and a button from the shirt of one victim are found. Bobby Yates is arrested on April 18, 2000, and charged with seven counts of murder in Spokane County and two in Tacoma's Pierce County. After an extensive search, the body of one victim is found buried outside his bedroom window.

ON FEBRUARY 28, 2001, at 10:54 a.m., the Puget Sound area suffers a severe magnitude 6.8 intraslab earthquake, similar to the 1965 event. The Juan de Fuca plate is feeling frisky.

Several hundred are injured; one person dies of a heart attack; $1 billion to $4 billion in damage occurs. The Alaskan Way Viaduct, the elevated highway running along Elliott Bay, cracks. It's ultimately removed, replaced by a tunnel costing several billion dollars and designed to withstand a quake with a magnitude of 9—perhaps the only infrastructure in the area that will.

WITHIN THE SPACE of a few years, several killers are caught. After Smiley Face Yates is arrested in 2000, Green River Gary is finally apprehended in November of the following year.

Gary has long been derided by co-workers as "Wrong Way" for his frequent on-the-job errors at Kenworth, but he's nonetheless made a mockery of the task force assigned to catch him.[60] He pleads guilty to forty-eight charges of first degree murder but is suspected of killing upward of seventy-eight girls and women over a twenty-two-year period. He tells officials that he's taken the skulls and bones of two victims and placed them in Tigard, Oregon, south of Portland, to throw police off the scent.[61] He leaves another on Tiger Mountain, the altar of the OWL, in a nod to his colleague Ted Bundy.[62]

NOBODY KNOWS IT YET, but Fort Lewis will eventually be included on the Tacoma–Pierce County Health Department's list of areas most affected by the ASARCO smelter plume.[63] Like most military bases, it's been generating its own toxic waste for decades, resulting in a Superfund site.[64] The base shares with Tacoma a remarkable association with multiple serial killers, to which it has added the distinction of hosting war criminals, mass murderers, and suicides.[65] Incidents of domestic violence are endemic. No less an authority than *Stars and Stripes* calls Joint Base Lewis–McChord "the most troubled base in the military," pointing to a string of scandals, dozens of suicides, flagrant mental breakdowns, war crimes, and murders.[66]

The base has long been a true-life Grand Guignol, a theater of horrors starring Ann Rule's old friends from the 1970s, Rodger Thompson and Phillip Van Hillman, and continuing on with Israel Keyes, George Water-

THE TOWERING INFERNO

field Russell Jr. (who spends months there as a child), and Robert Lee Yates Jr. Joseph Edward Duncan III, child rapist, has grown up next door in the suburb of Lakewood. John Allen Muhammad, born and raised in a trailer near the Mississippi River bayou, five miles south of an Exide Baton Rouge lead smelter, spends years at Fort Lewis, eventually training a teenage boy to join him in committing the 2002 sniper attacks in the Washington, D.C., area, killing seventeen. Their first murder takes place in Tacoma.

DAVID BRAME, Tacoma's lauded young police chief—the man who investigates Muhammad's local killing—is a murderer too. On April 26, 2003, after being accused of domestic violence by his wife, Crystal, thirty-five, Brame shoots her in view of his two screaming young children, eight and five. Then he shoots himself. He dies instantly. She lingers in a coma for days and then dies.

On earlier occasions, he has pointed his gun at her, choked her, and threatened her, telling her he can snap her neck. He's been credibly accused of rape, a charge known at the time of his appointment. Until he shoots his wife and himself, he's prone to admiring his image in the mirror and saying, "I love me."[67]

Born in 1958, David Brame grew up in Tacoma in a house his father built the year he was born, at 2250 East 34th Street, yards from the Puyallup River and close to the Commencement Bay tidal flats that had already been a toxic stew of industrial wastes for decades, dotted with Superfund and brownfield sites and home to the Tacoma Tar Pits. The tar pits were created when a former coal gasification plant dumped coal tar, creating what one geologist determined to be a series of stratigraphic layers: "Plank Roads and Pilings, Smelter Slag, Auto Wrecking Units with sub units of fluff, acid, oil, and coolant, PCP [pentachlorophenol] waste oil, Rail Waste, Coal Tar and Hair Tar. The Hair Tar was the waste tar that was used to strip the hair off of hogs."[68] The geologist was not present, he noted, when investigators encountered the blood layer.

The Tacoma smelter plume has earned a map all its own, and the pins on this particular crazy wall are something to see. In 2003, Gregory L. Glass, an environmental scientist hired by the state Department of Ecology and the Tacoma–Pierce County Health Department, publishes a 139-page report compiling "Credible Evidence" of the plume site, complete with two exquisite maps. The first is adorned with pinpoints identifying the maximum arsenic concentrations at sample locations throughout Tacoma, Seattle, Vashon Island, and Mercer Island; the second shows maximum lead. Red and salmon-colored dots mark the highest accumulations, an angry rash covering North Tacoma, Skyline, and Vashon; the dots on Mercer Island are puce, for medium. Puget Sound is robin's-egg blue, and the land is rendered in the off-white of a well-known VW Beetle.[69]

The Department of Ecology will eventually develop its own block-by-block and home-by-home GIS (geographic information system) maps of lead and arsenic contamination as part of a program called "Dirt Alert."[70] The largest covers the massive fallout from the ASARCO Tacoma Smelter, but there are four plumes in all. The others map the ASARCO Everett Smelter plume, the former orchard lands of central Washington (including the city of Wenatchee), and the Upper Columbia River and Lake Roosevelt Cleanup Site. Every one of those plumes, including the most remote and least populated site on the Columbia, has hosted the activities of one or more serial rapists or murderers.

Chapter 13

The Fog Warning

——◇——

This is the Hour of Lead—

—Emily Dickinson, 372
("After great pain . . .")

Above the sofa in my father's house hangs a copy of a painting by Winslow Homer called *The Fog Warning*. The house is gone, the painting is gone, and my father is gone. But they're still there, in my mind.

We have him cremated, but he lives on, like Sam McGee in the fiery furnace. Paradoxically, it turns out, you can demolish whatever you want, but the furniture of the past is permanent. The cuckoo clock, the Dutch door, the daylight basement—humble horsemen of the domestic apocalypse. The VWs, parked in the driveway.

I never see her here. My mother died years ago, after he worried her to death. If she'd left him, she could have lived in her own house on Queen Anne Hill, with her little bags of sewing and knitting, her happy kindergarten shapes cut out of felt. The bells she sewed to the tops of Christmas stockings, the sequins. Her greeting cards, her nice shoes, her tidy handwriting. As it turns out, you *can* kill someone with your mind. Toward the end, my father closes off the main floor of the house to save on heat, so my mother spends the rest of her life buried alive in the daylight basement.

Homer's painting is dark and foreboding. It shows a man straining to row a large dory by himself, the stern weighed down by an enormous fish, the catch of a lifetime but one that must be discarded if he's to make headway. He's desperate to beat the fogbank massing behind him. The sense of doom is palpable.

Here are a few things we find in my father's house after he dies of gangrene as a result of his foot falling off, rotting flesh being indifferent to Mary Baker Eddy's sophistry:

- Several sets of my parents' false teeth. (I scream when I open the box.)
- Images of Japanese devil masks for warding off evil spirits and pollution.
- A list of my father's "healings" (spurious) and an inventory of twenty-five of his favorite positive recollections, none of which have anything to do with his children.[1] At the bottom is written the phrase "Ship still drifts, No land in sight." It reminds me of a book he's fond of, *Sailing Alone Around the World*, by Captain Joshua Slocum, an international bestseller in 1900.

That's all he ever wanted to do: sail off by himself, into the void. And he would have, but for his wife and family hanging around his neck like albatrosses.

Things we don't find:

- The letters he wrote to my mother before and after their shotgun marriage. He'd already told me he burned them, to frustrate me. "Don't flatter yourself," I told him.
- Tanuki the Bad Badger. Tanuki is nowhere to be found. Of course, he's not really a badger. He's a raccoon dog, *Nyctereutes procyonoides*, a species related to the fox common in East Asia. Like me, he's escaped, somehow. He's last seen on the world stage in a wet market in Wuhan, China, just before a plague breaks out, killing millions.

THE FOG WARNING

THE FEVER BREAKS. Lead levels in American children and adults are seen to be declining rapidly, beginning in 1992. At the same time, the crime rate falls, the largest plunge in recorded history. Epidemiologists superimpose graphs of lead and crime over each other, the lines rising and falling in tandem so closely that a theory is born: the lead–crime hypothesis.[2]

As a graduate student living near Harvard Square in the late 1990s, in an old house with flaking paint, Jessica Wolpaw Reyes is considering ideas for her Ph.D. dissertation in economics at Harvard. She's pregnant, and she's worried about the paint.[3]

She attends a talk by a University of Chicago economist, Steven D. Levitt, who's proposing a theory about how crime rates fall after abortion is legalized, reducing the number of children born to mothers ill-prepared, due to youth and poverty, to care for them. It's a correlation that holds true, Levitt argues, even in other countries. Studies show that Australia and Canada have experienced similar declines after legalization, a theory Levitt elaborates in a chapter of his 2005 book, *Freakonomics*, co-authored with Stephen J. Dubner.

A competing theory, one beloved by police associations around the country, holds that intensive investment in policing since the passage of the Clinton-era crime bill has made steady inroads into violence in the inner city. Police boosters want to take credit for that.

But after Levitt's talk, Reyes starts thinking about lead. She calls multiple states to collect emissions data, finding that "state-specific reductions in lead exposure" could be used to identify the effect of childhood lead exposures on crime rates. The result, she writes in her dissertation, subsequently published in 2007 in a journal of economic analysis and policy, connects lead exposure to violent crime. The finding, she says, is "robust."[4]

She explains that lead peaked in the 1920s (from paint) and again in the 1970s (from gasoline). Then leaded gas was withdrawn from the market, disappearing by 1990. According to the state emissions data, violent crime (aggravated assault, robbery, murder, and rape) rose until 1980, declined, then rose again until 1991, reaching an unprecedented level. It dropped off precipitously after that. There's a twenty-two-year lag in such crimes after children are exposed to leaded gas, the average age of perpetrators being twenty-two. Lead exposure, she concludes, correlates with higher adult crime rates.[5]

ROGER STRAUS JR. dies in 2004, the same year as my father. He's a storied publisher, one of several Guggenheims who've managed to slide off the slag pile and cover his coattails in cultural glory. His mother is Gladys Guggenheim, daughter of Daniel Guggenheim and heir to a significant chunk of the family fortune. Gladys's husband, Roger Williams Straus, begins working for the family firm in 1914 as a clerk. Two years later, he's a director, eventually rising to president (1941) and chairman of the board (1947 to 1957). "The Guggenheims wanted a stooge on the board," he tells *Business Week* in 1956, "and I was married to a Guggenheim."[6] The initials of American Smelting and Refining are said to also stand for "American Sons & Relatives."[7]

Roger Sr. is a staunch anti-Communist, refusing company-wide collective bargaining and railing against officers of the International Union of Mine, Mill and Smelter Workers in 1949 for failing to file "non-Communist affidavits" and adhering to "the Communist party line."[8] ASARCO has a policy of supplying fair wages and proven benefits, he tells the Tacoma smelter manager, and "almost all AS&R employees are loyal Americans who want no part of the Communist Party."[9]

Roger Jr. spends much of his youth at Hempstead House, Daniel's mansion on the North Shore of Long Island, furnished with tennis courts, a nine-hole golf course, bowling alley, beach house, and swimming pool, but he doesn't care to work at the firm.[10] He marries Dorothea Liebmann, heir to a brewing fortune, and co-founds Farrar, Straus and Company in 1945 by borrowing $30,000 against his inheritance. He solicits money from well-heeled friends, including $50,000 from a scion of the Fleischmann yeast family, which has also underwritten *The New Yorker*.

THE FOG WARNING

Early on, Roger publishes *Metal Magic: The Story of the American Smelting & Refining Company*, a tribute to the "romance of mining," dedicated to the memory of Daniel Guggenheim.[11] It's not a major seller, but Farrar, Straus hits it big in 1950 with *Look Younger, Live Longer*, a diet book promoting better digestion, lower toilets, and the ingestion of blackstrap molasses. It bankrolls young Roger's taste for higher-brow literary fiction and Italian translations, and in time Farrar, Straus and Giroux becomes renowned for Nobel and Pulitzer Prize winners, its authors ranging from T. S. Eliot, Edmund Wilson, Flannery O'Connor, and Shirley Jackson to Aleksandr Solzhenitsyn, Isaac Bashevis Singer, Bernard Malamud, Robert Lowell, Joseph Brodsky, Susan Sontag, and Philip Roth.

Together with the Guggenheim Museum and family foundations devoted to subsidizing culture, Roger W. Straus Jr. completes the process of whitewashing the family name, intentionally or not. Two years before his death, *The New Yorker* publishes a flattering profile of him in which the origins of his family fortune are never mentioned. The profile lingers lovingly over his sartorial extravagance, in the form of cuff links, ascots, and cashmere jackets, and celebrates his European habit of kissing familiars on both cheeks.[12]

Daniel Guggenheim's name floats by, but the American Smelting and Refining Company is never named. Not a word about its suppurating Superfund sites, its asbestos lawsuits, its free hand with arsenic, or the lung cancer it has bestowed on communities all across the American West. Nobody wants to remember where the money comes from.

Whatever the Sackler family is trying to do by collecting art and endowing museums, lifting their skirts away from the hundreds of thousands addicted and killed by prescription opioids manufactured and sold by their company—Purdue Pharma—the Guggenheims have already stealthily and handily accomplished.[13]

BACK IN WASHINGTON STATE, Joseph Edward Duncan III, who at some point has begun styling himself online as "Happy Joe" and "Jazzy Jet," has had a checkered career in prison. He's always had crazy eyes, but now they look as if he's jammed a finger in a light socket.

He is first institutionalized at Washington's Western State Hospital, a large psychiatric facility on eight hundred acres in the historic Fort Steilacoom, south of Tacoma, initially home to an 1870s-era insane asylum and later rebuilt as a more modern complex. This is where Frances Farmer, a 1940s Hollywood star, spent five years after her arrests for drunk driving and erratic behavior, often bound in a straitjacket and subjected to electroshock therapy.

At the hospital, not far from his childhood home, Joseph is ordered to undergo medical and psychological testing and is enrolled in the Mentally Ill Offender Program, designed to assess and treat sex offenders. After almost two years he flunks out, having been caught peering in windows and masturbating in public while out on leave. He's sent to serve the remainder of his term in prison.

There he offends in a variety of ways, cited for hoarding contraband in his cell, including razor blades and child pornography. Nonetheless, after serving fourteen years, he's paroled in 1994 to a halfway house in Seattle, at the age of thirty-one.

On July 6, 1996, two young girls, Sammiejo White, eleven, and her nine-year-old half sister, Carmen Cubias, disappear while going to fetch cigarettes for their brother. They've been living in the Crest Motel, on Seattle's notoriously sordid Aurora Avenue, Highway 99. Seventeen months later, their bones and teeth are found in an abandoned barn in Bothell.

By March 1997, Joseph Duncan is in violation of his parole, having had contact with minor children. On March 27 he steals a friend's white car and bolts, leaving no information for his parole officer. A few days later, on April 4, ten-year-old Anthony Martinez is abducted in Beaumont, a city in Southern California, forced into a white car as his friends watch helplessly. Sixteen days later, a forest ranger finds the boy's remains, stripped of clothes and bound, some seventy miles east in the desert.[14]

Joseph bounces in and out of prison on charges of failing to register as a sex offender. Released in 2000, he ends up in the Midwest and in 2004 is arrested after molesting boys near school playgrounds in Fargo, North Dakota, and in Detroit Lakes, Minnesota. In April 2005 he's released on bail after writing a check for $15,000; the check bounces. He buys night-vision goggles and a video camera at Walmart, rents a red Jeep that he never returns, and heads for the Northwest. He has with him a shotgun and a claw hammer.

On I-90, he drives right through Kellogg, home of the shuttered Bunker Hill smelter complex, where the EPA is spending $200 million to treat the second-largest Superfund site in the country. The smokestacks are gone, demolished in 1996. Outside Coeur d'Alene, Joseph happens to spot two children playing outside a house on a frontage road. He pulls off.

For a day or two he spies on the family, using his night-vision goggles. He covets the youngest children, Dylan, a nine-year-old boy with strawberry-blond hair, and his sister, Shasta, eight. Their parents, Brenda and Steve Groene, are divorced. Brenda, forty, owns a housecleaning business called Maid to Order. Her boyfriend, Mark McKenzie, thirty-seven, works at a stainless-steel-sink-manufacturing company in nearby Spokane. They live with the two young children and Brenda's older son, Slade, thirteen.

They have a barbecue on the afternoon of May 15, 2005, and later that night, after the guests have left, Joseph Duncan enters the house. Wielding his shotgun, he ties up the adults and Slade with zip ties and duct tape, binding their ankles and yanking their wrists behind their backs. He beats them to death with the claw hammer. Their bodies are left lying on the floor in pools of blood. When police enter the house the next day, having been alerted by a neighbor to blood on the porch and doorway, the two younger children are missing.

Joseph drives east on I-90, pulling off in St. Regis, Montana, a town of a few hundred, peeling off on a logging road into the Lolo National Forest. There he sets up camp in a thicket of alders and ponderosa pines. For the next month and a half he tortures and molests the children, visiting particular cruelty on Dylan, whose execution he stages, tying him up, threatening to shoot him, and stopping at the last moment. At some point,

Duncan follows through and shoots Dylan, first in the stomach, then in the head. He burns the body in a campfire and throws the remains into a nearby culvert.

On July 2, at two o'clock in the morning, he's sitting with Shasta in a Denny's restaurant in Coeur d'Alene, eating onion rings and chicken strips, when their waitress, twenty-four-year-old Amber Deahn, recognizes Shasta from the posters and media coverage that have blanketed the state for the past six weeks. Asking the manager to call 911, Amber brings the child crayons and coloring paper and slow-walks a milkshake to delay their departure. Two customers recognize Shasta as well and call police with details of the vehicle.[15] Duncan is arrested without incident, and two days later, on July 4, working with information provided by the young girl, authorities find a fragment of Dylan's skull near the campsite, the only part of his remains to yield identifiable DNA.[16]

"Extremely wicked, shockingly evil, and vile" are the words the Florida judge attached to Ted Bundy's Chi Omega murders and assaults. Superlatives from the realm of the supernatural—Edgar Allan Poe or Robert Louis Stevenson or David Lynch—seem inadequate. Loathsome, repulsive, debased, diabolic: Duncan is all that and more. In court he simpers at photographers with a flirtatious come-hither stare.

Yet the rapists and murderers coming out of the Northwest, and particularly Tacoma, that city of woes, merit such hyperbole on a regular basis, their baroque crimes establishing a record of extravagant deviance. Sixteen years before Duncan's 2005 murders, a child rapist with a long record of crimes in the area was freed from prison and immediately abducted and raped a seven-year-old boy in a Tacoma park, cutting off his penis.[17] In 1990, outraged citizens demanded passage of a state law requiring long terms for sex offenders and mandatory registration upon release from prison, but it did not stem the tide of atrocious transgressions.

During this era, the unimaginable becomes the norm. If in the wider world, the majority of sexual assaults are committed by spouses, partners, relatives, or acquaintances—and they are—at this time and in this place, torture and murder committed by utter strangers assume monstrous proportions, as if someone had scratched through to the underworld and released a savage wave of sulfur.

ASARCO FILES FOR BANKRUPTCY.

Copper prices are tanking. On August 9, 2005, as prosecutors are debating whether Shasta will be required to testify against Joseph Edward Duncan III, the behemoth acquired by a modest family of immigrant lacemakers from Switzerland appears before a court. With a straight face, after extracting billions out of burning rock, this poor corporation can now only limp along, its silver finery in tatters. It is a victim of brutal economic forces and environmental bullies, beset—or so it would have us believe—by strikes and low copper prices, three-quarters of a billion dollars in personal injury lawsuits over asbestos, the management of twenty Superfund sites, and net losses of more than $680 million since its merger with Grupo México. It cannot find the pocket change to pay for gasoline for its trucks, and soon it will accuse Grupo México of stealing its Peruvian copper mines.[18] Not since *Jarndyce v. Jarndyce* have so many attorneys wept so many crocodile tears.

But in the eyes of corporate polluters, ASARCO becomes a model of avoiding accountability. It has been sloughing smelters like skin cells, closing doors, blowing up stacks, and walking away. In a new multinational circle of hell south of the border, it is reborn and lives to burn another day.

By 2005 Israel Keyes has already killed some people. After his discharge from the Army in July 2001, he breaks up with his Colville girlfriend, a chaste relationship maintained long-distance, and moves in with another, Tammie, a member of the Makah Tribe at Neah Bay, a reservation at the battered tip where the Pacific pours into the Strait of Juan de Fuca, on the farthest shore of Washington State. Tammie, raised in chaos and poverty herself, has a lot in common with Israel, and after she becomes pregnant, she watches as "Iz" evolves into a stable and valued member of the community, working as a contractor.

Their daughter is born on October 31, 2002, and Tammie believes that the experience has changed Israel. She's touched by his devotion to the child. But their domestic situation falls apart when she develops an opioid addiction after surgery for uterine cancer and a hysterectomy. She's struck by his admission that he knew the Kehoe brothers and by certain dark things he's said, such as "I'm a bad person" and "I have a black heart."[19]

Their relationship breaks up in 2004, and Israel becomes involved with a traveling nurse, Kimberly Anderson, based in Port Angeles, on the outskirts of Olympic National Park. Anyone taking the scenic drive into the Olympics or to Washington's wild Pacific coast has driven along the shores of Lake Crescent, a deep, cold mountain lake rimmed by resorts and campsites. Israel has taken that drive many times but has never heard of the OWL, that "continuous lineament of great magnitude" beneath its north shore.[20]

Lake Crescent has a legend attached to it by the Klallam and Quileute peoples. They tell of a violent battle fought between tribes beneath Mount Storm King, a 4,500-foot peak on the south side of the lake. Angered by their impudence, the mountain hurls rock into the valley below, killing warriors, damming a river, and creating a lake of uncanny depths.

Officially, the lake is a glacial scar 650 feet deep, but rumor has it that there are spots reaching 800.[21] Others say it's bottomless. In 1940, the body of a barmaid who worked at a tavern on the lake, beaten and strangled by her husband in 1936, surfaces in a remarkable state, preserved by the cold and the peculiar composition of the water.[22]

Later, Israel will admit to killing at least four people in Washington State between 2001 and 2007, when he moves to Anchorage, Alaska, with Kimberly, taking his daughter with him. While living in Washington, he rents multiple vehicles and boats. He takes canoe trips in remote areas. He hikes with a .22, exercising his sniper skills. He murders a couple, male and female, sometime between 2001 and 2005, as well as two women who may or may not be together. He deposits one or possibly two bodies in Lake Crescent, using a boat purchased from Tammie's ex-husband. They haven't come up yet.

YEAR AFTER YEAR, scientific studies are fleshing out the ways in which childhood lead exposure is associated with aggression, psychopathy, and crime. In 2001, a study in a pediatrics journal examines homicide rates and air lead levels in all 3,111 counties of the contiguous forty-eight states. It finds that the incidence of homicide is nearly 4 percent higher in counties with high air lead concentration than in counties with no lead, an increase that's just enough to account for all manner of havoc.[23] The lead, it notes, comes from smelters, battery plants, and industry.

In 2005, in *Biological Psychiatry*, a group of researchers demonstrates for the first time that structural deficits in the prefrontal cortex—including a lower volume of prefrontal matter—can be seen in so-called unsuccessful psychopaths.[24] They're the ones who get caught.

Three years later, another group links lead exposure to volume loss in the frontal cortex, the part of the brain governing "cognition and behavior."[25] Between 1979 and 1984, the researchers have recruited infants from poor neighborhoods in Cincinnati, where many are living in houses contaminated by lead paint, into a long-term investigation, the Cincinnati Lead Study. They measure blood lead levels until the children are around six. Years later, when their subjects are between the ages of nineteen and twenty-four, they conduct MRI scans measuring adult brain volumes.

They find that lead exposure in childhood is linked to brain volume loss when their subjects reach adulthood, and that the effects are particularly notable *in men*. The greatest volume loss is found in males with the highest lead exposure, and the loss shows up especially in the anterior cingulate cortex, a part of the prefrontal region responsible for the executive functions, regulating behavior.[26] In images, large red and yellow gaps show marked volume loss. In scans of female subjects, red areas are relatively minor. Another Cincinnati study links structural abnormalities—reduced brain volume in males exposed to lead—to higher levels of psychopathy.[27]

As the authors note, such findings "might help to explain the higher incidence of antisocial behaviors among men than women."[28] Worldwide, men commit the vast majority of violent crimes. Only 8.6 percent of serial killers in the United States are women, and the number of "lust killers" among them is smaller still.[29] Men are more violent than women by a country mile. Maybe we should do something about that.

IN 2005, BTK joins the list of unsuccessful psychopaths. Dennis Rader may not have killed anyone since 1991, when he left Dolores Davis in a culvert with a porcelain mask on her face, but until February 25, 2005, the date of his apprehension, he's still thinking about it, constantly.[30] He is, in fact, stalking his next victim.

He clumsily engineers his own capture through renewed communications with the public and the police. In March 2004 he sends a letter to *The Wichita Eagle* signed "Bill Thomas Killman," BTK. In it, he claims credit for murdering Vicki Wegerle in 1986, a crime for which her husband has long been considered a suspect, sending a photocopy of her driver's license and his personal snapshots of the crime scene. The Wichita police have DNA collected from beneath Wegerle's fingernails and begin testing hundreds of local men, an event referred to locally as the "swab-a-thon."[31] But Dennis doesn't live in Wichita. He lives in Park City, a northern suburb.

Lusting for attention, Dennis begins leaving packages around town, often in cereal (serial) boxes, one of his childish jokes. One includes a letter with graphic details of the Otero murders; another, inserted into the return slot at the Wichita Public Library, contains a missive falsely claiming credit for the recent death of a Kansas man; a third contains drawings of children in bondage and a fictionalized autobiography, "The BTK Story."[32] Yet another, left in a local park, holds Nancy Fox's driver's license and a doll with its hands bound and a plastic bag over its head.[33]

THE FOG WARNING

Writing to police, Dennis naively asks if his identity can be traced if he sends a previously erased floppy disk. In a personals ad in *The Wichita Eagle*, the police reassure him that no such identification is possible. That, of course, is a lie.

In the meantime, a few people familiar with Dennis have noticed remarkable similarities between the apparently fictitious autobiography penned by the killer, published in newspapers, and Dennis Rader's real life. In this crude list, BTK claims to love trains, to have served in the military in the 1960s, to have a cousin in Missouri, a grandfather who played the fiddle and died of lung disease, and a father who died in World War II. Dennis served in the military during the 1960s, and he's always loved trains, living close to the tracks. His father served in the war but died later, of black lung disease. One of the people struck by the close correspondences on the list is Dennis's daughter, Kerri, but no matter how much she tries to make sense of it, she can't.

Kerri muses on her father's preoccupations with Pittsburg, where they still attend family reunions. She knows there were "strip pits around Columbus and Pittsburg where Dad lived as a young boy."[34] She recalls driving out to the hills with him to visit Big Brutus, an orange-and-black electric shovel, eighty feet long, used for ripping out shallow coal seams, the star attraction of the mining museum in West Mineral, Kansas. Dennis, Kerri, and her brother have posed in front of Big Brutus to have their picture taken. They've camped and canoed near old strip mines.

She tries to put BTK out of her mind. Her father sends a floppy disk to the police. He's overwritten one used at his church, Christ Lutheran, with BTK materials, and authorities quickly find metadata with the church's name. Their search of church functionaries reveals a president named Dennis. His vehicle, a black Jeep Cherokee registered to Dennis Rader, has been seen on surveillance footage at a site where a box was left.

In search of DNA, officials subpoena Kerri Rader's medical files at Kansas State University, where, as a student, she had Pap smears and a biopsy on a cervical polyp.[35] Her tissue sample reveals a 10/10 familial match to semen in Nancy Fox's home and to the material under Vicki Wegerle's fingernails, providing enough evidence to arrest her father. On his way home to have lunch with his wife, he's detained without incident.

Charged with ten counts of first-degree murder on February 28, he keeps silent for a short time but then begins singing like the proverbial canary, providing an exhaustive and exhausting confession that lasts for nineteen hours. He wants the lawmen to admire his accomplishments. He's proud of his murders, so proud that when he pleads guilty he rambles on at his sentencing hearing in an address that's widely compared to an Academy Awards acceptance speech.[36]

Since childhood, however—summers spent digging, diving, and swimming in lead—it's entirely possible that he has a little less brain than he thinks he does.

In 2009, the ASARCO bankruptcy ends after four years. In a stroke of luck for the government, its settlement agreements are accepted by a federal district judge in Texas just as copper prices are rebounding, refilling corporate coffers at the moment when the EPA presents its bill.

Federal agencies and states renegotiate with the company, and the largest environmental bankruptcy in American history yields a landmark settlement: $1.79 billion.[37] The money will go to nineteen states, but the largest pot, $435 million, is collected by Idaho's Coeur d'Alene Basin to clean up Uncle Bunker's mess, where 1,500 square miles of land and water have been carpeted with up to thirty tons of lead per square mile.[38]

Washington State gets $188 million, $111 million of it designated to address the Tacoma smelter plume. Everett will receive $44.7 million to remediate its arsenic problems, a legacy of the Rockefellers; $22 million will go to strip arsenic-laden slag out of a former woodyard on the Tacoma tidal flats, where it's been leaching into the water; and $10.8 million will clean up old mines around the state. However inadequate for these Augean stables, it's a bonanza.

But there's nothing in that black bag for Arlene Yoss, who has survived chelation therapy only to suffer severe headaches, memory problems, deep bone pain, and kidney damage throughout her life, maladies that her children inherit to some extent. Little is known about the heritability of lead poisoning, but experts confirm that "lead can indeed cross the placenta."[39]

Lost in the endless ASARCO soap opera were the legal machinations the corporation had engaged in to try to limit its responsibilities to the people it had harmed and the environment it had ravaged. At one point, in 2002, after extensive negotiations with the U.S. Department of Justice, Grupo México—having acquired ASARCO's most valuable subsidiary, the Peruvian mines—offered to place a mere $100 million in a trust fund in order to meet its $1 billion in environmental liabilities: a sweetheart deal. "This is maybe one-tenth of a loaf," a Justice Department spokesman acknowledged at the time. "But it's better than no loaf at all."[40]

Chewing over the crusts was El Paso, which had been struggling with contaminated yards and playgrounds since the 1970s. The Texas Commission on Environmental Quality, a notoriously weak regulatory agency derided as "toothless and inert" and a "lapdog for polluters," had estimated that it would cost a minuscule $52 million to demolish the El Paso smokestacks and smelter buildings and to treat contaminated soil and water, restricting the cleanup to three kilometers from the smelter.[41]

But in February 2008, those same Texas commissioners who, in violation of state law, had been holding meetings with ASARCO attorneys from Baker Botts, the firm catering to the Bush political dynasty, granted ASARCO a permit to reopen the El Paso smelter. If it were ever allowed to get up and running, it would release 4.7 tons of lead into the air every year.[42]

CURIOUS THINGS ARE COMING to pass in Tacoma as well. Mike Cohen, a real estate developer known for building custom homes and casinos, has bought Ruston's former smelter peninsula, planning to erect a thousand high-rise condominium units, a 150-room resort hotel, a shopping district, a hundred thousand square feet of office space, and a mile-long promenade along the waterfront, built on slag. He also buys what he calls

"Stack Hill," where the smokestack once stood. There he builds thirty-five "high-end" homes looking out on the bay that the smelter polluted for nearly a century.

In buying the former plant, he's assuming its liabilities, paying $20 million to ASARCO, $5.5 million to the EPA (which has a lien on the property), and another $30 million for the remaining cleanup. Costs to build out the full ninety-seven-acre peninsula are estimated at $1 billion, potentially the largest project in the history of the county. It's to be called Point Ruston.[43]

Just as Cohen is poised to take the first steps in his construction spree, a real estate recession hits. Bill Baarsma, the former smelter worker, is now the mayor of Tacoma. In what Baarsma calls "the Big Betrayal," ASARCO, which has promised repeatedly to move the most hazardous waste off the Ruston site to a facility in eastern Oregon, shrugs its shoulders and walks away, inspiring one Tacoma resident to say, "As far as I'm concerned, Asarco is a corporate serial killer."[44]

So the local offal—arsenic and lead—is entombed in a gargantuan dump behind the condos and luxury hotel, held in what amounts to the largest garbage bag in the world: a three-ply plastic bag, officially dubbed an "on-site containment facility," consisting of a "containment cell . . . of multiple liners, a leachate collection system, and a leak detection system."[45] Inside the bag are the smelter's ancient arsenic kitchen and the remains of its Fine Ore Bins Building, as well as thousands of tons of arsenic-contaminated soil from the short-lived lead smelter in Everett. Incongruous monument, capped with topsoil, the toxic hump will sit there, perhaps forever, trespassers discouraged by chain link. Signage is terse, reading RESTRICTED AREA KEEP OUT. There's no further explanation.

IN ISRAEL KEYES, Ted Bundy is reborn. Israel sees Ted as his hero, and perhaps in homage he flies from Anchorage to Chicago on June 2, 2011, rents a car, and drives to Bundy's birthplace, Burlington, Vermont. It's less than a hundred miles from his property in Constable, New York.

THE FOG WARNING

As with his forebear, Israel's murders are sexually motivated, and he likes doubles. Israel, however, is bisexual: he enjoys raping and killing both men and women. He checks into a cheap motel in Essex, a suburb of Burlington, pays for a fishing license, goes fishing in a nearby park, and stops at a Lowe's hardware store to buy a portable camp stove. While fishing, he digs up a cache—a murder kit he stowed two years earlier in a buried Home Depot bucket. He has buried kits like this around the country, containing guns, ammunition, silencers, duct tape, zip ties, road flares, and Drano.

The night of June 8 is dark and rainy, and Israel, dressed in black and equipped with a headlamp, stakes out an apartment building. He nearly snatches a man in the parking lot. Oblivious to the danger, the man is nonetheless a bit too fast for his abductor, and Israel is left, momentarily, without a victim.[46]

After midnight, he's casing a house a few blocks from his motel on a quiet residential street. He likes what he sees, judging that an older couple lives there, noting no sign of children or pets. He cuts the phone line, waiting for a neighbor to collect a barking dog.

At 2:00 a.m. he puts on a mask and breaks into the attached garage, slipping into the car to read the registration. It belongs to a Lorraine Currier, and a picture in the car shows a couple, a man and a woman. He's excited by the possibilities. He has plans for both of them.

The door from the garage into the kitchen is locked, so he breaks a window and reaches in to unlock the door, turning on the headlamp and heading for what he assumes is the master bedroom, the one room he's observed that has a fan running. Within seconds of entering the bedroom, he's holding a gun on Bill Currier, fifty, and his wife, Lorraine, fifty-five. Bill works as an animal care technician for the University of Vermont; Lorraine works there as well, in the financial services department of the health care center. They're groggy and confused, and he fires questions at them, asking if there's a gun in the house. Lorraine admits to having a .38 Smith & Wesson in her bedside table. He grabs it, ordering them to roll onto their stomachs. He ties their hands behind their backs with zip ties.

He tosses the place, finding lingerie for Lorraine to wear, stealing clothing, her purse and wallet, jewelry, an ATM card (he forces them to divulge the PIN), and prescription drugs. When he's done, he walks them to the garage and puts them in their car, belting them in, and drives off into the night. He tells them they're being held for ransom, that they'll be fine. They tell him they have only a hundred dollars in their bank account.

He's heading for an abandoned farmhouse he cased earlier. Once there, he stashes Bill Currier in the basement, tying him to a stool. When he returns to the car he sees that Lorraine is trying to run to the road. He chases her down, takes her upstairs, and ties her arms and legs to an old bedstead with duct tape and rope.

Down in the basement, Bill is yelling, "Where's my wife? Where's my wife?" and when Israel runs down there, he finds that his captive, a large man, has reduced the stool to shards. This infuriates him. "There's a specific way I wanted things done, [a] very specific way I want things to happen," he'll say later. "I have the whole thing planned out. I have everything I need to do it."[47]

What the plan is, he does not explain, but it involves boiling water on the camp stove. Bill is thrashing and fighting, so Israel retrieves one of his weapons, a 10/22 rifle outfitted with a noise suppressor, and shoots him multiple times, in the head, chest, neck, and arms, until finally he falls dead.

Upstairs, he slices off Lorraine's clothing with a knife, gagging her with paper towels reinforced with duct tape. He rapes her once, offering her a cigar to smoke afterwards. Then he rapes her again, choking her until she loses consciousness. He uses condoms but never says what the boiling water is for.

When Lorraine wakes up, he takes her downstairs to show her what's happened to Bill and then strangles her from behind. He pours Drano over their faces and hands to speed decomposition, pulls trash bags over their bodies, and shoves them in a corner, dumping wood scraps and debris on top of them. He's been thinking of burning the house down, but the sun is up, so he drives the Curriers' car to a parking lot and abandons it. Then he leaves in his rental.

ONE OF THE MOST breathtakingly beautiful and accessible mountain lakes in the western United States is Lake Coeur d'Alene. Driving west from Missoula on I-90, climb up and up. High in the mountains, stop for gas and a huckleberry milkshake at the St. Regis truck stop. Cross Lookout Pass, elevation 4,680 feet, alongside the big rigs grinding through their gears on a roller coaster from Mountain to Pacific time, dropping down through the scraped gray wastes of Kellogg and Smelterville.

Thirty-five minutes later, the lake suddenly appears on the approach to the city of Coeur d'Alene: come around a bend and there are flashes of deep blue off to the left. The Missoula Floods created it, twelve or fifteen thousand years ago. Now there's a dam nine miles downriver. The lake is twenty-five miles long, a hundred to two hundred feet deep. On the lake bottom are parked a number of Model T Fords, evidence of those who tried to drive across the ice in winter in the early years of the last century. In the summer sun, it's a sparkling gem.

It's lined with lead. At the bottom rest seventy-five million tons of poisonous sediments laced with arsenic, lead, cadmium, and zinc. And the waste keeps coming, despite nine hundred million state and federal dollars spent trying to clean it up. Every day, around four hundred pounds of heavy metals leach out of Bunker Hill's tailings into the South Fork Coeur d'Alene River. Every year, another four hundred tons of lead and seven hundred tons of zinc flow into the lake.

Part of the Bunker Hill Superfund Site, the lake looks fantastic, but that might not last. For years, oxygenated lake water has pressed down on the metals, keeping them from entering the water column and dissolving. But Kootenai County has doubled its population in the past few decades, growing from 70,000 in 1990 to 171,000 in 2020, one of the fastest-growing counties in the country. As thousands have moved to the region, building lakefront homes, restaurants, and resorts; burying septic tanks; and planting laws that they cover with pesticides and fertilizers, the oxygen content of the lake has gone down. As oxygen is depleted, phosphorus rises, a cause of toxic algal blooms.[48]

Should oxygen continue to dwindle at the current rate, the metals will dissolve in the water and rise up, like the return of the repressed. And when that happens, as it has already in heavily polluted lakes in China, such as Lake Tai, the water will turn from ultramarine to sickly shades of chartreuse. The surface will be matted by algae. It will smell like a dead body. Every other living thing will die: fish, frog, tadpole, duck, swan, and eagle. As it is, dozens of tundra swans die every year foraging for food in the slough, ingesting lead that fills their digestive tracts. They starve to death.

All those beautiful swans.

This is what Uncle Bunker has wrought. What does he deserve? Something bad. Something like murder.

On the night of February 1, 2012, at around 8:00 p.m., Israel Keyes is driving down a street in Anchorage when he sees a girl working alone in a coffee hut on the edge of a parking lot. It's Samantha Koenig. She's eighteen, a senior in high school. She has an oval face framed by long, gleaming brown hair.

He orders an Americano, and when she hands it to him, he pulls out a gun and plucks her like a piece of fruit. First he tells her it's a robbery. He orders her to turn off the lights, which she does. It's closing time anyway. She hands him all the cash in the register.

He tells her to get down on the floor, and she complies. He vaults himself through the open window, ties her with zip ties, gets her to swear that she hasn't hit a panic button, and stuffs her mouth with napkins. As he's marching her to his truck, parked at the IHOP nearby, she briefly breaks away, but he tackles her and presses his gun into her side. He'll kill her if she tries it again, he says.

He straps her into the truck and pulls the napkins out of her mouth.

THE FOG WARNING

Driving off, he tells her he's holding her for ransom. That's true, but it's not the whole truth.

For Israel, there's a time crunch: he's scheduled to leave within hours to fly to New Orleans to take a Carnival cruise in the Caribbean with his daughter. Nonetheless, he circles back to the coffee hut, making sure this time to steal Samantha's cell phone, clean up, collect the zip ties he's dropped, and lock the door. He has to stop at a park to let her pee. He has to stop to get gas. He's smoking a cigar with her, something he seems to feel is a friendly gesture.

He drives back to his home, leaving her tied up in the truck. Eventually he moves her, blindfolded, into a work shed in the backyard, lined with a tarp and heated with space heaters, with heavy metal playing loudly on a radio to drown out any noise she might make. He secures her to a rope screwed to the wall. He gets the PIN for her ATM card and goes to withdraw money, but when he gets to the machine, he's forgotten it. He has to go back and ask again. There's ninety-four cents in her bank account.

He returns to her at 3:00 a.m. and ties her up with the ropes more elaborately, as a form of bondage, and rapes her slowly, twice. Then he puts on leather gloves and strangles her. He stabs her in the back with a knife, but "it wasn't to make her die faster," he'll say later. "It was something else."[49]

He tidies up, rolling the body in a sleeping bag and a tarp, concealing it in a cabinet, and locking the shed. At 5:00 a.m., he takes a taxi to the airport and leaves for the cruise.

Two weeks later, on February 18, he returns. What was he thinking, leaving a body on his property for so long? "I was thinking it was twenty degrees outside and I didn't have anything to worry about," he'll recall.[50]

He waits a couple of days until his daughter's gone back to school, then he returns to his prize, finding the sleeping bag he'd rolled her up in soaked with blood. He burns the tarp and whatever's been in contact with Samantha's body in his fireplace.

Then he takes her pliant form, rigor long passed, and hangs her up in the shed with a rope around her wrists. He thaws her out until she's nice and warm, then puts her body on a table and has sex with it. "I guess I lost track of time," he'll recall fondly, and when his daughter knocks on the shed door, he realizes it's morning.[51]

Necrophilia is an acquired taste, and not many human beings acquire it. The desire to commit sexual acts with a dead body requires overriding the hardwired instinct against coming into contact with odors and substances associated with death, decay, and decomposition.[52] Yet some serial killers, almost universally male, develop that taste, and an astonishing number of them have spent time in the Pacific Northwest.

Over the next day or so, Israel prepares a ransom note demanding $30,000 and buys supplies, including a sewing kit. He's saved Samantha's makeup, from her purse. He sews her eyes open with fishing line, but her cheeks droop. He tries superglue; he tries tape. He applies makeup and braids her hair, the way he once did for his sisters. "She definitely didn't look alive," he'll say later, but he takes pictures anyway, with an *Anchorage Daily News* from February 13.[53] He puts the note and a scanned copy of the photo in a ziplock bag, tacking it to a bulletin board in a park. It's proof of life, and it fools the detectives.

She's starting to smell, and although he's loath to part with her, he cuts her up in pieces and puts them into bags. Over the course of several days, he goes ice fishing at Matanuska Lake, cutting a hole in the ice, which is twenty inches thick, with a chain saw, and erecting a shelter. As he prepares to drop the body parts in the hole, he attaches weights to them. Lead weights.[54]

CORPORATIONS CAN BE PEOPLE, and people can be killers, ergo, corporations can be killers. Take Cominco or, as it became after a 2001 merger, Teck Cominco, aka Teck Metals or Teck Resources, as it later restyles itself. World's largest lead smelter. Last seen in the atmospheric vicinity of Israel Keyes and the friendly Kehoe brothers.

After years of litigation over whether U.S. agencies such as the EPA

THE FOG WARNING

have jurisdiction over a Canadian corporation, it turns out they do. Teck Cominco acknowledges certain facts: Over the course of a century it has discharged massive quantities of toxins into the air and water, all of which follow the path of the Columbia River Valley. The discharges have denuded vegetation and caused "significant mortality" to everything from trout fingerlings to zooplankton.[55] Its black slag, which has formed an entire beach outside the town of Northport, is not benign, as it has long argued, but instead leaches hazardous substances into the water.

In related developments, in 2002 Teck is fined $270,000 by the Workers' Compensation Board of British Columbia when sixty-five employees test positive for thallium poisoning. Production is halted for two months, and the company loses $14 million.

Thallium is a toxic metal, an odorless, colorless by-product of lead and zinc processing, once used in rat poison. It can be absorbed through skin or inhaled in dust. It can cause convulsions and, with heavy exposure, death.

One worker present during the thallium exposure dies, for reasons that remain "not clear."[56] Another, twenty-three-year-old carpenter Dean Moon, who tests positive for high levels of thallium, develops tremors, headaches, dizziness, and fatigue. Unable to work, he's still being compensated for exposure nearly a year later.[57]

Around this time, a professional long-distance swimmer named Christopher Swain, who's fallen in love with the scenic glory of the Columbia, decides to swim the length of it, 1,243 miles, from the headwaters in Canada to the Pacific Ocean. Yearning for the days when Lewis and Clark first saw its undammed magnificence, "clear at every depth," he wants to bring attention to its "contaminated beauty."[58]

Since the water temperature is often in the forties, Swain has to wear a dry suit, and he swallows so many foul mouthfuls that he begins rinsing with hydrogen peroxide every twenty minutes. Interviewed by an NPR reporter, he says, "Today I can taste . . . mud, metal, sewage, fuel." He swims through pesticides, nuclear waste, human feces, mercury, arsenic, zinc, lead, and salmon. When the water is clear enough, he sees scrolling beneath him an extraordinary wasteland of cars, tires, chunks of concrete, metal, and, in areas where dams have buried towns, submerged sidewalks and streets. To pace himself, he chants, "Water, Mordor. Water, Mordor. Water, Mordor," recalling Tolkien's realm of ultimate evil. That's where the volcano is: Mount Doom.

ISRAEL KEYES'S COMPLICATED ransom scheme proves his undoing. He uses Samantha Koenig's debit card to make multiple withdrawals from her ATM account, an account now full of money donated by the community and being monitored by the FBI, and he's arrested on March 13, 2012, in Lufkin, Texas. He's been visiting his mother and sisters, who've joined a post-Waco religious cult.

Over the next nine months, FBI agents and federal prosecutors in Alaska question Keyes as he makes a number of videotaped statements. They receive a confession to Samantha Koenig's murder and to the killings of the Curriers in Vermont in exchange for supplying him with cigars, candy bars, bagels, doughnuts, and Americanos, of the type prepared for him by Koenig herself. He's demanding a quick resolution to his case, asking for the death penalty. He wants his daughter spared the publicity surrounding his murders, something he might have thought of earlier. But then, his reasoning, while demonstrative of a certain ratlike cunning, does not seem entirely rational.

He never gives up the names of other victims, describing the circumstances surrounding their deaths in such broad terms that it's difficult to pin them down.

Nonetheless, he's linked to an astonishing number of disparate crimes. He's thought to have abducted and murdered a resident of Hackensack, New Jersey, Debra Feldman, in April of 2009. He's a person of interest in a series of carjackings and murders in Florida and is known to have committed bank robberies in New York and Texas. He speaks of plans to torch churches, kill police, and commit a mass murder, perhaps one involving explosives.

THE FOG WARNING

Tiring of his captors' legalistic approach, he attempts a dramatic escape during a federal court hearing in Anchorage on May 23. Like Ted, he's resourceful, whittling pencils down to slivers and using them to pick the locks on his cuffs and leg restraints. As his lawyer addresses the court, he's guarded by U.S. marshals and FBI agents and thought to be secured by handcuffs and leg irons, but he nonetheless vaults out of his chair at the defense table and over a railing, leaping from chair to chair until a guard shoots him with a Taser. Despite this attempt, the local jail fails to take precautions.

On the night of December 1, 2012, Israel Keyes, unfathomably supplied with razor blades, commits suicide in his cell, slashing one wrist with a blade secured in a pencil and strangling himself with a noose fashioned from a bedsheet. When he's found in the morning, after hours have passed, his body is stiff with rigor. He leaves two cups and two milk cartons containing his congealing blood, a suicide screed written on a lined yellow tablet, and eleven drawings of skulls executed in blood, captioned WE ARE ONE.

With the death of Israel Keyes passes the era of murder, our hour of lead. The CDC again revises its strictures on blood lead levels, advising that no child have more than five micrograms per deciliter.[59] It's lowered again in 2021, to three and a half. There is no safe level.

Throughout the 1990s, nationwide there are 669 serial killers. In the 2000s: 371. From 2010 to 2020: 117.[60]

HEALTH AND INDUSTRY go hand in hand. The OWL lies quiet. It takes a worried man to sing a worried song, but our Cascade Range volcanoes remain at normal background activity levels. Small earthquakes are commonly detected. Suicide Lane and Raper's Road are erased from the maps.

As for Tacoma, the city's still not pretty, but there's little of the age-old aroma. Millions upon millions of dollars have been spent to scrub its bloody hands clean. The Washington State Department of Ecology has set its ideal cleanup level for arsenic in soil at 20 ppm, for lead at 250 ppm.[61]

Before ASARCO gave up, it sampled 2,800 properties and cleaned 1,600, but only those with arsenic measuring over 230 ppm.[62] The EPA and Ecology have done the rest, remediating more than seven hundred residential yards, parks, and school properties for arsenic over 100 ppm and for lead over 250 ppm. That's all they have money for.

At the former Ruston smelter site, condos rise from the slag, and units facing the water have sparkling views of Commencement Bay. Trees cannot be planted here, nothing with a significant root system. There's a central courtyard and fountain, and on any given morning, elderly retirees with dementia gather with a caretaker, rocking and swaying to piped-in music, singing "Puff, the Magic Dragon." He lives by the sea.

Giant octopuses are playing hide-and-seek under the Tacoma Narrows Bridge, frisking in the ruins of Lacey V. Murrow's dreams. They know what he did. Pods of orcas sky-hop, and the odd gray or humpback whale heaves herself out of the Sound and falls back.

But along the ragged edges of the shoreline, there are still dead zones where jellyfish drift, dispirited by whatever pockets of volatile chemicals they've wandered into. On the old pilings of Ruston Way's former lumber mills, there are no starfish or anemones. Only barnacles. At the bottom of the bay, lead and copper are allowed to rest, undisturbed.

In April 2023, a Trident Seafoods factory fishing vessel, old and poorly maintained, catches fire and burns for six days, combusting 55,000 gallons of diesel, nearly ten tons of Freon coolant, and a hullful of frozen pollack from the Bering Sea. The Freon alone amounts to a massive release of climate-changing gases, the equivalent of burning 1.7 million gallons of gasoline.[63] It's the second such fire in as many years. A shelter-in-place order is issued for Tacoma residents, and the acrid odor is back.

In the condominium compound of Point Ruston, history has been relegated to a dark hallway next to a plastic surgeon's office that leads to public restrooms. Newspaper articles are yellowing under glass, maps of major crimes involving fire, smoke, and rat poison creating a real-life crazy wall.

Atop the smelter's slag landform is Dune Peninsula, a park traversed by the Frank Herbert Trail, a walking, biking, and skateboarding route

THE FOG WARNING

connecting Point Defiance Park to a waterfront path along the bay. There's a ladle from the smelter tipped on its side: kids can run into it and rub the rough refractory cement, striated by fire. It's cold now.

Prairie grasses wave in the wind, alongside shoreline shrubs and succulents, but signs warn walkers not to step off: DANGER / UNSTABLE SLOPE AND SLAG EXPOSURE. Areas of rock are wrapped in plastic to keep the arsenic genie in the bottle. Plaques along the trail are embedded with thoughts from Herbert, who died in 1986 at age sixty-five of a pulmonary embolism after surgery for pancreatic cancer, a cancer now tied to lifelong exposures to fine particulate pollution.[64] One reads: THE HIGHEST FUNCTION OF ECOLOGY IS THE UNDERSTANDING OF CONSEQUENCES.[65]

Beside the trail is the Silver Cloud Hotel, where couples get married in front of water views. Behind the hotel is Ruston's high hump of toxic waste, sullenly huddled into the side of a hill. No one gives it a thought.

The age of burning is over, along with the profusion of our most distinctive murderers. Or so it seems. During the first Trump administration, EPA director Scott Pruitt signs a pact with a Canadian company to reopen Bunker Hill. It's time, the EPA says, for a "fresh start."[66]

Sure it is. There's still metal down there. Let's dig it out. Let's burn it. Throw the Domesday Book on the pyre. The monster is still alive, and there's nothing we can do, at the end of the movie, to kill it.

THOSE WERE THE DAYS, my friends, and they may or may not ever end. But take heart: I have a plan. I have an incantation.

I curse you, you corporate scribes and pharisees, you hypocrites, rubbing your hands over whited sepulchres full of dead women's bones. You think you're getting away with it. Just you wait.

I rewrite your Bible, restoring the Gospel of Judith, her with a sword.

I declare this: Do not be about your father's business. Your father's business is rape and murder.

Be a witch. Be a bitch. Get in the reversible lane and make time run backwards. Loot the Guggenheim: Cover the walls in stove black and ashes. Hand the engineers their heads; hang them from lampposts on a floating bridge. Smother a foundling after a great war.

Follow the corpse road after midnight under a full moon and meet yourself at the place where power lines cross in the cleft between two mountains, one Taylor, one Tiger. Boil tar and cast in it a bird's nest laced with blond hair. Stir with a crowbar. Sing backwards "(Don't Fear) the Reaper."

In the West, light the white sage smudge and cast our spell by sucking the smoke down the stack and going back, back, back to the days when girls are dragged away from washing their clothes and hitching their rides and sleeping in their beds. Help them back into their bodies. Give them a hand up out of the green river and the trash and the leaf litter. They don't belong there. For the love of all that's holy, strew their paths with daffodils. Let a little girl wake in the morning after rain, wearing her plea to Saint Christopher, and keep her door latched fast. Put the baby back in the basket. Unmelt the slag, unbreak the rock, unbreathe the air.

Now and forever, let it all be over.

ACKNOWLEDGMENTS

Mercer Island today is as beautiful as it ever was, the water on the lake as sparkling, the views as serene. But for some of us who knew it in a different time, it's slightly haunted by ghosts of the past, a drowned forest offshore, a sunken bridge, a shattered school gymnasium, long swept away. East Seattle School, built in 1914, the oldest public building on the island, was demolished for no good reason in 2021. Last time I saw it, all that was left was a muddy pit. There are places where money means more than history.

The high school is still there, extensively renovated, the "Islander" mascot with the bone through its nose long relegated to the annals of a backwards world. It wasn't all bad: there were extraordinary teachers for whom I'm still thankful, particularly Carol McFadden, who taught more than just English and journalism and encouraged ambition in many students, and Bob Maier, whose attention to the fundamental texts of American history and literature was an inspiration.

One could not ask for three better friends than the people to whom this book is dedicated. The incisive, affable Jeff Dreiblatt, a gifted artist, poet, and volunteer firefighter, obligingly read the manuscript, providing corrective notes. He and his brilliant husband, William Sterling Walker, have been havens of hospitality and pillars of moral support: I can't imagine life without them.

For years, ever since we met in a high school hallway, Sheryl Whitney has shared her friendship, cake, and conversation, a generosity that has

ACKNOWLEDGMENTS

extended to enlightening discussions of this project. Her discriminating intellect and calm confidence never fail to sharpen my own thinking, and I'm in awe of her dedication to public service and quiet expertise on the history and practice of social justice.

I cherish the person I've known longest outside my own family, Sue Warner-Bean, who graciously provided comments on passages involving her family. Her intelligence and empathy have guided her throughout a distinguished career in responding to transportation emergencies and helping families cope with disasters. For someone schooled in her childhood in Christian Science denialism, she's chosen an extraordinary vocation. Instead of renouncing the real world, she has, in the most profound way, embraced it.

Some twenty years ago, Sue became involved with PeaceTrees Vietnam, a Seattle-based organization devoted to building schools in Vietnam and to removing unexploded land mines and bombs. She helped raise funds to build and maintain a kindergarten in the remote mountain village of A Xing in Quảng Trị Province. In 2007, the David Howard Warner Kindergarten was dedicated on what would have been her brother's sixty-first birthday.

The archives held at the Tacoma Public Library's Northwest Room are a rich source of historical information, and I'm indebted to archivist Anna Trammell and librarian Spencer Bowman, who helped me navigate the ASARCO records and other materials when the library was largely closed due to the COVID-19 pandemic and renovation, arranging two site visits and the scanning of many documents that proved essential.

Bill Baarsma took time away from preparing for an imminent move to share his family's history at the Tacoma smelter and his hair-raising experiences during summers working there. Marianne Sullivan was wonderfully helpful as an expert on the Tacoma smelter. Anne Fischel and Lin Nelson, retired faculty members at Evergreen State College, whose website, Their Mines, Our Stories, is dedicated to the woes perpetrated by ASARCO in Tacoma, El Paso, and other sites, offered practical advice as well. At the Washington State Department of Ecology, Marian Abbett and

ACKNOWLEDGMENTS

Justin Zakoren patiently answered questions about the Dirt Alert program, a heroic effort to put right what the Tacoma smelter—and other corporate villains—did wrong. None of these professionals, of course, are responsible in any way for the Lynchian excesses of this book.

Staff at the Tacoma Historical Society, the Washington State Historical Society, and the Museum of History & Industry in Seattle, or MOHAI, helped me track down images, and Chris Staudinger of Pretty Gritty Tours in Tacoma walked me around the reformed slag peninsula one day, introducing me to the once and future landmarks of that strange realm. Thanks as well to Mercer Island historian Jane Meyer Brahm and to Jessica Prokop at *The Columbian*.

I can't really find any adequate way to thank Sara Bershtel, my editor since 1995, who has seen all four of my books (and countless others) to publication. Sara is everything you want in an editor: shrewd, perceptive, and unsparing yet always buoyant and supportive. This book was to have been published by Metropolitan, her imprint at Henry Holt for nearly thirty years, but in an act of unfathomable corporate mischief Metropolitan was abruptly dismantled in 2022, its staff laid off. There are places where money means more than, well, anything.

Happily, Sara found a new home at Penguin Press, and I'm grateful to the fine team there, including Scott Moyers for creative suggestions about the title and Casey Denis, who ably assisted in wrangling maps and images. I'm deeply grateful for the skills and patience of Will Palmer, the copy editor on this book, who worked wonders, improving what he found in ways large and small and asking searching questions. Thanks as well to Dianna Delling for special assistance with the notes.

Perspicacious as always, Don Fehr, my agent at Trident Media, offered invaluable guidance on many issues. Prudence Crowther at *The New York Review of Books* edited a review I wrote about true crime that proved essential in contemplating this book. She is a charming correspondent whose editorial skills and wisdom I prize. Harbour Fraser Hodder, with her own glancing Mercer Island history, remains a stalwart friend.

I have a snapshot of myself as a toddler, standing beside a road some-

ACKNOWLEDGMENTS

where, looking lost. My brother is bending over me, solicitous and anxious to help, as he has always been. For the personal sections of this book and for much else, I'm forever indebted to him and to his wife, who shared their warm hospitality and, in a somewhat more trying exercise, their memories of a difficult time. Along with my sister, they've been remarkably obliging, giving, and forbearing throughout. I hope this work might offer my niece and nephew a new slant on the Pacific Northwest of earlier generations and a reason to keep working for a more just and incorruptible future.

With every book I've written I've relied heavily on the astute editorial advice, literary savvy, emotional support, and practical judgment of my husband, Hal Espen. He contributed immeasurably to this one from beginning to end, offering lashings of encouragement and essential dissections of the morality of exploring such sensational material. More than that, he's the best company I know, a genius at putting things in perspective and recalling appropriate song lyrics for every occasion. He is more precious to me than any metal, and I'm thankful for him every day.

Working on this project I fell prey at times to brooding on lines from James Merrill's "The Broken Home," an intensely personal poem that's also universal. After eons of industrial vandalism, our planet is just that, a broken home, "Father Time and Mother Earth, / A marriage on the rocks." At the end, the poet wonders whether we will ever create a place where "Someone at last may actually be allowed / To learn something." Will we? It's a question that's still hanging in the air.

NOTES

Author's Note: Many of the documents used in my research are held in public records collections, such as those maintained by the FBI, the King County Archives, and the Tacoma Public Library's Northwest Room. Others are posted on websites such as Ted Bundy: A Killer in the Archives, currently hosted by Patreon at https://www.patreon.com/killerintheachives, or blogs such as *CrimePiper*, at https://crimepiperblog.wordpress.com, which collect photographs, video and audio recordings, transcripts, and documents gathered from police and other archives.

INTRODUCTION: Crime Scenes of the Pacific Northwest; or, The Crazy Wall
1. Kirsten Kendrick and Amelia Greim, "Why Are There So Many Serial Killers in the Northwest?," *Seattle Post-Intelligencer*, July 24, 2012.
2. "Which State Has Produced the Most Serial Killers?," Crime Capsule, crimecapsule.com/which-state-has-produced-the-most-serial-killers.
3. The quotation is attributed to FBI agent John Douglas. See "Serial Killers Who Lived in Northwest," *Seattle Times*, December 10, 2007.
4. According to the National Institute of Justice, an agency of the U.S. Department of Justice, serial killers are typically those who commit two or more murders on separate occasions. (Mass murderers are those who kill a number of people in a single event.) This list (by no means complete) is drawn from "Suspected or Convicted Serial Killers in Washington," *Seattle Post-Intelligencer*, February 19, 2003. It includes those who committed murders in the Pacific Northwest, encompassing Washington, Oregon, Idaho, Alaska, and British Columbia. The Want-Ad Killer is Harvey Louis Carignan (1927–2023), convicted of the murders of two women in Minnesota; he killed two teenagers in Washington and a woman in Anchorage, Alaska. The Boxcar Killer is Robert Joseph Silveria Jr. (b. 1959), who began killing in Salem, Oregon; he confessed to twenty-eight murders. The Lust Killer was Jerome Brudos (1939–2006), who murdered at least four women in Salem and Portland, Oregon. The Phantom Sniper is Gary Addison Taylor (b. 1936); he killed in multiple states (Florida, Michigan, Texas); one of his victims was killed in Enumclaw, Washington, in 1973. The Hillside Strangler murders were

committed by two men, cousins Kenneth Bianchi (b. 1951) and Angelo Buono Jr. (1934–2002), the majority committed in the Los Angeles area. The last two murders, committed by Bianchi alone, took place in Bellingham, Washington. Bianchi is serving a life sentence at the Washington State Penitentiary in Walla Walla, Washington. The Lewiston Valley Killer, who may have been responsible for the murders of four or five girls and women and one man in the Lewis Clark Valley of northern Idaho between 1979 and 1982, remains unidentified. The I-5 Killer is Randall Woodfield (b. 1950), who committed a series of violent rapes, assaults, and murders along the I-5 corridor between Washington, Oregon, and California; convicted of one murder, he may have committed more than forty. He is serving a life sentence at Oregon State Penitentiary in Salem, Oregon. The Coin Shop Killer is Charles Thurman Sinclair (1946–1990), who committed at least eleven homicides between 1980 and 1990, targeting coin shop owners and committing perhaps four murders in Washington State. He died in Anchorage, Alaska, shortly after being apprehended. The identity of the individual responsible for the Dismemberment Murders remains unknown; the case involves a series of three murders, of two men and a woman, whose bodies were dismembered and dumped in Snohomish County in the late 1980s and early 1990s. The Index Killer, responsible for up to five murders in 1988 in the remote Cascades town of Index, Washington, has never been found. The Happy Face Killer is Keith Jesperson (b. 1955), currently serving three life sentences in Salem, Oregon; he strangled at least eight women in the early 1990s in a number of states, including Washington and Oregon. Before he was apprehended, he was known for sending letters to the media signed with a happy face. The Eastside Killer is George Waterfield Russell Jr. (b. 1958), who killed three women in suburban communities east of Seattle during the summer of 1990; Russell grew up on nearby Mercer Island and is currently serving two life sentences. The Werewolf Butcher of Spokane is Jack Owen Spillman III (b. 1969), who murdered a nine-year-old girl in Okanogan County, Washington, in 1994 and a mother and her fifteen-year-old daughter in East Wenatchee, Washington, in 1995. The Beast of British Columbia is Clifford Olson (1940–2011), who abducted and murdered eleven girls and boys in Surrey, British Columbia, between 1980 and 1981. The Green River Killer is Gary Leon Ridgway (b. 1949), who pleaded guilty to forty-nine murders of women in Washington and Oregon from roughly 1982 to 1998. Apprehended in 2001, he claimed to be responsible for seventy-one murders and is imprisoned at the Washington State Penitentiary at Walla Walla.

5. See Wikipedia, s.v. "Olympic–Wallowa Lineament," last edited January 22, 2024, en.wikipedia.org/wiki/Olympic–Wallowa_lineament; see also Henry V. Lyatsky, "Significance of the Trans-Cordilleran Olympic-Wallowa Zone in Geologic Evolution of the Washington and British Columbia Coastal Regions," chap. 5 in *Continental-Crust Structures on the Continental Margin of Western North America*, Lecture Notes in Earth Sciences, vol. 62 (Berlin: Springer-Verlag, 1996), pp. 73–132, doi.org/10.1007/BFb0011445.
6. Erwin Raisz, "The Olympic-Wallowa Lineament," *American Journal of Science* 243-A (1945): p. 479.
7. Raisz, "Olympic-Wallowa Lineament," p. 479.
8. Raisz, "Olympic-Wallowa Lineament," p. 479.
9. Raisz, "Olympic-Wallowa Lineament," p. 480.

10. Richard Edes Harrison, "Obituary: Erwin Raisz," *Geographical Review* 59, no. 3 (July 1969): pp. 448–49.
11. See Donald U. Wise, "An Outrageous Hypothesis for the Tectonic Pattern of the North American Cordillera," *GSA Bulletin* 74, no. 3 (1963): pp. 357–62; G. A. Davis, *Tectonic Evolution of the Pacific Northwest—Precambrian to Present*, Preliminary Safety Analysis Report, WPPSS Nuclear Project No. 1 (Richland, WA: Washington Public Power Supply System, 1977), subapp. 2R-C, p. 46.
12. This quotation, often attributed to Will Durant, exists nowhere in his published writings, according to James Bishop of the Will Durant Foundation. The words, which Durant may have delivered in a speech, appear to reflect other remarks the author made on geology. See W. Winston Elliott III, "Will Durant, Geological Disaster, and Devastation in Japan," *Imaginative Conservative*, March 15, 2011, theimaginativeconservative.org.
13. A reference to the 2014 Oso mudslide, four miles east of Oso, Washington, in the foothills of the Cascades, which destroyed forty-nine homes, killing forty-three.
14. My paraphrase of lines in W. H. Auden, "As I Walked Out One Evening," *in Selected Poems*, ed. Edward Mendelson (New York: Random House, 1979), p. 62.

CHAPTER 1: The Floating Bridge

1. "Emerald City" is a marketing slogan derived from a 1982 competition run by the Seattle–King County Convention and Visitors Bureau. See David Wilma, "Seattle Becomes the Emerald City in 1982," October 24, 2001, historylink.org/File/3622.
2. Poster, ca. 1971, Museum of History and Industry, Seattle.
3. Robert Service, "The Cremation of Sam McGee," in *The Spell of the Yukon* (New York: Dodd, Mead & Company, 1907), p. 61.
4. John Soennichsen, *Bretz's Flood: The Remarkable Story of a Rebel Geologist and the World's Greatest Flood* (Seattle: Sasquatch Books, 2008), p. 192.
5. See, for example, Kim Stanley Robinson, *Red Mars* (New York: Bantam, 1993), pp. 546–49.
6. Derek B. Booth, Ralph A. Haugerud, and Kathy Goetz Troost, "The Geology of Puget Lowland Rivers," in *Restoration of Puget Sound Rivers*, ed. by David R. Montgomery, Susan Bolton, Derek B. Booth, and Leslie Wall (Seattle: University of Washington Press, 2003), p. 28. The phrase "big hole" is also referenced in Wikipedia, s.v. "Puget Sound Faults," last edited November 7, 2023, en.wikipedia.org/wiki/Puget_Sound_faults.
7. The crustal block known as Oregon is described as "rotating in a manner similar to a jack-knifing trailer" in Wikipedia, s.v. "Puget Sound Faults," last edited November 7, 2023, en.wikipedia.org/wiki/Puget_Sound_faults.
8. This phrase appeared in an early version of the Wikipedia entry on "Puget Sound Faults," last edited July 29, 2024; it has since been edited.
9. See Jon Krakauer, "Geologists Worry about Dangers of Living 'Under the Volcano,'" *Smithsonian*, July 1996.
10. See Blaine Harden, "A Dream of a Mountain, a Nightmare of a Volcano," *Washington Post*, August 11, 2003.
11. Judy Gellatly, *Mercer Island: The First 100 Years* (Mercer Island, WA: Mercer Island Bicentennial Committee, 1977), p. 85.
12. "Murrow's Rise like Alger Tale," *Seattle Sunday Times*, June 30, 1940.

13. Craig Holstine, "Lacey V. Murrow & His 'Upstanding' Bridges," *Columbia: The Magazine of Northwest History* 31, no. 1 (Spring 2017): p. 13.
14. Holstine, "Lacey V. Murrow," p. 16.
15. Several people filmed the collapse. See "Tacoma Narrows Bridge History—Art—Continuation," Washington State Department of Transportation, wsdot.wa.gov/TNBHistory/art-continues.htm.
16. "Tacoma Narrows Bridge, Collapse and History," Study.com, updated November 21, 2023, study.com/learn/lesson/tacoma-narrows-bridge-collapse-facts-causes-physics.html.
17. "Tacoma Narrows Bridge Twists in Wind like a Piece of Taffy," *Spokane Daily Chronicle*, November 8, 1940, caption on p. 2.
18. Priscilla Long, "Tacoma Narrows Bridge Collapses on November 7, 1940," HistoryLink.org Online Encyclopedia of Washington State History, last updated November 12, 2014, historylink.org/File/5048.
19. Professor F. B. Farquharson, "University Prof Last on Bridge," *Spokane Daily Chronicle*, November 8, 1940, p. 2; see also accompanying article, "Murrow Gives Views."
20. "No One Man Can Be Blamed, Says Lacey Murrow," *News Tribune* (Tacoma), November 9, 1940, p. 8; "Engineering Professor on Tacoma Span with Movie Camera; Escaped," *Bellingham Herald*, November 8, 1940, p. 1.
21. Chris Maag, "The Bridge," *Mercer Island Reporter*, November 11, 1998.
22. "Lake Bridge to Be Protested," *Seattle Times*, June 2, 1938; Associated Press, "Bridge Bill O.K. Forecast, despite Seattle Opposition," *Seattle Times*, January 18, 1939.
23. Associated Press, "Thousands View Bridge Opening," *Spokesman-Review* (Spokane), July 3, 1940, p. 9.
24. Lloyd D. Weir, "Keeping Up the 'Biggest Thing Afloat,'" *Seattle Times*, March 1, 1942.
25. C. B. Blethen, "I Go for a Ride," *Seattle Sunday Times*, June 30, 1940, p. 1.
26. Blethen, "I Go for a Ride."
27. "Lake Bridge Doesn't Budge in High Wind," *Seattle Times*, November 7, 1940.
28. "2 Hurt, 5 Cars Wrecked on Lake Span," *Seattle Times*, November 29, 1957.
29. Washington Toll Bridge Authority, *Lake Washington Bridge* pamphlet (Olympia: Washington Toll Bridge Authority, ca. 1940), unpaginated.
30. Tim Benson and Paul Knaebel, "An Overview of Washington State's Floating Concrete Pontoon Bridges," paper presented at Heavy Movable Structures' Ninth Biennial Movable Bridge Symposium, October 22–25, 2002), heavymovablestructures.org/wp-content/uploads/2017/12/0095.pdf.
31. Kit Oldham, "Washington Transportation Chronology," HistoryLink.org Online Encyclopedia of Washington State History, updated 2004, blog.historylink.org/wp-content/uploads/2012/05/Transportation-Chronology-Updated.pdf. See also *Twenty-First Biennial Report of the Director of Highways, 1944–1946* (Olympia: State of Washington Department of Highways, 1946), p. 49.
32. Benson and Knaebel, "Floating Concrete Pontoon Bridges."
33. "Five from B.C. in Holiday Deaths," *Vancouver Sun*, September 4, 1945.
34. "Diver Finds Boat Sunk Ten Years Ago," *Seattle Times*, May 12, 1955.
35. Associated Press, "Spokane Woman Loses Life as Car Plunges," *Spokane Chronicle*, March 15, 1949, p. 1.

36. Associated Press, "Spokane Woman Loses Life."
37. Associated Press, "Pacific Northwest Rocked by Impact of Frigid Blizzard," *Spokesman-Review* (Spokane), January 14, 1950.
38. Washington State Highway Commission, Department of Highways, *Lacey V. Murrow Memorial Bridge* (pamphlet issued on rededication of the bridge), June 30, 1967.

CHAPTER 2: The Smelter
1. Roxborough High School Yearbook (Philadelphia: Academies at Roxborough High School, 1942), p. 19, Alumni Room, Academies at Roxborough.
2. "Eleanore L. Cowell in the 1940 United States Federal Census," Ancestry.com, accessed December 2024, ancestry.com/discoveryui-content/view/24571656: 2442?tid=&pid=&queryId=135ff88f-aae9-483a-b61e-6f6776bc3421&_phsrc =54e1186654&_phstart=successSource.
3. Ann Rule reported that Ted Bundy had seen the name Lloyd Marshall on his birth certificate when he checked the records while visiting Burlington, Vermont, in 1968; see Ann Rule, *The Stranger Beside Me* (New York: Simon & Schuster, 2008), p. xxxiii. In fact, on Bundy's Standard Certificate of Birth, State of Vermont, signed and dated by a physician two days after his birth, "Father of Child" is listed as "Unknown." Louise Bundy apparently supplied the name Jack Worthington to Stephen G. Michaud and Hugh Aynesworth; see Michaud and Aynesworth, *The Only Living Witness* (New York: Simon & Schuster, 1983), p. 47.
4. Dorothy Otnow Lewis in *Crazy, Not Insane*, directed by Alex Gibney (New York: Jigsaw Productions, 2020), originally aired on HBO.
5. Rule, *Stranger Beside Me*, p. 9.
6. Theodore Robert Cowell, Standard Certificate of Birth, State of Vermont, signed November 26, 1946, Killer in the Archives.
7. Wendy Ruderman, Barbara Laker, and Dylan Purcell, "Danger in the Dirt," *Philadelphia Inquirer*, June 18, 2017, pp. A1, A15.
8. One of the closest lead smelters to the Cowells' home at 7202 Ridge Avenue, Philadelphia, was A. W. Cadman Manufacturing Co., a lead smelter at 18 West Chelten Avenue, Philadelphia. See also Michael J. O'Shea et al., "Lead Pollution, Demographics, and Environmental Health Risks: The Case of Philadelphia, USA," *International Journal of Environmental Research and Public Health* 18, no. 17 (2021): fig. 3. The zip code later assigned to the area where the Cowells lived (19128) shows interpolated soil lead ranging from a low of 1–100 to a high of 800–1,000.
9. Details regarding Samuel Cowell in this paragraph are drawn from Myra MacPherson, "The Roots of Evil," *Vanity Fair*, May 1989. MacPherson, relying on interviews with Dr. Dorothy Otnow Lewis, a psychiatrist who questioned Bundy in 1989 in connection with his final death row appeal, was the first to posit the theory that Samuel Cowell, Ted Bundy's grandfather, may have also been his father. Incest was disproved, however, in 2020, when Dr. Lewis reported the results of a DNA analysis. See Gibney, *Crazy, Not Insane*. MacPherson's account of Cowell's personality was challenged by Audrey Tilden, one of Samuel's sisters; see Christian Barth, *The Garden State Parkway Murders: A Cold Case Mystery* (Denver: Wild Blue Press, 2020), p. 249.
10. MacPherson, "Roots of Evil."

11. Advertisement, "Roxborough Nurseries, S. K. Cowell, Proprietor, 7202 Ridge Avenue, Philadelphia 28 Pa.," *Philadelphia Inquirer*, September 19, 1954.
12. Barth, *Garden State Parkway Murders*, pp. 264–65.
13. Handwritten emendation to Cowell, Standard Certificate of Birth, 1946, Killer in the Archives.
14. Murray Morgan, *Puget's Sound: A Narrative of Early Tacoma and the Southern Sound* (Seattle: University of Washington Press, 1979), p. 170.
15. The characterization of Commencement Bay as one of the five best harbors in the world occurs in "Tacoma and ASARCO," *ASARCO News* 4, no. 2 (Spring 1962): p. 1.
16. Irwin Unger and Debi Unger, *The Guggenheims: A Family History* (New York: HarperCollins, 2005), p. 13.
17. Isaac Marcosson, *Metal Magic: The Story of the American Smelting & Refining Company* (New York: Farrar, Straus and Company 1949), p. 27.
18. John H. Davis, *The Guggenheims: An American Epic* (New York: Shapolsky, 1989), p. 52.
19. Unger and Unger, *Guggenheims*, p. 27.
20. Marcosson, *Metal Magic*, pp. 63–64.
21. Promotional flyer, in Heather MacIntosh and David Wilma, "Northern Pacific Railroad Announces Tacoma Terminus on July 14, 1873," HistoryLink.org Online Encyclopedia of Washington State History, February 22, 1999, historylink.org/File/922.
22. Marianne Sullivan, *Tainted Earth: Smelters, Public Health, and the Environment* (New Brunswick, NJ: Rutgers University Press, 2014), p. 17.
23. "Ruston," *Daily Ledger* (Tacoma), August 14, 1906, quoted in Amber Brock, "Residents of Tacoma's Smelter District Vote to Incorporate as the City of Ruston on October 19, 1906," HistoryLink.org Online Encyclopedia of Washington State History, March 12, 2019, historylink.org/File/20738.
24. Steve Dunkelberger, "Tacoma's Rust Mansions—Lavish Living Followed by Rumors," SouthSound Talk, October 21, 2016, southsoundtalk.com/2016/10/21/tacoma-rust-mansion.
25. Craig Sailor, "History for Sale with Listing of Second Rust Home," *News Tribune* (Tacoma), July 29, 2015.
26. Sailor, "History for Sale." See accompanying video titled "Tacoma's (Second) Best Rust Mansion." Description of vestibule and air lock occurs at thirty-four seconds.
27. Details of Guggenheim's last hours are drawn from "Guggenheim, Dying, Sent Wife Message," *New York Times*, April 20, 1912. The time when he appeared in his evening clothes is given in a schematic plan of the boat deck in Walter Lord, *A Night to Remember* (New York: Henry Holt, 1983), p. xxii.
28. "Guggenheim, Dying."
29. Gordy Holt, "How Much Arsenic Is Too Much? Fear Poisons Lives of Many Residents," *Seattle Post-Intelligencer*, September 11, 2000, p. A1.
30. Angela Cookson, "History of the Tacoma Smelter and Its Workers," research paper (University of Washington, March 31, 1992), p. 2. Cookson had worked as a waitress at one of the venerable taverns near the Ruston plant and, for a college class, interviewed several "old-timers" who gathered there regularly. See also Anne Fischel and Lin Nelson, "Workers' Concerns about Health and Safety at ASARCO," Their Mines, Our Stories, February 4, 2020, theirminesourstories.org/post/workers-concerns-about-health-and-safety-at-asarco.

31. John Gillie, "Smelter's Founder Correctly Judged Plant's Potential," *News Tribune* (Tacoma), July 31, 1983, p. 3.
32. Sullivan, *Tainted Earth*, p. 23.
33. H. K. Rockhill, "Tacoma's Poison Factory Is Interesting Industry," *News Tribune* (Tacoma), April 26, 1927, p. 13.
34. F. G. Cottrell, "The Problem of Smelter Smoke," in *Transactions of the Commonwealth Club of California* 7, no. 1 (February 1913): p. 487.
35. Adam M. Romero, "The Alchemy of Capital: Industrial Waste and the Chemicalization of United States Agriculture" (PhD diss., University of California, Berkeley, spring 2015), p. 35.
36. "Meetings Are Held throughout State to Plan War on 'Hoppers,'" *Daily Plainsman* (Huron, SD), May 28, 1932, p. 12.
37. "Meetings Are Held."
38. "Recommends Way to Fight Blister Beetle," *Rapid City Journal* (SD), June 28, 1933, p. 6.
39. "Grasshopper Bait Kills Cows in Charles Mix Co.," *Daily Republic* (Mitchell, SD), November 12, 1968, p. 12.
40. Ann Rule, *Lust Killer* (New York: New American Library, 1983), p. 20.
41. Rule, *Lust Killer*, p. 20.
42. See Kristeen Cherney, "Everything You Need to Know about Arsenic Poisoning," Healthline, April 24, 2018, healthline.com/health/arsenic-poisoning#common-causes. Studies have also shown an association between arsenic exposure and fungal infections. See Ling-I Hsu et al., "Cumulative Arsenic Exposure Is Associated with Fungal Infections: Two Cohort Studies Based on Southwestern and Northeastern Basins in Taiwan," *Environment International* 96 (November 2016): pp. 173–79, pubmed.ncbi.nlm.nih.gov/27693976.
43. R. N. Ratnaike, "Acute and Chronic Arsenic Toxicity," *Postgraduate Medical Journal* 79, no. 933 (2003): p. 394.
44. Dashiell Hammett, *Red Harvest*, in *The Maltese Falcon, The Thin Man, Red Harvest* (New York: Everyman's Library, 2000), p. 437.
45. The passage in *The Maltese Falcon* concerning Tacoma has been dubbed by literary critics the "Flitcraft parable" and is drawn from real crimes Hammett read about in the newspapers. For more on Hammett's time in Tacoma and the influences it would have on his work, see essays by Tacoma historian Michael S. Sullivan, including "Dashiell Hammett's Tacoma," *Columbia: The Magazine of Northwest History* 23, no. 1 (Spring 2009): pp. 22–25, and "A Shooting," *Tacoma History*, August 8, 2016, tacomahistory.live/2016/08/08/a-shooting. For a critical discussion of the Flitcraft parable, see Claudia Roth Pierpont, "Tough Guy: The Mystery of Dashiell Hammett," *New Yorker*, February 11, 2002.
46. "Frameup Alleged in Rust Kidnaping," *News Tribune* (Tacoma), March 25, 1921, p. 1.
47. See "Kidnaper Admits He Was Unaided," *Tacoma Daily Ledger*, March 11, 1921, p. 2.
48. The Mattson home was at 4605 North Verde Street, Tacoma. Details are drawn from Daryl C. McClary, "Ten-Year-Old Charles F. Mattson Is Kidnapped in Tacoma and Held for Ransom on December 27, 1936," HistoryLink.org Online Encyclopedia of Washington State History, December 13, 2006, historylink.org/File/8028.

49. "$28,000 Ransom Sought by Mattson Kidnaper!" and "Word Picture of Abductor and Victim," *News Tribune* (Tacoma), December 28, 1936, p. 1; "U.S., State and Local Forces Join Hands," *News Tribune*, December 29, 1936, p. 1.
50. "Roosevelt Spurs Manhunt; Offers $10,000 Reward!," *News Tribune* (Tacoma), January 12, 1937, p. 1.
51. Anne Fischel and Linn Nelson, "Labor's Place in Community History: The Past Is Never Over," Their Mines, Our Stories, updated January 17, 2020, theirminesourstories.org/post/labor-s-place-in-community-history.
52. Cookson, "History of the Tacoma Smelter," pp. 2–4.
53. Cookson, "History of the Tacoma Smelter," p. 6.
54. Cookson, "History of the Tacoma Smelter," p. 6.
55. Cookson, "History of the Tacoma Smelter," p. 8.
56. Cookson, "History of the Tacoma Smelter," p. 8.
57. Cookson, "History of the Tacoma Smelter," p. 9.
58. For ASARCO's early activities in South America, see Marcosson, *Metal Magic*, pp. 169–70; rumors about copper dumped in Commencement Bay persist among locals to this day.
59. Mary V. Dearborn, *Mistress of Modernism: The Life of Peggy Guggenheim* (Boston: Houghton Mifflin, 2004), p. 26.
60. Peggy Guggenheim describes her plan to buy a picture a day in *Confessions of an Art Addict* (New York: Ecco, 1997), p. 22; for the number and list of paintings bought during this period, see the documentary film *Peggy Guggenheim: Art Addict*, directed by Lisa Immordino Vreeland (Dakota Group, 2015).
61. Amit Kumar et al., "Lead Toxicity: Health Hazards, Influence on Food Chain, and Sustainable Remediation Approaches," *International Journal of Environmental Research and Public Health* 17, no. 7 (March 25, 2020): 2179.
62. See, for example, John Noble Wilford, "Roman Empire's Fall Is Linked with Gout and Lead Poisoning," *New York Times*, March 17, 1983, p. A19, and Emily Sohn, "Lead: Versatile Metal, Long Legacy," Dartmouth Toxic Metals Superfund Research Program, sites.dartmouth.edu/toxmetal/more-metals/lead-versatile-metal-long-legacy.
63. John Cowell, unpublished memoir, archived at: yumpu.com/en/document/read/11501563/an-autobiography-followed-by-jon-john-r-cowell.
64. *Conversations with a Killer: The Ted Bundy Tapes*, part 1, directed by Joe Berlinger, aired in 2019 on Netflix.
65. Elizabeth Kendall, *The Phantom Prince: My Life with Ted Bundy*, updated and expanded ed. (New York: Abrams, 2020), p. 136. Kendall is the pseudonym of Elizabeth Kloepfer, her name at the time when she knew Bundy, as she acknowledges in the introduction to the updated edition of her memoir, p. ix.
66. Sullivan, *Tainted Earth*, p. 23; lead emissions for the Tacoma smelter's main stack were 226 tons in 1960. See Gregory L. Glass, *Tacoma Smelter Plume Site Credible Evidence Report: The ASARCO Tacoma Smelter and Regional Soil Contamination in Puget Sound Final Report* (Tacoma: Tacoma–Pierce County Health Department and Washington State Department of Ecology, September 2003), p. 26.
67. Sullivan, *Tainted Earth*, p. 126. Sullivan notes that air emissions from the Tacoma smelter were shown to be eighty-nine times higher than the U.S. average in urban areas. See also Glass, *Tacoma Smelter Plume Site*, p. 26.

68. U.S. Department of Transportation, Federal Highway Administration, and Washington State Department of Transportation, *SR 16 / Union Avenue Vicinity to SR 302 Vicinity: Final Environmental Impact Statement* (Tumwater, WA: WSDOT, January 2000), p. 3.16-7, books.google.com/books/edition/WA_16_Union_Avenue_Vicinity_to_WA_302_Vi/5sM1AQAAMAAJ.
69. Based on the recollections of Sandi Holt, a girl in the neighborhood whose brother Doug was Ted's best friend: *Conversations with a Killer: Bundy*, part 1.
70. See Tacoma Public Schools, second report for Theodore Bundy from third grade, March 1956, and third report from fourth grade, June 7, 1957, Killer in the Archives.
71. *Conversations with a Killer: Bundy*, part 1.
72. The Bundy family moved to the Skyline Drive house in 1953, when Ted was in the third grade, according to Steven Winn and David Merrill, *Ted Bundy: The Killer Next Door* (New York: Bantam Books, 1979), p. 105. From 1951 to 1953, the family lived at 1630 South Sheridan Avenue, Tacoma, approximately five miles from the Ruston smokestack.
73. Sullivan, *Tainted Earth*, p. 38.
74. Sullivan, *Tainted Earth*, p. 40.
75. See Sullivan, *Tainted Earth*, p. 21.
76. Randolph K. Byers and Elizabeth E. Lord, "Late Effects of Lead Poisoning on Mental Development," *American Journal of Diseases of Children* 66, no. 5 (November 1943): p. 477.
77. Gerald Markowitz and David Rosner, *Lead Wars: The Politics of Science and the Fate of America's Children* (Berkeley: University of California Press, 2013), p. xvi, citing John Ruddock, "Lead Poisoning in Children with Special Reference to Pica," *Journal of the American Medical Association* 82 (May 24, 1924): p. 1684.
78. Byers and Lord, "Late Effects," p. 477.
79. Markowitz and Rosner, *Lead Wars*, p. 10.
80. Byers and Lord, "Late Effects," p. 491.
81. Byers and Lord, "Late Effects," p. 490.
82. See Leif Fredrickson, "The Age of Lead: Metropolitan Change, Environmental Health, and Inner City Underdevelopment in Baltimore" (PhD diss., University of Virginia, May 2017), pp. 19–20.
83. Steven Johnson, "The Brilliant Inventor Who Made Two of History's Biggest Mistakes," *New York Times Magazine*, March 15, 2023.
84. Lydia Denworth, *Toxic Truth: A Scientist, A Doctor, and the Battle Over Lead* (Boston: Beacon Press, 2008), pp. 37–38.
85. Denworth, *Toxic Truth*, p. 37.
86. Jamie Lincoln Kitman, "The Secret History of Lead," *The Nation*, March 2, 2000.
87. "Science Board to Start Probe of Tetraethyl," *New York Daily News*, May 21, 1925, p. 35; see also Tim Harford, "Why Did We Use Leaded Petrol for So Long?," *BBC News*, August 28, 2017, bbc.com/news/business-40593353.
88. Gerald Markowitz and David Rosner, *Deceit and Denial: The Deadly Politics of Industrial Pollution* (Berkeley: University of California Press, 2002), p. 27.

89. "Death in Own Device," *Kansas City Star*, November 2, 1944, p. 1; see also Steven Johnson, "The Brilliant Inventor Who Made Two of History's Biggest Mistakes," *New York Times Magazine*, March 15, 2023.
90. According to experts, 10 percent of lead emissions from cars "settled within 100 meters of the road." See Rich Nevin, *Lucifer Curves: The Legacy of Lead Poisoning* (Pennsauken, NJ: BookBaby, 2016), location 616 of 1406, Kindle.
91. See "Maximum Lead Concentration at Tacoma Smelter Plume Sample Locations (King and Pierce Counties)" in Glass, *Tacoma Smelter Plume Site*, p. 121. The subsequent online "Dirt Alert" GIS map and website launched by the Washington State Department of Ecology in 2018 identifies 658 North Skyline Drive as qualified for soil replacement, the front yard measuring arsenic at 99 ppm and lead at 210 ppm, the backyard arsenic at 77 ppm and lead at 140 ppm; ecology.wa.gov/dirtalert/?lat=47.273840&lon=-122.500000&zoom=11.
92. See Jeff Guinn, *Manson: The Life and Times of Charles Manson* (New York: Simon & Schuster, 2014), pp. 65–72. Manson was held at McNeil Island from June 1961 to June 1966. After a brief transfer to Terminal Island, in San Pedro, California, in 1966, Manson was released on parole in 1967.
93. Glass, *Tacoma Smelter Plume Site*, p. 121.
94. Mark Prothero with Carlton Smith, *Defending Gary: Unraveling the Mind of the Green River Killer* (San Francisco: Jossey-Bass, 2006), p. 112.
95. Ben Visser, "A History of Leaded Fuels," *General Aviation News*, January 27, 2020, generalaviationnews.com/2020/01/27/a-history-of-leaded-fuels.
96. Glass, *Tacoma Smelter Plume Site*, p. 26.
97. Prothero and Smith, *Defending Gary*, p. 105.
98. Micol Levi-Minzi and Maria Shields, "Serial Sexual Murderers and Prostitutes as Their Victims: Difficulty Profiling Perpetrators and Victim Vulnerability as Illustrated by the Green River Case," *Brief Treatment and Crisis Intervention* 7, no. 1 (February 2007): p. 78.
99. "Wooden Heart," recorded by Elvis Presley in 1960, based on a German folk song; a cover version by Joe Dowell became a hit in 1961.
100. Richard Bundy, the fourth son of Louise and Johnnie Bundy, was born on November 15, 1961.
101. For a description of youthful rape fantasies and their development in serial killers, see Chapter 4, "Childhoods of Violence," in Robert K. Ressler and Tom Shachtman, *Whoever Fights Monsters: My Twenty Years Tracking Serial Killers for the FBI* (New York: St. Martin's Press, 1992), pp. 102–26.
102. Rebecca Morris, *Ted and Ann: The Mystery of a Missing Child and Her Neighbor, Ted Bundy* (Seattle: True Books, 2013), p. 35.
103. Morris, *Ted and Ann*, p. 13.
104. Morris, *Ted and Ann*, p. 13.
105. Morris, *Ted and Ann*, p. 63; see also photos, p. 172.
106. Mark Higgins, "Expert Says Bundy Killed Girl, 8, When He Was 14," *News Tribune* (Tacoma), May 9, 1987, pp. B1, B2. In this article, Donald Burr, Ann's father, describes having seen a young man standing in the bottom of "a watery pit," stirring the water with his foot.
107. Transcript of interview with Ted Bundy conducted by Dorothy Otnow Lewis on January 23, 1989, the day before Bundy's execution, reprinted in Polly Nelson,

Defending the Devil: My Story as Ted Bundy's Last Lawyer (Brattleboro, VT.: Echo Point Books & Media, 1994), p. 273.

108. Morris, *Ted and Ann*, p. 75. See also Higgins, "Expert Says Bundy Killed Girl," *News Tribune* (Tacoma), May 9, 1987, pp. B1, B2. On May 30, 1986, Beverly Burr wrote to Bundy to ask if he had killed her daughter. He replied, "First and foremost, I do not know what happened to your daughter Ann Marie. I had nothing to do with her disappearance.... At that time, I was a normal 14-year-old boy" (Morris, pp. 206–7). He claimed not to recall hearing of the abduction, which was front-page news in Tacoma. At least three of Bundy's victims were under the age of eighteen. Until the last forty-eight to seventy-two hours of his life, just prior to his execution in Florida on January 24, 1989, Bundy consistently denied all of his murders, including the ones for which he was convicted. He was particularly vehement in denying responsibility for rapes and murders of children, since he feared violent reprisals in prison. Until his final hours, he denied responsibility for his last abduction, rape, and murder, that of twelve-year-old Kimberly Dianne Leach, committed on February 8, 1978, the crime for which he was executed.

CHAPTER 3: The Reversible Lane

1. *Mercer Island, Washington: A Community Profile of Upper-Level Suburbia*, pamphlet, second of a series from *House & Garden* (New York: Condé Nast, 1961), unpaginated.
2. Robert A. Barr, "Man, Invalided by Span Crash, Dies," *Seattle Times*, February 11, 1969, p. 33.
3. "One Dead in Accident on Lake Span," *Seattle Times*, April 19, 1961, p. 14.
4. Rule, *Lust Killer*, p. 43.
5. "A Study of the Effect of Lead Arsenate Exposure on Orchardists and on Consumers of Sprayed Fruit," *Public Health Reports* 56, no. 4 (January 24, 1941): p. 131.
6. Clair C. Patterson, interviewed by Shirley K. Cohen, March 5, 6, and 9, 1995, Oral History Project, California Institute of Technology Archives, Pasadena, CA, p. 19.
7. Denworth, *Toxic Truth*, p. 111.
8. Paul B. Allwood, Henry Falk, and Erik R. Svendsen, "A Historical Perspective on the CDC Childhood Lead Poisoning Prevention Program," *American Journal of Public Health* 112 (September 2022), ncbi.nlm.nih.gov/pmc/articles/PMC9528639.
9. Sullivan, *Tainted Earth*, p. 46.
10. Sullivan, *Tainted Earth*, p. 47.
11. Sullivan, *Tainted Earth*, p. 21.
12. S. S. Pinto and B. M. Bennett, "Effect of Arsenic Trioxide Exposure on Mortality," *Archives of Environmental Health* 7 (November 1963): p. 590. See also Sullivan, *Tainted Earth*, p. 117.
13. Sullivan, *Tainted Earth*, p. 49.
14. Sullivan, *Tainted Earth*, p. 125.
15. "Hans Forster, Dairyman, Hurt in Auto Collision, *Seattle Times*, February 14, 1963, p. 6.
16. Robert A. Barr, "Evergreen Span to Get New Locking," *Seattle Times*, March 19, 1968, p. 5.
17. Herb Robinson, "Third Bridge Debate" in "Circulation of All Ideas Encouraged," *Seattle Times*, April 13, 1967, p. A2.

18. Sullivan, *Tainted Earth*, p. 56.
19. Philip Carlo, *The Night Stalker: The Life and Crimes of Richard Ramirez* (New York: Kensington Publishing, 1996), p. 137.
20. Carlo, *Night Stalker*, p. 138.
21. Carlo, *Night Stalker*, p. 144.
22. Carlo, *Night Stalker*, p. 142.
23. Carlo, *Night Stalker*, p. 143.
24. Carlo, *Night Stalker*, p. 140.
25. "Historical Documents Found," Recasting the Smelter, recastingthesmelter.com/?page_id=18#historical.
26. Philip J. Landrigan et al., "Epidemic Lead Absorption near an Ore Smelter—The Role of Particulate Lead," *New England Journal of Medicine* 292 (January 16, 1974): pp. 123–29. See also Lauren Villagran, "Before Flint, Before East Chicago, There Was Smeltertown," NRDC, November 29, 2016, nrdc.org/stories/flint-east-chicago-there-was-smeltertown.
27. Carlo, *Night Stalker*, pp. 150–51.
28. "Autoist Killed in Crash on Mercer Island," *Seattle Times*, May 25, 1963.
29. "Reversible Lane: 2 Hurt in Collision in Tunnel," *Seattle Times*, June 5, 1963.
30. "Three Injured in Mercer Isle 3-Auto Crash," *Seattle Times*, December 21, 1963.
31. Mike Wyne, "Two Die in Crash on Bridge; Another Critically Injured," *Seattle Times*, February 6, 1964; "Man Given Term for Burglary," *Seattle Times*, August 18, 1959, p. 5.
32. "Times Readers Have Their Say," *Seattle Times*, March 28, 1963.
33. "Reversible Lane to Be Discussed," *Seattle Times*, March 16, 1964, p. 7.

CHAPTER 4: The Island
1. Details in this account are drawn from Judy Gellatly, *Mercer Island: The First Hundred Years* (Mercer Island, WA: Mercer Island Bicentennial Committee, 1977), pp. 6–7.
2. See, for example, Bill Dietrich, "How Sleuths of Science Uncovered Seattle Fault," *Seattle Times*, December 8, 1992.
3. Kathy G. Troost and Aaron P. Wisher, "Mercer Island Seismic Hazard Assessment," City of Mercer Island, April 2009, mercerisland.gov/sites/default/files/fileattachments/planning/page/2001/seismichazard2009.pdf.
4. The Warners' home was located at 4005 91st Avenue Southeast, Mercer Island, Washington.
5. Sullivan, *Tainted Earth*, p. 141.
6. Brian Herbert, *Dreamer of Dune: The Biography of Frank Herbert* (New York: Tor, 2003), p. 147.
7. The apartment was at 2415 8th Avenue North.
8. Lisa Wick also told police that the assailant had a receding hairline, which would seem to rule out Ted Bundy. But again I refer to the fact that the room was dark.
9. James H. Willbanks, *The Tet Offensive: A Concise History* (New York: Columbia University Press, 2007), p. 45.
10. "A Brother Lost to War, a Life Brought Back 'Thread by Thread,'" *Mercer Island Reporter*, November 9, 2011.
11. "David Howard Warner," The Virtual Wall, April 6, 2013, virtualwall.org/dw/WarnerDH01a.htm.

12. *Ted Bundy Multiagency Investigative Team Report 1992* (Washington, DC: U.S. Department of Justice and Federal Bureau of Investigation, 1992), p. 15, archive.org/details/tedbundymultiagencyinvestigativeteamreport1992.
13. Peggy Reynolds, "Investigation Reveals Details of Tope Tragedy," *Mercer Island Reporter*, July 24, 1969, p. 2. See also "Doctor's Death Called Suicide," *Seattle Times*, July 17, 1969, p. 5.
14. Stephen L. Tope Jr., "Times Readers Have Their Say: Marmes Digger Protests," *Seattle Times*, March 3, 1969, p. 12.
15. Many of the articles in *Good Housekeeping* that appeared as "My Problem and How I Solved It" during this period were fictional essays written by Fredelle Bruser Maynard, a freelance writer and the mother of Joyce Maynard, writer and memoirist. See Joyce Maynard, *At Home in the World* (New York: St. Martin's Press, 1998), p. 24.
16. See, for example, Yuri Yasuda, "The Kachi Kachi Mountain," in *A Treasury of Japanese Folktales* (Tokyo: Tuttle, 2010), pp. 52–60.
17. "Mount Si," Snoqualmie Valley Historical Museum, accessed December 29, 2024, snoqualmievalleymuseum.pastperfectonline.com/bysearchterm?keyword=Mount+Si&page=23. A more extensive version of the story, "Moon the Transformer (Snoqualmie)," can be seen at historylink.org/File/2586.

CHAPTER 5: The Devil's Business

1. The description of the smelting process at the Tacoma plant is drawn from Karen Pickett, *Images of America: Ruston* (Charleston, SC: Arcadia, 2011), pp. 77–82; the potential exposure of workers in each department is drawn from *Health Hazard Evaluation Determination Report 77-36-540, ASARCO, Incorporated, Tacoma Plant, Ruston, Washington* (Cincinnati: U.S. Department of Health, Education, and Welfare, Center for Disease Control, National Institute for Occupational Safety and Health, 1978), p. 3, cdc.gov/niosh/hhe/reports/pdfs/77-36-540.pdf.
2. See interview with Rodger Jones, "Worker's Concerns about Health and Safety at ASARCO," Their Mines, Our Stories, updated February 4, 2020, theirminesourstories.org/post/workers-concerns-about-health-and-safety-at-asarco.
3. Brendan Kiley, "Text Message from a Toxic-Waste Site," *The Stranger*, May 26, 2009.
4. Bill Baarsma, interview with the author, June 20, 2023.
5. Baarsma, interview.
6. Stephen G. Michaud and Hugh Aynesworth, *Ted Bundy: Conversations with a Killer* (New York: New American Library, 1989), p. 14; Polly Nelson, *Defending the Devil*, p. 272.
7. According to Dorothy Otnow Lewis, Bundy told her this in their last interview before his execution, January 23, 1989.
8. Rule, *The Stranger Beside Me*, p. 11; Michaud and Aynesworth, *Ted Bundy: Conversations*, p. 15.
9. Rob Dielenberg, *Ted Bundy: A Visual Timeline*, 4th ed. (Motion Mensura, electronic version, 2018), p. 47.
10. Dielenberg, *Visual Timeline*, p. 66.
11. See Michaud and Aynesworth, *The Only Living Witness*, p. 57.
12. Sullivan, *Tainted Earth*, p. 52.
13. Sullivan, *Tainted Earth*, p. 52.

14. Minutes, Tacoma City Council meeting, May 23, 1967, p. 11, City Council Meeting Minutes, Northwest Room, Tacoma Public Library.
15. Testimony of Sybil Ferris, in Al Carlisle, *The 1976 Psychological Assessment of Ted Bundy* (Magna, UT: Carlisle Legacy Books, 2020), p. 62.
16. Ferris, in Carlisle, *1976 Psychological Assessment*, p. 64.
17. This account is drawn from Rule, *Lust Killer*, pp. 1–9, 159.
18. Rule, *Lust Killer*, p. 165.
19. Carlisle, *1976 Psychological Assessment*, p. 64.
20. Kendall, *Phantom Prince*, p. 24.
21. Richard W. Larsen, *Bundy: The Deliberate Stranger* (New York: Simon & Schuster, 1980), p. 9.
22. Holling Clancy Holling, *Pagoo* (Boston: Houghton Mifflin, 1957), p. 80.
23. The identity of the Zodiac Killer has never been established, but a number of suspects have been considered. Because the Faraday and Jensen murders are believed to be the first Zodiac cases, there has been speculation that the murderer might have lived in the vicinity of Benicia or Vallejo, near the Selby smelter. Arthur Leigh Allen, considered a leading Zodiac suspect by Robert Graysmith, author of the 1986 bestseller *Zodiac* (New York: St. Martin's Press), grew up in Vallejo. Another suspect, Paul Doerr, explored in Jarett Kobek's book *How to Find Zodiac* (Los Angeles: We Heard You Like Books, 2022), worked at Mare Island Naval Base for decades. Mare Island is adjacent to Vallejo and approximately five miles from the Selby smelter.
24. K. W. Nelson to D. H. Soutar, Vice President, Industrial Relations, ASARCO, September 11, 1968, cited in Marianne Sullivan, "Contested Science and Exposed Workers: ASARCO and the Occupational Standard for Inorganic Arsenic," *Public Health Reports* 122, no. 4 (July–August 2007): pp. 541–47.
25. Nelson to Soutar, in Sullivan, "Contested Science."
26. Anna M. Lee and Joseph F. Fraumeni Jr., "Arsenic and Respiratory Cancer in Man: An Occupational Study," *Journal of the National Cancer Institute* 42 (1969): pp. 1045–52.
27. "Blames Traffic for EP Air Pollution Problem," *El Paso Times*, April 17, 1969, p. 15.
28. The murders of Susan Davis and Elizabeth Perry on May 30, 1969, have never been solved. According to Christian Barth, in *Garden State Parkway Murders*, a number of suspects have been considered, including Ted Bundy, who has never been officially ruled out. For a time, Gerald Stano (1951–1998), a serial killer convicted of nine murders in Florida, claimed that he killed the women. His confession was discounted, however, when he could not furnish correct details about the crime scene to investigators. Stano was housed at Florida State Prison near Bundy and may have communicated with him about the case.
29. Barth, *Garden State Parkway Murders*, pp. 251, 253.
30. A. L. Carlisle, "Utah State Prison Psychological Evaluation, Bundy, Theodore Robert," assessment conducted June 2, 1976, Killer in the Archives.
31. Nelson, *Defending the Devil*, pp. 276–77.
32. Nelson, *Defending the Devil*, p. 277.
33. Larry Lewis, "'69 Killings near Parkway Unsolved, but Bundy Is Blamed," *Philadelphia Inquirer*, Local South Jersey ed., May 31, 1993. See also "Psychologist Says Bundy's Reign of Terror Started with '69 Parkway Slayings," *Daily Journal* (Vineland, NJ), January 26, 1989, p. 5.

34. Denworth, *Toxic Truth*, p. 77.
35. David Rosner and Gerald Markowitz, "Standing Up to the Lead Industry: An Interview with Herbert Needleman," *Public Health Reports* 120 (May–June 2005): p. 333.
36. Denworth, *Toxic Truth*, p. 79.
37. Denworth, *Toxic Truth*, p. 87.
38. Rosner and Markowitz, *Lead Wars*, p. 76.
39. Rule, *Lust Killer*, p. 181.
40. "Residences Where Lived," in U.S. Department of Justice and Federal Bureau of Investigation, *Ted Bundy Multiagency Report*, p. 9.
41. "Fatality Adds to Reverse Lane Toll," *Mercer Island Reporter*, February 15, 1973, p. 1.
42. Vincent Bugliosi and Curt Gentry, *Helter Skelter: The True Story of the Manson Murders* (New York: W. W. Norton, 1974), p. 177.
43. Kendall, *Phantom Prince*, p. 10.
44. Robert Gillette, "Poisoned Pastures and Bay Smelter," *San Francisco Examiner*, March 8, 1970, p. 1.
45. Gillette, "Poisoned Pastures," p. 19.
46. See Graysmith, *Zodiac*, pp. 134–40.
47. *Conservations with a Killer: Bundy*, part 1.
48. Kendall, *Phantom Prince*, p. 103.
49. Robert D. Keppel and Stephen G. Michaud, *Terrible Secrets: Ted Bundy on Serial Murder* (MT7 Productions, 2011), p. 115, Kindle.
50. See photo in Kendall, *Phantom Prince*, first photo insert, following p. 82.
51. Lorraine Boissoneault, "The Cuyahoga River Caught Fire at Least a Dozen Times, but No One Cared until 1969," *Smithsonian*, June 19, 2019.
52. "CDC Childhood Lead Poisoning Prevention: Timeline of CLPPP Highlights," Centers for Disease Control and Prevention, June 4, 2024, cdc.gov/lead-prevention/php/about-clppp/timeline.html.
53. Rule, *Stranger Beside Me*, p. 27.
54. Rule, *Stranger Beside Me*, p. 31.
55. Rule, *Stranger Beside Me*, pp. 31–32.
56. "Combined Monthly Progress Notes for May & June 2013, Warren Forrest," Washington State Department of Corrections Sex Offender Treatment Program, Monroe Correctional Complex—Twin Rivers Unit, August 1, 2013, pp. 1, 5–6.
57. Warren Leslie Forrest remains a suspect in the disappearance of Jamie Grissim. See Rachael Trost, "Sister Still Hoping for Answers in Jamie Grissim's Disappearance," NBC News, January 4, 2017; Jessica Prokop, "Missing Teen's Sister Hopes for Conviction in Warren Forrest Trial," *The Columbian* (Vancouver, WA), January 24, 2023.
58. Nelson, *Defending the Devil*, p. 280. See also Michaud and Aynesworth, *Only Living Witness*, p. 110.
59. Joel Kestenbaum in *Ted Bundy: Falling for a Killer*, episode 1, "Boy Meets Girl," directed by Trish Wood, aired in 2020 on Amazon Prime Video.
60. Dr. Scott C. Fraser, interviewed in October 1975 by Seattle police: see Seattle Police Department files, King County Archives, p. 420.
61. "Mrs. Bonnie Jo Freeman," obituary, *Spokane Chronicle*, May 16, 1972, p. 3.

62. Frederick Stoeger, "Idaho's Number 1 Murder Mystery," *True Detective*, April 1974, p. 49.
63. The murder of Bonnie Jo Freeman has never been solved; the case has never been linked to Bundy.
64. U.S. Department of Justice and Federal Bureau of Investigation, *Ted Bundy Multiagency Report*, p. 16.
65. Sullivan, *Tainted Earth*, p. 56.
66. David Bond, "Smelter Firm Put Price Tag on Lead Risk," *Spokesman-Review* (Spokane), July 21, 1990, p. A6.
67. Mike Cochran, "El Paso Fears 'Killer,'" *Victoria (TX) Advocate*, March 26, 1972, p. 1.
68. Sullivan, *Tainted Earth*, p. 63.
69. Cochran, "El Paso Fears 'Killer.'"
70. Sullivan, *Tainted Earth*, p. 124; see also p. 212n58.
71. Sullivan, *Tainted Earth*, p. 124.
72. Sullivan, *Tainted Earth*, p. 124.
73. Sullivan, *Tainted Earth*, p. 124.
74. Robert Keppel, of the King County Department of Public Safety and the head of the Bundy Task Force, interviewed Sandy Gwinn at length twice, the first time when she phoned him from San Francisco on September 8, 1975, the second time in person on October 15, 1975, when Gwinn accompanied Keppel on a drive around Issaquah, trying to describe where she and Bundy had driven while looking "for an old lady's house." It was during the second conversation that Gwinn described her first sexual encounter with Bundy, which took place near the Humptulips River; she clarified that she had cut off their relationship in June 1972, because of suicide threats made by Bundy's girlfriend, Elizabeth Kloepfer.
75. This description of "one of [Bundy's] first murders," concerning "a blonde in the vestibule of her apartment building," occurs in Polly Nelson, *Defending the Devil*, p. 170. It contains information elicited from Bundy during Nelson's interviews with him in preparing his death penalty appeals. Kerry May Hardy, who is said to have known Cathy Swindler (who briefly dated Bundy), disappeared in June 1972. May was both Hardy's middle name and her married name, after she wed James Garvey May in 1971; they were separated at the time of her death. James May's father owned property near where her remains were discovered. At one point, she was also considered to be a possible victim of Gary Ridgway. Kerry May Hardy's remains were found at Suncadia in September 2010; using a composite sketch and forensic DNA technology, investigators identified and reported the remains as hers in June 2011. See "Suncadia Remains Identified as Seattle Woman," *Daily Record* (Ellensburg, WA), June 3, 2011.
76. Dielenberg, *Visual Timeline*, p. 69.
77. In the Pacific Northwest, a long-held urban myth has circulated suggesting that Ted Bundy was driving Governor Evans's official car on the opening day of the North Cascades Highway (and thus was the first person to cross the new highway). The myth has been debunked by Solveig Torvik, "It Wasn't Ted Bundy: North Cascades Highway 40th Anniversary," *Methow Grist*, August 27, 2012, methownet.com/gristarchive/features/highway_notbundy.html.
78. *Ted Bundy: Falling for a Killer*, "Boy Meets Girl."
79. See "Bundy, Theodore Robert, Work History," in Ted Bundy, Seattle Police Department files, King County Archives, pp. 700, 749.

80. Rodger Jones, "Arsenic: Our Problem" and "Arsenic: What Do We Really Know? An Interview," *The Smelterworker*, vol. 1, no. 1 (Dec. 1972), pp. 1, 5–8.
81. Jones, "Arsenic: Our Problem," pp. 7, 8. See also Malcolm MacNey, "Smelter-Area Tests Show 'Unsafe' Arsenic Residues in Children," *News Tribune* (Tacoma), November 15, 1972, p. 1.
82. Environmental Protection Agency, "EPA Requires Phase-out of Lead in All Grades of Gasoline," press release, November 28, 1973, archive.epa.gov/epa/aboutepa/epa-requires-phase-out-lead-all-grades-gasoline.html.
83. *Ted Bundy: Falling for a Killer*, "Boy Meets Girl."
84. In October 1975, officers in the Seattle Police Department were assigned to investigate rumors of a paper on "sexual violence" authored by Theodore Bundy during his stint at the Crime Commission. They found no such paper but learned from Donna Schram that she and a colleague, Philip G. Sherburne, had produced a preliminary report at the Law and Justice Planning Office containing a section entitled "Forcible Rape in Seattle—1972." That section, consisting of pages numbered 84 to 94, along with five pages titled "Preliminary Recommendations for Reduction of Rape," appears in the Seattle Police Department files devoted to the Bundy case, held in the King County Archives.
85. Schram and Sherburne, "Forcible Rape," p. 94.
86. "Fatality Adds to Reverse Lane Toll," *Mercer Island Reporter*, February 15, 1973, pp. 1, 28. The article includes statistics on reverse lane accidents kept since 1969 by the Washington State Patrol.
87. "Reverse Lanes Chalk Up Another," *Mercer Island Reporter*, March 1, 1973, p. 2.
88. See Winn and Merrill, *Killer Next Door*, p. 112.
89. Rule, *Stranger Beside Me*, p. 36.
90. Kendall says Bundy bought "a brown Volkswagen of his own" in early 1973 but may have been confusing the color of the vehicle with that of another VW he borrowed around that time; see Kendall, *Phantom Prince*, p. 43. The Department of Justice and FBI's *Ted Bundy Multiagency Report* describes the 1968 VW purchased by Bundy in 1973 as "tan in color with sunroof" (p. 11). In Utah, Detective Jerry Thompson described it as "white or light gray"; see Michaud and Aynesworth, *Only Living Witness*, p. 141.
91. "Molly's Story," in Kendall, *Phantom Prince*, p. 201.
92. "Molly's Story," in Kendall, *Phantom Prince*, p. 201.
93. "East Seattle's School Safety Patrol," *Mercer Island Reporter*, May 10, 1973, p. 5.
94. In the last days of his life, Bundy confessed this murder to Robert Keppel, one of the original investigators for the King County homicide task force in 1974. See Rule, *Stranger Beside Me*, pp. 481–82; see also U.S. Department of Justice, Federal Bureau of Investigation, *Ted Bundy Multiagency Report*, p. 19.
95. Liz Kloepfer, interview with Detective Kathleen McChesney, September 8, 1975, King County Department of Public Safety, King County Archives, p. 618.
96. Kendall, *Phantom Prince*, p. 63.
97. According to the Charley Project, an online clearinghouse for information on missing persons, Ted Bundy remains a suspect in Vicki Lynn Hollar's disappearance: https://charleyproject.org/case/vicki-lynn-hollar.
98. Gordon W. Schultz, "Evans' Re-election Aide Says He Spied on Rosellini," *Seattle Times*, August 29, 1973, p. 1.

99. Schultz, "Evans' Re-election Aide."
100. Donna Schram in *Ted Bundy: Falling for a Killer*, "Boy Meets Girl."
101. *Ted Bundy: Falling for a Killer*, "Boy Meets Girl."
102. Michaud and Aynesworth, *Only Living Witness*, p. 71.
103. Rule, *Stranger Beside Me*, p. 39.
104. Elaine Crafton, in "Ted Bundy," video, posted August 9, 2013, by Kansas City Police, YouTube, 3:58, youtube.com/watch?v=gwxiZJo-xaA.
105. Bond, "Smelter Firm."
106. "Handwritten Memo Concerning Potential Cost of Continued Smelter Operation after Bag House Fire," approximate date September 1973, plaintiff's exhibit in Yoss et. al. v. The Bunker Hill Company, et. al., Civ. No. 77-2030 (D. Idaho, 1981). See also Bond, "Smelter Firm"; Bradley D. Snow, *Living with Lead: An Environmental History of Idaho's Coeur D'Alenes, 1885–2011* (Pittsburgh: University of Pittsburgh Press, 2017), 114.
107. Snow, *Living with Lead*, p. 114.
108. Michaud and Aynesworth, *Only Living Witness*, p. 72.
109. Fred N. Howell, "Some Phases of the Industrial History of Pittsburg," *Kansas Historical Quarterly* 32, no. 3 (May 1932): pp. 273–94; republished online by the Kansas Historical Society, kshs.org/p/some-phases-of-the-industrial-history-of-pittsburg/12545.
110. Columbus, Kansas, had its own strip pits, the "Columbus coal beds," located about a mile northeast of town: W. G. Pierce and W. H. Courtier, "Geology and Coal Resources of the Southeastern Kansas Coal Field in Crawford, Cherokee, and Labette Counties," *State Geological Survey of Kansas*, bulletin 24, September 1, 1938, kgs.ku.edu/Publications/Bulletins/24/index.html. Pittsburg's last coal-fired smelting plant closed in 1915. In 2009, the EPA began testing sites there for lead contamination. See Brett Dalton, "Local Smelting Dates Back to 1870s," *Morning Sun* (Pittsburg, KS), February 22, 2009. Ultimately, of 155 Pittsburg properties, including homes, businesses, and several day-care centers, 50 were found to have lead levels over four hundred parts per million and were thus determined to be in need of remediation. See Brett Dalton, "EPA Releases Soil Testing Results," *Morning Sun* (Pittsburg, KS), May 27, 2009. Populations of wild birds have recently been found to suffer from a "toxic concentration of metals" derived from the history of mining, milling, and zinc smelting in the Tri-State Mining District surrounding Pittsburg; see W. N. Beyer, J. Dalgarn, S. Dudding, and John B. French, et al., "Zinc and Lead Poisoning in Wild Birds in the Tri-State Mining District (Oklahoma, Kansas, and Missouri)," *Archives of Environmental Contamination and Toxicology* 48, no. 1 (December 2004): pp. 108–17.
111. Katherine Ramsland, *Confession of a Serial Killer: The Untold Story of Dennis Rader, the BTK Killer* (Lebanon, NH: University Press of New England, 2016), p. 44.
112. Ramsland, *Confession of a Serial Killer*, p. 55.
113. Ramsland, *Confession of a Serial Killer*, p. 54.
114. Ramsland, *Confession of a Serial Killer*, pp. 60, 63, 58, 131, 168.
115. Dennis Rader in Ramsland, *Confession of a Serial Killer*, p. 162.

CHAPTER 6: The Daylight Basement
1. "Seattle," a song composed by Hugo Montenegro, with lyrics by Jack Keller and Ernie Sheldon, served as the theme for the 1968–1970 ABC comedy *Here Come the*

Brides, about the nineteenth-century campaign to recruit marriageable women from East Coast cities to Seattle. The show was based loosely on the historic "Mercer Girls," named for Asa Mercer, one of the founders of Seattle. Perry Como and Bobby Sherman each recorded versions in 1969; Como's became a Top 40 hit.

2. M. F. Szabo, M. P. Esposito, and P. W. Spaite, *Acid Rain: Commentary on Controversial Issues and Observations on the Role of Fuel Burning*, report prepared by PedCo Environmental, Inc., and Paul W. Spaite Co., Cincinnati, Ohio, for U.S. Department of Energy, March 1982, p. 8, osti.gov/servlets/purl/5318799.
3. "Acid Rain in Washington," USGS, revised May 21, 2007, pubs.usgs.gov/gip/stones/acid-rain.html.
4. Key chain, catalog identification no. 2012.48.190, Washington State Historical Society, Tacoma, washingtonhistory.org.
5. Michaud and Aynesworth, *Only Living Witness*, p. 72.
6. Jill Sederstrom, "Ted Bundy's First Known Victim Believes a Random Coincidence Saved Her Life," Oxygen True Crime, October 4, 2020, oxygen.com/true-crime-buzz/what-does-ted-bundy-victim-karen-sparks-believe-kept-her-alive.
7. The weapon used remains something of a mystery. Early accounts, including Ann Rule's in *The Stranger Beside Me*, described it as a metal piece of the bed frame without explaining how it had been removed. Crime scene photos, however, show the mattress resting on the floor, with no bed frame in the room. Sparks's roommates later recalled seeing a piece of rebar on the ground outside the basement door.
8. See Karen Sparks Epley in *Ted Bundy: Falling for a Killer*, "Boy Meets Girl."
9. Accounts differ as to where he saw the dog's paw prints. One author says the killer saw them on the dirt floor of the garage; see Stephen Singular, *Unholy Messenger: The Life and Crimes of the BTK Serial Killer* (New York: Scribner, 2006), p. 48. Rader himself recalls seeing them in the snow outside, in Ramsland, *Confession of a Serial Killer*, p. 27.
10. Ramsland, *Confession of a Serial Killer*, p. 27.
11. Ramsland, *Confession of a Serial Killer*, p. 29.
12. Ramsland, *Confession of a Serial Killer*, p. 29.
13. Ramsland, *Confession of a Serial Killer*, p. 31.
14. Singular, *Unholy Messenger*, p. 53.
15. Associated Press, "Violent Crime Jumps in State," *Spokane Chronicle*, November 19, 1975, p. 11.
16. No. 605, "Average Annual Wages and Salaries and Wage Supplements per Full-Time Equivalent Employee, by Industry, 1960–1974," *Statistical Abstract of the United States: 1976* (Washington, DC: Bureau of Statistics, 1976), p. 378.
17. Associated Press, "98 Per Cent Gain Reported in Crime," *Spokane Chronicle*, July 24, 1961; Alexia Cooper and Erica L. Smith, *Homicide Trends in the United States, 1980–2008* (Washington, DC: Bureau of Justice Statistics, 2011), p. 2.
18. Federal Bureau of Investigation and Department of Justice, *Uniform Crime Reports for the United States, 1974* (Washington, DC: Government Printing Office, 1975), table 4, p. 71; and Federal Bureau of Investigation and Department of Justice, *Uniform Crime Reports for the United States, 1960* (Washington, DC: Government Printing Office, 1961), table 2, pp. 36–37. The 1960 Uniform Crime Report did not offer a line item for violent crime; for Washington State, it tallies 61 murders, 168 rapes, 809 robberies, and 441 aggravated assaults, for a total of 1,479.
19. "Man Poisoned by Gas," *The Smelterworker*, January 1974, p. 1.

20. Rodger Jones, "Editorial: What Hazard?," *The Smelterworker*, January 1974, p. 2.
21. Scott Framke, "Hospital Committee Report," *The Smelterworker*, May 1974, p. 5.
22. "Ragnar Stenstrom," obituary, *News Tribune* (Tacoma), February 14, 1974, p. 6; name corrected, February 15, 1974.
23. Framke, "Hospital Committee Report," p. 4; "George J. Maas," obituary, *News Tribune* (Tacoma), December 30, 1973, p. 22.
24. Richard Lerner, "Nixon Tries to Assert Control," *Seattle Times*, January 31, 1974, p. 1.
25. Larsen, *Bundy: Deliberate Stranger*, p. 14.
26. Drawn by Irwin Caplan, copyrighted 1968 by Marshall Field, and sold at the local department store Frederick & Nelson, the Seattle skyline poster was ubiquitous in the city throughout the late '60s and early '70s.
27. See snapshot in *Ted Bundy: Falling for a Killer*, "Boy Meets Girl."
28. Robert Keppel, statement, King County Department of Public Safety, January 6, 1975, Seattle Police Department files, King County Archives, p. 20.
29. Re: Dante's Tavern, see list of dates and locations matching "missing girls in the Puget Sound area" and "the whereabouts of one Theodore Robert Bundy" in Seattle Police Department files, King County Archives, p. 753.
30. Details of Bundy's abduction and murder of Lynda Ann Healy are drawn from the hypothetical third-person confession Bundy gave to Stephen Michaud on April 4, 1980. A transcript of Bundy's remarks can be found in Michaud and Aynesworth, *Ted Bundy: Conversations*, pp. 84–90.
31. Michaud and Aynesworth, *Only Living Witness*, p. 21.
32. Paul Henderson, "After She Put Out the Light, What Evil Crept In?," *Seattle Times*, February 13, 1974, p. B2.
33. Henderson, "After She Put Out the Light."
34. All details and quotations in this account are drawn from the initial police interview with the victim, dated March 2, 1974, and their follow-up report, March 4, 1974, Seattle Police Department files, King County Archives.
35. Skeletal remains of a young female victim, including a skull and shoulder-length brown hair, were found on August 29, 1978, by fishermen in the foothills of Mount Rainier, near Eatonville, Washington. Items of clothing were also found, including a striped shirt; the skull had suffered "a non fatal blow to the head," according to reporting some twenty years later: Victor M. Gonzales, "Parents: Skeleton Not That of Apparent Ted Bundy Victim," *News Tribune* (Tacoma), February 3, 1998. Manson's parents denied that the striped shirt belonged to their daughter, and police allowed the remains to be destroyed before dental records could be compared. In 1989, Bundy confessed to killing Manson but claimed he had removed her head and burned it in Liz Kloepfer's fireplace. See also "Bundy Murder Still Captivates Officers," *The Olympian*, January 26, 1998.
36. Bundy provided this list of animals to Michaud and Aynesworth, *Ted Bundy: Conversations*, p. 106.
37. Richard Bach, the author of *Jonathan Livingston Seagull*, is a Christian Scientist. See "It's a Bird! It's a Dream! It's Supergull!" *Time*, November 13, 1972; and Ron Charles, "Richard Bach's New Spiritual Memoir, 'Illusions II,'" *Washington Post*, February 8, 2014.
38. Richard Bach, *Jonathan Livingston Seagull: A Story* (New York: Macmillan, 1972), p. 62.
39. Roughly paraphrased from Kendall, *Phantom Prince*, p. 48.

40. Ramsland, *Confession of a Serial Killer*, p. 78.
41. Singular, *Unholy Messenger*, p. 56.
42. Ramsland, *Confession of a Serial Killer*, p. 84.
43. See the account in Rule, *Stranger Beside Me*, p. 62; also Michaud and Aynesworth, *Only Living Witness*, p. 23. In a statement Jane Curtis gave to the Central Washington State College Security Department, she said that her encounter with the man occurred on a Sunday night in April.
44. Larsen, *Bundy: Deliberate Stranger*, p. 38.
45. Transcript of *Guerrilla: The Taking of Patty Hearst, American Experience*, directed by Robert Stone, aired on PBS in 2004, pbs.org/wgbh/americanexperience/films/guerrilla/#transcript.
46. See extract from Bundy's résumé in Rule, *Stranger Beside Me*, p. 37.
47. Michaud and Aynesworth, *Only Living Witness*, p. 24.
48. Winn and Merrill, *Killer Next Door*, p. 12.
49. See Keppel and Michaud, *Terrible Secrets*, p. 98, Kindle.
50. Burl Barer, *Body Count* (New York: Kensington, 2002), p. 264.
51. Michaud and Aynesworth, *Only Living Witness*, p. 123.
52. Quotes from Bruce Johnson, "Slag from Smelter Now Being Marketed," *News Tribune* (Tacoma), May 20, 1974, p. 1. For later environmental restrictions, see, for example, the case of *Louisiana-Pacific Corp. v. ASARCO Inc.*, in which the U.S. Ninth Circuit Court held, on September 23, 1993, that "slag waste" is covered by the Comprehensive Environmental Response, Compensation, and Liability Act (CERCLA) as a "hazardous substance" with components including "copper, arsenic, lead and zinc": see Louisiana-Pacific Corp. v. ASARCO Inc., summarized by Environmental Law Reporter at elr.info/sites/default/files/litigation/23.21505.htm.
53. Bruce Johnson, "Tacoma Tradewinds: Smelter Slag Sails Inland Sea," *News Tribune* (Tacoma), August 28, 1974.
54. "Cascade Timber 3 POT, Tacoma Pierce County," Department of Ecology, State of Washington, apps.ecology.wa.gov/cleanupsearch/site/2693. The former Cascade Timber site along Maxwell Way between Port of Tacoma Road and Thorne Road was contaminated in 1982 when the lumber company deposited five hundred tons of ASARCO slag containing high levels of arsenic and other metals across an eleven-acre area of the property. In 1985, a study conducted by the Washington State Department of Ecology found high levels of metals in stormwater leaving the log yards and running directly into Commencement Bay.
55. Uses of smelter slag are described in an environmental impact report prepared in advance of road improvements in Tacoma: U.S. Department of Transportation, Federal Highway Administration, and Washington State Department of Transportation, *SR 16 / Union Avenue Vicinity to SR 302 Vicinity: Final Environmental Impact Statement*, pp. 521, 525.
56. Herb Robinson, "Mercer Island Bridge May Lose Its Bulge Soon," *Seattle Times*, May 20, 1974, p. 11.
57. Robinson, "Mercer Island Bridge."
58. Michaud and Aynesworth, *Only Living Witness*, p. 75.
59. Thomas Sampson, statement, October 29, 1975, Thurston County Sheriff's Office, in Thurston County case file on Donna Manson's disappearance, Killer in the Archives.

60. Michaud and Aynesworth, *Only Living Witness*, p. 74.
61. "Superfund Site: Alcoa (Vancouver Smelter), Vancouver, WA," U.S. Environmental Protection Agency, cumulis.epa.gov/supercpad/SiteProfiles/index.cfm?fuseaction=second.Cleanup&id=1000597#bkground.
62. The Forrest family lived at 4708 Northeast 40th Avenue, Vancouver, Washington, approximately five miles as the crow flies from the Alcoa aluminum smelter at 5701 Northwest Lower River Road, Vancouver.
63. Kendall, *Phantom Prince*, p. 97.
64. Phyllis Armstrong interview in *Ted Bundy: Falling for a Killer*, "Falling."
65. Phyllis Armstrong interview in *Ted Bundy: Falling for a Killer*, "Falling."
66. Michaud and Aynesworth, *Ted Bundy: Conversations*, p. 30.
67. Michaud and Aynesworth, *Only Living Witness*, p. 126.
68. Bob Leeright, "Officials Deny Smelter Poisons Horses," *Idaho State Journal*, June 2, 1974, p. 32.
69. Katherine G. Aiken, *Idaho's Bunker Hill: The Rise and Fall of a Great Mining Company, 1885–1981* (Norman: University of Oklahoma Press, 2005), p. 172.
70. Associated Press, "Metals Study to Be Expanded, Advanced," *Idaho State Journal*, June 4, 1974, p. 9.
71. Robert Keppel with William J. Birnes, *The Riverman: Ted Bundy and I Hunt for the Green River Killer*, rev. ed. (New York: Simon & Schuster, 2005), p. 20.
72. Keppel with Birnes, *Riverman*, p. 374.
73. See details about damage to the jaw in Keppel with Birnes, *Riverman*, p. 368.
74. For restricted areas off Whidbey Island see, for example, the nautical chart "U.S. West Coast, Washington, Puget Sound—Northern Part," NOAA, September 1989.
75. United Press International and Associated Press, "2 Million Egyptians Welcome Nixon," *Seattle Times*, June 12, 1974, p. 1, and Ross Anderson, "U.W. Coed, 18, Disappears on Way to Sorority House," *Seattle Times*, June 12, 1974, p. 1.
76. Bob Leeright, "Scenic Lakes Fall Victim to Man's Industry and Recreation," *Idaho State Journal*, June 12, 1974.
77. Leeright, "Scenic Lakes."
78. Sena Christian, "Bunker Hill Superfund Site Is Still a Toxic Mess, with Legacy of Suffering," *Newsweek*, June 12, 2016.
79. Sullivan, *Tainted Earth*, p. 77.
80. Leeright, "Scenic Lakes."
81. See Keppel with Birnes, *Riverman*, p. 378. Bundy told FBI agent William Hagmaier that he had severed the heads of "half a dozen" victims; see William Hagmaier interview with Ted Bundy, January 22, 1989, p. 3, Killer in the Archives.
82. Ted Bundy, interviewed by Robert Keppel, January 20, 1989, transcript, p. 26, *CrimePiper*; see also Keppel with Birnes, *Riverman*, p. 380.
83. See cover article, Al Gray, "There Is Rape after Death!," April 1974.
84. Carlisle, *1976 Psychological Assessment*, p. 185.
85. Carlisle, *1976 Psychological Assessment*, pp. 118–21.
86. This account is drawn from Kendall, *Phantom Prince*, pp. 49–50.
87. Kendall, *Phantom Prince*, p. 50.
88. Bill Dietrich, "Witness Says Krista Blake Met Suspect," *The Columbian* (Vancouver, WA), January 24, 1979, p. 11.
89. Bill Dietrich, "Mother Provides Alibi for Forrest," *The Columbian* (Vancouver, WA), April 19, 1979, p. 13.

90. Kendall, *Phantom Prince*, p. 51.
91. Kendall, *Phantom Prince*, p. 51.
92. Details of eyewitness accounts are drawn from police notes and an extensive "Summary of Event July 14 to September 7, [1974]," Case #74-123376, King County Police Department file on the Lake Sammamish abductions, King County Archives.
93. King County Police Department, "Summary," p. 1.
94. King County Police Department, "Summary," p. 2.
95. King County Police Department, "Summary," p. 3.
96. King County Police Department, "Summary," p. 4.
97. From a transcript of Stephen G. Michaud's April 23, 1980, interview with Bundy in Michaud and Aynesworth, *Ted Bundy: Conversations*, p. 134.
98. Gerard Schaefer was held on death row at the Florida State Prison alongside Bundy and later boasted of having traded details of killings with him; see Dielenberg, *Visual Timeline*, p. 110. Dielenberg reproduces the covers of the 1973 issues of *Inside Detective* and *True Detective* on this page.
99. Michaud and Aynesworth, *Ted Bundy: Conversations*, p. 133.
100. King County Police Department, "Summary," p. 5.
101. King County Police Department, "Summary," p. 6.
102. King County Police Department, "Summary," p. 7.
103. King County Police Department, "Summary," pp. 6–7.
104. Bundy told Michaud in his April 23, 1980, interview that he left Ott alive at the Issaquah site when he returned to Lake Sammamish; Michaud and Aynesworth, *Ted Bundy: Conversations*, p. 138. Keeping to the third-person hypothetical format he'd established with Bundy, Michaud asked, "Would the second victim see the first victim?" and Bundy answered, "Oh yeah, probably. In all probability." Michaud also asked, "Would the first victim be conscious?" and Bundy said, "In all probability."
105. Parts of Ott's and Naslund's remains were later found, on September 7, 1974, along with bones belonging to a third victim, later identified by Bundy as belonging to Georgann Hawkins. Bundy confessed to severing Hawkins's skull and burying it separately. Ott's jawbone was recovered, but her skull was never found. Naslund's skull was recovered, detached from the spine and ribs; it had sustained severe injuries to the cranium caused by a heavy object, possibly a tire iron. See Keppel and Michaud, *Terrible Secrets*, pp. 59, 56, 158.
106. Michaud and Aynesworth, *Ted Bundy: Conversations*, p. 135.
107. Kendall, *Phantom Prince*, pp. 51–52.
108. Associated Press, "Missing Woman Seen Leaving Picnic with Man," *Longview Daily News* (Longview, WA), July 18, 1974.
109. "Women's Bones Hint of Beheading," *Seattle Times*, March 27, 1975, p. 34.
110. See, for example, "Where 2 Women Disappeared," *Seattle Times*, July 21, 1974, p. 3; Lou Corsaletti, "Calls Rain in on Missing Women," *Seattle Times*, July 19, 1974, p. 8; Lou Corsaletti and Paul Henderson, "County's 'Most Bizarre' Case," *Seattle Times*, July 28, 1974, p. A10.
111. "Women's Bones," *Seattle Times*.
112. Hannelore Suderman, "Anatomy of Murder: Robert Keppel '66 Police Science, '67 MA Police Science," *Washington State Magazine* (Washington State University), magazine.wsu.edu/2009/09/30/anatomy-of-murder-robert-keppel-66-police-science-67-ma-police-science.

113. Emily Gillespie, "Survivor Recalls Night of Terror: Upcoming Parole Decision on Warren Forrest Prompts Woman to Tell Her Story from 1974," *The Columbian* (Vancouver, WA), April 17, 2014.
114. Emily Gillespie, "Survivor Reunited with Her Hero: Woman Who Says She Was Assaulted by Suspected Serial Killer Meets with Man Who Found Her," *The Columbian* (Vancouver, WA), April 30, 2014.
115. See Michaud and Aynesworth, *Only Living Witness*, p. 77; examples of police sketches of "Ted" can be seen in Lou Corsaletti, "Calls Rain in on Missing Women," *Seattle Times*, July 19, 1974, p. 8 and in "Police Issue New Sketch of 'Ted,'" *Seattle Times*, July 25, 1974, p. 31.
116. Michaud and Aynesworth, *Only Living Witness*, p. 77.
117. Kendall, *Phantom Prince*, p. 54.
118. Kendall, *Phantom Prince*, pp. 63, 73.
119. Dielenberg, *A Visual Timeline*, p. 112.
120. Field Investigation Report, Thurston County Sheriff Department, August 2, 1974, Complaint of Suspicious Person, Thurston County Case File on Donna Gail Manson, Killer in the Archives.
121. Field Investigation Report, Thurston County Sheriff Department, August 2, 1974.
122. Kendall, *Phantom Prince*, pp. 60–61.
123. Kendall, *Phantom Prince*, p. 62.
124. Rule, *Stranger Beside Me*, p. 99.
125. See Alan Stackhouse, "Teen Beauty Shot Three Times after Rape Ordeal!" *True Detective*, June 1974, pp. 38–41, 54–58.
126. Andy Stack, "Case of the Two Virgins and the Insatiable Sex Freak," *True Detective*, February 1974, p. 68; see also Ann Rule, *A Fever in the Heart: Ann Rule's Crime Files* (New York: Pocket Books, 1996).
127. See Andy Stack, "Murder for the Hell of It!" *True Detective*, March 1975, pp. 44–47, 52, 53.
128. Carol M. Ostrom and Susan Gilmore, "Murder on a Whim—Why Kill a Complete Stranger? Even the Suspect Doesn't Know," *Seattle Times*, July 15, 1990.
129. See Ann Rule, "Campbell's Revenge," collected in Rule, *A Rose for Her Grave; You Belong to Me; A Fever in the Heart* (New York: Pocket Books, 1997), pp. 269–93.
130. Donna Schram interview, *Ted Bundy: Falling for a Killer*, "Falling."
131. Donna Schram interview, *Ted Bundy: Falling for a Killer*, "Falling." The list is shown at 44 minutes, 17 seconds.
132. Kendall, *Phantom Prince*, p. 56.
133. Kendall, *Phantom Prince*, pp. 64–65.
134. Richard Nixon, resignation speech, August 8, 1974.
135. Jimmy Webb, "MacArthur Park," recorded by Richard Harris in 1968 and many others subsequently.
136. "Grant Awarded for Rape Study," *Seattle Times*, August 21, 1974.
137. Theodore Bundy, Department of Emergency Services resignation letter, August 30, 1974, *CrimePiper*.
138. The murdered hitchhiker has never been identified, her body never found. Ted Bundy to Jim Whitehead, Chief of Idaho Bureau of Investigation, Chief Investigator Russell T. Reneau, and Randall Everitt, criminal investigator with the Idaho Attorney General's Office, transcript of tape-recorded confession to Idaho killings, January 22, 1989, Killer in the Archives.

CHAPTER 7: The Bird's Nest

1. "Lead Found in Blood of Children," *News Tribune* (Tacoma), September 6, 1974, p. 8. See also Sullivan, *Tainted Earth*, pp. 84–85.
2. "Lead Found in Blood."
3. Associated Press, "Fear Casts Ominous Shroud in Kellogg," *Idaho State Journal*, September 16, 1974, p. 9.
4. Associated Press, "Fear Casts Ominous Shroud."
5. For this and a description of the Cutchins family's ills, see Sullivan, *Tainted Earth*, p. 86.
6. Associated Press, "Fear Casts Ominous Shroud."
7. David Horsey, cartoon accompanying editorial "The Awful Lesson of Bunker Hill," *Seattle Post-Intelligencer*, August 1, 1990.
8. Gregory L. Glass, Tacoma Smelter Plume Site, Final Report, April 2003, Trace Element Analyses for Selected Soil Samples, Vashon-Maury Island and King County Mainland, (Tacoma–Pierce County Health Department and Washington State Department of Ecology, 2003), p. 18. Results cited from Eric A. Crecelius, Carl J. Johnson, and George C. Hofer, "Contamination of Soils Near a Copper Smelter by Arsenic, Antimony and Lead," *Water, Air, and Soil Pollution* 3 (1974), pp. 337–42.
9. Glass, *Tacoma Smelter Plume Site, Final Report, April 2003*, p. 17; results cited from R. M. Statnick, Environmental Protection Agency, *Measurement of Sulfur Dioxide, Particulate, and Trace Elements in Copper Smelter Converter and Roaster/Reverberatory Gas Streams*, EPA-650/2-74-111 (Research Triangle Park, NC: National Environmental Research Center, Office of Research and Development, 1974).
10. "Lunch Box Check," *The Smelterworker*, February 1975, p. 6.
11. Charles Aweeka, "'I Knew It Was a Human Skull,' Said Finder," *Seattle Times*, September 8, 1974, p. 1.
12. Aweeka, "'Human Skull.'"
13. "Bones Not Missing Women's," *Seattle Times*, September 8, 1974, p. 3.
14. Keppel with Birnes, *Riverman*, p. 14.
15. Keppel with Birnes, *Riverman*, p. 367.
16. Keppel with Birnes, *Riverman*, p. 18.
17. Henry S. Pollock et al., "What the Pluck? The Theft of Mammal Hair by Birds Is an Overlooked but Common Behavior with Fitness Implications," *Ecology* 102, no. 12 (2021).
18. Keppel and Michaud, *Terrible Secrets*, p. 58.
19. Maximilian Hiram Cantu, "Animal Scavenging on Human Skeletal Remains in the Southwest United States: A Preliminary Model" (master's thesis, Louisiana State University and Agricultural and Mechanical College, 2014). See also W. D. Haglund, "Canid Scavenging/Disarticulation Sequence of Human Remains in the Pacific Northwest," *Journal of Forensic Sciences* 34, no. 3 (May 1989): pp. 587–606.
20. "Women's Bones Hint of Beheading," *Seattle Times*, March 27, 1975, p. 34.
21. Darren McGavin grew up in Puget Sound and went to school in Puyallup, where the Daffodil Festival remains a major event. See *"The Night Strangler*, Trivia," IMDb, imdb.com/title/tt0069002/trivia.
22. Parole hearing, State of Washington, Department of Corrections Indeterminate Sentence Review Board, July 18, 2017, p. 3.
23. Bill Dietrich, "Court Quiet as Rape, Stabbing Described," *The Columbian* (Vancouver, WA), January 31, 1979, p. 9.

24. Combined Monthly Progress Notes for May and June 2013, Warren Forrest, Washington State Department of Corrections Sex Offender Treatment Program, Monroe Correctional Complex–Twin Rivers Unit, August 1, 2013, p. 5. For a useful timeline of earlier abductions and murders in which Forrest remains a suspect, see Jessica Prokop, "Painful Memories on Display as Warren Forrest Murder Trial Gets Underway," *The Columbian* (Vancouver, WA), January 24, 2023.
25. Jessica Prokop, "After Late 20th Century Peak, Serial Killers Called to Account," *The Columbian* (Vancouver, WA), January 26, 2020.
26. Ted Bundy provided differing accounts of his murder of Nancy Wilcox. In 1980, he suggested to Stephen G. Michaud that he happened upon Wilcox near her home, raped her in a nearby orchard, and accidentally asphyxiated her: Michaud and Aynesworth, *Only Living Witness*, pp. 133–36. On January 22, 1989, the last day of his life, Bundy delivered a perhaps more accurate version to Detective Dennis Couch of the Salt Lake County Sheriff's Office, claiming he had picked Wilcox up near her house, restrained her, and taken her to his apartment, discarding her body the following day; he suggested that her remains were left at a site some hours south of Salt Lake City. See Bundy Utah confession, transcript, pp. 12–13. A transcript of the Utah confession can also be found in Kevin Sullivan, *The Enigma of Ted Bundy: The Questions and Controversies Surrounding America's Most Infamous Serial Killer* (Denver: Wild Blue, 2020), pp. 230–31. Wilcox's mother later recalled that Nancy had spoken of "flirting" with a "good-looking" man; see Pete Axthelm and Michael Ryan, "A Condemned Man's Last Bequest," *People*, February 6, 1989.
27. Mike Carter, "Utah Lawmen Exposed Bundy's Horrible Masquerade," *Salt Lake Tribune*, January 29, 1989.
28. Bundy Utah confession, January 22, 1989, p. 12; see Sullivan, *Enigma of Ted Bundy*, p. 234.
29. After Bundy's confession, Utah officials searched an area east of Capitol Reef National Park, finding some bones and a blouse, but these were later determined not to belong to Wilcox. See "Bones, Blouse May Belong to Bundy Victim," *Deseret News*, March 19, 1989; "Gatherers Say Goodbye to Bundy Victim," *Daily Herald* (Salt Lake City), July 2, 1990.
30. United Press International, "Bunker Hill's Plant Closes Two Weeks," *Idaho Free Press* (Nampa), October 4, 1974, p. 16. According to the article, the meeting took place on Wednesday, October 2, 1974.
31. Bill O'Neal, "Sheriff Discloses Identity of Bones," *The Columbian* (Vancouver, WA), October 23, 1974, p. 1. The remains of the other woman were not identified until 2015; they belonged to Martha Morrison. Warren Leslie Forrest was convicted of Morrison's murder in February 2023. See Jessica Prokop, "Clark County Serial Killer Warren Forrest Sentenced to Life in Prison in 1974 Murder," *The Columbian* (Vancouver, WA), February 17, 2023.
32. "Murray Smelters," UtahRails.net, updated November 29, 2018, utahrails.net/mining/smelters-murray.php.
33. "Everett Man Sentenced for Murder," *Seattle Times*, October 15, 1974, p. 48.
34. "Area Air May Get Even Dirtier Tomorrow," *Seattle Times*, October 15, 1974, p. 48.
35. Dielenberg, *Visual Timeline*, p. 128.
36. Ramsland, *Confession of a Serial Killer*, p. 90. Ramsland's ellipses are presented without brackets; the author's ellipses are within brackets.

37. Detective Ben Forbes, initial report, October 27, 1974, Salt Lake County Sheriff's Office, *CrimePiper*.
38. Dr. Serge Moore, postmortem examination by Utah State Medical Examiner, October 27, 1974; see also Forbes, Salt Lake County Sheriff's Office Report, October 30, 1974, *CrimePiper*.
39. For details regarding sperm and blood loss, see Detective Ben Forbes, follow-up report on results of toxicology tests on Melissa Smith, November 7, 1974, *CrimePiper*.
40. Kendall, *Phantom Prince*, p. 68.
41. Michaud and Aynesworth, *Ted Bundy: Conversations*, p. 91.
42. Michaud and Aynesworth, *Ted Bundy: Conversations*, p. 300.
43. Michaud and Aynesworth, *Ted Bundy: Conversations*, pp. 260–61.
44. Michaud and Aynesworth, *Ted Bundy: Conversations*, p. 262.
45. "Inside the Spooky Hotel That Inspired *The Shining*," *Today*, NBC, October 31, 2018, today.com/video/inside-the-spooky-hotel-that-inspired-the-shining-1358038595695.
46. From a report titled "Similar Transaction No. 2," prepared by Frank G. E. Tucker, District Attorney, and Milton K. Blakey, Deputy District Attorney of Pitkin County, Colorado, November 1977, *CrimePiper*.
47. Tucker and Blakey, "Similar Transaction ."
48. Larsen, *Bundy: Deliberate Stranger*, p. 47.
49. Statement of Margith Maughan, taken by Detective Jerry Thompson, Salt Lake County Sheriff's Office, February 20, 1976.
50. An accomplished forger of Mormon documents, Mark Hofmann killed two people in 1985 in separate incidents in an attempt to cover up other crimes; see Robert Lindsey, *A Gathering of Saints: A True Story of Money, Murder and Deceit* (New York: Simon & Schuster, 1988), p. 378. As a child, he grew up five miles from the Murray lead smelter and played on its abandoned grounds.
51. Details of Carol DaRonch's attempted abduction are taken from the statement she gave at the Murray Police Department later that night, November 8, 1974; from her testimony in *State of Utah v. Theodore Robert Bundy*, Third Judicial District Court, Salt Lake County, February 23–27, 1976; and from interviews featured in *Ted Bundy: Falling for a Killer*, "Gone Girls."
52. Viewmont High School's upcoming production of *Redhead* is mentioned in Kathy Adler, "Oden's Ode," *Davis County Clipper* (Bountiful, UT), November 8, 1974, p. 25.
53. "Written Statement of Raelynne Shepherd," November 10, 1974, Bountiful Police Department, Bountiful, Utah, Killer in the Archives.
54. "Written Statement of Raelynne Shepherd."
55. Photograph, *Eddas*, Viewmont High School Yearbook 1974–75, Bountiful, Utah, p. 36.
56. Orville Ryver, witness statement, "Supplementary Report, Attempt to Locate Missing Person," November 9, 1974, Bountiful Police Department, Bountiful, Utah, in Debra Jean Kent, Police File, p. 141.
57. *Eddas*, Viewmont High School Yearbook 1974–75, p. 39.
58. Ted Bundy, interview by Detective Dennis Couch, Salt Lake County Sheriff's Department, January 22, 1989, transcript, p. 9.
59. Statement of Margith Maughan, taken by Detective Jerry Thompson, Salt Lake County Sheriff's Office, February 20, 1976.

60. Bond, "Smelter Firm"; and Aiken, *Idaho's Bunker Hill*, p. 180.
61. Bond, "Smelter Firm."
62. "Letter to Mayor Hits Close to Home," *Seattle Times*, November 19, 1974, p. 40.
63. Jim Simon, "Islanders Expect Victory, by 1992, in Their Dusty I-90 War," *Seattle Times*, July 2, 1985, p. B1.
64. "It's Gasper!" *Mercer Island Reporter*, May 21, 1970, p. 1; Simon, "Islanders Expect Victory."
65. Laura Ann Aime, Decedent, Preliminary Findings of the Medical Examiner, State of Utah, Division of Health, November 27, 1974.
66. Larsen, *Bundy: Deliberate Stranger*, pp. 59–60.
67. William Blake, "The Sick Rose," available at poetryfoundation.org/poems/43682/the-sick-rose.
68. Robert Louis Stevenson, "The Strange Case of Dr. Jekyll and Mr. Hyde," *Dr. Jekyll and Mr. Hyde and Other Stories* (New York: Penguin Books, 1979), p. 95.
69. Stevenson, "Dr. Jekyll and Mr. Hyde," p. 95.
70. Stevenson, "Dr. Jekyll and Mr. Hyde," p. 95.
71. Aynesworth and Michaud, *Only Living Witness*, p. 13.
72. Stevenson, "Dr. Jekyll and Mr. Hyde," p. 90–91.
73. Stevenson, "Dr. Jekyll and Mr. Hyde," p. 95.

INTERLUDE: From Alamein to Zem Zem
1. Keith Douglas, *Alamein to Zem Zem* (Potomac, MD: Pickle Partners, 2015), p. 20.
2. Douglas, *Alamein*, p. 14.
3. Douglas, *Alamein*, pp. 21–22.
4. Douglas, *Alamein*, p. 22.
5. Niall Barr, *Eisenhower's Armies: The American-British Alliance during World War II* (New York: Pegasus Books, 2015), p. 413.
6. Barr, *Eisenhower's Armies*, p. 413. See also Wikipedia, s.v. "Benghazi Burner," last updated July 27, 2024, en.wikipedia.org/wiki/Benghazi_burner, or Jonathan Hanson, "Irreducible Imperfection: The Flimsy," Overland Tech and Travel, August 17, 2012, web.archive.org/web/20131203082114/http://www.overlandexpo.com/overland-tech-travel/2012/8/17/irreducible-imperfection-the-flimsy.html.
7. Douglas, *Alamein*, p. 14.
8. Douglas, *Alamein*, p. 7.
9. Thomas Robertson et al., eds., *Nature at War: American Environments and World War II* (Cambridge, UK: University of Cambridge Press, 2020), p. 16.
10. Robertson et al., *Nature at War*, p. 33.
11. Robertson et al., *Nature at War*, p. 33.
12. Robertson et al., *Nature at War*, p. 127.
13. Robertson et al., *Nature at War*, p. 88.
14. Robertson et al., *Nature at War*, p. 103.
15. "Timeline II—The War Years," From Superstar to Superfund, montana-aluminum.com/part-ii-the-war-years.
16. Robertson et al., *Nature at War*, pp. 91–92.
17. Robertson et al., *Nature at War*, p. 91.
18. Snow, *Living with Lead*, p. 37.

19. Marvin Brienes, "Smog Comes to Los Angeles," *Southern California Quarterly* 58, no. 4 (Winter 1976): p. 515; "Don't Cry! Smarting Gas Not Chemical War," *Daily News* (Los Angeles), July 27, 1943, p. 2. See also Roger W. Lotchin, *The Bad City in the Good War: San Francisco, Los Angeles, Oakland, and San Diego* (Bloomington: Indiana University Press, 2003), p. 186.
20. For more on these and other risk factors, see Adrian Raine, *The Anatomy of Violence: The Biological Roots of Crime* (New York: Vintage, 2013). For the concept of an epidemic, see Peter Vronsky, *American Serial Killers: The Epidemic Years, 1950–2000* (New York: Berkley, 2021), p. 5.
21. Vronsky, *American Serial Killers*, pp. 92 and 390n15, citing J. Robert Lilly, *Taken by Force: Rape and American GIs in Europe During World War II* (New York: Palgrave Macmillan, 2007), and Miriam Gebhardt, *Als die Soldaten kamen* (Munich: DVA/Random House, 2015, English version *Crimes Unspoken: The Rape of German Women at the End of the Second World War* (Malden, MA: Polity Press, 2017).
22. Keith Douglas, "Simplify Me When I'm Dead," in *Simplify Me When I'm Dead: Poems Selected by Ted Hughes* (New York: Farrar, Straus and Giroux, 1964), p. 21.

CHAPTER 8: The Lead Moon
1. Robert J. Cole, "Revere Files Petition for Chapter 11," *New York Times*, October 28, 1982.
2. David Franke, "Fifteen Best U.S. Suburbs," *Ladies' Home Journal*, August 1975, pp. 71–73.
3. See National Institute for Occupational Safety and Health, *Arsine (Arsenic Hydride) Poisoning in the Workplace*, pub no. 79-142, August 3, 1979, cdc.gov/niosh/docs/79-142/default.html.
4. Marvin Bidstrup, "Business Report: Stiff Upper Lip Maintained by Most Tacoma Industry," *News Tribune* (Tacoma), January 3, 1975, p. B13.
5. Cover, *The Ecologist* 4, no. 10 (December 1974).
6. Ruth Lumley-Smith, "Editorial: Can We Afford Lead Pollution?," *The Ecologist* 4, no. 10 (December 1974): p. 355.
7. Lumley-Smith, "Editorial," p. 356, citing Henry A. Schroeder, "Trace Elements in the Human Environment," *The Ecologist* 1, no. 11 (May 1971).
8. Lumley-Smith, "Editorial," p. 356, citing Tsaihwa J. Chow, "Lead Accumulation in Roadside Soil and Grass," *Nature* 225 (1970): pp. 295–96.
9. "Violent Crime Jumps in State," *Spokane Chronicle*, November 19, 1975, p. 11.
10. Kendall, *Phantom Prince*, p. 86.
11. Kendall, *Phantom Prince*, p. 86.
12. Kendall, *Phantom Prince*, p. 87.
13. Details of Campbell's murder remain unknown and speculative, aside from autopsy findings. Bundy himself was vague: see Michaud and Aynesworth, *Ted Bundy: Conversations*, pp. 182–83; Michaud and Aynesworth, *Only Living Witness*, pp. 95–96.
14. Ellen Fagg, "Utahns Knew and Liked U. Law Student," *Deseret News*, January 24, 1989.
15. See "Next Question: Cause of Heidi Peterson's Death," *Seattle Times*, January 25, 1975, p. 3; Mike Wyne, "Searchers Doubt They Overlooked Body," *Seattle Times*, January 25, 1975, p. 3.

16. Paul Henderson, "Police Move to Halt Heidi-Case Rumors," *Seattle Times*, January 31, 1975, p. 25.
17. "Police Weigh Heidi's Play Habits," *Seattle Times*, January 29, 1975, p. 11.
18. Keppel with Birnes, *Riverman*, p. 23.
19. Keppel with Birnes, *Riverman*, p. 24.
20. Keppel with Birnes, *Riverman*, p. 24.
21. Scott Brainerd interview in Sullivan, *Enigma of Ted Bundy*, p. 71.
22. Sullivan, *Enigma of Ted Bundy*, p. 98: Brainerd recalls the ESAR team consisting of some four hundred volunteers. Keppel suggests the number was "over 250": Keppel with Birnes, *Riverman*, p. 32.
23. Sullivan, *Enigma of Ted Bundy*, p. 99.
24. Keppel with Birnes, *Riverman*, p. 30; Keppel notes that his supervisors considered decapitation unlikely, given the absence of neck vertebrae, usually present in such cases. Keppel remarks, however, that "this logic was not infallible."
25. See Rule, *Stranger Beside Me*, p. 131.
26. See Winn and Merrill, *Killer Next Door*, p. 72.
27. See Rule, *Stranger Beside Me*, p. 130.
28. See Winn and Merrill, *Killer Next Door*, p. 73.
29. U.S. Bureau of the Census, 1950 Seventeenth U.S. Federal Census, Salem, Oregon, Ward 4, Enumeration District 24-15. The 1950 Census for Walter J. Woodfield shows the family residing at 482½ Bellevue Avenue, Salem, OR. Randall Brent Woodfield was born in Salem; see birth announcement in *Capital Journal*, December 28, 1950, p. 6.
30. See reports from Oregon's Department of Environmental Quality on the Salem Riverfront Park Project, deq.state.or.us/lq/ECSI/ecsidetail.asp?seqnbr=865, and "Environmental Cleanup Site Information (ECSI) Database Site Summary Report—Details for Site ID 4427, Boise Cascade Mill—Salem," deq.state.or.us/lq/ecsi/ecsidetail.asp?seqnbr=4427.
31. L. Jon Wertheim, "The I-5 Killer," *Sports Illustrated*, November 21, 2016, si.com/longform/true-crime/i-5-killer-green-bay-packers-randall-woodfield/index.html.
32. Andrew H. Malcolm, "Local Economy Sags as Volcanic Mount Baker Keeps Steaming," *New York Times*, November 17, 1975, p. 25.
33. "1975—Increased Heat and Signs of Activity at Mount Baker," USGS, November 1, 2023, usgs.gov/volcanoes/mount-baker/1975-increased-heat-and-signs-activity.
34. Malcolm, "Local Economy Sags."
35. There is no such thing as the Lead Moon.
36. Bob Boxberger, "Smelter Asks Planners to Allow More Slag Fill," *News Tribune* (Tacoma), March 15, 1975, p. 2.
37. Jerry Pugnetti, "City Grants Slag Fill Permit," *News Tribune* (Tacoma), April 8, 1975, p. 1.
38. "No End in Sight for Nightmare of I-90," *Mercer Island Reporter*, August 21, 1975, p. 1.
39. Liz Schensted, "The Nightmare Goes On . . . and On," *Mercer Island Reporter*, August 21, 1975, pp. 4–5.
40. "Woman Critical: Husband in Jail," *El Paso Herald-Post*, May 5, 1975, p. 23. According to her death certificate, Josefina Valles died May 15, 1975. In 1973,

Miguel and Josefina Valles were seriously injured in a gas pipe explosion outside their apartment building; their five-year-old son was killed, along with six others. See Bruce Bissonette, "Seven Die in Gas Explosion," *El Paso Times*, April 23, 1973, p. 1.

41. David Cross, "El Paso Police Release Murder Statistics from 1960 to 2018," KFOX14 (website), January 16, 2019. In 1960, the total number of murders in El Paso was eleven; in 1964 it dropped to five; in 1966 it rose to sixteen. In 1967 it was thirteen; in 1968, eighteen; in 1969, fifteen; in 1970, thirteen; and in 1971, sixteen. By 1975 it had reached twenty-one, and in 1977 it rose to thirty-one. See also Chart 2, "Crimes of Violence 1960–1970," showing violent crime up 156 percent, in *FBI Uniform Crime Reports for the United States, 1970* (Washington, DC: Government Printing Office, 1971). See also "FBI Reports Increase in Crime Rate," *El Paso Herald-Post*, December 29, 1971, p. 1; "FBI Reports Upward Trend in EP, Albuquerque Crime," *El Paso Times*, December 27, 1974.
42. Keppel with Birnes, *Riverman*, p. 410.
43. Norma Tirrell, "ASARCO Wants Bond Issue," *Independent-Review* (Helena, MT), May 6, 1975.
44. Ressler and Shachtman, *Whoever Fights Monsters*, p. 118.
45. Bob Boxberger, "Future Clouded for Tacoma Smelter," *News Tribune* (Tacoma, WA), May 16, 1975, p. 1.
46. Kendall, *Phantom Prince*, p. 88.
47. Dielenberg, *Visual Timeline*, pp. 164–65, based on interview conducted by Chris Mortensen; see also Mike Carter, "Utah Lawmen Exposed Bundy's Horrible Masquerade," *Salt Lake Tribune*, January 29, 1989, p. 3.
48. In his interview with Utah officials, Bundy denied abducting and killing Nancy Baird. See Bundy, interview by Couch, pp. 10, 20.
49. "Factory cripples" was a term in use during the industrial era, when child labor was common in Great Britain; see, for example, "William Dodd's Factory System Illustrated," *The Spectator*, June 4, 1842, p. 17.
50. Michael J. Buchanan-Dunne, "Where Is the Most Dangerous Place to Live in Great Britain?," *Murder Mile UK True Crime* (blog), July 5, 2017, murdermiletours.com/blog/where-is-the-most-dangerous-place-to-live-in-great-britain.
51. Burl Barer, *Body Count* (New York: Kensington, 2002), p. 12.
52. "Our History," ADT, adt.com/about-adt/history.
53. "The Question—Is the Smelter a Menace?," *News Tribune* (Tacoma), July 27, 1975, p. 3.
54. Marlowe Churchill, "Ruston: Some Fear Company Town May Become Tacoma Annex," *News Tribune* (Tacoma), June 28, 1984, p. 19.
55. See Emmet Pierce, "Retired Mayor Has His Heart in Ruston," *News Tribune* (Tacoma), January 9, 1982, p. 1.
56. Malcolm MacNey, "Smelter-Area Tests Show 'Unsafe' Arsenic Residues in Children," *News Tribune* (Tacoma), November 15, 1972, p. 1; "Is the Smelter a Menace?" See also Sullivan, *Tainted Earth*, pp. 122–23.
57. "The First Arrest, 1975," *Killer in the Archives* (blog), August 29, 2021, killerinthearchives.blog/the-first-arrest-1975.
58. Notation on phone call from Detective Forbes, August 19, 1975, Seattle Police Report, p. 535.

59. Keppel with Birnes, *Riverman*, p. 66.
60. Winn and Merrill, *Killer Next Door*, p. 87.
61. Winn and Merrill, *Killer Next Door*, p. 87.
62. Steve Govoni, "From Actual Court Records: How He Butchered the New York Beauties," *True Detective*, February 1975, pp. 26–31, 66, 70.
63. Winn and Merrill, *Killer Next Door*, p. 135.
64. Winn and Merrill, *Killer Next Door*, p. 91.
65. Report dated September 5, 1975 in Debra Jean Kent file, Bountiful Police Department, p. 44.
66. Dielenberg, *Visual Timeline*, p. 191.
67. Interview with Detective Jerry Thompson, in Al Carlisle, *"I'm Not Guilty!" The Case of Ted Bundy* (Magna, UT: Carlisle Legacy Books, 2020), p. 91.
68. Murray (Utah) Police Department, case no. 74-10181, lineup held at Metropolitan Law Building, Salt Lake City, Utah, October 2, 1975.
69. Associated Press, "Former Evans Aide Charged in Kidnap Case," *Daily Olympian*, October 3, 1975, p. 1; Associated Press, "Ted, Kidnap Suspect, Linked to Killings," *The Columbian* (Vancouver, WA), October 3, 1975, p. 9; "Police Want Bundy Files Scrutinized: Death Link Sought," *Spokesman-Review* (Spokane), October 11, 1975, p. 5.
70. "Is Utah 'Ted' the Seattle 'Ted?,'" *Seattle Post-Intelligencer*, October 3, 1975.
71. Rule, *Stranger Beside Me*, p. 146.
72. Larsen, *Bundy: Deliberate Stranger*, p. 93.
73. Associated Press, "Ted, Kidnap Suspect, Linked to Killings."
74. United Press International, "'Ted' Arrested for Salt Lake Crimes," *Idaho Free Press*, October 6, 1975, p. 9.
75. Associated Press, "His Friends Express Surprise," *Idaho State Journal*, October 3, 1975, p. 17.
76. United Press International, "Mother Shows Disbelief," *Idaho Free Press*, October 6, 1975, p. 9.
77. Ann Rule, "The Computer Error and the Killer," in *A Rose for Her Grave*, pp. 684–85.
78. Rule, "The Computer Error and the Killer," in *A Rose for Her Grave*, p. 672.
79. Cosden wasn't convicted of Devine's murder until 2002, after DNA linked him to the crime. Associated Press, "Man Sentenced to Life in Prison for 1973 Murder," *Seattle Times*, July 30, 2002. He remains a suspect in the murder of Brenda Joy Baker but has never been charged in that case: Ian Ith, "Prisoner Charged in Teen Girl's '73 Slaying," *Seattle Times*, March 9, 2002.
80. Besides Bundy, Forrest, Taylor, and Cosden, Washington state serial killers active in 1974 included James Edward Ruzicka and James Homer Elledge. Ruzicka murdered two West Seattle girls in February 1974; see Associated Press, "Rapist Vows He'd Be OK If Released," *News Tribune* (Tacoma), October 8, 1975. Elledge murdered a motel owner in Seattle in May 1974; he later murdered another Seattle woman in 1998 while on parole. See Ann Rule, "The Killer Who Begged to Die," in *Last Dance, Last Chance and Other True Cases* (New York: Pocket Books, 2003), pp. 361–98.
81. "Violent Crime Up 14 Pct in State," *Spokesman-Review* (Spokane), March 26, 1976, p. 10.

82. James Reston, "Something Has Gone Wrong with Our Common Purpose?," *Post-Herald and Register* (Beckley, WV), September 28, 1975. Reston published a related column two months later: "The Politics of Anarchy," *New York Times*, November 21, 1975, p. 43.
83. Markowitz and Rosner, *Lead Wars*, p. 41.
84. Ted Bundy to Ann Rule, October 8, 1975, Killer in the Archives.
85. Rule, *Stranger Beside Me*, pp. 180–81.
86. Associated Press, "308 Rapes in Seattle, but Only Six Convicted," *News Tribune* (Tacoma), December 10, 1975, p. 39.

CHAPTER 9: The Dutch Door
1. "Will Bridge Keep Afloat?," *Mercer Island Reporter*, January 1, 1976, p. 6.
2. "Thieves Foiled by Theft-Guard," *Mercer Island Reporter*, January 1, 1976, p. 18.
3. Regarding lead-based paint in the housing at Joint Base Lewis–McChord, see Fort Lewis Directorate of Public Works, "Final Environmental Impact Statement for the Fort Lewis Army Growth and Force Structure Realignment," Fort Lewis and Yakima Training Center, Washington, July 2010. The Logistics Center at JBLM became a Superfund site in 1990, according to the "Record of Decision for the Department of the Army Logistics Center, Fort Lewis, Washington," September 25, 1990. See also "Mapping Joint Base Lewis–McChord," Basewatch, sites.evergreen.edu/basewatch/mapping-jblm-jade. According to comments posted on a website devoted to military families, those moving into housing at JBLM are notified that lead-based paint may be present and are asked to sign waivers acknowledging the fact. See Shannon Prentice, "Military Families Face 'Unlivable' Conditions in Installation Housing around the Country," National Military Family Association, February 2, 2019. The page has since been removed, but an archived version can be found at web.archive.org/web/20220209195139/https://www.militaryfamily.org/military-families-face-unlivable-conditions-in-installation-housing-around-the-country/.
4. Affidavit of Marlin L. Vortman, September 17, 1987, Bundy v. Dugger, U.S. District Court for the Southern District of Florida, Fort Lauderdale Division, p. 3, Killer in the Archives.
5. Transcript, "State of Utah, Plaintiff, vs. Theodore Robert Bundy, Defendant, District Court of the Third Judicial District in and for Salt Lake County, State of Utah," p. 44.
6. Transcript, *Utah v. Bundy*, p. 466.
7. Jerry Pugnetti, "Smelter Withdraws Plans to Fill Waterfront Acres," *News Tribune* (Tacoma), March 11, 1976, p. 1.
8. "Death at the Smelter," signed "Concerned Smeltermen," distributed at 7:00 a.m. on March 25, 1976, American Smelting and Refining Company Records, Northwest Room, Tacoma Public Library. See also "Edgewood Man Electrocuted at Smelter," *News Tribune* (Tacoma), March 12, 1976, p. 2.
9. "Death at the Smelter."
10. See "death list," p. 1, box 3, "Steelworker & Miner Labor and Union Posters & Documents, 1970s," folder 2 of 2, ASARCO Records, Northwest Room, Tacoma Public Library.

11. "Death list," pp. 2–3; see also "Victor J. Hrvatin," *News Tribune* (Tacoma), July 22, 1959, p. 14; "James R. Todd," *News Tribune* (Tacoma), March 15, 1971, p. 27; "Robert Mataya," *News Tribune* (Tacoma), May 20, 1974, p. 8; "Allan Staples," *News Tribune* (Tacoma), October 18, 1973, p. 30.
12. "Death list," p. 1.
13. Anne Fischel and Linn Nelson, "Worker's Concerns about Health and Safety at ASARCO," Their Mines, Our Stories, September 7, 2019, theirminesourstories.org/post/workers-concerns-about-health-and-safety-at-asarco.
14. "Death list," p. 1.
15. S. S. Pinto et al. "Mortality Experience in Relation to a Measured Arsenic Trioxide Exposure," *Environmental Health Perspectives* 19 (August 19, 1977): pp. 127–30.
16. "Patty Is Guilty," *The Argus* (Fremont, CA), p. 1; "Patty Hearst Is Guilty; Shaken Bailey to Appeal," *Akron Beacon Journal*, March 21, 1976, pp. 1, 6.
17. Donald M. Hull, "Presentence Investigation Report," State of Utah, Adult Probation and Parole, March 1976.
18. Hull, "Presentence Investigation Report."
19. Ted Bundy, medical examination, Utah State Prison, examination of skull X-rays, Q. B. Coray, MD, diagnostic radiologist, April 21, 1976, Killer in the Archives.
20. Associated Press, "Appeals Court OKs EPA Regulatory Right," *Fort Worth Star-Telegram*, March 20, 1976, pp. 1, 2; see also Denworth, *Toxic Truth*, p. 95.
21. Associated Press, "Appeals Court."
22. Sullivan, *Tainted Earth*, p. 135. For a discussion of what was considered a "normal" or background level of arsenic for children, see pp. 122–23.
23. Marlowe Churchill, "Rustonians Aren't Rusty at Defending Themselves," *News Tribune* (Tacoma), March 18, 1976, p. 18.
24. "Psychological Evaluation of Theodore Bundy," tests administered December 18, 1976 and March 8, 1976, by Evan Lewis, Ph.D., counseling psychologist, University of Utah.
25. Carlisle, *1976 Psychological Assessment*, p. 64.
26. Carlisle, *1976 Psychological Assessment*, p. 66, 67.
27. Carlisle, *1976 Psychological Assessment*, p. 25.
28. Carlisle, *1976 Psychological Assessment*, p. 37.
29. Carlisle, *1976 Psychological Assessment*, p. 49.
30. Carlisle, *1976 Psychological Assessment*, p. 49.
31. Carlisle, *1976 Psychological Assessment*, p. 117.
32. Carlisle, *1976 Psychological Assessment*, p. 119.
33. Carlisle, *1976 Psychological Assessment*, p. 121.
34. Carlisle, *1976 Psychological Assessment*, p. 126.
35. Rule, *Stranger Beside Me*, p. 191.
36. Winn and Merrill, *Killer Next Door*, pp. 165–66.
37. Theodore Bundy to Judge Stewart Hanson Jr., June 13, 1976, *Killer in the Archives*.
38. Larsen, *Deliberate Stranger*, p. 186.
39. See "Girl Raped at Burbank," *Mercer Island Reporter*, July 1, 1976, p. 37. See also, on the same page, "Bob Tall, 16, Dies in Boat Accident on Lake Washington," "Vandals Break 14 Windows in Schools," and "Exposure Case in Park."

40. "Police News," *Mercer Island Reporter*, July 8, 1976, p. 2.
41. Catherine Owen and John Owen, "Mercer Island Police Commended," letter to the editor, *Mercer Island Reporter*, July 8, 1976, p. 4.
42. Sullivan, *Tainted Earth*, p. 135, see also p. 216n36.
43. Sullivan, *Tainted Earth*, p. 135, see also p. 216n36.
44. Jerry Thompson, detective, "Summary of Notes on Investigation of Theodore Robert Bundy," October 1975–June 1977, Salt Lake County police file, p. 37, Killer in the Archives.
45. "Smelter Is Shut Down," *South Idaho Press*, January 12, 1977, p. 10.
46. Ramsland, *Confession of a Serial Killer*, p. 109.
47. Peggy Reynolds, "Bulge Takes Two Lives" and "Two Killed on Bridge," *Mercer Island Reporter*, April 28, 1977, pp. 1, 12; Matt McVay, photo of Circus McGurkus, *Mercer Island Reporter*, April 28, 1977, p. 12.
48. Ted Bundy, 1974 Filofax notebook, *CrimePiper*. The book contains no notations other than phone numbers.
49. Liz Schensted, "Experts Tell Parents 'Pushers Are Your Kids,'" *Mercer Island Reporter*, April 28, 1977, p. 11.
50. "Accident Takes Two Lives on West Mercer," *Mercer Island Reporter*, June 30, 1977, p. 3.
51. O. Casey Corr, "Pete Dawson: No Bitterness," *Mercer Island Reporter* and *Bellevue Journal-American*, June 16, 1977, p. 12.
52. Dr. Mary Jean Brown, "Lead Poisoning Prevention Program," Centers for Disease Control and Prevention, April 4, 2011, https://archive.cdc.gov/#/details?q=Lead%20Poisoning%20Prevention%20Program&start=0&rows=10&url=https://www.cdc.gov/nceh/stories/lppp.html.
53. Items from police inventory of cell no. 5, Garfield County Jail, January 4, 1978, in "Investigation Report," on Bundy's escape, prepared by Michael J. Fisher, chief criminal investigator for the Ninth Judicial District, State of Colorado, serving Pitkin and Garfield Counties, pp. 10–18, Killer in the Archives.
54. Deniz Yeter et al. "Rural and Urban Ecologies of Early Childhood Toxic Lead Exposure: The State of Kansas, 2005–2012," *Kansas Journal of Medicine* 15, no. 2 (May–August 2022): p. 285.
55. Ramsland, *Confession of a Serial Killer*, p. 114.
56. Ramsland, *Confession of a Serial Killer*, p. 115.

CHAPTER 10: The Volcano

1. Re: "the Oak Club," see "Neighbors' Impressions: Ted Bundy Was 'Friendly, Aloof,'" *Seattle Times*, February 18, 1978, p. 5.
2. Gregory Jones, "Power Failure at ASARCO: Close Encounter of Worst Kind," *El Paso Times*, January 10, 1978, p. 1.
3. Michaud and Aynesworth, *Only Living Witness*, p. 211.
4. Nelson, *Defending the Devil*, p. 286.
5. The order in which the victims were attacked at the Chi Omega sorority has been the subject of debate, but Dielenberg provides a comprehensive analysis of available evidence suggesting that Bowman was attacked first, then Chandler and Kleiner, and finally Levy: see Dielenberg, *Visual Timeline*, p. 216.
6. In the subsequent police interview with Cheryl Thomas, conducted on January 31, 1978, by Detective Don Patchen at the Tallahassee Memorial Hospital, she

stated that she owned several pairs of pantyhose but rarely wore them and was wearing only a pullover sweater in bed on the night of the assault.
7. Nancy Gould, "School Vandalism Continues to Sock the Pocketbook," *Mercer Island Reporter*, January 26, 1978, p. 1.
8. "Problem Nationwide, Parents Told," *Mercer Island Reporter*, January 26, 1978, p. 1.
9. Ramsland, *Confession of a Serial Killer*, p. 120.
10. Ramsland, *Confession of a Serial Killer*, p. 112.
11. See Dielenberg, *Visual Timeline*; see also George R. Dekle Sr., *The Last Murder: The Investigation, Prosecution, and Execution of Ted Bundy* (Santa Barbara: Praeger, 2011), p. 9.
12. Ramsland, *Confession of a Serial Killer*, p. 120.
13. Ramsland, *Confession of a Serial Killer*, p. 120.
14. Ramsland, *Confession of a Serial Killer*, p. 121.
15. Inventory of items removed from orange Volkswagen, Sheriff's Office, Leon County, Florida, February 23, 1978, *Killer in the Archives*.
16. Transcript of interview with Don Patchen, Tallahassee homicide detective, in Sullivan, *Enigma*, p. 171.
17. Sullivan, *Enigma*, p. 165.
18. Sullivan, *Enigma*, p. 180; see also Keppel and Michaud, *Terrible Secrets*, p. 30.
19. Kendall, *Phantom Prince*, p. 176.
20. Kendall, *Phantom Prince*, p. 177.
21. Markowitz and Rosner, *Lead Wars*, p. 83. See also "Preventing Lead Poisoning in Young Children—United States," Centers for Disease Control and Prevention, cdc.gov/mmwr/preview/mmwrhtml/00000659.htm.
22. Landon Kite, Staff Assistant, the White House, to Mrs. Ruth Webb, April 21, 1978, in author's possession.
23. Stefan Lovgren, "King Tut Died from Broken Leg, Not Murder, Scientists Conclude," *National Geographic*, December 1, 2006, nationalgeographic.com/history/article/king-tut-died-from-broken-leg--not-murder--scientists-conclude.
24. "2 Die in Freak Dump-Truck Accident," *Seattle Times*, June 27, 1978, p. 1.
25. Erik Lacitis, "Postcard-Pretty Road Is a Sore Spot for Many," *Seattle Times*, July 1, 1978, A9.
26. Jon Nordheimer, "All-American Boy on Trial," *New York Times Magazine*, December 10, 1978, p. 46. Nordheimer misspelled Denise Naslund's name as "Maslund" and Carol DaRonch as "Carole." See pp. 114, 120.
27. Gacy's childhood home at 4505 North Marmora Avenue, Chicago, lies about three miles east of the 8213 West Summerdale address. He thus spent most of his troubled life in the lee of O'Hare.
28. *Conversations with a Killer: The John Wayne Gacy Tapes*, episode 3, "Sane Enough," directed by Joe Berlinger, aired in 2022 on Netflix.
29. Harold Schechter, cited in Christopher Beam, "Blood Loss: The Decline of the Serial Killer," *Slate*, January 5, 2011.
30. Peter Vronsky, *American Serial Killers: The Deadliest Years 1950–2000* (New York: Berkley, 2021), pp. 7–8.
31. Caroline Fraser, "In the Night, What Things Move," *Sleepy Tree: Book II* (Fort Worth, TX: Sleepy Tree Publishing, 1981), p. 4.

32. Richard A. Lemen, "Asbestos in Brakes: Exposure and Risk of Disease," *American Journal of Industrial Medicine* 45, no. 3 (March 2004): pp. 229–37, chlwlaw.com/images-pdf/Lemen-Brakes.pdf.
33. Darcy O'Brien, *The Hillside Stranglers* (New York: Open Road Integrated Media, 2014), p. 33.
34. "Renton Man Dies in Bulge Accident," *Mercer Island Reporter*, February 28, 1979, p. 1.
35. "Three Mercer Island Youth Die in High-Speed Crash," *Mercer Island Reporter*, March 21, 1979, p. 1.
36. "Two Killed in Motorcycle Accident on Island Crest," *Mercer Island Reporter*, May 2, 1979, p. A2.
37. See Nancy Gould, "Teen Travel: 'A Blast or a Bummer!,'" *Mercer Island Reporter*, January 17, 1979, p. B4; Peggy Reynolds, "Shelley McMillan: Such an Accident Should Never Happen, but It Did," *Mercer Island Reporter*, June 16, 1977, p. 15.
38. See Marie Kusters-McCarthy, "Murder by Mail-Order," *Crime Magazine*, June 13, 2013. Indle King Jr., Mercer Island High class of 1979, known as "Indy," grew up in a "loving home," according to *Crime Magazine*, son of two professors, and later became fixated on acquiring an "obedient" bride from the East. His first, Ekaterina, from Siberia, dumped him when he beat and threatened to kill her. The second, Anastasia Solovieva, from Kyrgyzstan, went missing in September 2000, her body later found on a garbage dump at the Tulalip Reservation. In 2002, Indy, 270 pounds and sporting a hairpiece, was convicted of her murder after it emerged that he sat on her while a friend strangled her. He was already in touch with a third prospective bride.
39. Joanne Doroshow, interview, in *Meltdown: Three Mile Island*, episode 4, "Fallout," directed by Kief Davidson, released in 2022 on Netflix.
40. "Aroma from Seattle," *News Tribune* (Tacoma), April 20, 1979, p. 6.
41. "Report on Copper Industry Stirs Controversy," *News Tribune* (Tacoma), April 8, 1979, p. 89.
42. Manuel Gomez, Richard Duffy, and Vincent Trivelli, *At Work in Copper: Occupational Health and Safety in Copper Smelting* (New York: Inform, 1979), pp. 167–68.
43. "Report on Copper Industry."
44. Amy Clancy, "New Allegations of Sexual Abuse at Tacoma Boys' Home," KIRO-TV, December 12, 2018, kiro7.com/news/local/new-allegations-of-sexual-abuse-at-tacoma-boys-home/887973058.
45. For details of Joseph Edward Duncan's early offenses, see Gary C. King, *Stolen in the Night* (New York: St. Martin's Press, 2007), pp. 90–91.
46. Ann Rule, *The I-5 Killer* (New York: Berkley, 2022), pp. 72–73.
47. Linda Daniel, "Volunteers Plod through Rain Looking for Girl Who Disappeared 'Like That,'" *Seattle Times*, December 2, 1979, p. 14.
48. Ann Rule, "The Vanishing," in *You Belong to Me and Other True Crime Cases* (New York: Simon & Schuster, 1994), p. 407.
49. Rule, "The Vanishing," pp. 412–14. See also Paul Henderson, "Mother Voices Relief; Stacy Didn't Suffer," *Seattle Times*, September 15, 1981, p. 1.
50. Margaret Good, in *Ted Bundy Tapes*, "Burn Bundy Burn."
51. Paul Kaplan, "Bundy: Attorney, Witness and Defendant," *Miami News*, July 6, 1979, p. 46.

NOTES TO PAGES 294–303

52. Affidavit of Margaret Good, September 15, 1987, *Bundy v. Dugger*, p. 4.
53. Raymond Crew, videotape of his cross-examination, July 9, 1979, State of Florida v. Theodore Robert Bundy.
54. Crew, videotape of his cross-examination.
55. Gene Miller and James Buchanan, "Bundy's Cool as He Tests Cop Who Found Bodies," *Miami Herald*, July 10, 1979, p. 104.
56. *Ted Bundy Tapes*, "Burn Bundy Burn."
57. "Accidents on I-90: Frequent Injuries, Property Damage Year after Year," *Mercer Island Reporter*, March 19, 1980, p. A5.
58. "Accidents on I-90," *Mercer Island Reporter*.
59. Accidents on I-90," *Mercer Island Reporter*; see Blauman's photo of the station wagon and the caption for a description of the Pinto.
60. "Mercer Island Woman Drowns in Accident at Bulge," *Mercer Island Reporter*, February 27, 1980, p. 1.
61. Steve Miletich, "Mystery Blast: Powerful Bomb Gouges Support to I-90 Ramp," *Mercer Island Reporter*, November 14, 1979, p. B12.
62. Ann Rule, "Young Love," in *True Crime: An American Anthology*, ed. Harold Schechter (New York: Library of America, 2008), p. 724. Rule has changed the names of Clark and other individuals in this piece.
63. Matt Benoit, "Heartbreak and the Girl from Perham Hall," p. 3, *LandEscapes*, Washington State University, 2013, p.3.
64. Benoit, "Heartbreak."
65. Rule, "Young Love," p. 730.
66. Benoit, "Heartbreak," p. 13.
67. Unger and Unger, *Guggenheims*, p. 471.
68. Unger and Unger, *Guggenheims*, pp. 491–92.
69. Unger and Unger, *Guggenheims*, p. 447.
70. Michaud and Aynesworth, *Only Living Witness*, p. 9.
71. Jean Reichenbach, "Teenage Suicide II: Portrait of Jason—One Who Succeeded," *Mercer Island Reporter*, February 25, 1981, p. A5.
72. John Lustig, "Book's Influence Cited in Teen's Suicide Pact," *Mercer Island Reporter*, May 21, 1980, p. A10.
73. Alan Guggenheim, *Spirit Lake People: Memories of Mount St. Helens* (Gresham, OR: Salem Press, 1986), pp. 1, 3; see also "Lawetlat'la Nominated as Culturally Significant," Forest Feature, Gifford Pinchot National Forest, fs.usda.gov/Internet/FSE_DOCUMENTS/stelprdb5411954.pdf.
74. Guggenheim, *Spirit Lake People*, p. 136.
75. Guggenheim, *Spirit Lake People*, p. 136.
76. Lawrence Roberts, "Forty Years Later, Lessons for the Pandemic from Mount St. Helens," *New York Times*, May 17, 2020.
77. Associated Press, "Evidence of 1980 Murders Hidden by Volcano," *New York Times*, October 18, 1981. Randy Woodfield was considered a suspect initially, but in 1990 Martin Sanders, a long-haul truck driver operating out of Montana, pled guilty to murdering two Spokane teenagers in 1983 and was implicated in the murders of Weatter and Allen. See Jim DeFede, "Suspect in Killings May Face Death Penalty," *Spokane Chronicle*, July 11, 1990, p. 3; Associated Press, "Convict Pleads Guilty to Raping, Killing Two Teens," *News Tribune* (Tacoma), December 28, 1990, p. 15.

78. *Seattle Post-Intelligencer*, May 8, 2000, cited in Greg Lange, "Mount St. Helens Erupts on May 18, 1980," *HistoryLink.org Online Encyclopedia of Washington State*, May 15, 2003, historylink.org/file/5457.
79. Guggenheim, *Spirit Lake People*, p. 136.

CHAPTER 11: The Green River

1. Apologies to John Milton, *On Paradise Lost*, in *John Milton: Complete Poems and Major Prose*, ed. Merritt Y. Hughes (Indianapolis, IN: Bobbs-Merrill, 1957), bk. 1, lines 209–10, 236–37.
2. Jeff Weathersby, "Study Concludes Asarco Pollutant More Harmful Than Thought," *News Tribune* (Tacoma), March 19, 1981, p. 3. For SO_x regulations at the time, see "Timeline of Sulfur Dioxide National Ambient Air Quality Standards," Environmental Protection Agency, epa.gov/so2-pollution/timeline-sulfur-dioxide-national-ambient-air-quality-standards-naaqs.
3. Weathersby, "Study Concludes," p. 3.
4. "Smelter Given Deadline," *Kitsap Sun*, November 13, 1981, p. 16.
5. "Acid Rain in the Mountains May Be Killing Lakes' Fish," *News Tribune* (Tacoma), July 9, 1981, p. 3.
6. Art Johnson, "Overriding Factor: Money, Above All Other Woes, Is the Reason Bunker Hill's Dying, Industry's in Such a Bad Way," *Spokane Chronicle*, November 13, 1981, p. 6.
7. Woodfield was never charged with Ayers's murder, but his DNA was found at the scene: Maxine Bernstein, "DNA Links 'I-5 Killer' to 1980 Slaying," *The Oregonian*, March 1, 2006.
8. Alan K. Ota and B. Evangelista Jr., "Homicide Rate Escalates: 'Storybook' Couple Meets Tragic End," *The Oregonian*, November 30, 1980.
9. The Highway Serial Killings Initiative was launched in 2009. See Ginger Strand, *Killer on the Road: Violence and the American Interstate* (Austin: University of Texas Press, 2012), pp. 166–67.
10. Strand, *Killer on the Road*, p. 163.
11. L. Jon Wertheim, "The I-5 Killer," *Sports Illustrated*, November 21, 2016.
12. "Police News: Car and Body Recovered from Lake; 13 Burglaries Cleared by Arrest," *Mercer Island Reporter*, September 16, 1981, p. A5.
13. Jeff Weathersby, "Smelter Stack Sitters Come Down," *News Tribune* (Tacoma), October 16, 1981.
14. Jeff Weathersby, "12 Taken to Hospital after Smelter Coughs Arsenic Dust on Road," *News Tribune* (Tacoma), January 8, 1982, p. 1.
15. The Kenworth plant where Ridgway worked is located at 8801 East Marginal Way South, Tukwila, next to the old Boeing Field, now King County International Airport.
16. Ann Rule, *Green River, Running Red* (New York: Free Press, 2004), p. 377.
17. "Throat-Slashing Murder Trial Under Way," *The Columbian* (Vancouver, WA), November 9, 1982, p. 17.
18. See Ann Rule, "Campbell's Revenge," in *Rose for Her Grave*, p. 278.
19. "Charles Campbell, Death Row's Poster Child, Feared and Loathed," *Kitsap Sun*, May 8, 1994.
20. Theodore Bundy, "Segregation Psychological Assessment," June 22, 1982, Inmate Master File, Florida State Prison, Starke, Florida; see also "Chronological Record

of Outpatient Health Care," State of Florida, Department of Corrections, notes on June 22, 1982; August 2, 1982; and October 8, 1982.
21. Rule, *Green River*, p. 3.
22. The description of Frank Linard's discovery of Debra Bonner's body is drawn from Carlton Smith and Tomas Guillen, *The Search for the Green River Killer* (New York: Penguin, 1991), pp. 5–7.
23. Keith Ervin, "A Mother Fights to Forgive," *Seattle Times*, December 4, 2001.
24. Rule, *Green River*, p. 18.
25. Christy Scattarella, "Holdouts Haunt Ghost Town—Homeowners Reject Port's Buyout Offer near Sea-Tac Airport," *Seattle Times*, February 18, 1992.
26. Smith and Guillen, *Search for the Green River Killer*, pp. 176–77.
27. See Rule, *Green River*, pp. 49–51.
28. Norm Maleng, "Prosecutor's Summary of Evidence," undated, circa 2003, State of Washington v. Gary Leon Ridgway, Superior Court of Washington for King County, p. 80.
29. Maleng, "Prosecutor's Summary of Evidence," p. 40.
30. Associated Press, "State's Crime Rate Declines 2.6 Percent," *Bellingham Herald*, November 24, 1983, p. 10. Cotton's remarks did not acknowledge another notorious crime in Seattle in 1983, the Wah Mee massacre, a mass shooting in Chinatown on February 19 that left thirteen dead.
31. "Police News: After Eluding Police Two Weeks, Fugitive Captured," *Mercer Island Reporter*, June 7, 1983, p. 9; see also Jack Olsen, *Charmer: The True Story of a Ladies' Man and His Victims* (New York: Avon Books, 1994), pp. 47–48.
32. Olsen, *Charmer*, p. 47.
33. Dan Voelpel, "Black Particles from Asarco 'Pepper' North Tacoma Homes, Cars," *News Tribune* (Tacoma), June 9, 1983, p. C1.
34. Voelpel, "Black Particles," p. C1.
35. "Boat Owners near Smelter Outraged by Apparent Fallout," *News Tribune* (Tacoma), July 5, 1983, p. A4.
36. Boat Owners," *News Tribune* (Tacoma), p. A4.
37. Maleng, "Prosecutor's Summary of Evidence," p. 71.
38. Smith and Guillen, *Search for the Green River Killer*, pp. 153, 265, 442.
39. R. Steven Pappas et al., "Toxic Metal Concentrations in Mainstream Smoke from Cigarettes Available in the USA," *Journal of Analytical Toxicology* 38, no. 4 (May 2014): pp. 204–11.
40. Sandra Sugawara, "EPA Trying to Ease Out of a Leaden Box," *Washington Post*, May 21, 1982.
41. Al Gedicks, *The New Resource Wars: Native and Environmental Struggles against Multinational Corporations* (Montreal: Black Rose Books, 1994), p. 41.
42. Ronald Reagan, "Radio Address to the Nation on Welfare Reform," February 15, 1986, reaganlibrary.gov/archives/speech/radio-address-nation-welfare-reform.
43. Sullivan, *Tainted Earth*, p. 147.
44. John Gillie, "Stronger Controls on Smelter Favored by Most in TNT Poll," *News Tribune* (Tacoma), July 24, 1983, pp. 1, 3.
45. Jack Pyle, "Asarco Workers Plan Own Survey," *News Tribune* (Tacoma), July 31, 1983, pp. 1, 6.
46. Joan Didion, *Democracy* (New York: Knopf, 1984), p. 100.

47. Paul Henderson, "Protesters Charge County Police 'Playing Games,'" *Seattle Times*, March 17, 1984, p. A7.
48. Henderson, "Protesters Charge," p. A7.
49. Lewis Kamb, "How a Crime Lab Missed Evidence That Could Have Stopped the Green River Killer," NBC News, March 3, 2023, nbcnews.com/news/us-news/gary-ridgway-green-river-serial-killer-washington-rcna67794.
50. Later formulations of Imron are lead-free, but commercial and industrial uses of lead paint, such as automotive paint, were exempted from the 1978 U.S. lead paint ban. For the lead chromate content of earlier formulations of Imron, see, for example, "MSDS No. 7RS, Material Safety Data Sheet Imron Polyrurethane Enamel," E.I. du Pont de Nemours & Co., Automotive Products Department, Wilmington, Delaware, May 1, 1988.
51. Henderson, "Protesters," *Seattle Times*, March 17, 1984.
52. Newhouse News Service, "Serial Killers New Murderers," *Montana Standard*, August 11, 1984, p. 13.
53. Newhouse News Service, "Serial Killers," p. 13.
54. Newhouse News Service, "Serial Killers," p. 13.
55. Newhouse News Service, "Serial Killers," p. 13.
56. Newhouse News Service, "Serial Killers," p. 13.
57. Associated Press, "Serial Killers under Target," *Daily Advertiser* (Lafayette, LA), July 11, 1984, p. 44.
58. Philip Jenkins, *Using Murder: The Social Construction of Serial Homicide* (New York: Walter de Gruyter, 1994), pp. 67–74.
59. Jim Wilson, "Science: The Chemistry of Violence," *Popular Mechanics*, April 1998, p. 42. See also Adrian Raine, *The Anatomy of Violence: The Biological Roots of Crime* (New York: Pantheon Books, 2013), p. 227.
60. "Editorial: A Lonely Man's Fears Created a Nightmare," *Telegram-Tribune* (San Luis Obispo, CA), July 25, 1984, p. 6.
61. Wilson, "Science."
62. Raine, *Anatomy of Violence*, pp. 227–28.
63. Associated Press, "Bundy Escape Attempt Linked to Prison Guards," *Palm Beach Post*, August 11, 1984, p. 28.
64. This was Westley Allan Dodd, who murdered three young boys in 1989; see Timothy Egan, "Illusions Are Also Left Dead as Child-Killer Awaits Noose," *New York Times*, December 29, 1992, p. A1.
65. See Theodore Bundy, Florida State Prison, Department of Corrections Daily Record of Segregation, August 1–November 17, 1984, Killer in the Archives.
66. Dekle, *The Last Murder*, p. 216.
67. See Keppel with Birnes, *Riverman*, p. 180.
68. Keppel with Birnes, *Riverman*, pp. 184, 504.
69. John Ellingson, "Asarco Won't Be Whistling Fire Alarms in Ruston," *News Tribune* (Tacoma), January 22, 1985, p. 13.
70. Keith Ervin, "Asarco Bids a Foul Farewell," *Pacific Northwest*, April 1985, pp. 19–21.
71. "Reported Crime Numbers & Crime Rates, Los Angeles County, 1985–2022," *Los Angeles Almanac*, laalmanac.com/crime/cr01.php. See also Federal Bureau of Investigation and the U.S. Department of Justice, *Uniform Crime Reports for the United States, 1985*, (Washington, DC: Government Printing Office, 1986), p. 350.

72. "CDC's Recommended Terminology When Discussing Children's Blood Lead Levels," Centers for Disease Control and Prevention, November 2022, https://stacks.cdc.gov/view/cdc/122750.
73. Ramsland, *Confession of a Serial Killer*, p. 147.
74. Kim Severson, "Friend Consumed by Dark Fantasies: Sentencing Set Today for Man Twice Convicted of Raping Girls," *News Tribune* (Tacoma), September 18, 1987, p. 22.
75. Suki Dardarian and Dan Voelpel, "Ex-Con Charged in Sex-Torture of Runaway Girl: Lakewood Man Served Time for 1960 Rape," *News Tribune* (Tacoma), June 9, 1987, p. 1.
76. Suki Dardarian, "Runaway Portrayed as Prostitute," *News Tribune* (Tacoma), August 4, 1987, p. 9.
77. Dardarian and Voelpel, "Ex-Con Charged."
78. For "Little Detroit," see the documentary *Been Down So Long*, directed by Gilda Sheppard (Passion River, 2020); see also Dick Ferguson, "Super Challenge Faces Auburn with Boeing Growth," *News Tribune and Sunday Ledger* (Tacoma), February 6, 1966, p. 26.
79. "Redlining in Tacoma," video, posted August 25, 2020, by Tacoma Public Library, YouTube, 8:39, youtube.com/watch?v=FE7o3b_DjAg.
80. Rob Carson, "Crime Coils around the Military Bases," *News Tribune* (Tacoma), August 10, 1993, p. 21.
81. Washington State Department of Ecology, "Tacoma Smelter Plume—Extended Footprint Lead Concentrations," flickr.com/photos/ecologywa/9675276742/in/album-72157635377531447.
82. Ramsland, *Confession of a Serial Killer*, p. 154.
83. For more on the origins of Lecter, see Harris's introduction to the twenty-fifth anniversary edition of *The Silence of the Lambs* (New York: Arrow Books, 2013); see also Tim Ott, "Alfredo Ballí Treviño: The Killer Doctor Who Inspired the Character Hannibal Lecter," *Biography*, May 14, 2024.
84. *Manhunter*, directed by Michael Mann (De Laurentiis Entertainment Group, 1986).
85. Michael Gilbert, "Bloody Tacoma: City on Record Homicide Pace," *News Tribune* (Tacoma), February 15, 1988, p. B1.
86. Gilbert, "Bloody Tacoma."
87. Suki Dardarian, "Mayor's Murder Baffles Ruston," *News Tribune* (Tacoma), January 19, 1988, p. A12.
88. Kim Severson, "Murder Suspect Pleads Not Guilty," *News Tribune* (Tacoma), January 23, 1988, p. B1.
89. Debby Abe, "Ruston Mayor's Killer Sentenced to 18 Years," *News Tribune* (Tacoma), November 17, 1988, p. B1.
90. Nelson, *Defending the Devil*, p. 83.
91. Nelson, *Defending the Devil*, p. 155. See also testimony of Dr. Dorothy Otnow Lewis, competency hearing in Theodore Robert Bundy, Petitioner, v. Richard L. Dugger, Respondent, U.S. District Court for the Middle District of Florida, October 22, 1987, p. 297.
92. Hagmaier, interview with Bundy, p. 3. Without identifying all of the victims, Bundy confessed to eleven murders in Washington, two in Oregon, two in Idaho, eight in Utah, three in Colorado, three in Florida, and one in California.

93. Larry Lewis, "'69 Killings near Parkway Unsolved, but Bundy Is Blamed," *Philadelphia Inquirer*, March 31, 1993. See also Dielenberg, *Visual Timeline*, p. 60.
94. Hagmaier, interview with Bundy, p. 1; Michaud and Aynesworth, *Only Living Witness*, p. 111.
95. Michaud and Aynesworth, *Only Living Witness*, p. 106.
96. Nelson, *Defending the Devil*, p. 273.
97. Keppel with Birnes, *Riverman*, p. 399.
98. Charles Doud, "'I'm So Sorry,' Bundy Says," *News Tribune* (Tacoma), January 24, 1989, pp. 1, 14. Ellipsis in original.
99. Doud, "'I'm So Sorry,'" p. 14.
100. Molly Kendall, "Molly's Story," in Elizabeth Kendall, *The Phantom Prince*, pp. 207–8.
101. Roger Angell, "Comment," *New Yorker*, February 27, 1989, p. 24.
102. Angell, "Comment," p. 24.
103. Olsen, *Charmer*, p. 90.
104. Olsen, *Charmer*, p. 139.
105. Olsen, *Charmer*, p. 134.
106. Olsen, *Charmer*, p. 131.
107. See photos and description in Robert D. Keppel and William J. Birnes, *Serial Violence: Analysis of Modus Operandi and Signature Characteristics of Killers* (Boca Raton, FL: Taylor & Francis, 2009), pp. 164–68.
108. Olsen, *Charmer*, p. 186.
109. See Keppel and Birnes, *Serial Violence*, pp. 168–70.
110. Keppel and Birnes, *Serial Violence*, p. 10.
111. Keppel and Birnes, *Serial Violence*, pp. 170–71.
112. Feliks Banel, "Bizarre Lake Washington Disaster Struck Thanksgiving Weekend 1990," *MyNorthwest*, November 25, 2015, updated July 28, 2022, mynorthwest.com/150242/bizarre-lake-washington-disaster-struck-25-years-ago.
113. Banel, "Bizarre Lake Washington Disaster."
114. Peyton Whitely and Nancy Montgomery, "New Bridge in Danger—It's a Commuter's Nightmare," *Seattle Times*, November 26, 1990, p. 1.
115. Chuck Taylor, "State Reeling under Massive Flooding from Record Deluge," *Seattle Times*, November 26, 1990, p. A1.
116. Terry McDermott, Carlton Smithe, and Ric Nalder, "Questions Abound over Bridge Sinking—Access Holes, Waste Water Left in Pontoons Criticized," *Seattle Times*, November 27, 1990, p. A1.
117. McDermott et al., "Questions Abound."
118. Terry McDermott, "Bridge's Status Blows in Wind—Why Take a Chance with Floating Bridges?," *Seattle Times*, November 29, 1990, p. A1.

CHAPTER 12: The Towering Inferno

1. Dante Alighieri, *The Inferno*, trans. Robert Hollander and Jean Hollander (New York: Doubleday, 2000), p. 221.
2. Special Agent Dale Cooper, one of the lead characters of *Twin Peaks*, provides this fictitious location in the first episode of the series: *Twin Peaks*, season 1, episode 1, "Northwest Passage," directed by David Lynch and Mark Frost, aired April 8, 1990, on ABC.

3. The character Benjamin Horne, who owns the Great Northern Hotel, offers this bromide in *Twin Peaks'* first episode, "Northwest Passage," April 8, 1990.
4. Olsen, *Charmer*, p. 267.
5. Katherine Leal Unmuth, "Dolores Davis," in "10 Lives Ended by Dennis Rader," *Wichita Eagle*, June 28, 2005, p. 6.
6. Ramsland, *Confession of a Serial Killer*, p. 173.
7. Ramsland, *Confession of a Serial Killer*, p. 176.
8. "CDC's Recommended Terminology When Discussing Children's Blood Lead Levels," Centers for Disease Control and Prevention.
9. Mark Worth, "Stack's Demolition Windfall for Some; Others in Ruston Sad to See It Go," *News Tribune* (Tacoma), September 14, 1991, p. 8.
10. Linda Woo, "Saying Goodbye: Champagne, Hats and a Tear or Two," *News Tribune* (Tacoma), January 18, 1993, p. 4.
11. Worth, "Stack's Demolition," p. 8.
12. Worth, "Stack's Demolition," p. 1.
13. Margaret Riddle, "The ASARCO Smokestack—Once the World's Largest—Is Demolished at the Company's Old Copper Smelter in Ruston, North of Tacoma, on January 17, 1993," *HistoryLink.org Online Encyclopedia of Washington State History*, August 26, 2008, historylink.org/File/8744.
14. Worth, "Stack's Demolition," p. 8.
15. U.S. Department of the Interior and State of Washington, "Injury Assessment Plan for the Upper Columbia River Site, Washington," Prepared for the Upper Columbia River Trustee Council, Confederated Tribes of the Colville Reservation, Spokane Tribe of Indians, May 7, 2012. See also "Upper Columbia River Lake Roosevelt Site," Washington State Department of Ecology, apps.ecology.wa.gov/cleanupsearch/site/12125.
16. Karen Dorn Steele, "B.C. Smelter Dumped Tons of Mercury," *Spokesman-Review* (Spokane), June 20, 2004, pp. 1, 8.
17. Dee Riggs, "A Serial Killer Emerges," *Wenatchee World*, April 25, 2005.
18. J. L. Pirkle et al., "The Decline in Blood Lead Levels in the United States. The National Health and Nutrition Examination Surveys (NHANES)," *Journal of the American Medical Association* 272, no. 4 (July 27, 1994): pp. 284–91.
19. See, for example, *El Paso and Dona Ana County Metals Survey Sampling Report*, Contract No. DACA56-01-D-2001, Task Order No. 0002, Work Authorization Directive 005-Subtask 3, August 17, 2001, prepared for U.S. Environmental Protection Agency, Region 6 Dallas, U.S. Army Corps of Engineers Tulsa District.
20. C. Richard Bath, "U.S.-Mexico Experience in Managing Transboundary Air Resources: Problems, Prospects, and Recommendations for the Future," *Natural Resources Journal* 22, no. 4 (Fall 1982): p. 1147.
21. See Bath, "U.S.-Mexico Experience," p. 1150; Bath refers to the "arithmetic mean for benzene solubles found in the particulates analyzed."
22. Bath, "U.S.-Mexico Experience," p. 1151.
23. "El Paso Smelter Still Poses Lead-Poisoning Peril to Children in Juarez," *New York Times*, November 28, 1977, p. 22.
24. Corinne Chin and Erika Schultz, "Disappearing Daughters," *Seattle Times*, March 8, 2020, projects.seattletimes.com/2020/femicide-juarez-mexico-border.

25. For statistics and details of women killed between 2004 and 2007, see "Updated List of Murders of Women in Juárez and Chihuahua City," WOLA, June 25, 2007, wola.org/2007/06/updated-list-of-murders-of-women-in-juarez-and-chihuahua-city.
26. "Updated List of Murders," p. 1.
27. Ellas Tienen Nombre, ellastienennombre.org/mapa.html.
28. James Alan Fox and Marianne W. Zawitz, "Homicide Trends in the United States: 2002 Update," Bureau of Justice Statistics Crime Data Brief, U.S. Department of Justice, November 2004, p. 1, bjs.ojp.gov/content/pub/pdf/htus02.pdf.
29. John Dilulio, "The Coming of the Super-Predators," *Weekly Standard*, November 27, 1995.
30. The study was Marvin E. Wolfgang, Robert Figlio, and Thorsten Sellin, "Delinquency in a Birth Cohort in Philadelphia Pennsylvania, 1945–1963," Inter-university Consortium for Political and Social Research, 1986.
31. Marisela B. Gomez, *Race, Class, Power, and Organizing in East Baltimore: Rebuilding Abandoned Communities in America* (Lanham, MD: Lexington Books, 2013), p. 225; Jim Haner, "Experts Fault Enforcement of City Lead Laws," *Baltimore Sun*, December 24, 1999, p. 1.
32. "Pang Gets 35 Years for Deadly Warehouse Fire," *Kitsap Sun*, March 24, 1998.
33. See "Orchard Lands," GIS map at Dirt Alert, Washington State Department of Ecology, https://apps.ecology.wa.gov/dirtalert/orchard?lat=47.996860&lon=-119.948198&zoom=9.
34. Thelma F. Wilson's February 1, 1972, marriage certificate to Charles Dwayne Milner gives his address as 1040 1st Street, Wenatchee, Washington, a property one block south of a contaminated orchard and several blocks north of Washington Park, also contaminated. See Orchard Lands map, Dirt Alert.
35. Dee Riggs, "An Escalating Evil: Seeds of Deviancy Planted in Childhood, Experts Say," *Wenatchee World*, April 24, 2005.
36. Vernon J. Geberth, *Sex-Related Homicide and Death Investigation: Practical and Clinical Perspectives*, 2nd ed. (Boca Raton, FL: CRC, 2010), pp. 404–5, 408–9.
37. Geberth, *Sex-Related Homicide*, p. 405.
38. Associated Press, "Pickup Tied Man to Deaths," *Spokesman-Review* (Spokane), April 21, 1995, p. 6.
39. Riggs, "Escalating Evil."
40. Questions remain about the authenticity of letters purportedly sent by Jack the Ripper, but the "From Hell" letter is considered to be genuine by many Ripperologists. See Stewart P. Evans and Keith Skinner, *Jack the Ripper: Letters from Hell* (Gloucestershire, UK: Sutton, 2001), pp. 58–64.
41. Alexis de Tocqueville, *Journeys to England and Ireland*, trans. George Lawrence and K. P. Mayer, ed. J. P. Mayer (New Brunswick, NJ: Transaction, 1988), pp. 107–8.
42. Charles Dickens, *Bleak House* (1853; New York: Penguin Books, 1971), p. 49. Rick Nevin, *Lucifer Curves: The Legacy of Lead Poisoning* (self-pub., BookBaby, 2016), loc. 771 of 1406, Kindle. Nevins quotes from Charles Dickens, "A Small Star in the East," *All the Year Round*, December 19, 1868.
43. Wendy Lyons Sunshine, "Bituminous Coal Characteristics and Applications," ThoughtCo., January 29, 2020, thoughtco.com/bituminous-coal-characteristics-applications-1182545.

44. Nevin, *Lucifer Curves*, loc. 732–745 of 1406.
45. "She's Not There," by Rod Argent, recorded by the Zombies, 1964.
46. Herbert L. Needleman et al., "Bone Lead Levels and Delinquent Behavior," *Journal of the American Medical Association* 275, no. 5 (February 7, 1996): p. 368.
47. Denworth, *Toxic Truth*, p. 197.
48. Lizz Giordano, "Many Everett Families Still Live amid Arsenic and Lead," *HeraldNet* (Everett, WA), June 26, 2018; Associated Press, "Asarco to Buy 20 Homes at Old Site," *News Tribune* (Tacoma), February 10, 1994.
49. Maureen Callahan, *American Predator* (New York: Viking, 2019), p. 189.
50. Callahan, *American Predator*, p. 188.
51. Jim Lynch, "Double Amputee Vanishes from Home," *Spokesman-Review* (Spokane), March 14, 1996, p. 17.
52. "Trail of Death Follows White Supremacist Gang Led by Chevie Kehoe," *Intelligence Report* (Southern Poverty Law Center), December 15, 1998.
53. See Callahan, *American Predator*, pp. 249–52.
54. Associated Press, "Company News; ASARCO Signs Merger Pact with Grupo Mexico," *New York Times*, October 26, 1999.
55. Burl Barer, *Body Count* (New York: Pinnacle Books, 2002), p. 23.
56. The address given for Robert L. Yates in the 1969 and 1973 Oak Harbor, Whidbey Island, telephone directories is 3038 East 300th, near the entrance to the naval base. The address no longer exists after streets were renamed, but older maps of Oak Harbor show 300 Avenue East directly north of Pioneer Way and adjacent to the base; see "Street Map of Oak Harbor, North Whidbey Island," Island County Historical Society.
57. "Site Profile: Naval Air Station, Whidbey Island (Seaplane Base), Whidbey Island, WA," Environmental Protection Agency, cumulis.epa.gov/supercpad/Site Profiles/index.cfm?fuseaction=second.Cleanup&id=1001127#bkground.
58. Bill Morlin and Jeanette White, *Bad Trick: The Hunt for Spokane's Serial Killer* (Spokane, WA: New Media Ventures, 2001), p. 161.
59. Morlin and White, *Bad Trick*, p. 158.
60. Rule, *Green River*, p. 437.
61. Maleng, "Prosecutor's Summary of Evidence," pp. 75–77. Ridgway took the decomposed remains of Denise Bush and Shirley Sherrill to Oregon in April 1984 on a camping trip.
62. Sara Jean Green, "Remains of a Green River Killer Victim Found near Issaquah," *Seattle Times*, November 23, 2005. The skull of Tracy Winston, killed in 1983, was left on a logging road off Highway 18. Ann Rule asserted that Ridgway "knew a lot" about Bundy: Rule, *Green River*, p. 501.
63. "Tacoma Smelter Plume: What Areas Are Most Affected?," Tacoma–Pierce County Health Department, tpchd.org/healthy-homes/dirt-alert-tacoma-smelter-plume/what-areas-are-most-affected.
64. "Superfund Site: Fort Lewis Logistics Center, Tillicum, WA," Environmental Protection Agency, cumulis.epa.gov/supercpad/cursites/csitinfo.cfm?id=1001131.
65. In addition to the serial killers associated with Fort Lewis described in this book, Duane Elton, a Fort Lewis GI, murdered two women at the base in 1984; Timothy Burkhart, a native of Parkland (the neighborhood adjoining Joint Base Lewis–McChord's north end), murdered two girls and two women in Pierce County between 1986 and 2001; Benjamin Colton Barnes, formerly a soldier at JBLM, shot

four at a party on January 31, 2012, and the following day shot and killed a park ranger, Margaret Anderson, at Mount Rainier National Park; in March 2012, Staff Sergeant Robert Bales, based at JBLM and deployed in Kandahar Province, Afghanistan, on his fourth combat tour, killed sixteen civilians in a massacre. This is a partial list.

66. Derek Turner, "Joint Base Lewis–McChord Rocked by Scandal," *Stars and Stripes*, December 27, 2010.
67. Paul LaRosa, *Tacoma Confidential: A True Story of Murder, Suicide, and a Police Chief's Secret Life* (New York: Signet, 2006), p. 4.
68. Dan McShane, "The Grassy Knoll—Tacoma's," *Reading the Washington Landscape*, May 13, 2010, washingtonlandscape.blogspot.com/2010/05/grassy-knoll-tacomas.html.
69. Gregory L. Glass, "Maximum Arsenic Concentration at Tacoma Smelter Plume Sample Locations (King and Pierce Counties)" and "Maximum Lead Concentration at Tacoma Smelter Plume Sample Locations (King and Pierce Counties)," *Credible Evidence Report*, pp. 120–21.
70. Links to all four Dirt Alert plume maps can be found at Dirt Alert, Washington State Department of Ecology, ecology.wa.gov/dirtalert/?lat=47.273840&lon=-122.500000&zoom=11.

CHAPTER 13: The Fog Warning

1. See afterword in Caroline Fraser, *God's Perfect Child: Living and Dying in the Christian Science Church*, 20th anniv. ed. (New York: Picador, 2019), pp. 525–26.
2. David O. Carpenter, Rick Nevin, "Environmental Causes of Violence," *Physiology & Behavior* 99 (2010), pp. 260–68.
3. Kevin Drum, "Lead: America's Real Criminal Element," *Mother Jones*, January/February 2013.
4. Jessica Wolpaw Reyes, "Environmental Policy as Social Policy? The Impact of Childhood Lead Exposure on Crime," *B.E. Journal of Economic Analysis & Policy* 7, no. 1 (2007); see abstract.
5. Reyes, "Environmental Policy"; see pp. 19–21 and figs. 2, 3, and 4.
6. "Asarco Bids to Be a Giant in Mining," *Business Week*, November 24, 1956, p. 114.
7. "Asarco Bids."
8. R. W. Straus, Chairman of the Board, American Smelting and Refining Company, to Mr. John Clark, President, and Mr. Reid Robinson, Vice President, International Union of Mine, Mill and Smelter Workers, letter, May 3, 1949, American Smelting and Refining Company (ASARCO) Records, Northwest Room, Tacoma Public Library.
9. Straus to Clark, May 3, 1949; see also Roger W. Straus to Mr. Earl R. Marble, Manager, American Smelting and Refining Company, Tacoma, Washington, letter, May 11, 1949.
10. For Hempstead House, see Unger and Unger, *Guggenheims*, p. 179.
11. Marcosson, *Metal Magic*, dedication page and p. 1.
12. Ian Parker, "Showboat: Roger Straus and His Flair for Selling Literature," *New Yorker*, March 31, 2002.
13. "In Numbers: Sackler Family, Purdue Pharma and the US Opioid Crisis," *BBC News*, September 16, 2010, bbc.com/news/world-us-canada-49718388.

14. John Miller, "Killer Tied to Seattle Sisters' Deaths," *HeraldNet* (Everett, WA), January 23, 2007.
15. Sam Verhovek, "Missing Girl Found with Sex Offender," *Los Angeles Times*, July 3, 2005, p. A8.
16. Details of Duncan's final crimes are drawn from Gary C. King, *Stolen in the Night* (New York: St. Martin's Paperbacks, 2007), pp. 122–26; see also Susan Drumheller, "Deputy: Duncan Stalked Family," *Idaho Spokesman-Review*, July 13, 2005, pp. 1, 4.
17. Debby Abe, "Sex Suspect Denies Guilt," *News Tribune* (Tacoma), May 23, 1989, pp. 1, 16.
18. Les Blumenthal, "U.S. Company Says Its Owner Stole Peruvian Copper Mines," McClatchy DC, May 25, 2007, mcclatchydc.com/latest-news/article24460858.html.
19. Callahan, *American Predator*, p. 198.
20. Erwin Raisz, "The Olympic-Wallowa Lineament," *American Journal of Science* 243-A (1945): p. 480.
21. Ron Judd, "Our Deep Lakes Incite Curiosity and Conjure Legends," *Seattle Times*, August 8, 2014.
22. See Mavis Amundson, "Lady of the Lake," *HistoryLink.org Online Encyclopedia of Washington State History*, June 5, 2008, historylink.org/File/8599.
23. P. B. Stretesky and M. J. Lynch, "The Relationship between Lead Exposure and Homicide," *Archives of Pediatrics & Adolescent Medicine* 155, no. 5 (May 2001): pp. 579–82.
24. Yaling Yang et al., "Volume Reduction in Prefrontal Gray Matter in Unsuccessful Criminal Psychopaths," *Biological Psychiatry* 57, no. 10 (May 15, 2005): pp. 1103–8, pubmed.ncbi.nlm.nih.gov/15866549.
25. Kim M. Cecil et al., "Decreased Brain Volume in Adults with Childhood Lead Exposure," *PLoS Medicine* 5, no. 5 (May 2008), ncbi.nlm.nih.gov/pmc/articles/PMC2689675.
26. Travis Beckwith et al., "Reduced Regional Volumes Associated with Total Psychopathy Scores in an Adult Population with Childhood Lead Exposure," *Neurotoxicology* 67 (July 2018), pp. 1–26.
27. Travis J. Beckwith et al., "Criminal Arrests Associated with Reduced Brain Volumes in an Adult Population with Documented Childhood Lead Exposure," *Environmental Research* 201 (October 2021). See also Feyza Sancar, "Childhood Lead Exposure May Affect Personality, Mental Health in Adulthood," *JAMA Network* (March 2019), jamanetwork.com/journals/jama/fullarticle/2729713.
28. Cecil et al., "Decreased Brain Volume."
29. Taylor Stacy, "Putting Methods to the Madness: Serial Killer Statistics," March 4, 2023, sites.lsa.umich.edu/qmss/2023/03/04/serial-killer-statistics.
30. In 2023 it was announced that Dennis Rader is now considered the prime suspect in two unsolved murder cases, one involving a sixteen-year-old girl who disappeared in 1976 from Pawhuska, Oklahoma, and the other a twenty-two-year-old woman whose body was found in 1990 in Missouri; see Remy Tumin and Derrick Bryson Taylor, "B.T.K. Killer Named as Prime Suspect in Two Unsolved Cases," *New York Times*, August 24, 2023.
31. Kerri Rawson, *A Serial Killer's Daughter: My Story of Faith, Love, and Overcoming* (Nashville: Nelson Books, 2019), p. 192.
32. Ramsland, *Confession of a Serial Killer*, pp. 194–95, 198–99.

33. Ramsland, *Confession of a Serial Killer*, p. 201.
34. Rawson, *Serial Killer's Daughter*, p. 127.
35. Rawson, *Serial Killer's Daughter*, p. 192.
36. Jodi Wilgoren, "BTK Killer Is Sentenced to Consecutive Life Terms," *Deseret News*, August 19, 2005.
37. Office of Public Affairs, U.S. Department of Justice, "Largest Environmental Bankruptcy in U.S. History Will Result in Payment of $1.79 Billion Towards Environmental Cleanup & Restoration," press release, December 10, 2009.
38. Daniel Jack Chasan, "Asarco's Unlikely Boon to the Environment," *Crosscut*, February 17, 2010; Julie Titone, "Bunker Hill Landmark Demolished; Baghouse Had a Dubious History during Silver Valley Contamination," *Spokesman-Review* (Spokane), March 21, 1995.
39. Matt Hongoltz-Hetling, "Babygirl," Weather Channel, March 23, 2021.
40. Melissa del Bosque, "Dirty Money," *Texas Observer,* October 31, 2008.
41. Melissa del Bosque, "Back in Business?," *Texas Observer*, October 31, 2008.
42. The El Paso smelter did not reopen; its smokestacks were demolished in 2013. See "A Look at Asarco through the Years," *El Paso Times*, September 22, 2020.
43. John Gillie, "The Path to Point Ruston," *News Tribune* (Tacoma), February 3, 2008.
44. Bill Baarsma, interview with the author, June 20, 2023; Susan Gordon, "Neighbors Give Mixed Reviews to Asarco Plan," *News Tribune* (Tacoma), January 10, 2003, p. B1.
45. City of Tacoma Public Works Department, "Final Supplemental Environmental Impact Statement to the ASARCO Smelter Site, Master Development Plan Final EIS," prepared for Point Ruston, March 2008, sec. 3.4-2.
46. The following account of Israel Keyes's abduction and murder of Bill and Lorraine Currier is drawn from a series of FBI interviews with Keyes and from Callahan, *American Predator*, pp. 148–59. See also Michelle Theriault Boots, "Unsealed Interviews Detail Two Lives of Alaska Serial Killer Israel Keyes," *Anchorage Daily News*, May 19, 2018. This article contains links to audio interviews conducted with Keyes by the FBI, interviews that were unsealed after Callahan sued for their release in federal court in Alaska.
47. Callahan, *American Predator*, p. 156.
48. Peter Waldman, "The EPA Can't Wait to Reopen the Mine that Poisoned North Idaho," *Bloomberg Businessweek*, November 12, 2018.
49. Callahan, *American Predator*, p. 112.
50. Callahan, *American Predator*, p. 112.
51. Callahan, *American Predator*, p. 116.
52. There's "limited empirical work" on necrophilia, according to Jens Foell and Christopher J. Patrick, authors of "A Neuroscientific Perspective on Morbid Paraphilias," in *Understanding Necrophilia: A Global Multidisciplinary Approach,* eds. Lee Mellor, Anil Aggrawal, and Eric Hickey (Solana Beach, CA: Cognella, 2017), p. 183.
53. Callahan, *American Predator*, p. 118.
54. Callahan, *American Predator*, p. 122.
55. Kelly T. Wood, "Teck in its Tweens: An Update on 12 Years of Litigation over the Canadian Smelter," Northport Project, Northport, WA, November 28, 2020.
56. "Overdose, Not Thallium, Killed Worker," *Vancouver Sun*, August 21, 2002, p. 9.

57. Adrienne Tanner, "Tremors Leave Carpenter, 23, Unable to Return to His Trade," *The Province* (Vancouver, BC), April 21, 2002.
58. Tom Goldman, "Swimming the Columbia River," *Morning Edition*, NPR, June 26, 2003; Christopher Swain, "Christopher Swain, Columbia River Swimmer," *Grist*, June 11, 2002.
59. "CDC's Recommended Terminology When Discussing Children's Blood Lead Levels," Centers for Disease Control and Prevention.
60. M. G. Aamodt, *Serial Killer Statistics*, report based on the Radford University/ FGCU Serial Killer Database, September 4, 2016, Serial Killer Information Center, maamodt.asp.radford.edu/serial%20killer%20information%20center/Serial%20Killer%20Statistics.pdf.
61. Washington State Department of Ecology, "Frequently Asked Questions: Tacoma Smelter Plume: Cleanup Levels & Action Levels for Soil Arsenic and Lead," October 2016, apps.ecology.wa.gov/publications/documents/1109095.pdf.
62. Washington State Department of Ecology, *Tacoma Smelter Plume Annual Report, Fiscal Year 2020*, pub. 20-09-082, (Olympia, WA: Washington State Department of Ecology, Southwest Regional Office, 2021), p. 19, apps.ecology.wa.gov/publications/documents/2009082.pdf.
63. Cliff White, "Coast Guard, Firefighters Still Battling Blaze Onboard Trident Seafoods' Kodiak Enterprise," Seafood Source, April 13, 2023, www.seafoodsource.com/news/supply-trade/coast-guard-firefighters-still-battling-blaze-onboard-trident-seafoods-kodiak-enterprise.
64. Chit Ming Wong et al., "Cancer Mortality Risks from Long-Term Exposure to Ambient Fine Particle," *Cancer Epidemiology, Biomarkers & Prevention* 25, no. 5 (May 1, 2016), pp. 839–45.
65. Frank Herbert, *Dune* (New York: Berkley Books, 1965), p. 294. The wording on the plaque differs slightly from the text in the book, which reads: "The highest function of ecology is understanding consequences."
66. Waldman, "The EPA Can't Wait." See also Environmental Protection Agency, "Department of Justice, EPA Reach Agreement with Two Idaho Mining Companies to Secure Wastewater Treatment and Remove a Barrier to New Mining Operations: Settlement Paves the Way for Fresh Start with New Mine Operator," press release, March 12, 2018.

IMAGE CREDITS

Page 1, top: Tacoma Booklet, 1911 #2002.20.1, Washington State Historical Society, Tacoma (Wash.)

Page 1, bottom: Tacoma Historical Society

Page 2, top: Northwest Room at The Tacoma Public Library, Richards Studio D9946-10

Page 2, bottom: Museum of History & Industry, Seattle, Post-Intelligencer Collection, 1986.5.36878.1

Page 3: Library of Congress, LC-USZ62-46682

Page 4, top: U.S. Army Military History Institute

Page 4, bottom: Northwest Room at The Tacoma Public Library, Richards Studio D41635-2

Page 6, top: Courtesy of Rebecca Morris

Page 6, bottom: Family archive

Page 7, bottom: *The News Tribune*, December 12, 1972. Photo by Warren Anderson. All rights reserved. Used under license.

Page 8, bottom: King County Archives

Page 10, top: FBI

Page 10, bottom: *Miami Herald*. Photo by Bill Frakes. Bettmann Archive via Getty Images

Page 11: United States Geological Survey

Page 12: Courtesy of Museum of History & Industry, Seattle, Post-Intelligencer Collection 2000.107.166.17.01. Photo by Dave Potts.

Page 13, top: King Couty Sheriff's Office courtesy of Wikimedia Commons

Page 15, top: Los Angeles Police Department courtesy of Wikimedia Commons

Page 15, bottom: FBI

Page 16, top: EPA / Alamy Stock Photo

Page 16, middle: Washington State Department of Ecology

Page 16, bottom: Courtesy of Rick Nevin

INDEX

Abersold, John, 98–99
acid rain, 64, 124, 268, 306, 316–17
ADT (American District Telegraph), 226–27, 330
Age of Aquarius, 96–97
Aime, Jim, 197
Aime, Laura, 188–89, 196–98, 212
Aime, Shirleen, 189, 197, 242
air pollution, 46–47, 351–53
    Bunker Hill smelter, 119–21, 154, 173–75, 247, 255
    Clean Air Act, 62, 93, 104, 318–19
    Cottrell's paper on smelters, 39
    El Paso smelter, 65–66, 98–99, 108–9, 247, 267–68, 352–53, 385
    in England, 224–25, 359–60
    EPA and, 317–19, 351, 386
    Hammett's Poisonville, 42–43
    Herbert's vision, 70
    Ruston smelter, 40–43, 44–45, 49–50, 61–62, 70, 77, 93, 109–10, 112–13, 124, 163, 183, 220, 223–24, 227–28, 244, 247–48, 253, 290–91, 305–6, 308–9, 316–17, 318–19, 332, 368, 369–70
    World War II and, 203–4
"Air That I Breathe, The" (song), 137
Alamein to Zem Zem (Douglas), 200–202
Alaska gold rush, 16, 36, 111
Alaskan Way Viaduct, 367–68
Allen, Katherine Jean, 303
Allen, Robert, 195
All the President's Men (Woodward and Bernstein), 158
Alphabet Murders, 287
Alsos, Judy, 61

Altig, Douglas, 307
aluminum, 148, 201, 202, 211
Amalgamated Copper Company, 34
American Brake Shoe Foundry, 286–87
American Fork Canyon, 196–97
American Smelting and Refining Company (ASARCO), 64, 65–66, 190, 202, 374–75.
    See also specific smelters
    bankruptcy of, 379, 384–85
    founding of, 34–35
    name change of, 210
    pollution and environmental issues, 39, 44–46, 59, 62, 98–99, 108–10, 124, 211, 220–21, 223, 227–28, 244–45, 247–48, 253, 267–68, 306, 316–19, 369–70, 379, 385–86, 396
    public campaigns and litigation against, 38, 223–24, 247–48, 308–9, 319, 379, 384–85
    sale to Grupo México, 364–65, 379, 385
    valuation of, 45–46
    worker injuries and deaths, 112–13, 175, 223–24, 243–45
American Society of Civil Engineers, 20
Anaconda Copper Mine, 34, 98, 202
Anderson, Kimberly, 380
Anderson, Margaret, 449*n*
antimony, 66, 90, 181, 203
Apollo 1, 72
Apollo 11, 77, 79
Armstrong, Phyllis, 148–49, 150, 155
arsenic, 40–42
    applications, 38–39
    OSHA standards, 59*n*, 211, 223–24, 291
    Pinto's study, 62, 93, 98, 112, 113, 130, 244–45

INDEX

arsenic, (cont.)
   soil cleanup, 395–96, 397
   smelter operations, 31, 38–39, 40–42, 49–50, 90, 120, 175, 223–24, 253, 291, 309, 319, 349–50, 353, 361, 384, 386, 389
   toxicity, 39, 41–42, 49–50, 59–60, 91, 112–13, 130, 204, 223–24, 228, 244–45, 248, 253, 291, 309, 316, 319, 348, 349, 361, 370, 386, 389
Arsenic and Old Lace (play), 59–60
"arsenic showers," 50, 248
Arsenic Trioxide Site, 42
Aryan Peoples Republic, 363–64
ASARCO. *See* American Smelting and Refining Company
asbestos, 64, 287, 375, 379
Astor, John Jacob, 37
Ayers, Cherie Lynn, 307
Aynesworth, Hugh, 299–300

Baader-Meinhof Gang, 211
Baarsma, Bill, 91, 117, 386
Baarsma, Clarence, 117–18, 244
Bach, Richard, 139–40, 301–2
Baird, Nancy, 224
Baker, Brenda Joy, 235
Baker Lake, 219
Bales, Robert, 449n
Ball, Brenda Carol, 149, 215, 216, 309
Barnes, Colton, 448–49n
Bartholomew, Wynn, 214
Bascom, Clifford, 283–84
Bastian, Jennifer, 331
Battle of El Alamein, 199–200
Baum, L. Frank, 41
Bax, James, 173–74, 181
Beast of British Columbia, 1, 404n
Beatles, the, 126, 289–90
Beethe, Carol, 340–41
Bell Curve, The (Murray and Herrnstein), 354
Bell, Eddie Wayne, 335
Bellevue bombing, 296–98
Bellew, Jim, 165–66
"Benghazi boiler," 200
benzene, 15, 31, 65, 204, 352
Bianchi, Kenneth, 1, 262, 277–78, 286–88, 328, 403–4n
Bianchi, Nicholas, 286–87
Binam, Lowell D., 130
Black Angus, 339, 340
Blake, Krista Kay, 157, 165
Blanchard, Lawrence, Jr., 247–48
Blauman, Byron, 116, 296
Blauman, Owen, 253, 296
Bleak House (Dickens), 359–60
Bonner, Debra "Dub," 312
Boone, Carole Ann, 147, 263, 299
Boston Strangler, 293
Bountiful, Utah, 183, 187, 192–94, 224, 231
Bowe, Joyce, 70

Bowman, Margaret, 269, 270, 295–96
Boxcar Killer, 1, 403n
Bradley, Fred, 35–36
Bradley, Maria, 347–48
Brady, Ian, 225
Brainerd, Scott, 216
Brame, David, 369–70
Brattain, Walter Houser, 350
Bremerton Navy Yard, 22
Brendle, Paul, 343
Bretz, J. Harlen, 17
Bridges, Doss, 319
Brigham Young University, 196, 224, 249
Bright, Kathryn, 140–42, 184–85, 276
Bright, Kevin, 141
Brisbois, Kathy, 366
Broom (magazine), 40
Browne, John Henry, 279
Brudevold, Peter, 326, 334–35
Brudos, Jerome "Jerry," 41–42, 59, 94, 100–101
B.T.K. *See* Rader, Dennis
Bullat, Jerry, 143
Bundy, Carol, 204
Bundy, Johnnie Culpepper, 48–49
Bundy, Louise Cowell, 28–32, 47–49, 94, 102, 336
   son's execution, 338
   son's murders, 234–35, 296
Bundy, Theodore Robert "Ted"
   Ann Rule and. *See* Rule, Ann, relationship with Bundy
   arrest of 1975, 228–36
   arrest of 1978, 278–79, 280
   birth and paternity of, 28–30, 407n
   colleges and universities, 92–95, 99, 107–8, 110, 113–14, 115, 119, 135, 140, 143, 147
   death row, confession, and execution of, 311, 337–39
   early life of, 30–32, 47–49, 53, 54–56, 89, 91–92, 336
   escapes and escape attempts, 259–60, 262–63, 265–67, 324–25
   Gary Ridgway compared with, 314
   jobs of, 75, 93–94, 101, 103–4, 105, 112, 147
   Liz Kloepfer and. *See* Kloepfer, Elizabeth "Liz," relationship with Bundy
   murders, 2–3, 55–56, 70–71, 92, 93, 94, 99, 107–8, 110–11, 117, 118, 121, 125–26, 133–39, 143–44, 144–45, 148–52, 154–55, 157, 159–64, 175–77, 180–86, 188–89, 193–95, 196–98, 212, 213–14, 220–21, 222, 224, 250, 253, 268–71, 275–76, 280, 292, 338, 345
   murder attempts, 136–37, 179–80, 190–93
   police composite sketch of, 166–67, 170
   police surveillance of, 180, 232–34
   politics and, 95, 111–12, 117, 118, 234
   trial of 1976, 241–43
   trial of 1976 presentencing, 245–47, 248–51
   trial of 1979, 292, 294–96

INDEX

trial of 1980, 298–300
trial appeal of 1989, 335–38
Bunker Hill Mine and Smelting Complex, 35–36, 39, 129–30, 150, 173–75, 195, 397
    air pollution, 119–21, 154, 173–75, 247, 255
    shutting down, 306
    temporary shut down, 181
Bunker Hill Superfund Site, 377, 389–90
Buono, Angelo, Jr., 262, 287–88, 403–4n
Burgoyne, Art, 45–46
Burkhart, Timothy, 448n
Burr, Ann Marie, 2–3, 54–56, 135, 250, 338, 345–46, 413n

cadmium, 31, 66, 90, 108, 120, 146, 175, 181, 240, 291, 317, 323, 324, 349, 350, 353, 361, 389
Calder, Alexander, 298
Caldwell, David, 283
Caligula, 20, 47
Campbell, Caryn, 213–14, 232, 241, 253, 259
Campbell, Charles Rodman, 168–69, 311, 361–62
cancer, 60, 62, 131, 347–48, 397. *See also* lung cancer
Capote, Truman, 123
Carlisle, Al, 249–50, 338
Carnegie, Dale, 53
Carrie (King), 141–42
Carrillo, Gil, 328–29
Carson, Rachel, 211
Carter, Jimmy, 281
Carter, Rosalynn, 284
Cassidy, David, 115
Castle, Jamie, 115–16
Catalinich, Mary, 309
Catlow, William, 287–88
CCC (Civilian Conservation Corps), 41
CDC (Centers for Disease Control), 61, 353
    lead poisoning, 51n, 279–80, 330, 347, 395
Central Washington University, 142, 143
Cepeda, Dolores "Dolly," 277
Chandler, Karen, 269–70, 271
Chapman, Marcia, 312–13
Chapman, Mark David, 336
Charley, Mindy, 339–40, 346
Cherberg, Johnny, 151, 281
Chi Omega, 268–71, 292, 294–96, 300, 378, 437n
Christian Science, 82, 97, 139, 178–79, 251, 254, 256, 281, 290
chromium, 175, 212, 218, 349
Churchill, Winston, 201
Cincinnati Lead Study, 381
Circus McGurkus, 258
Citizens' Committee on Air Pollution, 61
Ciudad Juárez, 66, 108–9, 352–53
Clapton, Eric, 137
Clark, Lisa, 296–97
Clean Air Act, 62, 93, 104, 318–19
Cle Elum, 4, 110–11, 112, 156
Clinton, Bill, 354
Clinton, Hillary, 354–55

Clutter family murders, 123
Coatsworth, Leonard, 23
cocaine, 116, 301, 321, 326, 329, 332, 334
Coeur d'Alene, Lake, 154, 389–90
Coeur d'Alene River, 154, 389
Coffield, Wendy, 312, 313
Cohen, Mike, 385–86
Coin Shop Killer, 1, 404n
Coleman, James, Jr., 336–37
College of Puget Sound, 32, 47
Columbus, Kansas, 122, 420n
Colville Reservation, 349–50
Cominco, 348–50, 363, 392–94
Commencement Bay, 32–33, 35, 69–70
Connally, John, 158
Cooper, D.B., 106
copper, 64, 98–99, 203, 211, 243–44, 291, 379
Corbitt, Tarayon, 366–67
Corll, Dean (aka Candy Man), 299
Cosden, William Earl, Jr., 204, 235
Costello, Elvis, 300
Cotton, Eugene, 315, 442n
Cottrell electrostatic precipitator, 244
Cottrell, Frederick Gardner, 39, 244
Countryman, Norma, 165
Courson, Gregory, 289
Cowell, Edna, 133, 236
Cowell, John, 32, 47, 48–49, 95, 236
Cowell, Samuel, 30, 31–32
Cox, Archibald, 121–22
Crafton, Elaine, 119
crazy walls, 6–7, 29, 396
"Cremation of Sam McGee, The" (Service), 16
Crescent, Lake, 380–81
Crew, Raymond, 294–95
crime-lead hypothesis. *See* lead poisoning, crime hypothesis
crime rates, 129–30, 211–12, 222, 235–36, 315, 329–30, 373, 433n, 442n
Cronkite, Walter, 76
Cubias, Carmen, 376
Culver, Lynnette, 222
Cunningham, Julie, 220, 222
Currier, Bill, 387–89, 451n
Currier, Lorraine, 387–89, 451n
Curtis, Jane, 142
Curtis, Susan, 224
Cutchins family, 174
Cuyahoga River fire of 1969, 104, 317
cyanide, 31, 148, 218

Daffodil Festival, 178
Daffodil Princess, 150–51, 281
Dahmer, Jeffrey, 284
Dark Shadows (TV show), 179, 239
DaRonch, Carol, 190–93, 194, 212, 232, 233, 241–43, 246
Davis, Dana, 350–51
Davis, Dolores, 347, 382
Davis, Penny, 350–51, 356, 358

457

INDEX

Davis, Ross, 117, 118, 234
Dawson, Pete, 260–61
DDT, 60
Deadwood Gulch, 120, 173–74, 306
Deahn, Amber, 378
DeAngelo, Joseph, 204
DeFreeze, Donald, 142
Denver, John, 168
De Rocco, Eddie, 115–16
Devine, Katherine Merry, 235
Diamond, Neil, 254–55
Díaz, Porfirio, 65
Dickens, Charles, 359–60
Didion, Joan, 320
Dietz, Park, 322
Dilulio, John, 354–55
Dirty Harry (movie), 144
Dismemberment Murders, 1, 404*n*
DNA, 333, 346, 358, 378, 382, 383
Dobson, James, 338
Dr. Strangelove (movie), 7, 204
D'Olivo, Kathleen, 143
Domesday Book, 7
Doty, Donna, 66–67
Douglas, Keith, 200–202, 205
Dubner, Stephen J., 373
Duncan, Joseph Edward, III, 228, 291, 369, 375–79
Dune (Herbert), 69–70
Dune Peninsula, 396–97
Duniway Park, 217–18
Dunn, Roger, 176
DuPont, 51–52, 60, 100, 204, 321
Durant, Will, 405*n*
Dust Bowl, 41
Duwamish River, 87, 312
Duwamish Tribe, 25, 58, 68

earthquakes, 3–4, 18, 19, 44, 69, 219, 302, 367–68, 395
East Channel Bridge, 20–21, 24, 63, 67, 315
East Helena smelter, 223
East Seattle School, 80, 253–54
Eastside Killer. *See* Russell, George Waterfield, Jr.
Eastwood, Clint, 144, 158
Echo Lake Cutoff, 215
ecology, use of term, 69
Eddy, Mary Baker, 82, 97, 178–79, 245, 301, 372
Edwards, Diane, 93, 106, 117, 119, 122, 125, 250
Ehrlichman, John, 210–11
election of 1968, 76, 77, 95, 97
election of 1984, 323
Eliot, T. S., 285
Elizabeth Lund Home for Unwed Mothers, 29–30, 31
Elledge, James Homer, 204, 434*n*
Ellis, Connie LaFontaine, 367
Ellison, Harlan, 255–56, 289
El Paso smelter, 64–66, 385

air pollution, 65–66, 98–99, 108–9, 247, 267–68, 352–53, 385
electrical power failure of 1978, 267–68
shuts down, 353
Elton, Duane, 448*n*
Emerson, Cassie, 362–63
Emerson, Marlene, 362–63
EPA (Environmental Protection Agency), 317–19, 377, 392–93, 397
air pollution, 59*n*, 174–75, 317–19, 351, 386
ASARCO and, 220, 384, 386, 396
leaded gasoline, 113, 247, 351
lead poisoning, 53*n*, 174–75, 317–18
Ernst, Max, 46
Ethyl Corporation, 52, 60, 247
Evans, Dan, 111–12, 115, 117, 118, 418*n*
Evans, Ellis, 271–72
Everett smelter, 36, 38, 370, 384, 386
Evergreen Point Floating Bridge, 59, 63, 135–36, 151, 343–44
Evergreen State College, 138–39, 147
Exorcist, The (movie), 184

factor X, 276–77
Fallon, Virgil, 130
Faraday, David Arthur, 97–98
Farrar, Straus and Company, 374–75
FBI (Federal Bureau of Investigations), 106, 130, 236, 241–42, 322, 325, 337, 394, 395
Highway Serial Killings Initiative, 307
Ten Most Wanted Fugitives list, 267, 276
Uniform Crime Reports, 211–12
Feinstein, Dianne, 329
Feldman, Debra, 394
femicides, 353
Ferraro, Geraldine, 323
Ferris, Sybil, 93–94, 249
Fix, Darcey Renee, 307
Flame Tavern, 149, 215, 309
Flaming Gorge, 155–56
Flanary, Robert, 58–59
Fletcher, Arthur, 95
floating bridges, 19–27
Florida State Prison, 299, 339
Florida State University (FSU), 267, 268–71, 294–96
Fly, The (movie), 105
Focus on the Family, 338
Fog Warning, The (Homer), 371, 372
Forbes, Ben, 185, 230–31
Forrest, Warren Leslie, 107, 148, 157, 165, 170, 180, 182, 204, 235
Forster, Hans, 63
Fort Lewis, 48, 168, 240, 332, 364, 365, 367, 368, 369, 435*n*, 448–49*n*
Fort Vancouver High School, 106, 148, 180
Fox, Nancy, 264, 272–73, 276, 382–83
Frank Herbert Trail, 396–97
Fraser Glaciation, 16–17
Fraser, Scott, 107, 116

458

INDEX

Frazier, John Linley, 204
Freakonomics (Dubner and Levitt), 373
Freeman, Bonnie Jo, 108
Friend, Gerald, 331–32
frontal cortex, 266, 336, 381–82
Funicello, Annette, 123, 127

Gacy, John Wayne, 204, 284
Gallagher, Owen, 227–28
Garcia, Lisa, 307–8
Garfield County Jail, 259–60, 262–63, 265, 266
Garland, Judy, 80
Garrow, Robert, 231
gasoline. *See* leaded gasoline
GASP (Group Against Smog Pollution), 247
Gates, Bill, III, 59
Gaye, Marvin, 320
General Cartography (Raisz), 4–5
General Motors, 51–52, 60
geology, overview of, 16–19
Georgia-Pacific, 287–88
Gifford Pinchot National Forest, 302–3
Gilchrist, Diane, 147–48
Giske, Mark, 316
Gjendem, Gerald, 67
glacial lake outburst floods, 17–18
Glass, Gregory L., 370
Glenwood Springs, 213, 220, 265
Go Ask Alice (Sparks), 116
Gohl, Billy, 111
Golden Gate Bridge, 22, 86, 329
Good Housekeeping, 81, 82, 116
Gorsuch, Anne, 317–18
Graham, Janice, 159, 160
Grand Coulee Dam, 19, 202, 349
Granger, Don, 184, 228
Grant, Gary Gene, 310
graphite, 33, 45
Great Depression, 42
Great Domesday, 7, 212
Green Bay Packers, 131, 218, 306
Green Lake, 155
Greenpeace, 247, 308–9, 319
Green River Killer. *See* Ridgway, Gary
Green River Task Force, 321, 325
Gregorich, Christine, 221
Gregory, Teri, 297
Grissim, Jamie R., 106–7, 147–48
Groene family, 377–78
groundwater. *See* water pollution
Grund, Kevin, 283
Grupo México, 365, 379, 385
Guggenheim, Barbara Meyer, 33–34, 40
Guggenheim, Benjamin, 34, 37–38, 46
Guggenheim, Daniel, 34, 38, 374, 375
Guggenheim, Gladys, 374
Guggenheim, Harry Frank, 40
Guggenheim, John Simon, 34, 46
Guggenheim, Marguerite "Peggy," 37–38, 46, 298

Guggenheim, Meyer, 33–35, 37, 38, 40, 46, 298
Guggenheim, Solomon, 34, 46
Guggenheim, William, III, 298
Gulf Resources and Chemical Corporation, 120, 195
Gumm, Jeffrey A., 288
Gwinn, Sandy, 110, 246, 250, 418n

Haakanson, Heidi, 265
Hadley, Homer, 20–23
Hagmaier, William, 337
Hair (musical), 96
Haldeman, H.R., 210–11
Hall, Gaylord, 254–55
Hammett, Dashiell, 42–43, 409n
Hanford Dam, 202–3
Hannibal Lecter, 333–34
Hanson, Stewart, Jr., 242–43, 250–51
Happy Face Killer, 1, 404n
Hardy, Kerry May, 110–11, 418n
Harmon, Tom, 348
Harp, Carl, 168
Harris, Julie, 362
Harris, Kevin, 260
Harris, Thomas, 333–34, 361
Hartz, Billy J., 343
Hawkins, Georgann, 148–49, 150–52, 154–55, 161, 177, 216, 220, 336, 425n
Hawn, Stacy, 366
Hawn, Stacy Elizabeth, 335
Hayward, Pete, 185, 230
Hayward, Robert, 228–30
Healy, Lynda Ann, 131–35, 147, 216, 217, 230, 236
Hearst, Patricia, 135, 142, 145, 245
Hearst, Randolph, 245
Heath, Bert, 26
Heath, Ginger, 133
Hedge, Marine, 330
Heidnik, Gary, 204
Heinlein, Robert A., 255
Hemingway, Ernest, 40, 131
Hendrickson, Barbara, 168, 169, 311
Herbert, Frank, 69–70
Herbert (Frank) Trail, 396–97
Here Comes the Brides (TV show), 420–21n
Hergesheimer, Randy "Hergy," 186–87
hermit crabs, 95–96
Hernandez, Maria, 326–27
Herrnstein, Richard J., 354
Hibernia Bank robbery, 142, 245
Hillside Strangler, 1, 262, 277–78, 286–88, 328, 403–4n
Hilltop Crips, 331–32
Hindley, Myra, 225
Hinds, Cynthia, 312–13
Hirst, Russell, 232–33
Hofmann, Mark, 429n
Hollar, Vicki Lynn, 118, 419n
Holmes, Ronald, 337–38

INDEX

Holt, Doug, 56
Holt, Sandi, 56
Homer, Winslow, 371, 372
Hood Canal, 153
Hood Canal Bridge, 59, 288
Hooker Chemical Company, 204
Hoover, J. Edgar, 44, 130
hot prowlers, 138–39
House of Wax (movie), 122
Howard, Frank, 52
Hrvatin, Victor Joseph, 244
Huberty, James Oliver, 323–24
Hudspeth, Cindy, 277–78
Huffman, Rita, 357
Hull, Donald M., 245–47
Hull, Shari, 307–8
Humphrey, Hubert, 76, 77
Hunt, Cookie, 321
Hurkos, Peter, 293

Idaho State University, 222
I-5 Killer. *See* Woodfield, Randall
Illusions (Bach), 301
Imron, 321, 443*n*
In Cold Blood (Capote), 123
Index Killer, the, 1, 404*n*
Industrial Rock Products, Inc., 297
International Women's Year, 210, 219
"In the Night, What Things Move" (Fraser), 285–86
IQ tests, 354
IRATE (Island Residents Against Toxic Emissions), 247
iron, 90, 201, 202, 203, 223

Jackson, Michael, 320
Jack the Ripper, 192, 358–60
Jefferson Airplane, 142
Jekyll and Hyde, 173, 197–98, 250
Jensen, Betty Lou, 97–98
John, Elton, 210
Johns, Kathleen, 103
Johnson, Lyndon, 79
Johnson, Sonja, 277
Johnston, David, 303
Joint Base Lewis-McChord, 332, 368–69, 435*n*
Jolin, Annette, 217–18
Jolly, Rita Lorraine, 117
Jonathan Livingston Seagull (Bach), 139–40, 301
Jones, Rodger, 89–91, 93, 112–13, 130
Joseph, Jennifer, 367
Joy of Sex, The (Comfort), 231, 233, 341
Juan de Fuca plate, 18, 367
Juan de Fuca Strait, 5, 86, 152–53

Kaczynski, Ted, 204
Kaiser Aluminum, 211, 367
Kanizsa triangle, 5
Kappa Alpha Theta, 148–49, 150–52
Karr, Day Bradley, 303

Kastin, Elissa "Lissa," 277
Kehoe, Chevie, 349–50, 363–64, 380
Kehoe, Cheyne, 349–50, 363–64, 380
Kehoe, Robert A., 60, 61
Kemper, Ed, 204, 223
Kennecott Copper, 36, 190, 318
Kennedy, John F., 77
Kennedy, Robert F., 96–97
Kenney, Michael, 297
Kent, Belva, 242
Kent, Dean, 193–94
Kent, Debi, 193–95, 196, 212, 224
Kent State University shooting, 103
Keppel, Robert, 166, 212, 235, 236, 305, 333, 358
    background of, 165–65
    police search of, 164–65, 176–78, 214–17, 418*n*
    Bundy and Green River Killer, 325
    Bundy's appeal and interview, 335–38
    Bundy's arrest, 230–31
Kestenbaum, Joel, 107–8, 166
Keyes, Israel, 368
    arrest and trial of, 394–95
    birth and early life of, 265, 348–50, 362–65
    murders, 362–63, 379–81, 386–89, 390–92, 394, 451*n*
Keyes, Jeff and Heidi, 265, 348–49, 364
King County Law and Justice Planning Office, 113–14, 169
King, Evelyn, 277
King, Indle, Jr., 439*n*
King, Martin Luther, Jr., 76, 96–97
King, Stephen, 141–42, 188
King County Police Explorer Search and Rescue, 176–78, 214–17, 219
Kinney, Greg, 289
Kirkpatrick, Brian, 69
Kissinger, Henry, 132
Kleiner, Kathy, 269–70, 271
Kleptotrichy, 177
Kloepfer, Elizabeth "Liz," relationship with Bundy, 103, 106, 117–18, 138, 140, 147, 171–72, 224
    colleges and, 104, 143
    initial meeting, 101–2
    last letter of, 338
    lies, 104, 117–18
    Molly's baptism, 148, 149
    police calls, 170, 186–87, 212–13
    police interviews, 232–33, 245–46
    police sketch, 166, 170
    police surveillance, 180, 232–33
    in Salt Lake City, 167, 182
    in San Francisco, 122, 125
    telephone calls, 182, 183–84, 189–90, 213, 279
    trial and sentencing, 236–37, 243, 245
    vacations, 155–57, 158, 163
Kloepfer, Molly, 101–2, 104, 115, 122, 138, 148, 149, 155–56, 167, 171–72, 224, 338
Knutson, Gloria, 149
Koenig, Samantha, 394

460

INDEX

Kolchak: The Night Stalker (TV show), 178–79
Kraft, Randy, 204
Kretzschmar, Ruben, 268

Labbe, Armand, 109–10, 223
LaBianca, Rosemary and Leno, 2
Ladies' Home Journal, 81, 210, 355
Lake, Leonard, 204
Lakes High School, 150, 216
Lake Washington Floating Bridge, 195–96, 239, 252, 283–84, 396
   accidents and deaths, 26–27, 58–59, 63, 66–67, 101, 114, 146–47, 221, 259, 283–84, 288–89, 296, 308
   the bulge, 26–27, 58–59, 67, 146–47, 195, 259, 288, 296, 308
   construction of, 20–23, 24–25
   disaster of 1990, 341–44
   I-90 expansion proposal, 63, 195–96, 221
   name of, 24
   name change to Murrow, 92
   reversible lane, 58, 66, 67, 101, 114, 195, 221, 259, 283
   Sparks and, 308
Landrigan, Philip, 109, 353
Lang, Fritz, 262
Lanyon, Robert, 122
Larsen, Richard, 111, 234, 250
LaRue, Ruth, 192–93, 194
Laura Lee (boat), 26
LaVey, Anton, 320–21
Leach, Kimberly, 275–76, 280, 292, 298–300
lead, 46–47, 59–60, 224–25
   biological effects, 50–52, 60–61, 324, 361. See *also* lead poisoning
   physical properties, 46–47
   prices, 129–30
   smelter operations, 31, 33, 34–35, 38, 39–40, 49–51, 90, 102–3, 124, 211, 349, 350, 352, 353, 359–60, 370, 386, 389, 395–96. See *also* specific smelters
   World War II and, 201–2, 203
lead arsenate, 41, 42, 60, 356
lead-based paint, 49, 50–51, 53n, 211, 240, 310, 316, 318, 321, 332, 360, 366, 373, 381
leaded gasoline, 51–54, 61, 113, 117, 130–31, 201, 221, 236, 241, 247–48, 261, 307, 317–18, 330, 351, 352
"lead line," 50
lead poisoning, 50–52, 119–20, 211
   in animals, 102–3, 390
   CDC definition, 51n, 279–80, 330, 347, 395
   in children, 98–99, 108–10, 173–75, 181, 211–12, 224–25, 248, 279–80, 347, 355, 361
   crime hypothesis, 211–12, 224, 279–80, 307, 310, 324, 352, 355, 360, 361, 366, 373–74, 381–82
   EPA standards, 53, 53n, 317–18
   exposure routes, 50–52, 60–61, 174–75

Needleman's study, 99–100, 318, 361
Patterson's study, 60–61
Leadville Mine, 34
Lee, David, 278
Lehi, 188–89
Leschi Elementary School, 69
Leung, Mei "Linda," 322
Levine, Andrea "Randi," 341, 346
Levitt, Steven D., 373
Levy, Lisa, 269–70, 294, 295–96, 300
Lewis, Dorothy Otnow, 336–37, 338, 407n
Lewis, Evan, 248–49
Lewiston Valley Killer, 1, 404n
lidar, 5–6
Liebmann, Dorothea, 374
Lightfoot, Gordon, 172
Linard, Frank, 312
Lindbergh, Charles, 43–44
Lindquist, Larry, 316
Linkletter, Art, 116
Linkletter, Diane, 116
Little Domesday, 7, 212
Loeb, Albert, 40
Loeb, Harold, 40, 131
Loeb, Rose Guggenheim, 40
Loftus, Elizabeth, 242
Long Tom River, 100–101
Lorre, Catharine, 262
Lorre, Peter, 262
Love Canal, 204
Lovvorn, Gisele, 314
Lowe, Nickie, 366
Lower Monumental Dam, 79
lung cancer, 45, 61n, 62, 98, 112–13, 223–24, 244–45, 287, 291, 319, 375
Lunneborg, Patricia, 107, 113–14
Lust Killer, 1, 403n
Lynch, David, 345, 378

M (movie), 262
McCaffree, Mary Ellen, 111–12
McDonald, Loy, 244
McDowell, Slim, 131
McGavin, Darren, 178
McKenzie, Mark, 377
McMillan, Shelley, 289
McNeil Island Corrections Center, 2, 53, 93
Maddock, Mitchell Guy "Mad Dog," 260
Makarsky, Lee William, 26
Maltese Falcon, The (Hammett), 42–43, 409n
Mandic, Karen, 286, 288
manganese, 202, 203, 218, 349
Manhattan Project, 65, 323
Manhunter (movie), 333–34
Mann Act, 53
Manson, Charles, 2, 53, 93, 101, 239, 349
Manson, Donna Gail, 138–39, 147, 336, 422n
maps, 1–2, 3–5, 7
   Pacific Northwest, 8–9
   Puget Sound, 10–11

461

INDEX

Marmes Rockshelter, 79
Marshall, Lloyd, 28–29, 407n
Martinez, Anthony, 376
Martin, Kimberly, 277
Mataya, Robert, 244
Mattson, Charles Fletcher, 44
Maughan, Margith, 182, 189–90, 194–95, 212, 246
Maynard Hospital, 58
Mercer Island, 57, 195–96, 210, 251–53
    bridges, 20–27. *See also specific bridges*
Mercer Island floating bridge, 57, 195–96, 210, 251–53
    bridges, 20–27. *See also* Lake Washington Floating Bridge
Mercer Island High School, 240–41, 254–55, 258, 289–90, 296, 301, 346, 355
Mercer Island Public Library, 210
Mercer Island Reporter, 114, 116, 221, 239, 252, 253, 259
Mercer Junior High School, 271, 301
Mercer, Melinda, 367
mercury, 31, 120, 175, 225, 240, 288, 349, 350
Messier, Frances, 278
Metal Magic (Roger), 375
Michaud, Stephen G., 299–300, 335, 337, 428n
Midgley, Thomas, Jr., 52
Milham, Samuel, 112–13
Miller, Judith, 262
Mills, Opal, 313, 317
Milner, Thelma, 355–56, 447n
Minnesota Multiphasic Personality Inventory, 248–49
Missoula Floods, 17–18, 389
Mitchell, Joni, 80
Mobley, Wonzel, 240–41
Mondale, Walter, 323
Monte Cristo mines, 36, 361
Montgomery, Bernard Law, 199–200
Moon, Dean, 393
Moors Murderers, 225
Moses, Robert, 196
Mota-Velasco, Larrea, 365
Mount Baker, 18, 218–19
Mount Baker Tunnel, 24, 66, 121, 241
Mount Rainier, 19, 331
Mount Saint Helens eruption of 1980, 302–4, 309
Mount Storm King, 380
Mueller, William Frederick, 363
Muhammad, John Allen, 369
Mullin, Herbert, 204
Murder Incorporated, 305–6
Murray, Charles, 354
Murrow, Edward R., 21, 22
Murrow, Lacey V., 21–23, 92
Murrow Memorial Bridge. *See also* Lake Washington Floating Bridge

Nakamichi, Taryn Marr, 296
Naon, Constance, 317
Napoleon Bonaparte, 20

Naslund, Denise, 162, 164, 175–77, 215, 425n
National Football League, 131
National Lead Company, 100
Navy, U.S., 24, 29, 48, 57, 153
Neary, Nita, 270, 292, 295
necrophilia, 273, 325, 337, 340, 355, 358, 392, 451n
Needleman, Herbert, 99–100, 318, 361
Nelsen, Jeff, 289
Nelson, Craig, 260
Nelson, Kenneth, 98, 109
Nelson, Polly, 336–37, 418n
Nero, 47
New Deal, 21
Newman, Paul, 266
New Yorker, The, 263, 339, 374, 375
New York Times, 38, 52, 235, 284, 298
Nicholson, Jack, 140–41
Night Stalker. *See* Ramirez, Richard
Night Strangler, The (movie), 178
Nisqually earthquake of 2001, 367–68
Nixon, Richard, 115, 118, 247, 317
    election of 1968, 76, 77, 95, 97
    resignation of, 171
    Sadat meeting, 154
    Saturday Night Massacre, 121–22
    Vietnam War, 101, 104
    Watergate, 132, 210–11
Norman, Art, 336–37
North African campaign, 199–202, 205
Northwest Orient Airlines Flight 305, 106

O'Connell, John, 232, 242
Ohio River Valley, 203
oil embargo, 122, 135, 140, 147
Okazaki, Dayle, 327
Oliver! (musical), 97
Oliver, Patrick, 225–26, 366
Oliverson, Denise, 220
Olmsted, Frederick Law, 32
Olson, Thomas, 260
Olympic-Wallowa Lineament. *See* OWL
OPEC (Organization of Petroleum Exporting Countries), 135, 140, 147
Oregon Pulp and Paper Company, 218
Oregon State University, 144, 216
Orlando, Tony, 267
OSHA (Occupational Safety and Health Administration), 59n, 223–24, 291
Otero family, 127–29, 140, 184–85, 276, 382
Ott, Janice, 160–64, 166, 172, 177–78, 215, 425n
OWL (Olympic-Wallowa Lineament), 3–6, 18, 69, 111, 156, 158–59, 215, 266–67, 300, 315, 380, 395

Pacific Car & Foundry Co. (PACCAR), 310
Pacific Crest Trail, 306
Pacific Resins and Chemicals, 211
Pagoo (Holling), 95–96
paint. *See* lead-based paint

INDEX

Palmer, Laura, 345–46
Pang, Martin, 355
Parents Without Partners, 309–10
Parker, Mildred, 248
Parks, Roberta Kathleen, 144–45, 216–17
Parmenter, Danny, 274–75
Parmenter, Leslie Ann, 274–75
Partridge Family, The (TV show), 115
Patches, Julius Pierpont, 72
Patterson, Clair, 60–61
Peanuts (cartoon), 61, 105
Pedline Surgical Supply, 104
Percich, Joe, 44–45
Perrine, Jason, 301–2
pesticides, 41–42, 60, 211
Peterson, Heidi Birgit, 135–36, 214
Petz, Susan, 231
Phantom Sniper, 1, 235, 403n
Philadelphia Tooth Fairy Project, 99–100, 318, 361
Pickton, Robert, 204
Pike Place Market, 97, 321
Pincus, Jonathan, 336
Pinto, Sherman, 62, 93, 98, 112, 113, 130, 244–45
Pittsburgh, air pollution, 203
Pittsburg, Kansas, 122, 420n
plate tectonics, 3–4, 266–67
Plath, Sylvia, 285
Plischke, Jacqueline, 161–62
Pohlreich, Mary Ann, 340, 346
Point Defiance Park, 331, 397
Point Ruston, 386, 396
pollution. *See* air pollution; water pollution
Pol Pot, 211
Poole, Brenda, 289
Powell, Sarah Elizabeth, 363
Presley, Elvis, 54
Prestwich, Emily, 80
Prettyman, Loretta, 326
Price, Vincent, 105, 122
Pruitt, Scott, 397
Puget Sound, 16–17, 18, 20, 59, 85
 earthquake of 2001, 367–68
 map, *10–11*
Puget Sound Air Pollution Control Agency, 77, 93, 183, 224, 227, 316, 318
Puget Sound Naval Shipyard, 21
Puyallup River, 86, 369
Puz, Jenny, 348

Queen Anne Safeway, 76, 95

race
 crime and, 332, 354–55
 IQ and, 354
 Reagan and, 318
Rader, Dennis, 184, 204
 at ADT, 226–27, 330
 arrest and trial of, 382–84
 early life of, 122–23
 Gary Ridgway compared with, 314
 murders, 126–29, 140–41, 184–85, 257–58, 263–64, 276–77, 330, 332–33, 347, 450n
 poetry of, 272–73
Rader, Kerri, 383–84
Rader, Paula, 126
Rafferty, Cheryl, 269
Rainier Brewery, 158–59
Raisz, Erwin, 4–5, 6
Ramirez, Josefina, 221–22
Ramirez, Julián, 64–66
Ramirez, Mercedes, 64–66, 287, 352
Ramirez, Miguel, 221–22
Ramirez, Richard, 287, 320–23, 352
 early life of, 64–66, 221–22, 261
 murders, 321–22, 326–29
 vandalism of, 261, 321
Rancourt, Susan, 143–44, 147, 215–16, 217
"Raper's Road," 314, 395
Ray, Dixy Lee, 304
Reagan, Ronald, 317, 318, 332
Red Dragon (Harris), 333–34, 361
Redford, Robert, 266
Redhead (musical), 192–93, 194, 224, 233
redlining, 332
Reed, Judy, 26
Reichert, Dave, 312–13
Reston, James, 235–36
Revere Ware, 209
Reyes, Jessica Wolpaw, 373–74
Reynolds, Peggy, 114
Richardson, Elliot, 121–22
Ridgway, Gary, 2, 325, 404n
 adult life of, 309–10
 arrest of, 368
 birth and early life of, 53–54, 204
 murders, 310, 312–15, 317, 321, 330–31, 404n
Ring of Fire, 88
Roberts, E. I., 146–47
Robertson, Shelley, 224, 231
Robinson, Herb, 146
Robinson, John E., 58
Rockefeller, John D., 36
Rockefeller, Nelson, 95
Rockefeller, William, Jr., 34–35, 36
Rockford Files, The (TV show), 278
Rogers, Freda and Ernst, 101
Rogers, H. H., 34
Rogers, Roy, 158
Rogulskyj, Anna, 224
Rommel, Erwin, 199–200
Roosevelt, Franklin Delano, 21, 44, 46, 201
Roosevelt, Lake, 349, 370
Rose, Eleanor, 175–76
Rosellini, Albert, 61, 111
Rosemary's Baby (movie), 320
Rosenblum, Bernard, 109
Rothschild, Louis F., 40
Rowlands, David, 93
Ruckelshaus, William, 122, 317–19
Rule, Ann, 217

INDEX

Rule, Ann, (cont.)
   arrest of Bundy, 234, 235
   initial meetings, 105–6
   police sketch, 167
   relationship with Bundy, 112, 115, 147, 236–37, 250, 263, 407n, 421n
   True Detective, 167–69, 183, 368
Russell, Bill, 240
Russell, George W., 289
Russell, George Waterfield, Jr., 289, 330, 355, 368–69
   early life of, 239–41
   murders, 339–41, 346, 355, 404n
   police charges, 259, 315, 316
   police search, 315–16
   vandalism of, 239, 252, 315–16
Russell, George Waterfield, Sr., 240, 289
Rust, Helen, 36
Rust, Henry, 36, 37, 43
Rust, Howard, 37
Ruston smelter, 211
   after shutdown, 369–70, 384, 385–86, 396–97
   air pollution, 40–43, 44–45, 49–50, 61–62, 70, 77, 93, 109–10, 112–13, 124, 163, 183, 220, 223–24, 227–28, 244, 247–48, 253, 290–91, 305–6, 308–9, 316–17, 318–19, 332, 368, 369–70
   demolition, 347–48
   founding, 35–39
   public defense of, 227–28
   public protests, 247–48, 308–9, 319
   shuts down, 319, 325–26
   skimmers, 89–91
   slag, 32–33, 90, 145–46, 220–21, 243–44, 316, 384, 385
   worker health and deaths, 90–91, 93, 112–13, 130, 175, 223–24, 243–45, 291
Ruston Way, 44, 220, 243–44, 309, 396
Rust, William, 35–38, 43
Ruzicka, James Edward, 434n
Ryan, Dennis, 35–36

Sadat, Anwar, 154
Sagebrush Rebellion, 317–18
St. Paul & Tacoma Lumber Company, 101
Salee, Linda Dawn, 100
Salerno, Frank, 328–29
Salt Lake City, 167, 172, 181–83, 187–88, 212–13, 228–29
Sammamish, Lake, 4, 16, 43, 110, 157–65, 170, 175–78, 236
Sampson, Tom, 147
Sanders, Martin, 440n
San Ysidro McDonald's massacre, 323–24
Sapp, Yolanda, 366
Satan (Satanic worship), 164, 197, 261, 320–21, 328, 349
Satanic Bible, The (LaVey), 320–21
Saturday Night Massacre, 121–22
Savage, Susan, 225–26, 366
Schaefer, Gerard John, 161, 204
Schensted, Liz, 221
Schirra, Wally, 158
Schram, Donna, 113–14, 118, 143, 169–70, 171, 237
Seaman, Hallie Ann, 168–69
Seattle Center, 76, 282
Seattle, Chief, 58
Seattle Crime Prevention Advisory Commission, 112, 147
Seattle Crisis Clinic, 105, 110–11, 112
Seattle earthquake of 1953, 69, 75
Seattle Police Athletic Association, 159
Seattle Police Department, 95, 114, 134, 162, 230, 339
Seattle Post-Intelligencer, 81, 96, 174, 234, 304
Seattle Public School District, 20
Seattle Rape Relief, 137
Seattle SuperSonics, 77, 240
Seattle-Tacoma International Airport (SeaTac), 2, 54, 106, 149, 167, 313, 317
Seattle Times, 20, 25, 63, 67, 79, 111, 118, 135, 146, 154, 166, 171, 175, 195, 234, 250, 283, 344
Seattle University, 179
Seattle Yacht Club, 93–94, 249
Segretti, Donald, 118
Selby Lead and Silver Smelting Works, 39–40, 97–98, 102–3
Selective Service, 101, 104
serial killers. *See also specific killers*
   gender difference, 382, 392
   overview of, 1, 204–5, 225, 284–85, 322, 395, 403–4n
Service, Robert W., 16
Shakespeare, William, 28, 57
Sharif, Omar, 97
Shawcross, Arthur, 204, 336
Shepherd, Raelynne, 193–94, 232, 233
Sherman Crater, 219
Sherrod's, 268–69, 273
Sherwood, Judy, 348
Shields, Mary, 173
Shipman, Harold, 225
Silence of the Lambs, The (Harris), 333
Silent Spring (Carson), 211
"Simplify Me When I'm Dead" (Douglas), 205
Simonson, Harold, 220–21
Simpson, Thomas, 58
60 Minutes (TV show), 299
skimmers, 89–91
Skyline, 2, 49, 53, 61, 62
slag, 54, 211, 349, 374, 393, 396–97, 423n
   Ruston smelter, 32–33, 90, 145–46, 220–21, 243–44, 316, 384, 385
Slater, Greg, 260
Slawson, Linda Kay, 94
Smeltermen's Local 25, 44, 112
"smelter nose," 91
smelters. *See also specific smelters*
   overview of, 30–31, 34–39
Smelterworker, The, 112, 130–31, 175
Smiley Face Killer. *See* Yates, Robert Lee, Jr.
Smith, Louis, 186, 242
Smith, Melissa, 183–84, 185–86, 196–97, 212, 233, 241

INDEX

Smith, Merton O., 67
smog, 200, 203, 351–52, 360
Souviron, Richard, 295
Soviet Union, 318
Space Needle, 86, 133, 178, 290, 310
Sparks, Karen, 125–26, 132, 134–35, 217
Sparks, Stacy, 292–93, 308, 344
Speck, Richard, 71, 204
Spillman, Jack Owen, III, 1, 350–51, 355–58, 404n
Sprague, David, 283
Sprinker, Karen, 100
Stalin, Joseph, 201
Standard Oil, 51–52
Stano, Gerald, 416n
Staples, Allen E., 244
Starr, Ringo, 126
Star Trek (TV show), 179, 255–56, 272, 289
Star Trek Convention (1977), 255–56
Stenstrom, Rags, 131
Stevenson, Robert Louis, 173, 197–98, 378
Stewart, Bill, 346
Stickney, John, 296–98
Sting, The (movie), 266
Storwick, Terry, 143
Stotland, Ezra, 112
Strange Case of Dr. Jekyll and Mr. Hyde, The (Stevenson), 173, 197–98
Strategic Minerals Task Force, 318
Straus, Isidor, 37
Straus, Roger, Jr., 374–75
Straus, Roger, Sr., 374
Stuth, Vonnie, 235
Suicide Lane, 58, 395
sulfur dioxide, 39, 61–62, 61n, 90, 98–99, 108–9, 124, 218, 223, 227–28, 305–6
sulfuric acid, 130, 223, 268, 350
sulfur trioxide, 267–68, 268n
Summer of Love, 93
Summers, Shawnda Leea, 314
Sun Also Rises, The (Hemingway), 40
Superfund, 42, 204, 317, 318, 348, 368, 369, 375, 377, 379, 389
Super Outbreak of 1974, 140
superpredators, 354–55
Sutcliffe, Peter (Yorkshire Ripper), 6, 204, 224–25
Suwanee River State Park, 275–76
Swain, Christopher, 393–94
Swindler, Cathy, 95, 418n
Swindler, Herb, 95, 214, 217
Swisher, Dawn, 301
Symbionese Liberation Army (SLA), 135, 142, 145, 245

Tacoma Narrows Bridge, 2, 21–23, 25, 49, 102, 146, 347, 396
Tacoma News Tribune, 23, 39, 211, 223, 227, 228, 237, 290–91, 325
"Tacoma process," 317
Tacoma Smelting and Refining, 35. *See also* Ruston smelter
Tacoma Yacht Club, 316

Takei, George "Sulu," 255
Tall, Bob, 252
Tanbara, Gregory, 348
Tanuki the Bad Badger, 83, 372
Tate, Sharon, 101, 239
Taylor, Gary Addison, 1, 235, 403n
Taylor Mountain, 88, 145, 214–17, 219, 236, 398
Teck Cominco, 392–94
Temple University, 99–100, 104
Testa, Joanne, 133
Tet Offensive, 73, 74
tetraethyllead (TEL), 51–52, 100, 247, 351. *See also* leaded gasoline
thallium, 393
Thomas, Cheryl, 268–69, 270–71
Thompson, Jerry, 212, 230–33, 241–42
Thompson, Rodger, 168, 368
Three Mile Island accident, 290, 309
Tiger Mountain, 88, 145, 215, 368, 398
Tilden, Audrey, 29, 99
Titanic, RMS, 37–38
Tocqueville, Alexis de, 359
Todd, James R., 244
Toledo, Jon, 288–89
Tomlinson, Deborah Lee, 121
Tony Lama Boots, 65
Tope, Stephen L., Jr., 78–79
Towering Inferno, The (movie), 229–30, 243
Travis, Lee, 109–10
Traylor Bros., 342, 343–44
Treasures of Tutankhamun, The (exhibit), 282
Trimble, David, 297
Trinity nuclear test, 65
True Detective (magazine), 115, 155, 161, 167–69, 183, 231
Truman, Harry, 281, 302
Trumbull, Lonnie, 70–71, 92, 93
Trump, Donald, 397
Tukes Mountain Park, 157, 165
tungsten, 202, 203
Turner, Patricia, 161
Twain, Mark, 195
Twin Peaks (TV show), 345, 445–46n

Union Metal, 323
United Steelworkers, 112, 163
University of Arkansas, 95
University of California, Davis, 102–3
University of California, Los Angeles (UCLA), 285, 296, 300–301, 320
University of Michigan, 266
University of Puget Sound (UPS), 92, 119, 133
University of Utah, 108, 115, 119, 143, 147, 167, 182
University of Washington, 16–17, 23, 93, 94, 95, 97, 107, 110, 113–14, 125, 132, 148, 151, 166, 272, 306
Utah Highway Patrol, 228–29
Utah State Prison, 249, 251

Vail, Colorado, 156, 219–20, 266
Valenzuela, Carol, 170, 181–82

INDEX

Valenzuela, Robert, 170
Valint, Sylvia, 159–60
Valle, Manuel, 324–25
Van Amburgh, Hugh, 43
Van Cise, Rick, 343
vandalism, 252, 271–72
Van Hillman, Phillip, 168, 183, 368
Verdon, Gwen, 192
Vian, Shirley, 257–58, 272, 276
Vietnam War, 73–76, 102, 103, 104, 148, 153, 164–65, 221–22, 323
Viewmont High School, 192–94, 224
Vikko, Stephanie, 100
Vincow, Jennie, 323
Violent Crime Control and Law Enforcement Act, 354
Volkswagen Beetle (VW), 93, 115, 117, 118, 119, 122, 131, 142, 148, 151, 154–55, 155, 166, 167, 170, 172, 180, 188–89, 216, 218, 229, 230, 233, 236, 241, 253, 260, 278–79, 370
von Braun, Wernher, 199
Vortman, Marlin, 117, 122, 236, 241–42
Voshall, Larry, 156, 250

Wagner, Lauren, 277
Wah Wee massacre, 442*n*
Want-Ad Killer, 1, 403*n*
Warner, David, 73–76
Warner, Robert, 74, 75
Warner, Susie, 69, 73–74, 75, 209, 210, 289, 290
Washington, George, 81
Washington, Lake, 16, 20–21, 24, 59, 157–58, 240, 251, 252, 288, 310, 343, 344
Washington Park, 179–80
Washington Park Arboretum, 166
Washington State Department of Ecology, 342, 361, 370, 395–96
Washington State Department of Highways, 21
Washington State Department of Transportation, 20
Washington State University, 164, 296–97
Washington Thoracic Society, 223–24
Washington, Yolanda, 262
Watergate, 132, 210–11
water pollution, 42, 90, 104, 148, 154, 203–4, 211, 240, 306, 342, 366, 384, 389–90, 393–94
Watson, Tex, 101
Weatter, Marsha Ann, 303
Weckler, Kristina, 277
Wedgwood Erratic, 17
Wegerle, Bill, 332–33
Wegerle, Vicki, 332–33, 383–84
Weisenburgh, Mike, 346
Welch, Michella, 331
Werewolf Butcher of Spokane. *See* Spillman, Jack Owen, III

Werner, Ben, 195–96
Werner, Joanne, 195–96
Wesner, B. George, 102–3
Western Plastics, 211
Western States Republican Conference, 234
Western Washington State College, 170–71
Western Washington University, 286
West, Fred, 204
Weyerhaeuser, George, 43–44, 215
Weyerhaeuser Timber Company, 1, 16, 281, 302
Whidbey Island Naval Air Station, 153, 365–66
white arsenic, 40, 40n
White, Sammiejo, 376
White, Tom, 306
Whitman, Charles, 71
Whitney, Jan, 100
Whittaker, Jim, 17
Wickersham Bridge, 226, 366
Wick, Lisa, 70–71, 92
Wicklund, Renae, 168, 169, 311
Wicklund, Shannah, 168, 311
Wightman, Daria, 179–80
Wilcox, Nancy, 180–81, 428*n*
Wilder, Diane, 286, 288
Wildwood Inn, 213–14, 231, 232
William the Conqueror, 7
Wilson, Roy. *See* Spillman, Jack Owen, III
Wizard of Oz, The (Baum), 41
Wizard of Oz, The (movie), 80–81
Women's Coalition to Stop the Green River Murders, 321
Woodfield, Randall, 1, 131, 218, 292, 306–8, 404*n*, 440*n*
Woodrow Wilson High School, 91–92
Woodruff, Frank, 120
World Trade Center, 115
World War I, 4, 281
World War II, 1, 22, 26, 46, 47, 199–205, 285, 310, 365–66, 383
Worthington, Jack, 28–29
Worthington, John, 29

Xerxes, 19–20

Yates, John Taylor, 365
Yates, Robert Lee, Jr., 144, 226, 335, 358, 365–67, 369
Yates, Robert Lee, Sr., 365–66
Yoss, Arlene, 174, 247, 306, 384–85
Yoss, Bill, 174
Yu, Tsai-Lian, 327

zinc, 39, 64, 98–99, 122, 349, 350, 389
Zodiac Killer, 79, 97–98, 103, 416*n*
Zwang, Michael, 289